THE BATTLE OF BRITAIN

THE BATTLE OF BRITAIN

Five Months That Changed History; May–October 1940

James Holland

St. Martin's Press New York

Printed in the United States of America. For information, address St. Martin's Press, 175 Fifth Avenue, New York, N.Y. 10010.

www.stmartins.com

Library of Congress Cataloging-in-Publication Data

Holland, James, 1970–
The Battle of Britain : five months that changed history, May–October 1940 / James Holland.—1st U.S. ed.
p. cm.
"First published in Great Britain by Bantam Press"—T.p. verso.
Includes bibliographical references and index.
ISBN 978-0-312-67500-4
1. Britain, Battle of, Great Britain, 1940. I. Title.
D756.5.B7H66 2011
940.54'211—dc22

2010040646

First published in Great Britain in 2010 by Bantam Press, an imprint of Transworld Publishers, a Random House Group Company

First U.S. Edition: March 2011

10 9 8 7 6 5 4 3 2 1

For Bro

Contents

Part II: Respite

Part III: *Kanalkampf*

Part IV: Battle Over Britain

Maps and Figures

GERMAN AND ALLIED OPERATIONS PLANS, May 1940

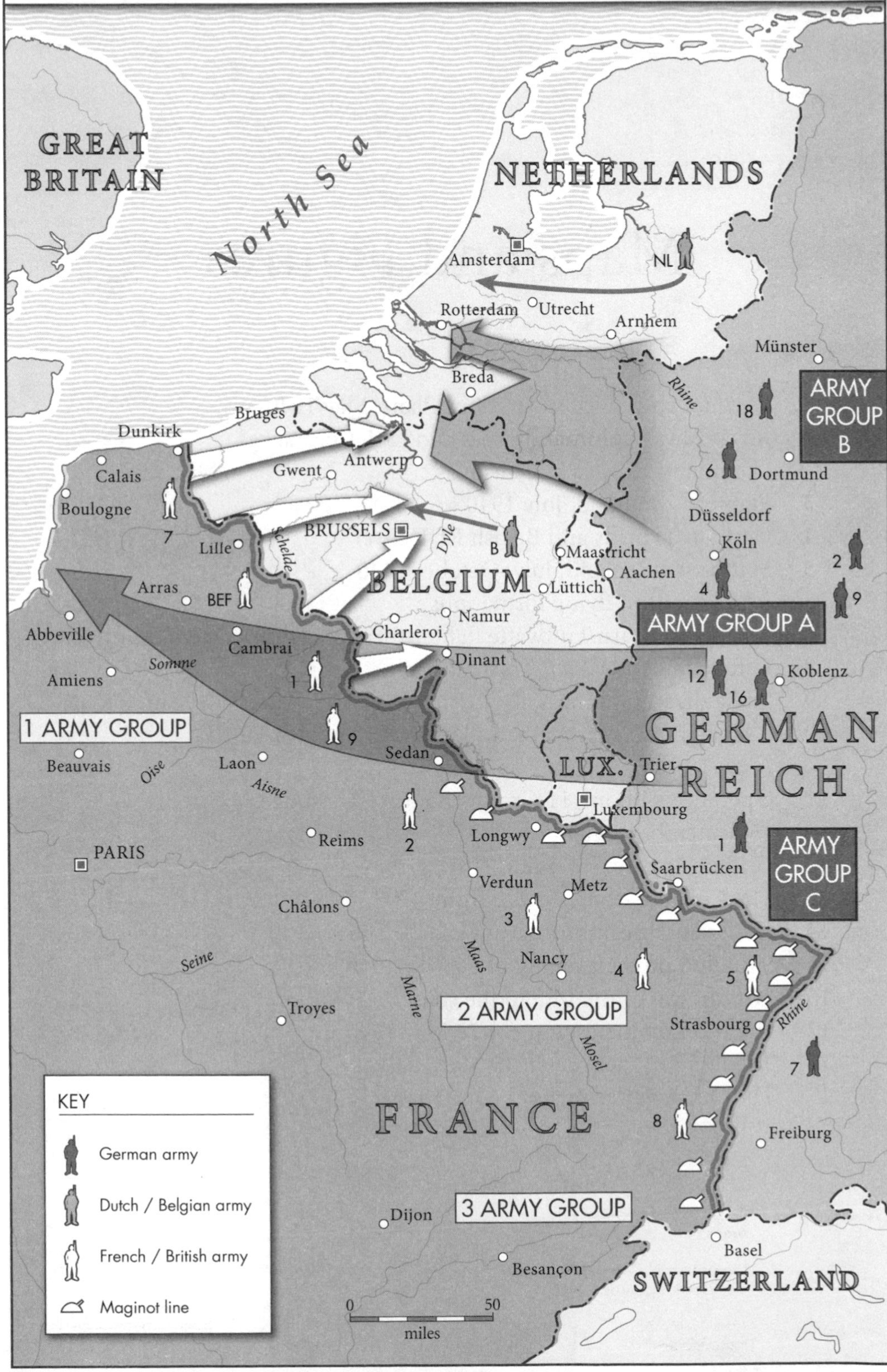

GREAT BRITAIN
North Sea
NETHERLANDS
Amsterdam
NL
Rotterdam
Utrecht
Arnhem
Münster
Breda
Rhine
ARMY GROUP B
18
Bruges
Dunkirk
Calais
Antwerp
Gwent
6
Dortmund
Boulogne
7
Düsseldorf
BRUSSELS
Lille
Scheldе
Dyle
B
Maastricht
Köln
2
Arras
BEF
BELGIUM
Aachen
Lüttich
4
9
Abbeville
Namur
Charleroi
ARMY GROUP A
Cambrai
Dinant
Amiens
Somme
1
12
16
Koblenz
1 ARMY GROUP
9
GERMAN REICH
Beauvais
Oise
Laon
Aisne
Sedan
LUX.
Trier
Luxembourg
2
Reims
Longwy
1
PARIS
ARMY GROUP C
Saarbrücken
Verdun
Metz
Châlons
3
Maas
Seine
Nancy
4
5
Marne
Troyes
2 ARMY GROUP
Strasbourg
Rhine
Mosel
7
FRANCE
8
Freiburg
Dijon
3 ARMY GROUP
Basel
Besançon
SWITZERLAND

KEY
German army
Dutch / Belgian army
French / British army
Maginot line

0 50
miles

ROYAL NAVAL COMMAND AREAS AND RAF COASTAL COMMAND GROUPS AND AIRFIELDS

ATLANTIC OCEAN
North Sea
ORKNEYS & SHETLANDS
No. 18 Group
Sullom Voë
201 Lerwick
Scapa
Kirkwall
ROSYTH
Butt of Lewis
Stornoway
Wick
Duncansby Head
Aberdeen
Cromarty
Kinnaird Head
Stornoway
Invergordon
Dyce
Aberdeen
ROSYTH
Montrose
No. 18 Group
No. 15 Group
ROSYTH
18 GROUP HQ
Leuchars
Rosyth
Glasgow
Lough Swilly
Bloody Foreland
Newcastle
Newcastle
Aldergrove
Thornaby
Belfast
No. 18 Group
Nore Rosyth Command
Boundary 13/11/39
No. 16 Group
Isle of Man
Liverpool
Liverpool
Grimsby
Humber
Dublin
Holyhead
Bircham Newton
Harwich
Cork
Milford Haven
Carew
NORTHWOOD
HQ GC
Harwich
Nore
NORE
Kinsdale Head
Pembroke
Cheriton
Cardiff
CHATHAM
16 GROUP HQ
Detling
Dover
Dover
Calais
WESTERN APPROACHES
PLYMOUTH
15 Group HQ.
Warmwell
Thorney Island
Portsmouth
No. 16 Group
Mountbatten
Devonport
Portland
PORTSMOUTH
Dieppe
Falmouth
Guernsey
FRANCE
KEY
ROSYTH Naval Commands
Dover Naval Sub-Commands
Newcastle Naval Sub-Command Headquarters
No. 16 Group Coastal Command Areas
Thornaby 220 Dispositions of Coastal Command Squadrons
ROSYTH Area Combined Headquarters
0 100
nautical miles

FIGHTER COMMAND, July 1940

North Sea
Irish Sea
English Channel
FRANCE
Grangemouth
Edinburgh
13 Gp H.Q.
Newcastle
Usworth
Catterick
13
Gp boundary
12
Leconfield
Church Fenton
M
Kirton in Lindsey
Manchester
M(W)
Digby
12 Gp H.Q.
Watnall
L
L(W)
K
Coltishall
J
Tern Hill
Wittering
K(W)
G
12
Gp boundary
10
Duxford
Martlesham
F
Debden
North Weald
E
Z
Stanmore
Stapleford
Rochford
Northolt
Hornchurch
Pembrey
W
10 Gp H.Q. Box
Hendon
Gravesend
Eastchurch
Croydon
Detling
D
Colerne
Kenley
Biggin Hill
West Malling
Manston
Middle Wallop
A
Boscombe Down
C
Hawkinge
B
Lympne
Y
Portsmouth
Westhampnett
Exeter
Tangmere
Warmwell
Thorney Island
Gosport
Lee on Solent (R.N.)
Roborough
10 11
Gp boundary
KEY
Group boundaries
Sector boundaries
Group headquarters
Sector airfields
Other fighter airfields
Coastal command airfield
Headquarters Fighter Cmd and A.A. Cmd
Sector Identity letters

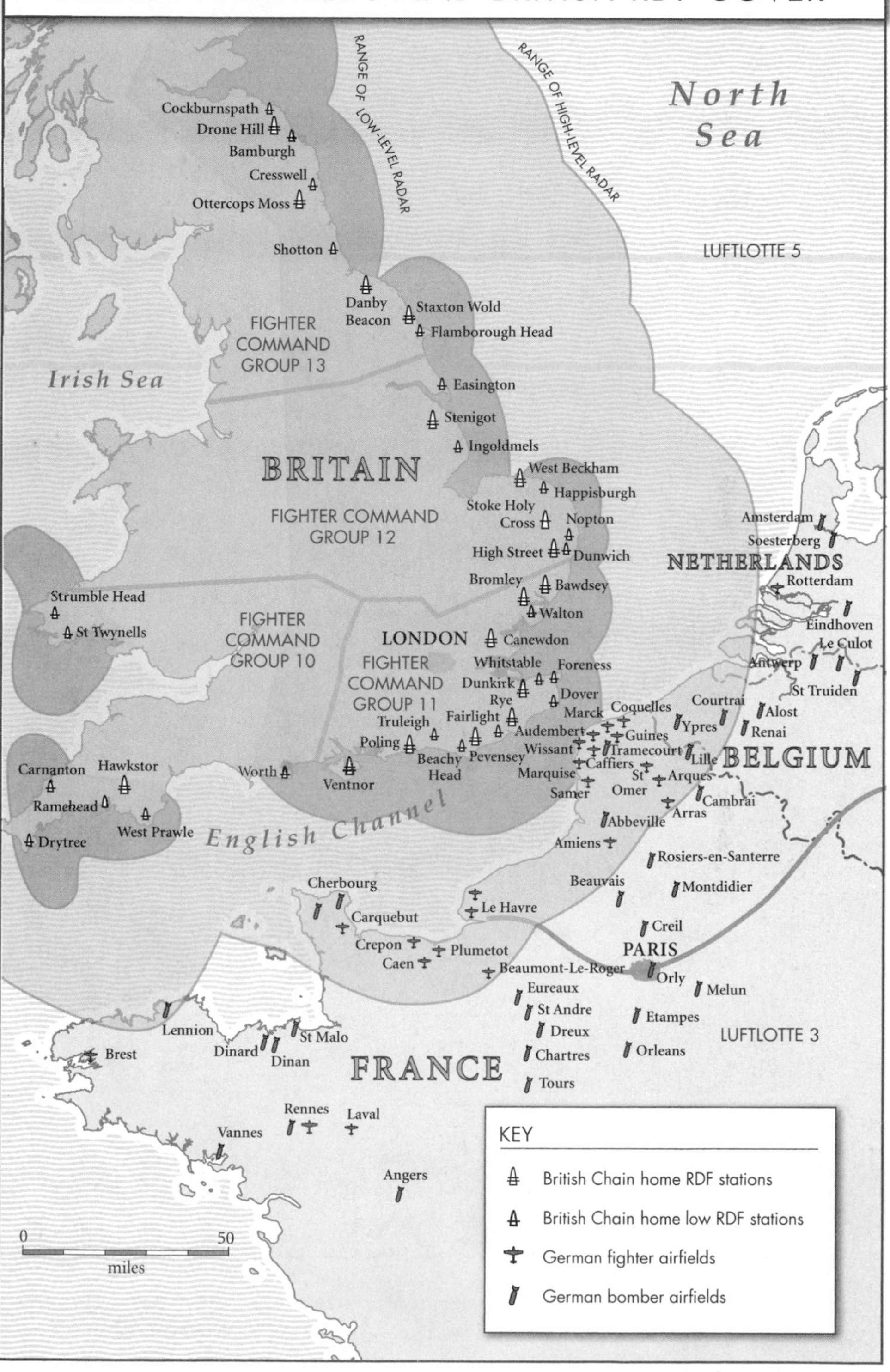

GERMAN AIRFIELDS AND BRITISH RDF COVER
RANGE OF LOW-LEVEL RADAR
RANGE OF HIGH-LEVEL RADAR
North Sea
Irish Sea
English Channel
BRITAIN
LONDON
NETHERLANDS
BELGIUM
FRANCE
PARIS
LUFTLOTTE 5
LUFTLOTTE 3
FIGHTER COMMAND GROUP 13
FIGHTER COMMAND GROUP 12
FIGHTER COMMAND GROUP 10
FIGHTER COMMAND GROUP 11
Cockburnspath
Drone Hill
Bamburgh
Cresswell
Ottercops Moss
Shotton
Danby Beacon
Staxton Wold
Flamborough Head
Easington
Stenigot
Ingoldmels
West Beckham
Happisburgh
Stoke Holy Cross
Nopton
High Street
Dunwich
Bromley
Bawdsey
Walton
Canewdon
Whitstable
Foreness
Dunkirk
Rye
Dover
Fairlight
Truleigh
Poling
Beachy Head
Pevensey
Worth
Ventnor
Strumble Head
St Twynells
Carnanton
Hawkstor
Ramehead
West Prawle
Drytree
Amsterdam
Soesterberg
Rotterdam
Eindhoven
Le Culot
Antwerp
St Truiden
Courtrai
Alost
Renai
Ypres
Lille
Coquelles
Marck
Audembert
Guines
Wissant
Tramecourt
Caffiers
Marquise
St Omer
Arques
Samer
Cambrai
Arras
Abbeville
Amiens
Rosiers-en-Santerre
Beauvais
Montdidier
Cherbourg
Carquebut
Le Havre
Creil
Crepon
Plumetot
Caen
Beaumont-Le-Roger
Orly
Melun
Eureaux
St Andre
Etampes
Dreux
Chartres
Orleans
Tours
Lennion
Brest
Dinard
Dinan
St Malo
Rennes
Laval
Vannes
Angers
0
50
miles
KEY
British Chain home RDF stations
British Chain home low RDF stations
German fighter airfields
German bomber airfields

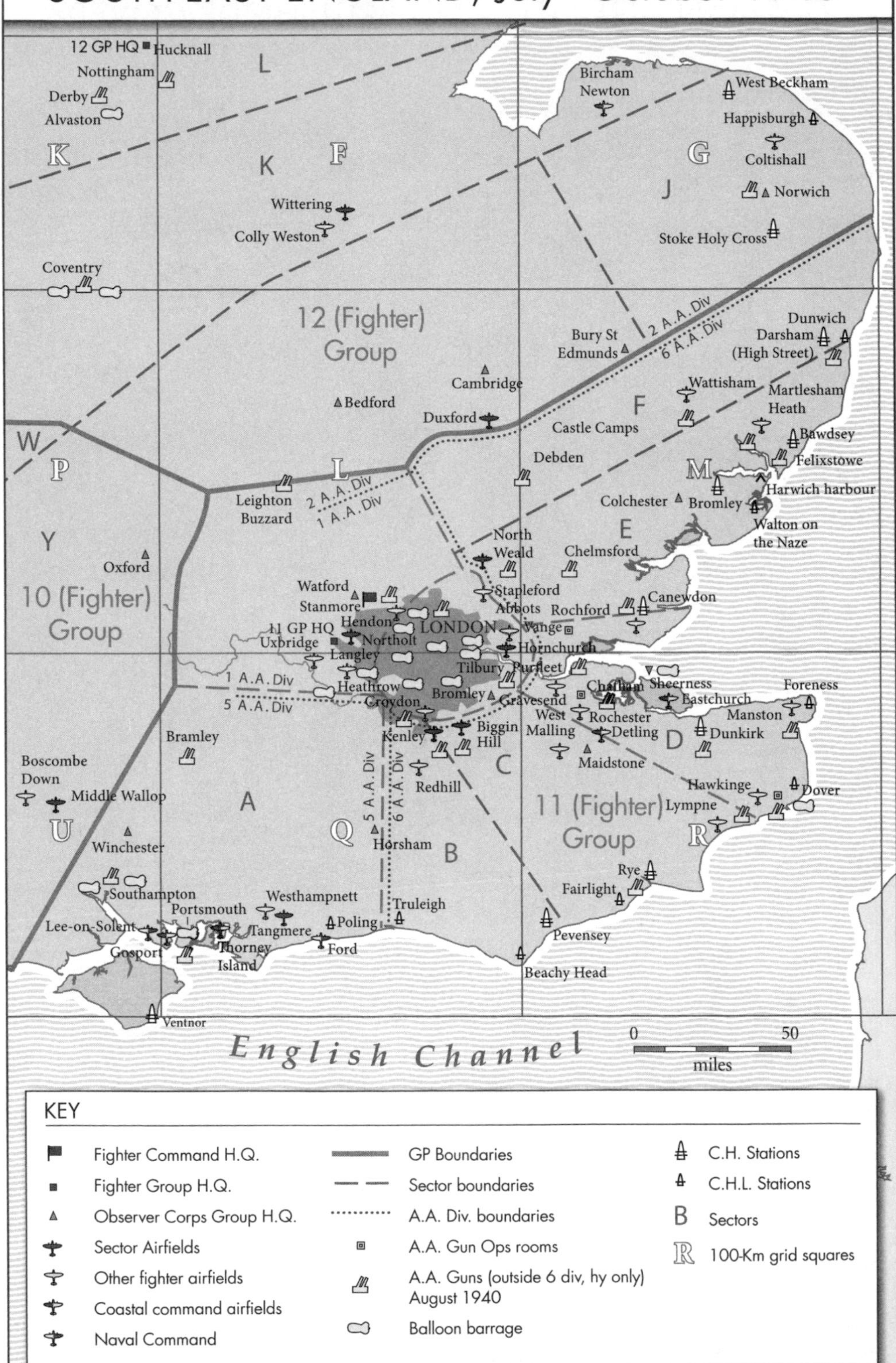
SOUTH-EAST ENGLAND, July–October 1940
12 GP HQ
Hucknall
Nottingham
Derby
Alvaston
L
K
F
G
J
Bircham Newton
West Beckham
Happisburgh
Coltishall
Norwich
Stoke Holy Cross
Wittering
Colly Weston
Coventry
12 (Fighter) Group
Bedford
Cambridge
Duxford
Bury St Edmunds
2 A.A. Div
6 A.A. Div
Dunwich
Darsham (High Street)
Wattisham
Martlesham Heath
Castle Camps
Bawdsey
Felixstowe
Debden
M
Harwich harbour
Colchester
Bromley
Walton on the Naze
W
P
Y
Leighton Buzzard
1 A.A. Div
E
North Weald
Chelmsford
Oxford
10 (Fighter) Group
Watford
Stanmore
Stapleford Abbots
Rochford
Canewdon
11 GP HQ
Uxbridge
Hendon
Northolt
LONDON
Vange
Hornchurch
Langley
Tilbury
Purfleet
Heathrow
Croydon
Bromley
Gravesend
Chatham
Sheerness
Eastchurch
Foreness
1 A.A. Div
5 A.A. Div
West Malling
Rochester
Manston
Kenley
Biggin Hill
Detling
Dunkirk
Bramley
D
Boscombe Down
Middle Wallop
C
Maidstone
Redhill
5 A.A. Div
6 A.A. Div
Hawkinge
Dover
A
11 (Fighter) Group
Lympne
U
Q
R
Winchester
Horsham
B
Rye
Southampton
Fairlight
Westhampnett
Portsmouth
Truleigh
Lee-on-Solent
Tangmere
Poling
Pevensey
Gosport
Thorney Island
Ford
Beachy Head
Ventnor
English Channel
0
50
miles
KEY
Fighter Command H.Q.
Fighter Group H.Q.
Observer Corps Group H.Q.
Sector Airfields
Other fighter airfields
Coastal command airfields
Naval Command
GP Boundaries
Sector boundaries
A.A. Div. boundaries
A.A. Gun Ops rooms
A.A. Guns (outside 6 div, hy only) August 1940
Balloon barrage
C.H. Stations
C.H.L. Stations
B Sectors
R 100-Km grid squares

RAF SQUADRON FLYING FORMATIONS

FIGHTER SQUADRON FORMATIONS

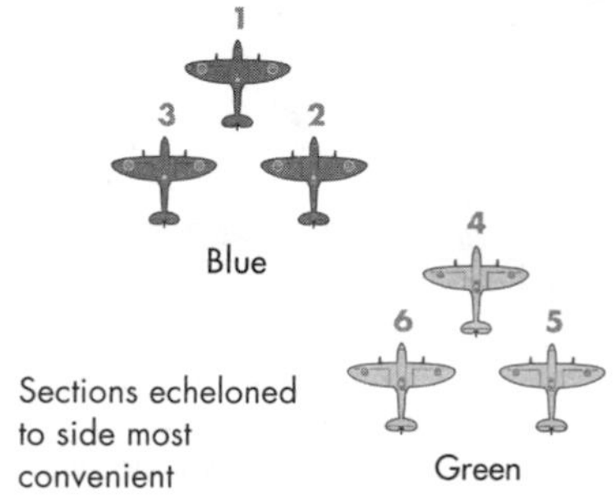

SEARCH AND CRUISE FORMATIONS

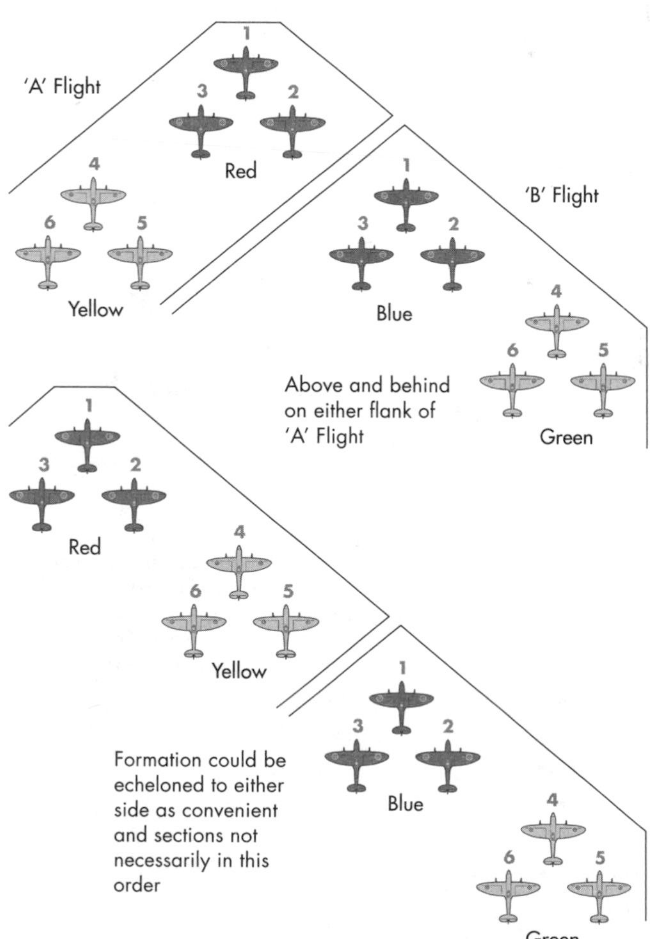

RAF FIGHTER TURN/LUFTWAFFE FIGHTER TURN

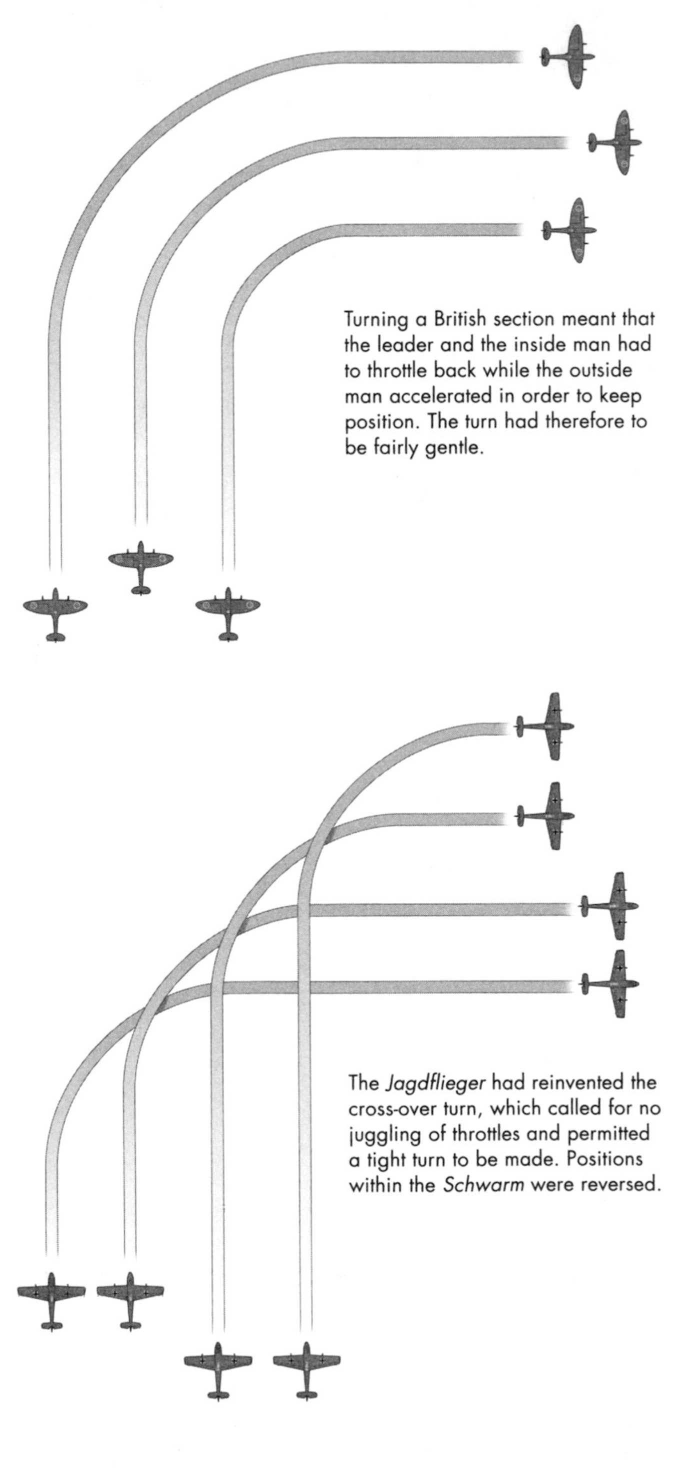

Turning a British section meant that the leader and the inside man had to throttle back while the outside man accelerated in order to keep position. The turn had therefore to be fairly gentle.
The *Jagdflieger* had reinvented the cross-over turn, which called for no juggling of throttles and permitted a tight turn to be made. Positions within the *Schwarm* were reversed.

LUFTWAFFE FIGHTER *STAFFEL* FORMATION

This shows a *Staffel* formation of twelve aircraft – although an operational *Staffel* often flew with fewer aircraft than this. The *Staffel* is made up of four *Schwarm*, and is lead by a *Staffelführer*. Each *Schwarm* is led by a *Schwarmführer*, and each pair, or *Rotten*, by a *Rottenführer*.

STAFFEL FORMATION

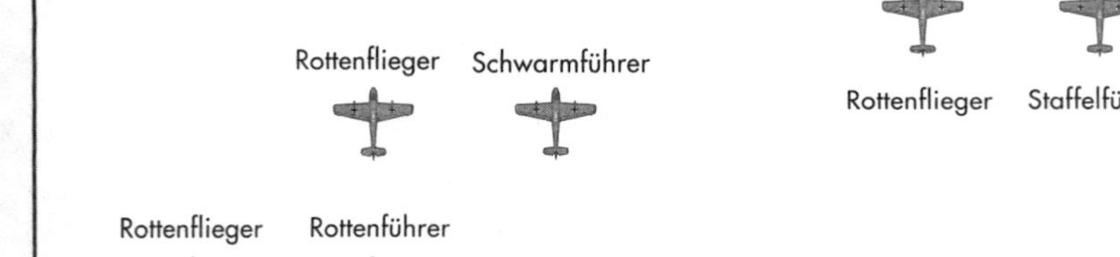

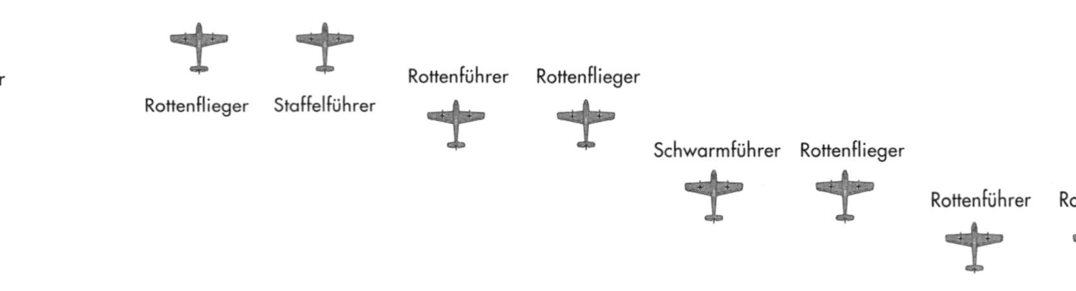

STAFFEL FORMATION FROM BEHIND

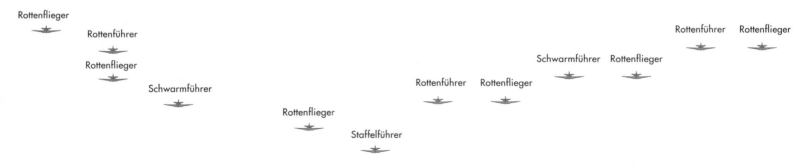

STUKA DIVE-BOMBING

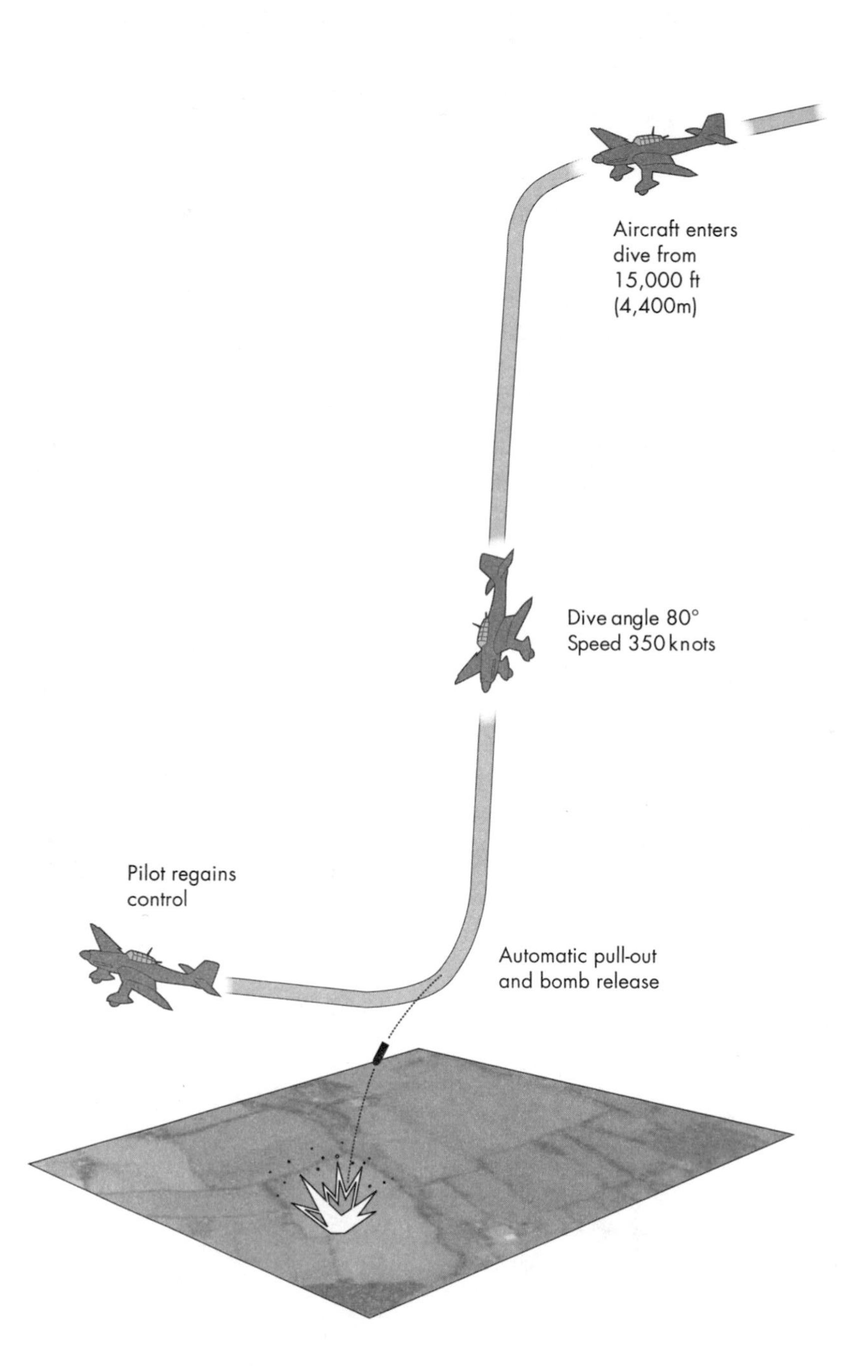

RAF FIGHTER COMMAND ORDER OF BATTLE

Groups and squadrons, 8 August 1940 (0900 hours)

(Sector stations in italic)

13 GROUP,
HEADQUARTERS NEWCASTLE

Wick

3	Hurricane	Wick
504	Hurricane	Castletown
232	Hurricane	Sumburgh (1 Flight only)

Dyce

603	Spitfire	A Flight Dyce B Flight Montrose

Turnhouse

605	Hurricane	Drem
232	Hurricane	Turnhouse
253	Hurricane	Turnhouse
141	Defiant	Prestwick

Usworth

79	Spitfire	Acklington (operational by day only)
607	Hurricane	Usworth
72	Spitfire	Acklington

Catterick

219	Blenheim	Catterick

Aldergrove

245	Hurricane	Aldergrove

12 GROUP,
HEADQUARTERS WATNALL

Church Fenton

73	Hurricane	Church Fenton
249	Hurricane	Church Fenton
616	Spitfire	Leconfield

Kirton in Lindsey

222	Spitfire	Kirton in Lindsey
264	Defiant	Kirton in Lindsey ('A' Flight Ringway)

Digby

46	Hurricane	Digby
611	Spitfire	Digby
29	Blenheim	Digby

Coltishall

242	Hurricane	Coltishall
66	Spitfire	Coltishall

Wittering

229	Hurricane	Wittering
266	Spitfire	Wittering
23	Blenheim	Colly Weston

Duxford

19	Spitfire	Duxford

11 GROUP,
HEADQUARTERS UXBRIDGE

Debden

17	Hurricane	Debden
85	Hurricane	Martlesham

North Weald

56	Hurricane	Rochford
151	Hurricane	North Weald
25	Blenheim	Martlesham

Hornchurch

54	Spitfire	Hornchurch
65	Spitfire	Hornchurch
74	Spitfire	Hornchurch
41	Spitfire	Hornchurch

Biggin Hill

32	Hurricane	Biggin Hill
610	Spitfire	Biggin Hill
501	Hurricane	Gravesend
600	Blenheim	Manston

Kenley

615	Hurricane	Kenley
64	Spitfire	Kenley
111	Hurricane	Croydon

Northolt

1	Hurricane	Northolt
257	Hurricane	Northolt

Tangmere

43	Hurricane	Tangmere
145	Hurricane	Westhampnett
601	Hurricane	Tangmere

10 GROUP,
HEADQUARTERS BOX,
WILTSHIRE

Pembrey

92	Spitfire	Pembrey

Filton

87	Hurricane	Exeter
213	Hurricane	Exeter

St Eval

234	Spitfire	St Eval
247	Gladiator	Roborough (1 Flight)

Middle Wallop

238	Hurricane	Middle Wallop
609	Spitfire	Middle Wallop
604	Blenheim	Middle Wallop
152	Spitfire	Warmwell

LUFTWAFFE ORDER OF BATTLE IN THE WEST

AUGUST 1940

LUFTFLOTTE 5—NORWAY

X Fliegerkorps
Long-range bombers
KG 26 Stab, I, III He 111
KG 30 Stab, I, III Ju 88
Fighters
ZG 76 I Me 110
JG 77 Stab, I, II Me 109

Coastal reconnaissance and mine-laying
Kü.Fl.Gr. 506 He 115
Long-range reconnaissance
Aufkl.Gr. 22 with Aufkl. Staffel Obdl.
1/F 120 } He 111 and Ju 88
1/F 121 }

LUFTFLOTTE 2—HOLLAND, BELGIUM AND NORTHERN FRANCE

I Fliegerkorps
Long-range bombers
KG 1 Stab, I, II, III
I, II, He 111; III, Ju 88
KG 76 Stab, I, II, III, Lehrstaffel
I, Do 17; II, Ju 88; III, Do 17
Long-range reconnaissance
5/F 122 Ju 88 and He 111
4/F 132 Ju 88, He 111, Me 110

II Fliegerkorps
Long-range bombers
KG 2 Stab, I, II, III Do 17
KG 3 Stab, I, II, III Do 17
KG 53 Stab, I, II, III He 111
Dive-bombers
II/St.G 1 Ju 87
IV/St.LG 1 Ju 87
Fighter-bombers
Erpro 210 Me 109 and Me 110

IX Fliegerdivision[1]
Long-range bombers
KG 4 Stab, I, II, III
I, II, He 111; III, Ju 88

IX Fliegerdivision—cont.
K.Gr. 100 (up to 16.8.40)[2] He 111
Naval co-operation
K.Gr. 40 Stab, I Ju 88
Mine-laying
K.Gr. 126 He 111
Coastal reconnaissance
K.Fl.Gr. 106 He 115 and Do 18

Long-range reconnaissance
3/F 122 Ju 88 and He 111

Jagdfliegerführer 2
Fighters
JG 3 Stab, I, II, III Me 109
JG 26 Stab, I, II, III Me 109
JG 51 Stab, I, II, III Me 109
JG 52 Stab, I, II, III Me 109
JG 54 Stab, I Me 109
ZG 26 Me 110

Jagdfliegerführer 1
In process of formation 22.8.40.

VIII Fliegerkorps
(Transferred to Luftflotte 2 29.8.40)

Dive-bombers

St.G 1 Stab, I, II,	Stab, Do 17 and Ju 87; I, II, Ju 87
St.G 2 Stab, I, II	Stab, Do 17 and Ju 87; I, II, Ju 87
St.G 77 Stab, I, II, III	Stab, Do 17 and Ju 87; I, II, III, Ju 87

Reconnaissance

II/LG 2 (at Boblingen, Germany)	Do 17
2/F 11	Do 17
2/F 123	Ju 88

Fighters

V/ZLG 1	Me 110

V Fliegerkorps

Long-range bombers

KG 51 Stab, I, II, III	Ju 88
KG 54 Stab, I, II	Ju 88

V Fliegerkorps—cont.

KG 55 Stab, I, II, III	He 111

IV Fliegerkorps

Long-range bombers

LG 1 Stab, I, II, III	Ju 88
KG 27 Stab, I, II, III	He 111
K.Gr. 806 (under St.G 3)	Ju 88
K.Gr. 100 (from 16.8.40)	He 111
St.G 3 Stab	Do 17 and He 111

Naval co-operation

KG 40 I	FW 200

Long-range reconnaissance

3/F 31 (from 8.7.40 to 12.8.40 under St.G 3)	Me 110 and Do 17

Jagdfliegerführer 3

Fighters

JG 2 Stab, I, II, III	Me 109
JG 27 Stab, I, II, III	Me 109
JG 53 Stab, I, II, III	Me 109
ZG 2 Stab	Me 110

Notes:

(1) Later IX Fliegerkorps.

(2) K.Gr. 100 Pathfinder and radio beam bombing unit.

Stab=Staff flight which was usually operational.

Night-fighter *Gruppen*, short-range reconnaissance *Gruppen* (Hs 126) and transports are not included in these lists.

OPERATIONS ROOM, 11 GROUP HQ, RAF UXBRIDGE, 15 September 1940

1 Sector name

2 Tote board

3 Colour-coded clock. Plot counters here changed to the corresponding colour on the clock every five minutes.

4 Balloon barrage heights in 1,000s of feet

5 Plotting table

6 P = Pilots
A = Aircraft
92 Squadron has nineteen pilots available on the morning of 15 September and twelve Spitfires

7 German 'plot' with approximate numbers of aircraft attached on top are squadrons intercepting, in this case 92 and 72.

8 Squadron state lights indicate which level, illuminated red, blue, yellow and green for each section

9 Cloud levels over each airfield

10 Visibility at each airfield

Note on the Text

So as not to cause any confusion, I have used German ranks, rather than English translations. I have also called German units by their German names, largely because when writing about something from the German perspective, it seemed odd not to do so. Thus I have called German motor torpedo boats S-boats – as in *Schnellboote* – rather than E-boats, as the British termed them.

Equally, I have referred to German air units in the German terminology, partly to help distinguish them from British units, but also because their units were not quite the same as those in the RAF. The largest Luftwaffe force was the air fleet, or *Luftflotte*, and within each *Luftflotte* were *Fliegerkorps* (air corps). Beneath that there could even be *Fliegerdivisionen*. However, the principal air unit was the *Geschwader*, which contained three *Gruppen*; each *Gruppe* then had three *Staffeln*. Thus 2/JG 2 was the second *Staffel* of the first group of Jagdgeschwader 2. A *Jagdgeschwader* was a fighter unit, a *Kampfgeschwader* a bomber unit. *Staffeln* were always labelled with Arabic numbers, *Gruppen* by Roman numerals. Thus III/KG 4, for example, was the third *Gruppe* of Kampfgeschwader 4. A fighter *Staffel* would have a theoretical establishment of twelve aircraft, but usually an operational number of nine. A bomber *Staffel* would have a theoretical establishment of nine, and an operational number of one or two less.

The RAF did not have an organization based on army structure, but rather was separated into commands, which from Britain were divided into Fighter, Bomber, and Coastal Commands. The principal unit within these commands was the squadron. Fighter squadrons had a theoretical establishment (IE or immediate establishment) of sixteen aircraft, of which at least twelve would be operational. They also had an IE of twenty pilots.

Introduction

'THE BATTLE OF BRITAIN began for me in the Autumn of 1939,' wrote Air Chief Marshal Sir Hugh Dowding in his despatch; after all, that was when Britain and Germany went to war. In the end, however, he opted 'rather arbitrarily' for 10 July 1940 as its starting point, the day the Germans first attacked southern England with a large formation of some seventy aircraft. Dowding was referring to RAF Fighter Command's role that summer and his despatch set the benchmark for how the great aerial clash over Britain has been viewed ever since.

Yet his Spitfires and Hurricanes first properly tussled with the Luftwaffe in May that year, over France, while the intense battle between the two sides was far more all-encompassing than an account of the clash in the air suggests. At every level, from the corridors of power to the man in the street, and from the Field Marshal to the private, or from the skies above to the grey swell of the sea, those summer months of 1940 were a period of extraordinary human drama, of shifting fortunes, of tragedy and triumph – a time when the world changed for ever. For Britain, her very survival was at stake; for Germany, the quick defeat of Britain held the key to her future. For both sides, the stakes could not have been higher.

The time has come to look at those critical months afresh. Dowding was possibly stretching the point too far in suggesting the Battle began with the outbreak of war. But it was with the launch of the western campaign that Britain began to face the worst crisis in her history, while for

Germany 10 May 1940 marked, inextricably, her crossing of the Rubicon. The point of no return.

In these five critical months, the battle encompassed warfare on land and at sea as well as in the air, whilst the British and German governments fought their own political and propaganda battles as well as one for intelligence, all of which had a profound impact on the unfurling events. In isolation, these differing aspects only present part of the story. Together, new and surprising perspectives emerge.

Truly, the Battle of Britain is an incredible story, and even more so when the full picture is revealed. Rarely has there been a more thrilling episode in history.

PART I

MIRACLES

PICTURE
POST

BRITAIN'S WAR-

HULTON'S
NATIONAL
WEEKLY

In this issue:

WAR: FACE TO FACE

MAY 25, 1940

Vol. 7. No. 8

3

1

First Flight

SUNDAY, 5 MAY 1940, a little after two that afternoon. A warm, sunny day over much of Britain, but above Drem aerodrome, a busy grass airfield some twenty miles east of Edinburgh, a deep blue sky was pock-marked with bright white cumulus drifting lazily across the Scottish headland on a gentle breeze. Perfect flying weather, in fact, which was just as well because Pilot Officer David Crook could barely contain his excitement any longer.

Dispersed around one end of the airfield, beside the concrete perimeter track, were the twelve Spitfires of 609 (West Riding) Squadron. Elsewhere, further along around the airfield's edge, were more Spitfires, as well as various other aircraft, including a number of Harvard and Magister trainers. Clutching his leather flying helmet and parachute, David followed his friend and flight commander, Pip Barran, from the wooden dispersal hut towards the line of Spitfires. Groundcrew were busy around several of them, including L.1083, a Mk IA, and one of four that had been delivered to the squadron at the end of the previous August.

David had missed their arrival, although he had seen the squadron's first two Spits land at 609's pre-war base at Yeadon in Yorkshire on 19 August – just a few days after their last peacetime summer camp had ended. Flying ageing Hawker Hind biplanes had been grand enough fun, but the news that the squadron was to convert to Spitfires had been greeted with euphoria by all concerned. Like any man or boy alive, David had wanted to fly one of these beautiful machines ever since he had first heard about them. With its powerful Rolls-Royce Merlin engine and sleek, curving lines, the Spitfire was an ultra-modern machine of barely imaginable power. Moreover, its heritage could not be bettered; Supermarine, its maker, had won the Schneider Trophy – the award given to the fastest aircraft in the world – a decade or so before for the third consecutive time.

Although an Auxiliary Air Force squadron made up of 'weekend fliers', 609 had been mobilized shortly before the outbreak of war. Yet while some of the more experienced pilots had headed straight to Catterick in anticipation of the beginning of hostilities, David and five other Auxiliary pupil pilots had been left behind, first to kick their heels for a month at Yeadon, and then to be sent to complete their flying training.

David had finished his training just a fortnight before, and his leave the previous day. Of the six that had been sent to Flying Training School (FTS), only four were now returning to 609. Two of them, Gordon Mitchell and Michael Appleby, had driven up to Scotland with David the day before, having all met up for lunch in Leeds. They had stopped again for dinner in Alnwick, before finally arriving at Drem in time for reunion drinks in the mess.

It had been good to be back amongst his old friends once more, although there were a number of new faces too, including three regular RAF pilots and four members of the Volunteer Reserve. At first glance they had seemed decent enough, however, and David had been pleased to notice that, despite a new CO, the old atmosphere of 609 was little changed. And Drem seemed like a good spot, with enough hangars and activity to whet the enthusiasm of any keen young pilot, and plenty of golf nearby, as well as tennis and squash courts. Furthermore, Edinburgh, with its mass of pubs and entertainments, was just a short drive away.

Best of all, however, was the prospect of spending many happy hours flying Spitfires. At last! And Pip had been quick to put him out of his misery. A half-hour flight in a Harvard in the morning and then he and the others had been given the all-clear to take the Spitfire up.

The wheels of the petrol bowser had left their impression in the grass and the smell of high-octane aviation fuel was still strong as David and Pip reached L.1083. The two groundcrew – the plane's fitter and rigger – were still finishing preparing the aircraft for flight as Pip led David around the Spitfire for the external checks, stepping carefully over the lead from the accumulator trolley that fed into the cowling. With his helmet now on, and his parachute strapped and dangling slightly from his backside, David then climbed on to the root of the port wing and, at Pip's instruction, hoisted himself over the half-door and down into the cockpit. Clambering on to the wing beside him, Pip then talked him through any unfamiliar aspects of the plane, reminded him of the settings, and then, with a cheery smile, jumped down and left him to it.

David kept the rounded canopy pushed back behind his seat as he clipped his radio leads on to his helmet. The cockpit was narrow – just three feet wide – but even for a man of decent height and build like David it did not feel cramped: he could move his arms easily enough, while his feet rested comfortably on the pale green metal pedals. The smell was distinctive – as it was in all aircraft; a mixture of oil, metal, hydraulic fluid, sweat, rubber and fuel. Not unpleasant at all; reassuring, rather.

Elevator set, rudder fully pushed to the right. Flaps up, artificial horizon set. With his left hand, David set the throttle next to his knee to the start-up position, switched on the radio button and then, with his right hand, turned the engine start isolation switch to 'on'. He unscrewed the priming plunger locknut and began priming the engine. Magneto switches on. Fuel selector on. Glancing out, he saw the groundcrew, then he leaned forward slightly to the bottom centre of the panel and with the index and middle fingers of his right hand simultaneously pressed the engine start and booster coil buttons. As the engine began to turn he vigorously worked the priming pump until, after a few seconds, and with a lick of flame and a belch of smoke from the exhaust stubs, the mighty Merlin roared into life. He carried out his magneto checks, then gave a nod to the groundcrew, who now pulled the chocks clear. A voice from control – he was clear to roll.

The noise was incredible. The airframe was shaking, the engine growling angrily, so that even though the sound was muffled by his tightly fitting flying helmet and earpieces, it was still a throbbing roar. In front of him, blocking his forward view entirely, was the engine cowling, pointing imperiously skywards, the propeller a faint whirr. Glancing out, he saw the groundcrew unplug the lead from the accumulator trolley and pull it clear. Then hearing the static-distorted voice of the ground controller give him the all-clear, he acknowledged, released the brakes and felt the Spitfire roll forward.

Zig-zagging slowly so that he could see what was ahead of him, he successfully manoeuvred the beast to the end of the grass runway and then paused one more time to check that everything was OK. Engine temperature was already 100 degrees – it had risen alarmingly quickly. He glanced again at the dials, tightened the primer locknut, and then opened the throttle.

The effect took his breath away. The engine powered up with a smooth roar and the Spitfire leapt forward like a bullet, the fuselage almost trying to twist from the huge torque from the Merlin. Easing the stick forward slightly as he'd been told to do, he felt the fuselage rise and the cowling lower so that at last he could see ahead of him. Then, before David barely knew what was happening, the Spitfire was hurtling at ninety miles per hour and then the shuddering along the ground stopped and he felt the plane slip seamlessly into the air. He had never known such power; it was like driving a Grand Prix racing car having just stepped out of an ageing Morris and for a moment he felt as though the machine was completely running away with him.

As he continued to climb, he managed to collect his scattered wits, raised the undercarriage, made sure the temperatures and pressure were stabilized, and then turned the propeller to coarse pitch. Glancing backwards, he was astonished to see the airfield already far, far behind him. It was hard not to smile.

After cruising over the Lothians for a few minutes, however, David began to realize that his Spitfire was perhaps not quite as formidable as he had first thought during the first breathless moments, so with his confidence rising he decided to take the plane back for a bumps and circuit. This he managed without too much difficulty, touching back down and then promptly taking off again and feeling altogether more comfortable.

Climbing high into the clouds in this remarkable new toy he swirled and pirouetted through the early-summer sky, performing gentle dives that saw his air speed indicator rise to as much as 400 miles per hour. It was fabulously thrilling, a brief time of unbridled joy. As he was very quickly discovering, it did not take long to become accustomed to the Spitfire's great power and speed, and once this adjustment had been made, it was an extraordinarily easy machine to fly and a quite superb aircraft for performing aerobatics.

After an hour he landed back at Drem, rolling the Spitfire across the grass to its dispersal around the perimeter. Having shut down the engine, he pushed back the canopy once more. He felt quite light-headed with exhilaration; his life irrevocably changed. 'Practically everybody who has flown a Spitfire thinks it is the most marvellous aircraft ever built,' he noted, 'and I am no exception to the rule.'

Not for nothing was the RAF known as the best flying club in the world. By the beginning of the war, flying was still a comparatively new phenomenon, and those fortunate enough to get their chance to take to the air found largely empty skies in which the world seemed to be their oyster. For David, a 25-year-old sport-loving Yorkshireman, the Auxiliary Air Force had meant that he could work in the family sports goods manufacturing business in Huddersfield by week and fly at the weekend with lots of like-minded friends. Although being in the air force had, with the onset of war, become a full-time occupation, David was enjoying himself enormously, despite having to leave his young wife at home. At FTS he had made even more friends, was finding flying as rewarding and exhilarating as ever, and now, at the beginning of May, had finally been given the chance of a lifetime: to fly the already fabled Spitfire. The war – and the prospect of one day fighting for his life in a bitter aerial conflict – was barely given a thought.

2

The Eve of Battle

David Crook flew L.1083 twice more on 6 May, and again on the 7th and 8th. On Thursday, 9 May, he practised both aerial attacks and formation flying, then was given the afternoon off, so with several of his friends from the squadron he went into Edinburgh for a 'grand evening' including a slap-up dinner and an uproarious variety performance at the Empire. Life in 609 Squadron could hardly have been more enjoyable.

As David had been carrying out his ninth and tenth Spitfire flights on that May Thursday, the world must have seemed a very calm and peaceful place. Through the light puffs of cloud, he would have seen Scotland stretching away from him, Edinburgh nestling against the Firth of Forth and then, to the north, the rolling coast and, inland, the mountains of Perthshire. The country looked a much smaller place from even 6,000 feet. He would also have seen the North Sea, deep, dark and forbidding, with ships, small lines of white wake following behind, dotting the vast expanse of water as they ferried freight around the British Isles. Fishermen, too, continued to head out to sea, making their way carefully through the channels between the extensive minefields that had been laid all along the Scottish and English east coast.

It would have been a scene that after four days back with the squadron would have already felt utterly familiar. It was almost as though the country were not at war at all. Yet, far across the sea, on mainland Europe, these were the last hours of calm. Some 900 miles away, in Berlin, Adolf Hitler, the Führer of the German Reich, was in his study dictating a proclamation to his forces gathering on the Western Front. The new Reich Chancellery that stretched all the way along Voss-strasse in the heart of the German capital had been designed by Hitler's architect, Albert Speer. Despite being more than 1,400 feet long and containing not only vast rooms and galleries but a massive underground bunker system, the new headquarters of the Reich had been completed in less than a year by 4,500 workers operating in shifts around the clock, for seven days a week. The Führer's study was naturally at the new building's heart, with five towering six-metre-high French windows looking out on to a tree-lined courtyard beyond. There was a large marble map table by the centre window, and a portrait of Bismarck – one of his heroes – above the fireplace, beneath which were a long sofa and a number of armchairs. At the other end of the room was Hitler's specially designed writing desk. Otherwise there was very little. Just space. Hitler's outsize study was 27 metres long and 14.5 wide.

X-Day – as the Germans called the start of Hitler's long-anticipated offensive in the West – had been set on 1 May for five days' time. Four days later, he postponed it until 7 May and then, finally, at the request of Feldmarschall Göring, his deputy and the commander of the Luftwaffe, he postponed it again for a further three days. But that would be it. No more postponements; the fateful hour would be dawn on Friday, 10 May.

Now, as Hitler walked the expanse of his study dictating to his secretary, there was less than eighteen hours to go. By the next morning, his air fleets would be raining bombs over the Low Countries, his armies marching forward, punching their way through Luxembourg, Holland and Belgium. 'The battle which begins today,' he concluded in his proclamation, 'will decide the fate of the German nation for the next thousand years. Now do your duty.'

It was Hitler's way to describe decisions as unavoidable do-or-die choices; his view of life was largely black or white, with few shades of grey. This also justified his gambler's approach. Yet, in this case, he really did have no choice. He had thought Britain and France were bluffing with their threats to uphold Poland's independence, that they were mere words. After all, they had stood by and watched when he moved back into the Rhineland, again during the *Anschluss* of Austria, and then once again during his occupation of both the Sudetenland and then the rest of Czechoslovakia. Why should Poland be any different?

It was Britain who had declared war first, on the morning of Sunday, 3 September. When Hitler heard the news he had sat immobile, gazing blankly before him. Eventually, he turned to his Foreign Minister, Joachim von Ribbentrop, and with a savage look asked, 'What now?' In the days that followed, he had time to answer that question for himself. It soon became clear that neither Britain nor France had any intention of going on the offensive – at least, not for the time being. That meant he would have to strike first. He had always known that at some point he would have to deal with the Western powers and Britain in particular. He had nothing but contempt for the French but he did admire the British and their Empire. Yet although he had gambled on her not declaring war over Poland, he had recognized that Britain would need subduing before he could continue with his expansion programme. The need for living space – *Lebensraum* – lay at the heart of his plans for the Third Reich.

Thus Britain was the most dangerous enemy. 'Our enemy Number One,' Hitler had told Speer, as early as 1937. It was Britain that had led the talks at Munich back in September 1938 and it was Britain that had been most vocal in her protestations against the German absorption of Czechoslovakia in March 1939. From that time onwards, right up until the outbreak of war, it had been Britain, more so than France, that had continued to denounce Hitler's plans; Britain that had first threatened to uphold Poland's independence. 'England is our enemy,' Hitler had told his Minister for Propaganda, Josef Goebbels, 'and the showdown with England is a matter of life and death.'

Nonetheless, since the outbreak of war, Hitler had been wracked by doubts. In the build-up to the invasion of Denmark and Norway in April, he had devoured kilos of pralines. 'They are nerve food,' he had said. Now, however, after months of nervous agitation, the Führer was confident and calm; the doubts that had tormented him continually since the invasion of Poland had been put to one side. In his opinion, he told his inner circle, France would roll over in six weeks, and then Britain would settle terms. She would have to. Continuing from such a weakened position would mean losing her Empire and that was unimaginable. Therefore, after France fell, Britain would sue for peace. Europe would then be subdued, allowing him to return to the process of building up strength before turning his attentions eastwards.

Even so, it was a huge gamble, and Hitler knew it. He had fewer men than the Western Allies, with 135 divisions compared to 151. He had fewer guns – 7,378 whereas the Allies could call on some 14,000, of which 10,700 alone were French. Germany had fewer tanks than France as well – 2,439 as opposed to the French army's 3,254. And Germany even had fewer operational aircraft than the Allies. Normal military practice is not to attack unless holding a superiority of numbers of at least three to one, and ideally higher than that. Hitler's forces had nothing like that advantage. But he did, he hoped, have surprise. And a strikingly original plan that he was increasingly confident would work.

Hitler might have been sure of its success, but this was because he had little operational or strategic understanding. How could he? His military career had ended on the Western Front in 1918, by which time he had risen no higher than corporal. Over twenty years later, despite his obvious intelligence and ability to absorb information, it was only his power and authority, rather than any military acumen, which qualified him to be a war chief.

Certainly many of his commanders had serious doubts, and with some reason. The plan was for one group of armies, Army Group B, to thrust their way across into the neutral Low Countries, drawing the French – and British Expeditionary Force – forward to meet the threat. At the same time, a larger force, Army Group A, spearheaded by panzer and mechanized divisions, would burst through the dense Ardennes forests, and cross the River Meuse. Then, having taken the French completely off guard, the panzers would charge forward towards the coast, thus isolating the majority of the French, British and Belgian forces in a massive encirclement. Most of the Luftwaffe were to operate in the north, supporting Army Group B, which in turn would help deceive the enemy into thinking it was in the north that the main German effort was coming.

The flaw in using the Luftwaffe in such a way was that it would leave Army Group A dangerously unprotected from the sky as it clawed its way through the Ardennes. The number of men, vehicles, horses and carts involved in the Ardennes thrust was staggering. Put toe to tail, the spearhead alone had a march movement length of nearly a thousand miles. For ten days or more, the roads passing through the Ardennes would be clogged with traffic, the juiciest of targets for any determined Allied bombers.

And that concern aside, the majority of the German commanders had neither understanding of nor faith in the tactical concept being suggested – namely that a fast, highly mobile tank force could be used to drive a far-reaching hole into the not inconsiderable French defences. To many, it seemed that only a miracle could possibly bring them victory.

*

The idea of this mobile thrust through the Ardennes had been put forward by General Erich von Manstein after considerable discussion with Generalleutnant Heinz Guderian, a dynamic and deep-thinking soldier who had already written *Achtung Panzer!*, a treatise on the employment of tanks in modern warfare, two years earlier. Jealousy and mistrust had ensured that von Manstein had long since been sidelined, but Guderian had not, and was now, on the morning of 9 May, preparing to lead Panzer Corps Guderian, containing three of the Wehrmacht's best armoured divisions, as the spearhead for the drive towards the Meuse and then, with luck, to the English Channel.

As one of the principal architects of the entire offensive plan, the 51-year-old Guderian had complete faith in its potential, but also considerable concerns as to whether his superiors would allow it to unfold in the way he hoped. An unusual and untested grouping of three corps – of which his was one – had been placed under the command of Generaloberst Ewald von Kleist, who, Guderian was well aware, was no great enthusiast for mobile warfare. Nor was Generaloberst Gerd von Rundstedt, commander of Army Group A. At planning conferences, Guderian's heart had sunk as it became clear that von Rundstedt had little idea about the potential of tanks. He also revealed his complete lack of understanding of the battle plan when he told Guderian and von Kleist that he preferred a more cautious approach to battle. Senior German commanders were far from singing from the same hymn sheet, yet since Guderian knew that it would be up to his three lead divisions to make the critical breakthrough over the Meuse at Sedan, he had done his very best to avoid consulting with his superiors, and to train his men in the way that he wanted; to prepare them for the task that he had envisaged.

At 1.30 p.m. that Thursday he received the orders to prepare to move. The task ahead was an enormous one. Everything depended on maintaining surprise and breaking through the main objective before the French caught wind of what was going on and brought up the substantial reserves they had at their disposal. That required sticking to a very tight timetable. It meant Guderian's spearhead had to reach the Meuse at Sedan and get across in just four days. Yet before he even reached the River Meuse, his men had to cross the Luxembourg border barriers, then the first Belgian fortification line, and, thirdly, the second Belgian fortification line. After these obstacles, there was the River Semois, which was bound to be defended, and finally there were the French border fortifications, which lay some six miles in front of the Meuse.

Despite this, despite the hindrances from above, and despite the very real threat of aerial attack, Guderian left his headquarters at Koblenz later that afternoon with spirits as confident as those of his Führer. He had complete trust in his commanders and knew his men were highly trained and ready; each man knew his task and what was expected of him. Nothing, he believed, had been left to chance. And yet for it to succeed, he would need good fortune. Plenty of good fortune.

Both France and Britain had been expecting a German offensive in the west for some time. Even though theirs was a modern world, the obvious campaigning season was spring and summer and so since the particularly harsh winter had ebbed away, they had been increasingly aware that Hitler could strike at any moment.

Nonetheless, in Westminster, the political capital of Britain, the attention of the nation's leaders was less on Germany, that May Thursday, and more on their own survival. Britain was in the midst of a drastic political crisis. For the past two days, a debate had been going on in the House of Commons over the Government's handling of the war to date and specifically the campaign in Norway, which had begun on 9 April. British forces, under-equipped and without sufficient air support, had been soundly beaten in their first clash on land with German forces, and in a subsequent vote of confidence the Prime Minister had suffered a crippling moral defeat.

Despite the numerous news programmes on the radio and the detailed accounts of the debate in the papers, however, these dramatic events seem to have passed over the heads of many in Britain that morning. Certainly, it made little impression on David Crook and his fellow pilots, for example. Young men with Spitfires to fly might have found all this politicking of little interest, yet there were few signs of it causing much of a stir in the Surrey village of Tadworth either. 'Out this morning,' wrote 37-year-old Daidie Penna, 'people didn't seem to have much to say of the Government's stormy passage. I think they've got into the habit these days of concentrating on their own lives and trying to exclude the unpredictable and rapidly varying international situations.' Although a housewife and mother of three, Daidie was also a writer and artist, intelligent and opinionated. She had a further particular interest in politics because an old family friend was a Labour Opposition MP, Herbert Morrison. Decidedly left of centre herself, Daidie was certainly no admirer of the Prime Minister, Neville Chamberlain, who she wished would be kicked out of office as soon as possible. Two days before, on 7 May, as the Norway debate had begun, she had wondered whether Chamberlain would be let off the hook, as it seemed to her he always was. 'If we allow him to remain in office,' she typed in her diary, 'I feel we might just as well save what we can and come to terms with Hitler at once. It is amazing – the blindness of this man – he seems so completely enveloped in the fog of his own complacency.'

A few days earlier, most in Westminster would have agreed with Daidie that Chamberlain had been unlikely to lose his job as a result of the debate. And yet what had begun as an attempt to censure the Prime Minister now looked to have escalated so much that, despite a whopping majority of more than 240 seats, the Prime Minister had been left fighting for his political life. Daidie was delighted – and even more so to read in the paper that Thursday morning that Herbert Morrison had been one of the politicians leading the attacks the day before.

Later that day, Daidie did find someone in the village who was willing to discuss the news with her, however – a neighbour and former pacifist Daidie called 'Mrs G'. Despite what the papers were saying, Mrs G told Daidie she still thought it very unlikely Chamberlain would go. 'You know how obstinate old people can be,' she said. Hitler had made him look silly. 'If he resigns it means that to all intents and purposes Hitler has got the better of him again.' Then Daidie asked her what she would do were there to be a German invasion of England. Her friend looked at her blankly for a moment then burst out laughing. 'Oh but that's absurd,' she said, 'a ridiculous idea.'

Watching the Norway debate from the Commons gallery was the 51-year-old United States Ambassador to Great Britain, Joseph P. Kennedy, a dapper man, with a broad face, pale eyes, a high forehead and round, horn-rimmed spectacles. Joe Kennedy had been posted to London two years before. An enormously wealthy businessman, he had made his fortune on the stock market and in commodity broking, before turning his hand to real estate, bootlegging from Canada during Prohibition, and then moving to Hollywood, where he created RKO Pictures. In the 1930s he had made a move into politics, providing much of the funding for Roosevelt's first successful bid for the Presidency in 1932. He had been rewarded, not with a Cabinet post, but with the position of the inaugural Chairman of the Securities and Exchange Committee. His reforming work in this post gained him wide respect, particularly at a time when America was emerging from the Depression.

His appointment as Ambassador had raised a few eyebrows both sides of the Atlantic, however. Although his bootlegging had never been proved, there was the faint whiff of the crook that accompanied him, while he was also known as mercurial and as something of a philandering Irish Catholic rogue, and a man who liked to call a spade a spade; his style was plain talking with no bull rather than the subtle language of diplomacy. Yet he was also undeniably energetic, ebullient and fabulously well connected. Furthermore, he had been accompanied to London by his bright, beautiful and apparently charming family – his wife, Rose, and their nine children. Very quickly the Kennedys had been embraced by British society. His second daughter, Kathleen, had been the 'most exciting debutante' of 1938, while Eunice, his third and no less beautiful daughter, had 'come out' in 1939. His elder sons, Joseph Junior and Jack, were clever and worldly and had become leading social figures, much photographed and discussed in the gossip columns and diaries of Britain's national papers.

Although vehemently anti-communist and unashamedly anti-Semitic, Kennedy most strongly believed that there should be peace at all costs, and that America should and could stay well out of European squabbles. Unsurprisingly, then, he had soon allied himself to Chamberlain and the appeasement policy that was dominating British politics at the time of his arrival as Ambassador. Indeed, he came to know Chamberlain well and considered him a good friend. Thus it was that he had watched the closing debate in the Commons with no satisfaction whatsoever.

The results of the vote of no confidence had been read out by the Speaker just after 11 p.m. Although Chamberlain was Prime Minister of a National (that is, coalition) Government of Conservatives, National Liberals, National Labour and Nationals, the majority were Tory MPs like himself. Only around forty Conservatives had voted against him, but a number had abstained, and with the votes of the Opposition the Government's majority had been cut to a mere eighty-one. That was nowhere near enough to bring down a Prime Minister in peacetime; but in times of war it was a very different matter.

The results had prompted, first, a gasp around the packed House, and then pandemonium had ensued.

An ashen and rather shell-shocked Chamberlain had walked stiffly from the Commons amidst jeers and taunts of 'Missed the bus!', 'Get out!'

and 'Go, in the name of God, go!', while another Tory rebel, Harold Macmillan, began singing 'Rule Britannia' before being silenced by irate supporters of the Prime Minister. A more sensitive man than his sometimes austere persona suggested, Chamberlain had been profoundly humiliated by events. 'Everybody was shocked,' Joe Kennedy wrote in his diary the following day. 'The Prime Minister looked stunned and although he appeared to carry it off, he looked to me like a definitely beaten man.'

In the lobby afterwards, Kennedy met Lady Astor, who told the Ambassador that she thought Chamberlain would have to fall and that Halifax, the Foreign Secretary, should take over. He then went to see the Canadian press baron Lord Beaverbrook, to get his slant on the situation. He too thought Chamberlain would go. The following morning, Kennedy spoke with President Roosevelt on the telephone and heard the news that Germany had just delivered an ultimatum to Holland. Later, at the Admiralty, he saw Winston Churchill, and the Minister for Air, Sir Samuel Hoare, and relayed the news about Germany. 'A terrible world this is getting to be,' Churchill told him. 'There really doesn't seem to be much hope anywhere, does there?' added Hoare.

Despite the predictions given to Kennedy the previous evening, the 71-year-old Prime Minister had woken early that Thursday morning, 9 May, determined to fight his corner. The Government whips had busied themselves trying to discover what concessions the Government would have to make to win back the rebels' support, while Chamberlain's Parliamentary Private Secretary invited leading back-benchers to No. 10 to discuss grievances. Chamberlain even offered Leo Amery, the man who more than anyone had landed the killer blow during the debate, a choice of the Chancellorship of the Exchequer or Foreign Secretary, but the Prime Minister's assassin refused.

Yet Amery was not the only Tory rebel in no mood for either concessions or olive branches; clearly the revolt had lost none of its momentum after a night of reflection. It was also becoming apparent that a consensus was emerging that a full cross-party coalition was needed – one that included Labour and the Liberals too. Chamberlain hoped he might yet lead this new administration but was conscious that neither Clement Attlee, the Labour leader, nor Arthur Greenwood, the other most prominent Labour MP, was likely to serve under him.

By 10.15 a.m., then, when Lord Halifax arrived at No. 10 to talk with him, Chamberlain knew that the hopes of dawn had been dashed and that he would almost certainly have to resign – and, as Lady Astor had suggested, hand over to Halifax. A former Viceroy of India, a hugely experienced politician and a man widely respected for his sound judgement, Lord Halifax was certainly top of Chamberlain's list as successor. In fact, he was the outstanding candidate. Most of the other leading Tories were either too young, lacked sufficient following, were too unpopular or were too inexperienced. There was, however, one exception: a man with unrivalled experience; a man who had held Cabinet posts over a forty-year parliamentary career that included the Home Office, Chancellorship of the Exchequer and the Admiralty; a man who had been a soldier as well as a statesman; a man who, despite eight long years in the political wilderness, had returned to the Cabinet on the outbreak of war and was one of the most dominant personalities in the country. He was Winston Churchill.

Nonetheless, despite his many favourable attributes, there was much mistrust of Churchill amongst many Conservatives. He was seen as a maverick, inconsistent and hot-headed; a man who drank too much. His methods were unorthodox. There was a lot of mud on him that he had been unable to shake off: he was the architect of the disastrous Dardanelles campaign of 1915, for example, and Chancellor during the General Strike of 1926. In more recent times he had fought hard against the Government over Indian independence, and against Chamberlain's appeasement policy with Germany; he had sided with Edward VIII during the abdication crisis of 1937, which had further distanced him from the establishment. And although he had largely avoided censure during the two-day debate, he had been the biggest advocate of the Norwegian campaign amongst the Cabinet. Thus for all his enormous energy, drive and undoubted oratorical skills, he was widely regarded as a man lacking sound judgement. And a man unsuited to the highest office.

Therefore most people assumed that, should Chamberlain go, it would be Halifax who took over. Safe, sound, solid. He could expect wide support from the majority of the Tories, but would also be acceptable to the Opposition in an all-party coalition. Of less importance, but not insignificant, was his close friendship with the King and Queen. Halifax had even been given a key to the Buckingham Palace gardens.

However, at their meeting that morning, Halifax – already aware that he was Chamberlain's and most others' preferred choice and feeling consequently ill with a psychosomatic bout of nausea – told the Prime

Minister he would be very reluctant to take over the reins. It would be difficult, he told Chamberlain, for a Prime Minister sitting in the House of Lords to have the necessary contact with the centre of gravity in the Commons. This, Chamberlain argued, could be resolved one way or another, and, in any case, in a coalition government there would be almost no opposition to deal with anyway. Even so, Halifax stuck to his guns, his stomach ache worsening.

He knew, however, as did Chamberlain, that whoever succeeded as Prime Minister needed to be acceptable to the Conservatives, to Labour and to the King. After this meeting it was obvious that the only other person who could possibly succeed was Churchill. If Labour refused to serve under him, or if the King put his foot down, then, Halifax conceded, he might be forced to think again.

Later that afternoon, Chamberlain had talks with his unpopular Chancellor, Sir John Simon, who offered to resign and suggested that, if it would help, then Sir Samuel Hoare, the equally unpopular Minister for Air, should also resign. With no final decision yet made, at 4.30 p.m. Chamberlain went into a meeting with the Chief Whip, Captain David Margesson, and also Halifax and Churchill, who had just arrived at No. 10. Margesson had already told Chamberlain that the Commons would prefer Halifax.

The four sat down and Chamberlain told them he had made up his mind that he should go but that he would be happy to serve under Halifax or Churchill. Margesson added that in the interests of unity he believed Chamberlain was making the right decision, although he did not say which of Halifax and Churchill it should be to succeed. Halifax, whose stomach ache started anew, then repeated his reluctance to take over, again citing the impotence he felt he would have as a peer while Churchill ran defence and, effectively, the Commons.

This was the nub of it. Halifax, rather than holding no ambition for office, believed that at this point he would merely be a lame-duck Prime Minister while Churchill took effective control. Far better for the country, he believed, if Churchill was PM while he, as Foreign Secretary, acted as a restraining influence from within the Cabinet. Yet while someone who felt sick at the mere thought of becoming PM was possibly not the best candidate, Halifax was aware of his own more pertinent shortcomings: he was not particularly interested in military matters; nor did he know much about them. Churchill, on the other hand, loved war and warfare and all matters military; he always had done and had a fine war record that had prompted talk of Victoria Crosses on more than one occasion. He had served at Omdurman, and in South Africa during the Anglo–Boer War, during which he had daringly escaped from captivity while a prisoner of war. Unlike Halifax, Chamberlain, or even Hoare and Simon, Churchill had served in the First World War too, commanding his battalion on the Western Front after resigning from Government in 1915.

The first hurdle over the succession was thus decided. Chamberlain left Halifax and Churchill to have a pot of tea together while he waited for the Labour delegation of Attlee and Greenwood to arrive. They did so at 6.15 p.m. Despite what he had said earlier about resigning, Chamberlain, still the Prime Minister, then asked them whether they would serve under him in a full coalition government, and, if not him, then somebody else. He did not name the someone else. Attlee and Greenwood told him they would ask the party's National Executive, who were in Bournemouth at their annual Party conference, although Attlee confessed bluntly that his own view was that Labour would not have him remain PM, and he added, 'I think I am right in saying the country won't have you either.' They left having promised to telephone through the answers as soon as they had them.

Meanwhile, Churchill had returned to the Admiralty. Later that evening, his son Randolph rang him from his Territorial unit and asked him the news. 'I think,' Churchill told him, 'I shall be Prime Minister tomorrow.'

Hitler had managed to maintain a high level of secrecy over his plans for the attack in the west, which was codenamed *Fall Gelb* – 'Case Yellow'. Even those in his close entourage had little idea what was afoot when, on the afternoon of 9 May, they were told to prepare to travel. Around 5 p.m., Hitler left the Reich Chancellery, climbing into an open-top Mercedes escorted by only plain-clothes detectives and members of the SD.* Following behind were various members of his staff, including the 32-year-old Christa Schroeder, who had faithfully been serving the Führer as one of his secretaries since 1933, when Hitler had first become Chancellor. At first she thought they must be heading to Staaken, but

* SD was the Nazi abbreviation of the Sicherheitsdienst, the Nazi secret intelligence service. On the whole, Germans preferred abbreviations to acronyms, unlike the British. 'Nazi' is also an abbreviation – of National Sozialistische Deutsche Arbeiter Partei, the German National Socialist Workers' Party.

then they drove on, past the airfield. Eventually, they came to a halt in the forecourt of the small station, where an unusual train stood waiting.

This was *Amerika*, the Führer Train – ten extremely long, dark green, armour-plated coaches pulled by two steam locomotives. Hitler was in a relaxed, confident mood still. Over the years, Christa had learned to tell his mood from his tone of voice, and now it was clear and exact, his face often breaking into smiles. The Führer had turned fifty-one just under three weeks before. A chronic hypochondriac, he felt sure his health was slipping away; it was one of the reasons he was in such a hurry – he needed to achieve his ambitions before it was too late. His pale eyes, however, were still bright, and his hair was still mostly dark, as was his distinct moustache, kept partly for its obvious identity value and partly to hide his large nose. 'My nose is much too big,' he had once said. 'I need the moustache to relieve the effect.'

Still Christa had no idea where they were headed. Nor, it seemed, did her fellow secretary, Gerda Daranowski, or Hitler's press chief, Otto Dietrich. At dinner in the dining car, Hitler's army adjutant, Generalleutnant Rudolf Schmundt, joked, 'Have you all got your sea-sick pills?' Christa immediately concluded they must be headed to Norway. Hitler then teased, 'If you are good, you might be able to bring home a sealskin trophy.'

Christa Schroeder may have been in the dark, literally and metaphorically, as *Amerika* puffed its way through the wide forests of northern Germany, but along the German border the men detailed to launch the great offensive were finally being briefed. Army Group A had just seven panzer and three mechanized divisions. Eight of those were in the specially formed Panzer Group Kleist, of which Guderian's corps was to provide the point of main effort. But while Panzer Group Kleist was to mount a second supporting crossing with General Georg-Hans Reinhardt's three divisions a little further north of Guderian's corps at Monthermé, a third was planned twenty miles north still, at Dinant, by two panzer divisions that were part of the Fourth Army and quite separate from Panzer Group Kleist.

One of these was the 7th Panzer Division commanded by a thrusting young Major-General named Erwin Rommel, who as an infantryman had won Germany's highest award for bravery in the First World War, the *Pour le Mérite*, or, as it was more widely known, the Blue Max. Rommel had been a late convert to mobile armoured warfare but since taking over

7th Panzer that February had embraced the tactics of Guderian and von Manstein wholeheartedly. Key to the operations of such units were the reconnaissance battalions, made up of motorcycles, armoured scout cars and half-tracks. Their role was to push forward some miles ahead of the rest of the division, scouting and probing for signs of resistance and points of weakness that could then be exploited. The emphasis was very much on dash and speed.

One of the company commanders in the 7th Armoured Reconnaissance Battalion was Hauptmann Hans von Luck, a 28-year-old career soldier from Flensburg. Despite his classical schooling – he could speak both Latin and Ancient Greek as well as English, French and Russian – his was a Prussian family with a long tradition of military service. Having left the Monastery School in Flensburg at seventeen, he had immediately joined the army. There he had remained ever since, serving under, amongst others, General Guderian, and later taking part with the rest of the division in the brief Polish campaign.

Although Hans and his comrades had been training hard all spring, they were equally uncertain as to when and in what precise form the offensive would take place. Not until a week earlier had they been given some warning that an attack was imminent, when they had been ordered to the Eifel mountains on the border of Germany and Luxembourg. The older and reserve officers amongst them who had served in the last war were quick to warn the younger ones such as Hans that France would not be a walkover like Poland. 'The French and British,' they said, 'are quite different opponents.' Hans listened but felt sure there neither would – nor could – be a return to the kind of static trench warfare of the Great War. 'We youngsters thought always of Guderian and his flashing eyes when he explained his tactics to us,' he noted. During exercises, Hans had soon concluded that Rommel was also the right commander for the task, despite his infantry background.

That evening, Hans and the other company commanders were summoned to see their commanding officer, Major Erdmann, who told them that in the morning they would be marching into neutral Belgium. Initial resistance at the frontier had to be quickly overcome; their goal was the River Meuse at Dinant. They would be amongst the spearhead through the Ardennes. 'Our reconnaissance battalion,' he told them, 'can take pride in being at the forefront of the division.' For Hans and all his comrades, that was a singular honour.

Also stationed in the Eifel region was the 24th Artillery Battalion, part of the 87th Infantry Division. Leutnant Siegfried Knappe, twenty-three years old, was another career soldier. Although his pre-war battalion had served in Poland, Siegfried had been one of 20 per cent of officers who had remained behind to form a new battalion. The forthcoming offensive thus promised to be his first taste of action – not that he had been in the slightest bit aware that an offensive was even imminent. Moving closer to the border a few days earlier had not aroused his suspicions because it was normal for them to move frequently; it helped prevent complacency.

Even so, Siegfried was one of the first to learn the news when he was summoned to see his CO, Major Raake, that evening, 9 May. 'Be ready to issue an alert at 5 a.m.,' Raake told him. 'This is not an exercise. It is the real thing. We are invading tomorrow.'

'Jawohl, Herr Major,' Siegfried replied. Although very surprised by this sudden turn of events, he quickly set about his tasks. As adjutant, it was his job to make sure that all the details and orders were correctly worked out and that everything went to plan.

To the north, the men of Army Group B were also being briefed for battle. Near the town of Walbeck, twenty miles or so west of Duisburg on the German–Dutch border, was the 171st Infantry Regiment, part of the 56th Infantry Division. Thirty-two-year-old Hellmuth Damm, a former teacher and choirmaster from Dresden, was an *Unteroffizier* – sergeant – in the 4th Machine-Gun Company of the 1st Battalion. Drawn into service as a reservist five years before, he had then been fully mobilized the previous August, three days before war began. Leaving his wife and young daughter in Dresden, he had joined his battalion and soon after found himself marching through Slovakia on his way to Poland.

As army reserves, they had not taken part in any fighting; the only shot his company had fired during the whole campaign had been when a cook killed a pig. In fact, having marched more than 300 miles, they had then been put on trains and transported back west, all across Poland and Germany until they reached the Eifel region along the Reich's West Wall. A further march north took them to Walbeck, where they had been training and helping to build border defences ever since.

Now, on the evening of 9 May, the battalion received the code word that told them they would be going into action. This would be no exercise. Immediately, Hellmuth and the rest of the company gathered their kit and set off, as they had trained to do, across a rough moor that led them to the Dutch border. In Hellmuth's *Gruppe* he had two MG08s, water-cooled heavy machine guns that had been the mainstay of the German army in the last war and were little more than a variation on the original Maxim gun, invented more than fifty years earlier. Old and cumbersome it may have been, but the MG08 was reliable, could fire 400 rounds per minute, and had an effective range of more than a mile. That made it a pretty useful weapon, even in the fast-developing world of 1940.

Reaching their forward positions, Hellmuth and his men halted. No-one was sure when they would be ordered to attack, but dawn the following morning seemed likely. The first big obstacle was the River Meuse – or Maas as it was called by the Dutch – and the task of Hellmuth and his men was to find a building whose first floor had a view of the river, set up their MG, and then provide cover for the assault engineers as they attempted to cross the water in rubber boats. Feeling tense, apprehensive and expectant, Siegfried found sleep hard to come by, even though it was a warm, still night.

It was now just a few hours until the static *Sitzkrieg* of the past nine months would be over. The point of no return had arrived. The clash against the might of Britain and France was about to begin.

3

The Go-for-Broke Gamble

AT HALF-PAST MIDNIGHT, the Führer Train seamlessly switched tracks, and instead of continuing north towards Hamburg began steaming west. Hitler had been on sparkling form, which had spread throughout the train creating a lively, buoyant atmosphere. Four hours later, *Amerika* finally hissed to a stop. It was still dark. The station had been stripped of its place name, but it was Euskirchen, a small German town between Bonn and Aachen, close to the Belgian border. Heading out into the clear, chill morning air, Hitler and his entourage clambered into a six-wheeled Mercedes. Christa Schroeder sat in the car as first light revealed nameless villages as they sped by. Eventually, they halted in a hilly, wooded region before a command bunker dug deep into the side of the hill, which, she soon learned, was to be Hitler's new temporary Führer Headquarters. Its name was Felsennet, and at some 1,200 feet high the hidden entrance held a commanding view towards the Belgian border less than twenty miles to the west.

Around the same time as the Führer Train had come to a halt, Siegfried Knappe was already up and ready, mounted on his horse, Schwabenprinz, checking the batteries to make sure the cooks had their fires going and the men were being roused before the alert was given. Half an hour later, at 5 a.m. exactly, Siegfried was able to report to his boss that each battery was in position and ready to move out the moment the orders arrived.

Siegfried would have a long wait, but for those in the vanguard of the advance, the moment had finally arrived. At 5.30 a.m., General Guderian crossed the Luxembourg border near Wallendorf in the company of his lead units in the 1st Panzer Division. Two minutes after that, Hans von Luck, in his armoured scout car and with his motorcycles ahead of him, crossed the Luxembourg border as well. Meanwhile, in the north, Generaloberst Fedor von Bock's Army Group B was also beginning its thrust into Belgium, supported by Luftwaffe paratroopers and more than 1,500 bombers and dive-bombers. From his position on the Dutch border, Hellmuth Damm heard the reams of bombers droning overhead. It was these aircraft that had done so much to help roll over the Poles the previous autumn, and with newsreels around the world relaying images of screaming Stukas and hordes of dark bombers dropping their loads, the Luftwaffe was very much a symbol of Germany's new military might. It had been the Luftwaffe, above all, that had shocked and awed the Poles, and it was expected that in the west it would do so again.

The Luftwaffe could call on 1,272 twin-engine bombers and 307 Junkers Stuka and Henschel dive-bombers as dawn broke that morning. As had been tried and tested, their first task was to neutralize the enemy's own air forces. Now ripping apart the early-morning quiet with the thunderous roar of aero engines from two air fleets, Luftflotten 2 and 3, these bombers were in the process of carrying out a large number of combined air attacks on airfields and communications throughout Belgium, Holland and northern France.

Amongst those now flying over the Dutch coast were Junkers 88 bombers of III/KG 4. Leading the 9th Staffel was Oberleutnant Hajo Herrmann, a square-jawed, pale-eyed 25-year-old, who already had over twenty combat missions to his name as well as considerable experience of flying in Spain during the Civil War. A supremely calm and cool-headed individual, Hajo had taken off in the dark just before dawn from Delmenhorst, near Bremen in Northern Germany. One of his aircraft had crashed on take-off, killing all four of the crew. It had not been an auspicious start, but soon the pale crest of light spread from the east behind them. Flying low out over the North Sea and across the East Friesian Islands, they then turned west and later, altering course, flew south-west parallel to the Dutch coast, the twin Jumo engines thrumming in the now bright early-morning sky. Climbing sharply to some 12,000 feet, Hajo then led his squadron in a right-angled turn in towards the coast, to the airfield at Bergen aan Zee that lay just beyond the coastal dunes.

From 12,000 feet they made a diving attack. 'We had achieved surprise,' noted Hajo. 'The Dutch fighters were unable to intercept us, and we left the dust behind without any damage to ourselves.' The systematic and thorough destruction of the Dutch air force had begun.

Meanwhile, at the Führer HQ at Felsennet, artillery could now be heard. Hitler gathered his staff around him. 'Meine Herren,' he said, gesturing to the west, 'the offensive against the Western powers has begun.'

Arriving at Felsennet at around 6 a.m. was General Franz Halder, the 55-year-old, crop-haired and bespectacled Chief of the General Staff of the army supreme command, the *Oberkommando des Heeres*, or OKH; the man, above all, responsible for the minutiae of the German operational plan of attack. At 7 a.m., the first reports began coming in. The Belgians, it seemed, had been warned of the attack at around 3 a.m., but the Dutch had been taken by surprise. Nonetheless, it seemed the Dutch had been quick to respond by blowing a number of bridges vital to the advance of Army Group B. Then better news: little resistance had been met at the Luxembourg border in the Ardennes, and border bridges had been captured according to plan.

It had been a particularly stressful time for Halder, who had been trying to manage the mercurial – and frankly, at times, insane – demands of the Führer, whilst also attempting to produce a plan for an offensive in the West that would not lead to the rapid annihilation of Germany. It was an extremely difficult hand to juggle, and one that had led him to consider leading a coup d'état and assassination attempt on Hitler. All positions of high command include their share of stresses and strains, but the pressure Halder found himself under was particularly intense. There were times when he had come very close to complete nervous collapse.

Born in Würzburg, in Bavaria, Halder came from a family with a long tradition of military service dating back some 300 years. Despite this, he had spent his career in a series of staff jobs, so that, although he had served throughout the First World War, he had never experienced frontline action or command himself. With a fastidious eye for detail and a reputation as an expert on training, he had first caught Hitler's eye during the army manoeuvres of 1937. A year later, in September 1938, he was asked by General Walter von Brauchitsch, the Commander-in-Chief of the OKH, to become Chief of the General Staff. In light of his well-known anti-Nazi attitude, he had to think hard about whether to accept the post. Von Brauchitsch, however, who had worked with him in the Training Branch in 1930, appealed to him to accept.

After some soul-searching Halder did so, and by the summer of 1939 had developed a strong team with which he and von Brauchitsch hoped they could rival the combined armed forces high command – the *Oberkommando der Wehrmacht*, or OKW – for influence. Halder was far from being alone in the army in his contempt for the Nazi High Command. Although both Feldmarschall Wilhelm Keitel, Chief of the OKW, and his Chief of Staff, General Alfred Jodl, were soldiers, they were considered yes-men, who were unable to curb Hitler and leading Nazi excesses. Not for nothing was Keitel known as 'Lakeitel' – lackey – a pun on his name.

Halder's plans for the Polish campaign had been exemplary. He had hoped that the swift success of the eighteen-day conflict might well convince the Western powers to come to terms; certainly, he was keenly aware that Germany was far from ready for a clash with Britain and France at that time. Defeating a militarily weak country like Poland was one thing; victory over Britain and France was quite another.

Thus it was a shock to learn that Hitler wanted to turn his attention on the West immediately. The Führer's gamble that Britain and France would not declare war if he invaded Poland had backfired. They had done as they had promised and now Germany was faced with having to deal with them. It was unavoidable, and as far as he was concerned the sooner he got on with it the better, before the Allies became too strong. Britain, especially, may have been slow to rearm, but that would surely be accelerated now. And both Britain and France had, thanks to their sea lanes and overseas possessions, far greater access to the raw materials needed for war than did Germany. The only way the Third Reich could match them was by further expansion themselves – in the east. Even Hitler understood, however, that it would be foolish to advance on Russia before the threat of the Western powers had been resolved.

And so it was that the Führer had found himself in a quandary entirely of his own making. Setting out his rather woolly intentions in a memorandum issued on 9 October, the Führer announced that his aim was to defeat as much as possible of the French army and of any forces fighting on their side, and at the same time to win as much territory as possible in Holland, Belgium and northern France from which they could successfully conduct an 'air and sea war against England'.

As Chief of Staff of the OKH it was Halder's task to draw up a plan of attack, and yet the very idea of such an attack so soon and with winter approaching appalled him. What the Führer had not fully realized was that despite their success in Poland, the eighteen-day campaign had showed up startling deficiencies, not least a severe shortage of just about everything, but especially vehicles and ammunition. It had also demonstrated that many of the divisions were far from fully trained. In many cases, discipline had been poor too. Yet now Hitler wanted to wage war with France, who had the world's biggest army, and Britain, who had the biggest navy, at the same time, and with winter on its way.

The majority of the Wehrmacht officer corps thought, as Halder did, that the plan was insane. Even Keitel, normally the first to kowtow to Hitler, urged the Führer to reconsider, and, when he refused, offered his resignation. This too was refused. Halder had tried to dissuade Hitler by producing a draft plan that, like the German advance in 1914, saw them making a thrust through Belgium to the coast. So unimaginative was it, he hoped it would show Hitler the senselessness of such an offensive.

It did nothing of the sort, however. Hitler stuck to his guns, and with mounting impatience. It was at this point that Halder took on the mantle of the central figure in Nazi resistance, hatching at Zossen, the headquarters of the OKH south of Berlin, a plan for a coup d'état and Hitler's assassination that involved a number of leading officers, including General Wilhelm Ritter von Leeb, commander of Army Group C, Admiral Wilhelm Canaris, the head of the Abwehr – the military intelligence service – and General Carl-Heinrich von Stülpnagel, Deputy Chief of Staff of Operations at OKH. For Halder, however, the plot produced a terrible crisis of conscience. He did not want to act without sufficient support – yet getting that support was an extremely risky task. Increasingly, he came to believe that assassinating the Führer was probably the best option and so through Canaris began planning to plant some explosives at one of his meetings with Hitler. He even took to carrying a loaded pistol in his pocket so that he might gun him down himself.

In the meantime, and with his nerves worn thin, he continued preparations for the Western offensive, producing a second plan at the end of October, which in essence was the same, but included a second simultaneous thrust further south. This was deliberate heel-dragging, and Hitler knew it. In the Reich Chancellery on 5 November, von Brauchitsch had tried to explain that his field armies were simply not ready for a major offensive in the west, only for Hitler to erupt into one of his uncontrollable rages. Von Brauchitsch had been left stupefied, and later confessed to Halder that he was unable to deal with Hitler's iron and maniacal will. Yet von Brauchitsch rarely stood up to Hitler, which was just as the Führer wanted it. In part this was because of his fear of Hitler but also because the Führer had agreed to pay von Brauchitsch's first wife a substantial divorce settlement that the army Chief had not been able to afford himself. He was thus literally in Hitler's debt.

Von Brauchitsch, like Keitel, offered his resignation, and as with the Chief of OKW, it was refused; Hitler, who mistrusted the OKH and had as much contempt for his generals as they did for many leading Nazis, had no-one obvious to replace him with. Instead, he recognized that the Commander-in-Chief of the army would not dare to stand up to him again. Like all bullies, Hitler had an innate ability to sniff out other men's weaknesses.

It was after von Brauchitsch's dressing down on 5 November that Halder had cut his ties with the resisters. On the return trip to OKH headquarters from the Reich Chancellery, von Brauchitsch, pale as a ghost, had told Halder that Hitler had raged against the 'spirit of Zossen'. Panicking, Halder mistakenly believed the Führer had somehow got wind of the plot and immediately ordered von Stülpnagel to destroy all the relevant documents.

It marked a significant turning point in Halder's life. Recognizing his total unsuitability as an assassin and revolutionary, he now decided to embrace the coming offensive wholeheartedly. If he could not prevent it, then at least he could do all in his powers to ensure it was as successful as possible.

Nonetheless, Halder was initially extremely dubious that a main thrust through the Ardennes had much chance of success. General von Manstein, during his time as Chief of Staff of Army Group A, had produced seven different drafts, which he submitted to OKH between October and January, and each draft contained the same essential concept: that if they could take the French by surprise and get across the Meuse, then a fast panzer thrust could blaze a way through France before the French troops could react.

It was a bold and daring plan that was dependent on far too many variables for comfort: that the extremely complicated logistic operation through the Ardennes would go to plan; that Allied air forces would not detect it; that the French would be surprised; that the French would not be able to recover sufficiently; that untried and untested panzer units could cut such a swathe. For the methodical, cautious Halder, this made it fatally flawed, and so he put von Manstein's memos to one side and did not pass them on to the OKW, knowing that if he did so the Führer would instantly latch on to such an adventurous idea purely because it was daring and because it ran counter to the more methodical approach Halder and the OKH had already put forward. Halder understood Hitler well enough to recognize that Manstein's plan would almost certainly appeal to the Führer's go-for-broke mentality. Furthermore, Hitler had even suggested a thrust through Sedan himself, not through any genius of military thinking, but rather because Sedan had witnessed the French surrender during the Franco–Prussian War in 1870 and had always fascinated him.

At the beginning of the year, however, two events happened that turned Halder's plans on their head. The first was on 10 January, when a German aircraft made a forced landing near Mechelen in Belgium. On board was a Luftwaffe operations officer with copies of the latest German offensive plans, which still held that a thrust through the Low Countries was to be the main point of attack. Realizing how important the documents were, the German officers hastily tried to burn them. They were captured, however, before the documents had been destroyed. Suddenly, the Allies had the details of the German plans laid out before them.

Hitler was incensed when he found out, but it soon proved to be of far greater benefit to the Germans than the Allies. The incident prompted a rapid response from the Allies, who began enormous troop movements, going on to the alert all along the front and moving reserves forward, all of which was watched and noted by Luftwaffe reconnaissance planes. And what this showed was that the Allies had been expecting a German attack exactly as outlined in Halder's plans.

The second event happened a few weeks later on 2 February, when General Schmundt, Hitler's military aide, visited Army Group A and was given copies of von Manstein's plan by Generals Günther Blumentritt and Henning von Tresckow. At the end of January, von Manstein had been sidelined by being given a phantom corps that had yet to be organized. Frustrated by such treatment of a man they greatly admired, Blumentritt and von Tresckow urged Schmundt to visit von Manstein and talk to him about his ideas, which he did right away. He then passed the plans to Hitler. Just as Halder had suspected, the Führer lapped them up immediately.

But by this time, however, the situation had greatly changed. The long winter months had proved more beneficial to the Germans than the Allies: ammunition stocks had been replenished, more tanks and aircraft had been built, training of raw divisions had been carried out. And spring was around the corner. The OKH had successfully managed to stall Hitler, their cause helped by a particularly vicious winter that even the Führer could tell was no help to offensive plans. Indeed, the excuse of poor weather came to Halder and von Brauchitsch's rescue time and time again; by 10 May, the attack date had been postponed no fewer than twenty-nine times. Even better, Hitler was also now considering an attack in Denmark and Norway first, before an offensive in the west. The Führer had recognized during the winter months the importance of Norway as the only route through which much-needed Swedish iron ore could reach Germany. This in turn meant the offensive in the west would take place in early summer, when conditions were far more favourable. Furthermore, rather than revealing German plans, the Mechelen incident had paradoxically shown Allied intentions instead, and that was something that could be used to the Germans' advantage.

And that wasn't all. War games at the beginning of February had shown Halder that Guderian's and von Manstein's plans for a deep panzer thrust might just work after all. Finally, the French, it seemed, had been very slow to respond to recent German regrouping movements along the front: intelligence suggested they had taken between ten and fourteen days to pick this up. Thus if the main French defences through the Ardennes could be reached in under that time, the French could be caught out. 'Surprise may now be regarded as assured,' he noted with confidence in his diary after a February Führer conference.

The methodical, careful, and rather unimaginative original plan would probably avoid any quick defeat. In fact, it would almost certainly lead to the long drawn-out attritional war that those veterans of the First World War so dreaded. The von Manstein–Guderian go-for-broke plan, on the other hand, might lead to a very quick and disastrous defeat. Yet, it might – *might* – just give them the emphatic victory they needed: certainly, Halder now realized, it was the only plan that had a possible chance of success. Thus by the end of February, when Halder submitted his latest plans for Case Yellow, he had completed his dramatic *volte face*: Army Group B would noisily thrust into Holland and northern Belgium with the support of the majority of the Luftwaffe, while the panzers of Army Group A would hurry through the Ardennes and attack the French across the Meuse. With luck, the Allies would be coaxed into a trap, rushing forward to meet the northern thrust, while the main German attack burst through the back door around Sedan, ensnaring the bulk of the Allies' northern front in a huge encirclement before they had time to effectively respond.

Halder might have been convinced, and so too von Brauchitsch, but it was palpably clear that the majority in the army believed it was a fatally flawed plan that had not one chance of succeeding. On 17 March, Guderian and the senior commanders of Army Group A had a conference with Hitler at the Reich Chancellery. Guderian was the last of the army and corps commanders to brief Hitler on his plan. On the fourth day after the advance began, he told the Führer and his army group superiors, he would reach the Meuse. By the end of the fifth he would have established a bridgehead across it.

'And then what are you going to do?' Hitler asked.

'Unless I receive orders to the contrary, I intend on the next day to continue my advance westwards.' He added that in his opinion he should drive straight to the Channel coast.

General Busch, who commanded Sixteenth Army consisting almost entirely of infantry divisions, said, 'Well, I don't think you'll cross the river in the first place!' He was speaking for almost all Army Group A's senior officers, including its commander, von Rundstedt.

Hitler, visibly tense, turned to Guderian, waiting for his response.

'There's no need for *you* to do so in any case,' Guderian replied. The last thing he wanted was slow, cumbersome, infantry divisions lacking almost any mechanized transportation getting in his way.

Not only were most of Army Group A against the plan, but so too was much of Army Group B. Its commander, Generaloberst von Bock, called in on Halder in his Berlin apartment and pleaded with him to abandon it entirely. 'You will be creeping by ten miles from the Maginot Line with the flank of your breakthrough,' he told Halder, 'and hope the French will watch inertly! You are cramming the mass of the tank units together into the sparse roads of the Ardennes mountain country, as if there were no such thing as air power! And you then hope to be able to lead an operation as far as the coast with an open southern flank two hundred miles long, where stands the mass of the French Army!' This, he added, transcended the 'frontiers of reason'.

There was much sense in what von Bock said. On paper, it looked hopelessly optimistic. And von Bock knew, as Halder knew, that of the 135 divisions earmarked for the offensive, large numbers were far from being the elite, crack units the rest of the world seemed to think they were. In the entire army, there were only ten panzer and six fully mechanized divisions. These mere sixteen divisions were the modern, fully equipped units of the German army. The other 141 were really rather old-fashioned, lacking mechanization and dependent on horses, carts and the oldest means of transport in the world – the soldier's two feet he stood on – to get from A to B. In the spearhead that would thrust through the Ardennes, there were only ten such modernized divisions: in Panzer Group Kleist, Guderian had three panzer divisions, General Reinhardt's corps two panzer and one mechanized (i.e. mainly lorried infantry), while von Wietersheim's corps had two mechanized divisions. Since there were not enough roads through the Ardennes for all three corps to advance at once, Panzer Corps von Wietersheim would be following behind the spearhead in any case. The remaining two panzer divisions in Army Group A were those of Panzer Corps Hoth, which included Rommel's 7th Panzer Division.

And yes, they were modern and well equipped, but the majority of their panzers were hardly the latest in cutting-edge tank design. Only Panzer Mks III and IV had decent-sized guns and there were only 627 of them. The remaining 1,812 were Mk Is, which had machine guns only, Mk IIs, which had a rather feeble 20 mm gun, and Czech 35s and 38s, which also had below-par firepower. In contrast, the Allies could call on some 4,204 tanks, almost double the amount in the German army. Of these, a significant number were bigger, better armed and better armoured than anything the Germans had.

Of the rest of the German army, only a quarter were active duty troops that could be used in the first wave of the offensive – that is, regular peacetime units reinforced with reservists, such as Siegfried Knappe's 87th Division. The second wave consisted of mostly younger fully trained reservists. After that were those reservists who had only been cursorily trained. Then there were the Landwehr units – territorials – who were mostly older, veterans of the Great War and barely trained at all since 1918.

This meant that only half of all German soldiers had had more than a few weeks' training, while more than a quarter were over forty. Nazi propaganda had kept this rather startling reality close to its chest.

Consequently, just ten German panzer and mechanized divisions – around 140,000 men – were being expected to do the lion's share of the main thrust, and drive a wedge through around 2.5 million French and

British forces all the way to the Channel coast. It was a very, very tall order indeed.

But what other choice was there? Hitler's invasion of Poland had got Germany in a terrible predicament. Do or die, a go-for-broke gamble, was the only chance she had of wriggling out of it.

On this Friday, 10 May, Case Yellow was finally underway. Germany would live or die by the sword. There could be no turning back. Hitler, at least, was confident of success. Guderian believed in it, and so did his men and his fellow commanders amongst the panzer elite. Von Brauchitsch and Halder *hoped* it might work. Most of the rest of the army command, however, did not share their Führer's confidence. They went along with it because they had no choice; only a miracle, it seemed, would save them.

At Führer Headquarters, reports were coming in regularly. Halder was reading them all, assiduously noting them down in his diary. By 10 a.m., news had arrived that Panzer Group Kleist was advancing according to plan; *Fallschirmjäger* (paratroop) units dropped into Holland to capture key forts and bridges similarly seemed to be progressing well. The railhead at Luxembourg, essential for the passage of supplies to the front, had been captured. So far, then, so good. But what of the enemy? Were the British and French northern armies moving into Belgium to meet the German onslaught in the north? For Halder, the man responsible for organizing the operation, these were desperately tense and long hours of waiting. And in the same building was the Führer, the man just a few months earlier he had planned to kill.

All morning and into the afternoon, Leutnant Siegfried Knappe and the rest of the 87th Division moved not an inch. Everything was ready, as it had been since 5 a.m.; ammunition loaded, guns jacked up to their carriages, the troops standing around in march order. Siegfried spent the time talking to Major Raake and the battery commanders, speculating about what lay in store. Would it be over quickly? Or would it soon bog down into trench warfare as it had a quarter of a century before? 'It was a very long day,' noted Siegfried, 'just sitting and waiting for orders to move out.'

Way ahead, at the spearhead of Army Group A, Panzer Corps Guderian was leading the race to the Meuse. Every man knew what was at stake. Since 0530, the clock had been ticking; every minute counted.

The General's three panzer divisions were the 1st, 2nd and 10th. He had warned his men they should not expect to get much sleep for three days and nights. With this in mind, the senior staff officer of 1st Panzer Division had ordered 20,000 tablets of Pervitin in an attempt to keep the men awake. No-one needed such stimulants this first day, however. Adrenalin alone saw to that. By 8.30 a.m. they had successfully passed through Luxembourg and swept aside Belgian defences at the town of Martelange. The next town on their route through the Ardennes, Bodange, proved a tougher nut to crack, but by evening they were through the main Belgian frontier defences. So far, the rush to the Meuse was on schedule, although Guderian was keenly aware there was still much that could go wrong between now and reaching the famous river. Belgium road demolitions, for example, needed to be cleared without delay.

In the north, it was the troops of Army Group B who were experiencing the most action as they thundered into Belgium and Holland. Unteroffizier Hellmuth Damm and his *Gruppe* – or half-platoon in a machine-gun company – of a dozen men realized the offensive was beginning when they heard aircraft droning overhead. At 6 a.m. came the order to attack. Just as they had trained, the battalion began moving forward: four companies, each of around 120 men divided into three rifle platoons and one machine-gun platoon. The rifle companies led the way, the machine-gun company following behind with their heavy gear. The two MG08s weighed over sixty kilograms each, and the gun mounts around thirty kilos. On top of that each man had to carry two twelve-kilo ammunition boxes, plus rifle, pouches, bread bags, spade, gas mask, pack, anti-gas cape, rations, hand-grenades, wire cutters and other personal gear. As *Gruppe* leader, Hellmuth also carried a message bag, a pair of binoculars and sighting equipment. It was quite a load.

Up ahead, Hellmuth soon heard gunfire, but he could not see any enemy. The word filtering back to them was that the Dutch troops had withdrawn behind the River Meuse.

Later in the morning, they reached the river. New orders arrived, and Hellmuth and his *Gruppe* were instructed to take up position on the first floor of a nearby house to cover the assault engineers as they attempted to cross the river in rubber boats. He soon found a suitable building, informing the bewildered and frightened inhabitants that he now needed to use their front-facing bedroom as a machine-gun post. Moving beds and furniture out of the way, he quickly got his two MG teams ready and radioed back to company headquarters that he was in position to fire. In the meantime, the artillery behind had arrived and unlimbered, and had begun firing. With shells hurtling through the air and with small arms beginning to crackle, Hellmuth was given the order for his men to open fire. Ahead, he watched the assault troops, crouching in their rubber boats, paddling furiously across the river. Soon the room was thick with the smell of cordite and oil. Through the haze of battle, Hellmuth saw white flags appearing from the enemy already as the assault troops began scrambling out of their boats and up the far bank, their flame-throwers and hand-grenades ready. More infantry were now pouring across the river, the signal for Hellmuth to dismantle his MGs and get his men across the water as well. 'To our surprise,' noted Hellmuth, 'the owner of the house invited us to a cup of hot coffee even though we hadn't exactly been polite to him.'

Quickly swigging back the coffee, they then found a couple of spare boats and made their way across the river. On the far bank, they came up against a large wire fence. Lying on his front, Hellmuth cut a hole and then his men hurried through the gap, lumbering their gear as quickly as they could. Ahead were the blackened remains of a Dutch concrete bunker. Prisoners sat around it and Hellmuth was surprised that no-one seemed to have taken responsibility for them. Shrugging to himself, he ordered his men forward, the infantry either side and in front of them.

During the rest of the day, Hellmuth's *Gruppe* never had cause to fire their machine guns again. Instead, they merely followed the advance, carrying their heavy loads through field after field, the sound of gunfire always up ahead of them. Late in the afternoon, they reached the village of Horst. There they learned they had achieved the day's objective – a distance of about twelve miles.

Hellmuth and his men were absolutely exhausted. His first day in action had left a strong impression on him. It was real war at last and yet they had been largely unhindered by the enemy, making it feel rather like a tight exercise carried out by the book.

Back at Felsennet, General Halder's anxious waiting game was far from over, but by nine o'clock that evening intelligence had arrived that motorized enemy columns were moving in the direction of Brussels. Just as he had hoped and prayed, it seemed the Allies were moving forward to meet the northern thrust. This part of the trap, at least, appeared to be working.

4

Hook, Line and Sinker

Gunner Stan Fraser was woken up in his billet near Arras at around 4.50 a.m. by the drone of aircraft. Wearing his pyjamas – a habit that amused his comrades no end – he slipped on his pumps, scampered down the steps of the loft over the large stable below and out into the yard, only to see three German bombers, the dark crosses on their wings clearly visible, streak across the sky against the dark glow of the rising sun. Almost immediately the regiment's heavy 3.7-inch anti-aircraft guns opened fire.

Hurrying back up into the loft, he hastily put on his trousers and began watching the opening salvoes of the German offensive from the window, gradually joined by his mates as they, too, were woken by the noise of bombs exploding and guns booming. From their window they could quite clearly see the regiment's batteries firing, and puffs of black smoke littering the sky as the shells exploded. Soon the raiders passed, the guns quietened down and they all clambered back into bed again. An hour later, however, there was a loud explosion nearby and the entire building shook, followed by several more blasts as bombs detonated. A keen amateur film-maker, Stan sprang out of bed once more as another wave of aircraft thundered overhead, and grabbing his cine camera ran down into the yard with two of his comrades, then sprinted up a shallow wooded hill behind their billet. As they crested the hill, machine-gun fire rattled out from an aircraft somewhere nearby. With his camera ready, Stan saw two aircraft suddenly roar into view through a gap in the trees. 'The last we saw of the planes,' jotted Stan, 'was when they were streaking away across the house tops of Arras.'

Not so far away from Stan and the rest of the 4th Heavy Anti-Aircraft Regiment was the Headquarters of the British Expeditionary Force. Habarcq, a pretty and normally quiet village of old brick farmhouses, lime trees and horse-chestnuts now in leaf, lay just eight miles west of Arras, amidst the wide, rolling arable countryside that some twenty and more years before had been at the heart of the Western Front. In the white-stoned chateau that served as General HQ, Major-General Henry Pownall was woken at 4.40 a.m. with the sound of four or five bombs exploding in the distance, followed by the boom of anti-aircraft fire. An hour later, Pownall, along with the rest of the staff officers, was washed, shaved and dressed, and anxiously awaiting news and orders from Général Georges's North-East Front, the French command under which the BEF had been placed.

It was Brigadier Swayne, head of the BEF's mission at Georges's HQ, who rang at around 5.30 a.m. with the instructions that Alerts 1, 2 and 3 had been given simultaneously. As Chief of Staff of the BEF, Pownall was with the British commander, General Lord Gort, when at about 6.15 a.m. a further message arrived from Général Georges's Headquarters. Orders had been issued by the French Supreme Command for the immediate implementation of Plan D, the forward movement of troops to occupy positions along the River Dyle in Belgium.

It could not be carried out quite immediately, however. The system of alerts, as devised by the French, was to warn the Allied forces along the front to prepare for various stages of readiness. Yet although they had been expecting a German offensive, the campaign in Norway of the past few weeks had distracted them somewhat, whilst during the previous days there had been the diversion of a political crisis not only in London, but in Paris too. Consequently, no alert of any kind had been issued in the last twenty-four hours and as a result no troops were ready to get moving right away. With this in mind, Gort announced that Zero hour for beginning the march into Belgium was 1 o'clock that afternoon, nearly seven hours hence.

In 1914, the British Expeditionary Force had been sent to France, and so it had again in 1939, following the outbreak of war. The name was telling; it suggested that the enterprise was an 'expedition', an adventure, rather than a force soon to be embroiled in a bitter and bloody war. That its name harked back to an earlier age was also indicative of a mindset that had not moved forward as much as it should have done.

In fact, the British Expeditionary Force was a large field army. An army can be called as such if it contains two or more corps. A corps, in turn, should contain at least two divisions. This latter is a major tactical and administrative unit that contains within its structure all the various forms of arms and services necessary for sustained combat, such as infantry, tanks, artillery, engineers and support troops. Divisions could have different emphases. An armoured – or panzer – division, for example, would have at its heart a couple of armoured brigades – or regiments of several battalions – while an infantry division would have as its core two or more infantry brigades (in the British example), or infantry regiments in the case of the German organization. The French system was also much the same, with infantry divisions comprising around 16,000–17,000 men in total and armoured divisions around 14,000.

The BEF contained about half a million men, and consisted of I, II and III Corps, with – on 10 May at any rate – three, four and two infantry divisions, and the equivalent of an armoured division attached to General Headquarters. In another echo of the previous war, British Headquarters had found a well-appointed French chateau in which to base itself, and an excessive number of staff officers. Its Commander-in-Chief, General the Viscount Gort, was also a hero of the First World War. His bravery was legendary – not for nothing did he wear the ribbons of an MC, two DSOs and Britain's highest award for valour, the Victoria Cross. As a man whose command abilities were widely believed to be suited to a division but no higher, he had been a surprise choice when he took over as Chief of the Imperial General Staff (CIGS) – Britain's top military job – in 1937, although no-one doubted either his work ethic or his enthusiasm. He was an equally surprising choice when, on 3 September, he stood down to take command of the BEF instead. Although, at fifty-three, he had age on his side, he was no intellectual nor even particularly experienced in command. The prospect of fighting once more was of great excitement, however. 'Here we go again,' he said with relish, 'marching to war,' then admitted, 'I can't expect everybody to be as thrilled as I am.' It seems likely that Gort himself pressed his case for the appointment. The problem, however, was that he and Henry Pownall, his Chief of Staff when he was CIGS, and who he insisted should accompany him to France, were the two soldiers with the greatest knowledge and understanding of British war plans. It might have made more sense had they stayed in London.

That Britain could field 500,000 men at all was some achievement. Having had the best army in the world by November 1918, Britain had, after the armistice, forgotten most of the lessons learned at the cost of so much of her young men's blood. Rapid disarmament went hand-in-hand with a reversion to its pre-1914 role: policing the Empire. Throughout the 1920s and 1930s, rebellions and upturns in violence in Iraq, Afghanistan and along the Northwest Frontier, for example, had kept British troops busy. Fighting against tribesmen, however, had not required many tactical advances. In any case, hadn't those long years of 1914–18 been the war to end all wars? In its aftermath, Germany had been disarmed, the Rhineland was to be permanently occupied by Allied troops, and a League of Nations had been formed to settle international quarrels by less violent means. Why would Britain need a large army or even air force any longer?

There was no money for maintaining large forces in any case. An assumption was made that there would be no major war for ten years and as each year passed, so the ten-year rule was moved forward too. No other country followed Britain's lead, however, although not until 1932 was this finally accepted and the ten-year policy abandoned. Even so, subsequent rearmament was painfully slow, and all the while not only was Hitler's Germany building up its strength, but so too were Italy and Japan; the latter was spending nearly half her national income on rearming. Suddenly, not just Europe was under threat, but British possessions and interests in the Middle East, Africa and the Far East were as well.

Although British rearmament began to gradually speed up, financial constraints as well as endless debate hampered progress, as did too many years of inactivity. By April 1938, the British Government considered that any future war with Germany should be conducted with primarily air and naval forces; another Continental land war was to be avoided. Not until Hitler marched into Czechoslovakia in March 1939, thus reneging on his promises at Munich the previous autumn, was it finally agreed that the Territorial force should be doubled and conscription introduced. Even so, the British Field Force (as the BEF was originally known) that headed over to France in September consisted of only two corps of four divisions. And there was the rub: it was all very well declaring war on Germany, but in 1939 there was no question of Britain taking the attack to the enemy. Britain's war policy was entirely defensive – at any rate, certainly until sufficient strength had been built up, and that, it was recognized, was not going to be any time soon.

If only Britain had carried the enormous technological and, ultimately, tactical, advances made during the First World War into the inter-war years! But there had been little attempt to maintain her traditional position at the cutting edge of technical and industrial development. Tanks, aircraft, and bigger, higher-velocity guns – even the thermionic valve that led to wireless telegraphy and portable radio communication – had changed the nature of warfare for ever. Yet instead of embracing this new technology and applying serious thought to how it could be developed and applied, too many senior officers had reverted to the traditions and mentality of the pre-1914 colonial army.

Certainly, the culture within the army hardly helped. The British regimental system was such that talking 'shop' was simply not done. In the mess, one discussed cricket, polo or pig-sticking, not how to improve the mobility and firepower of a tank. In the 1930s, most cavalry regiments were appalled that they should give up their horses for anything so vulgar as tanks. The Royal Scots Greys, for example, were so disgusted at the idea of mechanization that even in 1938 they were lobbying Parliament against such a move and taking their grievances to *The Times*. Yeomanry regiments – territorial cavalry for the young gentry of the shires – were also still on horseback by the summer of 1939.

Admittedly, publications such as the *Royal United Services Institute Journal* published forward-thinking essays, but little notice was taken of them. Of the big thinkers of the day, none were generals; of the best-known, John Fuller was a colonel and Basil Liddell Hart a journalist. Leslie Hore-Belisha, the extremely energetic War Minister, had tried to make the army more progressive and had heavily depended on Liddell Hart's advice. Rather than embracing such a dynamic figure, however, Gort had taken umbrage at his meddling and had used his influence to drive him out of office. And, in any case, Hore-Belisha was not an establishment figure; even worse, he was a Jew. Anti-Semitism might not have been so monstrously or violently articulated in Britain as it was in Nazi Germany but it was widely felt all the same.

Furthermore, in all parts of the army pay was low even at the highest ranks, so promotion was stripped of one of its great incentives. For many middle-ranking officers, it was easier to keep one's head down and make the most of what the army offered: good company, sport and a reasonable standard of living. It prompted a descent into complacency that could not be rectified overnight. The result was that initiative was stifled, while little thought had been given to how infantry, armour and artillery could operate together. Technology had moved on over the past twenty years, but not military thinking.

Nonetheless, it wasn't all bad, and although tactically the British army had barely moved forward, its kit was quite impressive. For starters, it was in relative terms far more mechanized than the German army. Its field and anti-aircraft guns were good, and most of the tanks were on a par with the majority of German panzers. The Bren light machine gun, of which there was one per section of ten men, was an excellent and reliable piece of kit, while the Short Magazine Lee Enfield rifle was as good as any in the world, with a short bolt that meant a reasonable marksman could fire twice as many rounds per minute as his German equivalent could with the Mauser K.98. Furthermore, the majority of soldiers in the BEF were now dressed in the modern 1937 pattern battle-dress, a warm and practical uniform that was light and allowed greater freedom of movement. Both German and French troops, on the other hand, were still dressed in traditional-style, heavily tailored tunics.

Yet because Britain had only lately decided to build up the strength of its army, the BEF's contribution – on the ground at any rate – was small. By May 1940, the BEF's nine divisions in France were fewer than the ten the Dutch had mobilized, and under half the twenty the Belgian army could field. The French, on the other hand, had three *groups* of armies on the North-East Front alone, containing no fewer than sixty-six divisions at the front with a further eighteen in reserve.

Since both Holland and Belgium, as neutrals, had made it clear they would remain so unless their countries were invaded, they had not become involved in any planning discussions about what should be done if Germany launched an attack in the west. Thus France and Britain, as allies, had prepared for a German attack together, while the Dutch and Belgians worked on their own, separate plans of action.

Yet there could be no doubting that in such preparations Britain was very much the junior partner. The BEF was effectively just one of five armies that made up Général Gaston Billotte's No. 1 Army Group, part of Général Georges's North-East Front. However, Gort was under the command not of Billotte, the Army Group Commander, but of Georges. Above Georges was Général Gamelin, the Supreme French Commander. Gort was ordered to carry out 'loyally' any instructions given to him by Georges in 'pursuit of the common object, the defeat of the enemy'. There was a get-out clause, however. 'If any order given by him appears to you to imperil the British Field Force,' his written instructions decreed, 'it is agreed between the British and French Governments that you should be at liberty to appeal to the British Government before executing that order.' It was an important proviso, and one that Gort would be eternally grateful for once the German offensive began.

Nonetheless, as far as preparing for a German attack went, the French were happy to pay lip-service to the British, but little more; indeed, the British Government had accepted that direction of any land campaign should be the responsibility of the French. The French war policy was much the same as the British – that is, to wait until she had built up her strength and then, and only then, to go on to the offensive. The great tragedy was that in 1939 France was in fact already more than strong enough. French forces were superior in numbers to the Germans in almost every department at the outbreak of war, and still would be by May 1940. Sadly for the entire history of the world, they had fallen for Nazi spin-doctoring, believing that even Hitler would not be crazy enough to risk war if his armed forces were not as invincible as had been made out.

In fact, the German Siegfried Line, or West Wall – the defensive system along Germany's western border – was underdeveloped and held by a mere skeleton force throughout the Polish campaign. As it was, the Germans nearly shot their bolt in Poland. Had the campaign lasted even a few days longer, front-line units would have found themselves without any ammunition at all. Had Gamelin mobilized his vast armies and marched over the Rhine in September 1939, Berlin would have been theirs for the taking and the war would indeed very likely have been over before Christmas.

It was not to be, however. From the moment the guns fell silent in 1918, France was determined that such a war should never happen on her soil again. Unlike Britain, her response had been not to disarm but to build such a strong defensive line that no attacker would ever again force its way through.

France had fewer colonies than Britain and had been far more traumatized than Britain by the experience of the First World War. The attrition of the trenches had proved to the French that concrete was king. It had also proved that the side with the stronger economy and the best defences would ultimately prevail. This view did not alter in the 1920s and 1930s. The Maginot Line, a series of interconnected reinforced bunkers mounted with heavy artillery and anti-tank and machine guns, and protected by layers of obstacles, was named after the French Defence Minister – a Verdun veteran – who devised the plan in the 1920s. Stretching from Switzerland to the Belgian border, it cost more than 7,000 million francs.

The Maginot Line was a reasonable deterrent along France's border with Germany, but there were still 250 miles along the Belgian border that were not so well protected. France would have liked to have stationed troops in Belgium but the latter refused them entry because of her strict adherence to her neutrality. Only when and if Belgium were attacked would she allow Allied troops on to her soil.

This left Gamelin with a conundrum. On the one hand, there were advantages to moving into Belgium to meet any German assault because the French line would be shorter and French forces swelled further by the thirty divisions of the Dutch and Belgian armies. Also, by moving into Belgium, the battle could be fought clear of France and her northern industrial area. On the other hand, if they stayed put on the French border, they would lose those benefits but gain the advantage of well-prepared defences. It was a tricky call.

Gamelin also had to decide where a German attack was most likely to come. Yes, he had considerable forces at his disposal, but he had to defend 500 miles of the French border, whereas the Germans could concentrate their forces at a point of their choosing. Thinking quite logically, he assumed that the Germans would probably not attack the Maginot Line. He also believed that a thrust through the Ardennes was unlikely. Although the Ardennes forest lay just beyond the northernmost point of the Maginot Line, the thick woods and deep valleys of this stretch of Belgium and Luxembourg were felt to be unsuitable for tanks. Furthermore, there was the major obstacle of the Meuse to cross as well. The Germans had made much of their panzer force and Gamelin again fell for the propaganda. Marshal Pétain, the French hero of Verdun in 1916, had called the Ardennes 'impenetrable'. Gamelin, too, had described the Meuse as 'Europe's best tank obstacle'. And so he reasoned that the Germans, as in 1914, would advance through the Low Countries, where they would be able to put their tank forces to best effect.

Gamelin had resolved his conundrum in his mind swiftly not least because intelligence suggested the Germans were planning an attack soon, and he asked Général Georges to produce plans for an advance into

Belgium that could be implemented the moment the Germans launched an attack. Georges was not enthusiastic about the decision but nonetheless delivered two options. The first, a short advance to the River Escaut, the first major water obstacle that ran as a natural line of defence across south-west Belgium, was known as 'Plan E'. The second was a further advance to the River Dyle, which ran from Antwerp all the way to Namur, where it linked up with the Meuse. This was called 'Plan D', and at a meeting of the Supreme War Council on 17 November was the one provisionally adopted.

Gort and his commanders were broadly happy with this plan. General Pownall thought Plan D much better than an advance to the Escaut. It would not be an easy move – some eighty miles in a bit of a hurry – and would require some serious logistical effort. 'But of course it can be done,' he noted, 'and if we can bring it off neatly it would be an excellent move.' Lieutenant-General Alan Brooke, commander of the British II Corps, was also receptive to the plan. 'If we can get there in time to organize ourselves properly to meet the German onrush,' he scribbled in his diary, 'it is without doubt the right strategy.'

Meticulous planning and preparations continued over the winter, but then, on 20 March, Gamelin added his so-called Breda Variant to the plan. Rather than try to link up with only the Belgians, Gamelin's new idea was to thrust further north from Antwerp to Breda in Holland so as to link up with the Dutch army too and thus make a continuous Allied front, just as in the Western Front of the First World War. On paper, this seemed like a small addition, but logistically it was a major revision. Breda was twice as far from the French border as it was from the German, and so in a race against the Germans the French could not hope to win. Also, the plan required considerably more manpower. In the original D Plan, ten French and five British divisions were to advance to the Dyle. The Breda Variant required thirty divisions. To achieve this, Gamelin moved the entire French Seventh Army north so that, when the moment came, it could move northwards towards the Dutch border; it had been Georges's intention to keep this army in reserve in the centre of his North-East Front.

It was this version of the D Plan that the Allies were putting into action this morning, 10 May. Général Gamelin was happy. At the French War Ministry, the Supreme Commander had been walking around with a broad smile on his face. Just as he had predicted, the Germans seemed to be attacking through the Low Countries. His forces were perfectly prepared. Indeed, the Germans were providing him with just the opportunity he had been waiting for.

Amongst the BEF, the 12th Royal Lancers, a forward screening force of armoured cars, were the first to move, getting going around 10.20 a.m. By 6 p.m., they had signalled over their No. 3 radio set that they had reached the Dyle. The infantry, however, were not so quick out of the blocks. General Brooke, the bespectacled, hawkish 56-year-old commander of II Corps, had spent the morning checking orders and ensuring everything was going to plan. II Corps was to hold a six-mile stretch of the River Dyle around the town of Louvain, some twelve miles east of Brussels. To its north would be the Belgians, to the south I Corps. Below it would be the French First Army. As far as Brooke could tell, everything appeared to be going like clockwork – there had been so many alarms and rehearsals no-one was short of practice – but the start of the move had not been hampered by enemy aircraft. Although plenty of aircraft had been flying over, it seemed the Luftwaffe had more pressing targets to bomb that day than the BEF. And it was a beautifully sunny and warm day. 'It was hard to believe on a most glorious spring day, with all nature looking quite its best,' noted Brooke, 'that we were taking the first steps towards what must become one of the greatest battles in history!'

Amongst those now moving up towards the Belgian border was Stan Fraser. Stan had joined the Headquarters of the 4th Heavy Anti-Aircraft Regiment just eleven days before. A 26-year-old Liverpudlian, he had joined up on the outbreak of war, realizing that he would soon get called up anyway, and thinking that if he volunteered he might get more of a choice. His father was already at sea and his younger brother, Babe, was in the RAF, but Stan preferred to join the army; thinking of his keen interest in the Scouts, he joined the 1st Army Survey Company of the Royal Engineers.

He had been posted to France before Christmas, but rather than surveying he had spent his time in a salvage unit instead, work that he soon found monotonous in the extreme. A bright and single-minded fellow, he had asked for an interview with his commanding officer, and having explained his frustration was told he might try to transfer to the Royal Artillery. On 30 April, the CO had appeared just as Stan was digging a new latrine. 'Well, Fraser,' he said, handing him a War Office communiqué, 'you are now to become a real soldier.' Although sorry to bid farewell to his friends, Stan had been greatly relieved at the posting, and even more so when on his arrival at 4th HAA Regiment he was told he would remain at Regimental HQ working with the surveyors. He soon found that his mapping skills from his scouting days were particularly useful.

There had been a noticeably restless air about Headquarters the previous evening, but now, with the offensive underway at last, the place had become a hive of activity. Halfway through a quickly snatched breakfast, orders for the entire regiment to pack up and move out had reached them. The heavy guns had been limbered up behind their lorries, while the men had loaded themselves and their equipment into trucks.

By one o'clock, they were nearing the Belgian border. From the back of his truck, Stan saw numerous border fortifications: trenches, wire entanglements, pill boxes and tank traps, and then an air raid siren droned. Stan found it quite a thrill to watch infantrymen scuttling into their trenches with their rifles and machine guns. Their own convoy pulled off the road, the vehicles taking cover under some trees. Grabbing ammunition and rifles the men clambered down. 'These precautions were in case the planes came low enough for our rifle fire to be effective,' noted Stan, 'and also in case they tried to land troops or spies by parachute.'

As they crossed the border into Belgium, they were greeted by waving and cheering civilians, scenes that followed them as they trundled along the dusty roads. Progress was slow because of the traffic, so that when they finally stopped at around 9.30 that evening, they were only just outside Tournai, less than twenty miles east of the French city of Lille. As they clambered out of their trucks and began unlimbering the guns, a flight of twelve German bombers flew over and were met by a hail of antiaircraft gunfire. Much to the gunners' delight, one of the planes was hit.

Back across the English Channel, the news of the German offensive was not slow in arriving. Neville Chamberlain had gone to bed the previous evening humiliated and defeated and knowing it was almost certainly his last night as Prime Minister. Yet when he was awoken shortly after 5.30 a.m., it was to be told the Germans had attacked and that there was now a new crisis. Winston Churchill, too, had been woken early, and he was immediately confronted with reams of telegrams pouring in from the Admiralty, War Office, and Foreign Office. At 6 a.m. and again twenty minutes later, he spoke to the British Ambassador in Paris. The news was that Belgium and the Netherlands had been invaded and that the French and British were now in the process of moving into Belgium, as had been planned, to meet the attack. Around 7 a.m., his son, Randolph, telephoned again and asked his father what was going on. Churchill told him. And what about becoming Prime Minister, Randolph then asked. 'Oh, I don't know about that,' Churchill replied. 'Nothing matters now except beating the enemy.'

The news spread fast. Up at Drem in Scotland, David Crook was woken by his batman with the words, 'Jerry's into Holland and Belgium.' David was astonished. At breakfast, he noticed everyone else was just as surprised, yet he also sensed a general feeling of relief too that the war had now really begun, and that as a result they would at last see some proper action. 'Now,' noted David, 'we could give the Huns a taste of their own medicine!'

In Surrey, Daidie Penna had also heard the news. Some friends of hers were holidaying in Biarritz and she wondered how they might get back. 'Now they'll be wishing they'd gone to Blackpool!' she noted. Everything seemed rather tense, although the mood in the village was calm if rather depressed. She also wondered what was going to happen to Chamberlain. The day before she had been excited by the prospect of his resignation. Now, however, she supposed he would probably carry on after all.

It was a thought that had occurred to Chamberlain too. Between endless meetings and briefings the War Cabinet met in emergency session three times that day: at 8 a.m., at 11.30 and then again in the afternoon, at 4.30. In the first of these sessions, the PM insisted that now was not the time for a change of leader and that he should at least stay on to see through the immediate crisis. Only Samuel Hoare rallied to this point of view. Kingsley Wood, a friend and long-time colleague of Chamberlain's, insisted that the German offensive only made it more imperative that he go; Halifax agreed. Still Chamberlain did not resign, however. There were more pressing military matters to deal with. Not until during the third Cabinet session – and it was the fifth item on the agenda – did Chamberlain reveal the news from Bournemouth. The Labour Party, he announced, had agreed to join the Government but not under the present leader. This, then, sealed the matter at last. Chamberlain announced that he would tender his resignation to the King.

One last effort was made to persuade Halifax, but he again demurred. At the Palace, the King was appalled and made it clear how grossly unfairly he felt Chamberlain had been treated. But, since this was the situation, he hoped Halifax would take over. Chamberlain explained that Halifax had already refused. That meant only one man could possibly take over. 'I asked Chamberlain his advice,' wrote George VI in his diary, '& he told me Winston was the man to send for.'

On this day of days, Britain had a new Prime Minister.

5

The First Clash in the Air

ADOLF HITLER'S PERSONAL TRAIN, *Amerika*, was impressive with its Pullman coaches, armour plating and accompanying flak wagons, but while the Führer liked to ensure he lived in the kind of style that befitted the leader of the German Reich, he was not a man overly bothered by luxury. The same could not be said of his deputy, the Commander-in-Chief of the Luftwaffe, Feldmarschall Hermann Göring, who stepped on to his own personal, and decidedly luxurious, train, *Asia*, that morning, 10 May.

No other leading Nazi embraced the opportunities for riches and extravagance that the regime presented as wholeheartedly as he. No other Nazi had so many self-designed uniforms; none had so flamboyant and extensive an estate as Göring had built for himself in the forests to the north-east of Berlin. Begun as a hunting lodge, it had greatly increased in size a few years before and had recently been massively extended yet again. It was now a huge pile of grandiose proportions: his study was now the original 'rustic' barn – which had been a house in its own right. There was a long, marble-lined 'Great Hall'; there were games rooms, gun rooms, an art gallery where he housed his ever-growing collection, and a library. The walls were lined with paintings, the furniture was exquisite. Inside and out, vast statues and sculptures lined corridors, entrance-ways or glades in the forest. And it was called 'Carinhall' after his dearly beloved and departed first wife; indeed, Carin's remains had been brought back from Sweden, where she had died in 1931, and reinterred in an equally extravagant underground tomb in the grounds.

Göring loved food, he loved wine, he loved collecting art, he loved hunting; he loved cars and he loved sailing too: he even had a luxury motorized yacht built, and called, unsurprisingly, *Carin II*. He *loved* luxury. His train, *Asia*, was also armour-plated, but, inside, the carriages were adorned with velvet upholstery and hand-produced wooden panelling. The walls were lined with tapestries and further works of art, while in the sleeping quarters Göring had a huge personal bathtub that would not have looked out of place in Carinhall. There was a darkroom for his own personal photographer, a hospital with six beds and an operating theatre, and his personal barber shop, which included hand mirrors, compacts, powder puffs, sun lamps, cologne and perfume atomizers. Göring was nothing if not a dandy. As well as the accompanying flak wagons, there were two flat wagons on which he kept an assortment of motor cars, which included American, French and German models, a shooting brake and a luxury Mercedes.

Although often portrayed as an overweight buffoon in the foreign press, Göring was in fact an extremely clever, wily and Machiavellian individual with a very high IQ and a canny ability to get his way through a combination of charm, guile and utter ruthlessness. Born in Bavaria in January 1893, the son of an upper-middle-class colonial official, he had been privately educated – even being sent to Rutland in England to study Greek – before entering military college and joining the Prussian army in 1912. After a stint in the trenches during the first year of the Great War, Göring transferred to the air force, first by becoming an unofficial observer for his lifelong friend Bruno Loerzer, but then, after being found out, obtaining a formal transfer. He went on to become a fighter pilot, to score twenty-two victories, to win the Blue Max and finally to lead the Richthofen Squadron, Jagdgeschwader 1, formerly led by the most famous pilot of them all, Manfred von Richthofen, the Red Baron.

After the war, he continued flying – barnstorming at air shows and then for the Swedish airline, Svenska Lufttrafik. As a highly decorated fighter ace with pale eyes and lean, dashing good looks, Göring soon made something of a splash in Swedish society. Clients included the wealthy Swedish explorer Eric von Rosen. It was through von Rosen that Göring met his future wife, Carin, Countess von Fock.

It was also at von Rosen's country estate at Rockelstad that Göring spotted the swastika symbol embellishing various places at the castle – von Rosen had found the emblem on various Nordic runes and had incorporated them into Rockelstad. It was supposedly Rockelstad that encouraged Göring to suggest to Hitler the adoption of the symbol by the National Socialists.

At this time, Göring already had political ambitions, and although he might easily have stayed in Sweden for ever, his affair with the married Carin and the gossip that surrounded them in Stockholm led him to return to Germany, where he met and befriended Adolf Hitler. Captivated by Hitler and his ideals, he became his new friend's right-hand man in the National Socialist Party, and head of the paramilitary Nazi organization, the Sturmabteilung, or SA.

Göring was badly wounded in the groin during the Beer Hall Putsch in Munich in 1923, and it was during his long period of recovery in Italy and Austria that he first became addicted to morphine, administered initially as an antidote to his extreme pain. This addiction had plagued him ever since; battles against the drug were won then lost but many of his more outlandish characteristics were most likely a direct result of regular morphine taking. A narcotic and highly addictive, morphine, besides relieving pain, also relieves fear and anxiety and produces euphoria. It plays havoc with a person's glands and hormones, and prompts outbursts of increased energy and vanity, as well as delusions. Extreme vitality is often followed by periods of languor and inactivity. All these symptoms were displayed by Göring.

In many ways, he was a contradictory character. A family man, he adored his first wife, Carin, but was equally devoted to his second wife, Emmy, and his young daughter with her, Edda. He loved art and nature, could be kind, generous and loyal, yet was also unscrupulous, demonic, vain and power-hungry. How much of this Jekyll and Hyde persona was a part of his natural make-up and how much was due to his drug addiction, it is impossible to know.

Certainly, however, in his moments of energy – and he was a highly driven, ambitious and determined individual before he had ever succumbed to morphine – Göring was to prove one of Hitler's most loyal and capable lieutenants. It was Göring who created the Schutzstaffel, or SS, set up initially as Hitler's personal bodyguard; and it was Göring who created the Sicherheitsdienst, the SD, of which the Gestapo, the Nazi secret police, was part. He was responsible for establishing the concentration camps. He became Speaker of the German Parliament, President of the Reichstag, Prime Minister of Prussia, President of the Prussian State Council, Reich Master of Forestry and Game (his hunting laws still exist), and creator of the new German air force, which, under his command, in 1935 became the Luftwaffe.

By this time, his position and standing within the Reich had never been higher. Hitler, the visionary, was no economist, but Göring was proving himself an adept businessman. In 1935, Hitler gave him control of Germany's oil and synthetic-rubber production effort, no small responsibility for a country so short of oil itself. The following year, in October 1936, he was given the post of Special Commissioner of the Four-Year Plan, over and above the Economic Minister, Hjalmar Schacht. His task was to completely reorganize the German economy: to continue rearmament and get ready for war, to build up resources, particularly of fuel, rubber and metal, to reduce unemployment, improve agricultural production, develop public works (including the building of autobahns), and stimulate coal and other industrial production.

By surrounding himself with top-level German industrialists and bankers and by using his considerable powers of charm and diplomacy, he concluded numerous bilateral deals in Yugoslavia, Romania, Spain, Turkey and Finland, enabling Germany to stockpile the kind of minerals – such as tungsten, oil, nickel and iron ore – that would enable the country to continue growing militarily. The Four-Year Plan revolutionized Germany's economy, run by Göring through his private cabinet of economic advisers and specialists brought into his Prussian Ministry.

Through bribes, favours and secret deals, he also created a vast industrial empire. Recognizing that iron ore and steel production was under-performing within Germany, he also set up his own iron and steel works, absorbing many of the independent iron works in the Ruhr Valley and in Austria – it was one of the reasons he was so in favour of the *Anschluss* – and so monopolizing the iron and steel industry in the expanding Reich until he had become one of the biggest industrialists in Europe, if not the world. His Hermann Göring Works, or HGW, became all-powerful. Furthermore, rather than ever becoming state-owned, HGW remained his own private concern. It was no wonder he could lavish such vast sums on Carinhall. Moreover, as the economic master of the Reich, he controlled Germany's entire foreign exchange reserves, while no corporation could purchase any imports without his say-so. Incredibly, he also established his own private intelligence service, the *Forschungsamt*, which similarly – and with Hitler's knowledge – remained in his own private control. Göring might have been willing to hand over the SS and SD to Himmler, but not the *Forschungsamt*, a listening service that bugged and tapped not only foreign leaders and businessmen but also almost every single leading Nazi. Thus in the political power struggles that were such a feature of the Nazi regime, Göring was always able to use political, military and industrial espionage to keep one step ahead.

Whilst building his industrial and economic empire, he was also developing the Luftwaffe, which, by May 1940, contained the majority of Germany's anti-aircraft forces as well as the *Fallschirmjäger* units – the airborne forces. Thus in addition to his economic and political interests, he also had a considerable number of air and land forces under his command. No other Nazi combined political and military power to such a degree.

Ironically, however, despite his military background, Göring was not particularly militarily minded – strategically or operationally so at any rate. His enormously forceful personality, and popularity in the early days of the Third Reich, had enabled him to attract the best men from both army and civil life into his fledgling air force. As the most powerful economic figure in Germany, he had also ensured that the Luftwaffe did not want for money. Indeed, its exponential expansion in just a few short years was an astonishing achievement. Persuasive, and infectiously optimistic, he truly believed that almost anything could be achieved. Yet his optimism often led him to ignore unpalatable truths, while his divide and rule policy for keeping his Luftwaffe General Staff in line – a feature of the Nazi regime – frequently proved itself to be counter-productive.

It is unlikely, for example, that as Göring boarded *Asia* on the morning of 10 May to meet his Luftwaffe commanders, he would have wanted to know the real state of the Luftwaffe's forces as the western offensive began. Dressed this morning in one of his specially designed summer white uniforms, his fingers bedecked with rings, he set out for the Air Staff's Permanent Headquarters at Kurfürst just outside the capital in a confident yet anxious mood. On paper, his Luftwaffe had an effective strength of some 5,446 aircraft. But strength on paper is not the same as actual strength, and actual strength is not the same as operational strength. For example, the third wing of the bomber group KG 4, in which Oberleutnant Hajo Herrmann commanded a *Staffel*, had an actual strength of thirty-five Junkers 88 bombers, but eight of those were not fit or ready for action. This was nothing unusual. Barely a single Luftwaffe unit could fly all the aircraft lined up at their respective airfields along the German borders that morning. Furthermore, out of the actual strength available to the Luftwaffe, a number were held back for home defence or were on service in Norway. What this meant was that, as the attack began, Göring had two *Luftflotten* available and a little over 1,500 twin- or single-engine bombers and just above 1,000 single- or twin-engine fighters. In other words, less than half what he thought.

'Among the high command,' wrote General Speidel, Chief of Staff of Luftflotte 2, 'above all in the case of the commander-in-chief of the Luftwaffe himself, he was only interested in the kind of strength figures he wanted to hear and he wanted to believe.'

Of course, there was one very quick way of reducing aircraft losses, and that was to destroy as many of the enemy's aircraft as soon as possible. Luftwaffe intelligence reckoned that in January 1940, the French Armée de l'Air had around 320 bombers and 630 fighters, while the RAF had 1,122 and 918 of each. Recognizing that Britain was hardly likely to throw all its available aircraft into France, the Luftwaffe planners were confident they could roll over the French air force easily enough and then the RAF in detail, by luring them a bit at a time into the fray. The Dutch and Belgian air forces were so small that it was reckoned a short, sharp strike should see them off.

German intelligence, however, was some way off mark. In fact, by 10 May, the French had over 5,000 aircraft of which 3,500 were combat machines, that is, bombers and fighters. It was true that there were only 879 French operational combat aircraft along the front lines, but there were also another 1,700 or so out of the line but combat ready and which, theoretically, could be put into action quite quickly. That they were not at the front on 10 May had been a deliberate policy to avoid them being destroyed on the ground should the Luftwaffe launch surprise air attacks. As such, it was quite a sensible idea.

German appreciation of the RAF's strength was closer to the mark, however. The RAF and Royal Navy had been the principal targets for Britain's rearmament programme, but even so there was a growing feeling in Britain that it was all too little and too late. This was one of the main reasons why when the 'German hordes', as Churchill referred to them, launched their attack with their apparently mighty forces, so many leading political and military figures were plunged into such despair. Privy to the endless arguments and prevarications over rearmament that had taken place over the past few years, they were keenly aware of Britain's military deficiencies. Hence their lack of confidence on 10 May.

However, because of its greater share of the rearmament cake, the RAF had nonetheless been obliged to make proportionally more of a contribution in the air than on the ground in France. The organization of the RAF forces in France was horribly complicated. Unlike the Luftwaffe, which was divided rather like ground forces, but into Air Fleets and Air Corps consisting of a mixture of aircraft, the RAF was divided into three home-based commands: Bomber, Fighter and Coastal. The problem was that aircraft for France had to be drawn from those commands and then placed in a new set-up, known as the British Air Forces in France. This was in turn then split in two. The BEF Air Component consisted of thirteen squadrons of Lysanders and Blenheims for reconnaissance, and Hurricanes for protection, and was to directly support the army, and so came under the control of General Gort. The Advanced Air Striking Force (AASF), on the other hand, was independent of both Gort and the French and was commanded by Air Vice-Marshal Playfair, answerable to Bomber Command HQ back in England. Should Gort want stronger bomber support than could be provided by the Air Component, he had to apply to the War Office back in London, who would then ask the Air Ministry, who in turn would order Bomber Command. They would then command AVM Playfair. It was hardly a system that encouraged the kind of quick response so often needed in the heat of battle.

There were around 500 front-line British aircraft on the morning of 10 May, although, as with the Armée de l'Air, there were more waiting in the wings – not least four more fighter squadrons that had been promised from the UK the moment an offensive started, and a bomber group from Bomber Command operating from England that had been put under command of the AASF.

Like everyone on the Allied side, the air forces had been expecting the offensive to begin sooner rather than later. At Senon airfield north-west of Verdun, however, the two squadrons at the airfield, 87 Fighter Squadron and 2 Squadron of Lysander reconnaissance planes, had been given something of a warning on the night of 9 May, when the Headquarters of the French air force's Operations Zone (North) received intelligence that Luftwaffe attacks were expected at dawn. Given the task of covering the northern part of the Maginot Line, these two squadrons had been temporarily severed from the rest of the RAF units in France and placed in a French area of operations. In fact orders were sent recalling them back to north-west France on the night of the 9th, but were then cancelled.

So it was that at 5 a.m. the pilots of 87 Squadron awoke at Senon to the sound of ack-ack guns and then, more menacingly, the intense crump of bombs exploding, which shook the ground and tents in which the pilots had been sleeping. Roland 'Bee' Beamont, nineteen years old, had already had an interrupted night as he had been feeling increasingly unwell, and had only just got to sleep when the explosions began.

'Ack-ack – 'ell!' shouted his tent partner, Johnny Cock, as more explosions sent the lamp in the middle of their tent swinging. A moment later, Johnny had disappeared outside. Clutching his stomach, Bee followed, to find a group of pyjama-clad pilots standing in a clearing in the trees beside the airfield, gazing up at the sky as a formation of German bombers thundered overhead.

Minutes later, the pilots were scrambled, hastily putting on flying gear over their pyjamas and running for their Hurricanes as the groundcrew started up their machines. There could be no flying for Bee, however, who, wracked by dysentery, was forced to return groaning to his camp bed; it was not the first time he or other pilots had suffered because of the poor standard of conditions at their airfields in France.

Bee may have been prostrate in his tent, but before 6 a.m., the rest of the 87 Squadron pilots were already engaged in fighting over Thionville near the Luxembourg border. 'The boys got four Huns before breakfast,' noted Bee, 'and Voase Jeff was attacked by an Me 109* while force-landing with a damaged radiator, but he got away with it.' Voase Jeff had been hit earlier by return fire from a Dornier 17.

To the west, at airfields spread through northern France behind the BEF, the main part of the RAF Air Component was also now hastily preparing to carry out its duty in support of the BEF. At Méharicourt to the south-east of Amiens in the Somme Valley, 18 Squadron of twin-engine Blenheims were slightly slower off the mark, however. Pilot Officer Arthur Hughes, a tall, lean-faced 24-year-old, was only woken at 7 a.m. when the wireless in his room was switched on. Still half asleep, he listened drowsily to the news until realizing that the announcer was

* From 1926 to 1938, Messerschmitts were given the abbreviation 'Bf', which stood for Bayerische Flugzeugwerke, the name of the aircraft-manufacturing company at which Professor Willi Messerschmitt was the chief designer. However, in 1938, the company was reconstituted as Messerschmitt AG, and from then on Messerschmitt aircraft were given the prefix 'Me'. Despite this, aircraft dating from the Bayerische Flugzeugwerke days were still known as Bf 109s and Bf 110s etc. In this book, however, I shall stick with 'Me' throughout.

talking about the invasion of Holland and Belgium. Jumping out of bed, he hurriedly dressed wondering whether it would be the last time he performed such a routine.

At the mess, no-one was quite sure what was going on, but as the pilots began to gather and there were still no orders, they decided to have breakfast. 'When we began at 8.10,' Arthur scribbled in his diary, 'we were at Readiness 1. By the time I finished at Readiness 2. At 8.40 a.m. I was ordered off on a photographic reconnaissance.' Rushing to flights, he felt a mixture of emotions: devil-may-care yet horribly scared and wildly excited all at the same time.

Having mentally prepared himself for immediate action, Arthur was then told that Pilot Officer Smith would be undertaking the visual recce instead – over Venlo, where Helmut Damm and the 171st Infantry Division were crossing into Belgium. Several tense hours followed, with Arthur and the other pilots hanging around near their flight, waiting for news. Smith got back at 11.30 reporting that Brussels was blazing fiercely, and that all of the bridges along the Moselle had been blown up. 'He also saw some nuns running frantically along the bank,' added Arthur. Smith had then been attacked by an Me 110, a German twin-engine fighter, and although hit, managed to evade his attacker by flying at only fifty feet off the ground at 285 mph, as fast as the Blenheim could take him. The only problem was that by flying so low, he exposed himself to enemy small-arms fire and was hit again. Fortunately, he managed to make it back to Méharicourt in one piece.

Meanwhile, further west, the pilots and aircrew of the Advanced Air Striking Force were also hurriedly being scrambled into the air. 1 Squadron, part of the Advanced Air Striking Force at Vassincourt to the south-east of Reims in northern France, had been woken at 3.30 a.m. and told to head straight to the airfield. With conditions considerably better than 87 Squadron's, the pilots were billeted comfortably in the nearby village of Neuville, with a splendid mess in the *Mairie*. Twenty-two-year-old Billy Drake was one of the 1 Squadron pilots who hurried straight from his digs to the *Mairie*, where a lorry was waiting to take them all to the airfield. Ever since April had turned to May, they had heard rumours that something might soon be afoot and now, on this Friday morning, they heard aircraft overhead as they approached the airfield.

Hurrying from the lorry, they headed over to the dispersal tent and the 'A' Flight commander, Flight Lieutenant 'Johnny' Walker, immediately rang through to Operations to find out what was going on. With the kind of insouciance that was a feature of 1 Squadron in particular, Johnny returned laughing, reporting that Ops were in a hell of a stew. 'Plots all over the board,' he grinned.

They did not have to wait long. At 5 a.m. the phone in the dispersal tent rang with orders for them to scramble and patrol Metz at 20,000 feet. They headed off in two flights, Billy with 'B' Flight led by Flight Lieutenant 'Prosser' Hanks. Having taken off, they formed up into two sections of three, maintaining the tight figure 'V' vics that they had trained at so assiduously, and with a further pilot following behind as 'arse-end Charlie' protecting their rear. Climbing through the thick early-morning haze, at around 5,000 feet they emerged into bright clear sunlight.

The problem was that with no controller on the ground vectoring them into position, they were now on their own. They could barely see the French countryside below; nor could they see any aircraft at all.

The pilots of the RAF and Armée de l'Air were very quickly discovering just how confusing air warfare could be and how all the balls were in the court of the attacker. Neither side had an early-warning system such as radar. This mattered less to the Luftwaffe because the pilots knew before they took off where they were heading and when. For the Allied airmen, however, it was a question of responding to visual reports – which invariably arrived too late – or of mounting patrols in the hope of spotting some of the enemy.

Eventually, however, 'B' Flight did spy a formation of Dornier 17s, which they attacked. 'Boy' Mould overshot and had his Hurricane riddled with bullets as a result, but Prosser Hanks managed to down one. Soon after, Billy managed to get separated from his section because he had been watching some Me 109s in the distance over Metz. Two 109s attacked him, but Billy managed to elude them and then get behind one of them himself. Closing in, Billy was almost within firing range, but the German pilot dived down towards the deck* and sped towards the German frontier. Following him, Billy crossed over into Germany only to watch the German pilot fly underneath some electric cables, hoping Billy would follow and hit them. Fortunately, he managed the same feat himself and opened fire with his eight Browning .303 machine guns. Much to his satisfaction, the 109 crashed in flames into a wood, exploding on impact.

* The 'deck' is the ground.

*

Although 87 Squadron had been tussling with the Luftwaffe, there was comparatively little enemy air activity over north-east France that day. The full weight of the Luftwaffe was reserved for the skies of Holland, Belgium and north-west France. Quite deliberately, as part of the German deception measures, the mass of bombers and dive-bombers – as well as airborne landings – took place in the north in support of Army Group B. Luftwaffe activity over the Ardennes was left primarily to the fighters, whose task it was to pounce on any unsuspecting Allied reconnaissance aircraft that dared to show its face.

Thus the beginning of the campaign was primarily the task of Luftflotte 2, under the command of Generaloberst Albert Kesselring. 'Smiling Albert', as he was known because of his even temper and willingness to break into a wide grin, was popular amongst both his superiors and subordinates, lacking as he did the patrician hauteur of many of the leading commanders in the Wehrmacht. There was certainly nothing particularly striking about him: his was a slightly bulky, rather bland, almost forgettable face. Yet underneath lay an iron will and a ruthless determination. Both efficient and pragmatic – as well as an unrepentant optimist – Kesselring was a cool-headed and intelligent man; precisely the kind of person a more flamboyant character like Göring needed to command one of his primary air fleets.

After the 1914–18 war, Kesselring had remained in the post-war army, demonstrating his aptitude as a staff officer, and where he steadily rose to the rank of Colonel with the command of a division. With the birth of the clandestine Luftwaffe in 1933, Kesselring was one of those drawn from the army by Göring to help build the new air force. Given a necessarily civilian post he set to work running the administration and airfield development of the Luftwaffe. He also taught himself to fly and worked hard to develop the Luftwaffe strategically and tactically. By 1936, he was back in uniform, both as a general and as the Luftwaffe Chief of Staff.

At the onset of war, Kesselring was in charge of the 1st Air Fleet that helped launch the blitzkrieg on Poland with such devastating results, and then had taken over as Chief of the Berlin Air Command. In January, the Mechelen incident had taken place, with Göring subjected to a considerable torrent of rage from Hitler as a result. He in turn called his senior commanders together to give them a severe dressing down. First the commander and Chief of Staff of Luftflotte 2 were sacked, and then the rest of his senior commanders were called in. After rollocking them all, he turned to Kesselring and snarled, 'And you will take over Luftflotte 2 – because there's no-one else.'

When Kesselring did take over in January, he was pleasantly surprised to find Luftflotte 2 in an advanced state of preparation already, yet the new commander recognized there was still much to do. Strenuous weeks from February to May were spent with staff conferences, plan revisions and operation rehearsals both on the ground and in the air. The thorny issue for Kesselring was the timing and co-ordination of the airborne forces to be used, of whom he had no real experience, with the bombers. Thus Kesselring had been understandably nervous that morning of 10 May. 'I breathed a sigh of relief,' he noted, 'when the first favourable reports came in.'

The aim of the airborne operations – the planning of which had greatly interested the Führer – was to catch the enemy off guard and to secure airfields and key defences in Holland and Belgium. To reach the drop zones, rather a large number of slow, poorly protected Junkers 52 transport planes and even more vulnerable gliders had to fly over much of Holland and Belgium and it was the task of fighters to escort them and give them as much protection as possible.

Amongst those accompanying the airdrops were the Messerschmitt 109s of the three fighter groups of JG 27. The second group were supporting paratroopers of the 7th Fliegerdivision in the Rotterdam area. Flying from Wesel in the Rhine Valley, the II Gruppe first flew over Holland covering one of the later waves of paratroopers. One of the pilots in the 6th Staffel, and flying his first combat mission, was Julius Neumann. Blond and good-looking, the 21-year-old Julius was the second of five children from Harzgerrode in the Harz Mountains. The son of a lawyer who had fought in the First World War, Julius was part of a close and happy middle-class family. His ambition, however, had originally been to join the army. In April 1936, he had joined the labour corps, the *Arbeitsdienst*, as an officer cadet attached to the 51st Infantry Regiment. After a year he was sent to the officers' school in Munich, but eighteen months later was transferred to join the Luftwaffe instead. 'Göring needed pilots,' he says. 'You had to be physically and mentally fit and intelligent enough.' Out of 600 at the officers' school, half were sent to flight school, and one of them was Julius. 'At the beginning of your time in the army, you had to sign a contract,' he adds, 'and wherever you were needed, you had to go.' Unusually for a young man, Julius had no particular interest in flying, but he accepted his fate and duly went to the pilot school in Werneuchen, near Berlin.

This was the A/B school for elementary flying training, which consisted of building up some 150 hours of flying in biplane trainers. It was a thorough and extensive course, and only at the end of it was Julius finally awarded his pilot's certificate and badge. It was also at this point that he was posted to train as a fighter pilot – after an assessment not only of his flying abilities but his character too. He was delighted. 'At fighter pilot school you found the same type of people,' he says. 'Fighter pilots are individualists.' Fighter pilot school lasted another three months in which he began flying the Me 108 trainer and then early models of the Me 109. With a further fifty hours to his name and having survived – the accident rate among trainee pilots on 109s was high – he was finally posted to a fighter group, JG 26, with around 200 hours in his logbook. There he had stayed until February, when he had been posted again, this time to Magdeburg as a *Leutnant* in the 6th Staffel of JG 27.

Not until the beginning of May were the 5th and 6th Staffeln moved to Wesel as the *Jagdgeschwader* made its final preparations for the offensive. Everyone had been both excited and apprehensive about what was to come. Now, at a little after half-past eight on the morning of 10 May, Julius was flying in combat for the first time, escorting Ju 52s as they ferried their second load of airborne troops to the drop zones.

Having completed escort duties of the airborne troops, however, JG 27's task was to then provide protection for the aerial artillery of VIII Fliegerkorps consisting principally of twin-engine Dornier 17s and the already world-famous Junkers 87 dive-bomber. Organizing the *Jagdgeschwader* on the ground was a highly frustrated 28-year-old *Hauptmann*, Adolf Galland, JG 27's adjutant. Desperate to get in the air and specifically in the cockpit of an Me 109, Galland had been a fighter pilot with the German Condor Legion that had been sent to Spain to support General Franco's Nationalists. There, he had led a *Staffel* of Heinkel He 51 biplanes operating in direct support of Franco's troops on the ground. In this he had been rather hoisted by his own petard, for he had performed the task so well that when he came back from Spain he had become an acknowledged ground attack expert. After a brief stint commanding a *Staffel* of the embryonic JG 52, then designated JG 433, he had been moved back to ground attack and given his own *Gruppe* of Henschel 123s. For someone as passionate about shooting and air combat as Adolf Galland, commanding yet more biplanes was clearly unacceptable. Managing to persuade a doctor to pass him medically unfit to fly in an open cockpit, he demanded a transfer to a fighter unit. This he was given, but as *Geschwader* adjutant the opportunities for flying had been limited, especially since JG 27 was a developing formation and right up until May was still working up to strength.

Thus on 10 May, 'Dolfo', as he was known, was busy supporting staff operations, liaising with General von Richtofen's VIII Fliegerkorps, and ensuring that each *Staffel* within the *Geschwader* knew exactly what it should be doing. Soon, though, he promised himself, he would get up in the air himself.

It was a hard first day of air fighting. At Méharicourt, only three Blenheims had been sent out on reconnaissance missions all day. Why so few is not clear, except that they were not achieving very much. After Pilot Officer Smith had returned with his aircraft damaged, Pilot Officer Geoff Harding had been ordered into the air. He had not returned. Later in the afternoon, after the airfield was bombed, Pilot Officer Dixon was sent off on another low-level recce mission. By evening, he had also failed to make it back. 'Two out of three!' wrote Arthur Hughes. Nor would they return: Geoff Harding's Blenheim had been shot down by an Me 109 near Venlo, while Dixon's had been hit by ground fire in the same area. Only one man out of the two three-man crews survived.

In the evening three Hurricanes of 79 Squadron landed, having been at Biggin Hill to the south-east of London in the morning, then sent to Manston on the tip of Kent and from there to France. They had been supposed to spend the night at Mons-en-Chaussée but, having chased a Dornier, got lost and so landed at Méharicourt instead. Arthur was amazed to see that one of the pilots was still wearing his pyjamas underneath his flying overalls.

Meanwhile, 87 Squadron had been ordered back to Lille-Marcq airfield this time, rather than Lille-Seclin where they had been before. Bee Beamont, still gripped with dysentery, had spent the morning lying on some bundles of kit while the groundcrew frantically packed up. The ambulance that was due to take him back to Lille never turned up and, after staggering around for it, he stumbled back to the airfield just as it came under attack once more. The rest of the pilots, having a last drink before leaving, dived for the cover of the neighbouring wood as the bombs began falling, so that almost every other tree had a prostrate form behind it. 'It was an interesting experience,' noted Bee, 'listening to the whistle of the bombs and having guessing competitions with one's next-door neighbour as to where the next one would land, while a nightingale would absolutely on no account be diverted from his solo in an oak overhead.' After the raid, Bee eventually secured a lift to Lille from their French interpreter, Capitaine Lasseud of the Armée de l'Air.

At Vassincourt, 1 Squadron had also had a busy day. After his first victory, Billy Drake had safely made it back and had then flown again around midday when 'B' Flight were ordered to provide cover for RAF bombers attacking Luxembourg. They never found the bombers, but did run into some Dorniers and, above them, some 109s. Recognizing that they were in a hopeless position to attack with the German fighters hovering above, Prosser Hanks ordered them not to attack. Just then a vic of three Hurricanes from a different squadron pounced on the Dorniers. A moment later, the 109s were peeling down on them like hawks, and in a trice one of the Hurricanes was tumbling to the ground in flames.

Back on the ground again, the entire squadron was ordered to move, to nearby Berry-au-Bac. 'B' Flight took off again, and this time Billy and 'Boy' Mould shared in shooting down a Heinkel 111 bomber. Arriving back down at Berry, they were soon bombed again. Fortunately, although some of the bombs landed close to the prostrate pilots, most fell wide, killing a neighbouring farmer and his son. Later that evening they took off again on yet another patrol. Smoke was now rising from several towns and villages. The airfield at Reims Champagne had been badly bombed. Here and there, farmhouses burned, angry flames and smoke pitching into the sky. They eventually went to bed as dusk fell. At 2.45 a.m. they would be woken again. 'There was a feeling that total chaos was reigning,' says Billy. 'Germans were everywhere and we were constantly being bombed. In between we were flying four or five times a day.'

However exhausting it may have been, at least 1 Squadron's pilots were all still alive. The same could not be said for far too many of the pilots and crew of the Fairey Battle squadrons. During the winter and spring, Battles had already proved themselves unsuited to the task given them. Single-engine machines, they were designed as two-seater day bombers, but they were horribly under-armed with just one manually operated Vickers machine gun to the rear and one machine gun on the right wing, much the same armament as a later First World War aircraft. Even without their bombs they were too slow and sitting ducks for modern fighters. Despite their obvious uselessness for a modern war, they had been sent into action on this first day. The first target that morning had been a German column advancing through Luxembourg, and attacking low at just 250 feet, the first eight Battles sent into action met a hail of small-arms fire. Three were shot down immediately. More Battles were sent into action later in the day and fared no better. Of thirty-two despatched over the battle area, thirteen were destroyed and every single one damaged to some lesser or greater degree. It was a high cost in return for negligible results.

It was a sobering day for the Allied air forces, which were new to this kind of war. The RAF was in France primarily to offer close air support to the forces on the ground, yet official policy within the RAF was to avoid direct air support; after all, most of Britain's air rearmament programme was dedicated to the home-based Fighter, Bomber and Coastal Commands. Of course, if there were no doctrine for close air support, it follows that there should have been little training in such practice either.

What was already self-evident was that not enough planning or thought had been put into RAF air operations in France. There could be no benefits to low-level reconnaissance, for example, if none of the aircraft sent on such missions ever came back, as in the case of 18 Squadron. Others did make it home, but their reports were often sketchy. Equally, vainly patrolling in the hope of finding the enemy was hardly an efficient way of fighting an air war either. Worst of all was the lack of communication and co-ordination. At midday, the AASF had been asked to bomb the German airborne troops at Waalhaven, but at the same time six Blenheim fighters – rather than bombers – had been sent from Manston in Kent to attack the same Dutch airfield. Intercepted by Me 110s, only one made it back. The RAF conducted just thirty-three bomber sorties on 10 May. One sortie represents a combat flight of one aircraft, so a bombing mission of six Blenheims is six sorties. Thirty-three sorties all day from more than 220 bombers hardly represented maximum effort.

By May, 85 per cent of the Armée de l'Air's aircraft were modern types, but its organization was poor. Its forces were divided into areas of command called Zone d'Opérations, each of which had its complement of all types of aircraft. The commander of each zone, however, was independent of the others, which made it very difficult to bring a concentration of air power to bear in the way that the Luftwaffe had been doing. Once again, the lack of control and co-ordination on the ground meant the Armée de l'Air could never hope to fulfil its potential. The Luftwaffe, as it intended, could deal with them a bit at a time, chipping away at those they encountered in the air and bombing airfields, aircraft and communications on the ground before the Allies knew what had hit them.

The RAF in France suffered sixty-one aircraft lost or damaged, with a further fourteen casualties from the UK. Of those, twenty-six would be repaired and flown again. The Armée de l'Air suffered seventy-four lost or damaged, of which eighteen would fly again. These were serious but not yet critical losses. For the Dutch and Belgian air forces, however, 10 May was truly a day of infamy as their weak air forces crumbled under the weight of Luftwaffe attacks. The Dutch lost half their aircraft.

As far as Göring and his commanders were concerned, the air war was going very much to plan. Experience in the Spanish Civil War and then in Poland and more recently Norway had proved that their tactics were right. Yes, they had expected stiffer opposition from the Allies than they had from the Poles, but the enemy did not appear to have known what had hit them. Careful planning and co-ordination, combined with initiative, had seen to that.

Yet it had not gone all the way of the Luftwaffe on 10 May. Admittedly the assault on the Belgian forts of Eben Emael had been a great success – even though the Belgian defenders would not finally surrender until the following day – and airborne landings around Rotterdam were also largely successful, yet the occupation of The Hague by airborne troops failed with horrendous losses of transport planes and of paratroopers.

Although the 2,500 aircraft the Luftwaffe could call on was a great number, losses on that opening day of the offensive were, in fact, appalling. For all its supreme confidence, the Luftwaffe had 192 fighters and bombers lost or damaged that day, of which only sixty-six would fly again. But that figure did not include the staggering 244 Junkers 52 transport planes and gliders crashed, shot down and destroyed that day – more than half the number that had been available that morning. In all, no fewer than 353 German aircraft and 904 pilots and crew would never fly again – a huge total for one day of fighting. In the German aircraft factories in April, only 310 fighters had been built, and 338 bombers. That might also sound like a large number but it soon wouldn't be if the Luftwaffe continued to sustain losses at even a fraction of the rate suffered on that first day.

Although there had been sporadic small-scale aerial engagements over the previous autumn, winter and spring, and although the RAF and

Luftwaffe had faced each other in an unequal contest in Norway, it was 10 May that really marked the beginning of the aerial clash between Britain and Germany – a clash that would continue all through that long summer and autumn of 1940, and would have far-reaching and decisive consequences for the rest of the Second World War. In terms of bare-faced courage, that opening salvo showed that the two sides were evenly matched. But courage would not be enough for the men of the RAF or the Luftwaffe. What they both needed were planes – good planes suitable for the task given them – aircrew and pilots. Plenty of trained pilots.

6

Breakthrough

'MORNING REPORTS SHOW further extension of objectives attained,' scrawled General Franz Halder on the morning of Sunday, 12 May. So far, so good. The German Sixth Army had linked up with the German airborne troops at Eben Emael and the Belgians there had surrendered; the Albert Canal, a key obstacle that ran from Antwerp to Liège, had been crossed. The Dutch army had fallen back on Rotterdam, while the French Seventh Army had been met and forced back from Tilburg towards Antwerp. That meant that most of Holland was now in German hands. Intelligence had also reached the Germans that the British and French were moving up towards the Dyle position, just as Halder had hoped.

Dutch resistance crumbled even more during the ensuing day, with German troops reaching the shores of the Zuyder Zee. The French Seventh Army, its forward units more than a hundred miles from the French border, was also struggling against one of the few German panzer divisions in the Army Group B and also the attentions of the Luftwaffe. The Belgians were stumbling too, and were now falling back to desperately try to link up with their French and British allies along the Dyle position. Meanwhile, although the BEF was now dug in along the Dyle, Général Blanchard's French First Army was struggling against the mounting tide of refugees and incessant Luftwaffe attacks to reach its allotted positions. By dusk, only two-thirds of Blanchard's men had reached the Dyle.

Nonetheless, as Halder was well aware, it was in the south, in Army Group A's sector, that the critical battle would be played out.

Hauptmann Hans von Luck and his company in the 7th Armoured Reconnaissance Regiment had reached the River Meuse at Houx, a few miles to the north of Dinant that evening, 12 May, incredibly, ahead of schedule. The advance had been through difficult terrain but they had not met any great resistance. Now, from the high ground that rose away from the east bank of the great river, they could see the valley below. The Meuse was more than a hundred metres wide. On the far side, wooded, craggy slopes rose sharply. There were also broken bridges, which they had hoped to take intact. Hans and his men felt their way slowly into the valley, but soon came under well-directed small-arms and heavy-artillery fire.

In fact, it was the Werner Advance Detachment, troops of the 5th Panzer Division, that had first reached the Meuse, although, because 7th Panzer was so far ahead of the rest of 5th Panzer, these men had been put under Rommel's command. Luftwaffe aerial support had reported that the bridge at Yvoir, some seven miles north of Dinant, was still intact, so the Werner Detachment had hurried on towards it. At 5.25 p.m., two German scout cars sped on to the bridge and were halfway across when the frantic Belgian engineers managed to blow it, sending the structure and the Germans on it into the water below.

Although that crossing attempt had been scuppered, it was later discovered that less than a mile to the south at Houx, near to Hans von Luck and his men, there was a weir and a lock system, strung either side of an island in the middle of the Meuse. Incredibly, the footbridge over the weir and lock had been neither destroyed nor blocked. At 11 p.m., men of the Werner Detachment crossed the river at Houx and, although they soon attracted enemy fire, were able to establish a small bridgehead. The first German crossing of the Meuse had been achieved.

Even so, it would require more than one crossing point and one wider than a footbridge to get the entire division across. Rommel himself had reached his division's reconnaissance regiment just before first light on the 13th. Arriving in his six-wheeled armoured car he immediately asked them what the situation was.

'Held up by artillery fire,' Hans von Luck's commander, Major Erdmann, replied.

Rommel asked to be shown where it was coming from and, standing up in his car, peered through his binoculars. It was a little after 4 a.m. Eventually, his face still calm, he turned to the reconnaissance men and said, 'Stay put. This is a job for the infantry.'

From his position on the wooded, rocky heights above the Meuse, Hans watched the sun rising over the valley. Soon elements of the division's lead infantry, the 7th Rifle Regiment, began scurrying down the hill, accompanied by engineers with rubber dinghies. Further to the south, at Dinant itself, Hans learned that the 6th Panzer Grenadier Regiment was also about to attempt a crossing.

'Hardly had the first boats been lowered into the water,' noted Hans, 'than all hell broke loose.' Opposite them, on the far bank, and occupying some positions prepared by the Belgians, were French troops of the 5th and 18th Infantry Divisions. French snipers and heavy artillery pasted the defenceless men struggling to cross the river in dinghies. Their own tanks and guns were counter-firing but the French were too well screened for them to make much impact. 'The infantry attack,' noted Hans, 'came to a standstill.'

Rommel hurried to Dinant, but his men were struggling just as badly there. He needed smoke canisters to create a screen, but he did not have any. Instead, he ordered some houses by the river to be set on fire. The breeze soon carried the smoke across the river, giving the struggling infantry the cover they needed to get across. The general then rejoined the crossing at Houx later that afternoon, organizing covering fire once more, which succeeded in knocking out several French positions, and then personally taking command of the 2nd Battalion of the 7th Rifle Regiment in an effort to try to inspire his men. He was one of the first across, and joined those who had crossed at the weir the night before. Immediately, he ordered a ferry to be built by his engineers. Making it back over to the other side, he was subsequently the first to cross on the ferry in his command armoured car.

By evening, two bridgeheads had been formed – at Houx with the 5th Panzer Division, and at Dinant. All day, Rommel's men had come under intense artillery and small-arms fire. The noise in that valley had been terrific as the sound echoed off the rock. But smoke, highly trained men, and the inspiring leadership and determination of their commander had enabled the Germans to get over that all-important obstacle. Throughout the night, Rommel's engineers worked hard to build pontoon bridges, and, with the ferries, to get tanks, half-tracks and guns across.

A crucial bridgehead had been made; it was now essential to exploit and widen those gains as quickly as possible.

The French opposite Rommel had been badly caught out that day. Dinant was in Belgium and although the French Ninth Army had begun moving forward to the Meuse position once the offensive had begun, its commander, Général André Georges Corap, had reckoned on the Germans – should they attempt an assault there – taking at least ten to fourteen days before they could attempt to cross the river. That gave the French all the time in the world to reach the Dinant area, dig in and build up strength. The weir at Houx was also, bizarrely, the boundary between two French corps – the II and the XI. Coincidentally, it was the precise place that German troops had crossed back in 1914. Why a corps boundary had to be at such an obvious weak spot is not clear; but it explains why, when the Werner Detachment crossed, they found a surprising lack of enemy troops on the night of the 12th. They had inadvertently hit upon a French troop vacuum.

As it happened, the French soldiers from II Corps to the north of Houx had already arrived by the 12th but had not dug in with any urgency at all. To the south, only five of the nine infantry battalions of the 5th and 18th Infantry Divisions had reached the Dinant area. In other words, two German panzer divisions had taken considerably less time to travel the seventy kilometres of their attack than the French divisions had for their almost entirely undisturbed fifty-mile approach. Guderian and von Manstein had always recognized that it would be a race to the Meuse, and at Dinant the Germans had emphatically won hands down.

Further south, near Sedan, Guderian was also managing to keep to his strict three-day timetable and by the evening of the 12th his three divisions had smashed their way through the five major obstacles that barred their way to the Meuse, the last of which was the French border posts some six miles to the east of the river, which had fallen by the afternoon. His men had done all he had asked of them: charging hell for leather, without a break, pumped up on stimulants, and supported by a meticulously planned and unique logistical system. This included pre-prepared fuel dumps and inserting lorries full of laden jerrycans in with the spearhead that could roll past handing out petrol without stopping. Relief crews had also been transported with the lead panzers. These measures had been simple, effective and ingenious.

They had also had little interference from the air. Guderian's lead

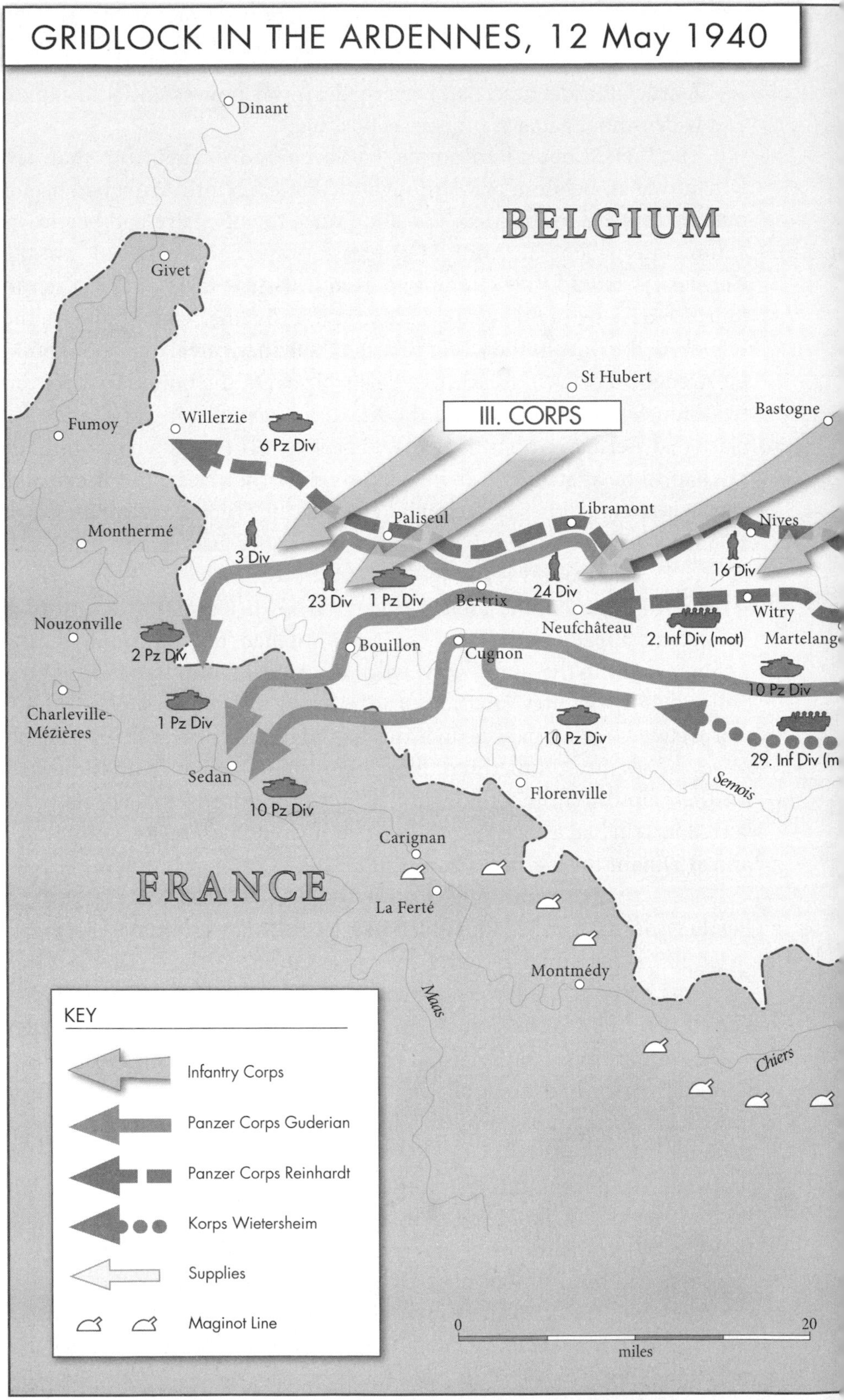

GRIDLOCK IN THE ARDENNES, 12 May 1940

Dinant
BELGIUM
Givet
St Hubert
III. CORPS
Bastogne
Willerzie
Fumoy
6 Pz Div
Libramont
Paliseul
Nives
Monthermé
3 Div
16 Div
24 Div
23 Div
1 Pz Div
Bertrix
Witry
Neufchâteau
Nouzonville
2 Pz Div
Bouillon
2. Inf Div (mot)
Martelang
Cugnon
10 Pz Div
Charleville-
Mézières
1 Pz Div
10 Pz Div
29. Inf Div (m
Sedan
Semois
10 Pz Div
Florenville
Carignan
FRANCE
La Ferté
Montmédy
Maas
Chiers

KEY
Infantry Corps
Panzer Corps Guderian
Panzer Corps Reinhardt
Korps Wietersheim
Supplies
Maginot Line

0 20
miles

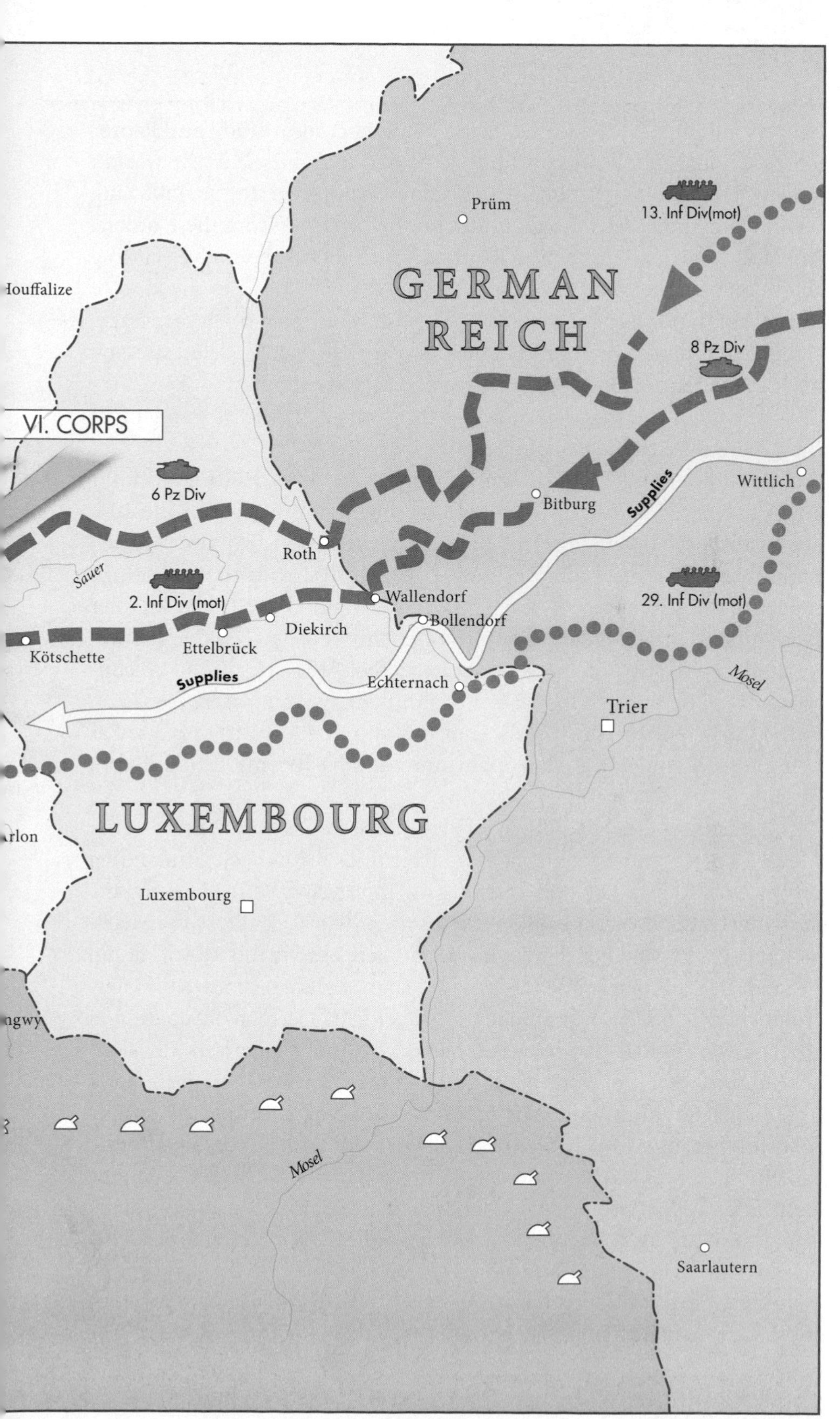

Prüm
13. Inf Div(mot)
GERMAN
REICH
Houffalize
8 Pz Div
VI. CORPS
6 Pz Div
Wittlich
Bitburg
Supplies
Roth
Sauer
2. Inf Div (mot)
Wallendorf
29. Inf Div (mot)
Bollendorf
Diekirch
Kötschette
Ettelbrück
Supplies
Echternach
Mosel
Trier
LUXEMBOURG
Arlon
Luxembourg
Longwy
Mosel
Saarlautern

panzers might have benefited from being the spearhead, but Panzer Corps Reinhardt, following behind, had soon found itself in the world's biggest gridlock as the infantry divisions supposed to be following behind and along strict march routes began deviating from these orders. In places, divisions competing for road space found themselves cutting across one another – or trying to, at any rate – which led to the kind of traffic jam that would make the M25 in rush hour seem like a race track. General Reinhardt's divisions became increasingly separated and split up; his lead 6th Panzer Division was shredded as no fewer than four infantry divisions following tried to cut across its advance. By the morning of 13 May, there were traffic jams some 170 miles long.

Yet although the bulk of Army Group A was thus a sitting duck for any Allied aerial attack, no such assault came. On the night of the 10th and again the following morning, Allied reconnaissance aircraft spotted a number of German columns going through the Ardennes. Although reported, this was not taken seriously. On the night of 11/12 May another recce pilot reported lengthy columns of enemy vehicles, but this too was treated sceptically. On the afternoon of the 12th yet another reconnaissance pilot reported the same, but although his claims were passed on to the intelligence section of the French Ninth Army, it was dismissed as being absurd. And so a golden opportunity to smash Army Group A went begging . . .

While the Allies had obligingly played ball in Guderian's drive to the Meuse, he was now having a few difficulties with his commanding officer, von Kleist, who was insisting on interfering with plans for the crossing. Guderian accepted von Kleist's order to attack across the Meuse at 4 p.m. on 13 May, but disagreed about where exactly this attack should be made. He was determined to cross at Sedan, a place he knew intimately from when he had been stationed there during its German occupation in the last war. Von Kleist, however, demanded that Guderian's divisions should cross at Flize, some eight miles west of Sedan. There were good arguments for both sites, but Guderian resolved this spat by simply ignoring his superior – a high-risk strategy should his crossing attempt fail. But there was less he could do about von Kleist's interference with the Luftwaffe support promised. Guderian had acted entirely autonomously, going straight to Generalleutnant Bruno Loerzer, Göring's old First World War flying chum and now commander of VIII Fliegerkorps in Luftflotte 3 to ask for air support. His big problem was a lack of artillery, most of which was still struggling its way through the Ardennes. The

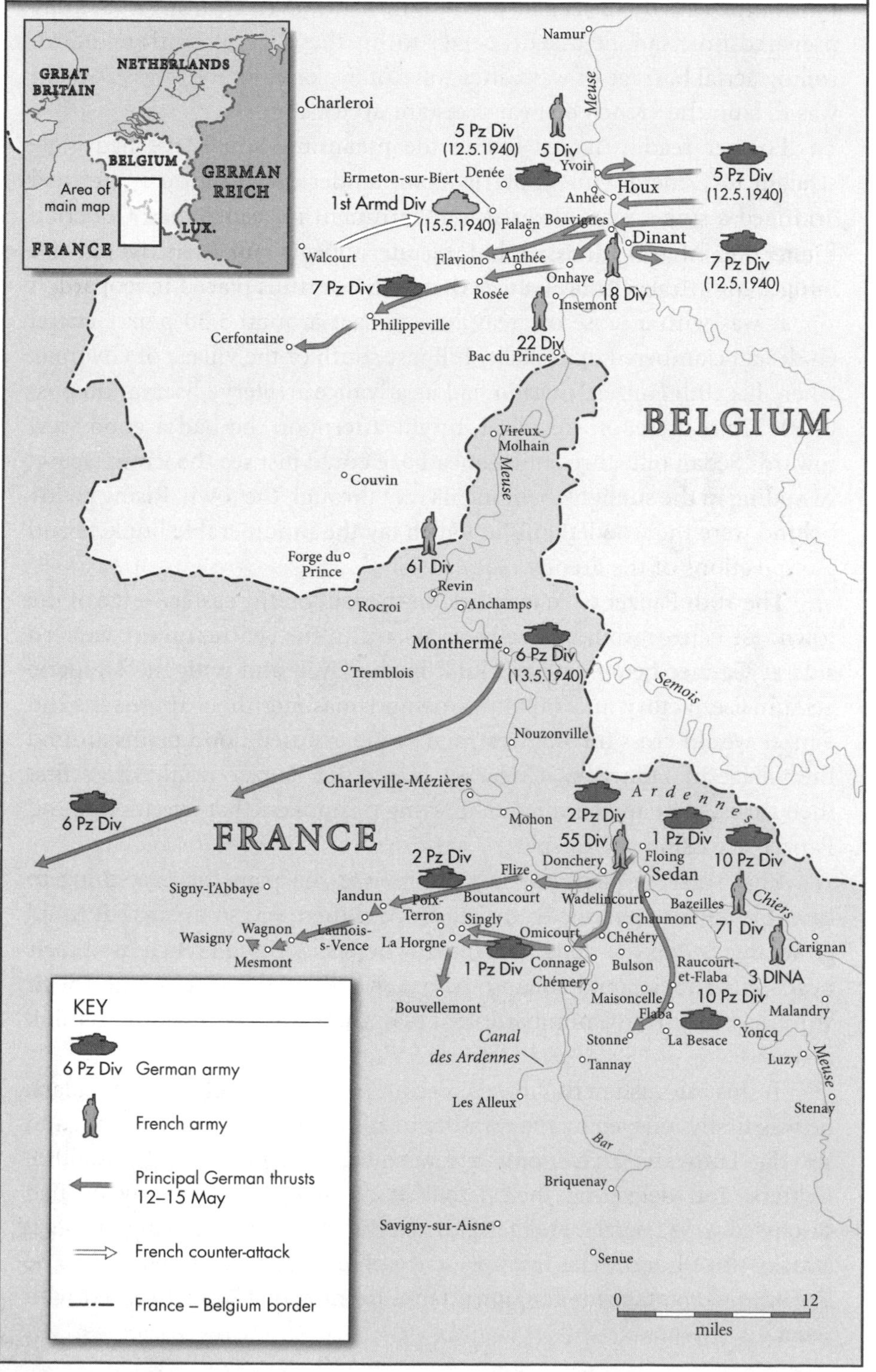

COLLAPSE OF THE MEUSE FRONT, 12–15 May 1940
GREAT BRITAIN
NETHERLANDS
BELGIUM
GERMAN REICH
Area of main map
LUX.
FRANCE
Namur
Meuse
Charleroi
5 Pz Div
(12.5.1940)
5 Div
Yvoir
5 Pz Div
(12.5.1940)
Ermeton-sur-Biert
Denée
Houx
Anhée
1st Armd Div
(15.5.1940)
Falaën
Bouvignes
Dinant
Walcourt
Flavion
Anthée
7 Pz Div
(12.5.1940)
Onhaye
7 Pz Div
Rosée
18 Div
Insemont
Philippeville
Cerfontaine
22 Div
Bac du Prince
BELGIUM
Vireux-Molhain
Meuse
Couvin
Forge du Prince
61 Div
Revin
Rocroi
Anchamps
Monthermé
6 Pz Div
(13.5.1940)
Tremblois
Semois
Nouzonville
Charleville-Mézières
6 Pz Div
Ardennes
Mohon
2 Pz Div
55 Div
1 Pz Div
FRANCE
10 Pz Div
2 Pz Div
Floing
Donchery
Sedan
Flize
Signy-l'Abbaye
Jandun
Poix-Terron
Boutancourt
Wadelincourt
Bazeilles
Chiers
Singly
Chaumont
71 Div
Wasigny
Wagnon
Launois-s-Vence
La Horgne
Omicourt
Chéhéry
Carignan
Mesmont
1 Pz Div
Connage
Bulson
Raucourt-et-Flaba
Chémery
3 DINA
Maisoncelle
10 Pz Div
Malandry
Bouvellemont
Flaba
Yoncq
Stonne
La Besace
Canal des Ardennes
Luzy
Meuse
Tannay
Stenay
Les Alleux
Bar
Briquenay
Savigny-sur-Aisne
Senue
0
12
miles
KEY
6 Pz Div German army
French army
Principal German thrusts 12–15 May
French counter-attack
France – Belgium border

Luftwaffe could do the artillery job for him, however. Drafting a carefully prepared fire plan, he asked Loerzer to hit these targets with a kind of rolling aerial barrage of wave after wave of Stukas and bombers. The aim was to stun the French by near-constant attacks.

Loerzer readily agreed but in the meantime von Kleist had gone straight to General Hugo Sperrle, commander of Luftflotte 3, and had arranged a single massed aerial bombardment instead. When Guderian found out, he was incensed, but despite appeals von Kleist would not budge. 'My whole attack,' Guderian noted, 'was thus placed in jeopardy.'

It was with a sense of great anxiety that around 3.30 p.m. General Guderian clambered up a chalky hill just south of the village of Givonne, where his 10th Panzer Division had its advance artillery observation post (OP). From there, on this clear, bright afternoon, he had a good view towards Sedan only three miles ahead. He could just see the River Meuse, twinkling in the sunlight, bending its way through the town. Rising gently behind were the wooded hills in which lay the innumerable bunkers and gun positions of the French.

The 10th Panzer were to attack on the left, on the eastern edge of the town. 1st Panzer would make their assault in the centre, on the western side at Gaulier before a sharp kink in the river, and with the Draperie Sedannaise factory and buildings behind masking their approach. 2nd Panzer would cross further west, across the exposed flood plains around the village of Donchery. Guderian hoped 1st Panzer would cross first then thrust west and eliminate the string of bunkers that overlooked 2nd Panzer's crossing at Donchery.

That was the plan, but how often was the plan the first thing to crumble the moment the battle began? And there was so much that could go wrong. Sedan was dense with enemy defences; if the French used their heads, his attack could collapse before it had barely started – and with von Kleist's Luftwaffe bombardment plan there was every reason to think it would.

To his astonishment, however, as he peered through his binoculars, he was firstly relieved by the number of his own guns firing, and then to see the Luftwaffe arrive, only a few squadrons, protected by Me 109 fighters, and delivering their lethal loads in exactly the way he had discussed with Loerzer. He then learned they had been carrying out such attacks since noon. 'The flyers were doing exactly what I believed to be the most advantageous for our attack,' he recorded, 'and I sighed with relief.'

At twenty minutes to four, the Luftwaffe then delivered a massive raid, which targeted the loop in the river at Sedan itself, where 10th and 1st Panzer were about to attack. The town now disappeared behind a mass of smoke and dust. Hurrying back down the hill, Guderian reached his command car and hurried to Gaulier where 1st Panzer were about to start their crossing. Like Rommel, some fifty miles to the north, Guderian wanted to be in the thick of it, at the front and leading his men across the water.

One of those flying over Sedan at four o'clock that afternoon was Oberleutnant Siegfried Bethke, a 23-year-old fighter pilot with the 2nd Staffel of JG 2. It was his third sortie of the day escorting the VIII Fliegerkorps bombers. So far he'd barely seen an enemy plane. 'We're almost disappointed,' he noted.

This was because nearly all the available Allied aircraft were flying over what they still believed was the main German attack across the Low Countries. It had been a bruising few days, in which the Allied airmen always seemed to be flailing around the sky, reacting to rather than dictating the air battle. The Luftwaffe always maintained the initiative, deciding when and where to attack and in what number. What efforts the Allies made to respond to the various crises always seemed to come too late, achieving little other than mounting losses. On the 11th, for example, desperate attempts had been made to destroy the bridges at Maastricht and across the Albert Canal. The Belgian air force had also had the misfortune to have a number of Fairey Battle squadrons. Ten out of fifteen Battles were destroyed as they desperately tried to bomb bridges at Maastricht and across the Albert Canal. Later, eight Air Component Blenheim bombers were sent over; three were lost and two more badly damaged. The RAF Battles also continued to drop like flies. Eight of them were ordered to carry out a low-level attack on a German column in Luxembourg; they never made it. Only one pilot returned – having turned back before they had reached the target.

The next day, 12 Squadron's Battles were given what was now clearly a suicide mission to attack two bridges over the Albert Canal. 'B' Flight of 1 Squadron Hurricanes had been ordered to fly protection cover but there was ten-tenths cloud cover over the target. 'All we saw was ten/tenths Bf 109s and we could not do a thing,' noted Billy, 'so we pissed off.' Below the cloud, with what was tragic inevitability, all five aircraft were destroyed, although one crew staggered back. The others were killed or captured. Pilot Officer McIntosh had been in a group of three led by Flying Officer Garland attacking the bridge at Veldwezelt. He was the second Battle to approach the bridge at a ridiculously low level. With his aircraft already on fire, he dropped his bombs and then crashed. Still alive, he was dragged out of the wreckage and taken into custody. 'You British are mad,' his captor told him. 'We capture the bridge early Friday morning. You give us all Friday and Saturday to get our flak guns up in circles all round the bridge, and then on Saturday, when all is ready, you come along with three aircraft and try and blow the thing up.' Garland and his observer, Sergeant Gray, who were both killed, were awarded the RAF's first VCs of the war.

At Méharicourt, Pilot Officer Arthur Hughes had still not been sent out on a reconnaissance mission; he was one of the lucky ones. Three out of four aircraft sent out on the 11th had not returned. By the evening of the 12th, 18 Squadron had made seven individual recces since the battle began. Of those, four crews had not been seen since, two had force-landed and the other had been shot at. 'And I am next on the list,' noted Arthur. 'I am not really panic stricken, but at intervals a horrid fear seems to seep into my entrails and my stomach grows hollow.' Who could blame him?

The RAF fighter pilots were feeling slightly more upbeat: at least they had some speed and firepower on their side, even if their Hurricanes were not as fast as the Messerschmitt 109s nor their eight Browning machine guns as powerful as the German cannon and machine-gun combination. Most of the French and British fighter squadrons were putting in decent numbers of claims. Indeed, although the Luftwaffe had not suffered anything like the losses of the opening day, sixty-eight aircraft had been destroyed on the 11th and fifty-four on the 12th. Another thirty-five were shot down on the 13th. But the Allies were losing similar numbers too, and it was not only bombers that were being knocked out of the sky.

By the 13th, Billy Drake's personal score was four and a half confirmed kills and one unconfirmed, making him very nearly an 'ace', an accolade that was awarded after five confirmed victories. After only ten minutes' flying, he developed a problem with his oxygen supply and so over the R/T he told the others he was returning to base. He was on his way, at a height that did not require any oxygen, when he spotted a formation of Dornier 17s. Getting in behind them, he fired off a short burst and saw one erupt into flames and begin to fall away, when suddenly he heard a loud and stunning bang and in an instant flames had started to engulf his Hurricane. Frantically glancing round, he saw a Messerschmitt 110 on his tail and, to his horror, still firing.

Initially, he panicked, and although he managed to undo his radio leads and harness and got himself into position to bale out, he had completely forgotten to open the canopy. 'By now,' he noted, 'I was covered in petrol and glycol and there were flames everywhere.' He began trying to pull back the sliding canopy but whilst doing so, the Hurricane obligingly turned over on its back and at that moment all the flames, which had been billowing upwards, were now drawn away from him. With the canopy at last open, he fell out of the plane, and pulled the ripcord on his parachute. 'Still the 110 was shooting at me,' he wrote, 'and then he was past and gone.'

Floating down gently, he now became aware that he had been wounded in the back and also the leg. In fact, he had had a miraculous escape and not just from the flames. Only a short time before, the CO, Squadron Leader 'Bull' Hallahan, had decided that all the squadron's Hurricanes should be fitted with armour plating behind the pilot's seat. This had duly been done despite the risk to the aircraft's balance and performance. A bullet had passed underneath this plating and, having hit his harness, wounded Billy in the back. But another bullet had struck the plating directly behind his head. Without it, he would have been dead.

Drifting down into a field, Billy soon discovered that his wounds were not his only problem. With blond hair and blue eyes and wearing peacetime overalls, he looked decidedly teutonic. Frenchmen arrived on the scene armed with scythes and pitchforks, convinced they had captured a Boche. 'With a little difficulty,' noted Billy, 'I was able to persuade them that I was indeed a "pilote anglais", whereupon they all embraced me.'

Taken to some French medics, he was patched up, put in a schoolroom with a number of wounded Frenchmen, and then finally rescued by his fellow 1 Squadron pilot Paul Richey, who arranged for him to be taken to hospital in Chartres. Billy had been lucky. He would fly again.

As at Dinant, it was the infantry within the panzer divisions that actually made it across the Meuse, destroyed the mass of French bunkers, and established a tentative bridgehead. Reaching the bank of the river at the Draperie Sedannaise, Guderian was delighted to see that a number of men had already safely made it to the other bank. Quickly jumping in a dinghy himself, he followed, and clambering up the other bank was met by Oberstleutnant Balck, commander of the 1st Rifle Regiment.

'Joy riding in canoes on the Meuse is forbidden!' he said with a grin. The joke was not lost on the general; he had used the very same words during an exercise in preparation for the operation a month before.

Fierce fighting was now raging around both crossing points in Sedan, while to the west 2nd Panzer were struggling to even reach the river. The town itself was burning, smoke billowing into the sky. Heavy gunfire boomed through the valley, while small arms chattered constantly. Yet in many ways, although the crossings were principally being made by a handful of German infantry divisions, the key encounters were being engaged by just a handful of men. As the 1st Rifle Regiment pressed forward to relieve the pressure on 2nd Panzer's crossing, for example, it was Oberleutnant Günther Korthals with only around seventy men from the 43rd Assault Engineer Battalion who managed to achieve the decisive breakthrough. His highly trained men worked their way from bunker to bunker, using the lie of the land as cover and making the most of blind spots in the bunkers' embrasures to creep up upon them, and then, with a combination of explosives and flame throwers, destroyed one after another, including the key Casement 103, which stood sentinel over a bend in the river and barred the way of both 1st and 2nd Panzers' advances. Korthals did not lose a single man; it was an astonishing achievement.

Possibly even more valiant was the performance of Feldwebel Walter Rubarth and his *Gruppe* of fourteen men. In 10th Panzer's sector, the crossing attempt seemed to have stalled dead until Rubarth and his men, under heavy fire, managed to get across the river and destroy a number of key bunkers. In doing so, he and his men enabled the rest of the infantry to successfully make the crossing.

As evening approached, the bridgeheads began to link up, yet it was another key moment that sealed the day. 1st Panzer's objective for the day had been Hill 301, a crucial feature overlooking Sedan which held a number of further French positions that were ranged over all three bridgeheads. With the village of Frenois at the foot of the hill captured, Oberst Balck saw his men were exhausted, but he also recognized that the stunned French were now in disarray. Recalling an episode in the First World War when his unit had failed to exploit a hard-won encounter, he urged his men forward. 'Something that is easy today,' he said, 'can cost us rivers of blood tomorrow.' Dusk was falling as his weary men began

GUDERIAN'S BREAKTHROUGH AT SEDAN, 13 May 1940

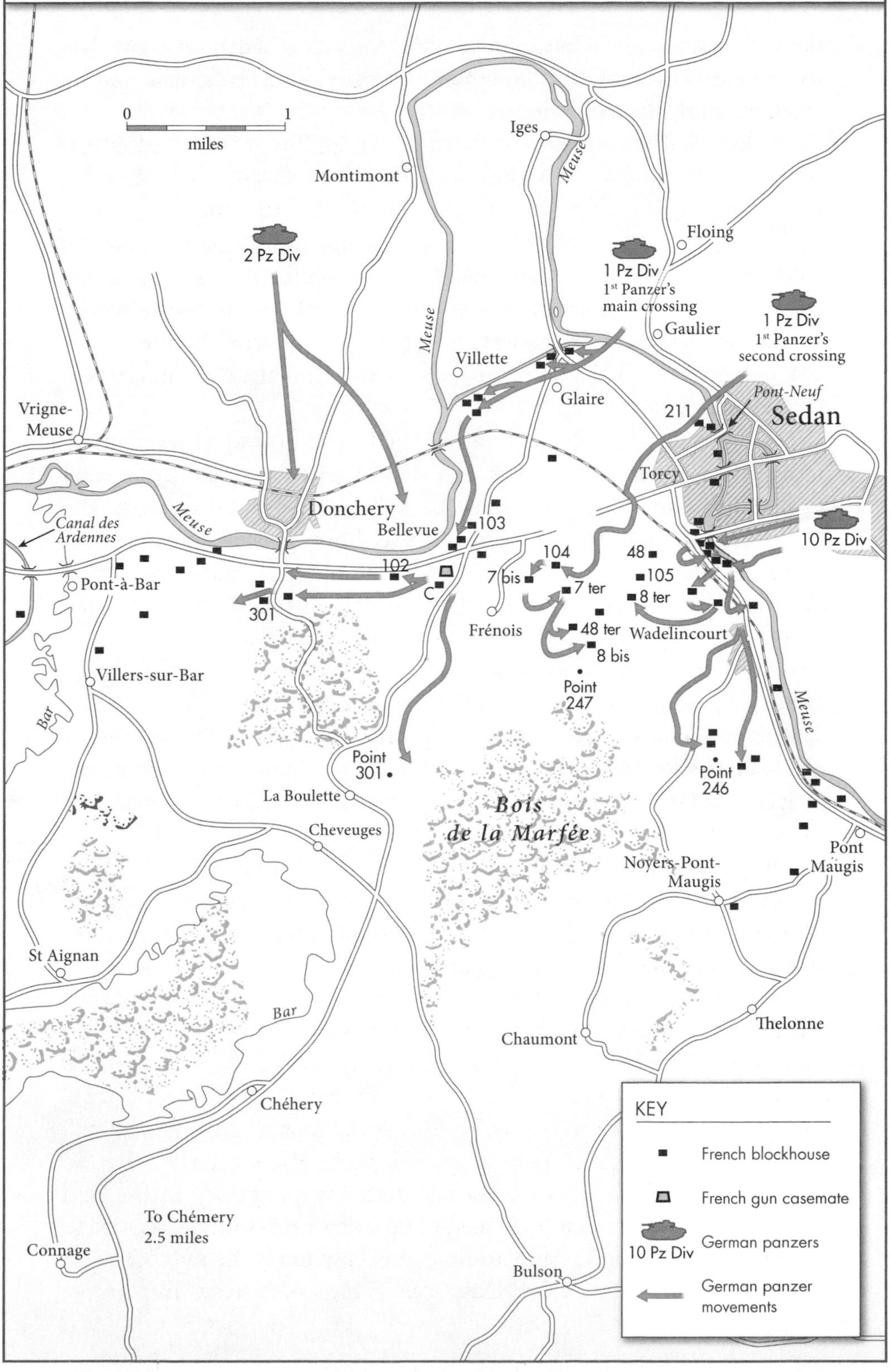

0 1
miles

Iges
Meuse
Montimont
Floing
2 Pz Div
1 Pz Div
1st Panzer's
main crossing
1 Pz Div
1st Panzer's
second crossing
Gaulier
Meuse
Villette
Glaire
Pont-Neuf
211
Sedan
Vrigne-
Meuse
Torcy
Donchery
Bellevue
103
Meuse
Canal des
Ardennes
10 Pz Div
104
48
102
7 bis
105
Pont-à-Bar
C
7 ter
301
8 ter
Frénois
48 ter
Wadelincourt
8 bis
Villers-sur-Bar
Point
247
Bar
Meuse
Point
301
Point
246
La Boulette
Bois
de la Marfée
Cheveuges
Pont
Noyers-Pont-
Maugis
Maugis
St Aignan
Bar
Thelonne
Chaumont
Chéhery
To Chémery
2.5 miles
Connage
Bulson

KEY
French blockhouse
French gun casemate
10 Pz Div
German panzers
German panzer
movements

their assault up the slopes of Hill 301. But Balck had been right. His second battalion took the strongpoint on the summit by storm, and by 10.40 p.m. the hill was theirs.

Below, Sedan continued to burn as the gunfire at last died down. Behind, in the rolling hills and farmland to the south of that historic town, the French were panicking. A rumour had started that the panzers were already across and heading towards them. Soon it had spread like wildfire. First the artillery retreated, then so too did Général Lafontaine, commander of the 55th Infantry Division that held the Sedan sector. Before long, waves of troops were falling back in disarray. By the time it was realized that the rumour was false, it was too late: the damage had been done.

As darkness fell, General Guderian, a proud and relieved man, returned to his command post and there he finally spoke to General Loerzer, thanking him for keeping the air plan they had discussed. 'The order from Luftflotte 3, which turned everything upside down,' replied Loerzer, 'came, let us say, too late. It would only have caused confusion among the air groups. That is why I did not forward the orders.' Guderian had not been the only one to disobey senior commanders that day.

And thirty miles to the north, at Monthermé, Panzer Corps Reinhardt, despite the huge traffic problems they had faced in the Ardennes, had also managed to gain a toe-hold across the Meuse. At nightfall on the 13th, all three crossings over the Meuse had been made: at Sedan, at Dinant and at Monthermé, just as Halder and Guderian had planned.

But it was still a long way to the Channel, and although the infantry had made it across, the race was now on to get both panzers and artillery over the river as well before the French brought their enormous reserves to bear and pushed them back again. Much still hung in the balance.

7

Inside the Third Reich

IT WAS TRUE THAT THE vast majority of Americans instinctively felt that the war in Europe was no affair of theirs; after all, the war-mongering of Hitler posed no immediate threat to them on the far side of the wide Atlantic Ocean. Yet the United States was not entirely inward-looking in its view, particularly not the President, Franklin D. Roosevelt, who had played his part in trying to avert war during the previous spring and summer, and who had, since the September, led from the front in persuading Congress to modify the Neutrality Acts of 1935–7, which had decreed that the US should neither export goods to any foreign belligerents nor grant them any kind of loan or credits.

The new measures, whereby America would allow belligerents of their choosing to procure goods on a cash-and-carry basis, became law on 4 November. It showed, at least, that the United States wanted the Allies to win. And while polls consistently revealed that around 95 per cent of the population was against American entry into the war, this did not mean there was a lack of interest; on the contrary, the newspapers, magazines and newsreels were full of it, which was why there were so many newspaper and radio men – and women – over in Europe, including London, Paris and Berlin.

The broadcasting company CBS was one of the biggest radio stations, having been formed in 1928 when its owner, William S. Paley, bought a collection of sixteen independent stations which he formed into one and renamed the Columbia Broadcasting System. By the early 1930s it had developed its news division and began hiring among the best journalists and writers around. One of those was Ed Murrow, who, at twenty-nine, had been sent to London as CBS's Director of European Operations.

One of the first people Murrow hired in Europe was William L. Shirer, who since 1934 had been in Berlin reporting for Hearst's Universal News Service. When UNS folded in 1937, Shirer was taken on by Hearst's other wire service, the International News Service, then promptly laid off once more. So when Murrow called and suggested a meeting, the timing could not have been better. Murrow needed an experienced journalist on the Continent and offered Shirer a job on the spot, subject to approval of a trial broadcast for the CBS directors back in the States.

CBS duly hired him, despite his flat, slightly reedy voice – albeit largely at Murrow's insistence, who knew that Shirer's fluency in languages, contacts and sources would be invaluable. And so they proved when Shirer, the only American journalist in Vienna at the time of the *Anschluss* in March 1938, secured a major scoop. The late thirties were still early days for radio news, however, and Shirer's regular broadcasts did not begin until shortly after, when, following the *Anschluss*, CBS asked him and Murrow to produce a *European Roundup* programme of news. From then on, Americans would regularly hear Shirer's distinctive timbre from all over Germany, but particularly Berlin, where he was based. 'Hello, America,' he would usually begin. 'Hello, CBS. This is Berlin.'

By May 1940, Shirer was thirty-six, balding, with a round, genial face, spectacles and a trim gingery moustache. Although married, he and his wife Tess agreed that after the birth of their daughter it would be safer for her to move with baby Inga to Switzerland, from where she could run the Geneva office of CBS. Although Shirer lived in some comfort in the Hotel Adlon next to the Brandenburg Gate at the heart of the city, he had a deep dislike of the Nazis and felt keenly the sense of menace that pervaded the capital. His room was bugged, while he suspected staff at the Adlon of being Gestapo informers. 'The shadow of Nazi fanaticism, sadism, persecution, regimentation, terror, brutality, suppression, militarism, and preparation for war,' he jotted in his diary soon after getting the CBS job in September 1937, 'has hung over all our lives, like a dark, brooding cloud that never clears.'

Although the Nazis allowed print journalists to cable their pieces uncensored, that was not the case for broadcast journalists. Each piece had to be submitted not only to Goebbels's Propaganda Ministry but also to the Foreign Office and OKW, a routine annoyance that never ceased to rankle with him. In his broadcast on 10 May, he was allowed to announce that the offensive had begun, and to express the surprise of most Berliners, who had not been expecting it at all. 'The people in Berlin, I must say,' he added, 'took the news of the beginning of this decisive phase of the struggle with great calm. Before the Chancellery an hour ago, I noticed that no crowd had gathered as usually happens when big events occur. Few people bothered to buy the noon papers which carried the news.'

In his personal diary, he noted that the memorandum issued from the Propaganda Ministry justifying the invasion of the Low Countries set up 'a new record, I think, for cynicism and downright impudence'. He was also struck over the ensuing days by the apathy shown by Berliners for the offensive. Most Germans he had talked to were sunk deep in depression at the news. 'The question is,' he noted, 'how many Germans support this final, desperate gamble that Hitler has taken?' Discussing it with fellow correspondents at the Adlon, they agreed that most did, yet that did not mean they had to like it.

Of course, Shirer, as an educated middle-class, democratically raised American, would find the totalitarian Nazis offensive. Yet despite the undoubted gloom within Germany about the war, Hitler's approval rating and popularity were still massive. He had brought employment, prosperity and pride. The turn-around in such a short period of time was truly astonishing. And he had started to make Germans feel secure once more. Without a shot fired, he had built up her armed forces, and expanded the Reich, bringing former German peoples back into the nation. Most Germans thought the claims on the Danzig corridor, which would link the Baltic outpost of East Prussia to the eastern border and make Germany whole once more, were entirely justified – after all, it was mainly German people living there anyway.

There was also another benefit from absorbing the eastern half of Poland: it created a buffer against the westward expansion of the Soviet Union. Bolshevism was painted as an evil and Stalin a bloody tyrant in much the same way that Nazism and Hitler were perceived in Britain and the West.

Else Wendel's attitude was typical of many Germans. Raised in Charlottenburg, an affluent part of Berlin, she was an educated and intelligent young mother, but with little interest in politics. Although not a Party member, her ex-husband, Richard, was, and indeed, when he fell in love with the lead violinist of the Brandenburg City Orchestra, of which he was conductor, the Nazi ideology that denigrated church and religion made a divorce from Else far easier and more acceptable than it would have been before Hitler had come to power. Nor did he make any further financial contribution to either Else or their children, which was also acceptable according to Nazi law. 'There are lots of women left for younger girls today,' a kindly doctor had told her. 'I know it's part of the superman idea.'

As a result, she had been forced to go back to work and to place the older boy, Wolfgang, in the care of her cousin and his wife, and baby Klaus with foster parents until she could afford to look after them herself once more. Both could have been placed in a *Kinderheim* – a state children's home – but the thought of having them raised by party members and becoming institutionalized did not appeal to her at all.

Else worked in the Department of Art in the *Kraft durch Freude* (KdF) – Strength Through Joy – organization, based at the Headquarters of the German Labour Front, in two large, four-storeyed houses in the Kaiserallee in west Berlin. She worked directly for one man, Herr Wolter, and their job was to organize art exhibitions in factories – part of the Nazi cultural plan to make workers more interested in art. Else had been lucky to get a job in a government institution without being a Party member, but because of a shortage of suitable staff she had been given a temporary post and then proved so adept they kept her on. Her boss was a Party man, however, although this did not stop him making numerous jokes about the leading Nazis. Nonetheless, like Else, Herr Wolter was a great admirer of Hitler and all his achievements and he certainly believed that the German invasion of Poland had been entirely justified.

'But up until now,' Else had retorted, 'Hitler has done everything peacefully. I do admire his foresight and diplomacy, as long as it means peace. But this is war!' In this she was reflecting the view of the vast majority; very few wished to risk a repeat of the disastrous 1914–18 war. There was certainly no euphoria as there had been in 1914. Herr Wolter had laughed, however. The war, he assured her, would be over in a flash.

A few days later, Else had been at her parents' house with her younger sister, Hilde, and brother Rudolf, helping her mother fit blackout sheets across their windows. Hilde had worried that the war might last longer than they all thought.

'Nonsense,' said their mother. 'Of course it will be over. Surely the Führer knows what he is talking about.'

Most people, on the whole, tend to accept the decisions of their leaders, assuming, as Else's mother did, that they are informed by a great deal more information than a member of the public can ever know. Faith in Hitler remained widespread through the first nine months of the war. When in September there had been a particularly fine spell of little rain and sunshine, Else and her fellow Berliners referred to it as 'Führer weather', as though Hitler's magic could even influence the skies above them.

Of Else's circle of friends and family there was only one person who was vehemently anti-Nazi, and that was her Aunt Fee, who lived in the country to the east of Berlin. Else had visited her at Christmas and while she was there Fee openly admitted to her that she listened to foreign radio broadcasts, something that was strictly *verboten* in Germany. Else was appalled, and horrified when her aunt accused the Nazis of repeatedly lying to the German people. 'This wicked man,' Fee said of Hitler, 'will lead Germany to her doom.'

Else was genuinely shocked; she felt sure her aunt was wrong.

'You are supposed to be an educated woman,' her aunt fumed, 'and you have two sons. Why don't you find these things out? You're hopeless. You are just as childish as the rest of Germany. You have a leader and that is all you ask. Can't you ever take any individual responsibility at all?'

'We were so young,' says Hilda Müller of those early months of the war, 'we didn't really understand the political background.' In May 1940, Hilda was not quite seventeen, but had already left school, done her compulsory year's service in the *Reichsarbeitsdienst* (Reich Labour Service), and had just begun her first proper job, working for Siemens, the world-renowned electrical engineering company. Her father was deeply wary of Hitler and the Nazis, but since he was something of a drunkard, Hilda had learned not to take his views too seriously.

In fact, Hilda had a lot to be grateful for to the Nazis. She was from a working-class family from the Hohenschönhausen suburb of east Berlin, and lived in a very small house her father had built on their allotment back in the early thirties to save money. Hilda was an intelligent girl but before the Nazis took power she would not have been able to stay at school, and would have left at thirteen. However, in Nazi Germany, she had been able to take an exam to remain a further two and a half years and because her family could not afford it, the State paid. Now, because of her education, she was being trained by Siemens and paid 75 marks a month, a good wage at the time for someone of her age.

Siemens had supported the Nazis, and their two factories in Berlin – Siemens Schuckert and Siemens-Halske – were both producing war material, yet Hilda thought little of it. As far as she was concerned, the Nazis had brought employment and prosperity. There were great celebrations too; Hilda had taken part in the opening ceremony of the Berlin Olympics in 1936, and had enjoyed the festivities to mark the 700th anniversary of Berlin in 1937. The following year there were the 'Happy Folk' celebrations, then in June 1939 there had been a festival to mark the summer solstice. The Nazis liked such public celebrations.

Yet there was also no doubting that a lot of the gaiety had gone out of life since the beginning of the war. From the outset, there were nightly blackouts, for example. Cafés, bars and dance halls were no longer allowed to remain open all night either. For someone like Hilda who loved dancing, this was a great blow. At night, the lights had all gone out and Berlin had become a place of darkness. During her year's service with the RAD, Hilda had been helping in the house of well-to-do Nazi members, looking after their children. They had a number of rehearsals for air raids, despite Göring's repeated assurances that no enemy bombers would fly over German air space. 'I would practise taking the children down to the cellar,' says Hilda. 'We always had to have a pail of water in the cellar in case of fire.' Gas masks were also issued.

There was rationing, too, introduced the previous August, and it was far more stringent than it was in Britain. Each person was issued with colour-coded ration cards – such as a red one for bread – which were valid for twenty-eight days. This meant the authorities could alter the amounts rationed at short notice. Bread, cereals, meat, fats, butter, cheese, milk, sugar, and eggs were all rationed from the outset of war, and the amounts permitted depended on age and the kind of work someone did. Clothing was also rationed, with further different coloured cards – brown for teenage girls, for example, and yellow for men. Germany's lack of resources had a big impact on the amount of clothes available. 'The truth is,' noted William Shirer, 'that having no cotton and almost no wool, the German people must get along with what clothing they have until the end of the war.' A great deal of what they did have was devoted to making incredibly elaborate and over-tailored uniforms for the armed forces;

there was nothing like the simple and spare British battledress in the Wehrmacht.

Rationing was relaxed over Christmas – everyone was given an extra quarter-pound of butter, a hundred grams of meat and four eggs – but many of the shops were tantalizing, displaying wonderful pre-war goods that were no longer for sale. Germans – even under the irreligious Nazis – loved Christmas and any town would normally have been twinkling with festive cheer, but the first Christmas of the war had been notable for the lack of lights and gaiety. Else Wendel, forced to spend it without her children, found it a particularly depressing time.

There was also a real shortage of coal, which, combined with the dark, the reduction in food, the menfolk being away and the uncertainty of Germany's future now that she was at war, made life very tough for many people. '1939 to 1940 was very hard,' says Hilda Müller. 'My toes were frozen a lot of the time. I often went hungry.'

Of less concern to most Germans were the lurking presence of the secret police or the strict regulations decreed by a totalitarian party like the Nazis. William Shirer may have resented the fact that his room was bugged, but so long as you were not foreign, Jewish, overtly homosexual, communist, or mentally or physically handicapped, the majority were left to get on with their lives without too much interference. The more unsavoury aspects of life under the Nazis were tolerated because most recognized that National Socialism had brought very obvious and rapid improvements. Hilda's father, for example, had resented the swastika and portrait of Hitler that had to be put up in the block of flats in which they used to live. 'We had to have them,' says Hilda, 'we had them at school too.' It didn't bother her particularly; it was simply a fact of life.

And, of course, now that it was early summer, life began to improve once more for most; certainly Hilda believed she had reached a turning point. She was greatly enjoying her time with Siemens, being trained to do something and being paid a decent wage. It also gave her a chance to escape from her moody, volatile father. 'It enabled me to be independent,' she says. And with the days lengthening and the weather warm, and with Berliners getting used to wartime life, the city no longer seemed quite as drab, cold, and lifeless as it had just a few months before.

One of the reasons why William Shirer had found Berliners so calm and subdued on 10 May was that Josef Goebbels, Reich Propaganda Minister, had insisted that the start of the offensive should not be marked by any great fanfare. There should not be excessive optimism; nor should initial successes be exaggerated.

Goebbels held a 'ministerial conference' every morning at the Propaganda Ministry just off Wilhelmstrasse – a stone's throw from the Reich Chancellery. His closest collaborators would attend, and the minister would brief his team and issue instructions for the forthcoming day. It was here, above all, that the image of the mighty Third Reich was created. In Goebbels, Hitler had found one of his most effective and loyal acolytes.

Despite the jokes that went around about Hitler and the Nazi leadership, Hitler remained phenomenally popular. Much of this was due to the enormously effective Nazi propaganda machine. Propaganda had been an integral part of Nazi politics from the outset, and was to a large degree the responsibility of the Reich Ministry for Popular Enlightenment and Propaganda, under its chief, Josef Goebbels. The son of a shop assistant and clerk, Goebbels had proved himself an intelligent pupil at school and despite his humble upbringing had attended the universities of Bonn, Freiburg and Heidelberg. At first he had had thoughts of becoming a teacher, but then turned to journalism; however, it was a career path that led nowhere. Instead, he turned to politics, joining the Nazis in 1922. Rising steadily up Hitler's party hierarchy, by 1928 he had been elected to the Reichstag. Marriage in 1931 to Magda Quant, a society divorcee, gave him the kind of money and status he had always yearned for but never attained. Doors now opened, with his elegant home in Berlin's west end becoming a regular Nazi meeting place before their ascendency to power. When that happened in 1933, Goebbels was given the post of Propaganda Minister, a position he had held ever since. Almost immediately, he announced that his prime goal was to achieve a 'mobilization of mind and spirit' in Germany. The traumatic end in 1918 could never be repeated; the Germans of the future had to be mentally tougher, which was where propaganda could play a large part. 'We did not lose the war because our artillery gave out,' he said in a speech in 1933, 'but because the weapons of our minds did not fire.'

Goebbels faced several challenges. The first was to mobilize the German people towards military expansion and war and to maintain morale. This had been achieved, although most Germans had needed little convincing that those lands lost by the terms of the Treaty of Versailles should quite rightly be part of Germany once more. However, they had all been achieved peaceably; war was a different matter. More thorny was the sudden *volte face* over the Soviet Union. Having spent the pre-war years ratcheting up anti-Bolshevism to fever pitch levels he had been faced with a particularly tough PR task trying to convince Germans of the wisdom of such a move whilst at the same time ensuring that belief in the Führer remained as high as ever. 'He must be very busy this morning,' Herr Wolter had told Else Wendel on 24 August, 'burning all the leaflets and books in which he thundered against the Russians, and told us so carefully why and how they were such barbarians. This morning they are our blood brothers.' Else had laughed as hard as her boss. From that moment on, Goebbels had had to try to persuade the nation that it was, after all, necessary to go to war.

The second main task was to present to Germans and potential enemies alike an aura of ever-increasing military strength and invincibility, with the aim of, first, persuading Germans that a war could and would be won and, second, trying to cow these enemies. At the same time, it was the Propaganda Ministry's job to ensure the population received practical advice about rationing, possible gas attacks, air raid protection and other wartime considerations, whilst at the same time maintaining morale.

Although Goebbels was one of the best-known Nazis both at home and abroad, he did not have complete domination of propaganda by any stretch of the imagination. It was very much Hitler's divide and rule style to encourage jealousy and back-stabbing amongst his senior acolytes, so he decreed that foreign propaganda should be handled by von Ribbentrop's foreign office and that military reporting be left to the OKW's propaganda department. Meanwhile, Hitler's Reich Press Chief, Otto Dietrich, although officially subordinate to Goebbels, was very much a part of the Führer's inner circle and produced daily directives to the press. Needless to say, Goebbels repeatedly tried to persuade Hitler to bring all propaganda under his control but the Führer refused to be budged.

Even so, Goebbels was able to get round most of these frustrating blocks to his control. The Propaganda Ministry maintained a large foreign section despite von Ribbentrop's separate role in that area. Dietrich's authority, for example, bizarrely only ever extended to the press, not the radio and news services. Unlike in Britain, however, there were few national newspapers – nearly all were regional, and although newspapers continued to be read widely, it was the radio, above all, that was used to convey the message of the Third Reich;

the Nazis had, from the outset, been particularly radio-conscious.

Although radio saw a world-wide expansion in the 1930s, the Nazis, particularly, had made sure that radio sets were both cheap and accessible. In 1933, the *Volksempfänger* ('people's receiver') had been put into mass production, and this was later followed by the DKE (*Deutscher Kleinempfänger* – 'German little receiver'), which was even more affordable. While across Germany some 70 per cent of the population owned radios by 1940, this was still not considered enough, so communal listening points were set up: all restaurants, cafés and bars had radios, while many were installed in blocks of flats, factories and other workplaces. There were radios at the Siemens factory where Hilda Müller was being trained, for example. Loudspeakers were also erected on pillars in towns and cities. The density of radio coverage was greater in the Third Reich than in any other country in the world. Radio wardens coaxed people into listening to key speeches and programmes, while propaganda broadcasts were broadcast between a heavy diet of light music and popular entertainment to ensure people kept tuned in.

Goebbels also went to great lengths to develop his foreign-language radio. By May 1940 his propaganda broadcasts were going out in twenty-two different languages. English-language broadcasts targeted the British working classes, while the broadcasts of the Irish national, William Joyce – or Lord Haw-Haw, as he was known – had millions of regular listeners. French broadcasts equally aimed to undermine morale – 'Why die for Danzig?' was an oft-repeated refrain. It was also up to Goebbels to release newsreel footage to foreign press and media organizations. Again, repeated film of panzers, burning villages, waves of bombers and, of course, the appropriate sound effects of Stukas dive-bombing, their 'Jericho trumpet' sirens wailing, ensured that most in the west duly believed Germany to be the military power-house it liked to make out. Goebbels had a simple dictum that he always stuck to: 'Propaganda means repetition and still more repetition!' And on the whole, it seemed to work.

One of Goebbels's most repeated messages was that Britain was the 'Number One' enemy. On 10 May, at his daily conference, he told his team that any gain of ground should be presented merely as 'getting nearer to the "principal enemy", the British'. Earlier, at the outbreak of war, he had issued very clear press directives to this effect. 'Britain is the true aggressor in the world,' he wrote on 1 September. A few weeks later he sent out a directive to all Party leaders making broadcasts with guidelines about tone and emphasis. 'Make clear that we are engaged in the fateful struggle of the German people which was imposed upon it by the English plutocracy,' he wrote. 'The English warmongering aims to destroy the German Reich.' In his concluding comments he added, 'Speakers must strictly avoid any polemics against France.'

Nazi leaders, whether it be Hitler, Göring or Goebbels himself, duly made repeated attacks on Britain and the Jewish-led 'plutocracy' during their many broadcasts and speeches. In November, for example, in Munich, on the anniversary of the Beer Hall Putsch, Hitler used an hour-long speech to rant against Britain. When, shortly after he had left the Bürgerbräu beerhall, a bomb exploded, it was immediately blamed on the British.

'All we want is peace,' announced Göring in another broadcast. 'Peace with honour, Mr Chamberlain. We do not want to fight the English people. Nor do we want one inch of France. It is the English who are inciting war. Remember, you Frenchmen, what England has said in the past: We will fight to the last Frenchman! Not the last Englishman, mark you!'

And once again, the message seemed to be getting through. On a press visit to see the German fleet in Hamburg, William Shirer was continually asked why the British fought Germany. Earlier, he had made a study of what German people were reading. One of the most popular was *Look Up the Subject of England*, a propaganda book against the country. At a family lunch, Else Wendel's undemonstrative mother declared, 'England hates us. She's jealous, that's all. It was just the same in the last war.'

By May 1940, one message that appeared to have got through was that Britain, not France, or even the Soviet Union, was Germany's most bitter enemy.

8

A Battle Against Time

WHAT WOULD BE AN email sixty years later was, in May 1940, a handwritten note using a favourite fountain pen. Winston Churchill, the new Prime Minister, had scribbled such a letter to the former PM, Neville Chamberlain, soon after returning from the Palace on the evening of 10 May, thanking him sincerely for promising to stand by him 'at this extremely grievous and formidable moment'. The two had repeatedly clashed during the preceding years, particularly over Chamberlain's appeasement policies, yet now Churchill was determined to show considerable magnanimity towards him. 'The example that you have set of self-forgetting dignity and public spirit,' wrote Churchill, 'will govern the actions of many and be an inspiration to all.' As if to underline the sincerity of his feelings, Churchill even offered to remain at Admiralty House, rather than make the Chamberlains move out of No. 10.

And Chamberlain, still bruised and humiliated, was flattered. 'I must say that Winston has been most handsome in his appreciation of my willingness to help and my ability to do so,' he wrote to his sisters. 'I know that he relies on Halifax and me and as he put it in a letter, "My fate depends largely on you." '

Churchill was no doubt sincere in his attitude towards Chamberlain, but there was no doubting that he needed two of the biggest names in British politics on his side, not least because large numbers of the House and particularly those within the Conservative Party still believed the new Prime Minister was a dangerous maverick unsuited to the top job at any time, but especially not in the middle of a national crisis of potentially catastrophic proportions. Moreover, Churchill was already making a number of decisions that would give him greater power and control than any previous Prime Minister – changes that would surely be questioned by some.

First, he decided to make himself Defence Minister. This had been an unknown post but it now gave Churchill the freedom to oversee the British war effort as not only Prime Minister but also specifically as the man in charge of defence policy. His right-hand man, as Chief of Staff, was not a politician but Major-General Hastings 'Pug' Ismay. A highly experienced intelligence and staff officer at the War Office, Ismay also became Deputy Secretary (Military) to the Cabinet and, crucially for Churchill, a fifth member of the Chiefs of Staff Committee. Headed by the Chief of the Imperial General Staff (CIGS), it also included the three service chiefs and was responsible for assessing and advising on all courses of military action and, once approved by Churchill or the War Cabinet, putting them into action.

While Churchill deliberately did not define Ismay's powers too closely, his intention was for his new Chief of Staff to be his eyes and ears, and the person who enabled him to maintain very tight reins on all aspects of British war policy and direction. It was a very different approach from that of Chamberlain, who, like Halifax, was the first to admit that he had little understanding of military matters. Not only did war fascinate Churchill, but he had also spent a lifetime reading and studying it. Yet he recognized that under Chamberlain there had been a lack of central control; that there had been co-ordination between the Chiefs of Staff and the Government but not firm direction. That would now change as he became generalissimo and effectively Commander-in-Chief of Britain's armed forces. As such, he was acting more like an American president – or even Hitler – than a Prime Minister. And he had made these fundamental changes without the approval of Parliament.

By 13 May, Churchill had filled all the major posts of his new Government, but two of his first appointments were those of Chamberlain and Halifax. The former continued as Leader of the Conservative Party and became Lord President of the Council. The latter agreed to continue as Foreign Secretary. More importantly, both would be part of the War Cabinet – whose number Churchill cut from eight to just five. The other two members were the Labour men Attlee and Greenwood. There were also posts for other supporters and anti-appeasers, such as Anthony Eden, who returned to the wider Cabinet as Minister for War, and Duff Cooper, who took over as Minister of Information. Sir Archibald Sinclair, the Liberal leader, took the important Air Ministry from Sir Samuel Hoare.

That Monday afternoon was Churchill's first appearance in the House of Commons as Prime Minister. There to witness his performance was Harold Nicolson, a 53-year-old former diplomat and journalist and, since the last election, a National Labour MP. Like Eden and Duff Cooper, he was an anti-appeaser and a supporter of Churchill. Married to the Bloomsbury poet and author Vita Sackville-West, he was also both well-off and well-connected.

The previous Friday, he had gone to bed believing the Germans might invade at any moment; he and his wife had agreed that should the country be overrun by Germany they would both rather die and were preparing lethal pills with which to kill themselves. As one of those trying to force Chamberlain out, he had also been struck by the dignity with which Chamberlain had made his resignation broadcast. 'All the hatred I have felt for Chamberlain,' he noted, 'subsides as if a piece of bread were dropped into a glass of champagne.'

He was not alone in such thoughts. Indeed, many Conservatives were appalled by what had happened – and by what they had done – and on that Monday afternoon, three days into the German offensive, Chamberlain had been cheered, not booed, as he re-entered the House. The applause for Churchill had been muted. The Prime Minister stood up and asked the House to approve the new Government. 'I have nothing to offer but blood, toil, tears, and sweat,' he told them. 'We have before us an ordeal of the most grievous kind. We have before us many, many months of struggle and suffering.' What was now their aim, he asked them rhetorically. 'I can answer in one word. It is victory. Victory at all costs – Victory in spite of all terrors – Victory, however long and hard the road may be, for without victory there is no survival.'

The House was hardly swept away by Churchill's rhetoric. 'Winston makes a very short statement,' noted Harold Nicolson, 'but to the point.' The formal backing of the new Government was passed without incident, but there was no doubting the anxiety in the Commons. There were many who now had a horrible sinking feeling that the revolution to oust Chamberlain might have been a terrible mistake, while few doubted that making Churchill leader in this moment of deep crisis was a massive risk and fraught with uncertainty; it was not only the Germans who were gambling at this time. Across the corridor in the House of Lords, Chamberlain's name was received with cheers and Churchill's with silence. Gossiping and griping was already rife amongst the corridors of Parliament, with the new appointments being heavily criticized by many. After the vote, Harold Nicolson talked to another Churchill supporter, Harold Macmillan, who had in turn been talking to a member of the new Cabinet, Brendan Bracken. Macmillan had asked Bracken what Churchill's mood was like. 'Profound anxiety,' Bracken had replied. It was nothing less than what Harold and many of his parliamentary colleagues were feeling.

'I spent the day in a bright blue new suit from the Fifty-Shilling Tailors,' noted the 25-year-old Jock Colville, 'cheap and sensational looking, which I felt was appropriate to the new Government.' Jock was one of several of Chamberlain's secretaries who had been kept on by Churchill. He was fond of Chamberlain and felt his boss had been unfairly treated, but he was deeply worried about the prospect of Churchill as the new Prime Minister. He rather thought that it had been Churchill's impetuousness that had led to the debacle in Norway, and had heard plenty of rumours about how difficult a man he could be; as far as he was concerned, the new PM was little more than an adventurer with friends unfit to be trusted with positions of high office and authority at such a time of national crisis. The thought of Churchill running the show sent a chill down his young spine.

The son of well-to-do and well-connected parents, Jock had left Trinity College in Cambridge in 1936, having had three fabulous and hedonistic years. He then travelled to Russia, crossed Asia Minor and travelled back through Europe, teaching himself French and German in the process. Once back in London, he realized it was time to settle down to some work, but a life in the City like his two elder brothers had not appealed. However, it turned out that his combination of intelligence and languages enabled him to sit the exhaustive exams for entrance into the Foreign Office. Much to his surprise, he won a place and was allotted to the Eastern Department, where his specific concern was Turkey and Persia. Then, soon after war had been declared, he was asked if he would like to join No. 10 as one of the Prime Minister's secretaries. He was promised it would be long hours and often very boring, but Jock accepted all the same; the chance to be 'in the know' at a time of war such as this seemed too good to pass over. So it was that on Tuesday, 10 October, Jock started his first day at Downing Street.

Now, seven months on, he had a new boss. Jock might not have thought too much of Churchill but he had to admit the man had drive. Whatever happened, he felt certain the new PM would get things done.

The same day, the US Ambassador, Joe Kennedy, saw Lord Halifax at the Foreign Office, and congratulated him on being in the new Cabinet. 'Confidentially, I wish I weren't, Joe,' Halifax told him. The Foreign Secretary was critical of those who had deserted Chamberlain. Kennedy then interrupted him, pointing out that Britain's real problem was not politics but a shortage of aircraft, plain and simple. The lack of them, he argued, threw everything else out of balance and made it impossible for her to wage a modern war. Halifax did not disagree. He then asked Kennedy if he thought it would be a short war.

'Definitely,' Kennedy told him.

There was another man in Britain who was deeply concerned about the shortage of aircraft, although it was the paucity of single-engine modern fighters that was his prime concern. At the start of the war, production levels were so low that on average just two Spitfires and Hurricanes were being built per day. It was, the Commander-in-Chief of RAF Fighter Command reckoned, probably just about enough to prevent unescorted bombers flying from Germany from causing large-scale havoc over mainland Britain. However, should the Luftwaffe overrun the Low Countries, then they would be able to fly over Britain with an escort of protective fighters, and that was an entirely different proposition. To meet that threat, Britain needed every single modern fighter she could lay her hands on and more, not waste them on the Continent. 'There could be no illusions,' wrote Air Chief Marshal Sir Hugh Dowding, 'concerning the wastage which would occur if we came up against the German fighters in France.'

Already, by 13 May, Dowding's worst fears were being realized. The previous summer, it had been agreed by the Government and the Air Ministry that Fighter Command should grow to fifty-seven squadrons, of which five would be used for shipping protection and in Northern Ireland, so leaving fifty-two squadrons for the home defence of mainland Britain. Not all these squadrons had been formed, however, and at the outbreak of war Dowding could still only call on thirty-two squadrons, of which just twenty-two were equipped with Spitfires and Hurricanes. The rest were biplanes, Blenheims or other obsolete models. It was simply not enough.

Over the ensuing months, Dowding had repeatedly pleaded his case, demanding more modern fighters and squadrons, but although more squadrons were promised, by 10 May Fighter Command was still ten short of the fifty-seven that had been pledged. What's more, two of his squadrons were earmarked for Norway and four to join the six already in France. In other words, Dowding actually had twenty fewer squadrons for home defence than had been promised him. Aircraft production had risen to 177 fighters per month by March and to 256 by April, but that was nothing like enough to bring Fighter Command up to the strength that had been agreed would be necessary to keep the Luftwaffe at bay, and make good the losses that would inevitably occur in France.

Three more squadrons had been sent the moment the offensive began. On this fourth day of the battle, he had been told that a further thirty-two pilots and aircraft – the equivalent of two squadrons – were also ordered over to France. Nor were his home squadrons idle. Four a day were leaving England for offensive patrols, landing and refuelling in France, and completing a second patrol before heading home.

For Dowding, who had so single-mindedly and determinedly built up the home defence of Britain, the loss of each aircraft over the Continent made him wince in horror. Yes, he understood the political necessity of the RAF's contribution in France, but to him the greatest single priority was the survival of Great Britain, and that could only be achieved with adequate home defence. 'The continued existence of the nation and all its services,' he had written to the Air Ministry back in October, 'depends upon the Royal Navy and the Fighter Command.' The argument that nothing should be allowed to interfere with the creation of a fifty-squadron Fighter Command was a line he had consistently taken since the previous July, when it had first been agreed that fighters should be sent to France in the event of war. It was a message that had cut no ice with the Chiefs of Staff; if anything, the more Dowding repeated this heartfelt opinion, the less impact it had. But Dowding was now beginning to think the worst. Already there was talk of an invasion. If the Luftwaffe struck any time soon, Britain, he feared, would not have a chance.

Hugh Caswall Tremenheere Dowding had been born in Moffat, Scotland, in 1882, although his father had been a Wiltshire man. Educated at Winchester College, he left school and went to the Royal Military College at Woolwich and from there was commissioned at the Royal Garrison Artillery in 1900. His early army career took him to India, Ceylon and

Hong Kong, but on his return to Britain he decided to qualify for his private pilot's certificate. He gained this in 1913 then undertook a further three-month course with the Royal Flying Corps to gain his wings. Returning to the artillery he was nonetheless obliged to transfer permanently to the RFC upon the outbreak of war in 1914. He rose to become commander of 16 Squadron but clashed with General 'Boom' Trenchard, then head of the RFC and later the father of the Royal Air Force, as it became in April 1918. The argument was over Dowding's belief that pilots needed resting from non-stop combat flying. He lost the debate and was sent back to England, his combat flying career over.

Nor was he initially needed in Trenchard's post-war Royal Air Force, although Dowding's commanding officer at the war's end eventually secured him a permanent commission as a Group Captain. By 1930, he was at the Air Ministry as Air Member for Supply and Research, and less than five years later he was given further responsibilities as Air Member for Research and Development. Both jobs had placed Dowding at the heart of development and expansion of Britain's fighter and bomber forces and also the country's air defences that began in 1934. During his time as head of research and development, Dowding oversaw the introduction of the Hurricane and Spitfire and of the Stirling four-engine heavy bomber, and the development of radar. Admittedly, under his tenure, hopeless combat aircraft such as the Battle and rear-armed Defiant had also seen the light of day; yet there is no question that he got much more right than he got wrong.

Dowding was a deeply intelligent, quietly spoken, rather stiff individual; this somewhat brusque and outwardly cold demeanour led to his being given the nickname 'Stuffy'. Yet he was not really stuffy at all because that suggests he was both conventional and narrow-minded, and he was neither. Rather, he was forward-thinking, deeply pragmatic and full of sound common sense. During the First World War, for example, he was one of the first people to advocate the use of radio communication in aircraft. In the early 1930s, Dowding was advised that biplanes were preferable because two pairs of wings provided greater lift and strength than one. Dowding replied by asking why, in that case, a monoplane had won the internationally coveted Schneider Trophy air speed contest. He had recognized, when many others had not, that speed was of the essence for fighter aircraft.

And although his detractors thought him stubborn and overly prickly, he would have argued that he simply knew his own mind. While others went along with the widely held belief that the bomber would always get through, for example – as the former Prime Minister, Stanley Baldwin, had put it – Dowding preferred to draw on his own experiences during the last war, when he had seen that a bomber force could be decimated unless supported by a sufficiently superior escort. Furthermore, he recognized that isolated incidents such as the destruction of Guernica in northern Spain should be viewed in context. 'I have never accepted ideas because they were orthodox,' he said, 'and consequently I have frequently found myself in opposition to generally accepted views.' Unfortunately, this did make him enemies within the corridors of power in Whitehall and amongst other men of power and influence within the RAF.

That said, while it was true that Dowding could have a waspish tongue and he certainly did not suffer fools, he was nonetheless courteous, modest and a good listener, and, when given the chance, had a quick wit. There were also some interesting quirks to this highly dedicated individual. He was, for instance, a fiendishly good skier and polo player, two extrovert sports that were seemingly at odds with his outwardly dour personality; he had even been President of the Ski Club of Great Britain in 1924–5. Perhaps the slightly gaunt, winsome expression he wore belied the personal tragedy in his life. Twenty years before, he had lost his beloved wife, Clarice. In that, if nothing else, he had something in common with Göring.

Hermann Göring had announced the birth of the Luftwaffe to the world in March 1935, and although rearmament in Britain had begun a year earlier, this, combined with German boasts that it had already achieved air parity with Britain, sent the British Government under Ramsay MacDonald into an outbreak of nervous anxiety.

The RAF had not been well served during this time by its Chief of the Air Staff, Air Marshal Sir Edward Ellington, and the Secretary of State for Air, Lord Londonderry. The former had been hopelessly over-promoted, was deeply conservative when dynamism and forward thinking were much in need, and was far too wedded to the Trenchard view that the bomber was pre-eminent. Londonderry, on the other hand, was a fabulously wealthy aristocrat with almost no political muscle whatsoever. They made a desperately ineffective pair.

Despite the widely held opinion that the best way to prevent a German attack was the threat of even bigger force of bombers dropping bombs over Germany, little effort had been made to create this mighty force. Too many committees, too much discussion and too much penny-pinching as Britain struggled to emerge from the Depression had seen to that. In fact, it was Neville Chamberlain, then Chancellor, who had pressed hardest for the build-up of home defence through fighter squadrons and who had argued that the money should be found through reductions in navy and army budgets. Incredibly, Ellington suggested this was an unnecessary over-reaction. Fortunately, Chamberlain, as the man controlling the purse-strings, had insisted on increasing the size of what was then called the Metropolitan Air Force. It was Chamberlain, more than any other individual, who had given the green light to expansion of the RAF.

Increased numbers was one thing but they would not add up to a hill of beans unless they could take on the best the enemy had to offer. The Air Ministry, in a brief moment of enlightenment, had in 1931 issued Specification F7/30, calling on aircraft designers to produce a new day and night fighter to replace the Bristol Bulldog biplane. The remit included a minimum speed of 195 mph in level flight at 15,000 feet, metal construction, armament comprising four .303 machine guns, and a service ceiling of at least 28,000 feet.

Nearly all the British aircraft manufacturers put forward designs, although it was widely held that Supermarine in Southampton would be the likely winners. Although they were primarily makers of seaplanes, it was their sleek, fast monoplane seaplanes that had won three consecutive Schneider Trophies – victories that ensured the trophy remained in Britain for evermore.

Yet the Type 224 produced by their chief designer, R. J. Mitchell, had been a huge disappointment: too slow, with a poor rate of climb, a fixed undercarriage and wings as thick as trees. Dowding, who had been involved in the F7/30 order from the outset, was also disappointed with Supermarine's effort, but then none of the other designs put forward had amounted to much either. There was even talk of importing a Polish-built fighter instead, although eventually the contract was awarded to the Gloster Gladiator biplane, an aircraft that was serving in France in May 1940 but by then was quite obsolete.

However, R. J. Mitchell, having recovered from an operation on a first bout of cancer, had, by the summer of 1934, returned to work on the Type 224. What soon began to emerge were more than mere changes; rather, he was designing an entirely new aircraft altogether, which he renamed the Type 300 and reckoned would have a top speed of 265 mph. So different was it that the Air Ministry, with Dowding's backing, decided it should be separate from the original F7/30 specification and instead given backing and funding as an experimental aircraft.

By the autumn of 1934, the Type 300 been given another boost. Supermarine had maintained a close relationship with engine makers Rolls-Royce – the Goshawk engine had powered the Schneider-winning seaplanes – but now, as Mitchell was designing his all-new airframe, a new, bigger, more powerful engine, in development for the past two years, was almost ready. The PV12 was a 27 litre power plant that was expected, with a bit of tinkering, to provide more than 1,000 h.p. Suddenly, Mitchell had an engine that could give his fighter design in excess of 300 mph. Supermarine had been given official backing from the outset, but the PV12 – soon renamed the Merlin – was an entirely private venture on the part of the enlightened men at Rolls-Royce. On 5 December 1934, at a conference held at the Air Ministry and headed by Dowding, it was formally agreed that the Merlin should be used in the Type 300.

At the beginning of 1935, the Air Ministry issued another specification, the F10/35, which called for a fighter capable of at least 310 mph and the firepower of no less than six but preferably eight machine guns. By this time, Mitchell had already decided on the ultra-thin, elliptical wings that would give his machine such a distinctive design and it seemed that his new aircraft, now married to the Merlin, would fulfil all the F10/35 requirements without the Air Ministry having to go through the cost and palaver of a formal tendering process. At the same time, at the Hawker company, the chief designer, Sidney Camm, was also working on a new design in response to yet another earlier specification, the F36/34. Suddenly it seemed likely that in both aircraft the RAF had found what it needed: modern, fast, single-engine monoplane fighter aircraft. By the summer, with official Air Ministry backing, the development of Hawker's and Supermarine's prototypes was accelerated.

By the time Göring was telling the world about the existence of his Luftwaffe, the British aircraft revolution was underway, but even so the path from prototype to full-scale production was a long one. It was entirely typical of the top-heavy bureaucratic Government of the time that its response to the existence of the Luftwaffe should be to set up a committee entitled 'Sub-Committee on Air Parity'.

The difference with this latest committee, however, was that chairmanship was given not to the Air Secretary, Lord Londonderry, but to the Colonial Secretary, Philip Cunliffe-Lister, a tough, decisive Conservative who immediately injected the kind of clear-sighted drive that had been absent from Government policy for so long. Quickly recognizing that governmental support was needed for Supermarine and Hawker, he urged the Cabinet to authorize production the moment the prototypes proved their worth; there was no time to dally on this matter. The Cabinet agreed.

When Baldwin took over as Prime Minister in June 1935, Londonderry was booted out and Cunliffe-Lister made Air Secretary in his stead, gaining the title Viscount Swinton soon after. The Air Ministry was infused with a new urgency and vigour under his leadership. He was determined not to let the development of new fighter planes lag or become mired in lengthy decision-making. The Hawker Hurricane, also powered by the Merlin, made its first successful test flight on 6 November 1935. The Supermarine Spitfire, as it was now called much to Mitchell's disgust, was delayed by a few months but took to the air on 5 March the following year. Reaching 335 mph, after a few minor tweaks it then reached 348 mph in level flight, close to the 350 mph Mitchell had hoped for. The Hurricane was slower, but still reached in excess of 310 mph, as had been required.

The decision to put the Hurricane and Spitfire into production was made by Swinton and Sir Wilfred Freeman, the new Air Member for Research and Development. Like Swinton, Freeman had no interest in Whitehall red tape. On 26 May, Humphrey Edwardes-Jones was the first RAF pilot to fly the Spitfire. Nearly crashing on his first landing, he remembered to lower the undercarriage only just in time, emerged unscathed and, as bidden, immediately rang Sir Wilfred Freeman.

'All I want to know,' Freeman asked him, 'is whether you think the young pilot officers and others we are getting in the Air Force will be able to cope with such an advanced aircraft.'

Edwardes-Jones took a deep breath and then gave his verdict. 'Yes,' he replied, 'provided they are given adequate instruction in the use of flaps and retracting undercarriage.'

Within a week, Freeman had placed an order for 310 Spitfires. A short time before, 600 Hurricanes had been ordered. Swinton had wanted to double the Spitfire order, but although Supermarine was owned by the much larger armaments manufacturer, Vickers Armstrong, the initial order was planned to be produced entirely by the small Supermarine factory at Woolston in Southampton and there were concerns over whether they would be able to cope with such an order.

While Hawker, a much bigger enterprise, dutifully got stuck into Hurricane production, Supermarine struggled. The Spitfire was a more complicated design and required new skills and new tools. The Hurricane had, in essence, the same airframe as many of Hawker's earlier biplanes, so the step up was not so drastic. By February 1938, not one production Spitfire had been completed, even though more than 80 per cent of its production had already been outsourced. A further order for 200 more merely added to Supermarine's woes. The production of the Spitfire, a plane much vaunted and publicized, was an utter mess, and on 14 May 1938, the very day the first production aircraft finally took to the skies, Lord Swinton was forced to resign.

However, before his fall, Swinton had developed what had become known as 'shadow factories'. These were factories set up to mirror the work of their parent plants in an effort to cope with the kind of mass production needed for rearmament. Swinton had been keen to bring Lord Nuffield into the shadow factory scheme as his Morris car company was probably the country's biggest mass producer. However, the two had fallen out and Nuffield had refused to play ball. Swinton's departure, however, paved the way for another approach to the notoriously prickly car magnate. A proposal was made in May 1938 that he build a huge new factory, in which he would mass-produce Spitfires – no less than an order of 1,000 to be going on with. It was the largest single order of any aircraft Britain had ever made. Nuffield agreed. A vast 135-acre site was chosen at Castle Bromwich on the edge of Birmingham and bought from the Dunlop Rubber Company; work began on developing the site almost immediately. It was agreed that sixty Spitfires a week would be produced once the factory was up and running.

The problem was that the factory had to be built from scratch, engineers had to be trained, and machinery built, and that all took time. In the long term, the Castle Bromwich factory would no doubt pay dividends, but what Britain and the RAF needed was Spitfires now and they weren't getting them from Lord Nuffield. The first four had finally entered service in August 1938 but fortunately, by that time, many of Supermarine's production problems had been resolved. Subcontracting issues had been ironed out, while the Woolston plant was now operating to its full capacity, with engineers there working an average of sixty-three hours a week. By the summer of 1939, 240 of the original order for 310 had been delivered. It was a start.

The reason why Dowding had not placed the first order for Spitfires and Hurricanes himself was that at the beginning of April 1936 he had been appointed the first Commander-in-Chief of the newly created RAF Fighter Command. With his now vast experience at the Air Ministry and his primary responsibility for research and development, he had been the obvious person for the post. Yet his was a massively daunting task if Britain was to be in any kind of position to withstand an all-out attack by a resurgent German air force.

He had been intimately involved with the development of radar – or RDF – but training personnel, pilots and aircrew to use it whilst bringing the chain of RDF stations to a sufficient level of operational efficiency had been yet another race against the clock. And radar was not sufficient on its own. The development of the Observer Corps, a tiny volunteer force, had needed to be hastened and expanded in conjunction with the chain of RDF stations. Finally, a system by which all this information could be filtered and passed on to the relevant stations and squadrons of Fighter Command had had to be developed, trialled and honed.

Also falling under his control were the anti-aircraft artillery and searchlight formations, although still part of the army. When Dowding had taken over as C-in-C Fighter Command, there had been only sixty usable but mostly obsolescent ack-ack guns and 120 searchlights. These numbers also needed to be dramatically increased. So too did the number of barrage balloons, which floated on wires above urban areas, key factories, ports, rail heads and other potential bombing targets. A further handicap was the lack of all-weather metalled runways, which had prevented pilots from carrying out much flying or training during winter months. The Air Ministry had argued that concrete airstrips made airfields more conspicuous from the air. Dowding persisted, however, and eventually got his runways.

The struggle to prepare Britain's home defences had been a constant battle against time. His doggedness and the not infrequent sharp rejoinders he used in his correspondence with the Air Ministry won him enemies – enemies who would later come back and haunt him. Yet by May 1940 he had believed Fighter Command was almost ready. *Almost.*

Now, though, it seemed as though everything that he had worked for was being frittered away. Despite the efficiency of his early-warning system, despite all the many changes he had implemented, the most important ingredient of all was aircraft and trained pilots, and these were being squandered uselessly over the battlefields of northern France and the Low Countries. Unless this stopped, and stopped soon, and unless something could be done to radically improve the rate of aircraft production, the hard-fought-for development of Britain's air defences would have been for nothing. For in an all-out clash with the Luftwaffe now, RAF Fighter Command would lose.

9

The Battle is Lost

On 13 May, General Lord Gort moved with his Chief of Staff, Henry Pownall, and a number of other select officers and staff to a new command post in a small chateau in the village of Wahagnies, ten miles south of Lille, but some thirty north-east of the rest of GHQ. In wishing to free himself from the cramped hubbub at Habarcq, Gort was revealing one of the fundamental problems of the BEF's set-up in France – that it was far too unwieldy and massively over-staffed. With his departure, some 250 staff were left at BEF's Headquarters under the effective control of two lieutenant-colonels. Communications were already poor in France: there were not enough radios, too many loops to go through to pass on whatever information there was, and too much dependence on an inefficient civilian telephone exchange. By moving to Wahagnies, however, Gort made the system even worse. In the crucial days that followed, vital information frequently failed to reach him or Pownall in time.

On the BEF's front, things had been quiet that day, but it was clear by evening that to the north of their positions the Belgians were struggling against the weight of the northern German thrust. 'All the Belgians seem to be in panic,' wrote General Pownall in his diary that night, 'from the higher command downwards. What an ally!' Incredibly, the news of the German crossings in the south had still not reached them.

Nor had the truth hit home at the Headquarters of the French High Command. 'It is not yet possible to determine the zone in which the enemy will make his main attack' was the conclusion of the final situation report at Gamelin's HQ. Only at Général Georges's Headquarters of the North-East Front was the penny beginning to drop. At around 3 a.m. on the morning of 14 May, Georges and his staff were gathered in the map-room, listening to reports coming in and staring aghast at the map spread before them. Georges, sitting in an armchair, looked deathly pale. 'Our front has been pushed in at Sedan!' he mumbled, briefly rising. 'There have been some failures . . .' He then slumped back into his chair and began to weep.

It was no good blubbing, however. All three bridgeheads across the Meuse needed to be expanded quickly, yet the situation at Dinant, Monthermé and Sedan was still very precarious for the Germans – especially at Sedan. Despite the mass panic by the French of the previous evening, it had principally been the rear echelon and artillery who had flooded back; much of the 55th Division's infantry still stood firm. Moreover, the reserve units of the French X Corps, including an armoured battalion, were ready and waiting to move forward, while a further cavalry division was also only a short distance away and could easily have been hurried forward to help at Sedan.

In contrast, the German infantry involved in the crossing were absolutely exhausted, having had no sleep to speak of since 10 May and having been involved in heavy fighting the previous day. Furthermore, it was not until around 7.20 a.m. that the first German panzers crossed the Meuse. The French armour was ordered up at around 4 p.m. on the 13th, to make a stand at a blocking position along a ridge that ran either side of the village of Bulson a few miles to the south of Sedan. The idea was that as the German panzers appeared, the French armour would be waiting for them. It would then open fire, and knock out the panzers, and then the French tanks and infantry would counter-attack, forcing the Germans back across the Meuse.

This was quite a realistic prognosis, but unfortunately, although the French tanks had only about twelve miles to travel, they did not reach the Bulson ridge until 8.45 a.m. on the 14th – some seventeen hours later – by which time the panzers were already there. Rather than the French lying in wait for the Germans, the opposite occurred – and the French were routed. By the time the French could have brought any more reinforcements forward, Guderian's bridgehead had been massively expanded. At 12.30 p.m., the general received news that the bridge across the Ardennes Canal had been safely captured. This was a huge coup, because the canal, to the west of Sedan, ran southwards, potentially blocking Guderian's intended westward thrust. With the bridge taken intact, there was nothing to stop him – nothing, that is, except for his superior officers, and even Hitler himself.

And it was at this moment that Guderian faced one of the biggest gambles of his life.

As the unfolding Allied disaster at Sedan was finally beginning to sink in, the French and British air forces were ordered to urgently bomb and destroy the newly built German bridges constructed overnight, and across which panzers were now rumbling in a steady stream.

Air Chief Marshal Dowding might have been worried about his precious fighter aircraft, but RAF Bomber Command could ill afford to lose large numbers of planes over France either. Tragically, however, this was precisely what was about to happen over Sedan. The flawed Allied air strategy was now about to reveal its shortcomings horribly above this key battleground. The use of RAF bombers in France had already caused no small amount of debate. Air Marshal Charles Portal, only since April the new head of Bomber Command, had voiced his concerns just two days before the German offensive had begun. He was convinced that using Blenheim medium bombers in direct support of the ground forces was a grave mistake. The enemy front would be swarming with fighters and he feared his bombers would suffer hideous losses. Really accurate bombing could not be expected and he doubted whether fifty Blenheims – which was what it amounted to – operating on information unavoidably some hours out of date could make enough of a difference to justify the inevitable losses that would occur. The problem was that these bombers, along with the squadrons of obsolescent Fairey Battles, had already been committed; they could not stand idle on their airfields, so the Air Staff back in London, despite Portal's grave concerns, had little choice but to commit them once the offensive began. But in so doing they were sending precious pilots to very early deaths.

Once again, the French seemed to be unable to respond to any crisis with anything like urgency. The Arméee de l'Air could only muster forty-three bombers to fly over Sedan, while the RAF sent seventy-three Battles and thirty-six Blenheims. Recognizing that the Allies would make a concerted effort to blow the bridges, Guderian had managed to bring to bear a staggering 300 anti-aircraft guns around his key crossing points. The aircraft of Luftflotte 3 were also there in force to protect the bridges, hovering above and waiting to pounce.

French attacks, made in dribs and drabs, began early in the morning but were hopelessly ineffective. Between three and four in the afternoon, the RAF arrived en masse, flung against the guns and aircraft waiting for them. It was a slaughter.

Oberleutnant Siegfried Bethke was one of the German fighter pilots lying in wait. His squadron had a field day, shooting down five enemy planes. He himself shot down a French Morane in the morning. 'A second was as good as right in front of my nose,' he noted, 'but I let it slip away in my excitement.'

Shortly before midday, Guderian's Army Group Commander, Generaloberst von Rundstedt, had arrived at Sedan. Guderian reported to him on the bridge at Gaulier, by the Draperie Sedannaise, with an air raid in progress. 'Is it always like this here?' von Rundstedt asked. Guderian replied that it was.

It was a beautiful early summer's day. Dark green pine forests and lush, vibrantly green meadows covered the countryside around Sedan. Almost incessantly, however, the dull explosions of bombs, the chatter of machine guns and the thudding flak guns boomed out over the valley, while, above, the roar and scream of aero engines seemed to be ever-present. The ground shook with the weight of ordnance. Long black plumes of smoke followed broken aircraft as they plummeted to the ground.

By early evening, the wrecks of Battles and Blenheims lay strewn, crumpled and charred, all over the wooded slopes around Sedan. Of the seventy-one aircraft that had set off for Sedan that afternoon, forty never returned. No RAF operation of similar size has ever suffered a higher rate of loss.

Meanwhile, Guderian, following his noisy chat with von Rundstedt, crossed back across the Meuse and hurried to Chémery, a small village near the bridge across the Ardennes Canal, where the 1st Panzer Division now had their command post. It was decision time. His orders were explicit: after establishing a bridgehead, he was to wait and build up strength in case of an expected counter-attack from the south. To charge on recklessly with the panzer force was considered by everyone from Halder to von Rundstedt and von Kleist as far too risky. Even Hitler, the arch-gambler, suggested the panzers should wait until sufficient forces still crawling through the Ardennes had caught up.

On the other hand, Guderian and von Manstein, when they had originally devised their plan of attack, had intended that the panzers go for broke, disregarding the danger to their flanks. They had always seen victory or failure in terms of a race against time. And Guderian did not now have time to wait for reinforcements. The French were reeling; it was time to exploit a favourable situation. The problem was that if he went ahead, he would be blatantly disregarding orders that went to the very top. It was a big call to make.

It was the 1st Panzer Division's Chief of Staff, Major Walther Wenck, who helped Guderian make up his mind, by reminding the General of one of his favourite sayings: '*Klotzen, nicht kleckern!*' – 'hit hard, not softly!' Guderian, his decisive, tough-guy reputation put on the line by a mere major, needed no further pause for thought. 'That really answered my question,' he admitted.

Immediately, he ordered 1st and 2nd Panzer Divisions west, leaving 10th Panzer to protect the bridgehead. The dash to the Channel had begun.

To the north, around Dinant, the 5th and 7th Panzer Divisions were also expanding the bridgeheads they had fought so hard to secure the day before. Hans von Luck heard that Rommel's command tank had been hit and knocked into a ditch. '"Is Rommel immune?" we asked ourselves.' Hans's reconnaissance battalion was once again at the front of the advance. 'Keep going, don't look to left or right, only forward,' Rommel had told them. 'I'll cover your flanks if necessary. The enemy is confused; we must take advantage of it.'

Once again, a slow response by the French allowed the Germans to burst out of the bridgehead. Both 5th and 7th Panzer Divisions had faced hard fighting on the 14th, but by the end of the day had begun breaking out because the French 1st Armoured Division, although on standby near Charleroi since the 13th, was not actually ordered forward until 2 p.m. on the 14th and then did not get moving for another couple of hours. Battling against roads crammed with fleeing civilians, it had gone about twenty miles when it leaguered for the night. Little did the troops realize that Rommel's lead panzers were also corralled for the night just a few miles away.

By morning, the Luftwaffe had bombed and destroyed several French fuel convoys, so the 1 Division Cuirassée (1st Armoured Division) was still in the process of refuelling near the village of Flavion when

Rommel's tanks spotted it and immediately opened fire. Meanwhile, anti-tank gunners and panzers from 5th Panzer Division had also arrived on the scene. Disengaging, Rommel ordered his panzers to push on while the remaining mass of the French armour fought a day-long battle with 5th Panzer Division.

Despite the superior firepower of the French tanks, the 1 Division Cuirassée, one of the best tank divisions in the French army, was destroyed, with burning wrecks littering the sweeping countryside much as RAF bombers were strewn around Sedan. The 1 Division Cuirassée had begun the day with 170 tanks. By the day's end, it had just thirty-six. By the morning of the 15th, that figure stood at sixteen. The 1 Division had been utterly destroyed.

That same day, 15 May, Panzer Corps Reinhardt also managed to break out from its bridgehead at Monthermé and thrust more than thirty miles. It was all the more extraordinary because only Generalmajor Werner Kempf's 6th Panzer Division had actually made it across the Meuse – the rest of the corps was still labouring through the gridlock of the Ardennes. The following morning, 16 May, Generalmajor Kempf met Guderian in the marketplace at the small town of Montcornet; the two Panzer Corps had linked up, some fifty miles west of Sedan.

Earlier, as Guderian had passed through an advancing column of the 1st Panzer Division, his men had cheered him. He had been worried that perhaps he had been pushing them too hard: the men were exhausted and ammunition was just beginning to run low. The day before he had seen Oberst Balck after a hard fight against 'a good Normandy infantry division and a brigade of Spahis', his eyes red and his face covered in dirt. Now, though, Guderian knew there must be no more hesitancy. 'The men were wide awake now,' he wrote, 'and aware that we had achieved a complete victory, a break-through.'

Guderian was right. The entire Meuse front had now collapsed. As the motorcycles, tanks, half-tracks and armoured cars of those half-dozen leading panzer divisions thundered through the dusty May roads, French soldiers, stunned to see German troops where no German troops could possibly be, surrendered in their droves.

For the Allies the realization that they had been well and truly humbugged came as a profound shock. In London, Churchill learned the news on the evening of 14 May, when the Cabinet received a message from M. Reynaud, the French Prime Minister, telling it that the Germans had broken through at Sedan, and asking for ten more fighter squadrons. Further messages from Gamelin and Georges revealed that the French C-in-C had been stunned by the rapidity of the German advance. At about 7.30 the following morning, 15 May, Churchill received a telephone call from Reynaud. 'We have been defeated,' he said. For a moment, Churchill did not say anything, so Reynaud added, 'We are beaten; we have lost the battle.' The Prime Minister tried to reassure him, but to no avail.

Soon after, he spoke to Général Georges, who seemed to have partially recovered from the previous day's breakdown. Georges admitted that there had been a serious breach of more than ten miles, but assured Churchill it was now plugged. In this, of course, Georges was hopelessly misinformed. In fact, the French Ninth Army had crumbled apart at the seams and a gap of some fifty miles had been punched in the line up to sixty miles deep. The French First Army had also had its front pierced on a 5,000-yard front. The BEF had repulsed all attacks along its stretch of the line, but the French Seventh Army had retreated west of the Scheldt in the north, while the Belgians continued to falter along their part of the line. By 11 a.m., news had arrived that the Dutch had surrendered. No wonder Reynaud had believed it was as good as over.

It is true that Gamelin had been completely fooled by the German deception plans – so much so that when reports of massed German columns in the Ardennes filtered through he repeatedly refused to take them seriously. Yet with an army of that size and armament, it should have been quite possible to prevent the German breakthrough. Just six panzer divisions could and should have been stopped in their tracks. But this had not happened.

There is no question but that France had been severely traumatized by the events of the 1914–18 war; all the combatants had, but it had been largely fought on French soil. This in itself, however, was not why the French had crumbled so spectacularly along the Meuse front. Rather, it was due to a completely different approach to battle from the German one, albeit one that had not developed at all since the last war; the only difference was that now they had better equipment and better defences.

Military doctrine centred around the concept of 'the methodical battle', whereby everything was prepared in great detail and carried out according to a prearranged plan. This led to very rigid centralization and an adherence to top-down orders, which in turn ensured there was little or no scope for initiative in low-level commanders. The result was that the French army was not equipped to deal with the unexpected. When the battle deviated from the prepared plan, the French did not know what to do. They simply hadn't been trained to take the initiative and to think for themselves.

Rather, military thinkers had believed that any new war would be dealt with by first sitting tight and waiting for the enemy to attack. From their bunkers they would halt the enemy with heavy fire, while local reserves were brought up, bringing any enemy attack to a standstill. Only once superiority had been achieved in men and materiel at the main point of attack would the French then go on the offensive. Thus, French armour, for example, was only ever conceived of as being infantry support, rather than an independent arm.

It was a cumbersome process designed for the long-haul attritional war of twenty years before, but while the French had pretty good tanks and guns, and a phenomenal amount of concrete, they lacked decent, properly thought-out logistics and disgracefully neglected developments in communications. As a rule of thumb, orders from Gamelin's HQ to the front usually took around forty-eight hours. There was not even a radio at Gamelin's HQ, for example; he believed they were too insecure, and could be easily listened in to by the enemy. Telephones were fine so long as the front line was not disrupted – which it inevitably was – while messengers were obviously horribly slow. It simply had not occurred to them that large, modern forces could or needed to be moved quickly. The speed at which the Germans reached the Meuse stunned them completely.

The lack of radio communication had been starkly revealed at Flavion when the 1 Division Cuirassée had been destroyed. Hardly any French tanks had radio sets and so they could not communicate with one another. The Germans, on the other hand, might not have had powerful guns in their turrets but they did have wireless sets. The Panzer Is and IIs, thanks to good communication, were able to lure the more powerful French tanks into traps of hidden anti-tank guns. It was these, rather than the panzers themselves, that had done most of the damage. And there were other little things: the French had been caught napping as they refuelled because it was such a long-drawn-out process. Fuel bowsers would laboriously go from one tank to another filling them up in turn. The Germans, in contrast, would deliver truckloads of jerrycans so that panzer crews could fill up simultaneously. And that, of course, saved time.

Poor French logistics were symptomatic of a system that was unwieldy in every way. The chain of command was also top-heavy and convoluted, with Gamelin as Commander-in-Chief, and then Général Georges as C-in-C North-East Front, then three Army Groups under him, and within Billotte's First Army Group no fewer than five armies, of which the BEF, with half a million men, was one. Furthermore, the French commanders were old. All were in their sixties and command veterans of the First World War. Commanding armies is an exhausting job at the best of times, but much more so during battle, when there are few opportunities for sleep; mental and psychological demands are intense. Army commanders need to be able to grasp information and intelligence quickly and then act decisively, something that is better suited to a man in his forties or fifties. Interestingly, nearly all the German commanders were of this age: Guderian was 51, von Kleist 58, Halder 55, Reinhardt 53, Rommel 48. Only von Rundstedt, at 64, was of a comparable age to the senior French commanders.

The entire French approach was defensive and negative – and a negative mindset takes hold in many counter-productive ways. The huge cost of the Maginot Line and the appeasement and non-aggression line of the French Government and political left also played an enormous part in formulating policy, but this endemic defensive attitude – this rigidity to the methodical battle plan – had ensured that there could be no French march into Germany when Hitler reoccupied the Rhineland in 1936, nor again when Germany invaded Poland in 1939. Had the French done so on either occasion, the Second World War would almost certainly have never taken place.

France's unwillingness to step out from behind her defensive system had also unwittingly proved to keen-eyed observers like Heinz Guderian that France was not offensively minded and that her commanders were overly cautious. It suggested they hoped to avoid a serious clash of arms, which was absolutely the case.

No matter how obvious it might have seemed to the conservative Gamelin that the German main attack must come through the Low Countries, the failure to prepare for other eventualities was seriously negligent. Nowhere was this carelessness more manifest than at Sedan.

The town effectively formed the hinge between the top of the Maginot Line, which ended twelve miles to the east at La Ferté, and the mobile north-east part of the line that had swung up into Belgium at the start of the offensive. Clearly, if this hinge could be broken, the two halves of the French line would be critically severed in two. With this in mind, it would perhaps have been sensible to err on the side of caution and make sure this stretch of the line was exceedingly well-defended.

It was not, however. There had been frantic bunker-building in the area over the winter so that by May there were 103 in all, but many were only half finished, lacking steel gun port shutters and doors, and still surrounded by their construction pits. Most of the construction work had been carried out by infantrymen rather than engineers; instead of training for combat they were busy building bunkers. As it was, the 55th Infantry Division was a second-rate division made up mostly of reservists. When the crunch came, and determined German troops were storming their positions, far too many realized they had no idea what they should do, so large numbers either fled or surrendered.

And there was another curious French practice that was a hangover from the last war. The individual infantry companies were constantly being rotated between construction work of various kinds, even agriculture, and infantry training. Once back in the line, they rarely returned to their former sector, but took over the positions of the company they were relieving. This meant they never got to know any stretch of the line particularly well. In the static attritional war along the Western Front, rotation had been more important than local knowledge, but that was not the case in 1940. Furthermore, by rotating companies in such a way, these units had become separated from their parent battalions. One company might be at one end of the sector, another in the middle, sandwiched between two companies from entirely different battalions. As a result cohesion – and hence strong communication – had been crucially lost between units.

Guderian had chosen his principal crossing point at Gaulier next to the Draperie Sedannaise for a very good reason. First, his approach was hidden by a multitude of buildings, but, second, there was not one single bunker along the far bank of the Meuse at this particular part of the river. Even though this mile-long stretch lent itself very obviously to the siting of a string of machine-gun and anti-tank gun posts, there was nothing. This was incomprehensible and doubly so because it had been at precisely that point that the German army had crossed the Meuse in August 1914.

To make matters worse, there was a complete absence of mines at Sedan, even though the narrow flood plains either side of the river were perfect mine-laying terrain, while the open countryside beyond should also have been pasted with them. Mines were comparatively cheap and easy to make – far easier to build and lay than bunkers – yet the 55th Infantry Division had been given just 422 for its part of the line. Most of these had not been laid, however, and those that had been, had been dug up and moved to a nearby depot to be re-greased to protect them from soil moisture. Needless to say, they had not been relaid by 10 May.

Curiously, it was a politician rather than a soldier – Pierre Taittinger, a member of the Parliamentary Army Committee – who first warned Gamelin about the poor defences at Sedan. 'In this region,' he told Gamelin in March, 'we are entirely too much taken with the idea that the Ardennes woods and the Meuse River will shield Sedan and we assign entirely too much significance to these natural obstacles. The defences in this sector are rudimentary, not to say embryonic.' His warning was not heeded.

Of course, once the bunkers were overrun, the poorly trained French infantry inside them did not know what to do. The Germans followed a 'mission command' principle, known as *Aufstragstaktik*. This meant that an officer or NCO would be given a mission or goal, such as to capture a specific bunker or to destroy an enemy gun position. How he then achieved it was entirely up to him. This was not a concept that the French – or British for that matter – understood at this time. Oberleutnant Korthals of the 1st Panzer Division was given the order to destroy a key bunker overlooking the Meuse, but not told how to do it. Using his initiative, he then went on to destroy a large number more.

Guderian, Rommel and Kempf led from the front – almost recklessly so in the case of Rommel – but by being near the action they were able to inspire their men at crucial moments and also see for themselves how the battle was going. At Sedan, Général Lafontaine, commander of the French 55th Infantry Division, remained in a bunker built into a hidden quarry some eight miles south of the town. When the panic occurred on the night of the 13th, he hastily vacated his command post and moved even further back.

The French were not prepared for the unexpected. The last war had been about having the most concrete and the best guns; so this was what they had concentrated on developing during the intervening years. They were to be proved half right, but when they discovered they had been certainly half wrong, they could not adapt quickly enough. Instead they became like a rabbit trapped in headlights: scared, frozen to the spot and unable to respond.

*

On the evening of 16 May, the BEF was ordered to fall back to the River Escaut, the 'E' Line, just inside Belgium. It would be part of a collective retreat but was necessary to ensure the British kept a straight front between the Belgians to the north and the French First Army to the south. The move was to take two days, and they would pause the first night along the River Senne to the west of Brussels and then the second along the River Dendre, a further twenty-five miles back. At Gort's Command Post, his Chief of Staff, General Pownall, wondered wearily whether it would be possible. 'I don't see how we can get back again in two days in a hurry,' he scribbled in his diary, 'especially as the roads are badly blocked with thousands of refugees and we may be sure that we shall get properly bombed, which we didn't on the way up.' To make matters worse, the truth about the German breakthrough in the south had not become clear to all. 'I hope to God the French have some means of stopping them and closing the gap,' scrawled Pownall, 'or we are *bust*.'

10

Emergency Measures

FROM ALMOST THE moment the German offensive began, Britain had become gripped by enemy paratroop and Fifth Column fever. 'Preparing a hot reception for any parachutists' was the headline in a page of the British weekly magazine, *The War Illustrated*. Underneath was a series of pictures of the army preparing roadblocks, soldiers ushering a bus around a pile of sandbags, and a Tommy checking the papers of a motorist. 'Britain took immediate and vigorous steps to meet the possibility of invasion from the air,' ran the article. 'Though this method had been foreseen, some surprise was occasioned by the large scale on which it was carried out in Holland and Belgium by the Nazis and the measure of success which attended it.'

It was the German airborne drops on the Low Countries, above all, that shocked the British. It made them realize how very vulnerable they were. For millennia, Britain's island status had protected her: no invader had managed to successfully cross the Channel since William of Normandy in 1066, yet now it seemed that stretch of sea was no longer the barrier it had once been. Aircraft could now bring new levels of destruction; Baldwin's line about the bomber always getting through still haunted the thoughts of many. And aeroplanes could now deliver a new terror as well: hordes of parachutists.

On 10 May, the Air Ministry had circulated a memo about this new type of airborne soldier. 'German parachute troops, when descending, hold their arms above their heads as if surrendering,' it warned. 'The parachutist, however, holds a grenade in each hand. These are thrown at anyone attempting to obstruct the landing.'

How a paratrooper was supposed to hold the cords of his parachute and clutch, let alone throw, grenades at the same time was not made clear, but certainly it appeared a very real threat. After all, for so long Nazi propaganda had been declaring that Britain was the primary enemy, and it stood to reason that if German paratroopers could be dropped over Holland and Belgium with such apparent ease and with so dramatic an effect, there was little to stop them crossing the Channel and delivering them over England as well. By 11 May, the Home Office had already issued a warning that the arrival of parachutists should be reported to the nearest police station. This meant the Government was taking the threat seriously, and few among the public were prepared to question that. 'The parachute troops now seem to have taken precedence in catching the imagination of the people,' noted Daidie Penna after a day of hearing her friends and neighbours speak of little else. 'It is said that the downs and the roads near our station are being closely watched for possible landings.'

It was primarily as a means of combating the threat of an airborne invasion that the Government decided to recruit a home guard. The decision had been made the day after the offensive had been launched, and three days later, a very rough and rudimentary means of organization having been worked out, an appeal for volunteers was made by Anthony Eden, the new Secretary of State for War. Clearly, it would have been far better to have completed the organization of this new force first, but such was the sense of crisis, it was felt there was no time to lose; the muster needed to be called now.

On the evening of 14 May, Eden broadcast to the nation. 'I want to speak to you tonight,' he said, 'about the form of warfare which the Germans have been employing so successfully against Holland and Belgium – namely, the dropping of troops by parachute behind the main defence lines.' These troops were to disorganize and confuse as a preparation for the landing of troops by aircraft. The Government wanted to leave nothing to chance so was asking for men who were British subjects, and aged fifteen to sixty-five, to come forward and offer their services. The name of this new force was to be the Local Defence Volunteers. 'This name describes its duties in three words,' added Eden. 'You will not be paid, but you will receive a uniform and will be armed.' Anyone choosing to join simply had to report to their local police station and hand in their names, and then wait to be called.

The first volunteers had arrived at their local stations before the broadcast had even finished. Within six days, more than a quarter of a million had offered their services; there were more than a thousand on duty along the Kent coast by the evening of 17 May. The problem was that despite his promise to clothe and arm these volunteers, Britain had nothing like enough uniforms or rifles or any other kinds of weapon to fulfil that pledge. Instead, a call was made for people to hand in shotguns and pistols, which raised around 20,000 firearms. Those who had volunteered and who had rifles or shotguns tended to keep hold of them, but volunteers turned out with picks, axes, crowbars and anything else they could think of that might be used against a parachutist. Local – and zone and group – commanders were appointed by the military. Landowners and retired officers were obvious choices, and where they did not exist, local dignitaries and businessmen took command. In the first days, improvisation was the by-word.

As elsewhere, the response was enthusiastic in the village of Tadworth in Surrey. Daidie Penna met an early recruit the following morning. 'I hope they give me a gun,' he told her. 'I'm just dying to have a pot at one of them fellers comin' down!' The man's wife was rather indignant at not being given the chance to join too.

'Your job is to keep up the morale on the home front,' her husband told her.

'I'm doin' that all right,' she replied, 'on my knees.' Daidie assumed she meant scrubbing not praying. Later, her oldest son, Dick, came back from school and gave her a detailed account of the techniques and equipment of parachute troops. 'So Hitler had better look out,' noted Daidie. 'Reigate Grammar School is discussing him!'

While most LDVs had to make do without uniforms or rifles, there were some who were considerably better equipped than others, albeit hardly in the latest 1937 pattern battledress. There were a large number of cadet forces throughout the country, although they were a particular feature of the country's public schools. At Marlborough College in Wiltshire, the school OTC (Officers' Training Corps) almost immediately offered its services. Dressed in old-style Service Dress, peaked caps and puttees up to their knees, and armed with Short Magazine Lee Enfield No. 1 rifles, they were the envy of the local townsmen who had to make do with trilbys, cloth caps and the odd shotgun.

Boys were expected to join the OTC at the beginning of their second year, although the Master announced that only those who were seventeen or older could join the LDV and only once they had received the written approval of their parents. Two of those who wasted no time in doing so were Douglas Mann and John Wilson, both seventeen.

Although attending a boarding school in Wiltshire, both lived in Kent. Douglas's father was a successful London brewer, but also owned around 1,500 acres between Tonbridge and East Grinstead, part of which he farmed and part of which was leased to tenant farmers. He was a wealthy man, with servants, a chauffeur and all the trappings of someone of his standing at that time. 'You were living in Edwardian times really,' says Douglas, 'right up to the war.'

Douglas had three older brothers who had all gone to Marlborough too; so had his father and his grandfather before that. Public school could be harsh, but Douglas loved it – he was surrounded by friends and there was always plenty of sport to play. 'It suited me down to the ground,' he admits.

John Wilson was equally happy at the school too. He was the son of a distinguished officer in the Indian Police who had risen to become Inspector General of the Bombay Presidency. Like so many children of colonial officers, John had been brought up entirely in England, mostly by his grandparents, although his mother would return home for six months every year. 'She couldn't stand the summer heat,' says John. However, his father had retired in 1932, and returning to England had bought a large house in Hawkhurst.

Shortly after war had been declared, John had taken a telephone message for his father. 'Markover,' the voice had told him. 'That's all you need say, and the time of the message.' In fact, his father was on the reserve list for the security service and the message was the signal for him to report to London immediately. By May 1940, he was working in counter-intelligence at Wormwood Scrubs in west London.

And now his seventeen-year-old son was doing his bit too. The OTC was run by a retired Lieutenant-Colonel, Bill Harling. New recruits joined 'D' Company, then after the first year they entered their house platoon for further training. There were enough volunteers in the sixth form to base the Marlborough College LDV on the same house platoon system. 'I was in B3 House Platoon,' says John, 'which in the LDV had a strength of fourteen. And we were never split up.'

The boys were soon set manning roadblocks on the Bath Road and an OP (observation post) on Manton Down. The roadblock on the A4 was created by dragging an old threshing machine halfway across. As incoming traffic came towards them, they would make the vehicles halt, then check drivers' identities, ask a few questions about where they going to and why, and look underneath their vehicle. 'There was the threat from both Fifth Columnists,' says John, 'and from parachutists. They virtually turned the whole of Britain into an armed camp.'

Exciting though it was to begin with, the novelty quickly wore off for Douglas. 'It was awful really,' he says. 'You spent the night, two hours on and two hours off and so on, and then you had to go to lessons just the same and you had to fit your prep in.'

The term 'Fifth Column' had originated during the Spanish Civil War when Franco's Nationalist Forces were closing in on Madrid. The Nationalists claimed that in addition to four columns of troops in the field, they had a fifth column already inside Madrid. The expression caught on and had since been cleverly exploited by Josef Goebbels in particular, who had spread the word that Germany had large numbers of undercover spies operating in France and the Low Countries, spreading confusion and discord and preparing the ground for airborne troops. Certainly, the Abwehr, the Wehrmacht intelligence service, had spies in these countries but nothing like as many as Goebbels had made out.

Once this seed had been planted, Goebbels's work was done; the Allies themselves did the rest. The genius of the scam was that it made everyone suspicious. It was not the man with the upturned collar and hat lowered over his face that the public needed to be wary of, but those who looked otherwise completely normal. Suddenly, any stranger was a suspect; any unusual behaviour, or strange, throw-away comment, a matter of deep suspicion.

The Dutch Foreign Minister had claimed that many of the German paratroopers that had fallen on Holland had been disguised in Belgian, Dutch, French and British uniforms and even as priests, nuns and nurses. The rumours spread like wildfire and soon it seemed that everyone was vainly searching for German parachutists dressed as nuns. On 18 May, *The Times* ran a section on its letters page called 'Parachutes and Traitors – More Suggestions'. One man had written in proposing to arm 'anti-parachutists' with Winchester .44 repeating rifles and with shotguns using solid 'paradox' shot. 'A paradox ball,' he wrote helpfully, 'will stop big game at short range.'

The creation of the LDV was just one of the measures to counteract the fear of Fifth Columnists and parachutists. On 16 May, the War

Cabinet and the Chiefs of Staff Committee were presented with a memorandum by the Joint Intelligence Sub-Committee entitled 'Security Measures against Air Invasion', in which they urged the internment of all enemy aliens between the ages of sixteen and seventy, male and female, and the heightening of internal security particularly for all officers and civil servants. They also suggested that all ports should be treated as prohibited areas and that in the event of an invasion or imminent threat of a landing, complete military control of the United Kingdom should be put into force immediately.

This advice led to Churchill asking Chamberlain to discuss with ministers the security implications of disaster in France. The result was two bills that were hurriedly drawn up and duly passed through Parliament on 22 May. The first was the Emergency Powers (Defence) Act, which gave the Government the completely unprecedented authority to exercise control over property, business, labour and life of the nation. The second was the Treachery Act, which enabled the Government to round up and detain all enemy aliens – i.e. Germans and Austrians – between the ages of sixteen and sixty. That most of the 60,000 such people were Jews and political refugees cut no ice with the Government as it desperately tried to stem the tide of Fifth Column fever. At Chamberlain's suggestion, these people were rounded up and taken to camps on the Isle of Man, well out of harm's way. Other 'aliens' were also forced to surrender cars and bicycles and to adhere to a strict curfew between 10 p.m. and 8 a.m. The act also allowed the Government to fling in prison without trial anyone it considered in any way in cahoots with the enemy. That included Oswald Mosley, leader of the British Union of Fascists, and his wife, Diana; the following day, both were sent to Brixton Prison. Never in its history had Britain enforced such draconian measures; never had a Government wielded such far-reaching – and, frankly, undemocratic – power. As Harold Nicolson noted, 'We have today passed a bill depriving ourselves of all our liberties.'

It was on the 16th that Churchill had flown to Paris along with his Chief of Staff, General Ismay, and General John Dill, the Vice-CIGS. After a sobering visit to a lifeless British Embassy, they went to the Quai d'Orsay to see Reynaud, Gamelin and Daladier, the former Prime Minister and current Minister of Defence. They met in a large, beautiful and airy room that overlooked the palace gardens. Outside, bonfires were lit – the state papers were being burned. Gamelin could tell them nothing but bad news. Things were not as dire as they seemed, Churchill suggested. They had been in a mess together before and got out of it all right. 'Evidently this battle will be known as the Battle of the Bulge,' he said. 'Now, my General, when and where are you going to counter-attack?' Gamelin replied morosely that he had nothing with which to counter-attack. 'We suffer from inferiority of numbers, equipment, method and morale,' he said. In fact, he was only right on the last two points.

Churchill tried to maintain an outward cheerfulness, but he had been deeply shocked. Again and again, the three Frenchmen asked for more fighter squadrons. Fighter planes, above all, were what they needed; perhaps then the battle could yet be turned. Churchill told them he would seek the consent of his Cabinet; in his mind he was convinced Britain should do as requested, but he wanted the approval of his ministerial colleagues.

'Today the news is worse,' noted a morose Neville Chamberlain in London that same day, 'the French are giving way without fighting.' Churchill was in France trying to stiffen Reynaud's resolve, but in London the mood was almost as bleak as it was in Paris. In the afternoon, Chamberlain saw Joe Kennedy, who told him frankly that he believed French morale was broken and that they had no fight left. He didn't see how Britain could fight on without them. 'I told him I did not see how we could either,' added Chamberlain, who thought the only chance left if France collapsed would be for President Roosevelt to make an appeal for an armistice, though he knew it was unlikely the Germans would respond.

For his part, Joe Kennedy had been shocked by the appearance of his old friend. 'He is definitely a heartbroken and physically broken man,' Kennedy noted. 'He looks ghastly; and I should judge is in a frightfully nervous condition.'

It was when Kennedy saw the ashen expressions of men like the former Prime Minister and listened to the increasingly dire news from France that he felt doubly sure his predictions of a short war that would end favourably for Germany were correct. The previous day, he had been summoned to see Churchill.

Although the PM had yet to set off to France, he had by this time spoken with Reynaud and had realized that Britain might well soon have to face Germany alone. To this end, it was, Churchill believed, essential to bring the United States in on her side, not in terms of troops on the ground, but materially. Only the US had the industrial might to provide the kinds of armaments that he envisaged would be needed. He thus planned to appeal that day directly to President Roosevelt, but felt it worth sounding out Ambassador Kennedy first.

Kennedy arrived at Admiralty House late on the 15th. The building was already blacked out, and outside stood a guard of soldiers. Ushered through Churchill's outer office, he was then led into the Prime Minister's study, where three of his ministers, including Archibald Sinclair, the new Secretary of State for Air, were waiting. Churchill was sitting in a comfortable chair, a large cigar between his fingers and an equally large Scotch at his side.

The PM immediately asked him whether he had heard any news about Italy. Mussolini's imminent entry into the war was a growing concern. 'It could make the difference,' he told Kennedy. 'It certainly will decrease our chances.' However, Churchill said, echoing the words he had told the Chiefs of Staff earlier, come what may, Britain would fight on.

Churchill then asked whether the United States might be prepared to give Britain some more destroyers. The entry of Italy into the war would badly affect Britain's situation in both the Mediterranean and the Atlantic; the Italian navy was more developed than the rest of her armed forces. Some American destroyers could make a huge difference as they would fill a shortfall until those currently under construction in Britain had been completed.

'It isn't fair to ask us to hold the bag for a war the Allies expect to lose,' Kennedy told them. 'If we are to fight, under these circumstances it seems to me we would do better fighting in our own backyard. You know our strength. Right now our navy is in the Pacific, our army is not up to requirements, and we haven't enough airplanes for our own use.' Kennedy could see no point in involving themselves in a war that was likely to be over in the near future.

Despite his stance, Churchill insisted that he would be asking the President for forty or fifty destroyers, as many aircraft as the US could spare, more anti-aircraft guns and steel. Although the Allies were still fighting in northern Norway, the situation looked bad there too. 'We are going to be in a terrible situation on steel with Narvik cut off,' continued Churchill, 'trouble in the Mediterranean that will hit the supply of chrome from Turkey and with Mussolini going in, Spain may follow.' He paused for a moment then added, 'Regardless of what Germany does to France, England will never give up so long as I am in power, even if

England is burned to the ground. The Government will move if it has to and take the Fleet to Canada and fight on.'

Late that night, Kennedy reported his conversation to Washington and the following morning, 16 May, forwarded on to the President Churchill's letter requesting help. The Prime Minister and President had begun a correspondence the previous autumn, but this was the first time Churchill had written to him since becoming PM. He did not beat about the bush. How much Churchill himself believed in the threat of parachutists is not clear, but he was certainly prepared to try to use it as leverage. 'We expect to be attacked here ourselves,' he wrote, 'both from the air and by parachute and air-borne troops in the near future, and are getting ready for them.' The voice and power of the United States, he warned the President, would count for nothing if withheld too long. 'You may have a completely subjugated Nazified Europe established with astonishing swiftness, and the weight may be more than we can bear.' He pleaded with Roosevelt to declare non-belligerency against Germany so that she might help Britain in every way short of actually engaging armed forces.

He then provided a list of requests. In addition to the destroyers, aircraft, AA guns and steel, he also asked that America send a naval squadron to Ireland to try to deter a German invasion there, and offered the US the chance to make use of Singapore in an effort to keep the 'Japanese dog' quiet in the Pacific.

Later on the 16th, some hours after sending Churchill's letter, Kennedy cabled the President stressing his grave doubt once more that Britain could fight on alone. 'It is not beyond the realm of reason,' he wrote, 'that this crack-up can come like a stroke of lightning. In consequence, any action must be conceived now if it is to be effective.' Around midnight, the President's reply arrived. The destroyers could not be made available without an Act of Congress and now was not the moment to ask. As regard to aircraft and steel, Arthur Purvis, the head of the Anglo-French Purchasing Commission in the US, could expect continued co-operation. Sending a naval squadron to Ireland was not impossible but the US navy was firmly ensconced at Pearl Harbor in Hawaii, so making use of Singapore was, for the time being, out of the question.

Churchill was naturally disappointed, particularly about the destroyers, but Roosevelt was being forced to tread carefully. In America he was seen as a leading interventionist. There was no stomach for war in the US and the anti-interventionist lobby was a powerful one. Isolationist sentiment was also, crucially, strong in both houses of Congress. Nonetheless, despite the negative response to Churchill's requests, the President still rang Kennedy, anxious to know what the Prime Minister's reaction had been.

The following day, Churchill replied to Roosevelt, stressing the mounting gravity of the situation. 'We must expect in any case to be attacked on the Dutch model before very long,' he wrote. If American assistance was to play any part at all, he stressed, it would have to be available very soon.

It would not be the last time Churchill would plead Britain's case in such stark terms. He would continue chivvying and cajoling the President for as long as it took because he was sure – as certain as he could be about anything – that the United States held the key to Britain's eventual victory over Nazi Germany.

Right now, however, he faced an uphill battle. From London, Ambassador Kennedy was warning the President that Britain would soon be beaten too, and that to support her now would be to back a busted flush. His man in France, Ambassador Bullitt, was equally certain the current crisis was going to end in disaster for Britain. On 16 May, he had put to the President – in an off-the-record cable that was for Roosevelt's 'most private ear' only – a hypothesis that he believed had a likely chance of becoming reality: Britain would throw out the current Government, sue for peace and install Mosley and the British Fascists, who would co-operate fully with Nazi Germany. 'That would mean the British navy against us,' he wrote. To this end, he urged the President to speak with Mackenzie King, the Canadian Prime Minister, and the senior commanders of the British Fleet, and make sure that should the worst happen, the navy would sail for Canada.

Roosevelt wanted to see the world rid of Hitler and the Nazis. Unlike the anti-interventionists, he did not see the Atlantic as the great bulwark that would protect them. War against Germany, he believed, was inevitable. But he was not a dictator; he was a democratically elected head of state. In November there would be a Presidential election and, to be re-elected, he needed the support of the nation – a nation overwhelmingly opposed to war. To overtly help Britain and France further when their futures looked so bleak would be political suicide. For the time being, at any rate, he had to maintain his position as a reluctant, but necessary, neutral. Britain would have to find a way through this current crisis without the United States.

*

At around midnight on 16 May, Neville Chamberlain returned to his diary. A deeply troubling day had just got worse. Churchill had returned from France and clearly the situation there was worse than he had thought. 'Terrible message from Winston,' he scribbled. 'Effect is next three or four days decisive unless German advance can be stayed. French army will collapse and BEF will be cut off. Decided to throw in more air forces tomorrow.'

For Air Chief Marshal Dowding, the Commander of Fighter Command, this was terrible news, for those air forces were fighter aircraft, precious Hurricanes that would all too soon be desperately needed at home. Britain's air war had completely lost its direction. Urgent priorities needed to be made. Fast.

11

Learning the Lessons

OBERLEUTNANT HAJO HERRMANN had been one of the first Luftwaffe pilots to go to Spain. In fact, he had been sent as a punishment. A headstrong and highly intelligent young man, Hajo had only been in the Luftwaffe a year and had still not fully completed his training when he had incurred the wrath of his bomber group commander. Back in 1936, the vast majority of those in the one-year-old Luftwaffe had lacked much flying experience so it was not altogether surprising that even group commanders made flying mistakes.

This was the case during an exercise in July of that year when the entire *Kampfgeschwader* was flying in a diversion exercise. Hajo's *Staffel* was the last in the line, so when it came to land again it was with mounting frustration that he watched the commander, Major Maass, overfly the airfield for what was clearly going to be an extremely wide approach. In wartime, Hajo knew, everything depended on carrying out manoeuvres as quickly as possible, but by the time everyone had followed their leader in, he reckoned he might almost be out of fuel. So, instead, Hajo broke formation, performed a tight turn, and landed his Junkers 52 ahead of the rest of the group. He had already taxied to the edge of the field and was out of his aircraft as Major Maass's aircraft finally touched down.

Soon after, Hajo was called over and disciplined immediately. 'Sign here,' he was told as he was handed a piece of paper. 'General Franco has approached the Government of the Reich,' Major Maass said, 'and asked for assistance.' At first Hajo did not understand. He had never heard of

Franco, but it seemed as though the commander was trying to get rid of him for the insolent flying offence he had just committed. His fears seemed confirmed when Major Maass told him he would have to be discharged from the Luftwaffe in order to go to Spain.

Soon enough, however, all became clear. His temporary discharge was merely part of the clandestine nature of the mission. He and his crew were one of ten transport crews and the same number again of fighter pilots. A long train and sea journey took them to Cadiz and then on to Seville. From there, Hajo began his flying missions, ferrying Moroccan troops to and fro between North Africa and southern Spain. Republican warships would open fire from the Straits of Gibraltar and, once, Hajo's plane was hit. From then on, he would load lumps of stone and iron into the hold and would have them dropped on the ships below as they flew over. Later, he was given real bombs.

Help to Spain had initially been given in return for much-needed raw materials, particularly iron and tungsten, yet it also allowed the German pilots and aircrews to gain invaluable experience of flying in a combat situation and for the Luftwaffe to test and develop its aircraft and tactics. Some 15,000 pilots and crews would see service in Spain, and after its highly secret beginnings Luftwaffe involvement in the Spanish Civil War became more open with the creation of the Condor Legion in November 1936, although, to maintain the fiction of legality, all German members of the legion were 'volunteers' and arrived in Spain wearing civilian clothes as 'tourists'. Hajo was still there at that time. He finally returned to Germany in April 1937, having massively increased his flying hours and with it his experience. He had learned many important lessons during that time.

So too had the fighter pilots, who had begun their time in Spain with Heinkel 51 biplanes but had progressed on to the new Messerschmitt 109B and later Cs. These fighter pilots had soon learned that the best flying formation was not the tight three-plane vic as had been practised in the last war, but a two- or four-aircraft formation, with two *Rotten* together making a *Schwarm.* Experience proved that a formation could be most effective when spaced apart with about 600 feet between each aircraft; it ensured the lead aircraft could be protected by his wingman, but also meant that from a distance the formation was harder for the enemy to spot than a group of tight formation fighters. The extra space also gave them greater freedom to manoeuvre. It was Werner Mölders, commander of the fighter unit 3/J88, who did much to refine these

David Crook. A pre-war regular with 609 (West Riding) Auxiliary Squadron, David's transformation from carefree 'weekend flier' to battle-hardened fighter ace typified the entire squadron's transition as, over the course of the summer, they became one of the most successful units in RAF Fighter Command.

Above: Halifax (*left*) with Ambassador Joe Kennedy: the peace-monger and the arch-defeatist. Both men did little to help Britain's cause during the dark days of May and early June.

Left: Prime Minister and former Prime Minister. The two forged a surprisingly strong relationship once Churchill had taken over, and Chamberlain would play a crucial role during Britain's moment of greatest crisis.

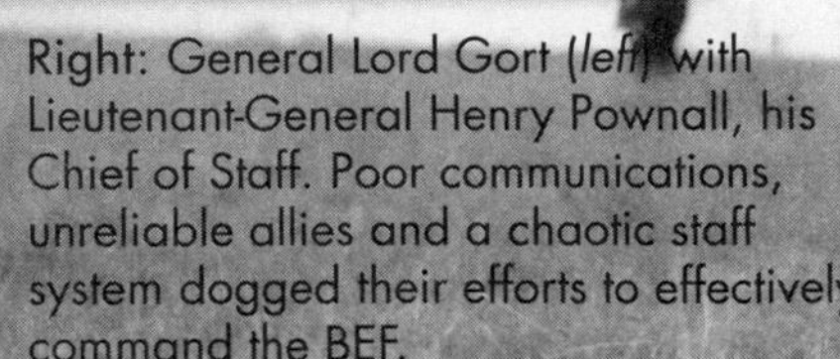

Right: General Lord Gort (*left*) with Lieutenant-General Henry Pownall, his Chief of Staff. Poor communications, unreliable allies and a chaotic staff system dogged their efforts to effectively command the BEF.

Above left: Hermann Göring, the second most powerful man in the Reich. Although chief of the Luftwaffe, he was a more effective and talented businessman and industrialist than military commander. Relishing the trappings of power, no man enjoyed being a leading Nazi more.

Above right: Franz Halder, Chief of Staff of the German Army, and no fan of Hitler. A brilliant staff officer, and the chief planner of the western campaign, he was nonetheless repeatedly frustrated by interference from above.

Right: This picture sums up well the uneasy relationship between Hitler and the Commander of the Army, von Brauchitsch (*right*). The Führer mistrusted the army and more than once reduced von Brauchitsch to a quivering wreck with his tirades.

Above: Rommel discusses his division's latest positions. A fearless commander who led from the front, he was by background an infantryman, and a late convert to mobile panzer tactics.

Right: General Guderian, one of the main architects of the panzer thrust through the Ardennes. Another commander never far from the vanguard of his troops, he was also prepared to repeatedly defy his senior commanders, and was one of the few men in the Wehrmacht to believe a rapid victory in the West to be possible.

Left and below: German forces had far more radios than the Allies and unquestionably better communications, a crucial ingredient of their success. However, despite the myth of the blitzkrieg, they had fewer tanks, guns, motorized transport and even troops than the Allies. Of 135 divisions to take part in the western campaign, only ten had any tanks, and only 278 of these were Mk IV Panzers like those shown below.

The reality. Most German troops got around on foot, on horseback (*above left*), or by bicycle (*bottom*) if they were lucky. The majority of panzers were Mk Is and IIs, under-armed and under-armoured. The men beside this Mk I (*top right*) are almost as tall as the tank itself, which was armed with nothing more than a machine gun.

Right: Gridlock in the Ardennes. Had the Allies responded to reports of large-scale traffic movement through the Ardennes, and sent their bombers over, the campaign could well have been over before it had barely begun.

Above: The Allies were stunned by the apparent might of the Luftwaffe, even though the Germans lost a staggering 353 aircraft on 10 May alone. This picture of Rotterdam, heavily bombed on 14 May, was taken by Julius Neumann from his Me 109.

Above: Feldmarschall Kesselring talks with Hauptmann Walter Rubensdörffer and the men of Erpro 210, one of the crack Zerstörer units.

Above left to right: Three of the Luftwaffe's best. A bomber pilot, Stuka pilot and fighter pilot: Hajo Herrmann, Paul-Werner Hozzel and Günther Rall.

Right: The charismatic Dolfo Galland, cap at rakish angle and ever-present cigar between his gloved fingers.

Below: Ulrich Steinhilper (*standing left*) and the men of 3/JG 52 outside their billet in France. Some of the unnecessarily wide array of Luftwaffe uniforms are on display here.

Above: Siegfried Knappe, his hand and wrist bandaged after being wounded in the final days of the Battle for France.

Above: Siegfried Bethke, his hand on hip, in the middle of a group of pilots and ground crew from 2/JG 2.

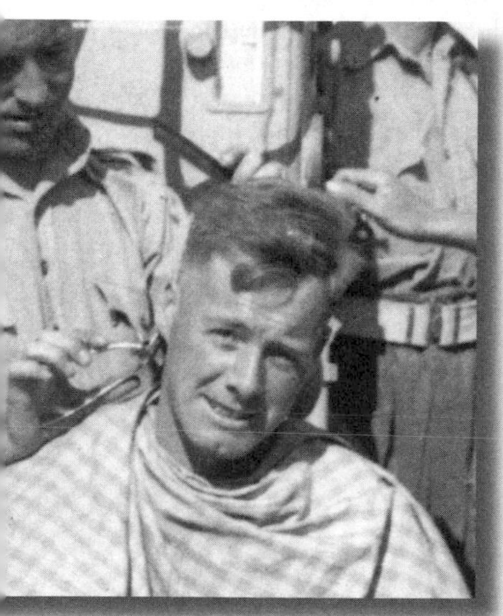

Above left to right: Stan Fraser, Arthur Hughes and Billy Drake. The Blenheim squadrons in France were decimated – Arthur was one of only four pilots from 18 Squadron to return to Britain and was wounded himself soon after. Billy Drake, although managing to score several 'kills', was lucky to survive when he was shot down on 13 May. The air fighting over France and the Low Countries provided a steep learning curve for all those involved.

A squadron of Hawker Hurricanes. Although a stable gun-platform and powered by the Rolls-Royce Merlin, the Hurricane was nonetheless outclassed by both the Spitfire Mk I and the Messerschmitt 109E.

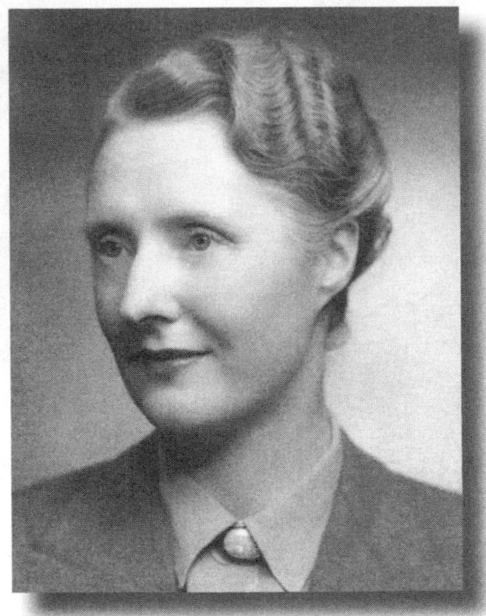

Above: Douglas Mann, who with friends from his school OTC joined the Marlborough Local Defence Volunteers to guard against invasion. Later, during the summer holidays back home in Kent, he found himself living directly under the heaviest of the air fighting over England.

Three of those on the Home Front: Londoner Olivia Cockett (*top*), and Berliners Else Wendel (*middle*) and Hilda Müller (*bottom*). There was a greater shortage of everyday goods in Germany than there was in Britain.

Below: Beware the enemy. Fear of German parachutists, especially, reached fever pitch in Britain in the panic of May and early June. Yet even by September, Göring had still not finally agreed to the deployment of any of his paratroop units in the SEALION invasion plans.

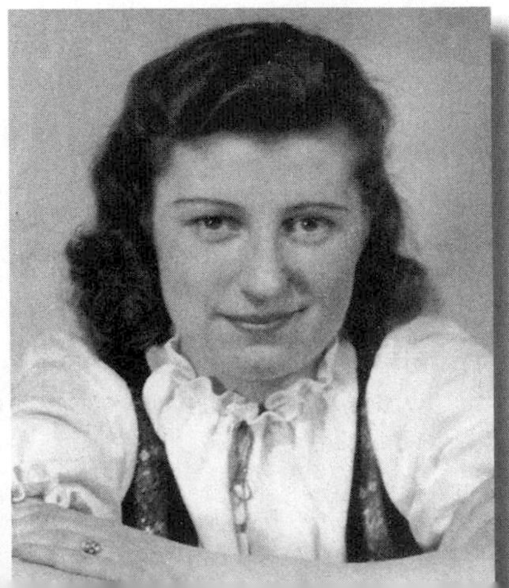

fighter tactics, introducing the idea of staggering the two pairs of a *Schwarm*: the *Schwarm* leader flew in the position of the tip of the middle finger, his wingman in that of the index finger; the second *Rotte* leader was represented by the third finger, and his wingman by the little finger – hence it became known as the 'finger-four'. He also introduced the cross-over turn, a manoeuvre the RAF had developed at the end of the last war. This got around the problem of trying to turn when the frontage of a *Schwarm* was some 600 yards: to turn through ninety degrees, the fighter on the outside pulled up and turned above the one nearest to him. The others followed in sequence, so that at the end of the manoeuvre the formation was the same but a mirror image of the order of aircraft before the turn had begun.

When the Spanish Civil War ended in March 1939 and the Condor Legion returned home, the lessons learned were put to immediate effect. Hajo Herrmann was not alone in being given time to prepare a full report of his experiences, which he then presented to the Chief of Staff of the Luftwaffe in Berlin. Training was made more realistic and practices such as the *Schwarm* and cross-over turn became normal procedure.

Another of the Spaniards – as the Condor veterans were known – who had written reports on his experience in Spain had been Hauptmann Dolfo Galland. It was largely because of what he had written that he had been pulled out of JG 52 and plunged back into the world of a biplane ground support *Lehrgeschwader* in order to bring the unit up to strength and then to lead it during the Polish campaign.

Dolfo Galland had been born in Westerholt, Westphalia, in March 1912, the second of four sons, whose father was land manager of the large, sprawling estate of Graf von Westerholt. Brought up as a strict Catholic despite the family's Huguenot origins, Dolfo had always preferred sport and the outdoor life to academia, although he had considerable practical skills, throwing his energy into making radio sets and model aircraft. At fifteen, he made his first glider with some school friends, and by the time he was nineteen had passed all three levels of his glider pilot's licence. Having matriculated from school, he joined the commercial flying school, run largely by the national airline, Deutsche Lufthansa, where he qualified as a pilot before being asked to enter the still illegal Luftwaffe. That had been in early 1933, but two years later, after he had joined the fighter unit JG 2, his career was nearly finished when he suffered a horrific accident flying a new Focke-Wulf 44 Stieglitz.

Recovering too late from a spin, his aircraft sliced into the ground. He was already in a coma when he was pulled out of the wreckage, and with multiple skull fractures it looked like he might never recover.

But recover he did, although there was little he could do about the serious damage to the cornea of his left eye. At his medical, he was declared unfit for flying, but fortunately for him his commanding officer at JG 2 decided to give him a chance to prove himself. This he did, demonstrating that, despite the glass splinters still in his eye, he could see – and fly – perfectly well. He also proved his marksmanship by being selected for the Luftwaffe clay pigeon shooting competition team which beat the best civilian team in the country.

Surviving another crash – and a second medical – he was eventually sent to Spain, where he flew over 300 missions. Opinionated, cocksure and undeniably fearless, Dolfo soon developed a considerable reputation, not only for his flying skill – which was considerable – but also for his individual style and strong personality. Good-looking with a neat film star moustache, he smoked cigars even when he was flying, and liked to decorate his aircraft with a picture of Mickey Mouse. It made him stand out.

Most of all, however, Dolfo Galland wanted to be a great fighter pilot. Now the war in the west had begun, it was to his frustration that he found himself largely desk-bound as adjutant of JG 27. Two days into the campaign, however, he decided to take matters into his own hands. On 12 May, as JG 27 was covering the Sixth Army's efforts to cross the Maas and Albert Canal, Dolfo attached himself to a patrol over Maastricht. Five miles west of Liège, and at a height of some 12,000 feet, he spotted eight Belgian Hurricanes a few thousand feet below. Diving down on them, he got behind one with ease; the enemy planes had not spotted him or his wingman. Much to his disappointment, he barely felt the adrenalin begin to flow; it was all too easy. 'Come on, defend yourself!' he thought, as soon as he had one of them directly in his sights. Closing further and still without being noticed, he opened fire. It was, he knew, at slightly too great a distance, but he still hit the Hurricane. A second burst saw bits of rudder and wings come away and, realizing he had got his man, Dolfo went after the other seven, who had now woken up to the presence of two Me 109s behind them. Closing in at a hundred yards, Dolfo followed a second through some cloud and opened fire again. The Hurricane stalled and fell out of the sky. So that was two.

Flying again later that afternoon, Dolfo shot down a third, but at the end of the day he felt no great sense of satisfaction, but rather a twinge of conscience. 'The congratulations of my superiors and my comrades left an odd taste in my mouth,' he noted. 'An excellent weapon and luck had been on my side. To be successful, the best fighter pilot needs both.'

In 1940, the best pilots also needed experience, and the Spaniards like Dolfo Galland and Hajo Herrmann had bucketloads of that. Inexperienced Belgian pilots did not have a chance against someone like Dolfo. Yet although these few could offer advice to those of lesser experience in the Luftwaffe, the fact was that the vast majority of German pilots flying over the western front had little if any combat flying time at all. Siegfried Bethke was very aware of the lack of gunnery practice he had had during his training and since joining JG 2. 'Young pilots have not had practice with air targets during training,' he noted, 'only with targets on the ground.' He keenly felt that he should have been shooting down more enemy aircraft in the encounters he had had during the first days of the campaign. Yet no matter how much training an individual might have done, real combat was a very different kettle of fish. Experience – hard combat experience – was unquestionably the best training of all.

One of those discovering this for himself was Leutnant Günther Rall, a pilot in the 8th Staffel of III/JG 52. The first week of the campaign had been quiet. III/JG 52 was part of Luftflotte 3 supporting Army Group A, but since the army had now broken through along the Meuse, the air force had begun going forward too. First, the group had moved closer to the German border, but now, on Saturday, 18 May, the 8th Staffel's ten serviceable 109s had been ordered to fly to a new airfield at Trier-Euren and then to rendezvous with a reconnaissance aircraft in the Nancy area and escort it home.

Günther, a 22-year-old from Stuttgart, had first joined the army four years earlier, but while at military college in Dresden had moved across to the Luftwaffe instead. 'I had a friend who was at the Air Force officers' school,' says Günther. 'We met every Saturday and he told me about his flying. That was more my thing, so I made an application for a change and I was accepted.' That had been in July 1938, and from the outset, he had been determined to be a fighter, rather than a bomber, pilot. Fortunately for him, he proved so good at aerobatics during his A/B training that having been awarded his military pilot's certificate and badge, and with 190 hours' flying on thirteen different types of aircraft, he was posted to the Werneuchen Fighter Pilots' School in Brandenburg a year later.

Taught by Spanish Civil War veterans, Günther completed his fighter training flying the new Messerschmitt 109D, or 'Dora' as it was known. Although he had flown a number of different types, he was unprepared – as David Crook had been during his first flight in a Spitfire – for the sudden surge of power and performance the 109 offered. 'The demands of this powerful machine are quite unlike anything I have flown before,' he noted, then added, 'the Messerschmitt is no docile carthorse, but a highly-strung thoroughbred.' In breeding it shared much with the Spitfire; but, for all its power, it was also a far less forgiving machine. For those who tamed it, the rewards were many; those who did not were soon thrown from the saddle.

When Günther joined JG 52 in September 1939, he had still not had any gunnery training and was yet to fire a shot from a 109. During the *Sitzkrieg*, JG 52 had remained at Böblingen, just ten minutes' flying time from the Rhine. Although Günther flew on a number of operational missions and continued training and familiarizing himself with the new 109E1s and E3s, by the time the offensive in the west began, he had become an experienced pilot but remained an inexperienced fighter pilot.

Now, at 18,000 feet over Nancy some time after 6 p.m. on 18 May, Günther was about to have his first combat action. Blessed with extremely sharp eyesight, he was the envy of his comrades, who believed he would be able to spot a target while it was still flying around the other side of the world. Needless to say, he was the first to spot the Heinkel 111 reconnaissance aircraft they were supposed to be liaising with. 'Twelve o'clock, five kilometres, same height,' he told the others over the R/T.

The Heinkel droned towards them like a lazy insect. The sun was low in the sky, spreading a soft, golden yellow light. Then suddenly Günther spotted some small black dots in the distance.

'Indianer!' he warned the rest of the *Staffel*. 'Indianer at twelve o'clock, Hanni six thousand five hundred! Ten or more!' They were 500 metres above the Heinkel.

'Viktor! Viktor! I have them!' replied Oberleutnant Lothar Ehrlich, the *Staffel* commander, a moment later. He gave them some orders and Günther and the rest of his *Schwarm* pushed forward the throttle and began climbing above the Heinkel, which continued on its same level course. Günther clicked the weapons safety catch, so that it moved forward to form a trigger: now, at the press of his finger, two MG17 machine guns above the engine, plus a 20 mm cannon firing through the propeller hub and a further two cannons in the wings, would pack a lethal punch.

In moments, the enemy aircraft were hurtling down towards the Heinkel. With their grey-green fuselages and red and blue roundels, Günther recognized them immediately as French Curtiss fighters. Seeing Ehrlich dive down on the French leader, Günther pulled his own aircraft into a steep dive and within seconds was sitting on the tail of one of the French leader's two wingmen. The French pilot immediately wrenched his Curtiss into a sharp turn, but not before Günther, having made a split-second judgement of distance and aim-off, opened fire and felt his Messerschmitt judder as bullets and cannon shells spat from his guns. The Curtiss was burning, but no sooner had Günther seen this than a loud clatter raked across his own plane. Gripped by a feeling of pure terror, he realized he had almost been shot down in turn by the French top cover. Hurling his plane around the sky in a desperate attempt to throw off his attacker, he made one turn so violent and steep that the automatic leading edge slots popped out of the wing and the Messerschmitt violently dropped as if it had been whiplashed. Günther cursed, but in truth, it had probably saved his life.

Suddenly, the sky was empty. As soon as he was able to pull his plane out of its involuntary dive he cast his head around, desperately looking for the rest of the *Staffel*. Sweat poured down his face from under his leather flying helmet; his heart pounded madly. He wondered whether his machine was still airworthy. A glance at the instruments in front of him calmed him: oil okay, coolant okay; fuel not obviously leaking. Temperature and pressure gauges normal, but the response to the control column was sluggish. He knew he needed to get her down soon – he had been flying for nearly an hour and after the intensity of the brief combat, the fuel tanks would soon be dry, even without being punctured.

With the rush of adrenalin seeping away, he managed to calm down and gather his bearings. Behind him on his port side was the setting sun. Below, he could now make out a small river and several large areas of water. They were familiar: he had to be somewhere near Sarrebourg in western Lorraine. Soon he would be over German territory. Breathing a sigh of relief, he headed to Mannheim.

It was at 7.15 p.m., and over an hour and a half after first taking off, that he finally touched down. After quickly refuelling, he took off again and eventually landed at their airfield at Ippesheim at around half-past eight, just as the light was fading for the day. There he reported to Ehrlich, who had been back some time, and learned that another of the pilots had seen Günther's Curtiss go down in a spin. He had his first confirmed aerial victory. He also discovered that the Heinkel had made it back safely too.

The pilots sat up late that night, talking about and discussing the action in fine detail. Only one of their number had not returned – Adolf Walter, who had been seen limping away from the fray having shot down a Curtiss himself. Some time after midnight, the phone rang and to the relief of the rest of the *Staffel* it was Walter on the line. He had belly-landed with engine trouble, but would make his way back the following day.

That first scrap above the skies of France had taught Günther three things. First, he could do it; he could recognize the enemy with plenty of time. He was cool-headed and shrewd enough to move himself and the *Schwarm* into the best position to give them the tactical advantage without being caught by surprise by the enemy. He could enter into an attack without crumbling with fear. And he had the ability to shoot the enemy down – not just a direct hit, but a deflection shot. That had given him confidence. He felt as though he were an athlete after winning a major sporting event.

Second, he realized that he was not invincible. He had dropped his guard and had nearly paid the price. 'Neglecting one's own safety in an attack will inevitably have fatal consequences sooner or later,' he noted. 'One of the most dangerous moments in aerial combat is that second immediately prior to opening fire.'

Finally, he recognized that he needed to master the Messerschmitt 109E yet further, to get a better feel and understanding of her idiosyncrasies. The savage turn had probably saved his life, yet he felt sure that the real art of flying was keeping one's head, even in a critical situation, and handling the controls smoothly at all times.

Few pilots had the kind of natural advantages of excellent sight and good marksmanship that Günther was blessed with. And few analysed their flying performance in such a pragmatic and rational manner. Yet consciously or subconsciously, the learning curve of the pilot rose exponentially the moment he found himself in combat. The key was to make the most of those lessons and absorb them as quickly as possible. As Günther had learned during that thrilling, frightening, sobering, exhilarating, first combat sortie, it was very easy for a fighter pilot to get himself killed.

Feldmarschall Hermann Göring had left Berlin for the front on 15 May, setting off in *Asia* with some extra carriages that housed his own personal general staff. These were mostly over-promoted young adjutants working personally for Göring and quite separate from the Luftwaffe General Staff headed by General Hans Jeschonnek. Supervising Göring's staff was Major Bernd von Brauchitsch, the son of the Commander-in-Chief of the army. It was von Brauchitsch's job to brief Göring on the daily operations.

Asia arrived nearby to Hitler's HQ and remained on a siding near a tunnel. A special wooden platform had been erected for Göring's personal use, but he rarely clambered down from the train, preferring instead to remain aboard his luxury carriages, where he ate sumptuously, drank even better, and commandeered the only properly functioning toilet for his own private use.

It is doubtful that Göring knew about the huge losses on the first day of the campaign, or that by 16 May the Luftwaffe had already suffered 621 aircraft wiped from the slate and 1,450 pilots and aircrew dead or captured – just over a sixth of its strength on 10 May. As far as Göring was concerned, the Luftwaffe had done everything that had been expected of it, sweeping all before it, destroying the Dutch and Belgian air forces and achieving almost total mastery of the sky, whilst at the same time providing crucial support to the ground forces. Hitler was delighted and, much to Göring's delight, lavished him with praise. Göring's assessment was correct; but it ignored the price that was being paid. It was a large one.

Working considerably harder than his outsized boss was the man who really ran the Luftwaffe, Generaloberst Erhard Milch. Officially, Milch was State Secretary for Aviation and Inspector General. In real terms, this meant he had operational control over almost every aspect of the Luftwaffe from training to air defence to the General Staff. With Göring kept busy with his plethora of other state positions and business interests, much was left to Milch. In effect, Göring was Chairman to Milch's CEO.

For several days, Milch had been at the front, beetling about in his personal Dornier 17 or the small, highly manoeuvrable reconnaissance aircraft, the Feisler Storch, flying over the front and visiting forward units to see for himself first-hand what was going on along the front and how his men were faring. He had insisted that the Luftwaffe maintain high levels of mobility, so that units could efficiently leapfrog over one another as the army began cutting swathes through the Low Countries and France. Siegfried Bethke, for example, and the rest of I/JG 2 had moved twice already by 16 May and would move forward again on 21 May. This ensured there were always plenty of aircraft operating over the front in support of the troops.

On 16 May, with Göring in his train now next to the Polch Tunnel, there was an 11 a.m. conference with the C-in-C, and then he was off again, visiting no fewer than six front-line units. Dynamic, untiring and deeply efficient, Milch liked to see what was going on for himself.

Milch was born in Wilhelmshaven on the North Sea coast in 1892. His father, Anton Milch, was a Chief Staff Pharmacist in the German navy. He was also a Jew. His mother, however, was a Protestant and that was what went on young Erhard's birth certificate. Göring was supposedly aware of Milch's Jewish blood and, although not much bothered, recognized that it could prove awkward, so a solution had been found. Milch's mother made a solemn declaration that her son was a product of an illegitimate affair with a minor German aristocrat, and the original birth certificate was withdrawn and a new one issued. Milch's origins were never to trouble him further.

He had joined the army, being commissioned in 1911 and serving on the Eastern Front until transferring to the Imperial Flying Service as an aerial observer and photographer, where he saw action over the Western Front. He ended the war a *Hauptmann*, left the army in 1920, and after a brief career with a police air unit in East Prussia joined the civil aviation company, Lloyd Eastern Flying Company. Two years later, he joined Junkers Airways Ltd, which took him all around the world, including to the United States, where the size of the Ford automobile works at Detroit left a lasting impression upon him of American industrial might.

He was a director of Junkers when, in January 1926, Junkers and Aero-Lloyd merged to become a single national airline, Deutsche Lufthansa. Milch, at just thirty-four, became one of its three directors, and was to become the driving force in ensuring that Lufthansa spread its wings throughout not only Germany but the rest of Europe too. By 1930, Lufthansa had established an air link to China and by the time of Hitler's ascent to power, had flights throughout the Baltic States and even into the Soviet Union – and Milch was its most senior figure, now one of only two directors.

These talents did not go unnoticed, and on 22 February 1933 he was invited by Göring to become the new State Secretary of Aviation. The two had known each other for some time; Milch had even helped Göring secure employment during the 1920s. Furthermore, Lufthansa had supported Hitler during his election campaign, providing him with flights all over Germany. Yet Göring also recognized that in Milch he had found a man who not only had a deep and expert knowledge of aviation and business, but who also had a rare talent for organization.

Milch did not waste any time. Although Göring had cleared the path for financing the Luftwaffe, it was Milch, together with Dr Hjalmar Schacht, then President of the Reichsbank, who hatched the plan to make it happen. Together, they found an old skeleton company, called the Metal Research Company, of which Schacht and Milch became directors. This cover company was then guaranteed by the Reichsbank and used to finance the growth of the Luftwaffe with its own bills of exchange. These were effectively a form of banknotes, a kind of IOU, but which, because they were guaranteed by the Reichsbank, were of effective value. The bills were given a validity of three months, but as soon as that time was up the Reichsbank extended them another three months, and another three months again and so on. They could also be cashed in early at the Reichsbank or they could be used as a form of payment to selected industrial concerns. It was hardly legal, but it worked, and it enabled Milch to plan a rapid and vast rearmament programme.

Key to this was the expansion of the aircraft industry. The main players were Junkers, Heinkel, Focke-Wulf, Arado, Dornier and the Bavarian Aircraft Company (later Messerschmitt). Milch sent the then Colonel Albert Kesselring to inspect the Heinkel works on the Baltic Coast. On the basis of Kesselring's visit, Heinkel were asked to open a much larger new factory at Rostock. Professor Willi Messerschmitt's Bavarian Aircraft Company was also given large orders to aid expansion. Only Professor Junkers was digging in his heels. A confirmed pacifist, he repeatedly resisted attempts by Milch and Göring to hand over the patents of his designs and control of his aircraft factories. But eventually, after threats of being prosecuted for treason, the ageing inventor and designer agreed, in October 1933, to hand over 51 per cent of his companies to the Reich. A major obstacle to progress had been overcome.

Plans for the establishment of a dozen specialized air-training schools for fighter and bomber pilots, bomb aimers, observers and air gunners were also drawn up and were to be completed within a year.

Factories making locomotives and shipping were converted to the production of aircraft. Junkers went from making eighteen Ju 52s a year with its 2,200-strong staff to being given an order for nearly a thousand. Milch had begun to envisage a larger air force than had ever been originally suggested – not a thousand aircraft strong but twenty times that size.

Both Göring and Milch had been fortunate to have one of the most talented of the army's staff officers as the new Chief of Staff of the Luftwaffe.* General Walther Wever had been on both von Hindenburg's and von Ludendorff's staffs during the First World War and joined the Luftwaffe with a superb reputation that he soon proved was entirely justified. A clear and realistic planner and thinker and someone who inspired both affection and respect, he was able to draw the best from those around him. Wever had believed, correctly, that the greatest threat to Germany came from the Soviet Union, so he planned to build up, first and foremost, a strategic bomber force that would operate separately from the army, and a solid air defence system. He also recognized, as did Milch, the importance of creating a solid General Staff in which its number were all imbued with a common purpose and who were very much singing from the same hymn sheet.

It was also General Wever and his staff who drew up the specifications for some of the key aircraft that were now flying over the Western Front: the Messerschmitt 109 and twin-engine 110; the Ju 87 'Stuka' dive-bomber; and the Ju 88. He had also, crucially, issued a specification for a long-range, heavy four-engine bomber. The Heinkel 111 medium bomber was also brought into production with a new large factory opened at Oranienburg just outside Berlin specifically for that task.

In May 1936, Wever had produced the first Luftwaffe training manual on air strategy, in which he made clear the importance of the strategic bomber force and the ability of a strong Luftwaffe to seize the initiative in any war. 'In a war of the future,' he said in an address to the Air War Academy in 1935, 'the destruction of the armed forces will be of primary importance. This can mean the destruction of the enemy air force, army, and navy, and of the source of supply of the enemy's forces, the armament industry . . . Only the nation with strong bomber forces at its disposal can expect decisive action by its air force.'

* Wever was appointed Chief of the Air Command Office when he joined the Luftwaffe in 1933, which made him effectively Chief of Staff. He was not, however, officially given that title at the time.

In this strategic thinking, Milch was in complete accord with Wever. Tragedy struck, however, when Wever, a new and inexperienced pilot, crashed his aircraft and was killed in June 1936. It was a simple mistake that did for him: failing to release the lock on the ailerons of his Heinkel 70, he had crashed almost as soon as he had taken off. It was an unfamiliar plane to him, and he had been in a rush to get back to Berlin for a funeral. Yet that fatal mistake had ensured that in a trice the Luftwaffe had lost its direction and, critically, its unity.

No-one could fill Wever's void; no individual shared his combination of military experience, strategic vision and likeability. It was Kesselring who was asked to take Wever's place, but although he had served in the army during the last war, he was seen as primarily a civilian managing director and was unable to earn the kind of respect Wever had enjoyed. Nor did Kesselring get on well with Milch. The former tried to increase the power and authority of the General Staff while the latter did his best to undermine Kesselring. Within a year, Kesselring had been replaced by General Hans-Jürgen Stumpff, who was only ever really seen as a stop-gap. In 1939, when still not quite forty, Oberst Hans Jeschonnek became the fourth Luftwaffe Chief of Staff in three years.

Only in the newly formed Luftwaffe, where speed of growth was everything and there was no tradition to complicate matters, could a man be a major-general at thirty-nine. He had been groomed for the job by Wever, although the latter had clearly never expected him to succeed quite so soon. A former fighter pilot during the last war, Jeschonnek was recognized as having a brilliant mind; yet his apprenticeship under Wever had been far from complete and he had certainly failed to learn his old boss's deep empathy for his colleagues.

Moreover, by 1939, he had fallen out with Milch. Originally Milch's principal staff officer, he had developed a close working relationship with his boss, but, with the death of Wever, Jeschonnek's ambition as well as clashes over policy had ensured that friendship had sunk to mutual contempt. When, in 1938, Jeschonnek had suggested to Milch that he replace Stumpff as Chief of Staff, Milch had dismissed the notion out of hand. Göring then went over Milch's head and promoted the young Chief of Staff. Milch understandably saw this as a direct blow to his authority – which it was; Göring did not like anyone becoming too powerful and threatening his own position.

A further undermining of his authority came when Ernst Udet became head of the Office of Air Armament, a new office created when

Göring restructured the Luftwaffe in early 1939. Udet had already been made head of the Technical Department, and he was woefully unsuited for both jobs. A bon viveur, talented cartoonist, former fighter pilot, colleague of Göring's and stunt pilot, Udet was a brilliant aviator but completely, utterly out of his depth in the dizzy, Machiavellian world of Nazi politics, and had almost no understanding of complex matters such as procurement, as he had freely admitted. 'I'm a flier and nothing else,' he had told Göring. 'I don't know anything about design and construction.'

'Neither do I,' Göring had replied. 'But when I announce that you're head of the Technical Board everyone will be happy and that's all I want.' Udet was a close chum of the Commander-in-Chief's, and that was qualification enough for Göring.

To make matters worse for Milch, Udet, in his new post, was directly responsible to Göring. Udet now had under his control five research establishments, most notably at Rechlin and Peenemünde, and although Milch was running almost every other aspect of the Luftwaffe, he now had no direct input on procurement and development whatsoever. Udet was left largely to his own devices since Göring had little time for offering any kind of supervision. When the two did meet on rare occasions, they hardly ever talked shop, instead spending their conferences reminiscing about the old days.

This breakaway of development and procurement was done purely to restrict Milch's power and it was very much to the Luftwaffe's loss. There had been big quarrels between Milch and Göring, and several times Milch, exasperated and at the end of his tether, asked to be relieved of his post, but this was always refused. Milch threatened to go sick; Göring countered that he would then be examined and, if fit, would be punished. 'Then I can commit suicide,' Milch threatened. 'That's the only thing left to you,' Göring replied.

Milch and Udet had been friends, however, and there is no doubt that in his new position Udet could have benefited greatly from Milch's knowledge and experience. Yet Udet was an insecure character, and feared that Milch would undermine him rather than the other way around, which was the reality. The two men became increasingly estranged.

By May 1940, the original four-engine bomber programme had long been consigned to dust. Jeschonnek was an ardent advocate of short, sharp campaigns in which the air force played a tactical role, that is, in direct support of the ground forces, rather than a strategic, independent mass-bombing role. He was little interested in air transportation and greatly favoured the dive-bombers, which he believed were the only types of aircraft capable of achieving precision bombing. The Junkers 87 Stuka had won the main dive-bomber contract, but from 1938 the priority for production and development was the Junkers 88, the Heinkel 177 and the Messerschmitt 210, an improved version of the 110. The Heinkel was a heavy, long-range bomber and had the unique design of four engines but only two propellers. The Ju 88 was a twin-engine machine, but had been conceived as a long-range, high-speed bomber. Both these aircraft suggested more of a strategic bombing role for the Luftwaffe, which was at odds with Jeschonnek's views of how air power should best be used.

Perhaps unsurprisingly then, both Jeschonnek and Udet were behind changes to the specifications for the Ju 88, which they agreed needed diving capability. This, however, shattered its original design aims. In fact, some 25,000 changes were made to the original design. The result was endless delays and an aircraft that, by 1940, had a flying weight not of six tonnes, as had been originally planned, but well over double that. The heavier it became, the slower it became; at 269 mph, it was only fractionally faster than the Heinkel and Dornier mainstays. High-speed it was not; nor were there many of them. Milch described it as a 'flying barn door'.

Thus it wasn't only the British who were struggling to get their best aircraft produced in enough numbers. The He 177 programme also fell behind because of the delays to the Ju 88, and the Me 210 was eventually scrapped altogether. Instead, the bulk of the bomber force was made up with Heinkel 111s and Dornier 17s, both of which were state of the art in the mid-1930s, but by 1940 were already beginning to seem a little under-armed and under-protected, as well as not manoeuvrable enough, and they were capable of carrying only comparatively small bomb loads.

The Me 109 had been given the nod for single-engine fighter production, even though Heinkel had produced a model, the He 112, which was 50 mph faster. When Heinkel protested, Udet's office forbade him to pursue the matter. The second-string fighter was to be the cumbersome twin-engine Me 110. It just so happened that not only was Professor Messerschmitt Hitler's favourite designer, but he was also a personal friend of Udet's. Development of the world's first jet-propelled aircraft, the He 178, whose maiden flight was in June 1939, was blocked by Udet; he had already promised jet development to Messerschmitt.

There were worrying production problems as well – a task that also fell within Udet's remit. Shortage of aluminium and steel was part of the problem; so too was competition for those raw materials from other areas of the armed forces. Hitler's refusal to mobilize the economy on an all-out war footing was another contributory factor. Udet's inadequate understanding of the industry, his lack of initiative and his poor leadership further frustrated production efforts. As a result, production of the major front-line aircraft throughout the winter of 1939–40 was pitifully small: in February 1940, for example, a paltry sixty-two Me 110s, seventy-six 109s, thirty Dornier 17s, fifty-eight He 111s, sixty-six Stukas and fifty Junkers 88s.

In May 1940, the Luftwaffe was headed by an over-mighty commander whose eye was only partly on the task in hand, and who encouraged dissension and rivalry between his immediate subordinates. Milch, the one man capable of infusing the Luftwaffe with the drive and unity it needed, was constantly battling to maintain his authority and to deflect the hostile stance of Jeschonnek, and increasingly Udet as well. Jeschonnek, in turn, found it hard to work with either Milch or Udet. Udet was simply out of his depth.

A house can have cracks so long as there is no storm. In May 1940, it seemed as though the Luftwaffe had the world at its feet, its power and strength undoubted. So long as France and Britain could be knocked out of the war swiftly, then the cracks would remain just that. Only if the battle continued would those cracks begin to widen.

But ten days into the battle, confidence amongst the Luftwaffe's command was sky-high. In that, its leaders, for once, were as one.

⊙ 12 ✠

What to Do for the Best

CERTAINLY THE RESIDENTS of Rotterdam had been left in no doubt about the power of the Luftwaffe. On the afternoon of 14 May, almost a hundred He 111s from KG 54 had thundered over the city in an effort to speed up the Dutch collapse. When they had gone again, Rotterdam was a smoking mass of rubble, its historic heart smashed from the face of the earth and unknown numbers of Dutch citizens left dead beneath the dust and debris. Truly, it seemed as though Armageddon had arrived. Early the following morning the Dutch duly surrendered.

The Luftwaffe had destroyed the Spanish Basque town of Guernica, much of Warsaw and now Rotterdam. In fact, casualties were not quite as high as had been first feared, but some 800 lost their lives and a further 78,000 were left homeless. Nonetheless, for the doomsayers, Rotterdam's destruction proved all their worst fears about the power of the modern bomber, fears that had begun with the prediction by an Italian colonel, Giulio Douhet, that no effective defence could stop the bomber and had been perpetuated by men in Britain like Air Marshal 'Boom' Trenchard and Stanley Baldwin. But for those at the Air Ministry and at Bomber Command it was the final justification they needed to begin a strategic bombing offensive inside Germany.

Although the 'medium' bombers of Bomber Command – the Blenheims and Battles – had been brought into action over the battle-field, there were still sixteen squadrons of 'heavies', consisting of Wellingtons, Hampdens and Whitleys – twin-engine aircraft comparable to the trio of German bombers, although the Whitley could carry more bombs than any of the German planes. They were 20–30 mph slower than the German bombers, however, and experience had shown that operations in daylight in the face of large numbers of enemy fighters would be suicidal. Under the cover of darkness, it was a different matter, and the Air Ministry held great faith in their ability to wreak havoc during night-time raids. Germany's lack of raw materials was well-known, even exaggerated by the British. Sixty per cent of her industrial output stemmed from the dense Ruhr Valley just the other side of the River Rhine, and within easy reach of the heavies. By hitting these targets as well as oil installations, the RAF believed it could strike at the very roots of the German war machine.

Throughout the winter and spring, the Air Staff had argued vociferously that they should begin a heavy-bomber campaign against the Ruhr the moment the Germans launched an offensive. The French, however, were having none of it. Openly, they refused to believe such attacks would have any substantial impact on the advancing Nazi hordes and insisted instead that the heavies would be better employed over or near the battlefield. Privately, as the British well knew, and in keeping with their intensely defensive mindset, they feared provoking a retaliation on their own cities.

The French had finally given way at the end of April, agreeing to British bombing of the Ruhr should Holland or Belgium be attacked, but since then it was General William 'Tiny' Ironside, the Chief of the Imperial General Staff, and Churchill and his War Cabinet, who had got cold feet. Air warfare was still new in 1940 and modern planes remained largely untested. When push came to shove, there was a horrible suspicion that heavy bombers were like some kind of super-weapon, which once unleashed would provoke large-scale tit-for-tat destruction and death. Leaders were understandably wary of instigating such carnage.

Yet in the cases of Guernica, Warsaw and Rotterdam, the Luftwaffe had always attacked in daylight, with good visibility, and with almost no enemy air opposition. Flying in darkness, depending on old navigational tricks such as dead reckoning, and over areas swarming with flak batteries, had no guarantees of producing Guernica-esque levels of destruction at all. Such considerations did not trouble the confidence of bombing's advocates within the RAF, however. And with the German bombing of Rotterdam the War Cabinet gave Bomber Command the green light to attack the Ruhr. This, it was recognized, might well provoke the Germans into retaliating over London and elsewhere in Britain; yet such a diversion could not come soon enough to help the French and Belgians. Through air power, if not on the ground, Britain could still play a decisive role.

That night, 15/16 May, 111 RAF heavies bombed sixteen different targets in the Ruhr. It was the first hundred-bomber raid of the war. Most of those who flew returned confident they had hit their mark. Reports from within Germany were less overwhelmed by Bomber Command's effort, however. A report from Cologne claimed that bombs directed at the IG Farben Werke at Dormagen hit only a large farm and killed a dairyman. Another report stated that he had switched on an outside light by mistake while on the way to the lavatory and that this provided a mistaken marker for a stick of British bombs. A further five were reported wounded in Cologne. It had hardly set the Ruhr alight.

False confidence was probably no bad thing for the men of Bomber Command, however. At 10 Squadron in Dishforth near Ripon in North Yorkshire, there was certainly a sense of relief – tempered with apprehension – that they were at last taking the fight to the enemy. Many of the crews had flown over the Reich before, but they had only dropped leaflets urging the Germans to lay down their arms. There had been cries of derision from the crews at the time, but as Leading Aircraftsman Larry Donnelly now recognized all too clearly, the lack of aggressive bombing operations had been a blessing in disguise, for it had given them much-needed experience.

More recently, they had been attacking airfields and other targets in Norway, a difficult task that had meant flying over long stretches of the North Sea, often through fiendish weather. Inadequate heating, oxygen facilities and clothing had created further unpleasant hardships for the crews. But now it was May and a hop over the Channel and then over the Low Countries to the Ruhr was seen as a more straightforward proposition. Furthermore, 10 Squadron had recently been re-equipped with new Merlin-powered Whitley Mk Vs, a considerable improvement on the earlier models. The wings also now had de-icing equipment, while the draughty one-gun manually operated rear turret had been replaced by a hydraulically operated, tightly sealed four-gun turret. Since Larry Donnelly was, as second wireless operator in the five-man crew, the person to fill that seat, he was delighted with the upgrade. 'I now felt,' he noted, 'I had a much better chance of giving a good account of myself should the occasion arise in future operations.'

Larry and his crew had been bombing rail and road targets – too late – at Dinant on the night of 15/16 May, but the following day they were told that they would be bombing Germany that night. The day had begun well because their skipper, Flight Lieutenant Richard Bickworth, had been awarded the Distinguished Flying Cross and the news had come through that morning. 10 Squadron was to fly along with 51 and 58 Squadrons to attack the oil storage depot at Bremen near the German north-west coast. Larry and his crew were airborne at 8.55 p.m. and around two and a half hours later were sneaking over the German coastline taking care to avoid the flak defences at the coastal ports of Wilhelmshaven and Bremerhaven. Following the silvery River Weser, they flew on towards Bremen, until over the aircraft's intercom Larry heard the men at the front of the Whitley report sightings of fires and heavy flak.

Their CO, Wing Commander Bill Staton, had told them at the mission briefing that they should attack from low level, dropping their bombs from between 2,000 and 6,000 feet. By the time Larry's crew arrived at the scene, the fires enabled Sergeant 'Nipper' Knapper, their observer, to pick out the aiming point and then begin their run-in, gliding in from about 4,000 feet. This was the worst moment for the crew. Flying straight and level in order to give the bomb aimer a steady bombing platform, they had to simply sit tight and hope for the best as they flew through an intense wall of flak. Bursts of anti-aircraft fire erupted all around them, knocking and shaking the Whitley. Tracer fire was also arcing up towards them. Larry, in the rear turret, found himself ducking involuntarily. Then suddenly a close shell burst would really buck the aircraft. Larry could feel himself tense with adrenalin. Finally, Nipper called out 'Bombs away!' and Bick, the pilot, took immediate evasive action and tried to get them away from the flak and weaving searchlights.

Setting a course for home, they safely managed to escape the fray although they soon realized the plane had been damaged. It was flying sluggishly and after a brief inspection they discovered that most of the fabric on the port wing had been shredded. As they flew on out over the North Sea, Larry clambered out of his turret to see the damage for himself. 'What I saw,' wrote Larry, 'wasn't reassuring, but the old Whitley did us proud and kept flying across the North Sea without losing height.' It was with great relief that they reached the English coast and even greater relief that they touched back down at Dishforth, nearly seven hours after they had left. As well as the wing damage, there were holes all along the fuselage and Larry found his bravado waning once he saw how close some of them were to his gun turret.

All fourteen planes from the squadron made it back that night although not a single Whitley had returned unscathed. The mood amongst the crews was buoyant; all believed they had dropped their bombs on target. They had done what the CO had asked of them and the next night were determined to go into Ripon and make the most of being alive.

In fact, the raid was nothing like as successful as Larry and his fellow squadron members had thought it had been. Six fires had been started, the largest of which was in two warehouses full of furniture confiscated from Jews. Thirteen people were killed and fifty-five injured. But the oil depot remained untouched.

On the 19th, the American journalist William Shirer was at Aachen, on his way, courtesy of Goebbels's propaganda department, to a visit to the front. Aachen, lying on the German–Dutch border, was one of the gateways to the Ruhr and Shirer had been expecting to see Germany's industrial heartland already rocked by RAF bombing. 'So far as I can see,' he jotted in his diary, 'the night bombings of the British have done very little damage.' He had also expected the attacks to have had an effect on the morale of the German people. 'But all afternoon,' he added, 'driving through the Ruhr, we saw them – especially the womenfolk – standing on the bridges over the main roads cheering the troops setting off for Belgium and France.' Bomber Command did not realize it yet, but it was far harder to accurately hit a target at night than they had supposed.

Even so, the strategic bombing war had begun.

In France, the pilots and aircrew of the RAF Air Component and Advanced Air Striking Force were still battling their way through the mayhem and confusion that had barely let up, except for a few precious hours of darkness each night, from the moment the offensive had begun.

At Méharicourt, Pilot Officer Arthur Hughes had finally flown his first recce, on 14 May. 'Oddly, I was no longer scared,' he noted, 'but relieved that action was at last imminent.' And he was lucky, first, because he was given a fighter escort of 57 Squadron Hurricanes, and, second, because his recce area was covered by cloud, giving them natural cover from enemy aircraft. He made it back unscathed.

Two days later, news arrived that the Germans were only thirty miles to the east. The squadron was given fifteen minutes to move, but having loaded all their gear into trucks and seen them drive away, they were then not given the order to actually fly out themselves. Later in the day, Sergeant Thomas was sent on a recce and got a bullet through his neck which passed out through his jaw on the other side, while his observer was hit in the arm. Incredibly, he made it back, but it was yet another of the squadron's crews that was now out of action.

By the following morning, the squadron still had not moved – no-one knew why; yet despite no longer having a toothbrush, change of clothes or any kind of washing facilities, Arthur had slept like a log. As he was discovering, war was an exhausting business.

Among those squadrons now flying daily to France were 32 Squadron, based at Biggin Hill, just south-east of London in Kent. On the 17th, Flying Officer Pete Brothers and the rest of the squadron flew to Manston on the tip of Kent, then across the Channel to Abbeville, flew a patrol of Lille and Valenciennes, then landed at Dieppe, flew back to Abbeville, did another patrol, then flew back to Biggin. The next day, they were over France again, this time in a tussle with Siegfried Bethke's I/JG 2 over Avesnes. It was the same the next day, 19 May, when they were based this time at Merville. During an offensive patrol over Le Cateau, Pete managed to shoot down his first Me 109. 'It was quite astonishing,' he says. 'I opened fire and half a wing came off and the thing caught fire, and I thought, Good Lord, did I do that?' He looked around in case it had been someone else, but there was no-one there. *That's going to infuriate all my friends*, he thought. *Where are they? They'll be after me.*

But Pete managed to get out of the fray and away in one piece. They were certainly operating at a frenetic pace. 'We'd go over at first light,' says Pete. 'Refuel, operate in France, come back in the dark to Biggin Hill; get a meal; fall into bed and be woken up almost instantly because there wasn't much darkness and we were off again. Dawn was beginning; there was just about enough daylight to see around.' When they reached France they had to refuel with tins by hand – there were no fuel bowsers. 'The French weren't organized to do anything,' says Pete. At one French airfield, they landed as a French fighter was practising his aerobatics. A moment later, they spotted a Dornier at 5,000 feet heading straight for them. 'We said to the colonel, "Tell that bloke there's a Dornier 17" and he said, "Today he is only authorized to do aerobatics." '

Aged twenty-two, from Prestwich in Lancashire, Pete had joined the RAF in 1936, having already taken his civil pilot's licence when still only sixteen. His father had wanted him to join the family chemical manufacturing business, but Pete had been set on flying and managed to get his own way. His first instructor had been a First World War Sopwith Camel pilot, who not only taught him a great deal about flying but a few tricks about being a fighter pilot as well. Now, four years on, Pete was a highly experienced pilot having flown almost 800 hours in the RAF on numerous types of different aircraft.

Flying over France had been an eye-opener in many ways. The squadron had been involved in recent tests on Britain's new RDF – or radar – defences, so now to find themselves operating across the Channel where there was neither radar nor ground control was something of a step back for them. Furthermore, having reached France, it was clear that no-one had much idea of what was going on. 'We'd just take off and see what we could see,' explains Pete. 'If you were lucky, you bumped into some Germans. Otherwise you just flew about the sky looking at what was going on down on the ground.'

Still at Lille-Marcq was 87 Squadron, which had now been joined by 504 Squadron from England. Bee Beamont had been passed well enough to fly again on 14 May, but it wasn't until the following day that he finally got into the air. Awake at dawn as normal, he and his fellow pilots had been shivering in the morning dew down at dispersal, but nothing happened. By eight, they were off duty and back to the mess for a large breakfast and a sleep until midday, when they were back on duty once more.

Not until 2.15 p.m. did the field telephone at dispersal ring with orders for Blue and Green sections plus a further section of 504 Squadron to patrol Louvain-Brussels at 10,000 feet. Frantically, Bee put on his parachute, helmet, goggles, and oxygen and R/T leads and sped to his Hurricane, its engine already throbbing. It was a lovely early summer's day with not a cloud in the sky as they climbed up towards their patrol area.

Like Günther Rall, Bee had much to learn about combat flying. Unlike Günther, however, he did not experience his first combat sortie of the campaign with the advantage of height. Instead, his flight spotted flak bursts and the tiny specks of aircraft above them over Louvain. Ordered into the line astern attack formation as prescribed by the RAF, they continued to climb towards the fray. But, by now, Bee was beginning to feel decidedly ropey again. 'I was having quite a difficulty judging my distance,' he says. 'I started to think, My God, when we get into action, how on earth am I going to be able to cope, feeling as I do?' Above them was a group of Dornier 17s, all now frantically moving into a defensive circular formation with the approach of the Hurricanes. Fortunately, Bee and the rest of the flight arrived before they could complete the manoeuvre. Equally fortunately, Bee somehow forgot about feeling ill the moment the action began; adrenalin had kicked in and was proving an instant antidote. Seconds later, he found himself firing his guns in anger for the very first time, but at the same moment another Hurricane cut in front of him, lucky not to be hit by Bee's bullets. The air was now thick with tracer but then a different twin-engine machine hurtled towards Bee from above and dead ahead. Yanking back the stick and pressing down on the fire button, Bee hammered a quick burst at him, and as the enemy plane zoomed past he recognized it as an Me 110. More were following, diving down on them right and left, and Bee just had time to half-roll out of the way of one that was about to pounce on his tail. Every time he tried to attack one plane, another seemed to be behind him. Rapidly tiring, he pulled his Hurricane into a tight turn, speeding around in a circle himself until finally another Dornier came slanting across his front, very close and looking very big. Rolling his Hurricane back after him, Bee started to attack, but completely forgetting to check what was behind him, he was now conscious of a feathery line of grey fizzing past him between his cockpit and his starboard roundel. 'It was an Me 110 up my backside busily pumping all he had at me and missing,' says Bee, 'and that put me off my stroke with this Dornier.' Rolling away, Bee dived down well out of the fray but then noticed another Dornier diving, trailing smoke, away to the north-east. Bee still had a few rounds left so decided to chase it.

He was soon catching up, too, because one of the Dornier's engines was hit and it was steadily slowing. Filled with excitement and with his adrenalin pumping, Bee opened fire at over 400 yards – 'too far really' – and continued firing until he ran out of ammunition. Even so, the Dornier began diving steeply, disappearing into a layer of low cloud. Still swirling around in a very hostile sky, but with no more ammunition, he realized his best option was to dive to the deck and, at just a few hundred feet off the ground, hedge-hop his way back to base.

He had begun to work himself on a course that would lead back in the direction of Lille when once again feathery lines of smoke began flitting past his cockpit. Sliding his canopy back in order to get a better look, Bee saw a Dornier on his tail. 'One of these cheeky bastards had decided he was going to chase a Hurricane with his Dornier!' says Bee. 'A bomber after a fighter!' For Bee, it was an indication of the very high morale of the Luftwaffe at that time. He was suddenly even more aware of his inexperience.

For a moment he couldn't think of what he should do, then remembered that a Hurricane was supposed to be able to out-turn a Dornier. He immediately yanked his plane into a very tight turn, as tight as he could fly it without blacking out, and pulled the 'tit', which increased boost for a short period of time. The Hurricane lurched forward and after only half a turn he began to see the rear quarter of the Dornier. 'So there were the two of us,' he explains, 'a bloody great Dornier in a vertical bank, and me in my Hurricane also in a vertical bank on his tail but with no ammunition.' Meanwhile the Dornier's rear-gunner had begun firing at him.

This, Bee knew, was not a healthy position to be in, but at least the enemy now knew the Hurricane had a superior turning circle. If he reversed the turn, he realized, the Dornier would never come after him. And nor did it. As Bee looked back, the Dornier was banking away from his own circle and beginning to level out in the direction of the German lines. 'And as he did so,' Bee recalls, 'he waggled his wings. He was saluting.'

The following day, Bee chased a 'Hun' and saw Brussels and Tournai burning fiercely. In the afternoon, the squadron was about to attack some Stukas when they were pounced on by Me 109s. Bee chased after one but found the Messerschmitt was too fast for him to catch. On the 17th, Bee's flight were about to go on patrol when the 'Raid approaching – all aircraft off the ground!' order came through. By now well-practised at this art, the best part of fifty Hurricanes at Lille-Marcq were all airborne inside five minutes. Once airborne, they carried out a mass patrol, but now presented too obvious a target and were soon being dived upon by more 109s. In a trice, two Hurricanes were plunging towards the ground.

So it continued: raids on the airfield, patrols, scrambles, some enemy knocked out of the sky, some of their number sent earthwards. On Sunday, 19 May, they were visited by Air Vice-Marshal C. H. B. Blount, the commanding officer of the Air Component. 'Having a good time, chaps?' he asked them. 'Which,' Bee pointed out, 'sounded rather strange to pilots who had been fighting and standing by to fight from dawn till dusk for eight days with about three hours' sleep a night and only spasmodic shifts for meals.'

*

One person who was certainly taking a pretty dim view of the mayhem the Hurricane squadrons were facing in France was Air Chief Marshal Sir Hugh Dowding. On 14 May, the Commander of RAF Fighter Command had outlined his views on whether a strategic bombing campaign against Germany should begin. In a letter to the Vice-Chief of the Air Staff, he made it clear that he thought it was the soundest of plans and that any operation that could undermine the Luftwaffe was worth trying. 'I want the Fighter Command to pull its full weight in this battle,' he added at the end of the letter, 'but I want it to do so by shooting down Germans in this country and not by being used as a reservoir for sending reinforcements to France.' At the time of writing, Dowding did not know that Reynaud, the French Prime Minister, had already asked for a further ten fighter squadrons, but he had got wind of the request before the day was out. Tearing his hair out with frustration, he asked to be allowed to state his case before the War Cabinet. This was granted.

Thus at the same War Cabinet meeting in which Bomber Command were given the go-ahead to attack the Ruhr, Dowding was able to speak lucidly and rationally, and make a convincing argument for not giving in to Reynaud's demands. Churchill and the Cabinet agreed: for the present, no more squadrons would go to France.

A day later, however, when the full scale of the collapse of the Meuse front had become clear, the French once again appealed for ten more fighter squadrons, recognizing that while Britain could offer little more in terms of ground troops, it still had the bulk of Fighter Command in England, as far as they were concerned, doing nothing. 'If they do not come,' warned Gamelin, 'the battle would be lost.' Gamelin was talking nonsense. Ten fighter squadrons were not going to make the difference between French collapse and a dramatic Allied recovery. Air Marshal Barratt and Lord Gort, both on the spot in France, also demanded more fighters be sent, and, in the face of logic, Ironside, Ismay and Pound on the Chiefs of Staff Committee supported the request.

So too did Churchill, whose affection for France and the French ran very deep indeed. He recognized that sending any fighters would be a grave risk but felt it was essential to do *something* that might chivvy French morale and which would give them a chance to recover their composure in the face of the German onslaught.

Thus, in an abrupt change of heart, the War Cabinet subsequently agreed to send four squadrons immediately with two more on standby.

Later in the day, Churchill rang from Paris having had his traumatic meeting with Reynaud and Gamelin, urging that yet six more fighter squadrons should be sent to France immediately. The Chief of the Air Staff, Air Chief Marshal Sir Cyril Newall, was against it but suggested instead that six Hurricane squadrons should be concentrated in south-east England and that three could fly over to France in the morning and then fly back and the other three could do the same in the afternoon. At a special War Cabinet chaired by Chamberlain, this scheme was agreed and put into effect the following day.

Dowding had written officially to the Air Ministry on 16 May, effectively repeating what he had said to the Cabinet the day before. Once the *volte face* had been decided, however, his letter unwittingly became a decisive protest against the frantic fighter squadron decisions that day. It has since become one of the most famous letters written during the war. 'I believe that, if an adequate fighter force is kept in this country,' Dowding concluded, 'if the fleet remains in being, and if Home Forces are suitably organized to resist invasion, we should be able to carry on the war single-handed for some time. But,' he warned, 'if the Home Defence Force is drained away in desperate attempts to remedy the situation in France, defeat in France will involve the final, complete and irremediable defeat of this country.'

Dowding was certainly not beating about the bush; his letter was quite deliberately stark and intended for wider circulation. He was also stating clearly and logically the terrible dilemma facing the British. It is important, however, no matter how memorable the lines, not to over-egg the influence of Dowding's letter. But it was the case that his superior, Air Chief Marshal Cyril Newall – despite offering home-based squadrons for France on the evening of the 16th – was, however, now firmly in accord with Dowding's point of view. The next day, 17 May, he circulated Dowding's letter with a memo of his own, in which he equally powerfully argued against sending any further fighters across the Channel. If they continued to do so, he warned, 'a time will arrive when our own ability to defend this country will disappear'.

Yet while it was clear that the Germans were winning in France, the French were not completely beaten yet. Despite the defeatism of Reynaud, Daladier and Gamelin, Churchill, for one, could not accept that France had passed the point of no return. After all, they still had vast numbers of troops, thousands of artillery pieces, and many, many tanks. If only a counter-attack could be quickly planned and executed, then surely the lightning German advance could be stalled. And while there was a chance, he believed Britain had a moral obligation to stand by her ally. On the other hand, if he was wrong, and it was too late for France, with every British fighter plane that was shot down across the Channel, Britain's own chances of survival were diminishing.

Such were the terrible, impossible conundrums facing the British in May 1940.

13

New Appointments

MAJOR-GENERAL HENRY POWNALL, Chief of Staff of the BEF, reckoned that 19 May was the most worrying day they had had yet. Very early that morning, accompanied by Major Osmund Archdale, liaison officer at French 1st Army Group, Général Gaston Billotte had come to see the British. The French commander was particularly downbeat. On the way over he repeatedly told Archdale, 'I am exhausted and against these German panzers I can do nothing.' When Gort had asked him what he could do to rectify the situation, Billotte had replied that he had 'no reserves, no plan, and little hope'.

Gort had tried to remain bullish over the previous few days, but Billotte's visit had shattered such optimism. As the morning wore on, liaison officers had arrived at Command HQ at Wahagnies reporting that the French had nothing left, that they were falling back, had disappeared or had given up the ghost. 'It seemed,' jotted Pownall, 'that there was a complete void on our right with only a disorganized mass of fag-ends from the First Army to fill it.' This was an enormous problem, because the BEF was now falling back to the River Escaut, as planned, but with no French right, it meant the British southern – or right – flank would have to be protected, otherwise the Germans could skirt around and attack them from behind. Gort and Pownall managed to move 50th Division south to deploy along La Bassée Canal, which ran roughly west–east along their flank, and had already created a scratch force of brigade strength hastily cobbled together under Major-General Noel

Mason-MacFarlane – the Director of Military Intelligence at GHQ rather than a field commander – called 'Macforce' and sent to cover the River Scarpe east of Arras.

Nonetheless, there was no getting around the problem that a huge gap was now developing between the British and remaining French units in the north and the French forces to the south of the River Somme. Maybe, if they managed to buck themselves up in lightning-quick time, the gap could be closed. But what if it couldn't? It was something Gort and Pownall had to consider and as far as they could see there was only one viable option should that be the case: to fall back to the coast, using the Douai–La Bassée–Aire Canal and other water obstacles to help them. 'But,' noted Pownall, 'the withdrawal ended at the sea at Dunkirk, from which hopes of evacuation of personnel were small indeed.' Gort summoned his corps commanders, General Brooke and General Evelyn Barker, and put them in the picture while Pownall warned the War Office in coded language for fear that the line was being tapped. Later in the afternoon, Pownall rang again and this time was emphatic. If the gap was not closed by an urgent, strong and co-ordinated counter-attack from the north and south, withdrawal to Dunkirk would become inevitable.

In these dark hours, the appalling paucity of information and the hopeless lack of communications was really debilitating Allied efforts. Reports arrived at Arras, then at Wahagnies, by despatch rider or by liaison officers in person. Journeys of ten to fifteen miles could take an age because by this time the roads were clogged with refugees. Arthur Hughes had been shocked by the sight of so many. So too had Henry Pownall. 'There are many most distressing sights,' he scribbled, 'the old women are indeed sad to see, poor old things – never a smile on the faces of many thousands I have seen. Why should there be indeed?' This, of course, made the co-ordination of the kind of forces necessary for such a counter-attack difficult. It also made it very hard to keep abreast of just precisely where the Germans were.

As it happened, the Germans hardly knew themselves. Since the collapse of the Meuse front, all three spears of Army Group A had sped west at an astonishingly untroubled rate. Hans von Luck and the reconnaissance troops of Rommel's 7th Panzer Division had been charging through the French countryside of Champagne. 'Keep going, don't look to left or right, only forward. The enemy is confused; we must take advantage of it' were Rommel's orders, echoing what Guderian and

General Reinhardt were urging upon their men a short distance further south. Hans and his men reached Avesnes on the 16th, some fifty miles from their crossing point on the Meuse; by dawn the next day, having pushed on through the night, they had reached another major obstacle, the River Sembre, a dozen miles further west. French troops moving forward to the front had no idea it had already reached them. Astonished to see German troops so far west already, they had not blown the bridges and Rommel's men had crossed the river with barely a shot fired. Half an hour later, Hans had reached the town of Le Cateau, nearly seventy miles from the Meuse.

'La guerre est finie, je m'en fou,' Hans heard French soldiers say as he and his men thundered past through the clouds of dust along the way. Apart from the orders they received, the reconnaissance troops had no idea what the wider situation was along the front; they only knew what they saw in front of them, and that was French troops being overrun and surrendering in droves. 'We had the feeling of being alone at the head of a division advancing tempestuously,' noted Hans. '"Forward!" was the cry.'

The same day, 18 Squadron, having finally moved airfields – to Crécy – was told its Blenheims were needed as bombers as well as reconnaissance aircraft. Their target was the 7th Panzer Division on the Cambrai–Le Cateau road. Arthur Hughes took off at around 10 a.m. Around Le Cateau, the country looked devastated to him. Here and there vehicles and buildings were burning. Spotting a load of motor transport along the road to the south-west of the town, he peeled down and dropped his four 250 lb bombs from about 700 feet. Suddenly, though, it seemed to him that the figures diving frantically out of the way of his attack were wearing khaki. He couldn't tell for certain, though, but he was sure that he had bombed the right place. Once again, Arthur made it back in one piece, but two other crews were not so lucky.

Whether he had hit Allies or Germans, Rommel's advance seemed in no way slowed. On the 19th, he captured Cambrai, the scene of a famous victory for the British in 1917 when they had used tanks in strength for the first time. Now it was German panzers that were doing the damage – or rather, a few lead elements. Fortune favours the brave, and in this case the French defenders saw a large cloud of dust approaching and fearing a far larger German force than was really the case, they fled with barely a fight.

Panzer Corps Guderian crossed the old Somme battlefield on the

19th, having successfully fought off counter-attacks by de Gaulle's tanks. It would have reached there earlier but Guderian had been once again discovering that his senior officers were a greater thorn in his side than the enemy. A whole day had been lost on 17 May when von Kleist, still concerned that his impetuous panzer commander might be overreaching himself, had ordered him to halt to allow the infantry to catch up. This had only been resolved once Guderian, outraged, had resigned and then hastily been reinstated. By the evening of the 19th, however, the panzer spearheads were all more or less now in line with one another. Guderian's 10th Panzer protected his southern flank along the River Aisne, while 1st and 2nd Panzer were poised to burst their way towards Amiens and Albert the following day. To the north Reinhardt's 8th Panzer Division had heroically made its way through the gridlock of the Ardennes and had caught up with 6th Panzer, while to the north of Rommel at Cambrai were 5th Panzer and 3rd and 4th from Army Group B. Furthermore, hot on Rommel's tails was the Waffen-SS Totenkopf Division. While most Wehrmacht infantry divisions barely had a couple of trucks to rub together, the Nazi military arm could pull all manner of strings that enabled inexperienced units like the Totenkopf to already be one of the best-equipped divisions in the entire German army. Placed under the direct command of Rommel, its resources were much needed at this latest critical moment in the battle.

Suddenly, the mad, frenetic panzer rush west was beginning to become a more solid, unified front, and thanks to their superior communications, the Germans were able to co-ordinate their actions and strengthen their line swiftly and efficiently. There were still isolated pockets of French resistance behind in the wake of the German advance but as the infantry began pouring out of the Ardennes, these were rapidly being mopped up. By dawn on the 20th, the Allies' chances of counter-attacking and successfully plugging the now gaping-wide gap were slipping away with every passing hour. They needed to act, and act fast.

By 19 May, there were only thirty-seven squadrons in Fighter Command ready for battle compared with the minimum of sixty that were required were the Luftwaffe to attack Britain in strength. This was some shortfall. Still, a corner had been turned, which was a great relief to Newall and Dowding: now that Gort was thinking in terms of evacuation, plans were put in place to get most of the RAF Component back to England too. No doubt Dowding and Newall's stark warning had made an impression, but it was the reality of the unfolding disaster that spoke louder than words. Thus the Prime Minister finally accepted that to send good after bad to France was a futile exercise. That same day, he sent a memo to Ismay ordering that no more fighters be sent to France but warning that, should it be necessary to evacuate the BEF, then a strong covering force would be needed from English bases. With this note, Churchill was reversing a trend that had placed Fighter Command in deadly peril since the outset. Instead of bolstering the position in France, all fighter resources were now to be used for what they had originally been designed for in the event of war: defending Britain and her armed forces only. Later that day, the eight half-squadrons sent to France began returning. The next day, most of the remaining fighter squadrons flew back to England. By the 21st, only three RAF Hurricane squadrons – those with the Advanced Air Striking Force – were still in France.

Bee Beamont had gone home on the 20th. It had come like a bolt from the blue. One minute he was watching a shot-down Hurricane plunge into the ground on the far side of the airfield, and almost the next his CO was offering him or one of the other pilots a flight home on a DC-2 that was about to take off. They tossed for it, and Bee won, finding himself a short while later on a Dutch KLM transport plane along with a number of other RAF fighter pilots.

He was landing back down at Hendon before the realization that he had been plucked from the maelstrom of war really sank in. From Hendon, he and a few others went into central London, its streets crammed with shoppers, buses, tradesmen and people going about their daily business with what seemed like no concern at all. They stopped at the RAF Club near Hyde Park Corner. Just a few hours before they had been in the heat of battle; now a group of dirty, unshaven pilots were standing in the middle of London with the nation's masses wandering past them as though there was no war on at all.

This was not really the case, however. Most in Britain were still half expecting German parachutists to float down from the sky at any moment. Daidie Penna saw a train-load of wounded troops pull into her local station on the 19th; she thought everyone out and about seemed very tense, although over the next couple of days the news seemed brighter. 'We seem to be holding the Germans at present,' she noted on the 21st.

In fact, Churchill, from the moment he became Prime Minister, was determined not to shield the public from the reality of the situation. This was sensible because should the situation deteriorate – and clearly it was doing so – then the public would have already been prepared, whilst at the same time it would be more likely to trust the Government. Certainly, his new Minister of Information, Duff Cooper, was very much of the same mind. Credible openness was to be the policy, while Churchill hoped that his rhetoric could stir the nation to fall in behind him. If Daidie Penna was hearing news that things were looking up in France then that was not because of any deliberate hoodwinking on the part of the Government, but because the BBC and the press, and in turn those running the War Office and at the Ministry of Information, were not fully in the picture at the time the news was given out. As Harold Nicolson noted on 21 May, 'The situation is terribly obscure' – and he was now working as Parliamentary Secretary for the Ministry of Information.

Nicolson had been asked to join the Ministry of Morale – as it was known – on 17 May, one of the last of the junior ministers to have been given a post. Having just heard the news of the calamitous German breakthrough at Sedan, he received a telephone call and a moment later the Prime Minister was on the line.

'Harold, I think it would be very nice if you joined the Government and helped Duff at the Ministry of Information,' the PM said to him.

'There is nothing I should like better,' Harold replied immediately.

'Well, fall in tomorrow. The list will be out tonight. That all right?'

'Very much all right,' said Harold.

'OK,' said Churchill and then rang off.

As asked, he was at work the following day at the Ministry's offices in Senate House at London University, and had been given the post of Parliamentary Secretary with the specific job of keeping tabs on civilian morale. There was a War Room, in which there was a large map full of pins and different-coloured wool marking out the positions of the armies and kept as up to date as possible. Twice a day there were conferences, at 10.30 in the morning and 5.30 p.m., and a press conference at 12.30 p.m. 'I have a nice sunny little room,' noted Harold, 'and if the bombing starts, I shall sleep here. They say that the shelter under our tower is proof even against a direct hit.'

Despite his excitement at being part of the Government and able to do something useful, Harold and his colleagues faced a difficult task. Unlike Churchill, Chamberlain's Government had insisted on bullish optimism. Both the defeat in Norway and now the unfolding disaster on the Continent had staggered the majority. 'It must be remembered that the defence of the Low Countries had been continually built up in the press,' ran one public opinion survey. 'Not one person in a thousand could visualise the Germans breaking through into France.' By 22 May, the Ministry had set up a Home Morale Emergency Committee to work on measures that might prevent a widespread break in morale. As Josef Goebbels well knew in Germany, propaganda was a key weapon of a modern war. The importance of the will of the people, in both a totalitarian state and a democracy, could not be underestimated.

There had been another key appointment in Churchill's new Government, and one that brought a glimmer of hope to Air Chief Marshal Dowding, and that was Max Aitken, Lord Beaverbrook, as the first ever Minister for Aircraft Production, complete with his new ministry. A Canadian from Ontario, he had made his first million, as a financier and investment banker, before he was thirty, then, in 1910, when still only thirty-one, had moved to England and become a Liberal Unionist MP, whilst at the same time buying large shares in the Rolls-Royce motor car and engine company. He sold out a few years later, and then embarked on building a hugely successful newspaper empire, which included the London *Evening Standard* and *Daily Express*.

By 1917, he was a peer, choosing 'Beaverbrook' after an area near his boyhood home, having played a key role in ousting Asquith as Prime Minister and helping Lloyd George to take over. By 1918, he was the first Minister of Information, and, although it was a short-lived post, throughout the 1920s and 1930s, with his ever-increasing power as the first real press baron of Fleet Street, his influence remained considerable.

He was also a close friend of long standing with Winston Churchill. As with all friendships, the two had drifted apart at times and they by no means saw eye to eye on everything. Beaverbrook had been notoriously opposed to war right up until the last moment, for example, but since then a closer relationship had returned. Back in November, Churchill, then at the Admiralty, had urged Chamberlain to bring his friend into the Government. 'When I talk to him,' Churchill wrote, 'I have a feeling of knowledge, force, experience, which I do not find – at my age – with most I meet. We need this kind of thing.'

Chamberlain had not heeded this advice, but by 10 May 1940 Churchill had decided that, personally, he very much did need this kind of thing. For all his gregariousness, Churchill was, in many ways, something of a solitary figure. He had many colleagues with whom he shared a close working relationship, but very few bosom friends. Most of his greatest pals were gone. Max was the only person in the political world with whom Churchill enjoyed spending considerable time, and whose enormous drive, drama, knowledge and vitality matched his own. Thus it was Beaverbrook with whom Churchill lunched and dined on 10 May; on the 11th they lunched alone together. On the 12th, Beaverbrook spent the afternoon with Churchill and stayed for dinner. Max was Churchill's intimate adviser, friend, right-hand man; unpopular with most within the Government but, now that Churchill was PM, one of the most powerful men in the country whether they liked it or not.

The political divisions of the past had been swept away. Now Churchill and Beaverbrook were as one on the fundamentals: saving Britain and helping to bring the United States into the war materially, at the very least. In fact, following the outbreak of war, Beaverbrook had given himself a self-appointed mission to travel to America, ostensibly to find out what the President really thought about the war. He learned little new, but did manage to charm Roosevelt, winning his confidence and establishing a firm relationship; Beaverbrook could speak for Britain but, as a Canadian, in the language of an American. Just as Churchill, since the beginning of the war, had opened a dialogue with the President, so too had Beaverbrook. With his understanding of business and finance, this access to Washington was invaluable.

Yet while Beaverbrook was to play a critical role as Churchill's man behind the scenes, the Prime Minister believed his friend could fulfil an even more important task. Before the war, Churchill had been one of those repeatedly demanding that production of aircraft could and should be speeded up. As in Germany, production was, in early May, still slow. What was needed, he felt, was a new ministry, separate from the Air Ministry. The Ministry of Munitions had been carved out of the War Office in the last war to resolve the shell shortage and had achieved miracles. With Max in charge of aircraft production, he saw no reason why the same could not occur.

He put this proposal to Beaverbrook on 10 May, but his friend did not agree immediately. He was over sixty, and his asthma was bad; he wasn't sure how much he could take on. Nonetheless, he wasted no time sounding out key personnel. On the 11th, he had a long discussion with Sinclair, the new Secretary of State for Air, and on the 12th spent most of the day interviewing men within the Air Ministry and businessmen whom he might recruit to the new ministry. Later that day, he told Churchill he would accept the job, which was officially announced two days later. On 17 May, the new Ministry of Aircraft Production, with a fanfare of very welcome publicity, came into being. It helped create the sense that something dramatic and dynamic was happening; that Churchill was immediately ringing the changes.

And so he was. It was true that shadow factories had already been set up; it was also true that back in April 1938 the Air Ministry had created a Supply Committee, which had effectively the same remit as the new Ministry of Aircraft Production. At the same time the post of Air Member for Research and Development (AMRD) had also been created with much the same responsibilities as the new minister. And it is also true that the Supply Committee had very sensibly been, since August the previous year, building up stocks of Swedish iron and steel, Perspex sheeting and other key aircraft materials. Furthermore, the Government's announcement of 'Scheme L' in April 1938, its latest programme for aircraft production, had been conceived without regard to financial limitations, the like of which had stymied production up to that point. In other words, no matter what it cost, the 12,000 aircraft planned in the scheme were to be built by the spring of 1940.

While these changes all made a huge difference, however, it was an altogether different kettle of fish bringing someone like Beaverbrook in at the top and unshackled from the Air Ministry, most of whose members still favoured the bomber as the best means of defence rather than the fighter. Beaverbrook wasted no time in going to see Dowding and immediately told him quite emphatically that his priority was to build aircraft for what was needed right now, in Fighter Command, to get Britain out of its immediate jam, rather than to continue with plans for the future. The two would speak every day. Beaverbrook would ask Dowding what he needed and would listen carefully to the answer. Whenever Dowding visited him, Beaverbrook would always personally walk him out of the Ministry building to his car below. The only other person he showed such attention to was Churchill.

On the 15th, Beaverbrook, in discussion with Sir Charles Craven, one of the old AMPD department men to remain in the new ministry, and the Air Ministry, agreed that production should be concentrated on five types of aircraft only, with immediate effect: the Hurricane and Spitfire, the Blenheim, and the Whitley and Hampden bombers. Nothing was to stand in the way of the maximum production of these types. Financial considerations, long-term plans, four-engine heavy-bomber projects – all were to be put to one side.

Within the first few days, Beaverbrook had established a new ministry that was like no other, and which was mostly funded by himself. The Supply Committee had been a sign of progress but it was still yet another committee of multiple people which needed consensus before anything could be agreed. Beaverbrook didn't like committees. In his office he had two notices. One said, 'Committees take the punch out of war', while the second read, 'Organization is the enemy of improvisation.' The buck stopped with him; he liked to be informed and then he made his decision. Scientists, businessmen, industrialists – men he respected and trusted – were all brought in and given loose job titles. 'They are all captains of industry,' Beaverbrook explained, 'and industry is like theology. If you know one faith, you can grasp the meaning of another.' There was little hierarchy, and Beaverbrook used his closeness to Churchill and his force of personality to cut through tedious red tape. Nor did he much like memos and letters for conducting business; the telephone was quicker. And while he was gracious to a point with men like Dowding, he was happy to make enemies should it be necessary. Nothing was to get in the way of speeding up aircraft production. Nothing at all.

Feldmarschall Hermann Göring had put one of his closest buddies in charge of the vitally important job of overseeing aircraft production, and so too now had Churchill. Whether this diminutive press baron, with his great experience, drive and authority, could achieve all that he, Churchill, and Dowding dearly hoped remained to be seen. But one thing was not in doubt: in almost every respect, the Canadian was the German's superior for the task.

14

Decisions

THE MIRACLE HAD HAPPENED. The gamble had paid off. Late on Monday, 20 May, having advanced more than 250 miles in ten days, troops of Panzer Corps Guderian had reached the Channel coast near Abbeville. Battles and campaigns rarely, if ever, go according to plan, least of all when they are carried out with so many pitfalls and obstacles to overcome, and when so reliant on luck and on the incompetence of the enemy. Yet, to all intents and purposes, that was what had happened.

Now caught in the mightiest encirclement ever in military history were more than 1.7 million men: the Dutch army, already in German hands, the entire Belgian army, one French army and large proportions of four others, and nearly all the British Expeditionary Force of half a million men – all trapped with their backs to the sea. And just ten divisions out of Germany's 135 available for the offensive were all it had taken to achieve this extraordinary panzer drive to the coast. The stupefied French, stunned to see German tanks and vehicles having advanced so far so quickly, seemed to have been powerless to stop them.

Guderian and his men were euphoric about their incredible achievement, but had no idea what they were supposed to do next. No plan had been made; neither von Kleist, nor von Rundstedt, nor von Brauchitsch or even Hitler himself had dared believe such rapid progress was possible. Thus he and his men had to impatiently twiddle their thumbs while they awaited new orders. Visiting 2nd Panzer Division he had asked an Austrian soldier how they had 'enjoyed' the operations to date. 'Not bad,' the soldier told him, 'but we wasted two days.'

While Guderian's men were kicking their heels near Abbeville on the 21st, the great Allied counter-attack was getting underway – except that it was barely a counter-attack at all; more a kind of demonstration. Only two British columns, each consisting of an infantry and armoured battalion, a battery of field artillery and anti-tank guns, and a few recce motorcycles, and a few French tanks were all that had been allocated for the task. In other words, less than a division, and rather than a pincer movement, it was thrusting south from the north only.

Since the French had planned their war in such a way that speed of movement was anathema to them, it was no real surprise that they had failed to come to the party. Gort had issued orders on the 20th for a thrust south of Arras to protect the town and his exposed right (southern) flank. It had not been intended as a counter-attack or part of any large-scale operation, and neither was he expecting French help. Soon after issuing this order, however, 'Tiny' Ironside, the CIGS, had arrived at Gort's command post with orders from the War Cabinet that the entire BEF should move south-west, 'attacking all enemy forces encountered'. Gort was incensed by this order. 'A scandalous (ie Winstonian) thing to do,' complained Henry Pownall, 'and in fact quite impossible to carry out.' Fortunately, once at Gort's command post, Ironside quickly realized this too, and so with Pownall in tow went off to see Billotte and Blanchard, commander of French First Army, at the latter's HQ in Lens, to discuss a co-ordinated counter-attack to retrieve the situation.

Although this had been imperative for several days and, since the day before, a matter of utmost urgency, absolutely nothing had been done by the French to prepare for such an action. The biggest sign of pro-action was the sacking of Gamelin, who had been replaced as Supreme Commander by Général Weygand – another Great War commander and now seventy-three years old. Ironside was shocked by Billotte's increasing hysteria. The French Army Group Commander kept repeating his by now well-rehearsed mantra that there was nothing he could do to stop the panzers. At one point, he became so overwrought, Ironside grabbed him by his tunic and gave him a good shake. While they were there, Gort telephoned and asked the French to help in the planned action for the following day. This was followed by a call from Général Weygand, who equally urged his commanders to pull their fingers out and get a grip of themselves. At last Billotte and Blanchard agreed to contribute two divisions. Since the French had at least eight in the area, this was not much of a contribution. 'Nobody minds going down fighting,' noted Pownall after this meeting, 'but the long and many days of defence and recently the entire lack of higher direction and action, have been terribly wearing on the nerves of us all.' It was an odd thing to say; after, all the battle was hardly a cricket match. The mayhem was getting to them all.

Despite their assurances, however, it soon became clear that neither Billotte nor Blanchard had any intention of taking part in the counter-attack at all. Billotte spent the rest of the day discussing whether an ammunition dump should be saved or blown up to prevent it falling into the hands of Germans, rather than marshalling his troops. At First Army HQ, Blanchard passed the buck to Altmayer, commander of French V Corps, but the latter informed his army commander that his men might be too tired to fight. Captain Reid, Blanchard's British liaison officer, visited Altmayer and found him sitting on his bed crying silently. Neither Reid nor Archdale at Billotte's HQ could then get hold of Gort or Pownall, so not until the following morning, a few hours before the attack was to begin, did the British learn that the French would not be contributing, save for a few tanks.

As it happened, the British thrust south of Arras seriously knocked Rommel's combined force of 7th Panzer and Waffen-SS Totenkopf divisions. At one point, as British armour was threatening to overrun Rommel's troops, the German general took personal command of an artillery battery sited in a quarry on the crest of a long shallow hill. The British were pushed back after a day of hard fighting, but it had given the Germans a severe shock. For the first time since crossing the Meuse, Army Group A had encountered some serious opposition. Von Rundstedt called it 'a critical moment in the drive', adding that, 'For a short time it was feared that our armoured divisions would be cut off.' Had the Allies managed to co-ordinate a combined counter-attack from both north and south, and in force, the Germans might yet have been checked. But it was not to be.

Not that Général Weygand, the spry septuagenarian brought in to put some steel back into the French, was giving up just yet – after all, he had not been brought in to do nothing. Nonetheless, matters hardly improved, and once again it was communications – or lack of them – that were one of the biggest problems. On the same day that the British were thrusting south of Arras, Weygand held a conference in the Belgian town of Ypres, now rebuilt since its destruction over twenty years before. By the time Gort finally got there, having been in the middle of a command post move and then struggling through the swathes of refugees clogging the roads, Weygand had already left. Billotte was also late, but, deciding to crack on with the conference anyway, the Belgians eventually agreed to fall back a short way, taking over part of the British northern line. Part of French First Army would also take over part of the British line, thus freeing troops to take part in the proposed counter-attack. By the time Gort eventually turned up, the plan was presented to him as a *fait accompli.*

It was a hopeless idea, not least because the main British lines of supply from the south had already been cut by the Germans. Gort's troops were already getting low on ammunition and food. Furthermore, the three British divisions earmarked for the attack were blatantly not enough for the task set them. Gort could have refused, but did not. Nonetheless, how Weygand could have thought that these complicated troop movements could have enabled an attack to be made the following day, only he could have known. As it was, Gort soon put the kibosh on that. First, he insisted that the BEF, which up to then had been keeping the Army Group B at bay quite successfully, should fall back to the French–Belgian border line on the night of 22/23 May. The following night, the Belgians would relieve one British division in the north of the line, and the French two in the south. That meant the three divisions needed for the attack that had been released would not be ready until 26 May at the earliest. No-one was happy. The British felt it was a pig of a plan, the Belgians suspected they were being abandoned, and the French felt not enough was being done. Then, as Billotte was driving back to Lens, he was involved in a car crash and later died. No replacement was found for him until 25 May. Why it took four days to appoint a new Army Group Commander was anyone's guess.

The next day, Wednesday, 22 May, the French did attempt a counter-attack at Cambrai, but it was beaten off, while German infantry was now catching up the panzers and together pressing hard on the beleaguered British units at Arras. The chances of there being any counter-attack at all on the 26th were diminishing rapidly. 'We are down to about two and a half days' rations and 3–400 r.p.g. [rounds per gun],' noted Pownall on the evening of the 22nd, 'enough for only one defensive battle. A very tight corner indeed.' By the morning of the 23rd, the BEF, along with the

French First Army, were stuck out on a limb, now that the Belgians had fallen back to the River Lys, which ran in a north-easterly direction, and the BEF had fallen back to the border, which ran in a south-easterly direction. German forces were pressing the BEF hard along its front, northern and southern flanks, and with Guderian's panzers now at the Channel it was in danger of being surrounded before it could fall back to the coast. The situation could hardly have been worse.

Yet it did not stop the Prime Minister, fresh from his latest trip to Paris, ordering Gort to counter-attack not on 26 May, but immediately, with eight British and French divisions and the Belgian Cavalry Corps on the right. 'Here are Winston's plans again,' railed Pownall. 'Can nobody prevent him from trying to conduct operations himself as a super Commander-in-Chief? How does he think we are to collect eight divisions and attack as he suggests? Have we no front to hold (which if it cracked would let in the flood?) He can have no conception of our situation and condition. Where *are* the Belgian Cavalry Corps? How is an attack like this to be staged involving three nationalities at an hour's notice? The man's mad.'

It was true the British and Belgians had been holding off the Germans reasonably well in the north up until then. But, of course, Army Group B was largely infantry and almost completely so now that two of its three panzer divisions had swung south. Thus it had to move mostly on foot and this took time. Unteroffizier Hellmuth Damm and his machine-gun company in the 56th Infantry Division had managed to commandeer some bicycles – they discovered there were many around – and that made life considerably easier for them. As *Gruppe* leader, he took a baker's bicycle, which had three wheels and a pannier on which he managed to set his heavy MG08s and ammunition cases.

The division had been part of Sixth Army but on the 19th it was attached to Eighteenth Army instead and so now was advancing almost due west towards Ghent and Dunkirk – and facing the men of the BEF. On the 20th, Hellmuth watched the unusual spectacle of the division's artillery marching past its infantry to take the vanguard of their advance. It then hammered the Belgian positions and the infantry followed. Hellmuth read this unorthodox practice as a sign of the Germans' dominance and their mounting confidence. He and his men then found themselves in a 'resting position' near Opdorp, some thirty miles east of Ghent, for a couple of days. It gave them a much needed respite. By the

22nd, they were moving forward again, however, this time to attack Ghent. The town fell to 56th Division the following day.

Leutnant Siegfried Knappe and his 24th Artillery Battalion were now in France at long last. As part of Army Group A, they had taken part in what had seemed like an impossibly long and exhausting march, which had begun near Cologne. Ahead of them, they had often been able to hear the sounds of battle, and as they passed first into Belgium and then France, they could see the evidence of fighting too: burned tanks, blown-up bridges, dead livestock. Pontoon bridges had already been built across most of the rivers they came to, and felled trees pushed from their path. At Bra, in Belgium, they had to leave behind their first horse. 'Other candidates for exhaustion,' noted Siegfried, 'were the battery blacksmiths.' This was how most of the German army moved: by horse, by bicycle and on foot.

Siegfried's battalion crossed the Meuse at Rommel's crossing point south of Houx then, once in France, was assigned to Panzer Group Kleist. The scenes of battle grew steadily worse. 'Dead cattle and other livestock were everywhere,' he noted, 'the victims of bullets, mortars, artillery shells and bombs. Their bloating carcasses lay in the fields with their legs sticking up. I learned that the smell of rotting flesh, dust, burned powder, smoke, and petrol was the smell of combat.' He was also shocked by the sight of his first dead soldier. They had been trained to deliver death quickly and efficiently and, of course, he knew that in wars people get killed. Indeed, comrades of his had died in Poland, but it had always had a clinical connotation for him; he mourned their loss, but now seeing a bloodied, stinking and mutilated corpse that had recently been a living, young human being was quite a shock. The men he saw were French Moroccans, their eyes and mouths open, limbs skewed in grotesque fashion. 'The experience was impossible to forget,' he wrote. 'From that moment on, death hovered near us wherever we went.' And he was also shocked by the numbers of refugees, traipsing along the roads with their paltry belongings and clearly without much idea of where they were headed. 'I felt sorry that we had to do this to them,' he noted. 'They were paying a terrible price because France had declared war on us.'

When Hitler heard the news that Guderian had reached the Channel coast he was beside himself with joy, and immediately began to occupy his thoughts with peace terms. 'We are seeking to arrive at an understanding with Britain,' Halder noted after a Führer Conference the following day, 'on the basis of a division of the world.' That same day, Hitler met

Grossadmiral Erich Raeder, C-in-C of the Kriegsmarine – German navy – and the admiral asked Hitler whether he had any plans for an invasion of England. Beforehand, the Führer had made it clear that he preferred an economic blockade and naval and air attacks to bring Britain to her senses. Nonetheless, Raeder had ordered a preliminary investigation into the feasibility of an invasion the previous November. So, too, as it happened, had OKH. For now, though, Hitler told Raeder not to think in terms of invasion, but to continue the economic blockade and to intensify naval warfare against the British Isles. In a directive a few days later, the Luftwaffe was given 'unlimited freedom of action' against Britain just as soon as sufficient forces were available. The Naval Staff certainly welcomed these directives. They 'indicate clearly the object of this war', noted the OKM War Diary, 'the annihilation of the main enemy, England. The way to her defeat lies through the destruction of France, her Continental sword, to the starvation of the British island empire and to the ruination of her economic fighting power.'

In the meantime, Hitler needed to finish off France, Belgium and the British forces there. Late on the 21st, Guderian at last received orders to continue his advance, now in a northerly direction with the capture of the Channel ports as his objective. This did not begin in earnest until the 23rd because the day before, 1st and 2nd Panzer had been ordered to secure the Somme bridgeheads and wait for the rest of von Wietersheim's mechanized divisions to catch up from Sedan, but the following day, in lovely early-summer sunshine once more, each of Guderian's panzer divisions was beginning its assault of the key Channel ports of Boulogne, Calais and Dunkirk. 10th Panzer, briefly taken out of his command the day before, had now been handed back once more, and so he ordered it to press on to Calais while 2nd Panzer attacked Boulogne and 1st Panzer made straight for Dunkirk, a mere twenty-five miles to the north-east. Three divisions, three towns. The arithmetic was very simple.

Guderian had good reason for optimism, even though the British troops trapped in Boulogne and Calais were fighting fiercely. Soon all three ports would surely be in German hands. And once that happened, there would be no chance of escape for the French, Belgian and British troops trapped in the encirclement.

Since the Allied commanders barely knew exactly what was going on half the time, it was not surprising that most on the ground had only a sketchy idea of what was happening, most of which was fed by rumour after rumour. At the farmhouse where the 4th Heavy Anti-Aircraft Regiment was now based to the south-east of Lille, Stan Fraser heard first that Amiens had fallen and then that Arras had too. In fact, Arras was not abandoned until the night of the 23rd, but Stan and his colleagues knew enough already to know that, whatever the truth, things were far from going well. They hastily busied themselves strengthening the defences of their farmhouse HQ, creating barricades with abandoned ploughs, a threshing machine and other farm implements.

Nor had they received any rations for several days. The farm was thus the best place to be as there were pigs and sheep to kill and cows to milk – which they did as often as they could to relieve the poor animals. The countryside around them was now deserted of civilians. More rumours arrived, this time that they could expect parachutists any moment; it was not only in Britain that parachutist fever had taken grip. Occasionally enemy bombers came over, in which case they opened fire, but with ammunition low they had to conserve what little they had. The rest of the time, they had to stay where they were and anxiously wait.

On the night of the 22nd/23rd, the northern flank of the BEF fell back to the French–Belgian border as planned. Second Lieutenant Norman Field, just twenty-three and newly married before he was posted to France the previous September, had just been appointed adjutant of the 2nd Battalion Royal Fusiliers. Part of 4th Division in III Corps, they had followed the lead units into Belgium and then had, bit by bit, retreated again. Occasionally they had seen some action, but nothing much. Neither Norman nor the rest of the battalion could really understand it. 'We merely had some skirmishes with the Germans,' says Norman, 'until we were told to withdraw again. We wondered why we were going backwards all the time.'

Now they were digging in again at Halluin, a village south of Menin on the French border. They were all exhausted, having marched thirty-one miles through the night all the way from the Escaut. The battalion was stretched over about one mile in a south-easterly direction with the canal in front of it until it linked up with the South Lancashire Regiment. The 23rd was spent consolidating their positions, preparing sangers and laying anti-tank mines. Civilians were encouraged to leave. There were some defences there already. 'We were back on the line we had previously prepared,' says Norman. Like the men of the 4th HAA Regiment, it was then a question of waiting for the enemy to catch up. By leaving during the night and covering such distances, they had given themselves a bit of time; it would take the Germans a while to gather their strength and move forward. A day, maybe two. Then the Fusiliers could expect a fight on their hands.

Also now fallen back along the French border was 1st Border Battalion, part of 42nd Division in I Corps. They too had had a long night march and by the morning of the 23rd were digging in either side of the village of Lezennes, just to the east of Lille. Now attached to 'C' Company was Sid Nuttall, a twenty-year-old Yorkshireman from Halifax. Sid had joined the Supplementary C Reserve before the war, created especially to establish a reserve of mechanics should it come to war. 'There were no camp duties, no training, no uniforms given out,' says Sid, 'but we would be the first people to be called up and put into the trade if and when they required us.' He had been duly called up shortly before the declaration of war and was soon after posted to 14th Army Field Workshops, part of the Royal Army Ordnance Corps, or RAOC.

Soon after, he found himself in France, but early the following year he got frostbite in his hands and toes whilst trying to recover a broken-down truck in freezing winter weather. 'My fingers had swollen up and were all touching each other,' he says. 'My feet were like balloons.' Packed off to hospital in Dieppe, several of his toes were nearly amputated but, by a piece of serendipity, the doctor was his same doctor from home in Halifax, evidently now called up too. Sid pleaded with him to save his toes, and Dr Hendry did just that.

But once passed fit again, Sid was not sent back to the 14th Army Field Workshop but posted instead to the 1st Border Battalion as a mechanic. As the battalion moved into Belgium at the start of the offensive, he accompanied it in that role, following behind the infantry with the B Echelon, the supply section of the battalion, and moving up by night to take away and repair trucks and Bren gun carriers. In the subsequent retreat to the Escaut, however, the battalion managed to lose most of its transport and so, no longer needed as a mechanic, Sid suddenly found himself being made into 'C' Company runner instead.

The only problem was that he had had absolutely no infantry training whatsoever. He had never even fired a Lee Enfield rifle. Nor did he have even a bayonet or an infantryman's webbing; instead, he had been issued with small First World War-era five-round pouches. The company was on the banks of the Escaut at Tournai when it came under fire. 'Can you use your rifle?' the company commander asked him.

'I can shoot a gun,' Sid replied, 'but I've never shot this one.'

'Do you know how to load it?' the captain asked.

'Yes,' Sid replied.

The CO then pointed out a house at the edge of a wood on the far side of the canal. 'If you see any German soldiers on that side,' he told Sid, 'fire at them. But only if you see them in that area.'

Sure enough, eventually he did spot a German, recognizing the distinctive enemy helmets. Taking aim, he squeezed the trigger and fired, but to Sid's surprise the German kept on walking; he never even ducked. The lance corporal hurried over. 'Have you just fired?' he asked. Sid told him he had.

'Did you hit him?'

'No.'

'Let's have a look at your rifle.'

Sid passed it to him and the lance corporal looked at it. 'Your sights are set to six hundred yards. That shot will have gone miles over his head.' He put Sid's sights back to one hundred yards.

Later, on the night of the 21st, 'C' Company had taken over positions held by the Lancashire Fusiliers. 'We were walking up in the middle of the night,' says Sid, 'and it was pitch black and suddenly a Lancashire voice comes out of the darkness, saying, "I shouldn't go up there, mate – they're killing one another."'

Now the battalion was back inside France and this time, when the enemy caught up, he would be at the sharp end, not behind with the rest of B Echelon. He'd only been an infantryman for a few days. His was a crash-course training, learning on the job.

Momentous decisions were now about to be made on both the German and British sides, decisions that would have far-reaching consequences in the days and weeks to come. Running south-east from Gravelines, just ten miles west from Dunkirk, lay the River Aa, which south of St Omer joined La Bassée Canal. This was the Canal Line that was protecting the southern – or right – flank of the BEF and the French First Army. By the morning of the 24th, Guderian's 1st Panzer Division had reached this line and by midday had secured crucial bridgeheads across it in three separate places. As at the Meuse, getting safely across a key water feature was the key to an operation; so as far as the buoyant Germans were concerned, the path to Dunkirk was now well and truly open, particularly since the bulk of the BEF was still south-east of the port. Calais and Boulogne had already been isolated and were expected to fall any moment, so it seemed to Guderian that the BEF and French First Army were now completely trapped with nowhere left to run.

Then, at 12.45 p.m., Guderian received an urgent order, from the Führer no less. North-west of Arras, all German forces were to halt along the line Lens–Béthune–Aire–St Omer–Gravelines. In other words, along the Canal Line. Hitler wanted 'all mobile units to close up'. First Panzer wasn't the only unit to have already won bridgeheads across the Canal Line. So, too, had the SS-Totenkopf Division at Béthune, for example. 'We were utterly speechless,' wrote Guderian. 'But since were not informed of the reasons for this order, it was difficult to argue against it.'

In fact, the origins of this fateful order could be found the previous day, when von Kleist had told Army Group A and OKH that his units were now quite widely spread, conducting attacks along the Canal Line and the Channel ports, and protecting their own southern flank. He told von Rundstedt that his panzer strength was down to 50 per cent, which was actually a far more pessimistic assessment than was the reality. He thus warned that if the enemy counter-attacked in strength then he believed his lead divisions might have some difficulties. However, there was no sign of any major counter-attack and nothing about the performance of the French or British suggested one was imminent.

Nonetheless, General Günther von Kluge was alarmed by von Kleist's message. Although commander of the Fourth Army, which included Rommel's 7th Panzer and Panzer Corps Hoth pressing north from Arras, he had also been given overall command of all the mobile forces on his left – i.e. all of Panzer Group Kleist. At 4.40 p.m. on the 23rd, he spoke to von Rundstedt and suggested a close-up order be issued, halting the fast-moving mobile forces while the infantry divisions such as 87th Division, of which Leutnant Siegfried Knappe was a part, caught up.

This was the same old concern that had repeatedly reared its head ever since the plans for the offensive had first been drawn up; and it represented the same doctrinal differences between the old-school conservatives and the progressives such as Guderian, Halder, Reinhardt and Rommel. Von Rundstedt, a conservative, agreed with von Kluge, and issued an order at 8 p.m. on the 23rd that the following day the panzers were to interrupt their advances for twenty-four hours while the infantry caught up. Most of the divisions already attacking the Canal Line were furious. Guderian's 1st Panzer largely ignored this order, however. After all, had he listened to the orders of von Kleist and von Rundstedt so far, they would have been yet to reach the coast.

Hitler would not have become involved, however, had Halder and von Brauchitsch not now become embroiled as well. Annoyed by von Rundstedt's decision, Halder came to the conclusion that Army Group A had become too unwieldy – it was now seventy-one divisions strong; 'I have a good idea,' he noted, 'its staff has not been energetic and active enough.' As a result, von Brauchitsch now issued an order that as of 8 p.m. on 24th May, the whole of Fourth Army, including all the panzers, would switch to the command of Army Group B, whose task it would be to finish the encirclement in the north, while Army Group A henceforth concentrated on confronting French forces to the south.

Needless to say, von Rundstedt took exception to this order and, when Hitler visited him the next day, made his disgruntlement clear. It was, however, the first Hitler had known about it: the decision had been taken by von Brauchitsch without his knowledge. Annoyed that such an important order had been issued without his say-so, Hitler immediately rescinded it and then confirmed von Rundstedt's close-up order of the previous evening.

The order prompted immediate and sustained outrage from nearly every single commander now pressing the Canal Line, as well as from Halder, whose plans were being badly compromised. Oberstleutnant Ulrich Liss, one of Halder's staff officers, saw his boss at the briefing that night. 'He was livid with anger,' noted Liss, 'such as I have never seen him before.' Their anger was justified. It was the southern British front that was vulnerable: the British left flank was now dug in along the border making the most of previously prepared defences and in good order. Along the right flank it was a different story altogether, and it was here that Halder's main strike force – his mobile forces – were now massing for their final strike. Yet more than that, it was abundantly clear that neither the British nor French were in any position to make a major counter-attack. German reconnaissance planes could sweep over the enemy corridor at will; the chaos within this pocket would have been all too apparent. And just where were the Allied troops there going to get their supplies from? Only Dunkirk remained. Cool, rational thinking should have revealed to von Rundstedt that the ammunition supplies of the enemy trapped there must surely be small indeed.

Yet von Rundstedt was demonstrating what he had made clear all along: that he neither understood nor approved of the kind of fast, mobile warfare Guderian and the progressives had been preaching. Hitler was showing – as if any more proof were needed – that he had no understanding of modern warfare either. His decision to rescind von Brauchitsch's order was made because he felt his authority had been challenged – how dare von Brauchitsch make such a decision without clearing it with him first! He had always mistrusted the OKH and now he had been humiliated in front of von Rundstedt. Incredibly, Hitler, a hair's breadth away from achieving one of the most complete and remarkable victories ever, was prepared to sacrifice this to his desire to impress his authority over his subordinates. His compulsion to put von Brauchitsch and Halder back in their boxes over-rode any sound military logic.

At any rate, the order to halt now had the written authority of the Führer, and this time Guderian had no choice but to abide by it. In so doing, however, the opportunity to annihilate the entire BEF, and with it very possibly to win the war, was lost.

'Our spirits rise and fall,' noted Henry Pownall, 'sometimes, most of the time, the position seems perfectly hopeless . . . then the clouds lift a little and there seems just a chance of seeing it through. It's a wearing existence.' The halt order was a godsend to Lord Gort, whose southern flank was now looking increasingly fragile. On the night of the 23rd, 5th and 50th Divisions were pulled back from Arras and the River Scarpe to the east of the city; it was these two hard-pressed divisions that were still earmarked for the great 'Weygand Plan' counter-attack on the 26th. Other troops had been shuffled around to shore up the fragile line closer to the coast around the town of Cassel. Rations were low, ammunition supplies critical, and the Luftwaffe had apparently complete mastery of the sky, making air-supply drops impossible. Gort and Pownall's task was to try to fill any breaches as the German forces pressed forward and tightened the noose around them.

But then an intercepted German message revealing the halt order gave them cause for one of their rises in spirits. 'Can this be the turn of the tide?' wondered Pownall. 'It seems almost too much to hope for.' It certainly gave Gort an option which would otherwise have been lost. On the 25th, news arrived that Boulogne had fallen, then that the Germans in the north had broken across the River Lys in parts. The Belgians were still clinging on to Courtrai, but a dangerous gap had appeared between the end of the British north flank and the Belgian army. Gort ordered his last reserves, one brigade and one machine-gun company, to help fill the gap, but it was clear that unless it was more amply filled, the Germans could easily push through and get in behind the British from the north.

To make matters worse, General Dill, the Vice-CIGS, then flew over with the news that the BEF was getting criticism at home. The icing on the cake was a copy of a telegram from Reynaud to Churchill in which he complained that the British withdrawal from Arras and the Scarpe had seriously jeopardized the plans for the counter-attack on the 26th and that, as a result, Weygand had given the order to call off the proposed attack northward from the south. This was disingenuous: Weygand had called off the northward thrust because his forces south of the Somme had not managed to get their act together in time.

Increasingly urgent messages arrived from General Brooke, commanding II Corps on the northern flank. The gap was widening between Menin and Ypres; captured German documents confirmed that the Germans were intending to attack heavily towards Ypres. By five o'clock, news arrived from the Belgians that they were unable to close the hole in the line.

By this time, Gort was already reaching one of the toughest decisions of his life. Between 5 and 6 p.m., he was alone in his small office at his Premesques headquarters, first staring at the map spread out on the wall and then sitting at his desk. Just before 6 p.m., news arrived that General Altmayer would be providing only one division for the next day's supposed counter-attack; unbeknown to Gort, Général Blanchard, who had finally taken over from Billotte, had already told Weygand that the French First Army was too weak to take part in a counter-attack. Weygand had responded by giving Blanchard complete discretion as to whether the attack went ahead or not. The Weygand Plan was thus already utterly dead in the water. As at Arras, the French were bottling it once again. Even worse, Moroccan troops had apparently bolted at Carvin, to the south of Lille. Two battalions from 50th Division had been rushed forward to plug the gap there.

By six o'clock Gort's mind was made up. Cancelling the proposed attack for the following day, he ordered 5th Division to move immediately with all speed to the gap in the north between Menin and Ypres. Whatever trucks were available were to be used to move them the thirty miles north. As soon as 50th Division could extricate themselves from Carvin, they too were to follow. It was a brave decision, taken without consultation and which involved directly disobeying the orders of his French superiors and his chiefs back home. But by doing so, he had given the British army a tiny, tiny glimmer of hope.

The die had been cast. There was now only one course of action left to the besieged British forces, and that was to fall back to the coast and to try to evacuate as many troops as possible. 'I must not conceal from you,' Gort warned the Government the following morning, having received provisional authorization to fall back on Dunkirk, 'that a great part of the BEF and its equipment will inevitably be lost even in best circumstances.'

And should his prediction be true, then the will of Britain to fight on would be severely, if not irremediably, damaged. For Britain, the situation could hardly be more grave.

15

Fighter Command Enters the Fray

THE BLENHEIMS OF 18 Squadron – or what few remained after ten days of battle – left France on 20 and 21 May. Arthur Hughes flew into Lympne in Kent, a Fleet Air station, and was immediately impressed by the hospitality of the Royal Navy. 'They ordered extra food,' he jotted, 'the petty officers ate bully beef so that our sergeants could have the hot meal; they arranged transport, fixed billets – and by midnight I was relaxing in the luxury of a hot bath at the Grand Hotel, Folkestone.'

Arthur was one of the lucky ones – in fact, one of just four pilots that remained. Pilot Officer Light, who had only been married a few days before, had failed to return; he and his observer – who had been Arthur's first ever in the squadron – were never heard of again. Pilot Officer Rees was shot down on his way back to England, although by a Spitfire of 610 Squadron; he and Sergeant Pusey and a squadron mechanic managed to escape unhurt, but the aircraft had to be abandoned along with three others left in France.

The squadron was sent to Watton, in Norfolk, but was still considered operational. Less than three days after arriving back in England, Arthur was called at 3 a.m. and told to fly down to Hawkinge in Kent and from there to fly a mission over France. Ground mist prevented him from carrying out the planned dawn take-off so it was not before 11 a.m. that he finally got going. By 3 p.m., he was in the air again, sent off on a recce of Boulogne. Going in south of the town over Berck-sur-Mer, he then turned and flew up the coast only to find himself coming under heavy anti-aircraft fire. Smudges of black smoke were blossoming all around him, but by taking fairly dramatic evasive action, he escaped, only to hit more flak over Le Touquet. 'To say that I was scared would be an understatement,' he noted. 'My stomach was a dead load of lead and my mouth was so dry that my breath rasped, while my heart was rattling like a Browning.' Again, however, he managed to escape the attentions of the German flak gunners, and then, somehow willing himself on, dropped lower to around a thousand feet to investigate some suspicious objects to the side of a road which he realized were camouflaged enemy trucks. Then spotting a larger park of some fifty enemy vehicles from Guderian's 10th Panzer, he shouted back to his observer, Joe Strong, 'Get a report back on this—' when he felt as though he had been smacked in the mouth with a wet fish and at the same moment saw his left hand appear to momentarily disintegrate. With a sense of horror and excitement, he muttered to himself, 'I am hit', then, stunned and not thinking clearly, flew on towards Abbeville.

Gradually, he managed to gather his wits. His microphone was shattered, his oxygen mask was full of blood and was dripping on his tunic, and his hand was badly wounded at the base of his left forefinger; the skin had peeled back like an orange, so that he could see the bone and tendons, which looked curiously black. Spotting a few enemy columns, he then banked and headed back for home. He could feel no pain – only relief that he was still alive, mingled with apprehension that the treatment might prove more painful than the wound. Odd thoughts flitted through his mind: concern that he might meet some Messerschmitts, pride that he was a wounded hero, hope that he might now get a few weeks off. 'We got back to Hawkinge without difficulty and I landed with no trouble at all,' he scribbled, 'having lost much less blood than the gory mess suggested.' Even so, an ambulance was called, his hand was bandaged, and then he was taken off to Shorncliffe military hospital. Another of 18 Squadron's pilots was now out of action – for the time being at any rate. That left just three.

The RAF might have been frantically pulling its squadrons back from France, but this did not mean the Battle of France would not continue to drain away Dowding's precious fighters. Far from it, the mantle of responsibility had now been handed over to Fighter Command. Spitfire squadrons were now being sent over to the Pas de Calais to provide protection for the first troops that were being despatched back to Britain: the evacuation of non-fighting troops had begun on 20 May, while a number of Hurricane squadrons – such as Pete Brothers' 32 Squadron – were rotated out of the fray having been operating almost non-stop since first flying over to France. Dowding had been desperate to keep his Spitfires away from the fighting, mainly because the supply situation was so bad that he knew he could not have maintained their existence had they been shot down in the kind of numbers he had suspected would – and indeed did – happen in France. But with the losses to the Hurricane squadrons and with the new demands on Fighter Command over the Channel ports, Dowding could no longer maintain that policy. 'The Spitfires,' he wrote, 'had to take their share in the fighting.' Although Fighter Command was now operating over France, it was, in helping to safeguard the BEF, more directly defending Britain, its stated role. There would be no more letters from Dowding urging that his fighters should be kept at home. In his mind, the Battle of Britain had begun.

Three squadrons were sent on offensive patrols over the Channel ports on 23 May, and two of them, 74 and 92 Squadrons, were equipped with Spitfires. Based at Northolt, to the west of London, 92 Squadron flew off at dawn to Hornchurch in Essex, refuelled, then flew on over the Channel. As they approached the French coast, 21-year-old Tony Bartley heard his flight commander, Paddy Green, tell him over the R/T, 'Stick to my tail and for God's sake keep a look out behind.' The son of an Irish scholar who had joined the Indian Civil Service for health reasons, Tony had been born in Bengal and then sent back to England and to boarding school. Good-looking, charming and a decent sportsman, Tony had left school fully expecting to follow his father into colonial service. This, however, required an apprenticeship at a firm of London chartered accountants, which he found soul-destroying to say the least. Quitting after a year, he was then playing rugby with an air force officer whom he greatly liked and admired and who suggested Tony join the RAF instead. After eight hours flying Tiger Moths at West Malling Flying Club, Tony was hooked. By May 1939, he was at No. 13 Flying Training School in Drem, Scotland.

By the time he was awarded his wings, shortly after war was declared, Tony looked set to join either Coastal or Bomber Command. This had been a great disappointment, but then, to his surprise, he was posted to 92 Squadron, a fighter unit then flying twin-engine Blenheims. Things improved further when, at the beginning of March, 92 Squadron had been re-equipped with Spitfires. So he was a single-engine fighter pilot after all and flying what he truly believed was the most perfect flying machine ever created.

Now, at around 11.45 a.m., Tony was given the chance to test the Spitfire's performance in combat. The first he knew about any enemy aircraft was as they crossed Cap Gris Nez and someone shouted over the R/T, 'Look out, 109s!' At the same moment, Tony saw a flight of eight 109s from 1/JG 27 and then they were swooping down upon them. Singling out one of the Messerschmitts, Tony closed in upon it but it then turned into a tight circle. Following him, Tony could see the German pilot crouched in his cockpit, looking back at him. With the enemy fighter filling his gunsight, Tony pressed down on the firing button and felt the Spitfire shudder as his eight Browning machine-guns began spitting bullets. They were hitting the fuselage and tail-plane of the 109 but then bullets were thumping into his own aircraft and another 109 flashed past. He had forgotten Paddy's warning.

Now his flight commander swung in front of him, opening fire on the 109 still in front. Bits of the Messerschmitt's wings flew off and then the pilot flick-rolled his plane and dropped out. Tony was close enough to see the German pilot's helmet fly off, and his face and billowing blond hair. 'He didn't pull the rip cord,' noted Tony. By now low on fuel, he radioed to Paddy that he was turning for home when he suddenly saw one of their own Spitfires blazing earthwards.

Also embroiled in this first dogfight was Pilot Officer Allan Wright. Tony may have been a gregarious extrovert, but Allan was a quieter, more softly spoken young man, equally popular within the squadron, who appreciated his gentleness and wry sense of humour. Fiercely bright, he had won a Prize Cadetship to the RAF College at Cranwell in 1938, commissioning with his wings the previous October. He too had got in a long burst of fire at one of the enemy planes although he was not sure whether he hit it or not.

He had also seen a burning Spitfire plunging to the ground but it was not until they were safely back at Hornchurch that he learned from fellow pilot Paul Klipsch that the stricken aircraft had been that of Pat Learmond, his best and closest friend. No-one had seen a parachute. Still dazed by the adrenalin of the first combat, Allan could barely take it in. In any case, all too soon, having rearmed, refuelled and had their damaged Spitfires hastily repaired, they were ordered to fly another patrol. This time they ran into a larger formation of enemy aircraft – some twenty Me 110s protecting a formation of fifteen Heinkel 111s and, above them, 109s.

Despite their being hugely outnumbered, their CO, Roger Bushell, ordered them to attack. Paddy Green's flight were to protect them and defend them against the 110s while Bushell and the rest went for the bombers. Tony Bartley managed to get on to the tail of one Me 110 that had shark's teeth painted under its engine cowling. The rear-gunner opened fire at him, but on Tony's second burst, the Messerschmitt flipped over on to its back and spiralled out of the sky, engines on fire. The 110s now formed a defensive circle with the Spitfires wheeling and circling and trying to get inside it. Allan Wright shot at about five different aircraft. The air was filled with tracer, arcs of flashing bullets streaming and criss-crossing the sky. Tony found himself crouching lower in his cockpit to make himself a smaller target. Allan meanwhile had latched on to one Messerschmitt, opening fire and following him down until both were hedge-hopping across France. Out of ammunition and low on fuel, he eventually turned for home.

By the time the squadron had landed back at Hornchurch once more, they were without a further four of their pilots. Roger Bushell had been shot down, although he had managed to belly-land east of Boulogne, where he was captured. Flying Officer Gillies had bailed out and was missing. Paul Klipsch had been killed, and Paddy Green had been wounded in the leg, and, having made it to Manston, had been taken to Shorncliffe, where he joined Arthur Hughes. Tony Bartley had scored his first confirmed kill, but his Spitfire looked like a colander. 'Back in the mess,' noted Tony, 'we downed unconscionable pints of beer.'

'It has been a glorious day for the Squadron,' the duty officer wrote in the squadron diary, 'with twenty-three German machines brought down, but the loss of the Commanding officer and the three others has been a very severe blow to us all.' It was as well they did not know the real score for the day: four aircraft and pilots lost and a fifth wounded and damaged in return for five enemy aircraft – that is, honours even.

Allan left the beer-drinking to the others and went and had a bath. It was only then, as he soaked in the comfort of the hot, steaming water, the enormity of what had happened and the terrible loss of his friend, Pat, began to hit home. He could not accept that his clever, brilliant friend, who had such a promising, fulfilling life ahead of him, was now gone. A desperate feeling of helpless loss swept over him. 'And then I broke down and wept,' says Allan. 'I wept in a way that I never had before or have since.'

*

That same day, the three *Staffeln* of I/JG 52 were also flying over Dunkirk for the first time. The 2nd Staffel had only reached Charleville that morning, having had a frustrating fortnight flying in support of Army Group A. 'I am doing very well,' Leutnant Ulrich Steinhilper had written to his parents on 15 May, 'however, I have not yet managed to get any Frenchies in front of my guns.' The next day he wrote again. 'Still no contact with the enemy.' Nor was there the day after that. Then orders arrived sending them into France. 'Now everybody is full of hope again,' he noted.

They finally reached Charleville the next day, but with no ground support or supplies Ulrich and some of the other pilots had decided to explore the town. Ulrich had been stunned by how empty the place was – the entire population seemed to have gone. Virtually everywhere they looked, notices had been pasted with 'Nicht Plünderen' and warning that any pillagers would be shot. When Ulrich's friend Kühle picked up and began looking at a pair of shoes, he began to feel a little uneasy. Then a guard came over and told them the rule applied to officers too. Apparently two privates had stolen some shoes, and were caught, summarily court-martialled and then executed.

By the afternoon, their groundcrew had caught up and the *Gruppe* were ordered on their first mission to the Channel coast. The pilots were all briefed beforehand, and warned that the British pilots and their aircraft were not to be underestimated. The weather was poor and visibility bad, and by the time they reached the coast, they had just fifteen minutes before they needed to turn back.

Even so, as they approached Dunkirk, the visibility improved and there ahead of them they saw the mass of smoke drifting up from the port. Ulrich could see Spitfires and Hurricanes attacking Stukas. 'It was immediately clear,' he noted, 'that we were up against very tenacious opposition.'

Ulrich was twenty-one, from Stuttgart, the son of a teacher. His had been a happy enough childhood, but the family had never had much money. Then, early in the summer of 1936, his school had been visited by officers from the Kriegsmarine and Luftwaffe. Both did good sales pitches, but Ulrich had been electrified by the possibility that a poor boy like himself could learn to fly. Immediately applying to join, to his great thrill he was asked to then attend the selection centre in Berlin, where he would undergo three days of tests. Confident he had done well enough in the examinations in speech and debate, he was less sure about the physical tests – kidney problems a few years earlier had excused him from sports and he knew he was not as fit as he might have been. Nonetheless, after two and a half days, ten names were read out, and his was one of them. He was in.

Three and a half years later, he was a lieutenant in a fighter squadron flying over Dunkirk; and as a pre-war regular with two years' flying since being posted to the fighter *Gruppe*, he was an experienced pilot too. What he lacked was combat experience. Over Dunkirk, it seemed that was about to change.

Helmut Kühle was leading the *Staffel*. A Condor veteran, he now held the others back from diving down on the mêlée below, instead circling carefully above. Ulrich was chomping at the bit. He had been waiting in the sidelines for so long and wanted his chance of gaining his first victory. 'As we wheeled around the dark cloud over Dunkirk,' noted Ulrich, 'Kühle cautioned us to stay well clear of its sinister billows.' If they wanted surprises, he warned them, there were plenty around the edges of the forbidding mass of cloud.

Their fifteen minutes up, they returned to Charleville having had a whiff of the action to come but once again without having fired their guns. Debates over tactics raged once they were back at their billet, but Kühle held his ground; he would only attack when there was a reasonable chance of success and equally the risk of losses was less. There was no point plunging down into the fray only to be outnumbered and shot down. His policy, he insisted, ensured that the *Staffel* would gain experience without suffering losses. However much Ulrich and his fellow pilots might have been itching to get amongst the enemy, Kühle's stance was a sensible one. They would all get their chance soon enough.

Back in London, the Ministry of Information had promised openness and that was what the British public were getting. In his broadcast on 22 May, Duff Cooper had admitted that not only was the situation 'grave', but it was also a fact that the enemy's intention was to take the Channel ports and from there 'launch war upon this island'. On the 23rd, the King broadcast to the nation and called for a National Day of Prayer to be held the coming Sunday, 26 May. The following day, Friday the 24th, *The Times* ran the headline 'Germans on the coast', while Beaverbrook's *Evening Standard* warned people that 'We would do better to prepare for the worst'. Nonetheless, most newspapers tried to remain as upbeat as possible, pointing out that the game was not up yet, that France was expected to rally, and that the RAF was blowing up targets and shooting down enemy planes at an impressive rate.

Even so, neither the news emerging from France nor the fact that the King felt an appeal to God was necessary was hardly encouraging. Most British people did appear to be keeping calm, but few could have doubted the seriousness of the situation, even if perhaps not just how grave it was. Daidie Penna, for one, was not sure what to think. On the 22nd she and her husband were wondering whether she should take the children back to Port Isaac in Cornwall, where they had evacuated to the previous autumn. The next day, things seemed brighter again. She met one man who said, 'Yesterday we reached rock bottom – now the tide will turn.' By the 24th, she felt even more encouraged. 'News fairly good,' she noted. 'Apparently we are holding them again and also cutting in on the spear-head of their attack.'

Those close to intelligence sources, however, were struggling to see much cause for hope. Britain appeared to be gripped by the biggest threat to her independence she had ever faced, one that was eclipsing the Spanish threat in 1588 and even that of Napoleon's France at the turn of the previous century. Deputy Director of Air Intelligence at the Air Ministry was Group Captain Tommy Elmhirst. It was Tommy's job to head the German Section, responsible for calculating the strength and potential of the Luftwaffe, a position he had held since the middle of January. This he had found a singularly depressing job, for by the spring the section had a reasonably accurate picture, albeit slightly over-estimated, of the German air force, its formations, reserves and, above all, its strength and the location of front-line units. Compared with the RAF, the Luftwaffe strength seemed so immense Tommy feared the outlook appeared very depressing.

His sources were mostly from signal intelligence, or 'sigint'. Since 1935, the RAF had maintained a radio intelligence service known as the 'Y' Service for listening in to and collating low-grade wireless traffic, usually between aircraft, low-grade radio and telephone traffic, and other signals traffic such as navigational beacons. More recently, the service had acquired high-grade ciphers encrypted by German Enigma coding machines. The Government Code and Cipher School (GCSC) at Bletchley Park had begun to break general Enigma traffic regularly during the Norwegian campaign and the Luftwaffe key fairly regularly since January. Luftwaffe Enigma traffic was not yet being deciphered with particular speed, but, combined with Y Service sigint, it had enabled Tommy and his team to build up a picture of the Luftwaffe that was disturbing to say the least. What worried Tommy was that should Britain be left to tackle the German air force on its own, the chances of the RAF beating it seemed slim indeed.

Aged forty-five, diminutive and quietly spoken, Tommy had a good-humoured face and large, bushy eyebrows that lent him an air of sagaciousness that was not without foundation. His background was naval – from ships he had been transferred to airships in the Royal Navy Air Service, and by the end of the last war found himself part of the newly formed Royal Air Force. And although an experienced pilot, since 1925 he had worked in intelligence, first under Boom Trenchard on the Middle East section, and most recently as air attaché at the British Embassy in Ankara.

A naturally positive person, he would attend his daily Air Staff meetings desperately trying to find something encouraging to say, but since the start of the Norway campaign in April he had struggled to find ways to lighten proceedings. 'The meetings,' he noted, 'were conducted in an atmosphere of unrelieved gloom.' His job as Deputy Director of Air Intelligence also meant a seat on the Joint Intelligence Committee (JIC) that met daily as well, and whose task it was to provide daily intelligence summaries for the Chiefs of Staff and War Cabinet as well as appreciations of Germany's probable intentions. As a member of the JIC, Tommy was thus amongst the very few to know the true state of affairs. Now, he felt more gloomy than ever. He simply could not see how the BEF could ever be evacuated. 'It looked,' he noted, 'as if the whole British field army, men, guns, vehicles, ammunition, tanks, everything, would cease to exist.'

It was armed with the kind of intelligence that Tommy and his colleagues were providing, combined with increasingly dire messages from France, that the Prime Minister and his Cabinet had lurched into a new, deeper level of crisis.

Saturday, 25 May, was another glorious day, 'if,' as Daidie Penna noted, 'one really noticed the weather'. Certainly the Prime Minister and his senior ministers had little opportunity to enjoy the early-summer sun. Weekends had traditionally been sacrosanct and kept free of politics but not any more. During the day, first at Cabinet, then at Chiefs of Staff meetings, and as reports and messages arrived, and finally at the Defence Committee meeting, it became increasingly clear that the French were not being entirely straight with them. As General Dill's report showed, Gort had kept Blanchard informed of all his decisions, which made it seem clear that the French had merely been looking for a pretext for cancelling the Weygand Plan and turning the blame on to Gort. 'The information given us by Weygand himself,' Chamberlain noted, 'as to the capture of Amiens, Albery and Peronne on May 23rd turned out to be false.' Reynaud's complaint about Gort of the previous day was looking rather hollow.

The truth was that neither Weygand nor Marshal Pétain were very keen on continuing the war. Pétain was a national hero in France, the saviour of Verdun in the last war, and newly appointed Vice-Prime Minister by Reynaud. It had been a move to try to stiffen the resolve of the French, but Reynaud now found himself faced with the two most powerful soldiers in the country presenting the united front of two Anglophobes who had been opposed to the Anglo-French alliance from the very start. Since both had been senior commanders in the 1914–18 war, both were indelibly scarred by the experience and agreed on one thing: the appalling loss of life could not be repeated. In Paris on the 25th, at a meeting of the Comité de Guerre, Weygand told Reynaud, Pétain and the President, Albert Lebrun, that the situation was hopeless. France had committed the immense mistake of entering into the war without the materiel or the military doctrine that were needed, he told them. He was right about the second point, wrong about the first. 'It is probable,' he added, 'that we will have to pay dearly for this criminal thoughtlessness.' Weygand, supported by Pétain, urged them to make a separate peace, which would go against the terms of the alliance with Britain. The rest of the Comité was not so sure. What was recognized by Reynaud was the need to explain the situation to the British. The next day he would go to London.

Of course, Churchill did not know about this discussion but it did not need a fly on the wall to know that the French will was crumbling and that they might soon seek terms. The Prime Minister put this to the second meeting of the Defence Committee at around 10 p.m. that night. 'If France went out of the war,' he told them, 'she must, however, make it a condition that our Army was allowed to leave France intact, and to take away its munitions, and that the soil of France was not used for an attack on England. Furthermore, France must retain her Fleet.' Clearly, both Britain and France had now accepted that there could be only one result in France itself. It was a question of when, not if. The alliance still stood, but both countries now had to look after number one. Gort thought most of the BEF would be lost; so too did Churchill. Then the mighty Luftwaffe would be unleashed against Britain. Would British will then crumble too? There were also the Italians to consider. On 16 May, Churchill appealed to Mussolini, the Fascist dictator, not to enter the war. 'Down the ages,' he wrote, 'above all other calls came the cry that the joint heirs of Latin and Christian civilisation must not be ranged against one another in mortal strife. Hearken to it, I beseech you in all honour and respect, before the dread signal is given. It will never be given by us.' Mussolini replied that Britain had entered the war to honour her treaty with the Poles and that Italy felt bound not to dishonour her treaty with Germany – the Pact of Steel, made back in March the previous year. 'The response was hard,' wrote Churchill. 'It had at least the merit of candour.' So that was that: Italy would soon be in too. The outlook was grim, very grim.

It was thus not surprising that certain men and leaders in Britain now began to think rather like Weygand and Pétain: that the situation was hopeless, and that surely it was better to come to terms with Germany – terms that might not necessarily be too bad – rather than drag the war on, with all its terrors and loss of life, especially when the outcome, now or later, looked so certain to end in German victory.

Earlier on that Saturday, Lord Halifax had met with Signor Giuseppe Bastianini, the Italian Ambassador in London. He had told Churchill what he was doing and the PM had agreed to the meeting so long as no word of the meeting got out, as that would be seen as a confession of weakness. They met that afternoon and, in a conversation shrouded in diplomatic euphemism, Halifax asked Bastianini whether there was any way in which Italy could be persuaded to stay out of the war. Bastianini replied that he would, of course, pass on any offer, then asked whether Halifax thought Britain might be open to a broader discussion not just with Italy but with 'other countries' as well. They were now talking about Germany. Halifax said that would be difficult while there was a war still going on. 'Once such a discussion were begun,' Bastianini told him, 'war would be pointless.'

Both agreed that their countries would be willing to discuss any settlement that protected European peace for the next century. Halifax, for one, was beginning to explore the chances of finding a way out. And he was not only the Foreign Secretary; he was also one of the most respected men in Britain.

16

Crisis

The American journalist William Shirer had been given a guided tour of the front thanks to Goebbels's Propaganda Ministry. On the 20th, he had been taken to the Albert Canal then on to Brussels and Louvain and across war-torn Belgium. He had seen close up the powerful effects of the German war machine. The next day he had even witnessed at first hand the fighting along the River Scheldt. 'You have to see the German army in action to believe it,' he noted. He was hugely impressed by the power of the Luftwaffe, by the fitness and high training of the infantry, and by Germany's machinery. 'All day long at the front,' he noted, 'you pass unending mechanized columns. They stretch clear across Belgium, unbroken . . . It is a gigantic, impersonal war machine, run as coolly and efficiently, say, as our automobile industry in Detroit. Directly behind the front, with the guns pounding daylight out of your ears and the airplanes roaring overhead, and thousands of motorized vehicles thundering by on dusty roads, officers and men alike remain cool and business-like.' Of course, this is exactly what Goebbels wanted him and other journalists to see and believe. The trip had been orchestrated very carefully. A single motorized division would have given William the impression of German mechanized might. And over Belgium, where the Germans had been pushing back the weak Belgian army, it was an easy task to make the conquerors look impressive. The German army was clearly better than any other they were up against, but that did not mean it was a superbly refined and highly mechanized fighting machine by any means. But the world believed in its military might and it was essential that they continued to do so. The psychological overpowering of their enemies remained an important weapon for Nazi Germany.

Gort had given the order for the evacuation of all 'useless mouths' through Boulogne, Calais and Dunkirk on 19 May. These were non-combat troops as well as the sick and wounded. At Boulogne, two Guards battalions had arrived fresh from Dover on the 21st to help cover the evacuation; then, when this was completed, and having fought a valiant rearguard, they re-embarked on the night of 23 May. Calais was also reinforced, with a battalion of the 3rd Royal Tank Regiment and 30th Brigade hastily despatched from England to hold the town, block the roads in, and then help relieve Boulogne. By the time 30th Brigade reached Calais on 23rd May, it was too late to save Boulogne and instead Brigadier Claude Nicholson began organizing the defence of the port. Later that day, Nicholson received fresh orders to try to force a desperately needed convoy of rations and fuel through to Dunkirk. By the following morning, with Guderian's panzers already surrounding the port, this too proved impossible. Instead, the order to evacuate the port was given in principle.

However, on the 24th, control of all the Channel ports was handed to Général Marie-Bertrand-Alfred Fagalde of the French XVI Corps and he immediately forbade the evacuation, which was upheld by Churchill. The old port now became something of a personal concern to the Prime Minister. To evacuate would be madness, he said. 'The only effect of evacuating Calais would be to transfer the forces now blocking it to Dunkirk,' he told Ismay. 'Calais must be held for many reasons, but specially to hold the enemy on its front.' This was relayed to Nicholson on the morning of 25 May, with orders that in essence told him he was on his own and could expect no reinforcements, but was to hold out for as long as possible.

Later that day, Guderian's 2nd Panzer sent a surrender demand to Nicholson. The brigadier replied stoically, 'The answer is no, as it is the British Army's duty to fight as well as it is the German's.'

Having enforced the halt decision on the panzers on the afternoon of 24 May, Hitler then gave von Rundstedt complete authority to lift the order whenever he saw fit. The outrage within the German units ranged along the Canal Line was intense. Von Bock, commander of Army Group B, was incensed. His infantry divisions, still mostly on foot despite the large number of captured bicycles, had to advance fifty miles to reach Dunkirk, and through organized and dug-in British divisions. The panzer and motorized divisions, on the other hand, were all lined up almost within spitting distance. General von Kluge, who had originally suggested the close-up, was as one with von Kleist that the order should be rescinded immediately. He had planned to push through the narrowest point of the corridor in which the BEF and French First Army were now trapped, capturing the low heights around the town of Cassel, then heading straight to Courtrai and linking up with Army Group B – and, in so doing, cutting off the British retreat to Dunkirk still some thirty miles to the north-west. Fully armed, highly confident panzers, a-brimming with supplies and ammunition against infantry low on rounds and increasingly hungry would have been no contest at all. The BEF would have been annihilated.

Even more galling was that for a number of units who had already made it across the Canal Line, the order was not a halt but, rather, a retreat, as they had to pull back across the water. Early on the 25th, Guderian visited the Waffen-SS Leibstandarte Division and found them crossing the River Aa in defiance of the order. Guderian crossed too and eventually found the commander, Obergruppenführer Sepp Dietrich, in the ruins of a castle on a well-placed hillock called Mount Watten. When Guderian asked him why he was disobeying orders, Dietrich pointed out that Mount Watten commanded a very strong position and that the task of crossing the Aa would be very much harder if it was in enemy hands. Guderian not only approved Dietrich's action, but ordered some of 2nd Panzer to move up in support.

Von Brauchitsch had been summoned to see Hitler on the afternoon of the 24th. It had been his chance to point out both the lunacy of the measure, and the golden opportunity now before them to finish off the battle in the north with the destruction of the BEF. When he arrived back at the OKH command post at 8 p.m., Halder found him shaken and humiliated; far from convincing Hitler, von Brauchitsch had been forced to listen to one of the Führer's furious rants. The Commander-in-Chief tried to put across his arguments, but failed. 'Apparently again a very unpleasant interview with the Führer,' noted Halder tersely.

However, while von Brauchitsch had been receiving his tongue-lashing from Hitler for daring to act independently, Halder had been working out how to get around the halt order. Late in the afternoon he had come up with a cunning plan and accordingly issued a message to Army Groups A and B. 'Expanding on the directives in the May 24 Army High Command order' he gave the 'go-ahead' for the continuation of the attack towards Dunkirk–Cassel–Estaires–Armentières–Ypres–Ostend – in other words, not the entire Canal Line, but just the northern half, which would shut the gate on the retreating British. This was clever wording; a 'go-ahead' was not the same as a new order, and it meant von Rundstedt need not lose face, nor the Führer order, strictly speaking, be disobeyed.

Incredibly, however, von Rundstedt dug in his heels and refused to forward on the message to von Kleist or von Kluge. Halder could scarcely believe it. 'This is a complete reversal of the plan,' he railed. 'I wanted to make AGp. A the hammer and AGp. B the anvil in this operation. Now B will be the hammer and A the anvil. As AGp. B is confronted with a consolidated front, progress will be slow and casualties high.' A crisis was now boiling over not just in Paris and London but within the German army too. Halder urged von Brauchitsch to try again to persuade Hitler to change his mind that morning, but Hitler was having none of it. The decision was to be von Rundstedt's Hitler told him, and von Rundstedt's only. And von Rundstedt, along with his Chief of Staff, General Georg von Sodenstern, was determined to keep the halt order in place throughout 25 May. This was more than just differences of military ideology – this was pure stubborn bloody-mindedness. That the Commander-in-Chief of the army was not permitted to move his forces as he saw fit was crazy.

Hitler's almost complete lack of military understanding was further proved with his indulgence of Feldmarschall Göring. On the 23rd, Göring had been sitting at a heavy oak table beside his train when the news arrived that the enemy was now almost entirely surrounded in Flanders. Banging his fist on the table, he declared, 'This is a wonderful opportunity for the Luftwaffe. I must speak to the Führer at once.' He then rang Hitler and told him that his Luftwaffe could set the Channel ports ablaze then destroy the British troops trapped in the encirclement. Hitler told him to do so, believing Göring's boast – this way, he reasoned, the army could be kept in its place but the end result would be the same.

Listening to the conversation was Hitler's army adjutant, Major Gerhard Engel, a 34-year-old career officer from Frankfurt an der Oder in east Germany, who had joined Hitler's staff two years earlier. As the

Führer's army adjutant, Gerhard was the intermediary between Hitler and von Brauchitsch and Halder. Although he was only a major, his access was considerable – all three of Hitler's service adjutants spent long hours at the beck and call of the Führer and would also accompany him on trips and at other functions. Gerhard was hardly a man to rock the boat, but even he was incensed by Göring's claims and by Hitler's agreement. Afterwards, General Jodl, OKW Chief of Staff, told Gerhard that Göring had bitten off more than he could chew.

Hermann did not think so, however. 'Our air force,' he told Milch, 'is to mop up the British. I've persuaded the Führer to hold the army back.' Milch immediately expressed his concerns: the Channel ports were at the limit of most of the fighter units' range, and they had already been involved in heavy and continual fighting since the offensive began. Furthermore, there was still a job to do supporting the army. Göring brushed aside such worries. 'The army always wants to act the gentleman. They round up the British as prisoners with as little harm to them as possible. The Führer wants them to be taught a lesson.' General Kesselring was as concerned as Milch about these new orders, and also pointed out the difficulty of such a task. Bombing Rotterdam into the ground had been one thing; destroying the Channel ports and the British was quite another. 'I pointed out to Göring that the modern Spitfires had recently appeared,' Kesselring noted, 'making our air operations difficult and costly.' Kesselring's misgivings also fell on deaf ears. Sadly for the Germans, Göring was revealing a lack of military acumen to match that of Hitler.

Nor did he help matters two days later when he visited the Führer. The two men went for a stroll around Felsennet, Hitler followed by his army adjutant, Gerhard Engel. 'Impression,' Gerhard jotted later in his diary, 'G. successfully stirred it up against Army. F[ührer] emphasised repeatedly the political reliability of the Luftwaffe in contrast to the Army.'

Now that both French and British commanders had accepted the inevitable, they began being more co-operative with one another again. Early on the 26th, Gort saw Blanchard, who was not only reconciled to the decision to fall back towards the coast, but positively helpful in drawing up lines of withdrawal to the north. The two agreed that certain roads should be used exclusively by the BEF. On the night of the 26th/27th, I and II Corps, having left rearguards at the frontier defences, were to swing back into the centre of the corridor while the French First Army prolonged the line. The following night, the bulk of the BEF was to fall behind the River Lys, with rearguards protecting the new line until the night after that. Thus his men were to fight by day and fall back under the cover of darkness. He did not have enough men to hold a continuous line along the southern flank along the Canal Line, so instead Gort decided to man the main villages, towns and high points and turn them into strongpoint redoubts.

Although Gort was careful not to mention anything about evacuation to Blanchard at this stage, he and Pownall were meanwhile making preparations for the defence of Dunkirk. Fortunately, a canal ran south from the port to Bergues, some five miles away. Running across Bergues, roughly east–west, was another canal, the Bergues–Furnes Canal, which went all the way to Nieuport, some twelve miles to the east. From Nieuport, a river ran two miles to the sea. These canals and rivers were to mark the boundary of the Dunkirk bridgehead. It was a strong defensive position. In front and behind lay a myriad of other dykes and irrigation channels that were difficult for vehicles to cross and easily flooded – which lessened the effect of shelling and made life even harder for motor transport. The Flanders countryside all around was flat as a board; only lines of poplars, small villages and red-tiled farmhouses interrupted the view. As a holding position, it wasn't at all bad.

Gort put General Ronald Adam in charge of preparing the port and the perimeter, relieving him of command of III Corps and sending with him the BEF's Quartermaster-General plus a bevy of other staff officers to help. How many troops – if any – would get away was still anyone's guess, however, and already Dunkirk was being heavily bombed. 'It is all a first-class mess-up,' noted Henry Pownall, 'and events go slowly from bad to worse, like a Greek tragedy the end seems inevitably to come closer and closer with each succeeding day and event.'

In Britain, it was the National Day of Prayer, as called for by the King, although for Britain's leaders there were more practical matters to attend to before they got down on their knees and appealed to the Almighty. The first War Cabinet of the day was held at 9 a.m., in the Cabinet Room at 10 Downing Street, although Churchill was still living further down Whitehall at the Admiralty. Also present were the Chiefs of Staff. Churchill began by telling them that the previous evening he had received a letter from his personal representative in Paris, General Sir Edward

Spears, which he then read out. The French were deeply pessimistic; the Weygand Plan had been cancelled. Blanchard's Army Group had lost all its heavy guns and had no armoured vehicles. Refugees hampered any movement. The Belgians, he warned them, were about to capitulate. That was not unexpected in the circumstances – after all, where could they go once they had fallen back to the sea? Nonetheless, it caused a further headache for Gort, who had just plugged the gap between the BEF and the Belgian army but would have to fill another hole in his line once the Belgians were out of the fight altogether. As Churchill pointed out – and this had still not been authorized by the War Cabinet at this stage – evacuation now looked like the only option. This being the case, there was a good chance, he told them, of getting off a considerable number of the BEF. There was little reason, however, for his optimism on that score.

Churchill then told them that Paul Reynaud would shortly be arriving and that the Cabinet should be prepared to hear from him that the French could not carry on the fight. The Prime Minister then announced that he had previously asked the Chiefs of Staff to prepare a document about what Britain should do if the French were to drop out of the war. 'What are the prospects of our continuing the war alone against Germany and probably Italy?' Churchill asked, reading out the remit he had given the Chiefs of Staff. 'Can the Navy and the Air Force hold out reasonable hopes of preventing serious invasion, and could the forces gathered in this Island cope with raids from the air involving detachments not greater than 10,000 men?'

The Chiefs of Staff made some comments in turn and then Halifax spoke up. 'On the broader issue,' he said, 'we have to face the fact that it is not so much now a question of imposing a complete defeat upon Germany but of safeguarding the independence of our own Empire and if possible that of France.' In other words, he now believed the Nazis were unbeatable. In this connection, he then told them about his meeting with Bastianini the day before. Mussolini's principal wish was to secure peace in Europe.

That would mean peace under German domination. 'That we could never accept,' said Churchill emphatically. 'We must ensure our complete liberty and independence. I am opposed to any negotiations which might lead to a derogation of our rights and power.'

None of the other War Cabinet members agreed or disagreed with either Halifax or Churchill, and after a few more comments on Italy's intentions, the eighteen-page aide-memoire prepared by the Chiefs of

Staff, entitled 'British Strategy in a Certain Eventuality', was handed out. Chamberlain then asked if it was possible to ask the French whether Italy could be bought off. 'This,' he pointed out, 'might at least keep matters going.'

'I agree that this point is worth bearing in mind,' said Churchill.

As Halifax glanced through the document he revealed his own lack of military understanding. Britain's ability to carry on, he said, depended on whether air superiority could be established over the Luftwaffe. No, Newall interjected, it depended on Britain preventing the Germans from achieving such air superiority as would enable them to invade this country. Halifax now blundered again. 'If France collapses,' he said, 'I assume that the Germans would no longer need large land forces. They will then be free to switch the bulk of their effort to air production. What effect would that have on the crucial question of air?' He was being naive about Germany's relations with the Soviet Union and also the difficulties of switching from one type of war production to another. Halifax then suggested that in the last resort they ask the French to put their factories out of gear.

Any undertakings of this case would be worthless, pointed out Chamberlain, 'since the terms of peace which the Germans would propose would inevitably prevent their fulfilment'.

'I agree,' said Churchill. 'It has to be expected, moreover, that the Germans would make the terms of any peace offer as attractive as possible to the French, and lay emphasis on the fact that their quarrel was not with France but with England.'

A clear split was emerging between Churchill, who was anxious not to become involved in any dialogue with Germany or Italy, and Halifax, who believed it was worth considering. The progression from this was either fighting on or suing for peace, as both men were well aware. For the time being, however, the discussions had to be put on hold. It was time to break up the meeting: the service at Westminster Abbey which was the centrepiece of the National Day of Prayer was due to start at 10 a.m. Churchill and Chamberlain then hurried down Whitehall to the Abbey. The King and Queen arrived punctually, both carrying gas masks and accompanied by Wilhelmina, the Queen of the Netherlands. Churchill, however, after staying for the first ten minutes or so, quietly slipped away to be ready to meet M. Reynaud.

Halifax had returned straight to the Foreign Office, where he was visited by Bastianini; the two achieved no more than they had the day before. Soon after, Churchill was lunching with Reynaud at Admiralty House. The French Prime Minister was, unlike Pétain and Weygand, an Anglophile, but although he had not, as Churchill had feared, come to tell them they were about to throw in the towel, he made it clear that the writing was on the wall. He personally would never sue for peace but a time might come when he was forced to resign; he now told Churchill about the depth of Pétain's and Weygand's defeatism. Even Reynaud admitted the war could no longer be won on land. Churchill told him that as soon as the north of France was cleared up the Germans would not turn south but immediately begin attacking Britain. Reynaud disagreed. 'The dream of all Germans,' he said, 'was to conquer Paris.'

'Whatever happens,' Churchill replied, 'we are not prepared to give in. We would rather go down fighting than be enslaved to Germany.'

Reynaud now remained at Admiralty House while Churchill returned to Downing Street for the second War Cabinet of the day. Now, at the second Cabinet, Halifax was more bullish. Since the morning session, all had read the Chiefs of Staffs' aide-memoire, in which the following scenario was envisaged: most of the BEF lost, France making peace with Germany, Italy entering the war, and Europe, from Norway to North Africa, either in German hands or under German domination. Britain *could* still hold out, but only if the United States gave full financial and material support, and if the Royal Navy and RAF managed to maintain a control over and around the country. At the back, in an appendix, were Tommy Elmhirst's estimates of Luftwaffe strength and that of the RAF. On 17 May, the RAF had just 491 fighters, including obsolescent Defiants. In contrast, he believed the Luftwaffe still had some 4,500 aircraft. Naval comparisons were more favourable: 319 of all types of ships for the Royal Navy compared with around a hundred for the Kriegsmarine. However, the Italian navy had some 400 vessels of all kinds, which then rather redressed the balance should the Italians come in with Germany, as it looked certain they would.

It was sobering stuff, and understandable that Halifax, for one, believed they were staring down the barrel. Their survival depended on so many ifs – 'eventualities' – that could in no way be even remotely guaranteed. Churchill had always been something of a warmonger; how could his judgement be trusted at this darkest hour?

Halifax now stated that he favoured an approach to Italy; Churchill said he doubted much would come of it but agreed that perhaps the War Cabinet should consider it. Soon after, the meeting broke up and Halifax

SITUATION ON THE EVENING OF 26 May 1940

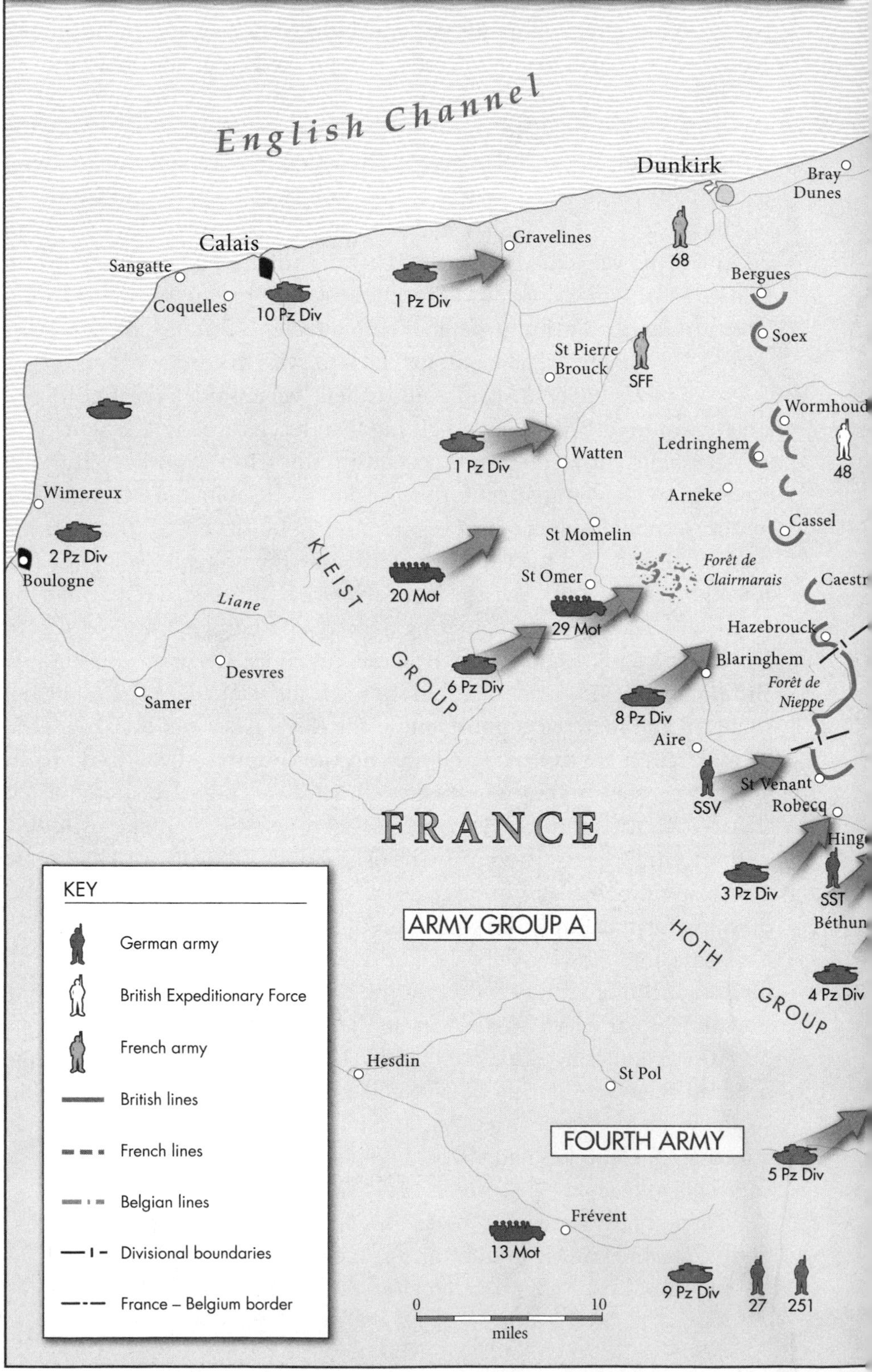

English Channel
Dunkirk
Bray Dunes
Calais
Sangatte
Coquelles
10 Pz Div
Gravelines
1 Pz Div
68
Bergues
Soex
St Pierre Brouck
SFF
Wormhoud
Ledringhem
48
Watten
1 Pz Div
Arneke
Wimereux
2 Pz Div
Boulogne
KLEIST GROUP
20 Mot
St Momelin
Cassel
Forêt de Clairmarais
St Omer
Caestr
Liane
29 Mot
Hazebrouck
Blaringhem
Desvres
6 Pz Div
Forêt de Nieppe
Samer
8 Pz Div
Aire
St Venant
SSV
Robecq
FRANCE
Hing
3 Pz Div
SST
Béthun
ARMY GROUP A
HOTH GROUP
4 Pz Div
Hesdin
St Pol
FOURTH ARMY
5 Pz Div
Frévent
13 Mot
9 Pz Div
27
251

KEY
German army
British Expeditionary Force
French army
British lines
French lines
Belgian lines
Divisional boundaries
France – Belgium border

0 10
miles

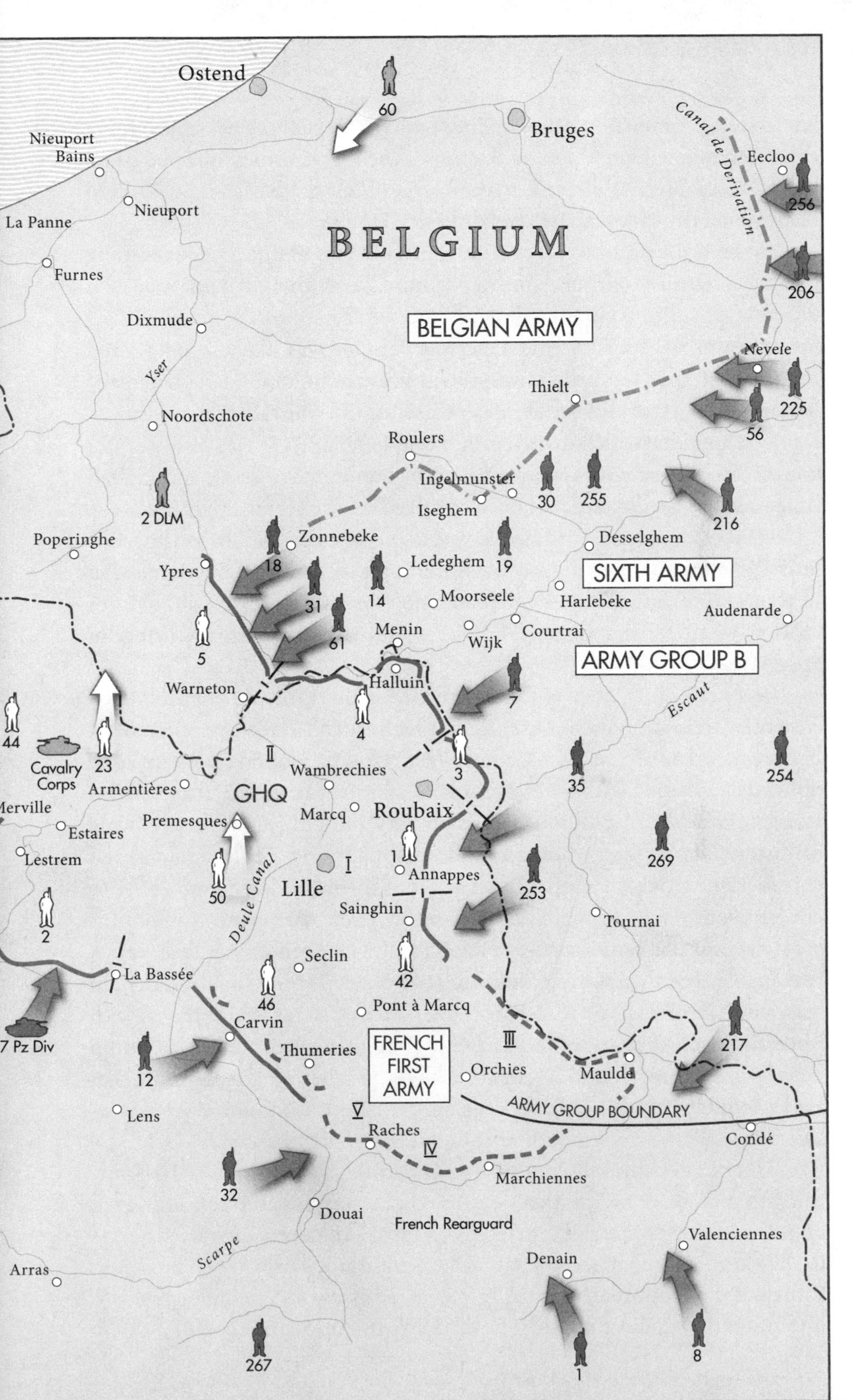

Ostend
60
Bruges
Nieuport
Bains
Canal de Derivation
Eecloo
256
Nieuport
La Panne
BELGIUM
Furnes
206
Dixmude
BELGIAN ARMY
Nevele
Yser
Thielt
225
Noordschote
56
Roulers
Ingelmunster
30
255
Iseghem
216
2 DLM
Zonnebeke
Poperinghe
Desselghem
18
Ledeghem
19
Ypres
SIXTH ARMY
31
14
Moorseele
Harlebeke
Audenarde
Menin
Courtrai
5
61
Wijk
ARMY GROUP B
Halluin
Warneton
7
Escaut
44
23
4
Cavalry
Corps
II
Wambrechies
3
254
Armentières
35
GHQ
Merville
Premesques
Marcq
Roubaix
Estaires
269
Lestrem
1
I
Annappes
50
Lille
253
Deule Canal
Sainghin
Tournai
2
Seclin
42
La Bassée
46
Pont à Marcq
Carvin
217
7 Pz Div
FRENCH
FIRST
ARMY
III
12
Thumeries
Orchies
Maulde
ARMY GROUP BOUNDARY
Lens
V
Raches
Condé
IV
32
Marchiennes
Douai
French Rearguard
Valenciennes
Scarpe
Arras
Denain
267
8
1

left to see Reynaud at Admiralty House and to discuss the possible buying off of Mussolini. Churchill and the rest of the War Cabinet followed some ten minutes later. At about 4 p.m., Reynaud left for Paris and Churchill reconvened the War Cabinet at Admiralty House.

By now, the argument between Churchill and Halifax was becoming more heated. The Prime Minister pointed out that Britain was in a different position to France. First, Britain still had, in her navy and air force, powers of resistance, and, second, France was likely to be offered reasonable terms, but Britain was not. 'If France could not defend herself,' he said, 'it is better that she should get out of the war rather than drag us into a settlement which involved intolerable terms.' He was also wary of going cap in hand to Mussolini with the French, as Reynaud had suggested, before Britain had been involved in any serious fighting.

Halifax disagreed that Hitler would necessarily ask for outrageous terms. 'We might say to Signor Mussolini that if there was any suggestion of terms which affected our independence,' he suggested, 'we should not look at them for a moment.' But he could see no harm in trying an approach.

Chamberlain, Attlee and Greenwood said little during this discussion. Churchill now recognized that he needed to tread very carefully. If the majority of the War Cabinet agreed with Halifax, he would be obliged to go along with them. In fact, if Chamberlain sided strongly with Halifax, Churchill's position would be very difficult; the former Prime Minister, the one man who had dealt personally with Hitler, still carried considerable clout, far more than Attlee or Greenwood, who were new to government. And Churchill was still only sixteen days into the job; his position was far from secure. Halifax's stance seemed, at face value, reasonable, and there was no doubting the gravity of the situation Britain was now in. However, Churchill knew that to try to bargain with Mussolini would be to set themselves down a path from which it would be very hard to turn back. In any case, he did not believe for a minute that Hitler would offer tolerable terms. There was thus no point in even considering it. They would fight on or die in the process.

'Herr Hitler thinks he has the whip hand,' said Churchill. 'The only thing to do is to show him that he cannot conquer this country.' However, he realized that some kind of concession to Halifax was now needed. He thus told the Foreign Secretary that he would not raise any objection to some kind of approach being made to Mussolini. The phrasing was intentionally vague; in reality he had no intention of making such a move. Halifax had already discussed a joint draft with Reynaud, which he now read out. Greenwood suggested Mussolini might demand Malta, Gibraltar and Suez. Chamberlain, crucially, said he suspected the Italian leader would demand more, and as part of a general settlement with Germany. The meeting ended with the five men agreeing that Halifax should, overnight, prepare a draft communiqué to Mussolini.

Later that evening, Churchill dined with Eden, Ironside – whom he had just sacked as CIGS, replacing him with Dill – and Ismay. He knew by then that Calais would surely fall and that, with it, would be lost all of 30th Brigade and the 3rd Royal Tank Regiment. Earlier, at 6.57 p.m., the signal had been given for the Royal Navy to begin Operation DYNAMO, the evacuation of Dunkirk. Much of the BEF would surely follow the Calais garrison into captivity. How else could it be otherwise? And the worse the news from France, the harder it would be to prevent Halifax from getting his way. That night, he barely touched his food or drink. Afterwards, he stood up, a sad expression on his face. 'I feel physically sick,' he said.

17

Black Monday

MEANWHILE, IN BERLIN there was no mention of the fact that the panzers had been brought to a pointless halt. Rather, William Shirer was given a communiqué that the fate of the Allied armies in Flanders was sealed. 'Calais has fallen,' he noted on 26 May. 'Britain is now cut off from the Continent.' There were even reports in the *Völkischer Beobachter* that the Luftwaffe had bombed south-east England.

The fate of the Allied armies in Flanders would have been sealed had von Rundstedt not been such a pig-headed fool. Not until 1.30 p.m. on the 26th did he finally lift the order; however, it was not until 8 p.m. that night that Panzer Group Kleist was finally given operational orders, and they were not to begin until the morning of 27 May. In other words, the panzers had been idle for three whole days. By then, Gort's men, as well as the French, had been organized and had dug in along the Canal Line. As Halder noted, 'On [the] left wing, von Kleist seems to encounter stronger resistance than expected.' He was still steaming.

The Royal Navy had not been idle since the opening of the offensive. Still heavily engaged around Norway, it had also been involved in blowing port installations and fuel depots in Holland to prevent the Germans getting their hands on them, ferrying Queen Wilhelmina to safety, and taking more troops and supplies to France and then evacuating them back to Britain too, whether it be from Cherbourg, Dieppe, Boulogne or Dunkirk; 5,000 refugees and nearly 3,000 troops had been lifted on 23

May, for example. There were also minelaying and minesweeping duties and coastal patrol work to be carried out.

Gort's warning on 19 May that the BEF might need to consider evacuation had been passed on to the Admiralty, where a meeting had immediately been held to discuss the matter. It had been decided that, should it come to it, an evacuation operation should be controlled by the Naval Sub-Command of Dover, under Vice-Admiral Bertram Ramsay. Representatives from the War Office Movement Control and Ministry of Shipping had met Ramsay at Dover on the 20th to discuss the many thorny problems involved in such an operation. The first was that the sleek destroyers and minesweepers that made up most of the navy's ships were filled with guns and depth charges and not designed to carry large numbers of men. That meant using merchant ships, fishing vessels, cross-Channel ferries and pleasure boats to carry out most of the work. Small boats would also be called upon, particularly to lift men from the gradually sloping beaches. Ramsay, for one, knew only too well from his experiences in the last war that the shoal-ridden coast off Dunkirk was rarely more than two fathoms deep and a notorious graveyard of ships.

The problems facing them on 20 May had multiplied by the morning of 27 May, when Captain Bill Tennant reported to Admiral Ramsay, some thirteen hours after Operation DYNAMO – as the evacuation had been called – had officially begun. Until 6 p.m. the previous evening, Bill had been Chief Staff Officer to the First Sea Lord at the Admiralty, but as something of a navigation expert – not least as Navigator on HMS *Renown* on the Royal world tour of 1921 and as a naval instructor at the Imperial Defence College before the war – Bill had been plucked from that job and sent instead to report to Admiral Ramsay in Dover. From there he was to be sent to Dunkirk to organize the shore end of the evacuation as Senior Naval Officer (SNO) there, where his navigation knowledge would prove invaluable. Lean-faced, with dark determined features, the 49-year-old had immediately packed a few things and by 8.25 p.m. had set out first for Chatham and then gone on to Dover.

It was not until 9 a.m., however, that he finally reached Ramsay's headquarters, a warren of rooms carved into the high chalk cliffs at Dover at the beginning of the last century by French prisoners of war, and at a time when Britain had last faced the threat of invasion. Ramsay's own office had a window and a small iron balcony overlooking the Channel; a cannon here had once pointed towards France, but now it was guns across the sea that could be clearly heard. Further inside the cliffs was a large chamber that in the last war had housed an electrical power generator, and so it was called the 'Dynamo Room'. Now, it was the nerve centre of the evacuation plans – hence Operation DYNAMO. It was here, at Ramsay's HQ, that Bill was briefed by the Vice-Admiral. When DYNAMO had been first conceived, Ramsay had expected to be able to use a number of Channel ports. Now, it seemed, they could barely use one. The port at Dunkirk had already been so badly hit that it was felt, for the time being at any rate, that it would be impossible to use the harbour. Instead, they would begin lifting troops from the long, ten-mile beach to the east of the port. This was difficult enough but, because of the secrecy of the operation, they had not been able to put out a call for boats and volunteer crews until it had begun – and this obviously took time. Thus on this morning of Monday, 27 May, only 129 of the Merchant Navy's 10,000 vessels were available. More were coming, but whether they would arrive in time was another matter.

And there was worse news. 'The Boche has got as far as Gravelines,' Ramsay told Bill. 'That's the worst blow yet.' There were key French guns at Gravelines, but with the coast west of Dunkirk now in German hands it meant the short thirty-nine-mile sea route from Dover to Dunkirk now lay within reach of powerful coastal batteries as well as from the air; some forty coastal guns were already operating by early that morning. Route Z, as it was called, would have to be abandoned. There were two alternatives. One, Route Y, was eighty-seven miles long and involved a dog-leg off Ostend and approaching from the east. The other, Route X, was fifty-five miles and hit the coast between Dunkirk and Gravelines. Route Y passed through minefields and Route X was as yet untested. Both, however, would have to be used. The crossings would take longer – much longer – but that could not be helped. They would have to do what they could, although that might well not be enough; Ramsay told Bill they could expect to lift only some 45,000 men of the BEF.

Accompanying Bill was a team of twelve officers and 160 ratings. They left Dover at 1.45 p.m. aboard the destroyer *Wolfhound* and following Route Y. The first Stukas attacked them at 2.45 p.m. and they were harried and bombed the rest of the way, although they managed to dodge and weave their way out of trouble. Above the din, Bill began organizing his men: each officer would have twelve ratings and was given a stretch of the beaches or part of the port to reconnoitre and manage. As they drew near Dunkirk, a vision of hell awaited them. The entire coast seemed to be ablaze. The oil refineries at St Pol were burning, thick black smoke pitching thousands of feet into the sky. Flames spewed from warehouses and buildings. Above, aircraft thundered over, bombs whistled down, and explosions erupted as bombs hit the ground and as guns boomed out. They finally pulled into Dunkirk harbour at 5.35 p.m., miraculously intact, as another stick of bombs fell on the quayside nearby.

Only once the raiders had passed did Bill disperse most of his men, then head off towards Bastion 32, the underground bunker of Admiral Jean-Marie Charles Abrial, the French *Amiral Nord* and naval commander at Dunkirk. Picking their way through rubble and shards of broken glass, burned-out vehicles and snapped tram wires, they reached Bastion 32 and were led through the heavy steel doors into a long, damp corridor lit by candles that took them to the Operations Room. Here Bill met with Brigadier Reginald Parminter from Gort's staff, Colonel G. P. H. Whitfield, the Area Commandant, and Commander H. P. Henderson, the British Naval Liaison Officer to Admiral Abrial. They all told him that there was no chance of using the harbour for evacuation. Bill asked how long they had got. Twenty-four to thirty-six hours was the reply. After that, the Germans would probably be in the town.

Dunkirk was in a bad way. The water supply had been cut off by bomb damage and there was only one telephone link left between the town and London. On that Monday alone, the Luftwaffe had hit the port with some 30,000 incendiary bombs and more than 15,000 high explosives. The railhead was largely destroyed and the docks and quays now lay ruined.

For those on the receiving end of this onslaught, Göring's boast to Hitler seemed justified, yet there was no denying the disquiet amongst the commanders carrying out this sustained aerial assault. Operations had begun against Dunkirk almost immediately Göring had given orders to Kesselring, but other demands upon his planes – Calais, Boulogne and operations in support of the army – meant that it was not until 26 May that the town became the main target. Even then, many of Kesselring's aircraft were too far back to be able to operate effectively over Dunkirk. On the 25th, General von Kluge had met with General Wolfram von Richthofen, commander of VIII Fliegerkorps, and had sarcastically asked whether he had already taken Dunkirk. 'No, Herr Generaloberst,' von Richthofen had replied, 'I have not yet even attacked it. My Stukas are too far back, the approach flights too long. Consequently I can use them twice a day at most, and am unable to focus them at one point of effort.'

And the weather was terrible. All month, one fine day had followed another but now the weather had turned. Low cloud hung over most of Flanders and that included Dunkirk. It made accurate bombing very difficult indeed. Furthermore, the Luftwaffe had now lost nearly a thousand aircraft since the campaign had begun. On top of that, a large number more were damaged or becoming increasingly hard to keep serviceable. Almost every single unit was operating below full strength, most at between half and three-quarters strength.

Stuka pilots were also finding that it was very difficult to successfully hit enemy shipping. It was one thing wreaking havoc on a concentration of troops in fine weather and with little opposition but quite another hitting a narrow destroyer that was pumping out anti-aircraft fire, as Major Oskar Dinort and the men of St.G 2 had discovered on the morning of 25 May, when they had been ordered to attack British destroyers off the coast of Calais.

Thick smoke had been the first obstacle but then, offshore, the air cleared and they saw the tiny thin specks below. Oskar felt a thrill at the prospect of attacking something new but he also wondered how they were ever going to hit their target. They had never ever bombed shipping before; they had not needed to. What was the procedure, he wondered? At thirty-eight, he was a hugely experienced pilot: he had begun flying gliders in the 1920s and held the world record for gliding for nearly fifteen hours. Joining the clandestine Luftwaffe in 1934, he had since seen action in Poland as well as earlier working with Udet in the Office of Air Armament. Now, though, despite his experience, he felt unsure how to carry out his mission. He screwed up his eyes; the diffused light off the sea was blinding.

'Attack by *Gruppen*,' the Stuka commander ordered over the R/T. 'Choose your own targets.' At this, the other two members of Oskar's section turned their machines in behind him. Throttling back, they began to lose height. Oskar knew that a dive on such small targets needed to be started as low as possible – the 12,000 feet at which they had been flying was way, way too high.

At what he judged to be the right height, Oskar rolled over his Stuka and began his dive, aiming for the largest ship. Almost immediately, his target disappeared out of his bombsight beneath his engine cowling. He decided instead to make a 'staircase' attack. This meant diving until he lost sight of the target, pulling out, re-sighting, then diving again. At last, he began his final dive, the target now thankfully larger but still horribly thin. As he hurtled towards it, his Jericho trumpet – the Stuka's distinct siren – screaming, the ship loomed ever closer, increasingly filling his bombsight with every nano-second. But then suddenly it moved, veering rapidly away. Oskar tried to follow but failed. Cursing, he knew there was only one thing he could do, and that was climb and dive again. He saw that most of the other forty Stukas were similarly struggling. Bombs were hitting the water, sending huge fountains of spray into the air, but none seemed to have hit the destroyers. A transport was claimed as hit but if true the damage seemed to be minimal.

Oskar made another dive but again failed, then ordered the *Staffeln* to re-form at sea level and head back south. This was the Stuka pilot's most dangerous moment. Speed was reduced and the pilot was distracted by reseating the diving brakes, reopening the radiator shutter, readjusting the bomb-release switches and changing the airscrew and elevator trim.

And at this moment, Oskar heard someone shout, 'English fighters behind us!' Immediately, he pulled his Stuka into a turn then craned his neck to look above him. High overhead, fighters were glinting in the sky, circling and weaving, but others were now diving down towards them. Oskar throttled back again and stall-turned to starboard, aware that he had no hope of escaping clear away from a fighter. It was a Hurricane of 17 Squadron bearing down upon him and the sleek machine now overshot and flew past; Oskar's trick had, for the moment at any rate, saved him. A few seconds later the Hurricane became engaged with a waiting Me 109 instead. Oskar made it safely back that day, but four other Stukas were destroyed. No doubt from the ships below, the sight of forty Stukas diving on them with their sirens wailing would have been terrifying; but the attack was not terribly effective. As Captain Bill Tennant had discovered on his trip across the Channel, a destroyer could get out of the way of a Stuka assault reasonably easily.

Even so, when Göring visited the Führer later that day, he was in a jovial mood and confident his Luftwaffe was doing all he had promised. 'Only fishing boats are coming over,' he joked with Hitler, 'I hope the Tommies are good swimmers.'

Just as British Hurricanes had often found themselves distracted from their main missions during the opening stages of the campaign, so too were Luftwaffe fighters as they now headed towards Dunkirk. On 26 May, I/JG 21 had been given the job of escorting Stukas to the port. Subordinated to JG 27 and part of von Richthofen's VIII Fliegerkorps, the

Staffel had barely formed up and was at around 12,000 feet over Cambrai when one of the pilots cried out, 'Enemy above!'

These were French fighter aircraft, some five US-built Curtiss Hawks and a dozen Morane 406s that happened to have been escorting a lone French reconnaissance aircraft. The French dived down on the Messerschmitts, for once able to begin a dogfight with the advantage of height. Forgetting their escort duties, each German pilot now found himself engaged in a fierce mêlée with the French attackers. Hans-Ekkehard Bob managed to get on the tail of one of the French Curtiss Hawks, but although his Me 109 was faster, the French pilot seemed to have the more manoeuvrable aircraft, turning and weaving so that Hans was unable to get a clear shot.

Hans was another of the Luftwaffe's pre-war regular pilots. Born and brought up in Freiburg in the Black Forest, the 23-year-old was an only son, but with four much older sisters. 'My youngest sister was seven years older,' he says. 'They all spoiled me.' Blond, good-looking and intelligent, Hans had grown up to become a confident, headstrong young man. He had first become interested in flying in 1927, when he had been just ten. One of his sisters had become friends with the famous stunt pilot Erich Haal, and he then invited her and her little brother to go for a flight in his biplane. It had been the most exciting thrill of his life, but it was another seven years before he flew again – and this time in a glider he had made himself whilst in the Hitler Youth. It was, then, hardly surprising that he volunteered for the air force after leaving school, and after three months' labour service began his training in December 1936. He soon proved himself to be a natural and extremely gifted pilot, taking his first solo after just seventeen flights. It had always been his intention to become a fighter pilot and that was what he did, joining his first *Staffel* in September 1938.

Hans knew he was a good pilot; knew he had plenty of experience too. He had flown every single mark of the Messerschmitt 109 and knew the latest model, the 109E, or 'Emil', so well that he could make his machine do what he wanted without even thinking about it. Now, more than two weeks after the start of the offensive, he had combat experience too: thirty missions and three aerial victories to his name. But the French pilot ahead of him was good too, and after twenty minutes of twirling and weaving through the sky without Hans getting a shot or the Frenchman able to get away, they had fallen so low that they were now flying over the treetops and spires of northern France. Hans was now beginning to tire and so decided to disengage. After another evasive manoeuvre from the Hawk, Hans did not try and follow but instead opened the throttle and turned east. Thinking his pursuer had given up, the Frenchman turned west.

However, seeing this, Hans decided to have another go. Turning 180 degrees, Hans opened the throttle and chased after the Hawk once more. This time the Frenchman failed to keep an eye out because creeping up below and behind him was Hans. When the Hawk filled Hans's sights, he opened fire with both his cannon and machine guns.

Belching smoke, the Hawk lost height rapidly and glided down, landing with his wheels up in a field. Hans circled the downed Hawk and saw that the pilot was alive but injured. Without a second thought, and safe in the knowledge that they were still in German-occupied territory, Hans lowered his undercarriage and touched down beside the Frenchman. Grabbing his first-aid kit, Hans clambered out of the cockpit, jumped out on to the ground and hurried over to the French pilot. Having tended to his wounds he then took the pilot's name – Sergent-chef Bés – and promised to write to his parents to let them know he was safe. This done, he clambered back into his Messerschmitt, took off and headed back to base.

'What I did was forbidden,' says Hans. 'I could have been court-martialled for that.' Even so, when he rejoined the rest of the *Staffel* he came clean – he had to explain why he had been so long. He was forgiven, however; after all, he'd scored another victory. 'I was euphoric,' Hans explains. 'I'd shot this aircraft down and then had landed beside him and saved him. If I'd stopped to think about it I'd have never done it. It was an instinctive thing.'

Nearly all the Luftwaffe's fighters were now operating over Dunkirk and the Channel ports – even units from Luftflotte 3 such as I/JG 2. On the 25th, Siegfried Bethke had patrolled the front above Panzer Group Kleist and had had clear and beautiful views all the way to the Channel. 'Saw England for the first time,' he had noted. The next day, he was flying over Dunkirk and Calais and encountered Fighter Command Spitfires for the first time, from 19 Squadron. 'Wild bunch,' he jotted in his diary afterwards, 'Wild firing again.' However, during the dogfight he managed to hit one with the best bit of shooting he had ever done – he had barely opened fire when first a belch of white smoke, then black smoke had burst from the Spitfire and it fell from 9,000 feet. Afterwards, he and the rest of the *Staffel* had been forced to land at a forward base to refuel. JG 2 were far from alone in operating at the limit of their range.

Siegfried now had three aerial victories, although that night as he wrote up his diary by the dim lamp by his bed, he chided himself for not having six or seven to his name. Seven letters from home reached him that day, but most were now quite old. Even his confirmed kill and the news that he had been awarded the Iron Cross Second Class could not shake his anxieties over what he believed was his lack of marksmanship. And he was getting tired, too; most days they were flying three, even four combat sorties, often for two hours at a time, and then becoming embroiled in heavy engagements. It was exhausting.

War *was* exhausting, whether one was a pilot, soldier, sailor or politician. There were some exceptions, of course. Hitler insisted on getting plenty of sleep; so too did Göring, even when his Luftwaffe was flying a maximum-effort operation. But the leaders of Britain, as they faced one of the biggest crises – if not the biggest – the country had ever known, could not relax for a moment. 'The blackest day of all,' Chamberlain had written in his diary on the night of the 26th. Monday the 27th was to be blacker, however. Halt order or no halt order, the future of the BEF looked horribly grim at dawn and even worse by nightfall. During times of particular strain, Churchill liked to recall quotations that matched his mood. He had asked one of his secretaries to find a line from George Borrow's 'Prayer for England at Gibraltar', and that morning was given it: 'Fear not the result, for either shall thy end be majestic and an enviable one, or God shall perpetuate thy reign upon the waters.' He was going to need that kind of stoic resolve during the days to come.

Yet if the fate of the British army rested in the besieged port of Dunkirk, the fate of Britain would most likely be determined within the buildings of Whitehall and the outcome of the split between Churchill and Lord Halifax. Much depended on Chamberlain, whose influence was still considerable. Should Chamberlain emphatically side with Halifax, Churchill would find it difficult to oppose both.

Already Chamberlain was a sick man, although the cancer that was taking hold of him had not yet been diagnosed. Nevertheless, he had been tireless since stepping down as Prime Minister; not for one moment had he shirked his new responsibilities. This was in large part due to his intense sense of public duty, but Churchill had also played his role, making it clear how much he depended upon Chamberlain and acting towards him with extreme graciousness.

The first War Cabinet that day was at 11.30 a.m. at Downing Street. To begin with reports were read out from France, which was followed by a discussion about what to tell the Dominions; it was well known that the Australian High Commissioner, for example, was a defeatist. Things were also still bleak in Norway. Not only had the British suffered a humiliating defeat in Central Norway, but it now seemed as though they would have to evacuate Narvik, which had been captured by a combined Anglo-French-Polish force two days before; it had been the only land success during the entire campaign, but, it now seemed, all for nought. Then Chamberlain gave an appraisal of the Chiefs of Staffs' 'A Certain Eventuality', pointing out that much depended on the United States. 'This was perhaps not an unjustifiable assumption,' he said, 'but we might not obtain this support in the immediate future.' This, as Churchill well knew, was true enough. The Prime Minister did, however, know that the aide-memoire was being discussed, questioning Group Captain Tommy Elmhirst's figures for Luftwaffe strength. The Vice-Chief of the Air Staff, Air Marshal Sir Richard Pierse, had been asked to produce new, more accurate figures, which he now presented. These showed a ratio of 2.5:1 in favour of the Germans, rather than 4:1, as in the aide-memoire. It still meant British airmen would have to shoot down three German aircraft for every one of their own that was destroyed. Halifax said little at this time. The mood in the Cabinet Room that morning was gloomy, to put it mildly.

The War Cabinet met again at 4.30 p.m. and this time it began with Halifax reading out his draft letter to Mussolini. Churchill then said he thought it would be better for Roosevelt to approach Italy rather than the British with the French. He suggested that, should France collapse, Germany might well give her good terms but she would have to be governed by men acceptable to the Germans. In other words, France would effectively become pro-German and anti-British. Chamberlain agreed, although he was still largely with Halifax and said that until France collapsed then Britain should go along with the approach to Mussolini so as not to let them down completely.

What Chamberlain was saying, Churchill pointed out, was that although nothing would come of an approach, it was worth doing so as to sweeten relations with a falling ally. What Reynaud needed was military and moral support, he said, not caving in to Mussolini.

Archibald Sinclair, who was attending in his capacity as Leader of the Liberal Party, agreed. 'I am convinced of the futility of an approach to Italy at this time,' he said. 'Being in a tight corner, any weakness on our part would encourage the Germans and the Italians, and it would tend to undermine morale both in this country and in the Dominions. The suggestion that we are prepared to barter away pieces of British territory would have a deplorable effect and would make it difficult for us to continue the desperate struggle that faces us.' Sinclair had hit the nail on the head and it now gave Churchill the opportunity to make clear what he really believed: that there should be no approach whatsoever. 'At the moment our prestige in Europe is very low,' he said. 'The only way we could get it back is by showing the world that Germany has not beaten us. If, after two or three months, we can show that we are still unbeaten, our prestige will return. Even if we are beaten, we shall be no worse off than we should be if we now abandon the struggle. Let us therefore avoid being dragged down the slippery slope with France. The whole of this manoeuvre is intended to get us so deeply involved in negotiations that we shall be unable to turn back.'

Halifax now lost his temper. He pointed out that the Prime Minister had, the day before, agreed to make a tentative approach to Italy but now seemed to have changed his mind. Nor did Halifax recognize any resemblance between the action he was proposing and the suggestion that they would be suing for peace with Germany. If Britain's independence was at stake then they could walk away from any talks, but if it was not, then he believed it was right to accept an offer that would save the country from avoidable disaster. Churchill reiterated his point that Hitler would be unlikely to offer any terms that were remotely acceptable.

This was what Halifax was finding so frustrating. *Unlikely*, yes, but not *impossible*; and this being so, it was, he believed, a mistake to rule out any chance of being offered reasonable terms. He simply did not buy the argument that to open any kind of dialogue was sure to lead only one way; he sensed Churchill was using his usual romantic rhetoric rather than common sense. So now he asked Churchill whether he would be prepared to consider any terms offered by Hitler, should he put them to France and Britain.

'I would not join France in asking for terms,' Churchill replied, 'but if I were told what the terms offered were, I would be prepared to consider them.'

Chamberlain now suggested a compromise. Hitler would most likely make a definite offer to France and when the French replied that Britain was an ally and that they could not sue for peace without her, Hitler would tell France that Britain should send delegates to the talks. In that scenario, Chamberlain said, Britain should refuse to do so. Halifax still insisted they should not send a flat refusal with regard to any talks to France.

And then he issued his bombshell. He told Churchill plainly what he thought of him and threatened to resign if the Cabinet insisted on stubbornly refusing to open any channel for talks whatsoever. This was a thunderbolt that none of the other members had expected, least of all Churchill. 'I can't work with Winston any longer,' Halifax told one of his Foreign Office colleagues afterwards. The split in the Cabinet was now threatening to plunge Britain into an even deeper crisis – one that, combined with the evacuation of the BEF, could prove catastrophic, and could easily bring down the Government. Should that happen, then a rudderless Britain, plunged into political turmoil, would find it very difficult to continue the fight.

Churchill now took his Foreign Secretary out into the garden at No. 10 for a private chat. At that moment, on the afternoon of Monday, 27 May, the fate of Britain, it seemed, depended heavily on these two men. Enormous, world-changing decisions were being made – both in Britain and amongst the Nazi command – by just a few men amongst all the many millions. And to a large extent these decisions boiled down to the differing characters and personalities of these individuals: Hitler's megalomania and irrational paranoia; von Rundstedt's military failings and stubbornness; Halifax's patrician logic and exasperation with his Prime Minister from whom he was so different; and Churchill's determined belief in the rightness of the stance he was making on behalf of his country.

Now, in the garden of No. 10, Halifax repeated his threat of resignation. It was Churchill's task to dissuade him. He certainly did his best to soothe him, apologizing repeatedly and 'full of affection'. Whether it worked or whether it was from some other deeper sense of duty, Halifax did not resign that day. The threat remained, however, because the essence of the split had still not been resolved.

There was a third War Cabinet that day, at 10 p.m., but it had been called to discuss yet another crisis. The Belgians had surrendered. As of midnight that night, they would no longer be in the fight. The north flank of the BEF was again desperately vulnerable and a mere 7,669 troops had been lifted from Dunkirk this first day of the evacuation. Whether Churchill could win over Halifax – and the rest of the War Cabinet – would have to wait another day. The stakes could not have been higher.

18

Dunkirk: The Beginning

'WE NOW ARE receiving very little news,' jotted Daidie Penna on 27 May, 'which may be a good thing.' She also wondered – with considerable perceptiveness – why the Germans appeared not to have made good use of their 'gap'. 'I should have thought they would have rushed troops through it,' she added, 'as fast as they could get them there.'

Very few people knew the true extent of the disaster, not even Harold Nicolson, who that morning at the Ministry of Information was also commenting on the paucity of news. He was soon put in the picture, however, when at a meeting at the Ministry later on that day he heard about the situation in France from General Mason-Macfarlane, just back from BEF Headquarters having commanded Macforce. 'Macfarlane tells us in blunt language that the BEF are now surrounded,' noted Harold, 'and that a disaster is bound to take place.' Macfarlane, as Gort's emissary, wanted the Ministry of Information to know that it was the Belgians deserting them – which was deeply unfair – and the lack of French fight that had caused the problems, and urged them to save the reputation of the British army by putting the blame on their allies instead. Harold and his colleagues called for their boss and Duff Cooper then explained that to take that tack with the French would be to shatter any hope of maintaining the alliance. The policy would be to prepare the public for the shock by not giving away too much information to the Germans.

This was further agreed upon at the late Cabinet that night, which Duff Cooper attended. He wanted the public to know something of the seriousness of the situation but Churchill was anxious that there should not be any detailed statement about the evacuation. In this moment of extreme crisis, the policy of openness was, for the moment, to be put to one side.

Communications – or the lack of them – had once again got the better of the Allies in their increasingly fragile pocket in Flanders. For much of the night, Gort and Pownall had been trying to speak with Blanchard to discuss the evacuation and the defence of the narrow corridor. Every time they followed a lead, they arrived to discover the French general had already moved on, without notifying Gort or his staff. Late that night, they even found themselves following a false trail to Dunkirk. 'Much of the town was in flames,' noted Henry Pownall, 'and falling houses blocked the roads, bodies of civilians were lying in the streets.' They also learned that the port had been destroyed and was thus unusable. It did not make them sanguine. Without ever catching up with Blanchard, they returned to the new HQ at Houtkerque at 3 a.m.

Plenty of troops were already moving that night of the 27th/28th, however, some back to Dunkirk, others to fill the gap left by the retreating Belgians. Even before news of their planned capitulation arrived it had become necessary to urgently plug the gap on the north-east part of the line. General Brooke, the commander of II Corps, which was now holding the northern British front, had held a conference with his commanders early that morning. His three divisions were spread out from west of Menin to the east of Lille, but now some complicated movements were needed. In the middle, 4th Division was to move back a short distance behind the River Lys around the village of Warneton. As the new battalion adjutant, Second Lieutenant Norman Field had an important role to play in getting the 2nd Royal Fusiliers back to the Lys as part of 4th Division's move. Vehicles were brought up and by 11 p.m. the companies along the Comines Canal around Halluin began to be thinned out. The rain helped keep the enemy at bay, although it made life miserable for the men.

Major-General Bernard Montgomery's 3rd Division, however, then at the bottom of II Corps's line, was to swing behind 4th and 5th Divisions and fill the hole on 5th Division's left flank. This was a major operation, which involved moving the entire division some fifty miles. In order to achieve this, it was decided to abandon its medium guns and for the infantry to do away with any kit that was not absolutely necessary so

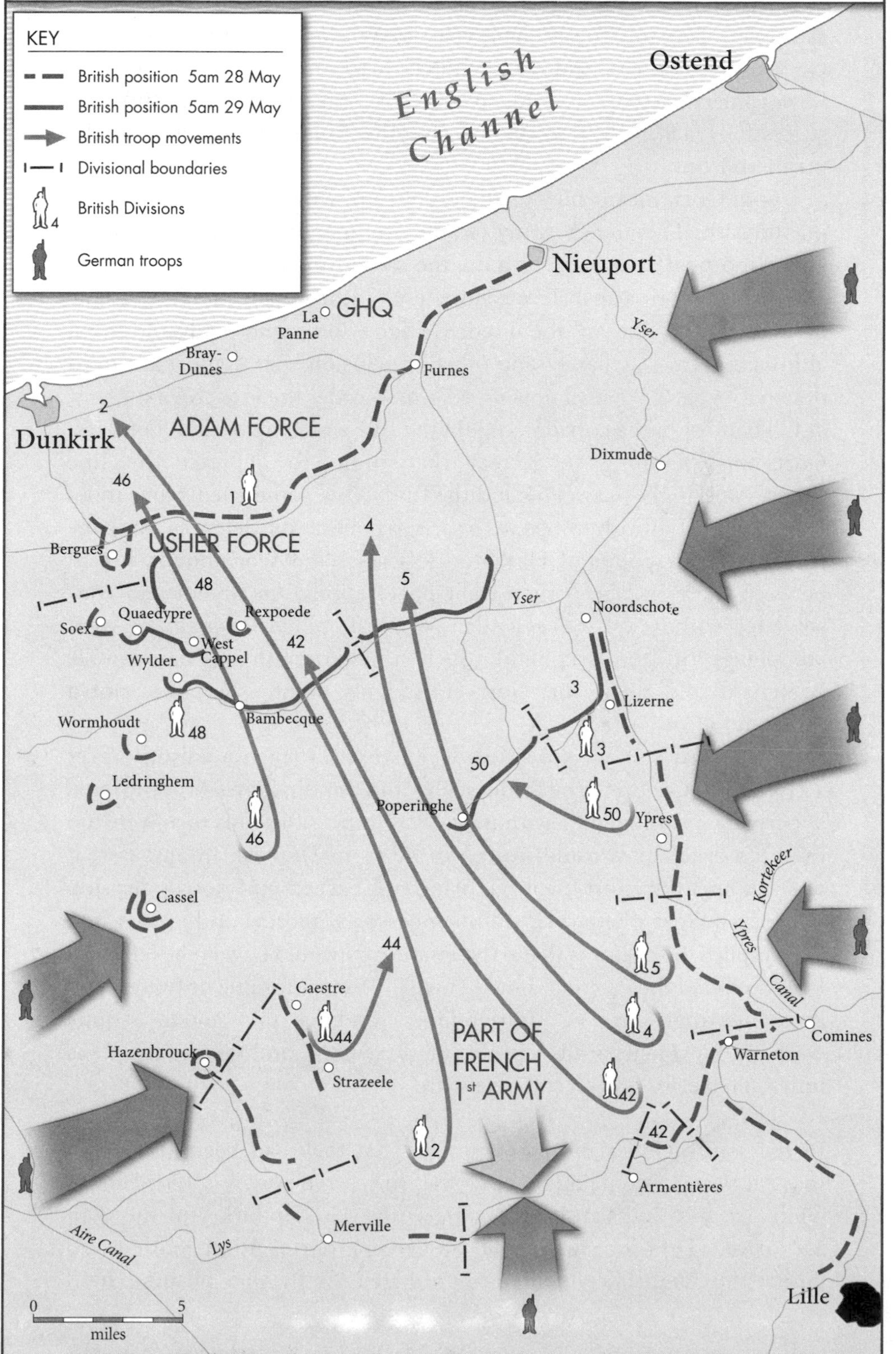
WITHDRAWAL OF THE BEF TO THE COAST
KEY
British position 5am 28 May
British position 5am 29 May
British troop movements
Divisional boundaries
British Divisions
German troops
English Channel
Ostend
Nieuport
Yser
La Panne
GHQ
Bray-Dunes
Furnes
Dunkirk
ADAM FORCE
Dixmude
Bergues
USHER FORCE
Yser
Noordschote
Quaedypre
Rexpoede
Soex
West Cappel
Wylder
Lizerne
Bambecque
Wormhoudt
Ledringhem
Poperinghe
Ypres
Kortekeer
Ypres Canal
Cassel
Caestre
Comines
Warneton
Hazenbrouck
Strazeele
PART OF FRENCH 1st ARMY
Armentières
Merville
Aire Canal
Lys
Lille
miles

as to cram them into the available vehicles. Passing under the noses of the Germans, on a wet and windy pitch black night, it was much to Montgomery's credit and his powers of organization that this was successfully achieved. It certainly gave the BEF a day's grace on the northern front.

Lord Gort, meanwhile, finally caught up with Blanchard at 11 a.m. on the 28th. The French Army Group Commander walked into Gort's command post at around 11 a.m., the same time as the Belgians were laying down their arms. He was horrified to learn that the BEF was now evacuating; no-one in the French High Command had told him, although there was barely any other conclusion that could have been drawn. Gort and Pownall now urged him to order the French First Army, at the bottom of the corridor, to join the BEF in falling back to Dunkirk. Gort was planning to retreat that night to at least the line Ypres–Poperinghe–Cassel behind the River Yser, some twenty-five miles from the coast. British troops were carrying out heroic defences along the southern strongpoints of Hazebrouck, Cassel and Wormhoudt, but in between there had been significant penetrations. An urgent and consolidated withdrawal was essential. 'Whereat,' noted Pownall, 'he went completely off the deep end.' Such a withdrawal was impossible, Blanchard told them, but Gort pressed his point. There was not a moment to lose.

Blanchard still felt the situation was useless when a liaison officer arrived from Général René Prioux, now commanding First Army. Prioux, apparently, also thought a withdrawal was impossible – his men were too tired; an evacuation could not be made from Dunkirk in any case; it wasn't worth the effort involved. Blanchard backed up Prioux's decision then asked Gort whether he still intended to withdraw on his own. Yes, Gort replied. So that was that – the First Army would have to be left to its fate. 'So ended the meeting,' noted Pownall. 'Except for one or two excited moments, there was no unfriendliness and we said goodbye quite cordially. But Blanchard is a professor, no general, and the situation was much too big for him to compete with.'

In the south, Guderian's panzers, now that they had been allowed to move forward, were taking a back seat. In reserve now was 10th Panzer, while 1st and 2nd Panzer pressed on towards Dunkirk and the 20th Motorized Division, with the SS-Leibstandarte Adolf Hitler and Grossdeutschland Regiments subordinated to it, was pushing hard against the British line. Guderian still hoped to reach Dunkirk, but his part in Germany's miraculous victory was now almost done. His panzers could play a supporting role, but it was infiltration by the infantry that was going to clear the kind of stubborn, dug-in defence they were now encountering. There were ugly scenes too. On the 28th, eighty POWs from the 2nd Royal Warwickshire Regiment were executed by Waffen-SS troops of the SS-Leibstandarte Adolf Hitler Regiment, while further south, near Merville, SS-Totenkopf troops also massacred ninety-seven men of the 2nd Royal Norfolks. Hans-Ekkehard Bob may have been suffused with a sense of knightly chivalry, but not so these men, many of whom had carried out multiple executions of Jews and others during the Polish campaign.

The Totenkopf was still part of Panzer Corps Hoth, but no longer subordinated to Generalmajor Rommel, whose 7th Panzer was pushing a wedge between the British 42nd Division – where novice infantryman Sid Nuttall was still fighting – and the French First Army to the north-west of Lille. Early that morning they had blocked the arterial road that led to Dunkirk – so Prioux's men would have had to fight their way north anyway. Hauptmann Hans von Luck had still barely stopped moving since 10 May, despite being wounded in the hand a week earlier. Having worn a sling for a few days, he had carried on regardless and by now was managing with just a bandage. He and his men were filthy – covered, as were their vehicles, in thick dust. It gave them the feeling that they were chewing dried biscuits all the time.

Hans and his men had just paused to have some breakfast when a runner arrived ordering Hans to go to Rommel's command post immediately. He hurried there as artillery shells began falling around them, not from the French, but from their own side – they had now almost linked up with the Sixth Army in Army Group B. Hans found Rommel at the edge of the town brushing dust from his uniform. Nearby, in front of a house lay a body, which Hans now saw was that of his commanding officer, Major Erdmann. The general looked upset.

'Von Luck,' he said, 'you will take over command of Panzer Reconnaissance Battalion 37 at once. You will receive fresh orders immediately.'

'General,' Hans replied, 'some of the company commanders are older than me. Does your decision stand in spite of that?'

'You're in charge, full stop. If the company commanders obstruct your orders, I will replace them.' Rommel had had plenty of opportunity to see Hans's mettle and liked what he saw, but, nonetheless, it was a big responsibility for a young captain to become a battalion commander. For Rommel, however, performance counted for more than seniority – and Hans had clearly performed.

In the north, Army Group B was also pressing forward, but with the sudden and dramatic collapse of the Belgians the German Eighteenth Army had to clear away the half a million prisoners and then move forward again, something that took time. In 56th Division, Unteroffizier Hellmuth Damm and his machine-gun platoon reached Dixmunde, still some dozen miles to the east of the Dunkirk perimeter. Hordes of Belgian companies were surrendering, wandering towards them in loose groups with their hands in the air, all of whom had to be cleared and corralled. Later that day they reached the old battlefields of the last war. 'We could still see some remains,' noted Hellmuth. Still, they would not be attacking the British that day. The next day, though, 29 May, Hellmuth and his men would be attacking them for the first time. The net was closing in. Gort had been right: for the BEF, there was not a moment to lose.

Back in Britain, there was, as planned, still no mention of the evacuation, although the newspapers were in no doubt about the gravity of the situation. 'BEF FIGHT HEROIC BATTLE FOR COAST' ran the headline in the *Daily Express*, '300 men with rifles hold off 100 Nazi armoured units. Fate of Calais uncertain.' Of course, by then, Calais's fate had become all too certain; it had been in German hands for two days.

In London, the grievous split between Churchill and Halifax had yet to be resolved. The morning Cabinet had been taken up, again, with the capitulation of Belgium and the implications of King Leopold's surrender. Churchill's magnanimity again came to the fore. In France, the finger of blame was being pointed squarely at King Leopold for deserting his allies, but the British Prime Minister refused to pass judgement on the Belgian monarch.

After the Cabinet, Churchill asked Chamberlain for a private talk. An opportunity for Churchill to show his loyalty to Chamberlain had conveniently arisen. Lloyd George, Prime Minister for much of the last war and the longest-serving MP in the House of Commons, had written to Churchill asking to be part of the Government, and Churchill now asked Chamberlain what he thought of the idea. Both men knew that Lloyd George was defeatist, admired Hitler, and hated Chamberlain. 'I replied that it was best to be frank,' Chamberlain noted. 'If he thought Ll. G would be more useful to him than I he had only to say so and I would gladly retire. But I could not work with him.' Churchill immediately replied that Chamberlain was of far more help to him than Lloyd George; there was no comparison. 'Winston and I were serving together,' added Chamberlain, 'and we would go down together.'

This renewed mutual commitment would be important for the next War Cabinet, although first Churchill attempted to shore up resolve by making a brief statement to the House about the fall of Belgium. There was no mention of the evacuation – he would put the House in the picture once the results of the present intense struggle were known. 'I have only one thing to add,' he concluded, 'that nothing which may happen in this battle can in any way relieve us of our duty to defend the world cause to which we have avowed ourselves; nor should it destroy our confidence in our power to make our way, as on former occasions in our history, through disaster and through grief to the ultimate defeat of our enemies.'

It was typically stirring stuff, but was, of course, precisely the kind of rhetoric Halifax and the Tory diehards despaired about – that still spoke of Britain having a moral duty to the world when logic suggested an opportunity to get out of their current dire fix should be grabbed with two hands. Nonetheless, when a Liberal member suggested the PM's words reflected the feelings of the whole House, no-one else demurred, even if no Conservative openly concurred.

The next War Cabinet met soon after in a room at the Commons, and it was then that the argument between Halifax and Churchill was reopened. Chamberlain felt it was a 'rather steamy discussion'. Certainly, Halifax and Churchill repeated their same arguments for and against mediation.

'The French are trying to get us on to the slippery slope,' said Churchill. 'The position will be entirely different when Germany has made an unsuccessful attempt to invade this country.'

'We must not ignore the fact,' Halifax replied, 'that we might get better terms before France went out of the war and our aircraft factories were bombed, than we might get in three months' time.' So it went on, back and forth, neither giving ground until, at 5 p.m., Churchill asked for an adjournment and to meet back again at 7 p.m. This was because he had already arranged to address the entire Cabinet – those not in the War Cabinet – in his rooms at the Commons.

A crucial moment had now arrived, for during his address to these senior ministers Churchill hoped to kill Halifax's proposals once and for all.

*

On his head, Captain Bill Tennant now wore a tin helmet with the letters 'SNO' cut out from the tinfoil of a cigarette packet and stuck on with sardine oil. It was makeshift, but then that was very much going to be the name of the game at Dunkirk. Indeed, it was this makeshift approach that had, by dawn on the 28th, given Operation DYNAMO a faint glimmer of hope.

Soon after arriving in Dunkirk the previous evening, he had signalled back to Dover asking for every available craft to head to the beaches east of the port, but it had been clear that taking soldiers to ships waiting offshore in rowing boats and other small craft was an extremely slow and laborious process. Then, at around 10 p.m. the previous evening, Bill had noticed something significant. The Luftwaffe had pounded the harbour and port facilities relentlessly, but not the two long moles that extended some 1,600 yards out into the sea. The western mole would be hard to get to but the eastern mole, running out from the seawall that linked the harbour entrance to Malo-les-Bains, was still easily accessible. Made of latticed concrete piles and topped with a narrow wooden walkway, it was, like its neighbour, a breakwater, rather than a quay suitable for mooring ships against. But what if it could be used in that way?

Taking two of his officers with him, he hurried over to conduct a quick survey. It felt sturdy enough, but whether it would take the strain of a large ship slapping into it with a three-knot tidal current behind it was another matter. Well, there was only one way to find out. Signalling to *Wolfhound*, which was now handling communications offshore, he asked her to send a personnel ship to the eastern mole to embark a thousand men. *Wolfhound* called for *Queen of the Channel*, in peacetime a cross-Channel steamer, and now offshore at Malo-les-Bains. She immediately hurried over, and eased her bow in at around six knots. Gently nudging first her stern against concrete piles, she slithered alongside. The mole had taken the strain without any difficulty at all. Tennant could breathe a sigh of relief – perhaps the east mole might offer the kind of lifeline they so desperately needed.

Less than an hour later, the *Queen of the Channel* was loaded with 904 men, and the captain was preparing to cast off. How many more could she take, someone shouted from the mole. 'It's not a question of how many more,' her skipper called back, 'but whether we can get away with what we already have.' The skipper's sixth sense was right. At 4.15 a.m., as dawn was breaking and halfway across the Channel, the *Queen of the Channel* was attacked by a lone enemy aircraft and bombs straddled the ship, breaking her back and main propeller shaft. By a stroke of good fortune, however, another ship en route to Dunkirk was able to stop and lift off all the troops before the *Queen* sank.

The *Queen of the Channel* might have been lost but the mole worked and that was an incredible fillip for Bill Tennant and all those trying to make it back to safety. At 4.36 a.m., Bill signalled asking for all vessels to go alongside the east pier rather than off the beaches. At 4.45 a.m., a second ship left the mole; at 9.55 a.m., a third ship cast off, packed with men. By mid-morning, the pier was crammed with men and the Luftwaffe were once again overhead, but offshore, the guns of destroyers were blasting into the sky. Furthermore, the burning oil tanks ashore were casting a vast pall overhead, which was being added to as houses within Dunkirk were hit and caught fire. Huge clouds of thick, dark smoke were unfurling over the town, which was making life difficult for the German bombers. The situation was still undeniably dire, but perhaps just a little less dire than it had seemed the previous evening. Even so, as more and more men began falling back on the town and long dunes and beaches spreading east of the port, the gargantuan task facing the navy began to hit home. 'There are at present 2,000 men on a Dunkirk beach,' signalled Bill Tennant at 9.35 a.m., his desperation all too clear, '7,000 men on a dune for which I have no boats available. They are now in need of water which army cannot supply. Unlimited numbers are falling back on this area and situation in present circumstances will shortly become desperate.' These figures would soon seem like small fry. Tens of thousands of men were now heading towards the beaches, and all were struggling with the dire shortages of food and especially water.

What were needed were more boats – ships of all sizes: large ones that could moor alongside the mole and smaller ones that could pull troops off the beaches. Even with little boats, the more that could make the trip across the Channel, the better. The problem was that because of the secrecy of the operation, the only ships that could be called upon were those of the navy, personnel and fishing vessels, barges and a number of Dutch skoots that had been brought back by the Royal Navy before the Dutch surrender. Private vessels could still not be drawn into the effort.

But those ships that could go were now heading to Dunkirk. The Royal Navy's reach was considerable, with Naval Commands in the Mediterranean, Middle East and Far East, so obviously none of those ships could be called upon. The British Isles were protected by five Naval Commands: Nore, Portsmouth, Western Approaches, Rosyth, and Orkneys and Shetlands, which were then divided into Sub-Commands. Dover was a Sub-Command in Nore. The ships operating in these Commands were the navy's largest force, the Home Fleet, commanded by Admiral Sir Charles Forbes, although the C-in-C's forces were already hugely stretched thanks to the continuing Narvik operation, the operations at Boulogne and Calais, in carrying out coastal patrols and across the North Sea, and in protecting Atlantic convoys. Nonetheless, the Admiralty was quick to direct a considerable proportion of the Home Fleet under Ramsay's charge.

One of the thirty-nine destroyers steaming towards Dunkirk was HMS *Icarus*, an 'Intrepid' class four-year-old destroyer. She had been in Plymouth, loading up with mines for a mine-lay when the orders were countermanded. 'And we dashed off to Dover,' says Andrew Begg, one of the ship's engine room artificers (ERAs), 'tearing up the Channel as fast as we could make it.' And it was pretty fast: Andrew and his fellows in the engine room could get 35 knots out of *Icarus*. 'She was exceptionally well built,' he says. 'The engine room was beautifully laid out and everything was handy. You could stand at one point in front of the controls and could read every gauge by doing a 360-degree turn. We had no trouble mechanically with her.' And that was despite the abuse such ships suffered at sea and despite already having had a very active war.

Very little might have happened in the air and on land before the Norwegian campaign, but at sea it had been a different matter: the Royal Navy had been busy from the outset and *Icarus* had been in the thick of it. She had helped sink a German U-boat back in November, had rescued survivors from a Norwegian ship in December, and then had been refitted as a minelayer, joining the 20th Destroyer (Minelaying Flotilla) in February. Throughout March, she had carried out minelaying operations in the North Sea and Moray Firth and then, in April, had been sent to Norway, originally to lay mines but then, when the Germans invaded, as a destroyer against enemy shipping. She and her crew acquitted themselves well, capturing a German supply ship, the *Alster*, of 8,500 tons. Andrew had witnessed that. He'd been off watch and up on deck when the *Alster* had been spotted. It was dark, around a quarter to midnight, but there was usually enough light on the sea to spot the silhouette of a ship. They dashed towards it, pulling in alongside and the boarding party leaping across as the for'ard decks were about the same height. Someone started firing and then there was a burst of machine-gun fire from *Icarus*'s bridge which brought the shooting to a stop. Suddenly, however, there was a loud explosion. The enemy had dropped a demolition charge over the side and blasted a hole in the side of the *Alster*.

'To us lot on board *Icarus*,' says Andrew, 'it was obvious that the German ship was starting to heel.' However, the boarding party had secured the ship and began towing her back to their oiling base in one of the fjords, albeit at only five knots. By seven the following morning, they had reached their fuel base and largely repaired the hole in the *Altser* so that it was once again floating on an even keel. It was a big prize, although they had no time to rest on their laurels, as they were immediately sent to the aid of a cruiser that had dashed itself on a submerged rock. They made it in time after a three-hour dash and rescued the crew.

After that episode, they had sunk an iron-ore ship and taken part in the Second Battle of Narvik on 13 April, which ended in the destruction of eight German destroyers and one U-boat. She landed British troops at Andalsnes and then carried out further minelaying duties at Trondheim. Barely had she made it back to Plymouth when the latest urgent call for her services was received.

Andrew Begg had volunteered for the Royal Navy Reserve back in March 1939. He had always intended to go to sea as a marine engineer, but wanted to learn his trade first and so had found work in a Glasgow shipyard near his home. But when conscription was first introduced, Andrew realized he was in the first group to be called and since he had a terror of being a soldier decided he should think about going to sea sooner rather than later, and so signed for the navy right away. In June, he was sent to Devonport, where he had to prove he was a competent fitter and turner, then pass a rigorous physical. He passed both and after basic training was posted to HMS *Victory* at Portsmouth before being posted to *Icarus*.

Andrew and the other ERAs and stokers took pride in keeping the engine room immaculate. There were three boiler rooms, each in its own watertight compartment. 'I don't think upper deck people envied us,' admits Andrew, 'but I found the job extremely absorbing.' The only thing that really worried him was the two huge steam pipes above his head. The pressure gauge showed that the steam in the pipes was 3,000 lb per square inch – or 675 degrees Fahrenheit. 'In any action,' says Andrew, 'I hoped nothing would come through the side and hit one of those.' *Icarus* had certainly been under fire before, but nothing like the degree she and her crew would face at Dunkirk. For men like Andrew, it was best to put such thoughts out of mind.

While HMS *Icarus* was speeding along the south coast of Britain, Winston Churchill was addressing his Cabinet – some twenty-five men from different parties, and all highly experienced parliamentary men. Churchill gave them a frank account of what had happened during the past fortnight and admitted the BEF was now being evacuated. He expected 50,000 to be lifted, although told them 100,000 would be a magnificent effort. The public needed to be prepared for bad tidings and what was happening in northern France was truthfully the greatest British military defeat for many centuries. Soon, the war would be turned against their island and they needed to prepare themselves for that. Nonetheless, an invasion would be an immensely difficult thing for the Germans to carry out. There was no point, he added, thinking Britain would get better terms from Germany if they tried to make peace rather than if they fought it out. Hitler would demand their fleet, naval bases and much else besides. A puppet government would be no doubt set up under someone like Mosley. On the other hand they had plenty of reserves, a strong navy, air defences that were easier to manage from home, and waters amply mined. 'We shall go on and we shall fight it out,' he told them, 'here or elsewhere, and if at last the long story is to end, it were better it should end, not through surrender, but only when we are rolling senseless on the ground.' There was a murmur of approval, and not one expression of dissent.

Churchill now had the support of his wider Cabinet, and, crucially, of Chamberlain. When the War Cabinet reconvened, Churchill recounted what had just happened and stressed the response. 'I cannot recall having ever before heard a gathering of persons occupying high places in political life,' he told them, 'express themselves so emphatically.' At this, Halifax mentioned Reynaud's proposed appeal to President Roosevelt and whether it should be a joint message; he said nothing more of an appeal to Mussolini. Churchill now dismissed even an American appeal out of hand. And that was that – no more was ever said on the matter.

Churchill had scored a great personal victory and in so doing had greatly increased his previously fragile authority. Britain was still in great peril but at least she now had a chance to fight on, to pit herself against the best that Germany could throw at her. The battle might have been lost in France, but the war was not over yet. In Britain, one major crisis, at least, had been averted.

19

Dunkirk: In the Balance

On the afternoon of 28 May, Lord Gort had moved his command post to the Belgian King's summer palace overlooking the dunes and sea at La Panne, just inside the Belgian border and some nine miles east of Dunkirk. 'And so here we are back on the shores of France on which we landed with such high hearts over eight months ago,' jotted Henry Pownall that night. 'I think we were a gallant band who little deserve this ignominious end to our efforts.' It was incredible to think they had been pushed back to the sea in just three weeks. 'For myself,' he added, 'I am still stunned. It seems all a bad dream from which I hope to wake.'

At least he had reached the beaches, which was more than could be said for the majority of the BEF. Most, however, would be on the move that night. Sid Nuttall and the 1st Border Regiment, still at the bottom of the British corridor to the north-west of Lille, had been given orders to withdraw by thinning out companies and then to rendezvous at Ploegsteert with the rest of the brigade using lorries abandoned by the Royal Engineers. Sid and his mates in 'C' Company still had no real idea of what was going on, although it hadn't taken much to realize things were going badly wrong. The battalion had also suffered a number of casualties and was, like everyone else in the BEF, struggling with the lack of ammunition and rations.

At around 3 p.m., the battalion began pulling into Ploegsteert, the trucks covered by a screen of Bren gun carriers from the Carrier Platoon. There was, however, no sign of the rest of the brigade, so it continued onwards to Poperinge, a few miles to the west of Ypres. There the troops found an artillery regiment. 'Whacking great guns they were,' says Sid. 'They were shooting their ammunition off because they were going to destroy the guns.' The battalion learned that the RV for 42nd Division was now Killem, a village just to the south of the Dunkirk perimeter. With the artillery booming and offering them cover, the men set off again. It was now evening and they finally learned that they were headed for Dunkirk. 'We began meeting more and more people,' says Sid, 'and seeing more and more abandoned vehicles.' These were the trucks, carriers and cars that had made the BEF one of the best equipped armies in the world – but they could not be taken back across the sea, so orders had been given to abandon them either at or near the perimeter of the Bergues–Furnes Canal, and then to destroy them. It was the men who needed to get home – soldiers with as little kit as possible. 'Some had been sabotaged and some hadn't,' says Sid. 'People were shoving sand and earth in and then running them, trying to ruin the engines.' A few were setting them on fire but that ran the risk of attracting enemy aircraft.

The battalion reached Killem some time after 9 p.m. and abandoned the trucks, but then, as darkness began to fall, Sid lost sight of his MT sergeant. 'So it was just me,' says Sid, 'and a chap called Middleton, the other vehicle mechanic, and "C" Company.' They crossed a bridge over the canal and then kept going until, at dawn, they found themselves at Bray Dunes.

The men of 4th Division were also moving back. It seemed that no sooner had the 2nd Royal Fusiliers safely crossed the River Lys than news had arrived of the Belgian surrender. With it came new orders to retreat, this time towards Dixmude. The problem was that many of the battalion's vehicles had been put out of action. For Second Lieutenant Norman Field, the battalion adjutant, this was a difficult time. Verbal orders – the battalion had no radio or telephone links – were issued for an immediate withdrawal but delivering them was tricky because enemy troops had managed to occupy some houses near the battalion's farmhouse HQ and now began peppering the building with small-arms fire. The British managed to subdue these troops, however, so that by 7 p.m. the battalion had pulled back successfully with hardly any casualties.

Its immediate rendezvous was on the Poperinge road, but it now seemed that half the BEF plus countless civilians were also using the road.

Nonetheless, the battalion managed to reach the town, more or less in one piece. The guns Sid Nuttall had seen earlier were now silent. Abandoned vehicles littered the roadside, as did bomb craters. Through this mayhem, the soldiers marched onwards until early the following morning they found the 12th Brigade commander, Brigadier Leslie 'Ginger' Hawkesworth, standing at a crossroads some five miles south of Furnes, issuing company commanders with their new orders, which for the Royal Fusiliers, was to hold the perimeter line around Nieuport, just inland from the coast. This was the easternmost point of the British defensive line. The problem was getting all the men there. 'We weren't very cohesive,' says Norman. 'There was so much traffic on the roads and all nationalities. Some people got lost.' By daylight, the entire battalion numbered just 280, about a third of its strength on 10 May.

Gunner Stan Fraser and the 4th HAA were among the last to fall back to the coast. On the 27th, they had been on the hills around Menin, providing cover for the retreat. They were not large hills, but on the flat plain of Flanders Stan had been able to see for miles – as far as Dunkirk and the fires and columns of smoke billowing above the town. He had also watched waves of bombers fly overhead. Mercifully, they had not dropped any bombs on them, but rather, it seemed to Stan, mostly on defenceless civilians trudging along the roads. In fact, the only thing to fall on them were leaflets, on which there was a map and the lines, 'British Soldiers! Look at this map: it gives your true situation! Your troops are entirely surrounded – stop fighting! Put down your arms!' In fact, the map showed a considerably larger stretch of coastline than was the reality; it had clearly been printed before the Belgian surrender. Stan and his mates had just laughed.

The following morning, he was up at dawn to deliver rations to the batteries, which were a few miles from Regimental Headquarters. Passing through a village that had just been bombed, he and his mate found an abandoned stash of rations and cigarettes in the village square. Helping themselves, they then continued on their way, successfully reaching the battery. On the return journey, however, they were caught in an endless stream of convoys – horses, lorries, guns, ambulances, troops, all making for Dunkirk. When Stan and his friend eventually reached their HQ camp, rumours abounded of another imminent move. Soon after, firm orders came not only to pack up but also to dump and burn everything except spare socks and a few other essentials. Everything, apart from their three trucks, was to be abandoned.

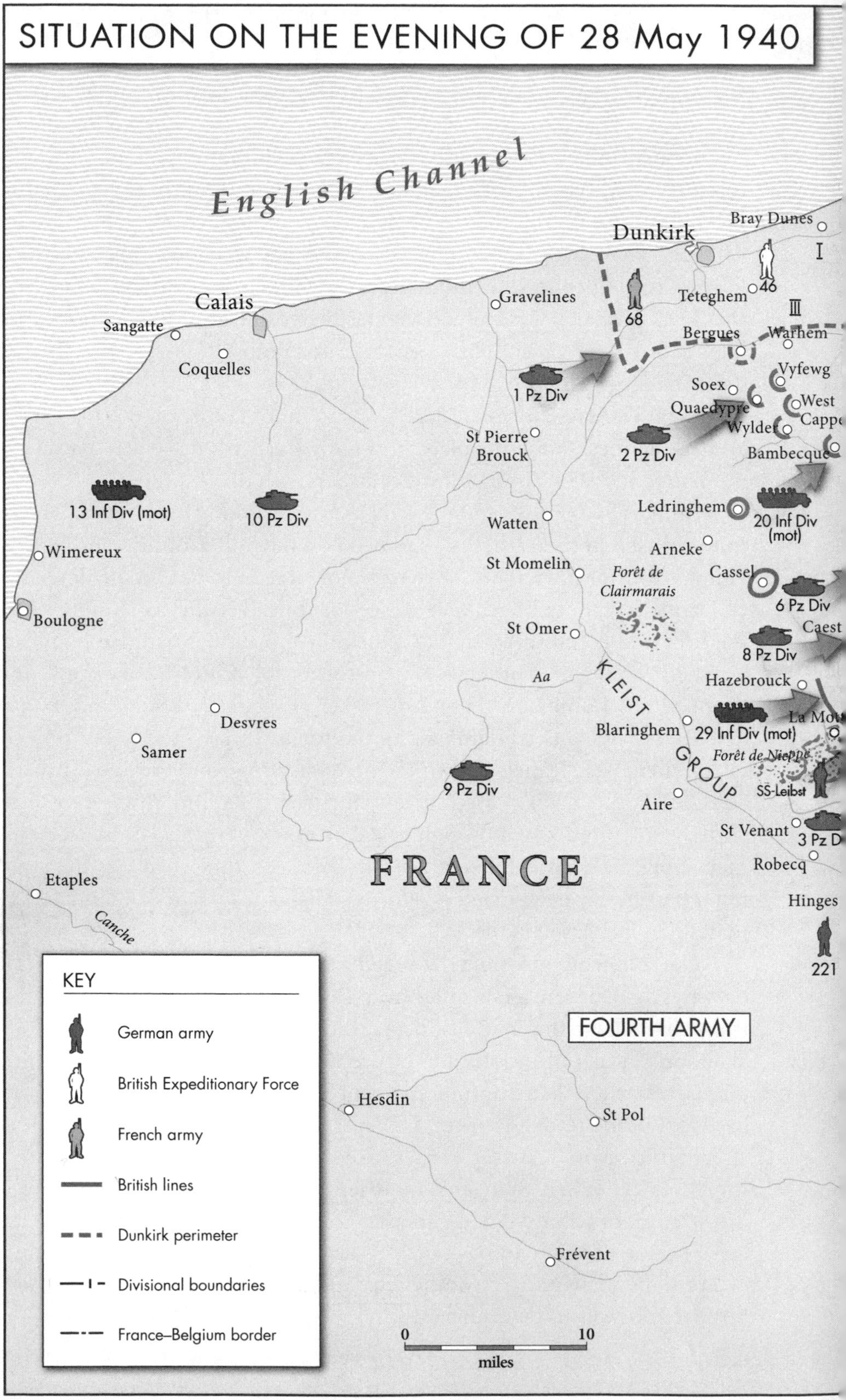

SITUATION ON THE EVENING OF 28 May 1940

English Channel
Dunkirk
Bray Dunes
I
46
Teteghem
III
Warhem
Bergues
68
Gravelines
Calais
Sangatte
Coquelles
1 Pz Div
Vyfewg
Soex
Quaedypre
West Cappe
Wylder
Bambecque
2 Pz Div
St Pierre Brouck
13 Inf Div (mot)
10 Pz Div
Ledringhem
20 Inf Div (mot)
Watten
Arneke
Wimereux
St Momelin
Forêt de Clairmarais
Cassel
6 Pz Div
Boulogne
St Omer
Caest
8 Pz Div
Aa
KLEIST GROUP
Hazebrouck
Desvres
Blaringhem
29 Inf Div (mot)
La Mot
Samer
Forêt de Nieppe
9 Pz Div
SS-Leibst
Aire
St Venant
3 Pz D
Robecq
FRANCE
Etaples
Hinges
Canche
221

KEY
German army
British Expeditionary Force
French army
British lines
Dunkirk perimeter
Divisional boundaries
France–Belgium border

FOURTH ARMY
Hesdin
St Pol
Frévent

0 10
miles

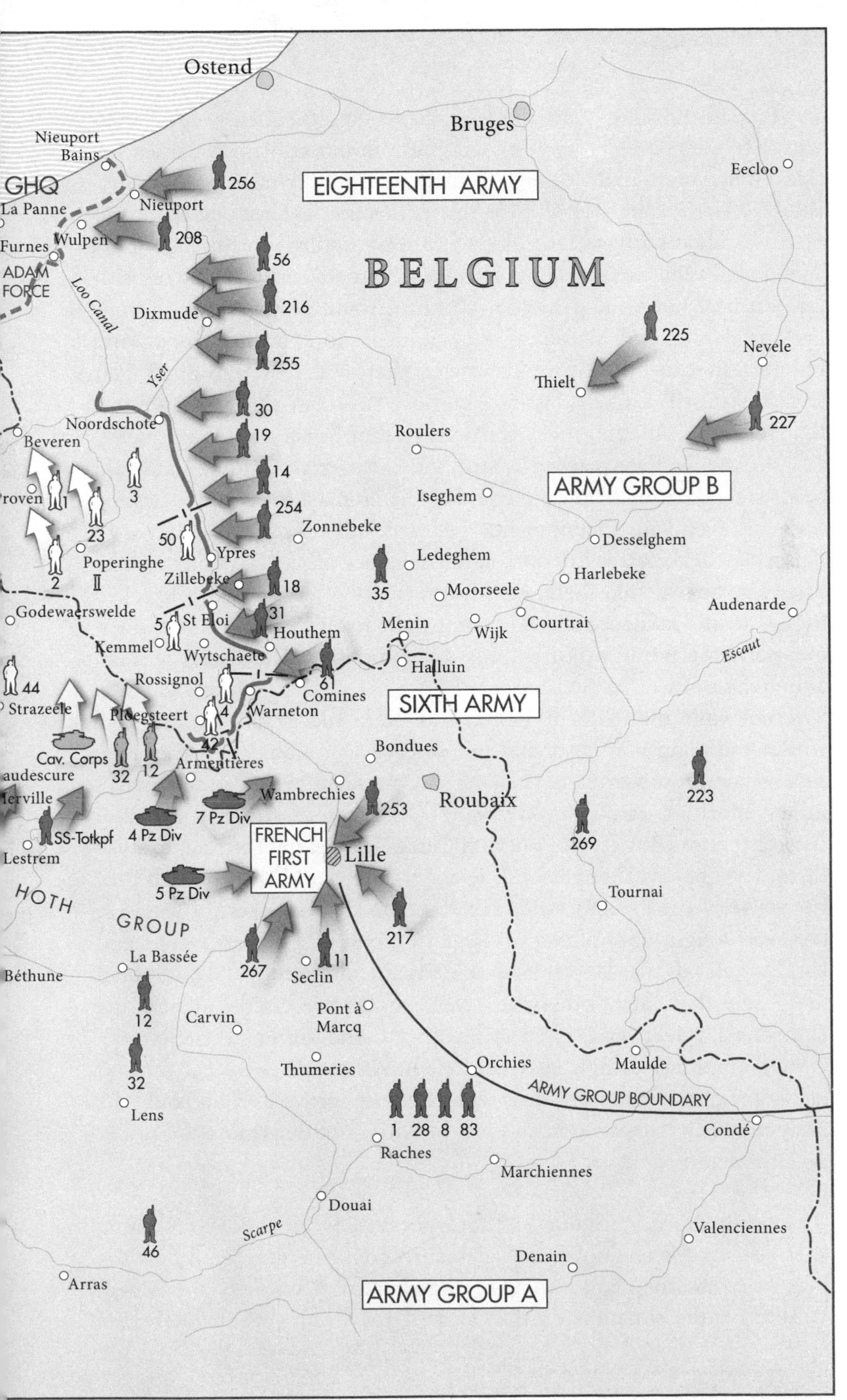
Ostend
Bruges
Nieuport Bains
GHQ
La Panne
Nieuport
Furnes
Wulpen
ADAM FORCE
Loo Canal
Dixmude
Yser
Noordschote
Beveren
roven
Poperinghe
II
Ypres
Zillebeke
Godewaersvelde
St Eloi
Kemmel
Wytschaete
Houthem
Rossignol
Strazeele
Ploegsteert
Warneton
Comines
Cav. Corps
Armentières
audescure
erville
SS-Totkpf
4 Pz Div
7 Pz Div
5 Pz Div
Lestrem
HOTH GROUP
La Bassée
Béthune
Carvin
Lens
Arras
Scarpe
EIGHTEENTH ARMY
BELGIUM
Eecloo
Nevele
Thielt
Roulers
Iseghem
ARMY GROUP B
Zonnebeke
Ledeghem
Desselghem
Harlebeke
Moorseele
Audenarde
Menin
Wijk
Courtrai
Halluin
Escaut
SIXTH ARMY
Bondues
Wambrechies
Roubaix
FRENCH FIRST ARMY
Lille
Tournai
Seclin
Pont à Marcq
Thumeries
Orchies
Maulde
ARMY GROUP BOUNDARY
Condé
Raches
Marchiennes
Douai
Valenciennes
Denain
ARMY GROUP A
256
208
56
216
255
30
19
14
254
18
31
61
35
225
227
223
269
253
217
267
11
1
28
8
83
12
32
46
44
42
4
5
50
3
23
2
1

By mid-morning the trucks were loaded and the men were on their way. 'God helped our retreat by sending a thunderstorm to darken the skies,' noted Stan, 'and although it made our journey rather uncomfortable, we were really thankful for this protection against the bombers.' Stan was shocked by what he saw as they trundled north: even more abandoned vehicles, stores littered across the road, corpses lying in fields and ditches, houses and buildings bombed and blazing. The journey became slower and slower as they joined more traffic, troops and refugees. Eventually, near the perimeter, they were forced to ditch their trucks. With rifles, one Bren and one Boys anti-tank rifle, plus as much food and ammunition as they could carry, they began marching.

Eventually, they reached a farmhouse where the colonel had told them to rendezvous – Stan and six others had remained behind to destroy the vehicles and other equipment. They were still not sure what they were doing but the Assistant Adjutant, now the senior officer, gave them a talk. The Germans, he told them, were now very close on all sides. He called for a vote of confidence and told them to be ready throughout the night to defend the farm until there was not a man left to do so. The men, although utterly exhausted, agreed.

But while the majority of the BEF were successfully falling back within the main perimeter and the defence line along the River Yser, some were not so fortunate. As those at Calais had sacrificed themselves in an effort to delay the advancing Germans, so too had the 2nd Gloucesters and 4th Ox and Bucks at Cassel and nearby Ledringhem. For three days they had fought off one attack after another. Although they had been eventually surrounded and cut off from the rest of the BEF, they had fought on, holding up large numbers of German troops and with it their advance, and thus enabled many more troops behind them to fall back than might otherwise have been the case. On the night of the 28th, the survivors attempted to break out, and although a few small groups eventually managed to reach Dunkirk, most were caught and taken prisoner. However, their epic defence proved what could be achieved when troops stood and fought with grim determination rather than fleeing in panic.

'Apparently the lack of news was not a good thing,' noted Daidie Penna, after hearing the news of the Belgian surrender. She wondered how the BEF could possibly be saved. 'Nothing short of a miracle,' she added, 'could save the situation on that part of the front now.' Nonetheless,

Daidie sensed a renewed feeling of determination – not just within herself, but amongst everyone. And she was enjoying the reports of the RAF's 'wonderful' performance. 'The daily bag of enemy planes,' she scribbled, 'is now almost a commonplace.'

Certainly Fighter Command had been playing its part in covering the evacuation. Air Chief Marshal Dowding had placed tactical control of his fighters with Air Vice-Marshal Keith Park. It had been an obvious step, because any fighters operating over Dunkirk would have to be based at airfields in the south-east of England; Fighter Command was divided into four groups – 10 Group in the south-west, 12 in the middle, 13 in the north and Scotland and 11 in the south-east, of which Park was commander. A New Zealander, Park was the son of a Scottish geologist. In the previous war, he had served in the artillery at Gallipoli, but later joined the British army and was moved to the Western Front. Wounded in October 1916, he recovered and applied to join the RFC. Accepted, he began life as a spotter then became a pilot, later commanding 48 Squadron, and finishing the war with fourteen victories, a couple of MCs, the DFC and the *Croix de Guerre.* One of the comparative few to receive a regular post-war commission in the RAF, he later served as Dowding's Senior Air Staff Officer at Fighter Command before being given command of 11 Group in April.

Tall, with a lean face, trim moustache and twinkly eyes, he was nonetheless a rather stern, austere figure: a tough, exacting man who suffered no fools – in many ways not unlike Dowding. He was also a great thinker and had done much to develop fighter tactics and the defence system during his time as Dowding's Chief of Staff. The two both liked each other and worked extremely well together. For Dowding's part, Park had repeatedly proved his competence. As a commander and leader, he trusted him implicitly – and with good reason.

For covering Dunkirk, Park had sixteen squadrons at his disposal out of the thirty-six now left in Fighter Command, the rest remaining as both a reserve and to protect other parts of the country. Like Kesselring, Park was also faced with the problem of range, although not so much from lack of fuel (although his fighters had a limit of forty minutes over the French port) but because it meant operating outside Britain's defensive system. There was no radar cover over Dunkirk so he was forced to rely on inefficient and exhausting standing patrols.

From the Admiralty came demands for constant fighter cover around the clock. Park was not sure this was the best use of his fighters, however. Flying over Dunkirk himself in his Hurricane, and then talking to pilots, he quickly became convinced that it was better to send over two squadrons for some of the time rather than one or half a squadron to provide non-stop cover. He was undoubtedly right, and by 29 May he got his way, Dowding authorizing him to use his aircraft as he saw fit, rather than how the Admiralty was demanding. It was one of the many benefits of the two men's close working relationship.

In order to try to keep all his squadrons at reasonable strength, Park also made sure he rotated them regularly. 92 Squadron, for example, had flown two missions over the French coast on the 23rd and one on the 24th, and then one Channel patrol on the 25th, before being posted to Duxford and out of the fray, while those who had earlier served in France, like Pete Brothers' 32 Squadron, were kept out of it altogether.

Squadrons were also moved around from other groups and placed temporarily under Park's charge. One of these was 616 Squadron, which until 27 May had been based in Leconfield in Yorkshire and hence part of 13 Group. That morning, the squadron had made the one-hour flight down to Rochford in Kent, relieving 74 Squadron. That same afternoon it had set off for a patrol over Dunkirk but had engaged nothing. Not so on its second patrol the following morning when, at around 9.45 a.m., it ran into around thirty Messerschmitts of JG 26.

The first Hugh 'Cocky' Dundas saw of these enemy aircraft was as the squadron approached the coast. Two Skuas of the navy's Fleet Air Arm were swooping past him in the opposite direction, clearly in a hurry. As he craned his neck, he saw why: five 109s, their black crosses and swastikas as clear as day, were diving away and behind to his right, and from the lead Messerschmitt came thin trails of grey smoke as the pilot opened fire. In a trice, the group had faded to specks, disappearing beneath the dense smoke cloud that rose above Dunkirk and spread like a shroud down the Channel as far as the eye could see.

Cocky had only the briefest moment to absorb his first view of this fearsome enemy because suddenly his section commander, George Moberley, was wheeling in a climbing turn. Following, Cocky heard the confusion of garbled voices over his R/T. Then there was another 109, curving round with a bright yellow nose. More feathery trails of smoke spat from it and lights of cannon fire flashed from the propeller hub. Red flashes of tracer arced lazily towards them then seemed to suddenly accelerate as they streaked above Cocky's wing. With a sudden stab of pure fear, Cocky realized he was being fired upon, so he banked his

Spitfire hard into a tight turn, the blood draining from his head from the force of negative gravity. The aircraft began to judder on the brink of a stall, but as it straightened out his head cleared and ahead of him he saw a mass of twisting, turning planes. More bullets and cannon shells seemed to be hurtling towards him, so he instantly flung himself into another turn. Coming out of it once more, a 109 sped across his windscreen and instinctively he opened fire, his plane juddering as his eight machine guns rattled.

Cocky felt close to panic in that first dogfight. Instinct made him keep turning and twisting his neck, but rather than a compelling urge to shoot down the enemy, it was a desire to stay alive that drove him. At last, he felt it safe to straighten out and was amazed, as so many pilots were in the first few engagements, to discover a sudden inexplicably empty sky. Panic now gripped him again and finding himself over the sea some miles north of Dunkirk his training and nerve deserted him. Rather than calmly thinking about the course he needed to take to get back to the Thames estuary, he blindly set out in what he thought was roughly the right direction. Driven by an overwhelming urge to land back on dry land, he pressed on, all calmness and good sense gone. He knew he was heading north and that that was the wrong direction so he turned around, vainly hoping that by returning to Dunkirk he would get his bearings. The sight of the French coast and two ships steaming below kicked some sense into him, however, and forcing himself to work out this simple navigational problem he managed to set a course west and soon the English coastline appeared ahead of him.

As he flew low down the estuary and past Southend pier, he realized he was soaked with sweat. And as he touched down at last, the abject fear and panic were, in an instant, gone, replaced instead by a sense of jubilation and exhilaration that, at the age of nearly twenty, he was now a fighter pilot who had tangled with the enemy – and survived.

And it was the young man back on land who wrote to his mother a few days later with the kind of nonchalance becoming of a fighter pilot. 'Dear Mummy,' he scrawled, 'No more major excitements since I last wrote to you. We are doing lots of offensive patrols over the battle area, always going across with all the machines we can get into the air and in company with several other squadrons: in fact, the air becomes black with Spitfires and Brother Bosche is not so ready to bomb our troops and ships.' He then gave her a breathless description of the action – 'he dived like a rocket and I pumped a lot of lead into his starboard mainplane' –

and finished his letter telling her there was no need to worry about him or his older brother, John, who was also a fighter pilot. 'I am quite certain that our Spitfires are the finest machines flying over Belgium now,' he added cheerfully. It is unlikely she felt very reassured.

While the vast amount of smoke was helping the British cause, so too was the weather. After weeks of largely fine, dry weather, a front was now inching over the Channel and northern France. By the evening of Tuesday, 28 May, visibility was deteriorating and with it came rain. Heavy cloud and rain – but no wind. The Channel remained flat as a board. The weather gods were smiling on the British.

Nearly 18,000 men were evacuated that day – almost 12,000 from the east mole, and nearly 6,000 from the beaches. Yet most of these had been lifted from the Dunkirk end, and now more and more men were pouring on to the beaches further along, particularly near Bray Dunes. Bill Tennant heard that there were now around 5,000 milling around the dunes and beaches there, so sent two of his officers and fifteen men to see what they could organize. They were staggered to discover not 5,000 but some 25,000 men already there, most exhausted, thirsty, hungry and leaderless. And there were nothing like enough boats offshore. 'I must stress the need for boats and motor launches at Bray,' they signalled. 'Much provisions for troops also needed.'

That same evening, Ramsay, from the Dynamo Room at Dover, asked that every available shallow-draft power boat should be sent to the beaches as soon as possible. Despite the embargo on the news of the evacuation, the Admiralty responded by combing the entire coast from Portsmouth to Norfolk for motor boats, lighters and barges, and, of course, their crews. And these were now heading to Dunkirk too.

HMS *Icarus* had now reached Dunkirk too, having reached Dover in the early hours and then steamed off with four other destroyers, including her sister ships *Ivanhoe* and *Intrepid*. They arrived at the mole at around 5.30 a.m. just as a personnel vessel filled with water and waiting outside the harbour for a berth hit a magnetic mine. 'She just erupted into a thousand pieces,' says Andrew Begg, who saw her go. The *Mona Queen* sank in about two minutes. Earlier, the destroyer HMS *Wakeful* had also sunk, hit by a torpedo on her return to Dover; more than 600 troops on board were drowned.

Only two hours after drawing alongside the mole, *Icarus* sailed away again with some 950 men on board, reaching Dover at around 11.30 a.m. Quickly unloading, she then turned round and sped back, this time heading not for the mole but for the beaches at Bray Dunes, where the shortage of shallow-draft boats was still causing major difficulties. 'It was chaos,' says Andrew Begg, 'because there was no way of getting large numbers of men out to the ship.' *Icarus* dropped two whalers and a motor boat. 'We couldn't anchor and daren't anchor because of the constant aerial activity,' says Andrew. 'There was continuous bombing and periodic dive-bombing. The Stukas would come over and have a go and so you had to keep moving – going round in little circles backwards and forwards.' They were there for about six hours – it had taken around four hours just to fill the two whalers and get the men on board. Then having taken 450 men from the Dutch skoot *Doggersbank*, they set off back to Dover once more.

By this time, Andrew was back down in the engine room, where he and his fellows had been joined by a couple of dozen troops. A number were in severe shock and shivering. 'They needed some heat,' says Andrew, 'and it was warm enough there.'

One of those watching *Icarus* was Sid Nuttall, who, with his fellows from 'C' Company, was amongst the 25,000 now at Bray Dunes. It was bewildering emerging through the dunes and suddenly seeing the scene before them: vast numbers of troops, ships out at sea, men firing wildly at any aircraft that flew over them. Smoke still billowed from the port and houses all along the seafront. At first, it seemed to be utter chaos, but actually there was some attempt being made to bring about some order. Someone was directing RAOC men to an assembly point, but Sid now felt more Border than RAOC, and so stayed put with his company. There were around eighty of them now, mainly from 'C' Company. Most were all very much worse for wear. Sid only wore his battledress on his top; his shirt had become infested with lice and although he'd been taught how to get rid of them, it got to be so bad he had thrown it away. He still had his rifle, but almost no other kit. His mates were in much the same boat. 'A regular officer came down,' says Sid, 'and told us no man from the Border regiment would be evacuated until he was in possession of a full set of equipment. We went on the scrounge and everything was there. We made up our kit from things people had thrown about.' Having done this, the officer inspected them again, and ordered them to shave, but with no water they had no choice but to use the sea. Eventually, the officer seemed satisfied. Bringing them into line, he marched them back into defensive positions in the dunes.

Sid noticed that a large number of men were drunk. Because there was no water, soldiers had been breaking into bars and cellars and had stolen beer, wine and spirits – anything they could get their hands on. Despite this, however, Bill Tennant's men had begun bringing some order to the beaches at Bray. Sid saw queues of people forming down to the waterline, and destroyers and other ships moored offshore. Overhead, the Luftwaffe seemed to be near-constant companions. 'The destroyers were being dive-bombed at regular intervals,' says Sid, 'but luckily most of the dive-bombing was being done on the ships.'

He had absolutely no idea how long they would be there on the beaches or what their chances were of ever getting away. There was no food and no water, and the beach seemed to be getting busier by the minute. All he and his mates could do was wait and hope for the best.

During the morning of 29 May, Lord Gort heard news that Général de la Laurencie's III Corps had decided to have a dash for it and had severed itself from the rest of the French First Army and was now heading towards Dunkirk alongside the last of the BEF. The rest of First Army, however, was now entirely surrounded, just as the BEF would have been had Hitler not sided with von Rundstedt in halting the panzers.

Henry Pownall had received orders that he was to set sail for England that evening, but first there were several 'flaps' to sort out. The first was that Admiral Abrial had not been told by his government that the British were evacuating. He had understood that non-combatants would be shipped home, but not fighting men. Furthermore, he told them, according to French practice, he was in charge of defending Dunkirk and he expected the British to pull their weight rather than leave it to the French. Patiently, Gort explained that British troops were now defending the perimeter, most of it, in fact, except for the area west of the port and the very north-west, which was held by the French. Had Abrial ventured out of his bunker at Bastion 32, he could have seen this for himself. Gort sent General Adam to explain this to Abrial in person then spoke to Dill and asked him to get Reynaud or Weygand to put the *Amiral Nord* in the picture properly.

Then came word that there were some 1,500 French soldiers on the beach at La Panne who were rushing the boats. Two little ships were so swamped by French soldiers they sank. Another air raid fortunately dispersed them, but as a result of this Gort now agreed that French soldiers should also be evacuated and that this should be done from the mole and around Malo-les-Bains in turn with the British troops there.

Most British troops were now within the perimeter. The policy of fighting by day and falling back by night seemed to have largely worked. The last line of defence south of Dunkirk held by 50th and 3rd Divisions had suffered heavily but the line had held. Throughout the afternoon, they began falling back across the River Yser, still held by the 42nd and 5th Divisions, and then, as evening came, it was time for them to fall back too.

Also now at Bray Dunes was Gunner Stan Fraser. The battalion colonel had not arrived during the night. The men had waited until 11 a.m. the following morning, then gave up and decided to head for the sea without him. The trek seemed to last for ever. It was bad enough trudging along with their kit, and taking turns with the Bren and Boys – the Bren weighed more than ten kilos – but with waves of German bombers flying over they were continually diving into the side of the road to take cover. And the sun was hot on their backs. At one point Stan found a cart horse in a field, so gave it some biscuits in the hope of befriending it. Managing to lead it back to the road, he then spent ten minutes trying to get on its back. Eventually, he got himself on, exhausted, but the beast was hard to ride bareback and after a mile or so he slipped off and continued on foot.

It was about four in the afternoon when they eventually reached Bray Dunes, only for another wave of bombers to drone over. They all flopped down into ditches and holes in the dunes whilst bombs whistled and exploded and naval guns and any artillery still functioning pounded away. When the raiders eventually passed, they stumbled on to the beach. Stan was also astonished by the vast numbers of men there. More bombers came over. Stan watched the bombs fall, and then the resulting spout of sand or water. 'When the bombs dropped close,' he noted, 'when we could hear the long whine as they descended, then we pressed down flat waiting – waiting for the explosion which sometimes lifted us off the ground.'

As dusk fell, a ship out at sea was ablaze, casting a flickering orange glow across the sky. Stan still had his sleeping bag, a piece of kit he'd not thrown away, and now was thankful for his foresight. Scooping out a hole in the sand, he laid it out and clambered in. Already he had written up his diary. 'I will never forget that day,' he wrote, 'as long as I live.'

20

Dunkirk: The Middle

THERE WAS STILL no mention of any evacuation in the British newspapers on Thursday, 30 May, although there was much about the heroics of the RAF and the bravery of the BEF still fighting in Flanders. There were, however, the usual listings: births, deaths, marriages. There was sports news – racing at Bath, and although there was no longer any first class cricket, the schools were still reported; the MCC was playing Winchester College. As in Berlin, the theatres were still running in London and West End shows were listed. At the New Theatre, George Bernard Shaw's new play, *In Good King Charles's Golden Day*, had opened, starring, amongst others, the well-known actress Margaret Rawlings.

It was a busy time for Margaret, who, just a few days short of her thirty-fourth birthday, had only finished her previous West End play, *A House in the Square*, five days before. Amongst her admirers was John Dundas, the older brother of Cocky, and she had arranged for him and two of his friends to see her in the play's final night. Afterwards, she had accompanied all three of them to a party. 'You looked your most beautiful last night,' John wrote to her the next day, 'and ever so you!'

The two shared an unusually close friendship. Ten years older than John, Margaret already had a failed marriage behind her, and was now having an affair with the playwright and novelist Charles Morgan, who was married and refused to leave his wife. There was another admirer, Robert Barlow, a businessman, who ran Metal Box Company, a tinning manufacturing business already turned over to war work, but he too was married and fifteen years her senior. If John minded this rather complicated tangle of lovers and admirers, he did not say so. Instead, he was grateful to have a friend and confidante from the glamorous world of the theatre, and someone who enjoyed intellectual debate as much as he.

John had got to know her two years before, having met her after a performance in Leeds, which he had been reviewing for the *Yorkshire Post.* Two days later he had written to her asking to see her again. 'Don't you think,' he had written, 'that on Monday we left a good many intellectual (or mainly conversational) loose ends lying around, which might be fun to pick up?' She had taken up his offer and he had duly become smitten. This beginning of their friendship had also coincided with his first solo flight with his Auxiliary squadron, 609 (West Riding) Squadron. The two experiences, he told her, 'have succeeded in raising the beat of my pulse (permanently I believe) by several strokes a minute'.

Their friendship had soon flourished. She enjoyed his company and loved him dearly, but they had not become lovers. In any case, he had barely seen her since the beginning of the war because he had been stationed at Drem near Edinburgh. He had written her reams of letters, but now that his squadron had been moved south, to Northolt, in north-west London, he was excited by the prospect of seeing more of her.

These past ten days, the pilots had been allowed into town as often as they liked in the evening, because although 609 Squadron had moved south on 19 May, it had yet to fly an operational patrol. Now, however, on 30 May, 609 Squadron was finally called to stand by for a patrol over Dunkirk. It had been a long time in coming, but it was time for 609's pilots to enter the fray. They hoped they were ready.

John Dundas's younger brother, Cocky, was also over Dunkirk again that day. The two were close – brothers amongst three sisters. Brought up in rural north Yorkshire, theirs had been a comfortable, idyllic upbringing in which sport and country pursuits had been an accepted way of life. Cocky certainly looked up to his older brother, first joining him at Stowe school and then hoping to follow him to Christ Church, Oxford. John had graduated with a first in modern history and an award that had sent him for a year to the Sorbonne in Paris and then to Heidelberg, but during this time abroad he had lived far too wildly and racked up excessive bills so that their father told Cocky he could only afford for him to go to Oxford on condition he won a scholarship. This he did, but to Trinity rather than Christ Church. In the end, however, his parents were worried that Cocky might prove as profligate as his brother and so encouraged him not to take up the place. Bowing to the wishes of his mother and father, Cocky instead became articled at a solicitor's firm, a job he loathed.

Meanwhile, John had joined 609 Squadron and Cocky had wanted to fly too. He had always been fascinated by war as a boy, although it was more because of the excitement of flying rather than the possible coming of war that had made him determined to join the Auxiliary Air Force. For some reason Cocky was never able to fathom, however, he failed his preliminary medical three times. Only on the fourth time did he pass, and although he was unable to join John in 609 Squadron as he had hoped, he was happy enough, in May 1939, to be sent to 616 Auxiliary Squadron at Doncaster as a pupil pilot.

A year on, he and his brother were fighting over Dunkirk.

Ambassador Joe Kennedy was very much with Halifax in believing that Britain's leaders needed to look at the rapidly unfolding events both rationally and pragmatically, yet he feared they were viewing the situation far too optimistically. As far as he was concerned, defeat by Germany still seemed heavily on the cards. Thus, he had spent some energy trying to encourage the Government to send its gold reserves to safety in Canada and to make contingency plans for the future, such as sending the Royal Family there and making preparations for the Government to move there should it be necessary. This suggestion was sharply rebuffed by Churchill, who said that even shipping valuables might make the public think the Government was in a panic. What concerned Kennedy was not only the gold reserves falling into German hands but particularly the Royal Navy – a worry shared by the President. Of course, Churchill understood this – he had even dangled the threat of losing the British fleet before Roosevelt in an effort to get more help from the United States. Luring America in remained a key policy for Churchill, yet the Prime Minister knew that Kennedy was not the man to facilitate this. Kennedy was sensing this too. 'My contacts with the Churchill Cabinet were certainly far less friendly than with the old Government,' he noted. 'Yet my first duty was to the United States and I had to tell them that they could not count on us for anything but supplies. And the worse the situation became, the harder it was to tell them.'

On the 30th, however, Kennedy visited the Palace to hand-deliver a letter from Roosevelt to the King. George VI was wearing his army uniform and looking fitter than Kennedy had seen him for some time. He told Kennedy that they had now lifted some 80,000 from Dunkirk, almost double what had originally been hoped. 'Just think,' said the King, 'all this death and destruction due to the whim of one man.'

The King was right: the evacuation was going far better than had been first hoped – more than 33,000 had been lifted from the mole alone the previous day – and was continuing all that morning. Helping them once again was the weather. From dawn, a fog and sea mist had rolled in over the Flanders coast and, with the still heavy smoke, made it impossible for the Luftwaffe to see any targets at all. Twice formations of Stukas took off and on both occasions were forced to return.

There was nothing to stop the ground troops pressing forward, however, although the Germans attacking the bridgehead were finding it hard going. The panzers had brought chaos with their speed and drive, and would have continued to do so had they sped up the coast behind the enemy's backs. But now they were facing determined troops well dug-in behind a considerable water obstacle, and the job of spearheading the attack had necessarily been handed back to the infantry with the artillery to help, just as it had been when they crossed the Meuse two weeks before. The gunners were doing a magnificent job, but many of the shells were falling in the waterlogged fields around the enemy positions and were thus not terribly effective. Mortars and small-arms fire were keeping up the pressure and night patrols were probing for weak spots, but this was old-fashioned attritional warfare. And it took time to wear the enemy down.

At OKH Headquarters, they were still livid about the missed opportunity of a few days before. Von Brauchitsch was in a foul mood, despite the remarkable victory his men would soon achieve. 'We lost time,' grumbled Halder, 'and so the pocket would have been closed at the coast if only our armour had not been held back. As it is, the bad weather has grounded our air force and now we must stand by and watch how countless thousands of the enemy are getting away to England right under our noses.' Nor was it helping that both Army Groups A and B were involved in the operation against the Dunkirk bridgehead, which, in the big scheme of things, was too small an area for two such large military machines to operate. Resentment was brewing. There was anger that the Luftwaffe could not do more, while, within Army Group A, the Fourth Army believed Panzer Group Kleist was not attacking hard enough, and that Army Group B was expecting Army Group A to do the lion's share of the fighting. Panzer Group Kleist, meanwhile, complained to the Fourth Army that its panzers were ill-suited to the task. When its 20th Motorized Division began attacking around Bergues, it reported that it was unable to break through. A lack of unity in command was hampering German efforts.

The men on the ground knew nothing about this high-level testiness, however. Certainly the men of the Eighteenth Army attacking the eastern end of the bridgehead believed they were doing all they could. The 56th Infantry Division was now pressing on the bridgehead either side of Furnes. The 171st Regiment was given the small town of Bulscamp, defended by the 9th Durham Light Infantry and 1st King's Own Scottish Borderers.

Amongst those attacking were Unteroffizier Hellmuth Damm and his men. Just the day before they had passed a number of freshly dug German graves and it had sent a chill down their spines. Neither he nor his men were under any illusion that the attack that day would be a walkover. It was now around 9 a.m. on the morning of the 30th. 'When we moved into the assembly position to attack,' noted Hellmuth, 'we saw Bulscamp and its church towers in the morning mist, roughly three kilometres away, in the uncanny silence.' Hellmuth was now company leader for the attack. His CO, Hauptmann Krusche, gave him company documents, maps, lists and orders. He put two stick grenades into his boot legs, checked his rifle and ammunition pouches and was then given the order to get into Bulscamp and establish a company command post as soon as possible which could then become the battalion CP. As the attack began, the infantry sped forward, running with covering fire, then falling behind any cover they could find, before moving forward again. Hellmuth's heavy machine-gunners still had to follow closely behind, giving the immediate fire support the infantry needed. As leader, however, Hellmuth was at the front of his men, and was surprised by the vast amount of abandoned material as they approached the town. Equally surprising was the lack of enemy fire.

Reaching the edge of the town, the accompanying artillery observation officer clambered into a church tower and Hellmuth followed him hoping to get a better view. Nearby was a large building, perhaps a monastery, he guessed; at any rate, it looked ideal for the new battalion command post. Back down on the ground, he and one of his NCOs inspected the building. It looked as though it had been a field hospital until recently – bandages and medical equipment were strewn everywhere. Hellmuth was not sure it should be the new CP, however, as it was facing west, towards the British, with large windows, and rather exposed. He was back out in the yard and was about to open a large garden door when artillery shells started hurtling over. A gable of the building was hit and Hellmuth was struck on the side. Immediately, he asked his comrade whether he had been hit by a brick on his back. 'No,' came the reply, 'but you have a hole in your jacket.' Reaching inside his breast pocket he felt blood, so rushed to find the medical officer. Ripping his jacket off, he saw blood running down the left side of his chest. The doctor grabbed some dressings and pulled him down on to the floor as another shell crashed into the chimney. The room was now full of choking smoke, dust and grime. The doctor began bandaging him and, as he did so, Hellmuth reached back behind him and pulled out a piece of shrapnel as big as his thumbnail. 'The shot had gone through my pay book, song book and machine-gun target data sheet,' he noted, 'all of which were in my left breast pocket, as well as through my jacket, jumper, shirt and left shoulder, without damaging my heart, lung or ribs.' He had been lucky indeed. The doctor pinned a wounded note on his shirt, 'Shot through chest.' Still able to walk, Hellmuth got up and hurried back to Hauptmann Krusche. 'I was hit,' he told him.

'How am I going to find another company leader?' Krusche asked him. 'You are already the fourth.' Hellmuth handed back the company documents. 'Find an aid station,' Krusche told him, 'then come back!'

Gingerly, Hellmuth went in search of the aid station, which he found in an abandoned restaurant across the street. There he rested in the basement with four other soldiers and a few civilians all afternoon until the firing at last began to die down and he hoped it was safe to leave the town and head back to the rear echelons. Hellmuth and the other wounded men staggered out into the street, and, taking bicycles, headed back out of town, dodging debris as they did so. 'I had a hard time of it,' noted Hellmuth, 'because I had to press my left arm on the wound and the bandage. I ignored the pain.'

Eventually picked up by an artillery unit, they were taken back to Regimental Headquarters , where they were given some hot pea soup and then taken in to the 56th Division Field Hospital. By late evening, Hellmuth was in the operating theatre. Injecting a local dose of anaesthetic around the wound, the doctor probed around the mess of his wound, until pulling out a wad of bloody pulp. 'I've seen many things,' he

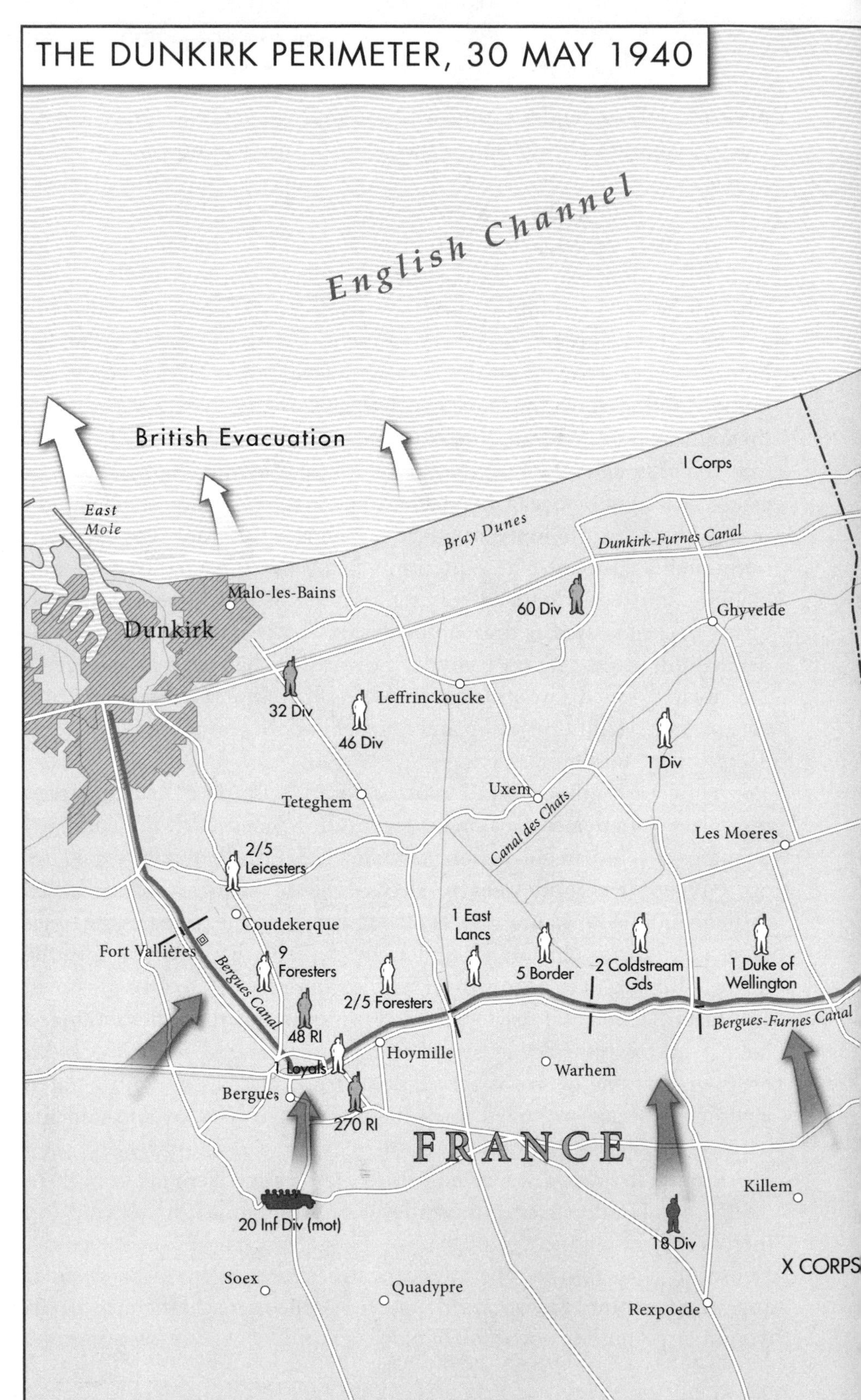
THE DUNKIRK PERIMETER, 30 MAY 1940
English Channel
British Evacuation
East Mole
Bray Dunes
Dunkirk-Furnes Canal
I Corps
Malo-les-Bains
Dunkirk
60 Div
Ghyvelde
32 Div
46 Div
Leffrinckoucke
1 Div
Uxem
Canal des Chats
Teteghem
Les Moeres
2/5 Leicesters
Coudekerque
Fort Vallières
Bergues Canal
9 Foresters
48 RI
2/5 Foresters
1 East Lancs
5 Border
2 Coldstream Gds
1 Duke of Wellington
Bergues-Furnes Canal
1 Loyals
Hoymille
Warhem
Bergues
270 RI
FRANCE
Killem
20 Inf Div (mot)
18 Div
X CORPS
Soex
Quadypre
Rexpoede

1 South Lancs.
Nieuport
2 Royal Fusiliers
1/6 Surreys
4 Div
256 Div
2 Duke of Cornwall's LI
2 Beds & Herts
2 East Yorks
Coxyde
La Panne
GHQ
1 Suffolk
Wulpen
4 Royal Berks
XXVI CORPS
II Corps
3 Div
2 Grenadier Gds
1 Coldstream Gds
1 Grenadier Gds
Adinkerke
Furnes
2 Royal Ulster Rifles
5 Div
23 Div
1 King's Own Scottish Borderers
EIGHTEENTH ARMY
9 Durham Light Inf
Moeres
Bulscamp
Loo Canal
5 Green Howards
6 Durham Light Inf
4 East Yorks
IX CORPS
4 Green Howards
Houthem
Wulveringhem
BELGIUM
14 Div
Hondschoote
KEY
German army
British Expeditionary Force
French army
British lines
Divisional boundaries
France–Belgium border
SIXTH ARMY
Beverem
0
2
miles

said, 'but I've never had to pull a man's pay book out of his body before.' With the wound cleaned, disinfected and dressed, Hellmuth was at last given a bed and the chance to sleep. For him, the battle was over.

It was not, however, for Lieutenant Norman Field. The 2nd Royal Fusiliers were now defending Nieuport, with their battalion HQ in an old German blockhouse from the last war that stood within a strip of woodland running west from the town and some 300 yards north of the Nieuport–Furnes Canal. It seemed solid enough, although they were now facing the enemy from the reverse side of its original design. Either side, the men had dug slit trenches. The previous night, German patrols had pushed forward, firing short bursts of submachine-gun fire, tempting the Fusiliers to respond and thus reveal their positions. By morning, the German guns had opened fire.

Heavy artillery, mortars and small arms were all firing upon their positions. From the outset, the only way for the battalion B Echelon to reach the forward positions was by Bren gun carrier. The Carrier Platoon had also been busy patrolling their right flank until the 1st East Surrey Battalion arrived to plug the gap.

Tragedy had already hit the Fusiliers that morning. Norman had been in the blockhouse with the remains of HQ Company and the Officer Commanding, Lieutenant-Colonel Allen. All had been desperately short of sleep, but Colonel Allen had dropped off and then, in a sleep-induced trance, had suddenly jumped up and yelled, 'Follow me! We've got to see these bloody Germans off!' and then run out of the blockhouse and started down the road to Nieuport. In seconds, a sniper had shot him in the head. 'He fell flat on his face on to the road,' says Norman. 'We got hold of his legs and pulled him in.' Allen was still alive, but only just – he would die two days later. It was a huge blow to the battalion; Allen – brother of the England cricketer Gubby Allen – had been a popular commanding officer. The men trusted him and looked up to him. Major Jack Lotinga, one of the company commanders, took over, but it was clear to everyone that they would be lucky to get out of there. The artillery behind them had just sixty rounds left per gun, while their own Bren and rifle ammunition was getting horribly low. It was only a matter of time before the Germans overwhelmed them.

In many ways, the 20,000 British soldiers now manning the perimeter were on something of a suicide mission. Short of supplies and, as the casualties mounted, increasingly short of men, their task was to keep the enemy at bay for as long as was humanly possible. It was a vital task: with every hour that passed, more soldiers were escaping from the mole and beaches. All along the front, epic stands were now taking place as the Tommies dug in behind the canal as the Germans shelled, mortared and shot at their positions. 'We were having a pretty tough time,' says Norman. 'They knew where we were and they were giving us hell with the shelling.'

Meanwhile the RAF was determined to do its bit to help the boys on the ground, despite the weather. Bomber Command Blenheims had been sent off to disrupt the Germans threatening the Fusiliers at Nieuport, but owing to the weather had been forced to abandon the mission. Later, they tried again and this time had more luck. Fighter Command also flew a number of patrols, including one by twelve Spitfires from 609 Squadron. David Crook was not amongst them – he had sprained his knee and was currently off flying – but John Dundas was. They saw little – there was ten-tenths cloud over the coast – but on that first combat patrol it was the weather that did for them. John was in Yellow Section and all three lost their bearings on the return trip. Desperately short of fuel, he and Joe Dawson eventually landed at Frinton-on-Sea in Essex, while Frankie Howell made it to Rochford. George Oakley was not so lucky, however. Although he reached the coast near Harwich, he then spun in and crashed, killing himself instantly. It was a sobering start.

On the beaches, some engineers from the 250th Field Company were using their ingenuity to create a makeshift pier off the sea at Bray Dunes. At around eight that morning, while the tide was out, they began collecting abandoned three-ton lorries and driving them out across the sand, and with the help of other soldiers created a 150-yard-long jetty. Bullets were fired into the tyres to anchor them, sand was shovelled into the back of them and the canvas covers were stripped from the superstructures and lashed to one another. Finally, decking panels from a bridging lorry were placed along the top of the trucks to create a walkway. More planks were found at a nearby timber yard. As the tide came in, smaller vessels were able to moor alongside it. Military Police ensured that only around fifty men used the jetty at any one time, but it was soon working very effectively.

Stan Fraser was not one of those being shepherded on to the lorry-jetty, but he and his mates were now down at the water's edge. One of

THE DUNKIRK PERIMETER, 1 JUNE 1940

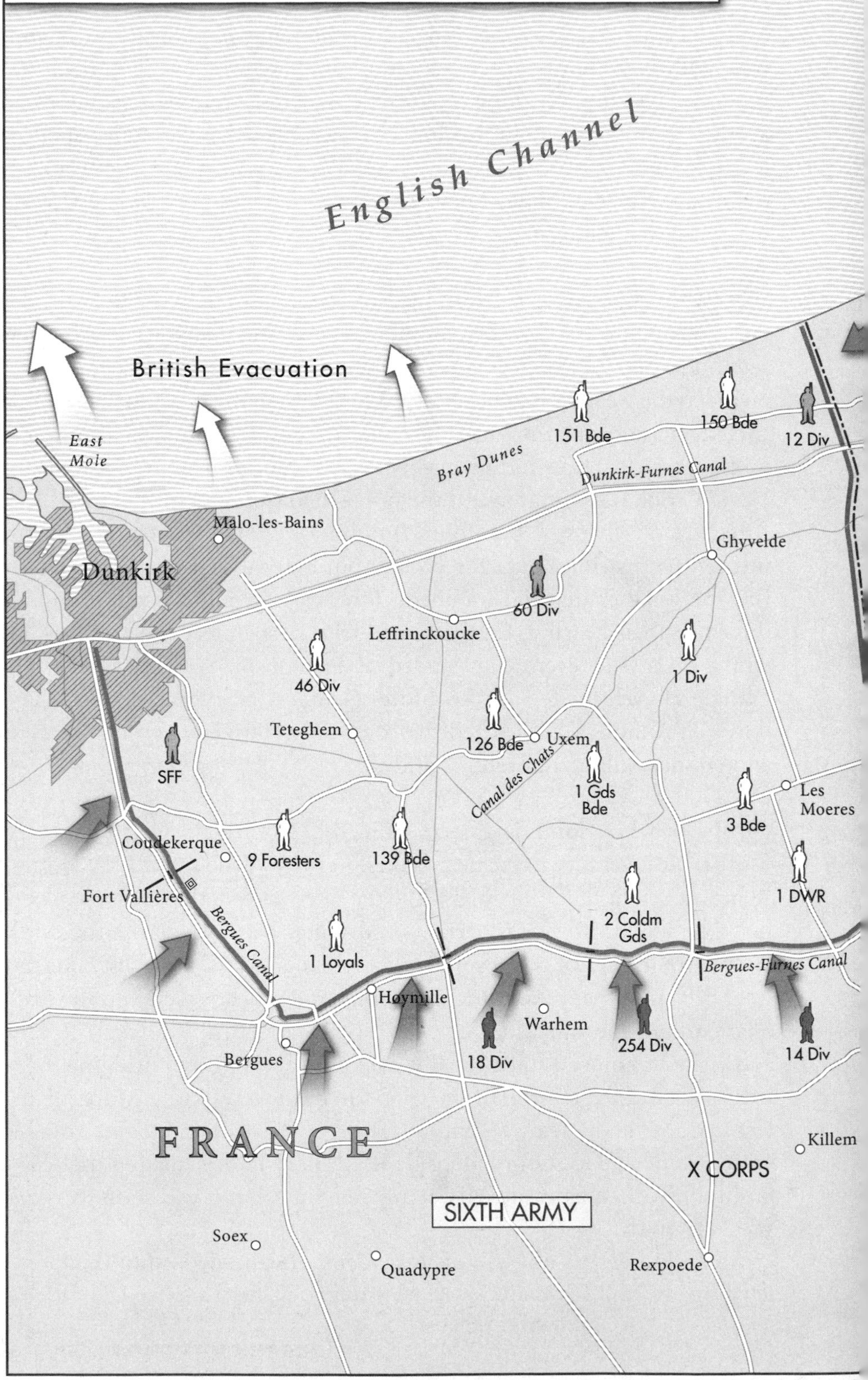

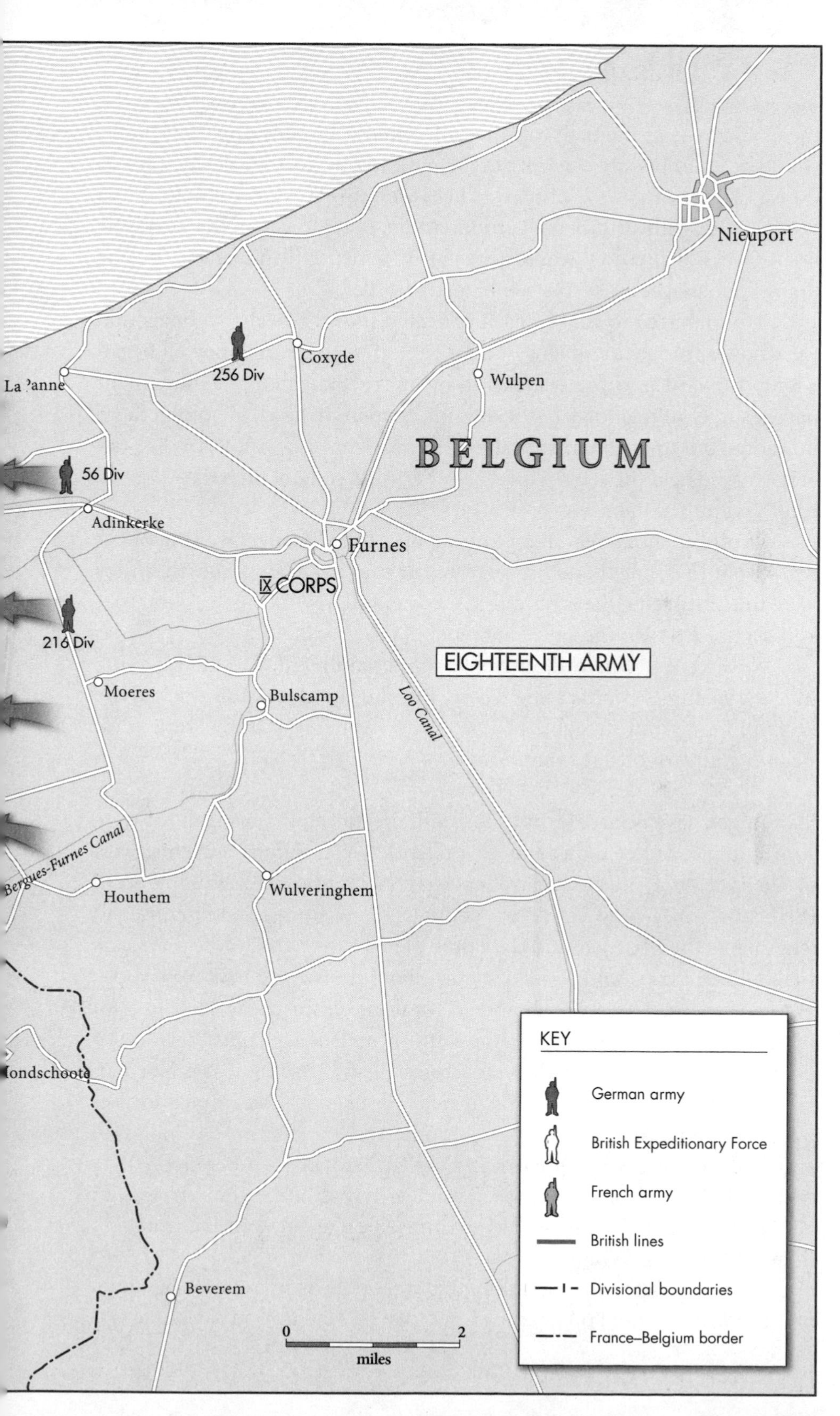

Nieuport
Coxyde
256 Div
La Panne
Wulpen
BELGIUM
56 Div
Adinkerke
Furnes
IX CORPS
216 Div
EIGHTEENTH ARMY
Moeres
Bulscamp
Loo Canal
Bergues-Furnes Canal
Houthem
Wulveringhem
Hondschoote
Beverem
0
2
miles
KEY
German army
British Expeditionary Force
French army
British lines
Divisional boundaries
France–Belgium border

their officers kept them all together but when it became apparent that it would be an impossible task to get them off in one go, they decided it was a case of every man for himself. There were officers now all along the water's edge, with Tommies all around them, eager to get on the next little boat. Occasionally they would threaten the men with revolvers, but by doing so managed to keep a semblance of order.

Stan managed to find himself allocated into the next two boats that were now approaching them. In their eagerness to get on, they all began edging forward into the sea, then a bit more. Stan thought they might have a surge on the boats but it did not happen. Instead, he joined them in wading out to the boat, until the water reached his waist. With the Staff Sergeant, he held the stern while the others jumped on, then they pushed it off and pulled themselves over the side.

An officer shouted at them to head over to a destroyer waiting out at sea. When they got there, officers on the ship yelled to them that they were full, but seeing the scrambling net was still down, Stan leapt on to it and clambered over the side. He had made it.

'Now, this is where the trouble starts,' muttered one of the ship's officers, gazing skywards as he did so. But the cloud was still thick, there was not an aircraft in sight, and soon they were away from France and steaming, untroubled, towards Dover.

Stan might have been safe, but those still defending the bridgehead were continuing to suffer under the now relentless German assault. Just west of Nieuport, the 2nd Royal Fusiliers were still desperately clinging on to their positions, however, even though by evening the enemy had lengthened their barrage and were now shelling the battalion rear areas as well, killing a cook and a Fusilier porter and destroying half their cooking equipment. There was, however, some cause for cheer. First, one of their second lieutenants turned up with three Fusiliers, and then so too did Captain Malcolm Blair. 'He was always the life and soul,' says Norman Field. 'He had everyone laughing. A marvellous man.' Malcolm, a former policeman and rugby player, had become separated from the battalion and had ended up at Dunkirk, where he had been ordered on to a destroyer. Whilst on board he had heard that the battalion was at Nieuport and still fighting so had got himself off again, waded ashore and then walked back to rejoin it.

As darkness fell the German guns were still once more. 'Very quiet night,' Norman jotted on a piece of notepaper. 'Had a good sleep.' He was up at first light, however, and had been sent to an alternative headquarters further back for messages. On his return, at around 5.30 a.m., the German shelling began once more. Taking cover in a slit trench, Norman could hear the shells landing around the blockhouse up ahead. When it finally lifted, Norman hurried back to the blockhouse. Outside in the slit trenches, he saw several men crouching as though sheltering from the rain. 'They had been caught by the shell blast,' says Norman. 'Still sitting there, but dead.'

The blockhouse had also taken a direct hit. As the Fusiliers now discovered, the rear of the building – the part now facing the enemy – was only made of brick and plaster. Inside, Captain Kit Bowring looked ashen. Malcolm Blair was dead. He'd been beside Kit when the shell had exploded. He had suffered only a slight wound, but Malcolm had been killed instantaneously. 'Tears came to my eyes when Kit told me about Malcolm,' says Norman. 'It was bloody awful.'

21

Dunkirk: The End

Lord Gort was now preparing to leave. He didn't want to; he wanted to stay to the bitter end. But he received a personal message from Churchill. 'On political grounds,' Churchill told him, 'it would be a needless triumph to the enemy to capture you when only a small force remained under your orders.' Before he departed, Gort was also ordered to make sure more French were evacuated – in fact, on a fifty-fifty basis from now on. After a cordial meeting and farewell with Admiral Abrial in the depths of Bunker 32, Gort then saw Fagalde and Général Blanchard, offering them both a chance to join him on the journey to England. Both declined; then they shared farewell toasts and promised to see each other in France soon, and Gort returned to La Panne.

There, Gort summoned Major-General Alexander, commander of 1st Division, who, he had decided, was to take over from him after his departure. Brooke had already gone; so too had Adam. General Barker, the commander of I Corps, whom he had originally had in mind, had seemed nervy at a conference the previous evening. His hands had been shaking and he'd made a bad joke about soon having dinner in a *Schloss* overlooking the Rhine. Alexander, on the other hand, was utterly imperturbable, as he proved when told of his new task. He would be serving under Abrial, Gort told him, but also gave him an important get-out clause: should any order which Abrial issued seem to him to be likely to imperil the safety of his men, he could make an immediate appeal to London.

Hans-Ekkehard Bob in France in June. A highly gifted fighter pilot, Hans flew throughout the long summer of 1940, both in the western campaign and over Britain. A companion throughout that time was his dog, Chica, here standing on the wing of his Me 109. Chica enjoyed nothing more than a trip in the cockpit with Hans, a treat he indulged her with whenever moving airfields.

Dunkirk. British soldiers wait to be lifted from the beaches. Most got home, but the majority of the BEF's equipment was left behind (*below left*), a loss that took a long time to recover, and which left Britain's army desperately weakened.

Right: Norman Field, who with the 2nd Royal Fusiliers was amongst those heroically defending the Dunkirk perimeter. Many of the wounded were left behind; Norman was one of the lucky ones to make it safely back across the Channel.

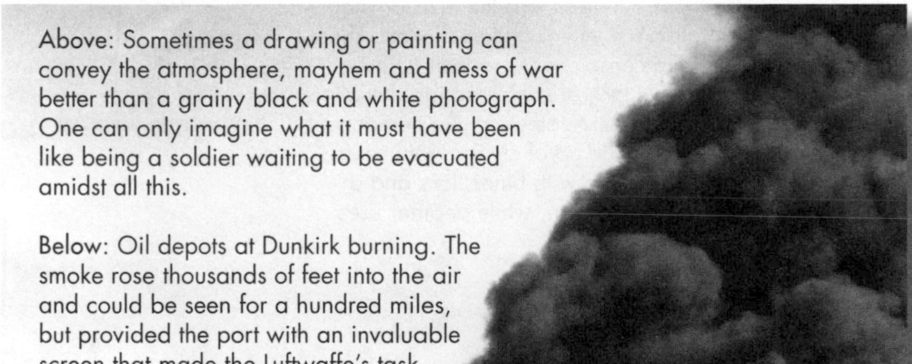

Above: Sometimes a drawing or painting can convey the atmosphere, mayhem and mess of war better than a grainy black and white photograph. One can only imagine what it must have been like being a soldier waiting to be evacuated amidst all this.

Below: Oil depots at Dunkirk burning. The smoke rose thousands of feet into the air and could be seen for a hundred miles, but provided the port with an invaluable screen that made the Luftwaffe's task that much harder.

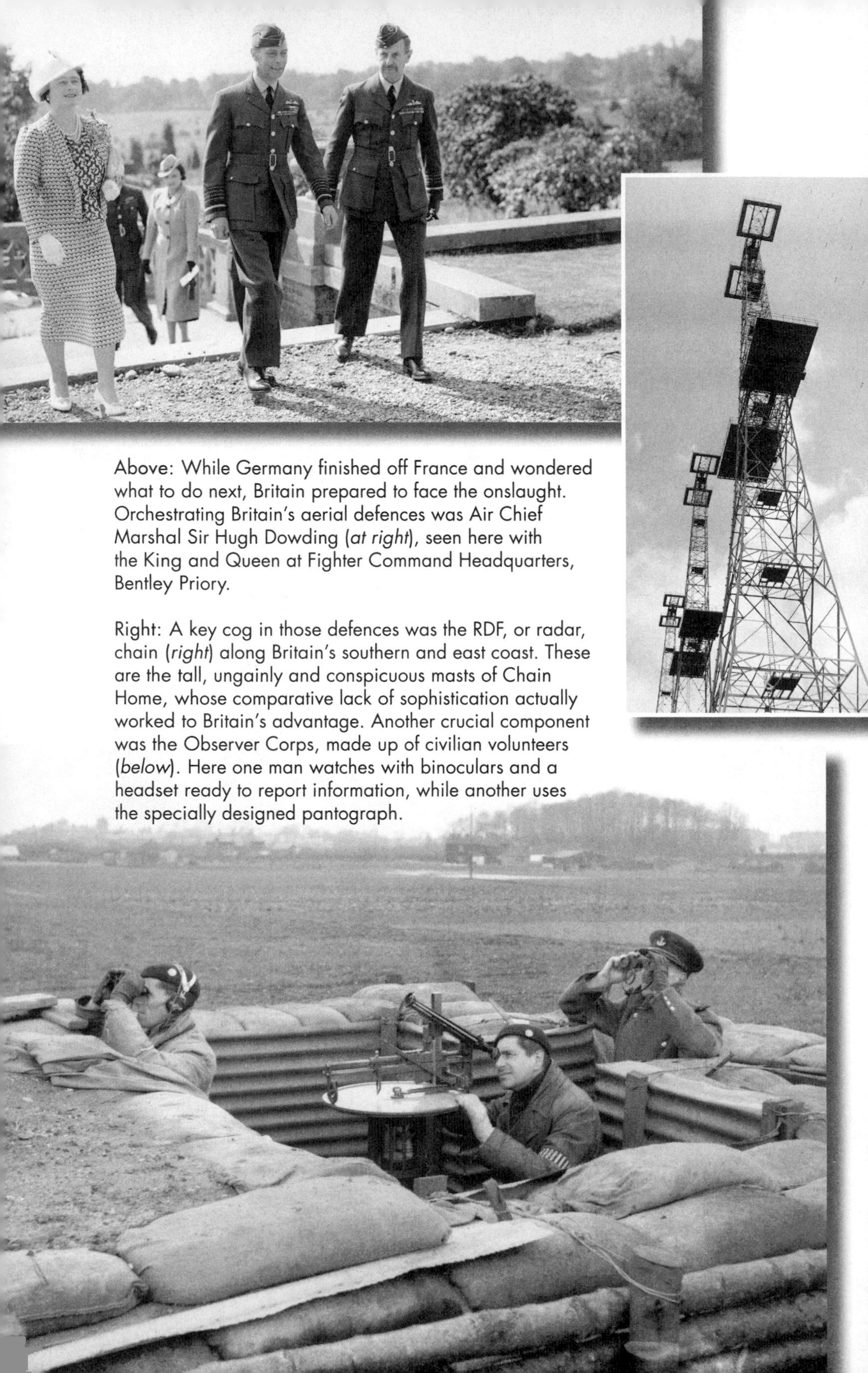

Above: While Germany finished off France and wondered what to do next, Britain prepared to face the onslaught. Orchestrating Britain's aerial defences was Air Chief Marshal Sir Hugh Dowding (*at right*), seen here with the King and Queen at Fighter Command Headquarters, Bentley Priory.

Right: A key cog in those defences was the RDF, or radar, chain (*right*) along Britain's southern and east coast. These are the tall, ungainly and conspicuous masts of Chain Home, whose comparative lack of sophistication actually worked to Britain's advantage. Another crucial component was the Observer Corps, made up of civilian volunteers (*below*). Here one man watches with binoculars and a headset ready to report information, while another uses the specially designed pantograph.

The Operations Room at Bentley Priory (*above*) taken from the gallery as the controllers look down on the plotting table and towards the tote board, while (*right*) WAAF plotters at 11 Group Headquarters in Uxbridge move plots around the table. Every operations room was set up in precisely the same way.

Below: A common sight along Britain's beaches in the early summer of 1940. Sandbags, mines and wire were laid along large stretches of the coast as Britain was gripped with invasion fever.

Above: Kurt 'Bobby' Fimmen, one of the S-boat aces, here receiving his Knight's Cross. The S-boats (*opposite, right*) were superb pieces of kit: fast, heavily armed and able to move safely over magnetic minefields. They wreaked havoc on the east-coast convoys, but as with the U-boats, could have been so much more effective were there more of them.

Left: Bee Beamont, a Hurricane pilot with 87 Squadron, who like many of his Luftwaffe counterparts fought throughout that long summer, both in France and over Britain.

Below: A British merchantman seen through the periscope of a U-boat.

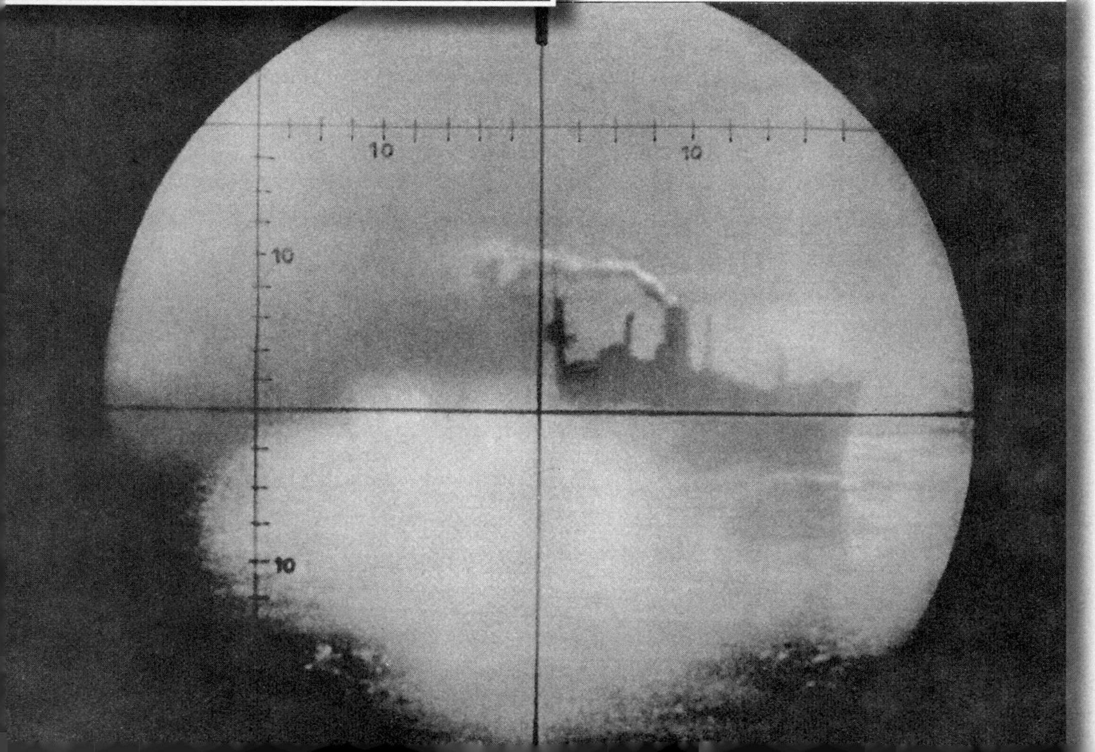

Right: Günther Prien, one of the greatest U-boat captains of them all. Famous all around Germany – and indeed the world – for having sunk the British battleship the *Royal Oak* at Scapa Flow, Prien and his boat, U-47, continued to sink gargantuan amounts of Allied shipping throughout the summer of 1940.

An east-coast convoy under attack. Although ocean-going convoys soon stopped using the Dover straits, coal trampers never did. Coal was what drove Britain's power stations and was absolutely essential were Britain to maintain her industrial war effort, not least the production of aeroplanes.

Above: The photograph of Hitler and Göring discussing the invasion of England taken secretly on 20 June by Gerhard Hartmann, a young guard at the Wolf's Ravine, the Führer's Headquarters in Belgium.

Below: William Shirer, the American CBS reporter, taps out another broadcast, somewhere near the front in June 1940.

Even before Gort had left, Alexander went to Bastion 32 to see Abrial, who was insisting on holding the perimeter indefinitely. He was also suggesting a different perimeter, in which French troops would hold a line from Gravelines to Bergues, and then a combined French and British force would hold a reduced line up the Belgian border. Alexander was taken aback by this suggestion to put it mildly. To start with, Gravelines had fallen four days earlier, and secondly the British were already in Bergues and all along the line to Nieuport in Belgium. In any case, a reduced perimeter in the east of the line would expose the beaches to German artillery, while holding the line indefinitely would be impossible because already those manning the bridgehead were suffering appalling casualties and running out of ammunition. Abrial was being urged to make this pointless stand by Weygand, who was even more out of the loop than Abrial was in his bunker. Calmly, Alexander instead proposed holding on to the existing bridgehead for the next day and then pulling out completely on the night of 1/2 June. Abrial, however, baulked at this suggestion and threatened to close the port entirely if Alexander did so. Already, it was time for Alexander to invoke his appeal.

By noon on Friday, 31 May, 165,000 men had been lifted from Dunkirk, as Churchill cheerfully told the French War Council in Paris on his latest trip there. It was an incredible number, achieved in part because of the still intact east mole, but also because of the determined resistance around the perimeter, and because the Luftwaffe had been far less effective than had been imagined by either side.

For the pilots and crews of the Luftwaffe, the poor weather the previous day had provided them with something of a respite. Most were now exhausted. 'I don't know what day of the week it is,' scribbled Siegfried Bethke the day before. He had just completed his fiftieth combat mission. He had now flown a number of sorties over the port. 'Dunkirk is all one firebrand,' he noted. 'Many ships on the beach, bombs, fires, anti-aircraft fire, Stukas.' All pilots were now familiar with the indelible images of destruction and carnage below. Julius Neumann, in 6/JG 27, was flying his seventh mission over the beaches around midday on the 31st. 'I could see Dunkirk from many miles away,' he says, 'the smoke from the oil tanks was burning continuously.' Cocky Dundas was also now all too familiar with the sight. That same day, he flew his sixth sortie there. 'The black smoke rose from somewhere in the harbour area, thick, impenetrable, obscuring much of the town,' he wrote. 'As it rose, it spread in patches, caught up in layers of haze and cloud. But still the greater part thrust upwards to a height of between twelve and fifteen thousand feet, where it was blown out in a lateral plume which stretched for many miles to westward, over Calais and beyond, down to the Channel.'

After the terror and exhilaration of his first combat sortie, Cocky was now finding these missions increasingly frustrating. The Squadron always seemed to arrive just before or just after an enemy raid. Sometimes he saw other planes, but swirling spectrally around in the haze it was hard to tell who or what they were. When they were engaged, they were short, sharp fights in which the squadron became split up. And, so far, Cocky had still not shot down a single enemy plane.

Back at Rochford, they had met some of the soldiers who had been evacuated and had been shocked to find that instead of thanks and praise they had been met with open hostility. 'Where the hell were you?' noted Cocky, 'that was the question we were often asked in a tone of anger and contempt.'

Of course, the reason the men on the beaches had not seen them was that they had been too high, often inland, and often up above the smoke and cloud. But they *were* there and suffering for it too: twenty aircraft had been lost on the 26th, for example, thirty the following day, twenty-five on the 28th and thirty-three on the 30th; 108 aircraft in just four days, most of which were from Fighter Command. It was a toll Dowding could not afford.

Yet the Luftwaffe was suffering too. In the same period, the Luftwaffe had lost ten more aircraft and 191 pilots and aircrew. Those figures were about to rise, as both Hajo Herrmann and Siegfried Bethke were soon to discover. Hajo and the other men of KG 4 had been operating almost continually since the offensive began and not least over Dunkirk, although their casualties had been slight compared to some other units – just two aircraft lost in the past five days. Hajo's vast experience had been put to good use a few days earlier. Flying a lone mission late over the port, by the light of the moon he had spotted a number of ships alongside the mole, with one just casting off. Banking, he positioned himself for an attack at right angles, with the moon ahead of him. Setting the fuse on his first bomb, he dived, and when almost over the target, pressed the release button and then pulled out. His rear-gunner reported the bomb had been ten metres short. Releasing bombs one at a time rather than in a cluster was considered far too risky – the rule was to strike hard and quick and then get away. Still, it was a trick Hajo had learned in Spain and he knew a bit more about operational flying since those days and, with the cover of darkness, fancied his chances.

Climbing again, he dived once more, but this time was twenty metres out. His observer suggested they should now release the last two bombs together and go home but Hajo, feeling irritated, insisted he would drop them one at a time. It was a decision that paid off. On his next dive, he hit the ship – there was a sharp flash from below. Climbing away, Hajo circled over it, watching the fire spread. He looked down over the other boats coming to its rescue, assuming the soldiers must all be jumping off into the sea. He still had one last bomb so this time dived even lower, hitting a smaller vessel. 'The vessel didn't catch fire,' noted Hajo. 'She sank.'

Now, on Friday, 31 May, early in the evening, Hajo had taken off from Schiphol near Amsterdam, where they were newly stationed, in a large formation. The weather had improved and although there were still dense smoke palls over Dunkirk itself, visibility was otherwise good. Their targets were the beaches and ships lying offshore, to be attacked from the land side. He was not flying his usual aircraft as it was unserviceable, but had not had a chance to test his replacement machine; it could not be helped. In any case, it seemed all right to him as they flew south across Belgium. As usual, they could see the smoke above the port way before they reached it. Above them were the fighter escort, so Hajo was happy to keep his steady position in the middle of the formation.

As they approached the diving line, puffs of flak began to smudge the sky. Hajo watched the lead aircraft begin to dive, then pulled his own brake lever, but the brake did not come out. Hurtling downwards, he sped past the leading machines. The slipstream whistled in a high-pitch screech past the cockpit and the plane began to shake and rattle. He pulled desperately on the brake, but nothing happened, so he pulled back the control column in a long curve in the hope that the aircraft would not break up. The rest of the formation were now over their targets and dropping bombs. Cursing to himself, Hajo decided to have another go but suddenly a Hurricane swept past and then another. Abandoning plans for another attack for the moment, Hajo climbed to the safety of the smoke cloud, which stank even from inside his Junkers. All too quickly he emerged out of the top, dropped back down and came out at the bottom of the pall once more. Suddenly a burst of fire raked the fuselage. Wires sprang out towards him from the instrument panel. He wondered whether to jettison his bombs but a brief glance either side of him told him that both his engines were still working. Dipping in and out of the smoke cloud, he thought he saw a French fighter but it disappeared again just as there was a bang and one of his engines packed up. The wireless operator cried out and the under-gunner groaned. Hajo could see a dark trail of smoke from his hit engine so now dived steeply, and noticed the enemy fighters were holding back – he couldn't understand why.

For a moment, Hajo couldn't decide what to do – land on the beach where the Tommies were? Or crash out at sea? Neither appealed, but with his aircraft spluttering and jolting he realized he did not have much choice. Diving down again, he picked out a ship, dropped his bombs but missed, then saw a Hurricane had followed him down after all. There was another bang as the bullets hit home, but the British pilot had overshot and now Hajo knew he had to ditch the plane. Crouching in his seat, he waited for the *coup de grâce* as he glided down towards the sea.

Water now burst through the cockpit. The urgent desire for survival made Hajo act fast. Ripping off his life-jacket, leads and overalls, he clambered out through the jettisoned canopy and on to the roof of the sinking aircraft. To his relief, three more heads appeared beside him. Hajo and his observer were unharmed but the wireless operator and gunner had cuts to their faces. All four were alive, however, and they now swam the short distance to the shore, dog-paddling then crawling up through the shallows and on to the shore. Hajo looked around and then saw a soldier, wearing a German steel helmet, emerge from the grass beyond the shore. Relief coursed through him. Clearly, he had ditched just to the west of the bridgehead – off the coast that was now in German hands. 'I'd made it,' he noted. 'That was my fortieth operation in this war, not counting the half-century in Spain.'

Around the same time, Siegfried Bethke was leading the *Staffel* over Amiens in support of Army Group A's southern push. It was his second flight of the day and they soon encountered a flight of French LeO 415 and Douglas Db-7 twin-engine bombers. Siegfried ordered them to attack, swooping down fast upon the enemy planes. Opening with his cannon he saw bits of the French bomber fly off and one of the engines catch fire, so he pulled back the stick and climbed out of the way to dodge the debris. All his pilots were now attacking in turn. He spotted one Frenchman bail out; one of the planes dived and glided in to land before being engulfed in flames, then another bomber was plunging earthwards. All four had been destroyed, no match for the 109s. Siegfried had just ordered his *Staffel* to reassemble over Amiens when he spotted two more

French aircraft flying low below them. Diving down, he attacked again, although this time only with his machine guns as he had already used up his cannon ammunition. Then suddenly he heard a loud crack from the front below his plane and in seconds thick smoke was swirling around the cockpit and flames were licking his feet. The control column was loose in his hands and he knew he needed to get out of his machine fast. Releasing the canopy, he managed to undo his harness and leads and somehow flip the Messerschmitt over so that he fell out. He was horribly close to the ground but managed to get the parachute open and briefly noticed a large cenotaph from the last war and large numbers of shell craters and dead strewn round about before hitting the ground. Knocked unconscious, he awoke as several soldiers were carrying him back to their positions. Not far away, Siegfried saw his plane, his 'No. 7', burning. His head throbbed, but he was alive. Like Hajo, his had been a lucky escape.

Back on the ground, the situation was becoming critical at the eastern end of the perimeter. It was here, against Nieuport and Furnes, that the German Eighteenth Army had hit hardest, and the Fusiliers, for one, were suffering under the weight of this onslaught. Their depleted number, armed with rifles, a few Brens and way too little ammunition, could only hold on so long against an enemy of massively superior man- and fire-power. Their remaining carriers had now been pressed into service as ambulances to take the wounded back to the Regimental Aid Post. Casualties were now critical so Major Lotinga ordered them to fall back 800 yards. Another second lieutenant and several NCOs were killed in the process. The new battalion HQ was little more than a ditch. 'It consisted merely of me,' says Norman Field, 'with a signaller equipped with a vital telephone.' Dribs and drabs found their way back and took cover in neighbouring water ditches.

The RAP, which had been operating in a house on a crossroads, was also ordered to pack up and fall back. It was just as well, because no sooner had they left than it was hit by six successive shells and reduced to rubble.

All along the eastern end of the perimeter, the Tommies were hanging on by a thread. Furnes had been heavily attacked all morning and looked likely to fall as the line between the town and the village of Wulpen began to collapse. A costly counter-attack by the Coldstream Guards managed to restore the situation but it was clear they would not be able to hold out much longer. Next to the Fusiliers, the 1st/6th Surreys were also suffering, although they had managed to stand firm. Late in the afternoon the Germans had been seen massing for another attack on Nieuport but it was at that moment that the Blenheims arrived, hitting them sufficiently hard for no further assault to come that evening.

General Alexander, meanwhile, had managed to get through to London and just after 8 p.m. received his instructions, which were to continue withdrawing his forces on the fifty-fifty basis with the French that had earlier been put to Gort. This was relayed to the French, who could do little but acquiesce. With Gort now gone, Alexander at least now had the authority to act as he thought fit, coming up against Admiral Abrial at every turn.

And it was clear that the eastern perimeter could not hold another day. In the ditch that was still the Royal Fusiliers' headquarters, orders were received at 9 p.m. that they were to pull back and embark at La Panne. The fighting had died down; the Germans never liked attacking much at night. Out of nearly 800 men who had marched into Belgium a fortnight earlier, only around 150 now remained. Gathering their remaining carriers, they collected themselves together and under the cover of dusk headed down the road to La Panne, now largely empty but pitted with shell craters and lined by houses and buildings reduced to rubble.

It was almost dark by the time they reached the town of La Panne. They abandoned their vehicles, immobilized them, then marched to a crossroads near the centre of town. There they were halted by Movement Control Staff for over an hour. As other units arrived, so their numbers swelled until the town was dense with exhausted soldiers. Then the German guns opened fire once more, and shells began to hit the town. Norman Field managed to take cover in a kind of cellar window below a house. 'It was all rather frightening,' he says. 'It's fascinating stuff, though, to see what happens when these shells burst on the road – like white tadpoles whizzing around because there are bits of white-hot metal.' Whilst crouching there, he felt his left hand move. Lifting it up, he could no longer move his fingers. 'I realized I'd been clobbered,' he says, 'but I didn't feel a thing, not then.' Shrapnel had ripped off the back of his hand. With the shelling, the bottlenecked men had been hurriedly dispersed down to the beaches, so Norman now got up and headed that way too, calling out, 'Royal Fusiliers! Royal Fusiliers!' Eventually a voice called out, 'Come and lie down here,' so he did and found himself next to Jock Cleghorn, a Fusilier captain on the brigade HQ staff, who then dressed

Norman's wound. Of the rest of the battalion there was no sign. The shelling continued, while overhead a plane circled, dropping flares that hung in the air and made the beach like daylight. The men lay flat, pressed against the sand. They no longer had any weapons, kit or anything – not even entrenching tools. 'The firing was so intense,' says Norman, 'and people were being hit all over the place and crying out. It was awful; a nightmare. We were worn out. We hadn't had any proper sleep for ages.'

This attack had brought the evacuation at La Panne to a halt. As the shelling intensified, the ships were forced to withdraw westwards, although it was hoped that later, when the guns quietened down, they would return and continue lifting the men, now numbering some 7,000 from 3rd and 4th Divisions. Desultory shelling continued. The night was absolutely black except for some tiny beach creatures which glowed at the shore's edge. The sea was still flat, so that in between the groans of wounded and dying men all that could now be heard was the gentle lapping of the waves.

Eventually the ships returned, the destroyer HMS *Worcester* and the minesweeper HMS *Hebe*; also anchored a little west of La Panne was another minesweeper, HMS *Speedwell*. Suddenly everyone was on their feet running down to the shore. There was chaos until two Military Police began firing Bren guns into the water to warn the mass to move back. With his wounded hand, Norman was one of the lucky few to be put on to one of the collapsible canvas rowing boats available to ferry men to the waiting ships. When Norman was hauled up on to *Speedwell*, he found one of his signallers lying on a stretcher. He had been shot in the stomach and thought he was going to die. 'Of course you're not,' Norman told him. 'I'll go and get a doctor.' He found one then lay down himself and fell fast asleep.

Norman might have got away, but it was clear there were nothing like enough small ships at La Panne. Because the eastern perimeter had been abandoned up to the French border, it was essential to have La Panne cleared by dawn. It was soon realized, however, that this would never happen so the beach was abandoned entirely as an evacuation point. The remaining men, utterly shattered, hungry and, above all, parched with thirst, were ordered to trudge up the coast to Bray Dunes and the port, the latter ten miles away.

At Dunkirk, the harbour entrance was thick with boats. Destroyers and other ships were lined up three abreast alongside the mole, while many of the little ships were also bobbing about off the coast at Bray and Malo-les-Bains and around the harbour. The mole was packed with men, British and French, a long dark column of weary troops patiently waiting their turn to embark. One of the ships reaching Dunkirk that morning was HMS *Icarus*, now on her sixth round trip.

With the weather much improved, the Luftwaffe hit Dunkirk hard that morning. Norman Field, on board HMS *Speedwell*, awoke to the sound of crashing glass. The ship was zig-zagging violently and above Norman glass bottles were falling off their shelves. He now heard the screeching sirens of Stukas and from the corner of his eye saw huge spikes of water exploding into the air. Wave after wave attacked her, dropping more than a hundred bombs. Miraculously, there were no direct hits, although some, as Norman saw for himself, were horribly close. Some forty-six men had been killed and many more wounded.

Once the raid had finally passed, Norman, unhurt apart from his badly wounded hand, gathered himself up and saw they were now speeding across the Channel. His signaller had died – as the man had foretold – and now the dead were buried at sea, a padre performing the burial rites. To his astonishment, Norman recognized him – he'd been in his house at Shrewsbury. He was equally surprised to see the ship was full of Frenchmen; he'd had no idea that, having left La Panne, *Speedwell* had picked up more men from the mole. And then, at long last, they neared England, finally pulling into Sheerness. From there, Norman was taken by ambulance to a hospital in Dartford. It would take some time for his hand to mend, but at least he was home. The same could not be said for far too many of his friends and colleagues, who would, like the young men of a generation before, be staying forever in Flanders.

Home seemed a long way away to those still manning the perimeter. Four German divisions now attacked the six British battalions continuing to man the Canal Line between Bergues and the village of Houthem. All these men fought with extraordinary bravery – as did the French in the east and to the west of the port, and as had those holding the line between Nieuport and Furnes the day before. One officer in the East Lancashires, Captain Harold Ervine-Andrews, managed to hold off an entire German attack by leading one of his platoons to the roof of a barn and personally shooting seventeen Germans with his rifle and many more with a Bren, despite being under continuous fire. Not until the barn was a charred wreck did he eventually fall back at round 4.30 p.m. that afternoon. For this action, he was awarded the Victoria Cross.

The RAF continued to send fighters over to cover this last stand. Both Cocky and John Dundas flew over Dunkirk this first day of June; John managed to hit a Heinkel 111. Cocky and the rest of 616 Squadron had been over the port by 5 a.m., this time along with three other squadrons, although their efforts could not prevent a heavy toll on the ships below. Four had been sunk before 7.30 a.m., including the destroyer HMS *Keith*. More followed: the destroyers *Basilisk* and *Havant*, while *Ivanhoe* was also hit, killing a number of men already loaded on to her. Sid Nuttall, who was still stuck on the beaches, saw the attack on *Keith*, *Basilisk* and *Ivanhoe*. One dive-bomber, attacked from the sea, finished up low over the dunes, where a number of soldiers took pot-shots. 'We saw a piece of plane fall off,' says Sid. 'He veered off and crashed into the ground beyond the town.'

Sid had been helping as a stretcher bearer since arriving at Bray Dunes, although mostly this had been at night. Nearby, the casualty clearing station at Malo was heaving with the wounded. He found it quite difficult lumbering these men out on to the boats, even with three others to help. 'We'd wade into the sea and had water up to our chests before a boat could reach you,' he says. 'Then you had to pass this wounded chap inside the boat.' He now had a thick line of salt around his battle dress. With no watch, Sid had lost all sense of time. He had no idea what day it was or when it might be his turn to leave; all he knew was that he'd now been on the beach at least three days. An eternity.

By mid-afternoon, the Canal Line was crumbling; Bergues, after a heroic defence by the Loyals, was finally given up at 5 p.m. Alexander had already accepted that morning that the evacuation would not be completed that night, but hoped that with the help of the French to the west and south of the town, his last few thousand fighting men might be able to maintain a small perimeter around Malo and ensure the remaining 39,000 British might yet be able to get away. The French were also defending equally heroically and putting up greater resistance than Alexander had anticipated and so, in agreement with Abrial, he decided to continue the evacuation through the night of 2/3 June.

Yet there was no doubt that the end was now near. Later that day, Sid Nuttall saw some French troops reach the beaches then spotted a German tank that began firing towards them until the guns of a destroyer offshore opened up and hit it. The proximity of the enemy and the confused nature of the fighting, combined with the shortage of communications, meant that Alexander was faced with making decisions based on what limited information he had. It was a huge responsibility, but one of the hardest decisions he had made was that no more wounded could be lifted off. Stretchers took too much room. It was, he decided, the fit that now needed saving. A hospital ship sent out that day was so badly bombed she was forced to return. So too was a second, but 1 June was undoubtedly the worst suffered since the evacuation had begun. The Luftwaffe had flown over a thousand sorties that day between 5.30 a.m. and 5.54 p.m. Thirty-two ships had been lost this day, not including further little boats, and a further ten badly damaged. It was a disastrous toll.

Captain Bill Tennant had watched the attack on HMS *Worcester* with both horror and anger. He had barely had an inch of sleep since arriving, but this attack was the last straw. Out of forty-one precious destroyers that had taken part in the operation only nine now remained – the rest were all sunk or damaged. Enough was enough; the price of daytime evacuation was becoming too great. 'Things are getting very hot for ships,' he signalled Ramsay at 6 p.m. 'Have directed that no ships sail during daylight. Evacuation by transports therefore ceases at 0300.' Then he added, 'If perimeter holds, will complete evacuation tomorrow, Sunday night, including most French. General [Alexander] concurs.'

There was salvation for Sid Nuttall, however. Now that there were no more stretcher cases to take out to the shore, he and his remaining mates in 'C' Company were sent that night towards the mole. With the onset of darkness, the evacuation was once more accelerated. In the early hours, Sid was near the end of a long line of men on the mole. Now arriving at Dunkirk on her seventh trip was HMS *Icarus*. It was just after midnight on the morning of Sunday, 2 June. Two destroyers were coming out in reverse as *Icarus* and HMS *Windsor* entered. Watching out on deck was Andrew Begg. 'There was no thought for safety,' he says. 'The skipper sat with his legs over the bridge yelling, "Come on! Hurry up! Get a move on!"'

Dunkirk was still blazing, great orange flames leaping angrily into the sky. It meant ahead of them, everything was swathed in an orange glow, but that behind it was pitch black. Now clambering aboard was Sid Nuttall, having first crossed the decks of the *Maid of Orleans* to which *Icarus* was moored. He heard the skipper urging them to load up quickly.

'The captain wanted to get off before the Stukas came down at first light,' he says. With a further 677 troops on board, *Icarus* cut her ropes and headed out of the harbour once more, but as she was clearing the harbour entrance astern, two more ships were coming in. *Icarus* then backed around out of the harbour and as she did so accidentally rammed a trawler, causing serious damage including to her gyro compass. Fortunately, she could still sail, however, and so set off for England once more.

Sid Nuttall collapsed on one of the lower decks, where he and his mates were given cocoa and thick bully beef sandwiches – both of which were most welcome after more than three days without food and barely any fluids at all. Sid drank and ate, blissfully unaware that because of the damage to the gyro compass *Icarus* managed to sail right through the middle of a minefield. Andrew Begg back down in the engine room had been told by the chief ERA. 'That's why we're going at five knots,' the ERA said in hushed tones. 'Don't let the rumour get around in case the soldiers panic.' For the next hour, Andrew wondered whether they would blow up at any moment, but then the signal came to increase speed and they were clear.

They reached Dover around seven that Sunday morning. It was *Icarus*'s last trip. In all she saved 4,704 men, one of whom was Sid Nuttall.

During Churchill's visit to Paris two days before he had promised the French that British and French troops would leave in partnership, arm to arm, and that it would be British troops that would form the rearguard and be last to leave, not the French. This pledge had not been passed on to Alexander and, in any case, would have been impossible such was the state of the last remaining Tommies. By that Sunday, and despite Alexander's preparations around Malo-les-Bains, it was the French who were holding the final defensive line around Dunkirk – and doing so with a kind of steel too infrequently shown during the previous three weeks. Carrying out a number of local counter-attacks, they forced the Germans briefly on to the back foot. The remains of the First Army were also fighting fiercely in their pocket at Lille, despite the hopelessness of the situation. It was all too little too late, but it gave the men at Dunkirk – the last of the BEF – the chance to lie low during the day and ready themselves for one last night of evacuation. No-one was quite sure how many men remained but Bill Tennant and Alexander reckoned there were about 5,000 Tommies still remaining and some 30,000 French.

During the day, a naval demolition party carried out its work on the surviving port equipment and arrangements were put in place to block the harbour entrance once the last ship had sailed. Meanwhile, at Dover, Admiral Ramsay's team had collected eleven destroyers, thirteen personnel ships, and a host of minesweepers, drifters, skoots and other little boats and these set sail around 5 p.m. that afternoon.

The first troops began boarding around 9 p.m., but already the harbour was under German artillery fire. Once again, the port was lit by the still-burning fires, which cast an orange glow over the column of troops inching their way along the mole. Miraculously, though, that narrow walkway had still not been hit, nor buckled under the strain of playing host to so many ships. At around 11.30 p.m., with the last British troops on board, Bill Tennant and General Alexander boarded a motor launch and began a last tour, first of the harbour, then along the beaches down to Bray, calling out to any last remaining British soldiers. Not one man replied. All that was left were the dark silhouettes of the abandoned lorry piers, other destroyed trucks, carriers and cars. Guns stood where they had been left on the beaches. That long strip of sand, in normal times filled with people enjoying the sun and the sea, was now littered with the debris of a proud army that had abandoned all but the men who fought within its ranks. Desultory shell fire continued, but otherwise the beaches were still.

It was time to go. Already Bill Tennant had sent his last signal to Admiral Ramsay, one of just four words. 'BEF evacuated. Returning now.'

Der Adler

HEFT 15 / BERLIN, 29 JU

Belgique Frs.
France Frs.
Portugal E
Roumanie
Suisse C

PUBLIÉ AVEC L
BORATION DU
DE L'AIR ALL

PART II
RESPITE

Édit
frança

Des coups destructeurs s'abattent dans l'est

Du haut d'un avion Heink
on voit les autres machine
He 111 attaquant les positi
qui, chaque jour, sont
grêle de bombes de
Cliché PK

⊙ 22 ✠

What Next?

THE RAF HAD continued to cover the evacuation right to the end, flying over at dawn and dusk when the lifting of men ended and began for the day. The fighter boys of 92 Squadron had flown their last Dunkirk sorties early on the 2nd, and they had been their most successful to date. For some reason Tony Bartley could not fathom, the fighter escort was hanging back, so the large formation of lumbering Heinkels posed a juicy target. And the pilots were learning, too. Over Dunkirk, they had cottoned on that it was best to dive down below a Heinkel then pull up and blast his underside at as close a range as possible. Without an under-gunner, the Heinkels could do nothing but take evasive action. They were also realizing that the more firepower they could bring to bear, the more likely they were to knock aircraft out of the sky. Tony's section had raked six Heinkels in turn. 'We silenced all six rear gunners,' noted Tony, 'and set five Heinkels on fire, before running out of ammo.' These were bombers from KG 54, and of those five only one managed to stagger home.

Cocky Dundas and 616 Squadron had also flown their last combat patrol over Dunkirk that day, while Cocky's brother John had flown his last the day before. On that sortie John had discovered just how hard it was for a single Spitfire to shoot down another aircraft. He had hammered away at a Heinkel, using up all his ammunition, 'but the wretch refused to come down'. Like all the squadrons, 609 had suffered over Dunkirk. Five pilots had been killed – a third of their number. The excitement and bravado with which they had entered the fray had gone. Any small group of men in a time of war are tied by a unique bond, but those men in the fighter squadrons had mostly known each other a long time. This was particularly true of Auxiliary squadrons such as 609 and 616, whose number were close friends drawn largely from the same part of the country. Allan Wright in 92 Squadron had also lost his best friend when Pat Learmond had been shot down and killed. The first losses in war can be the hardest to take, and yet all were equally aware that a long, hard fight lay ahead of them. The air fighting over France had only been the beginning. It was a sobering thought.

It was a sobering thought for Air Chief Marshal Dowding too. It was true that the Air Ministry had agreed to form three new Spitfire squadrons and it was also true that he had gained those squadrons that had been operating in France, which, on paper, meant an overall gain of eleven squadrons, bringing Fighter Command up to fifty-eight squadrons in all. However, these figures did not mask the fact that many of these units were unfit for operational service and that nearly all were now badly below strength. Cold statistics made for harsh reading: 106 fighters had been lost over Dunkirk, of which sixty-seven were Spitfires. In all, 396 Hurricanes had been shot down or destroyed in France. Two hundred and eighty fighter pilots had lost their lives or been taken prisoner. This meant that Dowding now only had 331 Spitfires and Hurricanes with which to defend Britain. Furthermore, the number of anti-aircraft guns was woefully inadequate. If the Germans attacked Britain right away, Dowding's forces would be hard pushed to keep them at bay.

And it was an attack right away that Britain's Chiefs of Staff thought most likely. On 29 May, they had put together a report on 'Invasion of the United Kingdom'. The Germans had two options – either to continue the battle against France in an effort to knock her out of the war at an early stage, or to stabilize the front in France and concentrate a major attack on Britain. A counter-attack of sufficient strength by the French now seemed to them unlikely. Britain was also, in their view, Germany's main enemy, and defeat of the United Kingdom would lead to the subsequent collapse of France as a matter of course. 'In our view, therefore,' they concluded, 'it is highly probable that Germany is now setting the stage for delivering a full scale attack on England' – an attack they believed they were neither prepared nor organized enough to repel. Their biggest fear was a lightning-fast Channel crossing of massed German forces in which they were able to establish a foothold. 'We have ample evidence,' they warned, 'of the difficulty of dislodging the German once he has established himself on enemy soil.' They recommended that the country be 'warned and roused to the imminent danger', that the army at home – and that included the LDV – be brought to a high degree of alertness, and that defence works along the coast should be improved without delay.

It was with this in mind that beaches were mined and laid with barbed wire, signposts were taken down in an effort to confuse the enemy should he land, pillboxes began to be built along the coast, by rivers and at road junctions in vast numbers, and a series of new coastal gun batteries continued to be constructed; by 12 June, the first batch of forty-six new batteries, each comprising two six-inch naval guns and two searchlights, had been put in place along the south-east coast. Even a Petroleum Warfare Department was set up in early June, with the idea of burning the invader back into the sea. Short stretches of road leading inland from likely landing places were lined with perforated pipes, each connected with a fuel tank hidden nearby. If the enemy got ashore, waiting members of the LDV would then flood the road with petrol and ignite it by hurling a flaming missile.

One of the biggest problems was the shortage of trained men and equipment. There had, in fact, been one more night of evacuation of French troops, so that by the morning of 4 June, when Operation DYNAMO officially came to an end, a staggering 338,226 Allied troops had been brought back to England since 20 May.* However, the best part of 70,000 British soldiers were either dead, prisoner, or still stuck further south in France, which was a massive dent in Britain's forces. On top of that, Britain had left behind nearly all her equipment. Having begun the campaign as the proportionally best equipped army in the world, she was now one of the worst. Sixty-four *thousand* vehicles were left, many of which were gleefully taken by the vehicle-starved Germans and continued to perform sterling service for years to come. In all, 76,000 tons of ammunition were lost; more than 400,000 tons of stores; 2,500 guns. This could not be replaced overnight. Far from it. The British army, in June 1940, was not good for very much.

Winston Churchill heeded the advice of the Chiefs of Staff when he finally addressed the House of Commons on Monday, 4 June, by giving a

* Figures vary slightly between those given by the War Office, the Dover Report and the Admiralty. The War Office figures are considered the most accurate and are the ones used here.

stark warning. There had been a 'miracle of deliverance', in bringing back so many from Dunkirk, he told them, but, 'We must be careful not to assign to this deliverance the attributes of victory,' he added. 'Wars are not won by evacuations.' There could be no doubting the extreme gravity of the situation, he told them, and an immediate assault upon Britain was now expected. Hitler, he said, was planning an invasion. He was, however, confident that such an invasion would be resisted. 'Even though large tracts of Europe and many old and famous States have fallen or may fall into the grip of the Gestapo and all the odious apparatus of Nazi rule,' he added defiantly, 'we shall not flag or fail. We shall go on to the end, we shall fight in France, we shall fight on the seas and oceans, we shall fight with growing confidence and growing strength in the air, we shall defend our island, whatever the cost may be, we shall fight on the beaches, we shall fight on the landing grounds, we shall fight in the fields and in the streets, we shall fight in the hills; we shall never surrender.'

Listening to this stirring defiance was Harold Nicolson, who believed it was the finest speech he had ever heard. 'The House,' he noted, 'was deeply moved.' So too was one of the Prime Minister's young secretaries, Jock Colville, who had been listening from the Gallery. 'It was a magnificent oration,' he wrote in his diary. From sceptic, Jock had turned into one of Churchill's most ardent admirers in the short time since the new PM's appointment. Churchill had only been Prime Minister for twenty-five days, but having won over the Cabinet, he was now beginning to galvanize the rest of the nation behind him too. Both Hitler and Churchill were fine orators, although with very different styles. The Führer had been able to mesmerize his people with his changes of tone – quiet one minute, angry the next, often building to a climax of shouted phrases accompanied by exaggerated sweeps of his hands. Churchill was altogether more lyrical, more measured, making the most of his love of the English language and his deep sense of history. Churchill was romantic; Hitler more prosaic. Both had the ability to instil determination, pride and self-belief into their audience. These were rare skills.

Certainly Daidie Penna was impressed too when it was re-run over the radio. 'I thought it was the finest bit of rhetoric I had ever heard,' she noted. 'Seems to have been received everywhere with enthusiasm. It's what the country has been wanting for years, and I am reminded of Auntie's remark when some months back, while inveighing against the hopelessness of the Chamberlain administration she said, "The time will produce the man," and by George, it has in Churchill.' She had noticed 'a great heartening-up going on', and felt an urge to somehow do her bit too. The nation was drawing together, and although she had absolutely no basis for thinking so, she felt, deep down, a conviction that Britain would undoubtedly win in the end.

Yet although the Government was now right behind Churchill in its determination to continue the fight, it was not so convinced by his belief that it should still help Britain's ally, France. Churchill was the man who had faced the French Comité de Guerre on 31 May, and had witnessed their desperation. His Francophilia was also deeply felt, but, furthermore, he worried that if France made a separate peace, Britain might be faced with a country not just out of the war but with a government actively hostile towards its former ally. He also knew that the longer the French held out, the greater the chances of British survival. At that time, it was unclear whether Germany would try to finish off France or turn straight to Britain, but if the French made that decision for them by capitulating immediately, that would not help Britain's cause. Already, one request after another was coming from Paris: for more troops, for twenty fighter squadrons, for a joint appeal to Roosevelt. 'The French,' noted Neville Chamberlain, 'are hysterical in their demands for assistance for the attack which they expect at any moment across the Somme.'

Chamberlain was not alone in feeling both weary and wary of the French. While there was no doubt Weygand, Pétain and others believed the British had cut and run and left them in the lurch, there was an almost unanimous feeling amongst Britain's political and military leadership that the French had badly let the side down with their feeble response to the German onslaught, their dithering, and their poor military leadership. The Cabinet was still fresh from hearing Henry Pownall's withering view of the French performance on his return from France when Lord Gort appeared and took an equally dim view. Everyone could see that France was now a busted flush. Only Churchill wanted to make an effort to keep them in the fight.

Not only did he propose sending three divisions via Normandy, but he also wanted to send over fighter and bomber aircraft, as requested. The Chiefs of Staff had already urged that no more squadrons be sent to France. Both Newall and Dowding, attending the War Cabinet, also argued strongly against such a move. Dowding even produced a graph showing that, on average, twenty-five Hurricanes a day had been lost in France from 10 to 18 May. Had more squadrons been sent there, he pointed out, there would have been no Hurricanes left by the end of the month. He told them that if the Germans launched an attack now, Fighter Command would be able to hold them for no more than forty-eight hours.

Despite these arguments and the opposition of both Halifax and Chamberlain to such a decision, Churchill insisted on helping the French. Both men and more aircraft would go to France.

On 5 June, Generaloberst Erhard Milch, number two in the Luftwaffe, flew over Dunkirk. He was struck by the enormous devastation he saw there: the thousands of abandoned vehicles and equipment, the charred rubble that had once been the old Channel port. What had surprised him more than anything, however, had been the absence of British troops.

That evening, he visited Göring aboard *Asia*. His boss had been back to Potsdam throughout the attack on Dunkirk but had now returned to France and was delighted that the BEF had been so routed.

'The British Army?' said Milch. 'I saw perhaps twenty or thirty corpses. The rest of the British Army has got clean away to the other side. They have left their equipment and escaped.' The British had suffered a major defeat, of that there could be no doubt, but there was no denying that they had managed to flee with almost their entire army. Göring asked him what the Luftwaffe should do now. Milch recommended sending all available aircraft in Luftflotten 2 and 3 to the Channel coast and then invading immediately. The Kriegsmarine would not be ready to take troops across yet, but the Luftwaffe could act right away. Paratroopers could capture vital airfields in south-east England and then they could fly in Stuka units to operate from them, just as they had in Norway. The remaining transport aircraft could ferry over perhaps two or three divisions of ground troops. It was, he realized, a gamble, but one worth taking because the British would be incapable of offering much resistance at the present time. The RAF had suffered and the army had no equipment; the time to strike, Milch argued, was now. 'If we leave the British in peace for four weeks,' he told Göring, 'it will be too late.'

Göring was unconvinced by these arguments. He had just one airborne division, rather than the four he had tried to create. 'Had I had these four divisions at the time of Dunkirk,' he said, 'I would have gone across to Britain immediately.' The Luftwaffe's failure to destroy the BEF and French forces at Dunkirk had been a disappointment, but in light of its enormous success in the rest of the campaign, Göring was not unduly concerned. Nor, it appears, was Milch, who despite urging an immediate attack against England seemed content to get on with the job in hand once Göring had dismissed such plans. Thus a golden opportunity to examine the real potential and capability of the Luftwaffe was passed over in the flush of success.

And there were telling lessons to learn too, had they chosen to take note of them. The dive-bomber, for example, was not quite as pinpoint accurate as had been expected, as Oskar Dinort could testify, and as revealed by the intact east mole and the large number of ships that had successfully flitted back and forth across the Channel. There was still a shortage of transport aircraft, whose losses had not been made good after the mauling they had suffered on the opening day of the campaign – and these aircraft would be needed should an invasion of Britain be necessary. Nor were there enough trained crew and pilots coming through to replace the losses.

Still, it was hoped an invasion would be unnecessary. France was all but beaten, that much was obvious, and Britain would surely follow. Hitler was by now convinced that Britain must sue for peace – logic demanded it – and Göring thought likewise. Not everything had gone to plan, but so what? They had still achieved a far greater victory than the Führer had ever dared believe possible.

So instead, while Milch beetled about, visiting airfields and attending conferences, Göring decided to enjoy the spoils of war, taking the opportunity to do a spot of art collecting. On 10 June, he was in Amsterdam, where he had just packed off twenty-six priceless works of art to Carinhall, including a number by Rubens, Rembrandt and Peter Breughel the Elder.

Despite the fears of Britain's leadership, there would be no immediate attack on Britain. Hitler had already decided on 24 May that they would finish France first. With the northern pocket finally clear, the second phase of the campaign in the west, Case Red, began on 5 June. The Germans had ensnared 1.7 million men in their giant encirclement, from which around half a million had managed to escape one way or another, although most via Dunkirk. Still, 1.2 million men was a huge number and included the cream of the French army. Now, Germany had the numerical advantage in manpower. Thanks to the distraction of Dunkirk and the fighting of the French First Army around Lille, Weygand had been given a bit of time to arrange his forces roughly east–west along the Somme and Aisne rivers, but both he and the rest of the French High Command had accepted that they could not hold the Germans for long.

Army Group B pushed south-west, across the Somme towards Rouen and Le Havre, while Army Group A pushed south and east. There were a few changes between the two army groups. Panzer Corps Hoth, with Rommel's 7th Panzer, was now in Army Group B, as was Panzer Group Kleist, albeit without Guderian, who had been given his own panzer group and had remained in Army Group A. His task was to wheel behind the French forces, heading for the Swiss border, and thus achieve another encirclement.

Amongst the French forces facing Army Group B were the last remaining British units, those that had been cut off from the rest of the BEF when the panzers had driven their wedge through to the coast. Le Havre and Rouen had been the BEF's main supply points and there were vast stores and ammunition dumps there, manned by Ordnance Corps and other base troops as well as a number of infantry battalions. The bulk of 12th Division had already been evacuated, but not so the 1st Armoured Division, Britain's only one of its kind, nor the 51st Highland Division, which had been taking its turn to man a portion of the Maginot Line when the offensive began and had only recently been sent back west. These had since been placed under the command of IX Corps of the French Seventh Army on the left wing of the French line. There were also the remnants of the Advanced Air Striking Force of six bomber squadrons and thirty battered Hurricanes.

The French had already made good use of these disparate British forces, flinging them pointlessly at Abbeville in an attempt to destroy the German bridgehead there. 1st Armoured had taken part in the failed counter-attack on 27 May, losing over a hundred tanks in the process, while the Highland Division had also suffered during another attempt on 4 June. The rest of the British units had been formed into a loose under-gunned force called Beauman Division, named after its hastily appointed commander.

The German attack, launched first by Army Group B, did meet stiffer resistance than they had been accustomed to from the French, and initially suffered heavy losses. One of the German units that managed to break through quickest was Rommel's 7th Panzer. Once again, Hauptmann Hans von Luck and his Reconnaissance Battalion were at the vanguard. To avoid the congestion of refugees, they advanced cross-country in open battle order, keeping clear of any major roads. They took the Somme bridges intact but then came up against the Weygand Line, the main French defences, and immediately found themselves under heavy enemy fire.

It was still early morning when, taking cover from French shelling, Hans heard a voice behind him say, 'Captain, your breakfast.' Hans turned around to see one of his runners clutching a tray of sandwiches. He had crawled through enemy fire carrying the meal, which had even been garnished with parsley and a napkin. Such was the confidence and high spirits of these lead units.

With the support of artillery and panzers, they soon managed to break through the French line. On 7 June, Hans and his men covered some sixty miles, blasting their way not only through the French but also between the two brigades of 1st Armoured Division. Rouen, recently pasted by the Luftwaffe, lay smoking ahead of them. They had assumed the next obstacle would be the formidable River Seine, but instead Hans received orders to swing north-west to the coast north of Le Havre. 'In the harbours between Le Havre and Dieppe there are said to be British units still waiting to be evacuated,' ran Hans's orders.

This was true. Both the 7th and 5th Panzer Divisions, by breaking through, had the British forces potentially trapped. The Highland Division had fallen back to the line of the River Bresle, some ten miles behind the Somme, on 6 June, but the German troops following them seemed in no hurry to push them back further. There was no point – they had most of IX Corps ensnared, a trap that would be complete once the panzers to the south wheeled round and reached the coast. Before the Germans had launched their attack, General Fortune, commander of the 51st Division, had recognized that by being on the coast, with the Havre peninsula behind them, they would be particularly vulnerable to an out-flanking movement, and had discussed possible evacuation from Le Havre with Brigadier Beauman. However, by 7 June, when such an encirclement first seemed likely, it was already too late for IX Corps to fall back – they simply could not organize themselves that quickly. And since the British troops were under French command they faced a simple choice: desert their French comrades or fight their way back with them step by step. Both honour and the political situation ensured they took the latter option.

As it happened, however, General Fortune had been given authority to fall back on Le Havre with all speed early on 8 June, but because of the usual communication problems that had been such a feature of the Allied effort it was not until late afternoon that he received these instructions. He did manage to send a covering force – 'Arkforce' – of two brigades to protect the approach to Le Havre, but the rest of the division and those French units on their right could only fall back as far as Dieppe.

On 10 June, Rommel's men reached the coast. 'Am at sea,' he signalled to Army Group B. Then calling his commanders together, he explained his plan. He was now going to drive up the coast to St Valéry sur Mer, but wanted Hans von Luck, with a battery of 88 mm guns, to push west towards the coastal town of Fécamp and secure the approach to Le Havre.

It was around 11 a.m. on the 10th that Fortune learned that the road to Le Havre had been cut. There was now only one exit route for him, and that was the tiny port of St Valéry, so what remained of his division and the French IX Corps fell back on the port and began digging in. Meanwhile, at Fécamp some British troops and a number of French had been captured by Hans von Luck's Reconnaissance Battalion, but most of Arkforce had managed to successfully escape back to Le Havre. They were the lucky ones. On the afternoon of 11 June, St Valéry came under fire. An attempt was made to evacuate the troops that night but rain and fog hampered efforts so that only 2,137 men were lifted.

At 8.15 a.m. the following morning a white flag was raised over the town, which Fortune immediately demanded should be taken down as he had no intention of surrendering – not yet, at any rate. His depleted forces still had heart – they would fight on. Yet Général Ihler, commander of IX Corps, had already accepted the hopelessness of the situation and called on Fortune to give up. By ten, Rommel's tanks were in the town but it was not until 10.30 a.m. that Fortune finally agreed it was over. Proceeding to the town square he discovered Général Ihler and his French commanders already there facing none other than Generalmajor Rommel himself.

'And what do you command?' Rommel asked Fortune.

'You, sir, should know that,' Fortune replied tersely.

Rommel laughed and invited Fortune to have a meal with him, which the British general declined even though he had no rations left.

'Dearest Lu,' Rommel wrote that night to his wife, 'The battle here is over.'

23

The End in France

AT 8 A.M. EXACTLY ON the morning of 6 June, three airmen, scanning the dark, grey-green waters of the North Atlantic from their inflatable dinghy, suddenly saw the outline of a low shape emerge through the heavy haze. Immediately, they took their flare pistol and fired a white star into the sky, then began waving and shouting madly. It was forty hours since they had sent a wireless signal that they had been attacked by a British Blenheim, that their pilot was badly wounded in the head, and that they were going to ditch their Dornier 18 flying boat and take to the rubber life-dinghy. Since then, the pilot had died, but another of the crew, Unteroffizier Stökinger, was also wounded. The three survivors were hungry and parched with thirst. They were exhausted too, having first smashed the floats on their aircraft to make it sink, and then having paddled east for nearly two days in a vain attempt to reach the Shetland Islands. But in all that time they had seen nothing but an empty grey sea, and now all hope had begun to slip away. Now, however, it appeared that salvation was at hand.

It was only a few minutes later that the grey vessel, scything gracefully through the mist, drew towards them. At first they thought it must be a British submarine, but then a voice – a German voice – called out to them. The men, overjoyed with relief, watched as the 220-foot-long boat drew alongside them. A couple of men were clambering down on to the deck, while above, on the bridge, stood the captain. He was easily identifiable with his white-top cap, battered leather jacket, black woollen scarf and the pair of massive 7 x 50 Zeiss binoculars. Painted on to the conning tower was a picture of a white snorting bull. This was U-47, the single best-known submarine in all of Germany, and its skipper, Germany's most famous submariner, the 32-year-old Kapitänleutnant Günther Prien. The first man in the Kriegsmarine to win the Knight's Cross.

Günther had been delighted to find the men. The signal to all U-boats in the area to look for the men had reached them at four o'clock the previous afternoon, and since then they had been searching hard, wasting precious time and fuel. That morning, there was hardly a breeze so the water was calm, but the haze meant visibility was limited. He had continued hunting, changing course from time to time, but was on the point of giving up when at last the flare had been spotted.

The airmen were lifted on to the deck and then taken down below, and Günther followed soon after. When he reached the cramped ward-room he found his off-watch men gathered round the airmen, plying them with sausage and drink. Crouching down by Stöckinger, Günther examined his wounds. 'One through the calf and a flesh wound in the shoulder,' he said. 'Nothing too serious.' That was good, for there was no way of getting the wounded man off again until the patrol's end – and that would not be for another month.

The crew had hoped that finding the airmen had been a good omen, but a whole week passed before they found any shipping. Crew morale quickly dipped in such circumstances. The Mk VIIB U-boat might look large enough from the outside, but, inside, the cigar-shaped pressure hull was only 142 feet long and ten feet wide, which for forty crew – five officers and thirty-five ratings – was claustrophobic to say the least. The men literally lived on top of each other since the boat sailed round the clock whilst on patrol, and crews would take turns to be on watch. Thus they shared what few facilities there were, side by side with the fourteen torpedoes, 220 88 mm deck-gun rounds, and the stores for four or five weeks of patrol; every nook and cranny was filled with nets of potatoes, tins of fruit, meat and condensed milk, coffee, sugar, cheese and hard-crusted black bread. From the innumerable pipes that ran along the boat, there hung vast numbers of sausages and sides of cured meat. By the end of a patrol, vegetables and cheese left over had often become mouldy, adding to the already foul stench on board, a stench of sweat, diesel oil, brine and food. There was only one toilet, for which there would often be a long queue and which smelled particularly repugnant. There was little spare water so the men hardly washed, and certainly never changed their clothes. Beards were the norm because shaving was a waste of water. Hair quickly became matted and greasy with oil and sweat. The heating rarely worked properly – it was always either too hot or too cold on board, but the fetid air nearly always clammy. And while on the surface, which U-boats were for most of the time because they could travel so much faster than when submerged, the boat would pitch, plunge and roll with the swell of the ocean. The men who manned the U-boats were tough, hardy and imperturbable. They needed to be.

When U-47 did at last spot a ship, on 14 June, they were way to the south, off the bottom coast of Ireland in a wolfpack along with nine other U-boats. Günther had immediately given the order to dive and was just lining up his first torpedo when the ship suddenly changed direction, veering straight for them, and forcing them to crash-dive and forego the shot. Following behind, however, was a huge convoy of some forty-two ships, a salivating prospect for a U-boat. The problem, however, was closing in on it; they were just too far away to catch the steaming vessels submerged. On the surface, U-47's seventeen knots was fast enough to catch a convoy that rarely travelled at more than around fourteen knots, but submerged the best it could manage was just eight. When they did finally have a chance to take a shot, they were nearly rammed a second time and had to crash-dive again. A further attempt was then thwarted by the arrival of a Sunderland flying boat swooping overhead.

Günther cursed, convinced the patrol must be jinxed, but then a straggler was sighted. Ordering the boat to dive, he waited, then closed in towards the weaving vessel. It was 11.58 – a couple of minutes before midday. At last, Günther, glued to the periscope in the control room, gave the order for Tube Five to fire. A loud hiss of compressed air filled the boat and the men felt the submarine shiver as the torpedo hurtled from its tube. For a few moments there was silence. And then they heard the sound of an explosion.

'Hit almost amidships,' said Günther triumphantly. He continued to give a running report as he peered through the periscope. The ship looked heavily laden; there were a number of crates on the deck. She was British, the *Balmoralwood*, about 5,000–6,000 tonnes, he reckoned. Men were lowering whalers and scrambling frantically down into them. Then the ship began to list and heel over, and then slipped down into the sea, a huge whirlpool sucking many of the men and the cargo down with it. Soon after, all that was left were a few crates bobbing on the surface. Some had burst open so that Günther could see what she had been carrying on her way to Britain. Aircraft – he could see the wings and fuselages clearly.

Hitler had never intended to subdue Britain by air and land alone. To beat Britain, to bring her to her knees, she needed to be strangled, her sea-borne lifeline cut off to such an extent that she simply would not be able to survive. To achieve that, he had belatedly realized, and as Rear-Admiral Karl Dönitz, commander of the Kriegsmarine's U-boat arm, had been urging upon his superiors for years, that Germany did not need vast battleships, cruisers and aircraft carriers. She needed U-boats. As Kapitänleutnant Günther Prien had proved all too well when he had sunk HMS *Royal Oak* the previous October, forty men in a small submarine could destroy a 1,200-man British battleship more effectively than any German surface vessel.

Günther and his crew need not have worried; there was no jinx on this, their sixth patrol. Rather, the sinking of *Balmoralwood* was just the beginning of a slaughter out on the Western Approaches. The U-boat men would call it the 'Happy Time'.

Back in France, the battle may have been over, but that did not stop Churchill sending more reinforcements. On the same day that the 51st Highland Division surrendered, the newly knighted General Sir Alan Brooke landed back in France, at Cherbourg, to lead the newly re-constituted BEF. He was there reluctantly, aware that it was a fool's mission doomed to fail. Receiving his orders had been one of the blackest moments of his life. Already half his proposed force – those trapped in the Havre peninsula – had gone. The 52nd Division had already landed and the 1st Canadian was on its way, and Dill had further promised him the 3rd Division, but organizing those into a coherent whole that could achieve anything whatsoever was going to be impossible. Three British divisions amongst the sixty-six French and more than 130 German was peanuts to say the least. 'All that I found on my return,' he noted, 'were the remnants of one brigade which had escaped capture, but were without much equipment and only fit for evacuation. My Corps Headquarters was dispersed all over England after its arrival back from Dunkirk. Chaos prevailed.'

Mercifully, however, Churchill had backed down over the sending of more squadrons to France, persuaded by the united stance of Halifax, Chamberlain, the Air Ministry and Dowding. Even so, it did not stop aircraft operating from England being sent over; on 6 June, no fewer than

144 fighters flew over France. The Prime Minister simply felt unable to abandon France completely, but that did not stop him becoming angry at their incessant demands or hurt by French accusations of inadequate support. 'Winston is justifiably angry with Vuillemin,' recorded Jock Colville, 'who referred to our tremendous air efforts in the first battle as "tardy, inadequate but nevertheless of some value".' This revealed one of the persistent inconsistencies of the French: blaming the British for deserting them but then criticizing them for their negligible contribution. British condemnation of the French for letting everyone down was equally vociferous; Churchill was amongst a minority who had a good word to say about them. Bad feeling between the two countries was mounting and these tensions were not just amongst the High Command. British prisoners had been attacked by French POWs for their 'desertion' at Dunkirk so that the Germans had to keep them separated.

On 10 June, Mussolini finally entered the war against the Allies, much to everyone's wrath, including Hitler's. The Führer had already told Mussolini that he did not want him coming in just yet. After all, Germany had done quite well enough without the Italians and he did not want them trying to cash in on easy booty now that France and Britain were on their knees. 'It is embarrassingly opportunistic,' noted Gerhard Engel from Hitler's headquarters, 'first of all they are too cowardly to fight with us and now they cannot join us fast enough to get their share of the swag.' Hitler had muttered that from now on he would have to be far more cautious in his dealings with the Italians. It was not exactly a cosy start to their military alliance.

But while Mussolini's timing was undoubtedly opportunistic, Italy's entry into the war created another massive headache for Britain and her interests in the Mediterranean and Middle East at a time when she least needed it. Indeed, barely had the declaration of war been made than Italian bombers were over the key British naval port of Malta, which had been left horribly under-defended. Italian troops were not considered any great threat but the Italian navy was; the British Mediterranean Fleet would be stretched. Rather than resenting Mussolini's opportunism – and, in any case, Hitler was strong enough to limit Italian involvement in the spoils of war – he should have welcomed such a strategically placed ally, however late her entry into the fray.

Jock Colville had to wake Churchill from his afternoon nap to tell him of the Italian declaration. It was not at all unexpected, but with the news that the French Government had now abandoned Paris, it put the Prime Minister in a foul mood. 'People who go to Italy to look at ruins,' he muttered, 'won't have to go as far as Naples and Pompeii in future.' Churchill was determined to strike at Italy right away by launching a bombing raid on the Fiat plant at Turin. So too were many British civilians. After the declaration, Italians living and working in Britain were attacked, ice-cream shops ransacked, restaurants damaged with bricks and stones. The next day, Churchill ordered that all male Italians between seventeen and seventy years of age resident in Britain for less than twenty-five years should be interned. 'Collar the lot,' he said, which amounted to more than 4,000. It was draconian but few British people baulked at the measure. Daidie Penna noticed that in her corner of Surrey, at any rate, there was something like relief at Mussolini's declaration. 'You mark my words,' the village grocer told her, 'in a month's time, he'll be a brick round Hitler's neck!' Another shopkeeper told her cheerfully, 'Now we can get the whole bag.'

RAF Bomber Command had been busy since beginning its strategic bombing campaign against Germany, although it had called a temporary halt to help with the evacuation of Dunkirk, attacking German positions every day of Operation DYNAMO. No fewer than 126 Blenheims and Wellingtons had bombed the enemy on 31 May, a considerable effort. Yet now that Italy was in the war, Britain was keen to strike immediately – a show of strength that demonstrated they took no truck with their latest enemy.

They had urged the idea of bombing Italy upon the Comité de Guerre at the end of May when it had become clear Mussolini would make his move sooner rather than later. Thus, an advance party of Bomber Command's 71 Wing had been sent to Marseilles to prepare for such a strike and had taken over two airfields, which would act as a base and refuelling stop for the Wellingtons. These aircraft were duly sent to Marseilles on 11 June but had barely touched down when the French informed them they were not to bomb Italy under any circumstances. Since agreeing to the plan, Général Joseph Vuillemin had thrown most of his southern fighters into the battle further north and the French were now worried that if the Italians retaliated, they would not have any means of defending themselves. Visions of Marseilles and other French cities being razed to the ground by Italian bombers loomed large.

The British were determined to press ahead, however, and ordered the Wellingtons to go ahead, so that a few minutes after midnight the first bombers were beginning to taxi into position. Yet, as they did so, a number of French trucks drove across the airfield blocking their way and preventing them from taking off. The Wing had no choice but to call it off.

Meanwhile, 4 Group's Whitleys had flown to the Channel Islands, where they refuelled and took off again without any hindrance. Thirty-six aircraft took off, including those from 10 Squadron. Larry Donnelly, now promoted to sergeant, was amongst the crews taking part. Their aircraft began its take-off down the short 800-yard airfield at Jersey at 8 p.m., reassured by the sight of the Whitley in front safely taking to the air. Even so, Larry was feeling particularly nervous about this entire trip. 'To say that I was feeling tensed up,' he noted, 'as I sat in the tail turret of the Whitley bumping its way along the take-off run was an understatement.' They took off without mishap but initially struggled to gain any height, laden as they were. From the back, Larry glanced out at the sea, keenly aware of how close it was.

Had they been amongst the first to take off, Larry and his crew might have made it to Turin, but unfortunately as they reached southern France they ran into heavy electrical storms. Ice began to build up on the wings, while lightning flashed around. The Whitley was bucked and thrown about the sky and then suddenly there was a blinding flash and an audible bang as they were struck by lightning. Their pilot, Enery, decided they could not go on, so they turned and headed back to the Channel Islands.

In fact, only nine aircraft managed to bomb Turin, dropping their loads from around 5,000 feet, and not on the Fiat plant, but on railway marshalling yards instead. To begin with the Italian ack-ack gunners fired way too high before eventually adjusting their range, but they were unable to shoot any of the Whitleys down. Two further bombers attacked Genoa by mistake.

Larry and his crew made it safely back to Jersey and from there to Dishforth. Four days later, Turin was bombed again, this time by Wellingtons; the much feared retaliation had not brought the death and destruction the French had feared. In the meantime, however, 10 Squadron, along with the rest of 4 Group, had German positions and communications in France to bomb. The end for France was coming, but while the fighting continued, Bomber Command would do what they could to help.

*

The second part of Case Red, the attack by Army Group A, was launched on 9 June. Once again, Hitler was unable to resist interfering with Halder's plans, insisting that Army Group A first secure the iron ore basin in Lorraine, the source of France's armament industry, before turning on the bulk of the French forces. What Hitler failed to understand was that by destroying the French army, there would be no more armament industry.

As it happened, the French now collapsed so quickly that both Halder's and Hitler's aims were achieved at the same time. On 11 June, Churchill flew to France with Eden, Dill, Ismay, and his representative in France, Edward Spears, to Weygand's new headquarters in Briare on the Loire. That night they met with the Comité de Guerre, Churchill urging them on and promising twenty and more divisions in 1941. Weygand said they needed that number in hours, not next year. Later, over a brandy man to man, Reynaud confessed to Churchill that Pétain believed the time had come to seek an armistice.

They prepared to leave the following morning, having agreed nothing but an undertaking to try to organize some kind of redoubt in Brittany. At the rather desolate airfield at Briare, Hastings Ismay tried to dissuade Churchill again from committing any more troops to France, but the Prime Minister would have none of it. Ismay, like so many others, felt the French had found it all too easy to blame the British for everything that had gone wrong. He also expressed his belief that Britain would be better off without the French. Churchill, his spirit and optimism for once deserting him, replied that in three months' time, he and Ismay would both be dead.

His prophecy was nearly fulfilled that morning. With nine-tenths cloud, it was too dangerous to have a fighter escort. Churchill, impatient to return to London, decided they should fly anyway. As they flew out towards the coast, they spotted two German aircraft bombing ships below. By enormous good fortune, the German pilots never looked up.

Thirty-six hours later, Reynaud asked Churchill to fly out again, this time to Tours, where he had now based the Government. The weather was bad once again, but the Prime Minister brushed aside concerns and flew anyway, taking Ismay, Halifax and his close friend Max Beaverbrook with him. They met in a small prefecture, Reynaud looking ashen and aged in that brief day and a half. Weygand wanted to surrender, Reynaud told them, but still hoped he might persuade them to fight on if only the Americans would agree to join the fight. If they would not, would Britain agree that it was now impossible for France to continue? Churchill told him that Britain would fight on. She would never surrender. Churchill felt deep sympathy for France's agony but could not agree to a French armistice. In the courtyard below, a number of French commanders and politicians gathered to see the British go. Amidst embraces, handshakes and tears, the Prime Minister and his entourage left France for the last time.

Paris fell the next day. Between 8 a.m. and 3 p.m., Leutnant Siegfried Knappe and his gunners in the 87th Division marched thirty miles, before taking up a position along the Marne River; in the distance they could see the Eiffel Tower. At 9 p.m., they were suddenly ordered to a position on the Ourcq Canal, where apparently some French sailors drafted in for the defence of Paris were still resisting. Siegfried went forward with the infantry, who were being pinned down by small-arms fire from the basement of a house on the far side of the canal beside a bridge. Siegfried called up one of his 105 mm guns, and from the cover of a building on their side of the canal the gun was brought up and readied. 'At my command,' Siegfried told his men, 'we will push the gun around the corner and I will aim the gun and give the order to fire. Everyone understand?' His men nodded. 'Let's go!' shouted Siegfried.

As they pushed it round, pinpoints of fire flashed from the building opposite. Quickly, they aimed the gun and pulled the trigger, then flattened themselves on the ground. Siegfried knew he had been hit on his left wrist, but as he looked up only smoke now came from the basement. The French firing had ceased. Siegfried now looked at his wound. A bullet had passed through the back of his hand and out by his wrist. It was oozing blood, but felt numb. He then noticed a hole through the side of his jacket, his sleeve and his map case, and realized he had been extremely lucky. 'The bridge was now open to us,' noted Siegfried, 'and the next morning the division was in Paris.'

In brief moments between his duties for the PM, Jock Colville was reading *War and Peace*. He never seemed to be able to finish it, but on the day Paris fell had got to the point where the French were entering Moscow. It was, he felt, in some ways analogous. He also seemed taken with Churchill's idea for a Breton Redoubt, drawing his own Napoleonic analogy. 'If the French will go on fighting,' he jotted, 'we must now fall back on the Atlantic, creating the new lines of Torres Vedras.'

Jock and Churchill must have been just about the only two people who thought there was any mileage in this whatsoever. Certainly General Brooke did not. That day, he had seen both Weygand and Georges, who told him that it was all over. The French army, Weygand said, had ceased to be able to offer organized resistance. Georges concurred and it was agreed that the Breton Redoubt idea was impossible. Brooke rang Dill and told him this and then began making preparations to get the 52nd and Canadian Divisions to Brest and Cherbourg, and remaining troops to Nantes and then to various ports to be evacuated.

Around 8 p.m., Dill called from Admiralty House and then put Churchill on the phone, who said that he did not want his troops evacuated. He told Brooke that they had been sent to France to make the French feel that Britain was supporting them. 'I replied that it was impossible to make a corpse feel,' Brooke noted. The conversation went on for half an hour, Churchill arguing vociferously for their continued presence in France, but Brooke, unmoved, stood his ground. And eventually the Prime Minister said, 'All right, I agree with you.'

So began the Royal Navy's latest series of evacuations. Thanks to Brooke, over the next few days, a further 200,000 men were lifted from Cherbourg, Brest, St Nazaire and La Pallice. It meant that more than half a million men were brought back from France in all. Half a million men who could continue the fight.

On 16 June, Reynaud again asked that France be released from its obligation to Britain and be able to seek terms with Germany. The War Cabinet replied that they would do so only if the French fleet sailed to British ports. Meanwhile, Général de Gaulle, one of the few French generals refusing to throw in the towel, had flown to London. He urged Churchill to propose a formal union between Britain and France, which the War Cabinet had been ruminating over for several days. The offer was clearly born of desperation and although it was sent to Reynaud, and Churchill was all set to go to France to discuss it, the French Prime Minister refused to see him again. Indeed, that night, Reynaud resigned. Had he held on, he could have formed a government in exile, but it was not to be. He did, however, perform one last service for the Allied cause by agreeing that all France's arms contracts in the USA should immediately be transferred to Britain. That was something at least.

Meanwhile, those men of speed, Guderian and Rommel, had continued their full-throttle hurtle through France. On 17 June, Rommel's men advanced a staggering 160 miles, while that same day Guderian reached the Swiss border, sending a message back to OKW that he was in Pontarlier. A reply came back: 'Your signal based on an error. Assume you mean Pontailler-sur-Saône.' Guderian answered: 'No error. Am myself in Pontarlier on Swiss border.'

It was also the day the French asked for an armistice. Reynaud had resigned and Pétain taken over, ordering his soldiers to lay down their arms. Hitler, from his new HQ in Brûly-de-Pêche in southern Belgium, now flew to Munich to meet with Mussolini. 'Reply will be held until then,' noted Halder. 'Nothing is known as yet about Britain's reaction.' In the meantime, the German forces pushed on, Rommel reaching Cherbourg in the west, the swastika rising over Strasbourg in the east. Halder busied himself preparing for the peacetime organization of the army now that the war was all but over; it would be reduced from 165 divisions to 120.

The Germans offered the armistice terms on 21 June and it was signed the next day at Compiègne, in the very same railway carriage in which the Germans had been forced to sign the surrender in 1918.

Britain now seemed terribly alone. Turkey, who had pledged to enter the war on Britain's side should Italy come in, had reneged on that promise. So too had Egypt. Anti-British feeling was also growing in Iraq, so that British interests in the Mediterranean and Middle East suddenly looked very shaky indeed. Roosevelt and the United States were still a long way from entering the war, and despite Spain's claim of non-belligerency there was mounting concern that she, too, would come in on the side of the Axis. At any rate, Franco's Spain was certainly sympathetic to Germany. This meant that the entire coast from the Arctic Circle to the west coast of Africa was either Nazi or pro-Nazi. Not even during the Napoleonic invasion threat had Britain been confronted by such a wall of hostility. To make matters worse, it looked very unlikely that Britain would be able to get her hands on the all-important French Fleet, or on the American destroyers she so desperately needed. For Britain, the future looked bleak indeed.

Neville Chamberlain had finally vacated No. 10, having moved next door to No. 11 Downing Street instead. He was glad to still feel of use to Churchill at this hour of need, 'But,' he wrote to his sister, 'if we suffer greater disasters we may all go down. I haven't begun to hang my pictures yet . . .'

24

Hitler's Dilemma

WHEN HITLER HEARD the news that the French wanted an armistice, his secretary, Christa Schroeder, saw him slap his thigh and laugh out loud with joy. She then listened to Keitel hail him as the greatest warlord of all time. What a victory it had been! They could scarce believe it. The French had suffered around 120,000 dead and missing, the Belgians, 7,500, the Dutch 3,000 and the British around 5,000 killed in action with a further 70,000 prisoners and missing. Over 1.5 million men had been taken prisoner. The Germans, on the other hand, lost 49,000 dead and missing, and 60 per cent of those losses had occurred during the last ten days. Incredibly, the 1st Panzer Division, the very spearhead of the entire campaign, had lost just 267 men killed in action, a little over 2 per cent of its number.

William Shirer was one of the journalists invited to witness the official armistice signing at the clearing in the woods where the railway *wagon-lit* stood. He was a little way away, but through binoculars watched Hitler step out of his car and stride towards them. 'I observed his face,' wrote William. 'It was grave, solemn, yet brimming with revenge. There was also in it a springy step, a note of the triumphant conqueror, the defier of the world.'

By the terms of the armistice, France was divided. The north and western seaboard would be occupied by the Germans, while the south would be left as a puppet state headed by Pétain, with its government in the small but elegant Auvergne spa town of Vichy. All France's overseas possessions were also to be governed by Vichy. Much to his disappointment, Mussolini was not allowed to have the French fleet, but nor were the British. Germany, now fully convinced that U-boats were the key to naval success, agreed that the French navy should remain in port, inactive, although, of course, Hitler could always change his mind about that at a later stage.

Declaring the end in France to be the 'most glorious victory of all time', Hitler ordered that bells should be rung in the Reich for a week and that flags should be flown. The Third Reich was to celebrate. 'How many mothers and wives will thank God that the war with France has ended so quickly,' wrote Christa Schroeder. In Berlin, Else Wendel's life had not much improved – she was still estranged from her sons and without the love of a good man – but even she was swept along by the carnival atmosphere of victory. 'What stupendous successes!' she wrote. 'All my fears disappeared for there was hope again. I loved that spring and summer, and so did everyone in Berlin. Victory flags, victory music, victory gaiety. Everything was all right in Germany.' She also thought it was brilliant of Hitler to sign the armistice in the same railway carriage as had been used in 1918. As far as she was concerned, France and Britain had asked for and got it. Germany stood once more in her true place in Europe. 'A great people,' she added, 'who had proved themselves more than equal to the rest of the world.'

Hilda Müller, still training for Siemens, had been following the war carefully. It was unavoidable, for at the Siemens office there was a large map on which glass-headed pins were moved every time the Germans advanced. The radio would also be on. 'We listened to the radio at work,' she says. 'It was known as Goebbels' Gob.' A loudspeaker had been set up, so that everyone could hear it. Whenever there was a success, there would be a special announcement on the radio and a Franz Liszt prelude would be played, followed by an announcement.

Hilda was pleased that the war seemed to be nearly over, but best of all was the announcement that the dance halls were to be reopened. 'To be honest,' she says, 'France wasn't so important to me as the fact that I could go dancing again.'

Hitler was determined to take a short break too, visiting the battlefields where he had served during the First World War, and to Dunkirk too, where he was delighted to find so much intact British kit strewn all over the place. 'They thought only of their skins,' he said contemptuously.

'They can certainly beat their colonial subjects with whips, but on the battlefield they are miserable cowards.' He also made a brief visit to Paris. 'F. talked again about trip to Paris,' noted Gerhard Engel, 'which had impressed him deeply; praised Napoleon and French kings, who had really thought and planned on the grand scale.'

But what was the world's greatest warlord going to do about Britain? The war was not over – not until Britain gave up the fight as well. He felt sure she would sue for peace, and in the flush of victory he was feeling generous. He told Mussolini he had no intention of breaking up the British Empire and said he would offer generous terms – a few possessions and an acceptance of the German position in Europe. Yet he was also clearly worried about a risky invasion. On 17 June, the day before his meeting with Mussolini, the OKW had told the Operations Staff of the Kriegsmarine that the Führer had not yet expressed any intention to make a landing in Britain, 'as he fully appreciates the unusual difficulties of such an operation'.

Three days later, he was feeling more bullish. Von Brauchitsch had met with him at the Wolf's Ravine, as the Führer Headquarters was known, to discuss winding-down operations. He advised the Führer that it was absolutely necessary to negotiate a peace with Britain or prepare to invade and quickly so. Hitler, however, was sceptical. He considered Britain was now so weak that major operations on land would hardly be necessary after the Luftwaffe had bombed her into submission. The army would then cross the Channel merely as an occupation force. Out at sea, ready to pounce on Allied shipping in the Western Approaches, were Admiral Dönitz's wolfpacks. Soon, his fast, agile motor torpedo boats, his *Schnellboote*, would be operating from along the Channel coast too. One way or another, he told von Brauchitsch, Britain would back down.

That same day, Gerhard Hartmann, a young soldier in the Grossdeutschland Panzer Grenadier Division on guard duty at the Wolf's Ravine, overheard a conversation between Hitler and Göring as the two men strolled through the woods outside the Headquarters. The young man could not help but hear; the two men paused just yards away from him. Göring told Hitler that the Luftwaffe was already prepared to attack England, at which the Führer began talking about an invasion. 'What he has in mind,' recorded Gerhard, 'is a fifty-kilometre strip of land that can be secured by the Luftwaffe.' As they moved on again, Gerhard moved so that he was hidden by a tree and then surreptitiously took a photograph of these two giant figures plotting the course of history.

Also on that day, Hitler told his secretary, Christa Schroeder, that he intended to address the Reichstag and in the speech make an appeal to the British. 'If they will not quit, he said, he would go ahead ruthlessly!' she wrote in a letter. 'I believe that he is sorry to have to wrestle the British to the ground; he would apparently find it preferable if they would be reasonable about it.' Of course he would – it was far easier to conclude a peace treaty without having to go to the trouble of mounting an assault by air and sea.

He believed he had already done enough to bring Britain to the peace table. Britain's army had been trounced and her ally crushed, and Germany had proved that its army and air force were superior in almost every way. Britain stood alone. It did not make sense for her to continue the fight.

Only Britain now stood in the way of Hitler pursuing his bigger agenda, the showdown with the Soviet Union. It is easy to think that Germany started the war largely because the megalomaniac Hitler craved power and land, and because the German people, cowed and humiliated after the First World War and the harsh terms of the Treaty of Versailles, were prepared to go along with a man who seemed to be literally offering them the world. It was, of course, a lot more complicated than that.

Hitler viewed Stalin and the Soviet state as an evil, blood-stained tyranny that had deliberate aims of spreading westwards. In this, he was largely correct. At the heart of his ideology – as outlined in his book, *Mein Kampf* – was the struggle against the Jewish-Bolshevik. World Jewry was a malevolent force that needed to be crushed, but so too was Bolshevism. Indeed, Communism in Germany was painted in much the same way as Nazism was portrayed in Britain, that is, something dangerous that had to be stopped. Hitler's hatred of Bolshevism was shared by the military aristocratic elite, who still believed that the Kiel Mutiny in 1918, which had hastened the end of the First World War, had been led by communist elements. It had ensured that in the post-war army it was only aristocrats who had reached the highest command. It was for this reason that the Wehrmacht of 1940 still had so many men from traditional German military families in key positions – men such as von Rundstedt, von Brauchitsch, von Kleist, von Kluge, von Richthofen and even von Manstein. These men allied themselves to Hitler and the Nazis partly because he represented the antithesis of Bolshevism, but also because he promised massive military rearmament, which was felt to be necessary if Germany was to protect herself.

And it was this vulnerability, this insecurity about Germany's central geographical position in Europe, which was the nub of Hitler's ability to drive such an aggressive foreign policy. In the 1930s, Germany was still a very young state that had been created only in 1871. As such, it remained a nation of German peoples rather than the German nation. It was also a part of Europe that had a long history of bloody wars, from the terrible Thirty Years War in the seventeenth century, to the Napoleonic Wars of the early nineteenth century, to the catastrophic First World War. With a comparatively small coastline along only her northern border, Germany was vulnerable to attack from all other sides. After Versailles, she was more vulnerable than she had ever been.

There was another factor in Germany's geographical position, however. The Reich lacked oil and sufficient supplies of iron and other key ores, and had only comparatively small coal seams. These could be gained either by foreign trade agreements or by expansion. If Hitler could attack and destroy the Soviet Union, then he would kill two birds with one stone. First, he would eliminate the Soviet threat to Germany, and with it Bolshevism, and, second, he would have vast lands that could supply the Reich with all the minerals, farmland, and manpower he needed to ensure Germany's long-term future. This was his *Lebensraum* policy. It was not an original idea; the concept had been around in Germany since the end of the nineteenth century. Another word for it was colonization, and that was as old as the stars.

Before he turned to Russia, however, there was expansion closer to home to attend to. In many ways, Hitler's massive rearmament policy and early territorial expansionism were entirely understandable. Certainly, megalomania played a part, but he also believed, like most Germans, that those German-speaking territories were rightly part of Germany. Furthermore, he needed to make Germany more secure, by creating a greater protective ring around the country – a kind of buffer. The stronger the Reich, the less vulnerable it would be to foreign aggression.

And his early expansionism was phenomenally successful, which gained him ever more popular support. The Rhineland was reoccupied; Austria was absorbed; so too was the Sudetenland; and then, in March 1939, so was the rest of Czechoslovakia. And all without firing a shot. No wonder the Germans loved him. He had given them pride, jobs, prosperity and nearly all the land stripped from them in 1919, and all peacefully. It was nothing short of a miracle.

Nearly all, but not quite. The last remaining piece of pre-1919 German territory now lay in Poland, and it was to this new country that Hitler turned his attention in the spring of 1939. In 1919, the new Polish state had been granted a strip of land between the German province of East Prussia and the rest of Germany that gave them access to the Baltic Sea. Hitler wanted this largely German-peopled strip of land returned and had assumed that Poland could be threatened and bullied into ceding the Danzig 'corridor' back to Germany. This done, he believed Poland would then become a virtual German satellite and ally when he eventually launched an attack on the Soviet Union.

The Poles, however, had no intention of being bullied and flatly rejected German proposals to cede the corridor despite threats of military action. It was at this point that Britain, and then France, made their pledge to honour Poland's territorial rights. Few countries involve themselves in the affairs of others purely for the wider good. Foreign intervention is always rooted in self-interest, albeit this self-interest might be shared with a number of other states. Thus Britain, under the Prime Minister, Neville Chamberlain, and Foreign Secretary, Lord Halifax, had in March 1939 given a public guarantee of Poland's territorial rights, not because they were feeling altruistic towards Poland but because they thought this would be the best way to deter Hitler from ideas of further expansion. They assumed that Hitler, with his despicable totalitarian Nazi ideology, would, if encouraged, slowly try to conquer all of Europe and then even the world, in which case Nazi Germany was clearly a threat to Britain too. Thus he had to be stopped. That might well have happened in the long term, but in 1939 Hitler's aims were still ultimately directed towards the Jewish-Bolshevik menace in the east.

Since Hitler ignored this threat and invaded Poland anyway, the policy was clearly a failure. What might have been more effective would have been an alliance with the Soviet Union, which both Britain and France actively pursued at the same time as von Ribbentrop. Ironically, however, Britain and France's Polish guarantee had already ensured that a deal with Russia was out of the question, because Stalin wanted his hands on Poland just as much as Hitler did.

The wooing of their sworn enemy was an extraordinary success that had followed on from a series of failures. For some time before, von Ribbentrop, Hitler's Foreign Minister, had tried to bind both Italy and Japan into a military alliance. An Axis coalition that ran through the heart of Europe, the Mediterranean and the Far East would have been a nightmare for Britain and may well have deterred her from declaring war. However, Japan and Italy were not prepared to go to war with the Western powers – not at that time, at any rate. So Germany had turned to the Soviet Union instead.

Hitler suspected Britain and France's pledge to Poland was nothing more than bluff. However, in case it was not, it was clear that he had to avoid an alliance between France and Britain in the west and Russia in the east, because as he moved to Poland, it would be easy for Stalin to start becoming nervous about German intentions. In 1939, Germany's armed forces were big enough to risk war with Poland, but not the Soviet Union.

It was von Ribbentrop who was the prime mover in approaching the Russians and securing a non-aggression pact, eventually signed on 23 August 1939. That Germany was prepared to sign a treaty with an implacable enemy was certainly cynical in the extreme, but hardly unique. It meant Hitler could invade Poland and secure the corridor in the safe knowledge that the Soviet Union, at any rate, would not object.

Despite the German military might carefully depicted on the newsreels, Germany was only just strong enough to attack humble Poland in September 1939. Her air force was her biggest asset, but the army was under-trained and, worst of all, she faced a massive ammunition shortage. Yet Hitler was in a hurry; time, he believed, was not on Germany's side, because her economy was faltering and, thanks to the inherent shortages of fuel and, especially, iron ore, his rearmaments programme had almost ground to a halt.

It was after Munich that Hitler had begun to realize that a showdown with the West was probably inevitable. His long-term strategy was still very much the establishment of *Lebensraum* in the east and the conquest of the Soviet Union, but the threat of the Western powers would clearly have to be dealt with first. In September, Generalmajor Georg Thomas, the Wehrmacht chief economist, was told to prepare for war against Britain in 1942. A fortnight later, on 14 October 1938, Göring announced a further rearmament programme that was to dwarf the earlier, yet still considerable, military growth. The Luftwaffe was to increase fivefold to some 21,750 planes, including 7,000 Ju 88s and more than 800 He 177 heavy bombers. The navy was to begin a fleet-building programme, called the Z Plan, which would include six new battleships and hundreds of U-boats and other vessels that would make it comparable in size to the Royal Navy within six years. The army, too, was to expand yet further with large numbers of new guns and panzers and the production of new explosives.

These plans were the stuff of make-believe, however. To start with, the Germans did not have the industrial capacity or raw materials to build so many aircraft or ships. Entire dockyards and naval bases, for example, would need to be built before they could even begin. Even if built, they would never have the fuel needed to operate such a gigantic air force or fleet.

And nor did they have the cash. The existing rearmament programme had already pushed Germany to her economic limits. Indeed, by the end of 1938, Germany was facing a massive cash squeeze and something of an economic crisis. The German market had briefly rallied after Munich in the belief that long-term peace had been assured. The announcement of even greater rearmament, however, ensured that confidence fell. When the Reichsbank tried to raise another vast loan, it was unable to find the necessary investment. There was a further problem. So much energy had been spent on rearmament that foreign exports were massively down. There was little foreign exchange coming into the country and what there was had already been spent. Financially, Germany was in trouble by the beginning of 1939.

In May that year, Generalmajor Thomas presented a clear analysis of the balance of forces between Germany and the Western powers. Thomas was against any premature war against Britain and France but nonetheless his figures were alarming. In 1939, Germany was spending 23 per cent of its national income on rearmament, whereas France was spending 17 per cent, Britain 12 per cent and the USA just 2 per cent. On top of that, Britain could count on the entire Empire for raw materials as well as on the USA thanks to the 1938 trade agreement between the two countries. Since Britain had a similar-sized economy to Germany's, there was clearly scope for Britain to expand her rearmament. As for the USA, it was a country that with its vast industrial power could be in a league of its own should it so choose.

Thomas had hoped his analysis would deter Germany from war, but actually it did quite the opposite. Germany had a head start over Britain, America and even France, particularly with its air force – and in the 1930s it was air power that was feared above all. It was also ahead of the Soviet Union, whose military capabilities had been greatly affected by Stalin's purges of 1936–7 in which the Red Army's command and officer class had been decimated. Yet because of the economic crisis, Germany's rearmament programme was beginning to slow while everyone else's seemed to be increasing. Thomas's figures were particularly alarming for the Luftwaffe. Aircraft production was on the decline, not the rise, and although they had been rapidly expanding ever since 1933, and so had a large material advantage at present, this would not last, particularly since British aircraft production, already in the spring of 1939, matched that of the Luftwaffe. Thus there was no time to lose. Hitler needed to make the most of his air force and army before the Western powers caught up. And despite the chronic ammunition shortages his air force and army were sufficiently powerful and ready to enter into a quick war with Poland.

Many of Hitler's generals were against war in 1939. Rearmament and military might were seen as weapons of deterrence, whereas war could lead only to disaster. Even Göring was of the same mind. Logic suggested that it was mad to risk throwing everything away with a war that few believed could ultimately be won. Yet, to Hitler, the logical option was war because otherwise the Western powers *and* the Soviet Union would become too powerful and Germany would be destroyed all over again. Hitler was not under the illusion that Stalin would not one day attack Germany. In this, he was almost certainly right. 'We have nothing to lose, everything to gain,' he told a gathering of his commanders at Berchtesgaden on 22 August 1939. 'Because of our restrictions our economic situation is such that we can only hold out for a few more years. Göring can confirm this. We must act.'

The next day, Hitler was still in Berchtesgaden, at the Berghof, his villa on the Obersalzburg in the Bavarian Alps. After supper, he and his close entourage stepped out on to the balcony. Beyond and above the mountains a rare natural spectacle could be seen. In a particularly intense display, the Northern Lights were casting a deep red light across the Untersberg mountains on the far side of the valley, while the sky above shimmered with all the colours of the rainbow. Hitler's face and hands were bathed in the same red light. He became suddenly pensive. 'Looks like a great deal of blood,' he said at last. 'This time we won't bring it off without violence.'

How right he was, although most of the blood spilled had not been German. It was a trend that needed to continue, for if Germany was to win it could only be achieved by a single decisive blow, Hitler believed, at the earliest available opportunity. Another whole winter might give Britain, particularly, the edge in the arms race, which was why he had been so determined to strike in the west in the autumn of 1939.

The winter, however, had, ironically, been more beneficial to Germany than to either Britain or France. Large aircraft orders from the USA had not reached them yet; nor had rearmament levels in Britain sufficiently increased to threaten Germany's head start. However, the winter had enabled Germany to improve its cash flow and improve the critically low production of ammunition. Hitler had demanded that all German resources be channelled towards the one decisive blow and that meant the German people had to shoulder that burden.

Although most Germans had been delighted by the end result in Poland, the war was unpopular, not because of the loss of life that war brought but mainly because of the downturn in the standard of living. Hitler's urgent need for cash had been resolved by reducing civilian consumption and beefing up the amount of labour, raw materials and industrial capacity that could be directed to the production of arms. By May 1940, the share of national output devoted to military production went to a third, a big increase on an already high proportion. This was why Else Wendel and William Shirer when Christmas shopping found almost nothing to buy. The shops were largely empty, while rationing became more strict. With nothing to spend money on, household consumption dropped massively and the surplus flowed into the German war economy instead. 'We cannot win the war against England,' Hitler said, 'with cookers and washing machines.' He believed that the German people would soon forget these hardships in the flush of victory.

On top of that, supplies of raw materials were beginning to flow back into the country, largely thanks to the large trade deal made with Russia as part of the non-aggression pact. These benefits did not happen overnight but by the beginning of 1940 were making themselves felt. Furthermore, overall steel production in Germany was increased. It was a risk because it meant Germany would increase the rate at which it exhausted its own stocks of iron ore, but Hitler's single throw of the dice was a gamble that had to be applied to everything. It was do or die industrially as well as militarily. If Germany won the decisive blow, she could rape the resources of France and Britain and the rest of western Europe. If she lost, the fact that her own resources would be critically depleted would be irrelevant.

How the tables had now turned. In the autumn of 1939, Nazi Germany had been economically and politically isolated as never before, but now, at the end of June 1940, it was a very different picture. Nearly all of

Europe was now harnessed to Germany and with it much of the ores essential for Germany's increased armaments production. From neutral Sweden, iron ore was now arriving in plentiful amounts and thanks to the occupation of Norway, through which Swedish ore flowed, would continue to do so. No less important was a new trade deal with Romania. On 27 May, as the Luftwaffe had pounded Dunkirk and Britain had wavered on the cusp of pursuing terms, Germany had completed a historic oil-for-arms pact. Making the most of Romania's fear of Soviet aggression, Germany had offered protection, even though it was against an ally. Germany gave Romania large numbers of weapons – mostly taken from the Poles – in return for a monopoly of oil supplies. In many ways it was a double coup. Oil to Britain had accounted for almost 40 per cent of supplies from Romania's Ploesti oilfields. By the beginning of July, it was all going to Germany instead. From now on, Britain would not get a drop while Germany's chronic oil shortage had now been considerably eased. Furthermore, 'reparations' from Denmark, Norway, Belgium, Holland, Luxembourg and especially France also bolstered Germany's shortage of foreign cash. France was now obliged to pay 20 million *Reichsmark* a day, a gigantic fund of cash.

No wonder Hitler and the Nazi hierarchy were made giddy by the fruits of their astonishing victory. Hitler's incredible high-stakes gamble had paid off spectacularly. Victory on the Continent had been achieved; all that remained now was Britain – a Britain that had lost over a thousand aircraft, whose navy had taken a battering in Norway and at Dunkirk, and whose army was in tatters.

Still, now was not the time to take one's eye off the ball. Logic might suggest Britain would sue for peace, but from her Prime Minister were coming words of defiance. In two speeches that month, Churchill had pronounced that Britain would fight on come what may. Perhaps it was bluff, but it was important Hitler did not wait too long to launch an all-out attack on Britain.

Back in March, Generalmajor Thomas had been talking with Hitler's new Armaments Minister, Dr Fritz Todt, the man who had built the autobahns. 'Führer has again emphasized energetically,' noted General Thomas following that conversation, 'that everything is to be done so that the war can be ended in 1940 with a great military victory. From 1941 onwards, time works against us (USA potential).'

This war aim still held true. Defeat of Soviet Russia remained Hitler's principal goal, yet despite Germany's new-found riches he could not afford to fight a war on two fronts, and neither could he compete, in the long term, with Britain, the Empire and the United States. He still needed to knock out Britain and, with her, the threat from the United States. And soon. His victory had been remarkable but it was not yet complete. For Germany, the stakes were still critically high.

25

All Alone

IN BRITAIN, THE NEWS that France was out of the war prompted mixed reactions. Harold Nicolson, whose principal task at the Ministry of Information was to monitor civilian morale and keep the public informed with advice about the possibility of invasion, was feeling pretty low in morale himself, albeit he was calmly resigned. The prospect of fighting alone filled him – and his colleagues – with gloom. At the Ministry, he had meanwhile helped write a leaflet called *If the Invader Comes*, which was issued to every household in the country.* It was all commonsense advice, such as not believing rumours or spreading them, staying put, keeping watch, and telling the Germans nothing. 'Think before you act,' it concluded. 'But think always of your country before you think of yourself.' For a nation already expecting German parachutists to land at any moment, this pamphlet did little to allay fears.

Harold certainly feared the worst. He felt it would be impossible to beat the Germans and that, with France's surrender, Britain would be bombed and invaded. He and his wife, Vita, had both agreed that should Germans land and Britain fall, they would kill themselves – they had even obtained cyanide capsules for the purpose. 'I am quite lucidly aware,' he

* There is some debate over who wrote this. Harold Nicolson claimed to have penned it, but then so did the art historian Kenneth Clark, one of his colleagues at the Ministry of Information. The original document, however, seems to have been written by Nicolson, but then refined by Clark.

recorded, 'that in three weeks from now Sissinghurst may be a waste and Vita and I both dead.'

Olivia Cockett was stunned by France's capitulation. A south Londoner, Olivia was a bright, intelligent woman of twenty-seven who worked as a payroll clerk at New Scotland Yard for the Ministry of Works. The news had been broadcast on a radio at work and for the rest of the day she could barely speak, let alone concentrate on the job in hand. She felt shaky and tearful and in the evening, still in a state of shock, met up with her 'man', Bill Hole. He too was in despair, although calm. 'He felt we should give in,' she noted, 'which had not occurred to me, but which seemed reasonable at the time.' Bill had to leave her soon after; despite an intense affair that had lasted ten years already, he remained a married man with a family to return to. Still unable to eat, she went home, did some gardening and had a hot bath and slept better than she imagined she would do. The following day her dark mood of despair had gone.

In Surrey, Daidie Penna noticed people seemed more cheerful now that France was finished. 'Although I will grant a certain amount to the Nazis,' she heard a man say in the pub, 'they've got to be stopped. And I believe they will be stopped by something which is in the nature and genius of our species.'

'Spirit,' suggested Daidie.

'Yes,' said the man, 'spirit. That will win!'

The next day she saw the grocer and they wondered what would happen next. Without France, he wanted to know where the next battlefield would be. Daidie suggested there might be another Battle of Hastings. 'What, all around our coast?' he said, then added laconically, 'Be all right, wouldn't it?'

A number of the pilots who had flown over France were now being given brief stints of leave. Hugh 'Cocky' Dundas was allowed four days. In his own village of Cawthorne in Yorkshire and in every village round about he found all the middle-aged and elderly men formed into units of Local Defence Volunteers. His 63-year-old father was pondering the respective merits of handing over his shotguns to help the local LDV unit or hanging on to them for his own use should it come to it. All the signposts had already been taken down, whilst on the very few flat areas in that part of England, obstacles had been set up to prevent aircraft landings.

Further south, Arthur Hughes, now out of hospital, had gone to spend a week's leave with his second brother, Dave, and his wife, Joan, at

Old Sarum near Salisbury. Dave was also a pilot, but the two of them managed to drive down to Dorchester to take their young cousins out from school. On the way back, with no signposts, they got lost. 'But this was due solely to the lack of a large map,' noted Arthur. 'Any invader would be well provided with these, and probably air photographs as well.' It was a fair point.

They heard the news of the armistice on the radio. 'So now it is England versus the rest,' he wrote. 'We'll show them!' He was due for a medical and fully expected to be passed fit to fly once more. He hoped to get a transfer to fighters, like his brother Dave, who flew Hurricanes with 238 Squadron. At Biggin Hill, Pete Brothers and the men of 32 Squadron had been delighted when they heard France had finally thrown in the towel. 'I remember cheering when France collapsed,' he says, 'and saying, right, thank God, we're on our own now.' Like Arthur, he felt confident they would fix the Germans. It was now just a question of waiting for the onslaught to begin.

A man supremely conscious of history, Winston Churchill was keenly aware that he had been given a lead role at a time of deep peril for his country. Britain's current predicament was as grave as any she had faced. It was a matter of life and death, in which the nation was the last bastion of the world, fighting freedom's battle against tyranny, the forces of light against those of darkness. 'Hitler knows that he will have to break us in this island or lose the war,' he said during his speech to the Commons on 18 June, a stark yet accurate assessment. 'If we can stand up to him,' he said, 'all Europe may move forward into broad, sunlit uplands. But if we fail,' he added, 'then the whole world, including the United States, including all that we have known and cared for, will sink into the abyss of a new dark age made more sinister, and perhaps more protracted by the lights of perverted science.' He called upon everyone to do their duty at this momentous time, so that a thousand years hence future generations would look back and say, 'This was their finest hour.'

It was wonderful rhetoric but Churchill knew as well as anyone that just because their cause seemed a noble one, that did not mean the odds of survival were any better. Britain was staring down the barrel, as he was all too aware. However, brilliant oratory could help galvanize the nation. Not everyone puffed their chests out a little further or stood slightly taller, but many did. And while Churchill led the way, he was ably assisted by the country's press and media. People grumbled at the classist BBC broadcasters, at the patronizing posters issued by the Ministry of Information, and continued to spread rumours galore, but the message of defiance was getting through. The radio broadcasts of the writer J. B. Priestley were particularly popular, for example, with his observations about the inherent decency of the British character and the evil of the Nazis. The newspapers, too, unfailingly praised the heroism of Britain's armed forces, while also breathing heart into their readers. On 17 June, for example, the London *Evening Standard* announced that Britain was to transform itself into a fortress. The sea, it claimed, was still their strength. No-one denied the seriousness of the situation, far from it, but the stoicism and defiance – the spirit – that Daidie Penna was discovering in her Surrey village was beginning to take root.

But while uniting the British was of great importance, so was stirring the United States into action. Churchill had deliberately included America in his speech on 18 June, words of warning that were broadcast and printed throughout Britain and her Dominions as well as the United States. Bringing the US into the fight was still a key part of his strategy despite the cold shoulder Britain had received earlier in May. The President had spoken out against Italy's entry into the war, and promised all material support for those prepared to defy the Axis and to speed up American rearmament and their own means of defence. 'I call for effort, courage, sacrifice, devotion, the love of freedom,' he said in a speech on 10 June. 'All these are possible.' This was music to Churchill's ears, who wasted no time in re-opening a dialogue with the President, and stressing that the fight against Nazism was America's fight too. 'I send you my heartfelt thanks,' he wrote, 'and those of my colleagues for all you are doing and seeking to do for what we may now indeed call a common cause.' He once again asked for '30 or 40' American destroyers to be sent over immediately, and also told Roosevelt that US entry into the war was the only possible means of keeping France fighting. This Roosevelt rejected out of hand; on the question of destroyers, he did not reply.

Churchill's efforts to wed America to the 'common cause' were infuriating the US Ambassador in London. Joe Kennedy had never had much truck with Churchill. He mistrusted him, thought he drank too much and was too prone to cronyism. Since Churchill had become Prime Minister, Kennedy had also felt increasingly snubbed by the new Government, shut out from the kind of access that he enjoyed during Chamberlain's premiership. He had finally secured an appointment to see Churchill at 7 p.m. on 10 June, but his nose had been put further out of joint when he was kept waiting half an hour. The fact that Churchill was frantically busy with the current crisis, and that Kennedy's own isolationist and defeatist stance was neither helping British interests nor endearing him to the Prime Minister, did not seem to occur to him.

When he was finally ushered in to see the Prime Minister, Churchill immediately offered him a 'highball'. Kennedy told him he didn't drink.

'England is next on Hitler's list,' Churchill said, 'but we will fight to the end and give him plenty of trouble. How about those destroyers? We need them badly.'

'The President can't do anything with Congress lined up against him,' Kennedy replied, 'and Congress won't act unless it feels that the American people are behind it.'

'The American people will want to come in when they see well-known places in England bombed,' Churchill retorted. 'After all, Hitler will not win this war until he conquers us, and he is not going to do that. We'll hold out until after your election and then I'll expect you to come in. I'll fight them from Canada. I'll never give up the Fleet. But some other government might turn over anything Hitler wanted in order to save England from destruction.' Inciting a unity of purpose and then posing sinister warnings as to what might happen if Britain lost was very much Churchill's technique in this latest attempt to lure in America; so too was going straight to Roosevelt and keeping Kennedy at arm's length as far as possible. Nothing the Prime Minister said, however, could convince Kennedy that Britain was heading for anything other than defeat. 'To fight the kind of war that Hitler wages,' Kennedy reported to Washington, 'Britain's condition of preparedness appears to be appallingly weak still. Aside from some air defence, it is my opinion that the real defence of England will not be with arms but with courage.' And that, he was certain, would not be enough.

What worried Kennedy was sending American arms and aid to support a country he reckoned was already beaten. As with Dowding's view of sending more fighters to France, he felt it was pointless throwing in ships and destroyers that could be better used at home; if it ever came to a fight with Germany, Kennedy believed they should do so in their own back yard not somebody else's. Roosevelt, on the other hand, thought quite the opposite – that it was in America's interests to fight the battle as far away from their own shores, and as indirectly, as possible. Nor was he convinced that Britain was beaten – not just yet, at any rate.

*

It was to get a second opinion on Britain's chances of survival that Roosevelt and the State Department had decided to send Colonel Raymond Lee back to London as military attaché and Head of Intelligence. A 54-year-old dashing, good-looking bon viveur from Missouri, with a raffish moustache and a reputation for diplomacy and sound judgement, Lee had already spent four years in the post before being sent home at the outbreak of war to help train American soldiers. By the beginning of June, however, he was told he was going back. Aside from his normal attaché's duties, he was to spend time at the War Office, to which he would have access, and travelling around the country, and then reporting back on whether he thought Britain would prevail.

Before he went, Lee was thoroughly briefed. Kennedy, he was told, was still being defeatist, although according to Herbert Feis, the State Depertment Advisor, that was only because the war was lowering the stock market and affecting the Ambassador's securities. Nonetheless, Lee was taken aback by how much defeatist talk there was. He felt there was a pathological assumption that it was all over bar the shouting and that it was too late for the United States to do anything. 'Well, it boils down to this,' Lee said in his briefing, 'that the President and the State Department want to be just as helpful to the Allies as the public opinion of this country will permit, and the latter is changing very rapidly.' Yes, he was told, in a nutshell that was it.

He arrived in England on 21 June, having flown via Lisbon. London had changed a great deal in the nine months since he had last been there, and seemed 'as dark as a pocket'. Many of the familiar streets now had piles of sandbags along them, or barricades of wire. Everyone at the Embassy seemed pleased to see him back, however, even Kennedy, who nevertheless wasted no time in emphatically telling him that Britain was beaten and that he was against American intervention. Lee, however, was not going to allow himself to be swayed by the Ambassador. Rather, he preferred to judge the situation for himself.

One person who could understand the defeatist talk in America was the photographer Cecil Beaton. He had reluctantly left England shortly after the German offensive had begun, full of remorse for leaving at such a time of peril for his country, but nonetheless conscious that he had a large tax bill in arrears and so was financially unable to turn down the £2,000 from Pond's Cream to take some advertising pictures for them.

Since he had been away, however, the news had grown progressively worse and worse, so that despite the sumptuous amounts of unrationed food and the bright lights of New York, and despite the luxury and comfort of living in a city untouched by war, Cecil was wracked with anguish. ‘Every hour,’ he wrote, ‘the radio bulletins told of further tragedy. Nowhere could one find solace from the prevalent gloom. One’s worst fears were confirmed each hour by friends and news bulletins.’

By the time war had broken out in September 1939, Cecil was thirty-five and, with recent commissions to photograph the Queen, his reputation had never been higher. He had turned to photography as an amateur after dropping out of Cambridge, but had soon risen to prominence through his daring portraits of the young, rich and fashionable. A certain notoriety from his association with the Bright Young Things – a group of young aristocratic men and women who had scandalized London society with their camp theatrics and extravagance – did him no harm. More work followed; then trips to Hollywood, contracts with *Vogue* and, finally, commissions from the British Royal Family. For someone who worshipped beauty and glamour as much as Beaton, his was a thrilling lifestyle: friendships with artists, movie stars and the richest in the land; and near-constant travel – to New York, Paris, Hollywood, Rome.

It was also a lifestyle that came to a crashing halt with the outbreak of war. Hearing the news that Germany had invaded Poland had been ‘like a death knell’, and affected him profoundly. Rather than mourning the passing of a way of life, however, he discovered he no longer had an ‘appetite for the sort of things that had been fun. They were remote.’ Rather, his concern came primarily from his fear for Britain’s future. His reaction was entirely typical of most people of his age, who could no longer rely on the callowness and naivety they had possessed at nineteen or twenty. To the middle-aged man, war spelled doom. To the younger man, still flushed with youth, thoughts of potential death and destruction registered less acutely.

Cecil Beaton had very quickly begun to feel both frustrated and ashamed. ‘This war, as far as I can see,’ he confided to his diary, ‘is something specifically designed to show up my inadequacy in every possible capacity.’ He offered his services as a driver, then as a camouflage designer, and finally took work as a telephonist at an Air Raid Precaution unit. It did not last long, however, and soon he was back to photography and theatre work.

His work in New York was now done, however. His friends tried to persuade him to stay. 'England will probably be invaded any day now,' they said, 'and there can't be much resistance.' Surely it made more sense to stay where he was? Although tempted, Cecil knew that at this 'worst moment' in Britain's history he had a duty to return home – and there to do something that might actually be of real use to the war effort.

There had still been one more evacuation for the Royal Navy to perform. Between 19 and 23 June, just under 23,000 British subjects were taken from the Channel Islands. It had been accepted that, because of their proximity to France, the islands could not be held and sure enough, on 30 June, the first German occupiers arrived. It was ironic that for all the anxiety about British interests in the Far and Middle East and over Malta and Gibraltar, the first British territory to be lost should be part of the British Isles itself, but there had been no practical alternative to letting them go.

A further mounting concern was the Republic of Ireland, independent of Britain since 1922, but still a part of the Commonwealth. Despite this, it was decidedly hostile towards Britain, and following the fall of France the idea that German troops might use Ireland as a springboard for an assault on Britain and as a base for U-boats began to take hold. Raymond Lee had barely arrived back in London before he heard plenty of such talk; it certainly seemed plausible to him. Part of the 1922 treaty had been to allow the Royal Navy to use Irish ports, but Chamberlain had let this right go in 1938. At the beginning of the war, Churchill, as First Lord of the Admiralty, had briefly considered using force against Ireland to get it back. Nothing had come of such plans, but it was now Chamberlain, in something of a *volte face*, who suggested force might be used to get Ireland to give up its harbours. To complete the see-saw change in approach, it was now Churchill, fearing US opposition, who opposed the idea. He was, however, keen to secure use of these crucial Atlantic-facing ports, partly to prevent the Germans using them and partly so that the navy and RAF would have bases from which to take the attack to the U-boats. As a quid pro quo for their immediate use, he proposed offering de Valera, the Irish president, the post-war unification of Ireland. British Northern Ireland would be sacrificed for this more pressing need. Churchill gave the job of leading the deal to Chamberlain.

Yet despite being handed Northern Ireland on a plate, and despite the offer of protection against any German invasion, de Valera was having nothing of it. Chamberlain cursed his obstinacy. 'The moment the Germans land,' Chamberlain noted, 'he will ask for help but not a second before; in fact, his people would fight us if we came first.'

But however hemmed in and threatened Britain may have felt, she was not entirely alone. Ireland was an exception; the weight of the Dominions was behind the mother country. Canada, Australia, New Zealand and South Africa had all declared war on Germany. Canadian troops were already in Britain – they had even made their aborted trip to Normandy. Pilots were arriving from the far corners, and not just from Commonwealth countries. Some from the United States had volunteered to fly for the RAF. There were others, too, from Poland and Czechoslovakia, for example, who were determined to fight for their broken countries' honour and to have their chance for revenge.

Among those arriving in England during these tumultuous days of late June was Jan Zumbach. Although the 25-year-old was of Swiss origin and nominally a Swiss citizen, his family, birth and upbringing were Polish and he considered himself very much a Pole at heart. Brought up on a large estate in the north of Poland, near Brodnica, Jan had had an idyllic, privileged childhood, paying little attention to his school books and more to the cowherd's daughter, whom, at seventeen, he managed to get pregnant. Immediately packed off to school, he returned two years later, having dutifully passed his exams and determined to join the Polish air force, an ambition he had held since a child. With his father dead, he had to overcome the opposition of his equally strong-willed mother, who was vehemently opposed to the plan. Eventually, recognizing that she would not budge, he opted for deception instead, forging her authorization for his enlistment. When she discovered what he had done, she was distraught but too much of a patriot to cancel his enlistment, and so he had got his way. 'All this,' he noted, 'for the right to get myself shot down in flames instead of sliced up by sabres!'

By the time war broke out, Jan had been a pilot for more than three and a half years, and had become a highly experienced one at that. He had been trained well, but a flying accident in the spring of 1939 and a long convalescence meant that he was only just about to return to operational duties when the Germans invaded. Unaware that 80 per cent of the Polish air force had been knocked out on the first day of the war, Jan never did catch up with his squadron. However, he and a number of other pilots were ordered to an airfield on the Romanian border. Initially mystified, he then learned that Russians had invaded from the east. Trapped between Russian and German troops they now had no alternative but to escape; and unlike the tens of thousands of refugees jamming the roads, Jan and his colleagues were fortunate enough to have a means of getting away.

It was far from plain sailing, however. Trouble with Romanian border guards meant that Jan, along with two other pilots as passengers, hastily took off again, heading south until running out of fuel some twenty-five miles from Bucharest. They eventually reached the city and from there, via Constanza and Beirut, to Marseilles. It was now the end of November 1939, and at Salon-de-Provence Jan and his two Polish friends joined the French Armée de l'Air.

Their services were hardly required, however. They were told there was a shortage of aircraft, which was nonsense, so spent idle days in the bistros and brothels of Lyons, where they were stationed. Eventually, they were formed into a Polish Squadron, but remained on the Lorraine front, behind the Maginot Line. Jan and three other Polish pilots were then transferred to another squadron in a fighter group made up of a motley assortment of pilots and aircraft and stationed near Tours. He had still barely flown even once the German offensive began. On 6 June, the pilots were in the middle of lunch when reports of German aircraft reached them. Jan and his fellow Poles immediately jumped up. 'What's the hurry?' said their French commander. 'We haven't finished eating.'

Jan's squadron was eventually given a modern Morane 406 and on 10 June they finally flew their first proper combat sortie over France. They were soon tangling with a mass of Me 109s, and horribly outnumbered. Although Jan managed to shoot one down, he and his three fellow Poles were shot down themselves, and he was the only survivor – and only just. Having safely bailed out he was then surrounded by a bunch of hostile French soldiers who in the nick of time realized he was Polish and thus on their side.

Jan was eventually given a new plane on 13 June – an American Curtiss P-36 – but by harmonizing and testing his guns at one end of the airfield, he caused panic. Mistaking his gun test for Germans attacking them, the rest of the fighter group began taking off. Such was the prevailing mood of defeatism; it only needed a spark and panic quickly spread.

As France crumbled, Jan and his colleagues made their way to Bordeaux, where, joining forces with a Polish artillery officer and his battery, they managed to get a ride to Plymouth on a Polish collier. They landed in England on 22 June. About a hundred of the men on board were Czech and Polish airmen – pilots and groundcrew. Their journey was still not over, however. Bundled on to a train, they were taken north to Blackpool and there put into quarantine. Checked and interrogated and medically examined, they discovered there would be no immediate transfer into the RAF.

They also found themselves constantly at cross-purposes. Jan knew 'yes' and 'no' but that was the limit of his English. A friend of his was asked whether he had VD. The Pole had no idea what he was being asked, but the doctor looked very solemn. 'So he took a chance,' noted Jan, 'answered yes, and was promptly hauled off for a vigorous massage of the prostate which left him white with rage.'

For Air Chief Marshal Dowding, in desperate need of pilots, these men were potential gold dust. After all, few now in Britain were more ready and willing to try and shoot down Germans. This, however, was not yet understood or appreciated, and so for the next three weeks Jan and his fellows would remain under guard in Blackpool.

But their time would come. All too soon Fighter Command would need every fighter pilot it could lay its hands on.

26

Getting Ready

As one of the Prime Minister's secretaries, Jock Colville was fortunate enough to meet and get to know most of Britain's war leadership. For an intelligent and observant young man such as himself, it was fascinating to be allowed to listen to the debates and arguments of the Cabinet and Chiefs of Staff, or to find himself, as he did, quite casually on the evening of 18 June, talking to men such as Professor Frederick Lindemann, a brilliant scientist, trusted friend of Churchill's and now the PM's Chief Scientific Adviser. For a brief while they gossiped on the steps of the Foreign Office, discussing Général de Gaulle.

Later, after dinner, Jock returned to No. 10, where Churchill's inner circle was gathered. Everyone was in a bad mood, unsurprising in light of the collapse in France. Beaverbrook told Jock that Sinclair was a hopeless Air Minister and that the whole Air Ministry was rotten. General Ismay, meanwhile, was complaining that the Chiefs of Staff were too old and too slow. The last straw for Churchill that day was the non-arrival of the morning newspapers, which he liked to see the night before. In his exasperation he spilled his whisky and soda over some of his papers, which put him in an even worse temper.

Yet despite these gripes, tensions and personal animosities, and despite the many concerns still facing Britain, the month of June was unquestionably giving her a fighting chance. The clock was ticking but, with every hour and day that passed, so Britain was strengthening her defences, not least with the addition of new fighter aircraft.

Even after just a fortnight in the job, Lord Beaverbrook's Ministry for Aircraft Production (MAP) had made startling improvements. In the first week he took over, around 130 new aircraft of all types had been built. By the third week of May, that had risen to 200, and by the last week of May it was around 280. Throughout June, weekly aircraft production remained at somewhere between 250 and 300 aircraft. In the week of 2–8 June, for example, eighty new Hurricanes and twenty-two Spitfires were built; in all, 446 fighter aircraft were produced in June. He had achieved this by allowing nothing to get in the way of that single goal: more aircraft. Red tape was dispensed with; so too were niceties. If there was a bottleneck anywhere, a senior member of MAP would be sent to the relevant factory and whatever the problem – such as mismanagement, lack of workers, shortage of parts – it would be assessed and resolved with extreme haste and the bottleneck cleared. He got rid of Lord Nuffield, whom he considered complacent and too full of his own importance, and sent Sir Richard Fairey, the eminent aircraft designer, up to the new specially built shadow factory at Castle Bromwich to assess why it was still not operating effectively nearly two years after building work had begun. Fairey found mismanagement was rife, that the workforce was slack, undisciplined and often poorly trained, and that many of the machine tools were the wrong ones for the job of building Spitfires. Paperwork was non-existent. The place was, frankly, a shambles. Vickers took over the running of the factory from Nuffield and matters soon began to improve. There would be no more slackness, not at Castle Bromwich, nor at any other factory working for MAP: workers were expected to toil seven days a week with a disregard for all labour regulations. That was how Beaverbrook worked himself and he expected everyone else to do the same. It was a wonder what could be achieved when everyone involved was focused entirely on the main task in hand.

But while new production figures were impressive, so too were those of repaired aircraft. Repair and salvage of aircraft had been outsourced from the RAF and was run by the Civilian Repair Organization (CRO), headed by Lord Nuffield and managed by Morris Motors. Needless to say, Nuffield went as soon as the Ministry of Aircraft Production took over. The principle of the system was a good one, with a chain of Civilian Repair Units, which were major repair workshops, but also depots at airfields, training schools and other warehouses.

Beaverbrook took the existing set-up but quickly made a number of changes. Before, aircraft damage had been categorized: 1, repairable by squadron; 2, repairable by contractor or at depot; or 3, recommended for parts salvage. Beaverbrook now re-categorized damage as 4, 5 or 6. Category 4 applied to aircraft that could be repaired within thirty-six hours. Category 5 was given to those aircraft safe to fly lightly, and which became known as 'fly-in' repairs; if a category 5 aircraft was repairable within twenty-four hours, for example, then the pilot could wait and fly it back. Finally, there was category 6, applied to any aircraft which would take longer than thirty-six hours to repair and which needed to be moved by road. Responsibility for transporting damaged aircraft to depots and CRUs was left to No. 50 Maintenance Unit.

All members of the CRO and Maintenance Units were as indoctrinated with the need for long hours and speed of response as those working in aircraft production. And, once again, Beaverbrook did not care whose feet he trod on in order to achieve results. He took over all aircraft storage units, normally carefully controlled by the Air Ministry, and his agents scurried around putting MAP padlocks on all the hangar doors. He even decided which aircraft would go where, a decision reached in consultation with Dowding and his commanders, such as Park. The Air Ministry was bypassed entirely. The effect was electric. In addition to nearly 300 new aircraft a week, in the last two weeks of June more than 250 were repaired and sent back to squadrons. In just a few weeks, the production of new aircraft had risen by 62 per cent, new engines by 33 per cent, repaired aircraft by a staggering 186 per cent, and repaired engines by 159 per cent. It was an astonishing turn-around.

Perhaps not surprisingly, Archibald Sinclair, Air Chief Marshal Newall and others at the Air Ministry did not take well to this whirlwind brand of unilateral decision-making, particularly on a number of matters such as stores and allocation where they believed they were better qualified for the job. But if Beaverbrook felt he was not getting the co-operation he required, then he simply threatened to resign, as he did on 30 June. 'I cannot get information which I require about supplies or equipment,' he wrote to the Prime Minister, putting on record what he had undoubtedly told him face to face. 'I cannot get permission to carry out operations essential to strengthening our reserves to the uttermost in readiness for the day of invasion . . . The breach which has thus been made between the Air Ministry and myself cannot be healed, although I have made many efforts.' Of course, Churchill refused to accept his resignation. The Air Ministry was told to be more co-operative. Beaverbrook had won even greater autonomy. 'Beaverbrook was an unpleasant bastard,' said Alex Henshaw, one of the principal Spitfire test pilots. 'But he was the right man in the right place at the right time.'

Funnily enough, Hitler would have approved of Beaverbrook. Going behind the backs of those on the same side, getting on the nerves of colleagues and displaying single-minded ruthlessness was the kind of attitude he liked to see from the Nazi leadership. And, in fact, Beaverbrook's short-termism, where future projects and reserves were put to one side in the interests of resolving the immediate crisis, was precisely the mindset Hitler had adopted in his preparation for war in the west. The big difference was that, unlike the RAF, the Luftwaffe had no Beaverbrook in charge of aircraft production.

It was true that Germany was suffering economically and from a shortage of raw materials during the winter and spring of 1939, but thanks to Hitler's go-for-broke orders the Luftwaffe was not struggling from a shortage of aluminium or other key components. Her aircraft factories were well-established and had, by 1940, considerable experience of producing large numbers of aircraft, unlike the RAF. Admittedly, there had been bottlenecks on the German railways which had held things up, but operating to all intents and purposes on a peacetime footing there should have been no excuse for the slow rate of production.

With Milch sidelined from the entire procurement and production process, it was left to Udet to whip the industry into an urgent, highly efficient organization that was operating to maximum capabilities. This, however, simply did not happen. Udet did not have Beaverbrook's drive, experience and understanding of how big business could operate. Individual manufacturers were largely left to their own devices, and although Udet regularly visited Heinkel, Junkers and others, he never seemed to check too closely on what they were actually doing.

He had also been hit hard by the continual delays to the Ju 88, but with an offensive against the west looming had, in the spring of 1940, urged Heinkel to speed up development of the four-engine He 177 heavy bomber. Production was now to be rushed, without adequate testing, so that by the spring Heinkel's factories were due to be producing 120 He 177s per month. Late in March, Udet visited Ernst Heinkel. The strain was showing; Udet was smoking continuously and seemed restless and edgy. 'I hope there won't be any trouble with the He 177,' he told Heinkel. 'The Ju 88 has caused enough difficulty for my taste. The He 177 has got to get into operation. We don't have any other large bomber that we can use against England. The He 177 has got to fly! It must!'

His anxieties seemed to leave him the moment victory was assured in France. Depression was replaced by euphoria. The war was over, and none of his plans over which he had worried so much mattered any longer. As a result, he was easily persuaded by Heinrich Koppenberg, the Director-General of Junkers, to downgrade the He 177 and make the Ju 88 the principal German bomber instead. 'All this planning,' Udet told Göring, following the fall of France, 'is garbage.'

Udet's lack of grip and urgency and the inability of the rest of the Luftwaffe High Command to do anything about it meant that aircraft production was now way below that of Britain. In June, 220 new fighters were built and 344 bombers. In July, those figures would fall even lower. Repair figures were worse. Just over a thousand Me 109s and just fifty-nine Ju 88s would be repaired and back in the air during the whole of 1940.

The Luftwaffe still had vastly superior numbers of aircraft compared to the RAF, but its might was not looking anything like as impressive as it had on 9 May. It had lost around a third of its operational strength since then and a fifth of its establishment strength. Its transport fleet had also not recovered from the mauling it had suffered on that opening day of the campaign – and neither would it when monthly production figures of the Ju 52 stood at just twenty-four in May. This was significant because without Ju 52s there could be no large parachute drops over England, and moving groundcrews and other personnel took much longer when carried out by road. And unlike Fighter Command, Luftflotten 2 and 3 had remained fully engaged in the battle right up until the end in France, which had cut down on the opportunities for rest and rebuilding. Siegfried Bethke, who had returned to 2/JG 2 in the middle of June, had been glad to get back to flying duties but the endless frenetic action and moving of airfields had taken its toll. 'We're all very fatigué!' he wrote in his diary as he waited on readiness in his 109. 'I am also about to fall asleep in my plane.'

On the first day of June, Dowding had had just 331 Spitfires and Hurricanes, but by the last day of the month had 587 ready and serviceable, with plenty more on their way. It still wasn't enough, but it was a vast improvement; the odds were getting better. More of a concern was the shortage of experienced pilots. There were, admittedly, well over double the number of pilots available for the number of aircraft, but Dowding was worried that the rate at which new pilots were being trained was slower than he had planned. This was largely due to the terrible winter, which had severely hampered the amount of flying training that could be done. Worse was the loss of nearly 300 pilots in France – pilots who had considerably more flying experience than the new boys now coming through.

Still, most of the fifty-five fighter squadrons had been able to build up their strength and make good earlier losses. Now back up at Leconfield in Yorkshire, 616 Squadron had returned to the old routine of readiness and convoy patrols along the north-east coast. Cocky Dundas felt no anti-climax, however. Rather, he was filled with a renewed sense of purpose in the knowledge that the Germans would launch their offensive at any moment. However, while 616 had not suffered too many losses over Dunkirk, in other squadrons the atmosphere now seemed very different. Tony Bartley and Allan Wright had been posted to Pembrey, in South Wales, where, with a new CO, 92 Squadron was resting and rebuilding after its baptism over Dunkirk. 'We were really glad to get our rest,' Tony wrote to his father. 'Some of us couldn't eat or sleep much after Dunkirk.' David Crook had noticed that quite a change had come over 609 Squadron. He finally rejoined them on 29 June, although unlike 92 Squadron, they were still at Northolt, in the front line of 11 Group. There was also a new CO as well as a number of new faces. 'The old easy-going outlook on life had vanished,' noted David, 'and everybody now seemed to realize that war was not the fairly pleasant affair that it had always seemed hitherto.'

Meanwhile, Pete Brothers and 32 Squadron were still based at Biggin Hill in 11 Group and on front-line duties, although those were little more than occasional combat sorties. One day, he and the squadron escorted Blenheim bombers over France and on another occasion some photo reconnaissance Blenheims, but in between there had been a chance to practise and to operate at a slightly less hectic pace. In Pete's case, it meant a chance to see his wife, who was still living in their little bungalow in Westerham, a few miles from Biggin.

Bee Beamont and the rest of 87 Squadron had been sent north, out of the fray, to Church Fenton near York. It took a while for the squadron to congregate again after the chaos of France. There were new faces and also new Hurricanes – the squadron had to be almost entirely re-equipped with new aircraft, but within a week they were operational once more. Bee found it took a little while to get accustomed to life on a normal RAF station having been abroad for eight months, and also to a calmer pace of life, but eased his way back by heading off with one of his squadron mates, Jimmy Dunn, in an old Avro Tutor biplane looking for possible invasion landing fields. Billy Drake was also back in England, although not with 1 Squadron. Although recovered from his wounds, he had been posted to 6 Operational Training Unit at Sutton Bridge as an instructor. It was Billy's job to make sure the pilots now coming through training were fit to be sent to operational squadrons. Most were Volunteer Reserves or overseas pilots. To begin with, he would take them up in a Harvard or Miles Master two-seater trainer, and when satisfied that they could handle themselves, would send them up in a Hurricane, following in his own. They would practise formation flying and then Billy would try and teach them rudimentary dog-fighting. His combat experience was invaluable.

Yet while it was the fighter aircraft that were to shoot down enemy aircraft, there were other weapons in Dowding's armoury – weapons that he hoped would greatly improve the efficiency, and chances, of his pilots. Now dotted along the British coast was a series of twenty-one high metal masts, as much as 360 feet tall like giant Meccano. Also standing sentinel looking out to sea were thirty shorter, more squat stations. These together were Britain's RDF, or radar, chain, a key component in Dowding's early warning system.

The genesis of such a system had begun six years earlier, in 1934, when Harold Wimperis, Director of Scientific Research at Dowding's then department in the Air Ministry, had set up a committee under the well-known physicist Henry Tizard, with the idea that it should investigate the possibilities offered by science to assist air defence. Wimperis immediately consulted Robert Watson-Watt, a Scottish scientist who had for many years been studying high-frequency radio and atmospheric research. Wimperis had asked Watson-Watt first about the possibility of developing a 'death ray'. This Watson-Watt thought unlikely, but he did have ideas about how radio wave reflections might be used to detect, rather than destroy, aircraft.

Watson-Watt put forward his theories on 'Detection and Location of Aircraft by Radio Methods' to the Tizard Committee. In essence, he argued that an aircraft meeting a short-wave radio pulse would act as a kind of radiator, and reflect the signal, which, if powerful enough, could be picked up. The time lag, measured in microseconds, between the emission and reception of this reflected signal could be shown on a cathode ray tube as a blip of light on a fluorescent screen. Thus once a suitable time base was established, the distance of the aircraft from the radio base could, in theory, be worked out. The Tizard Committee was impressed and asked Dowding for approval to spend development money. Dowding replied that if it could convince him of its possibilities, he would arrange for the necessary funding.

On a cold, wintry day in Northamptonshire in February 1935, Watson-Watt carried out the first of his experiments. A BBC short-wave radio transmitter, some six miles away in Daventry, provided a continuous radio beam. The pilot of an RAF Heyford aircraft from Farnborough was told to fly along a railway line to a point twenty miles away and then back again, keeping close to the line provided by the beam. He made three runs, and although on the first he did not fly close enough to the beam, from the second and third there were clear echoes from the bouncing-back of the transmission.

Dowding was delighted by the results and immediately authorized the necessary development money. 'We now have an embryo,' Wimperis wrote to Dowding a week after the experiment, 'a new and potent means of detecting the approach of hostile aircraft, one which will be independent of mist, cloud, fog or nightfall.'

An experimental station was hastily established at Orfordness on the Suffolk coast. Within six months, Watson-Watt's Radio Direction Finding – or RDF, as he called it in an effort to dupe the enemy – was detecting aircraft at forty miles. It was, however, impossible with one radio mast to assess the bearing of any incoming aircraft. Only with two or more could a picture of the position of a plane at any given moment be achieved. Simple geometry then made it possible to track any oncoming aerial traffic with an accuracy that improved significantly with experience and as the system was extended.

Initially five radar stations were ordered to be built. Watson-Watt and his team moved to Bawdsey, south of Orfordness, in early 1936, by which time aircraft were being detected as far as sixty-two miles away. All of the five stations suffered various time-consuming snags; it did not seem possible to achieve anything with the kind of urgency Dowding required. A radar training school was set up at Bawdsey in early 1937, and the actual RDF station there opened in May that year. In July, Dover Chain Home – or CH – station opened, followed by Canewdon in August in time for Dowding's Fighter Command air exercises that same month. Despite inevitable errors, the results were encouraging. Aircraft were now being detected at up to a hundred miles away, and immediately afterwards the Air Ministry authorized the establishment of a twenty-station chain around Britain's coast.

Chain Home, however, had its limitations. It was rudimentary in many ways, as Watson-Watt and his team were well aware. Transmitter antennae floodlit the airspace directly in front of them with pulses of radio energy. If these pulses hit an object – such as an aircraft – they would rebound and be sent back, rather like an echo. These pulses were high-frequency beams of a broad wavelength of 10–13.5 metres, which required large antennae capable of enough power to achieve the flood-light effect. Thus, CH stations required four 360-foot masts, 180 feet apart, with antenna wires strung between them for transmitting the pulses, and then four different antennae of 240-foot masts for receiving the echo-like reflections. This made them pretty big and very obvious to any German who cared to look at them through his binoculars on the other side of the Channel. Furthermore, because the antennae were static, rather than rotational, they could only transmit – and receive – on the section of the coast directly in front of them. Nor did it work over land. They could detect what was coming towards them over the sea, but once the raiders had passed, they could offer nothing more.

A further limitation was that aircraft could fly under the masts completely undetected. This, however, was resolved by the addition of a second string of radar stations, known as Chain Home Low, which then proved to have another benefit, namely a more accurate measure of the size of an enemy raid. While the RAF had been developing Chain Home, the Admiralty Research Laboratory had also been carrying out research for its own needs and had developed coastal defence and gun-laying radars known as CD, which could measure ships' ranges accurate to about twenty yards using a rotating antenna. These were much lower frequency and sent out on a shorter wavelength of just 1.5 metres. These were copied and developed for the RAF and became Chain Home Low (CHL). Much smaller, they were effectively a searchlight of rays rather than a floodlight, and could be manually rotated by an operator using cranks. A similarly hand-rotated receiver would then pick up the echoes. The CHL programme was only implemented in the autumn of 1939, and that thirty stations had been built and were operating by June the following year was largely down to frantic compulsory purchasing of land and a lot of red tape being cut; aircraft production was not the only area where bureaucracy could be overcome when minds were focused. Britain's radar chain was rudimentary and lacked finesse but it was the best that could be achieved within the time that had been available. But it worked: approaching aircraft could be detected up to 120 miles away. More than that, its rudimentary nature had worked in Britain's favour too.

In fact, the Germans had also developed radar, and earlier than Watson-Watt. They called it *Dezimator Telegraphie*, or *DeTe* for short. Dr Rudolf Kühnold, Chief of the Kriegsmarine Signals Research Department, had been working on bouncing underwater sound waves – which became sonar – when it occurred to him that the same principles could be applied to radio waves above ground. This he developed into a radar that could be used for ship detection and gun ranging, either from land or from a moving ship. A prototype was developed which could change its range and accuracy by altering the frequency it used. This became known as 'Freya', and its shorter-range version, which was fitted to surface ships, was called 'Seetakt'.

'Freya' and 'Seetakt' had been made by the Gema company, but in the meantime Telefunken, a rival company, had developed a small, mobile radar capable of plotting aircraft up to twenty-five miles away. The 'Würzburg', as it was called, was highly sophisticated, mechanically rotated and elevated, and capable of guiding both anti-aircraft gunners and fighters on to targets. And since it was rotational, it could operate on a 360-degree setting and on land.

Thus when the Germans thought of other countries developing radar, they assumed they would be small, rotational, sophisticated pieces of kit like the ones they were developing, and not huge rows of iron lattice towers staring out from the cliffs for all the world to see. And spot them they did. German 'tourists' were packed off to Britain to go 'sight-seeing' around Bawdsey, and then in May 1939 General Wolfgang Martini, head of the Luftwaffe signal organization, persuaded Milch to allow him to fly over one of the old Zeppelin airships to have a look. The airship, he believed, with its ability to drift slowly and presenting a large object, would be perfect to try and find out whether these masts were indeed some kind of primitive British radar, or something quite different altogether. The Zeppelin duly went over, approaching Bawdsey then turning north and heading along the east coast. Expecting to hear some kind of response from their radio receivers, the crew were surprised to hear nothing but a loud continuous crackling sound. What they were hearing was high-frequency static, but because they had already discounted high frequency for radar – they were using very-high-frequency

(VHF) and ultra-high-frequency (UHF) ranges – it did not occur to them that they were in fact picking up beams from a radar network.

The Zeppelin had been picked up immediately by one CH station after another, its course plotted and tracked carefully. Going into cloud, it actually drifted over Hull, well into British airspace, but despite the temptation to send a radio signal telling them so, those charting its movement decided to keep shtum. Soon after, the Zeppelin turned for home, with General Martini none the wiser. Convinced there must have been some kind of technical defect with the airship's own kit, Martini sent it over again. In August, in bad weather, the Zeppelin came over a second time. This time, however, it picked up nothing at all, not even static. By sheer fluke, the radar chain had been turned off that day to sort out some minor malfunction.

Less than a month later, war broke out and any further investigations into the strange high towers dotted along the British coast were put on hold. This did not unduly concern Martini, however, or any of the Luftwaffe High Command. Because of their size, shape and use of high frequency, the masts had been discounted as being radar. Unwittingly, the crude, rather ungainly appearance of these monster masts had worked very much in Britain's favour.

Just to put the seal on it, they discovered a British mobile radar set that had been abandoned near Boulogne. Although rather like the German 'Freya', this was even more rudimentary. Instead of being impressed by their find, the Germans who examined it were delighted to discover the British had such crude pieces of kit and were operating a *DeTe* set so technologically behind their own.

Now, as they looked across the Channel to the high masts perched above the white cliffs of Dover, they still had no clear idea what these pylons were for. Soon enough, though, once they were over England, they would find out.

27

Trouble at Sea: Part 1

'TOMORROW AT DAWN, we put into operation a plan called CATAPULT,' jotted Jock Colville on 2 July, 'which entails the seizure of all French ships in British ports, and, later in the day, an ultimatum to the big French capital ships at Oran.' Concern about the French Fleet had been mounting in London. The Kriegsmarine on its own might not have been a match for the Royal Navy; the German and the Italian fleets together made a formidable enemy; but the German, Italian and French fleets could prove potentially disastrous. By the original terms of the armistice, the French Fleet was to assemble at French ports under German and Italian control, but Admiral Darlan, the French C-in-C, decided to send the bulk of the Fleet to its base at Mers-el-Kébir, near Oran, in French Algeria. The Germans did not object to this.

The British did, however. Both the British and Général de Gaulle made a plea for all French ships and forces to continue to fight and, in the case of the French navy, head for British ports. Some did, including two old battleships, several destroyers and a number of submarines. There were also several capital ships at Alexandria. These refused to join the British, so were immediately demobilized under British instructions.

Both Darlan and Marshal Pétain insisted that no warship would be allowed to fall into German or Italian hands, but however honourable may have been their intentions, Vichy France was now a German vassal state and their ability to enforce such a declaration was limited to say the least. From the British perspective, the risk of those ships being turned over to the enemy was simply too great. On 28 June, the Cabinet came to a difficult, but unanimous conclusion. The French Fleet at Oran and Algiers must surrender to the British or be attacked and destroyed. 'This was a hateful decision,' noted Churchill, 'the most unnatural and painful in which I have ever been concerned.'

The man given the job of confronting the French Fleet was Admiral James Somerville, now commander of the powerful Force H, hastily sent to guard the Western Mediterranean in the absence of the French. Somerville, like many in the Royal Navy, knew a number of his French counterparts well; indeed, many were friends. 'You are charged with one of the most disagreeable and difficult tasks that a British Admiral has ever been faced with,' came the message from the Admiralty, 'but we have complete confidence in you and rely on you to carry it out relentlessly.' In the early hours of 2 July, Somerville sent his ultimatum, which despite repeated appeals and negotiations was rejected. Thus, at 5.54 p.m. on 3 July, Somerville's ships opened fire. One French battleship blew up, another ran aground and a further battleship was beached. One cruiser escaped to Toulon, albeit damaged, as did those at Algiers. A few days later, the huge battleship *Richelieu*, at Dakar, was also put out of action. Over 1,200 French sailors, who just a couple of weeks before had been allies and comrades in arms, lost their lives.

When Churchill told Parliament what had been done, tears had streamed down his cheeks. On 5 July, Vichy France formally broke off relations with Britain. The sinking of the French Fleet at Mers-el-Kébir was a tragedy, but had, in a stroke, eliminated a serious threat. More than that, it showed the world that Britain had no intention of rolling over.

Group Captain Tommy Elmhirst and his colleagues on the Joint Intelligence Sub-Committee had been busy trying to collate and interpret intelligence regarding Germany's intentions. On 4 July, they submitted their latest appreciation, concluding that Germany was indeed preparing an invasion. There were reports of large-scale landing exercises, troop-carrying aircraft had been moved from training schools to front-line duties, aerial photographs suggested large numbers of rafts were being built at Kiel; dive-bombing units were being concentrated in Holland and north-east France. So it went on – a long list of compelling evidence that suggested invasion was imminent, although 'unlikely to take place before the middle of July'.

Meanwhile, General Ironside, C-in-C Home Forces, had been

putting together his own plan for the defence of Britain, which included more anti-invasion obstacles, anti-tank obstacles, and a 'crust' of troops protecting the coast with mobile reserves inland. 'In general, I find myself in agreement with the Commander-in-Chief's plan,' noted Churchill, then added, 'Until the Air Force is worn down by prolonged air fighting and destruction of aircraft supply, the power of the Navy remains decisive against any serious invasion.'

In this he was correct, but already a major strategy dispute had broken out between the Admiralty and Admiral Forbes, the C-in-C of the Home Fleet. Admiral Pound, the First Sea Lord, was determined that not only should imminent invasion be taken extremely seriously, but enough ships should be available to mount a crippling attack on an invasion force before it even set sail. To achieve this, he ordered that a strike force of four destroyer flotillas – some thirty-six ships – with cruiser support should be kept along the east and south-east coasts, all within the Nore Command.

This was overly cautious. As Dunkirk had proved, ships could be moved from bases as far north as Scapa Flow to the Channel within twenty-four hours, whilst even those out in the Western Approaches would be able to get there within a couple of days. For Admiral Sir Charles Forbes, it was a ridiculous suggestion. The 59-year-old veteran of Gallipoli and Jutland was a hugely experienced sailor who had commanded destroyer flotillas and battle squadrons, held senior staff positions at the Admiralty and with the Mediterranean and Atlantic Fleets, before being made C-in-C Home Fleet in 1938. Modest and unassuming, with a dry sense of humour, he was enormously popular with those who served under him. He was utterly imperturbable, never known to be rattled, and his calm, pragmatic mind was able to work through a number of myriad difficulties, whilst always maintaining a very clear sense of proportion. Charming and possessed of sound judgement he may have been, yet Forbes was not a man afraid to speak his mind, nor to stand up to his superiors if he believed they were wrong.

And he certainly believed Pound was wrong over the disposition of the Fleet. While others in London were awed by the German successes on the Continent, Forbes, from his cabin aboard HMS *Nelson* at Scapa Flow, was able to stand back and view matters slightly more logically. To him, an imminent invasion seemed unlikely. Germany had not yet won air superiority, which he considered a prerequisite for invasion, nor did the Germans appear to have anything like the number of surface vessels for such an operation. British experience in Norway showed how hard it was to transport and maintain a force without control of the air. Of course, he argued, it was always possible the Germans might be foolish enough to mount an invasion anyway. 'If so,' he wrote to Pound, 'we should welcome the attempt as being an excellent opportunity to inflict a defeat on the enemy, but we should not deflect our forces and energies into purely defensive measures to guard against it.' This was the nub of the matter. The Home Fleet did not have enough ships to both keep vigil in the Channel and adequately protect convoys as they drew towards the Western Approaches. Forbes believed that it made far more sense for the Germans to try and sever the transatlantic lifelines than attempt an invasion. In any case, he was certain that until the RAF had been destroyed, no invasion attempt could possibly be made without Britain knowing about it at least twenty-four hours earlier, thanks to radio intercepts and aerial reconnaissance of Continental ports. Should such an attempt be spotted, ships could hurry to the Channel in time. In the meantime, he believed his forces were far better used protecting convoys from U-boats and sweeping for mines.

Pound, however, was having none of it. Despite the calm logic of Forbes's arguments, the First Sea Lord declared them unconvincing. 'The JIC have appreciated that the enemy has plenty of military forces available for invasion,' he noted tersely, 'in addition to his other commitments.'

Even Pound, however, must have been troubled by the staggering numbers of ships that were now being sunk. Every week the Chiefs of Staff and Cabinet were presented with a list of shipping that had been lost; it made for sobering digestion. In the last week of June, for example, so much shipping had been sent to the bottom of the sea, it could no longer fit on the graph summaries that were produced by the Naval Intelligence Department. From 288,461 tons of shipping lost in May, the figure had risen to 585,496 tons in June. Since the beginning of the war, nearly 1.5 million tons of new shipping had been built but nearly 2.1 million tons had been sunk. At current rates, that discrepancy would soon rise to critical proportions. Strangling British sea-lines had suddenly become a very real possibility – particularly if the German U-boat force continued to grow.

When the then Kapitän Karl Dönitz had been appointed commander of the Kriegsmarine's submarine force in 1935, he had been disappointed by the post. A naval agreement had just been signed between Britain and

Germany, in which Germany had suggested limiting her naval strength to 35 per cent of that of Britain. It was a clever move, because it tested whether Britain was prepared to move away from the Versailles Treaty, whilst suggesting that Germany had no hostile intentions towards her. At the same time, because of the large size of the Royal Navy, 35 per cent still enabled Germany to build two large battle cruisers, the *Gneisau* and *Scharnhorst*, and the giant battleships *Bismarck* and *Tirpitz*. On the matter of submarines, Germany agreed a 45 per cent parity with Britain and promised to abide by the 1930 London Treaty Submarine Protocol, which barred unrestricted submarine warfare against merchant shipping. The agreement was a coup for Hitler. From having had a navy of just 15,000 men, Germany was now allowed to build a considerable force with the blessing of the world's largest naval power. It was British appeasement at its worst.

From Dönitz's perspective, however, the agreement showed that the Kriegsmarine's future lay in surface vessels, so for an ambitious 48-year-old, his new command seemed something of a dead-end. However, he had been a U-boat commander in the last war and, having thrown himself into his new job, became convinced that not only would Germany one day be at war with Britain, but that when such a time came to pass, submarines, not capital ships, would be the key to German naval success. In his view, U-boats had come very close to winning the war for them in 1914–18, and had they built more of them rather than battleships, the end result could have been very different. Submarines had come a long way since then. They were tougher and faster, could dive quicker – the Mk VII could dive in about thirty seconds – and had larger, more numerous torpedoes, warheads that were battery-powered and wakeless, thus making them harder to detect, and with ranges of up to three miles. Radio technology had also improved. The new U-boats were equipped with highly effective long- and short-wave transmitters and receivers. This meant that U-boats could not only communicate with their base but also with one another. Now, Dönitz realized, U-boats could operate together, and hunt for enemy shipping as a pack – a wolfpack as he called it. And while it was true that more advanced anti-shipping weapons, such as sonar, had been developed, Dönitz believed they were overrated – a threat, yes, but not a considerable one.

He made little headway in persuading Admiral Raeder, commander of the Kriegsmarine, the OKM, or the OKM staff, that U-boats were the way forward, however. Not only were they already committed to the existing building programme, they did not want to risk, at this stage, breaking the Anglo-German agreement. Furthermore, unlike Dönitz, they believed that modern technology and improvements in aircraft range and power put submarines at a severe disadvantage.

Following Munich and the instigation of the massive rearmament drive, the OKM produced the Z Plan, which although it called for 233 U-boats also proposed building six battleships, eight cruisers, four aircraft carriers and a number of surface vessels. The U-boats and battleships were to be completed by 1943, which was still five years away. The Z Plan was flawed for many reasons, but it missed an important truth. Germany's geography, with only a stretch of coastline in the narrow Baltic, made it very difficult for surface vessels, particularly large capital ships, to break out into the Atlantic, where any war on Britain's lifeline would have to be conducted. The English Channel was impassable in a time of war owing to mines, aircraft and British shipping, but the route into the North Sea and around the north of Scotland was also easy for the British to block. The only vessels that could adequately reach the hunting grounds of the Atlantic were U-boats. The Royal Navy had large fleets of surface vessels but their role was primarily to protect those lifelines, for which fast, powerfully armed surface vessels were well-suited. Germany's task would be to destroy as much merchant shipping as possible – and for that, Dönitz believed, U-boats were the best tool available. Furthermore, there was another massive advantage. Unlike battleships or aircraft carriers, U-boats were comparatively easy, quick and cheap to build. Lots of them could be produced in a comparatively short time. And they used less fuel.

By the summer of 1939, Dönitz was ever more convinced that the Germans would soon be at war with Britain. Germany had already publicly renounced the Anglo-German Naval Treaty and the hurried rearmament programme had been instigated because of the threat in the west, rather than the east. Britain had made its pledge to Poland. With war thus looking increasingly likely, Dönitz asked Admiral Raeder to convey to Hitler his continuing concerns about the size of his U-boat fleet, which had only twenty-seven ocean-going boats, of which just nineteen were ready for war. In contrast, Britain had fifty submarines and France, seventy. In July, Raeder conveyed Hitler's reply. 'He would ensure that in no circumstances would war with Britain come about,' noted Dönitz. 'For that would mean *finis Germaniae*. The officers of the U-boat arm had no cause to worry.'

Why Hitler was so anxious to keep his navy in the dark is not clear, but with the subsequent outbreak of war seven weeks later he soon began to recognize the important role U-boats could play, a role already outlined in some detail in a paper earlier submitted by Dönitz. Thus, in September, Hitler scrapped the Z Plan and ordered the beginning of a massive U-boat Command, with the emphasis on the Mk VIIs that Dönitz had been urging for several years. Indeed, such was the urgent importance of now building U-boats, they were to take priority over even key projects such as the Ju 88, while skilled shipwrights drafted into the Wehrmacht were to be sent back to the shipyards right away. Hitler wanted Britain out of the war and he now believed that the U-boats were the key to achieving this, more so than Göring's much-vaunted Luftwaffe. The new plan called for the production of U-boats at a rate of thirty to forty a month. Dönitz, it seemed, had been right all along, and, as if to prove the point, six weeks after the outbreak of war one of his U-boats made an emphatic statement of intent, with the sinking of just one boat. Not any old boat, however, but one of Britain's mighty 50,000-ton battleships: HMS *Royal Oak*.

The best submarine commanders had many crucial attributes but a cool head, decisiveness and intuition – a sixth sense – were essential. Günther Prien had them all, as well as a ton of experience: half his life had been spent on the sea, travelling the globe, where he had learned telegraphy, navigation, about weather, and, crucially, the art of leadership.

Making a periscope attack was not easy, as a number of considerations came into play. For a torpedo to successfully hit a target, a calculation had to be made taking into account the speed, range and course of the enemy ship, the submarine and the torpedo. The Mk VII had two periscopes, a sky periscope as well as an attack and night periscope. The Captain would look through the latter, and, with the help of a graduated ring around the lens, make a number of visual calculations. Range was calculated by reading the angle between the waterline of the target and its bridge or masthead. This was tricky because an estimate had to be made having already assumed the size and class of the ship, not an easy task when simply peering through a periscope. Although an estimate of speed was made visually, sonar helped with this calculation.

The Captain would call out his estimates, which would then be passed to the navigating officer, so that he could start to plot a course for a suitable interception. The crucial factor was working out the director angle (DA), or, in plain terms, the 'aim-off' needed in order to hit a moving target. The torpedo, effectively a mini-submarine itself, was most effective when hitting a target at somewhere close to ninety degrees. As the Captain continually refined his estimates, so the different information would be programmed into a kind of calculator, which would then produce the DA. As soon as the Captain was happy, he would give the order to fire.

All this needed to happen very quickly, and there is no doubt that the best way to assess range, course and speed was through snap assessments made by the naked eye. And this was where experience, allied to a calm, calculating mind and a dash of decisiveness made all the difference.

Making these calculations and decisions at two minutes to eight o'clock on the morning of 2 July was Kapitänleutnant Günther Prien of U-47. Still off the south-west coast of Ireland, U-47 had, for the past twenty-four minutes, been tracking a large liner. The U-boat had just one torpedo left – one that had been defective but, Günther hoped, had been successfully repaired by Peter Thewes, the Ober-Mechanikersgefreiter, the Torpedoman's Mate. Now peering through the attack periscope, Günther had already made a difficult decision. The ship filling the glass was a liner, and at first he had wondered whether it might be neutral, such as an American passenger liner. But then it had started to weave, which suggested it was British or steaming in British interests. Now, as it turned again, Günther gave the order to fire.

Günther Prien had been born with the sea in his lungs, at the Baltic port of Lübeck, one of three children and the son of a judge. His parents divorced when he was young, however, and they moved to Leipzig, but in the post-war economic crisis his mother fell on hard times, so in 1923, aged just fifteen, Günther left home and joined the merchant marine, having spent his last few marks on a three-month course at the Seaman's College in Finkenwärder. Beginning his life on the sea as a cabin boy on a sailing ship, he spent the next eight years in the merchant service, rising steadily through the ranks and learning much about seamanship but also how to look after himself. By the time he had his master's certificate, however, there were few captain's jobs going and he found himself out of work. Life soon picked up, however, as he learned that the expanding German navy was offering its officer candidate programme to merchant marine officers. He applied, was accepted, and so in January 1933, aged just twenty-five, he joined the German navy. Two years later, having been commissioned, married and had a baby daughter, he volunteered for the U-boat arm. There he prospered, going on to be the third – and youngest – commander of the new Type VII U-boats.

Although he had demonstrated his promise during war games before the war, it was in October that Günther really made his name. The British Home Fleet was berthed at Scapa Flow, its base in the Orkneys, but Günther managed to creep U-47 in and sink the *Royal Oak*. It was a huge coup for Germany and particularly Dönitz's U-boat arm, and Goebbels's propaganda team wasted no time in making the most of it. By the time U-47 arrived back in Wilhelmshaven on 17 October, Prien's name and that of his boat were known throughout Germany, and waiting on the quay were Raeder and Dönitz. The crew were then flown to Tempelhof in Berlin, where thousands waited to cheer them. From there they were bundled into a motorcade to the smartest hotel in town, their route lined by more cheering Berliners desperate to see the new naval heroes. There was even lunch with Hitler at the Reich Chancellery, where the Führer presented Günther with the new German award for extreme valour, the Knight's Cross of the Iron Cross.

Hitler had already been won round to Dönitz's persuasive arguments for more U-boats, but there is no doubt that it was the sinking of the battleship the *Royal Oak* that really caught the Führer's imagination and convinced him of the potential carnage large numbers of U-boats could cause.

Since those dizzy days, the U-boat arm had continued to sink plenty of ships – 177 in fact – but there were not yet enough U-boats to really make a difference. But in April the U-boats had been withdrawn from the Atlantic and sent to Norway instead, where U-47's fortunes – and those of the entire U-boat arm – had waned. Part of the reason was faulty torpedoes. U-boats kept firing only to find their torpedoes never exploded. Most of the torpedoes they used were detonated by a magnetic pistol, so that as they reached a target the magnetic force of the ship would detonate them. On 15 April, U-47 had been inside Vaagsfjörd and had discovered three large transport ships plus three smaller ones and two cruisers – a massive 150,000-ton target that would have eclipsed the *Royal Oak* by some margin. None of its torpedoes exploded, however. Later that night, Günther fired another four at targets that were sitting ducks. Again, not one exploded. He was outraged at this golden opportunity missed, but then insult was added to injury when U-47 ran aground. It managed to break free but cracked the starboard diesel engine in the process. This left Günther with no choice but to abort the patrol. On the way home, the U-boat came across the battleship HMS *Warspite*, escorted by two destroyers. Günther fired two torpedoes but neither hit, although one did explode, alerting the destroyers, which then peppered U-47 with depth charges. It was lucky to escape. On its return, Günther told Dönitz the men could not be expected to fight with a 'dummy rifle'.

'Prien's opinions were shared by the other U-boats' crews,' noted Dönitz. 'Faith in the torpedo had been completely lost.' Morale, which was so important for crews who operated in such physically and mentally stressful conditions, slumped. The problem was partly because the magnetic detonation pistols were too sensitive but also because the British had worked out a system of degaussing which reduced a ship's magnetic field. The other problem was that too many torpedoes were losing depth as they travelled through the water. The first problem was resolved when a British submarine was captured. Examining the detonation pistols on its torpedoes, they found them to be far more effective and so copied them exactly. The depth-keeping defect was also partly resolved. Thus having had six weeks off duty in which U-47 had been repaired and refitted, and armed with much improved torpedoes, Günther and his crew had once more set out for what U-boats were best suited to – hunting and destroying merchant shipping.

And they had had good hunting too. Since the sinking of *Balmoralwood*, U-47's luck had despatched a further six vessels, amounting to nearly 40,000 tonnes of enemy shipping. Now, on this grey July morning, a big 15,000-ton prize awaited it. All the crew were wondering whether the torpedo would blow. On board, there was silence, except for the voice of the Bootsmaat, the coxswain, counting the seconds as the torpedo sped through the water. Thirty, thirty-one, thirty-two, thirty-three – then Günther saw an eruption just below the forward funnel and a moment later heard the sound of the explosion dully ripple through the submarine. 'Bull's eye!' he called out. The crew cheered. Keeping the boat at periscope depth he watched carefully for the next quarter of an hour. The ship had stopped and was beginning to list.

Satisfied that the ship was finished, he ordered them to dive out of danger, resurfacing a little over half an hour later. 'No sight of the enemy,' he noted in the log. 'I assume that the vessel has been sunk.' His assumption was correct. All that remained of the liner, *Arandora Star*, was a wide patch of oil, bits of debris, and a few over-filled lifeboats and rafts. Günther had been right to assume it was a British vessel and thus fair game, but in fact the majority of the ship's number had been German and Italian prisoners. The Captain, twelve officers, forty-two crew, ninety-one British soldiers, and 713 POWs went down with the ship. But Günther was not to know.

On 6 July, U-47 returned to Kiel, drawing alongside the quay with '66,587 tons' painted on the conning tower above the snorting bull, and with a pennant depicting every one of the ships sunk on the patrol fluttering in the wind.

Despite the still comparatively small size of the U-boat arm, the submarines were beginning to cause havoc in the Atlantic. In the narrow confines of the Channel, however, lurked other dangers: mines, dive-bombers and what the British called E-boats. The Germans preferred another name: *Schnellboote.* Fast boats. And they were. Deadly fast.

28

Bringing It All Together

IN EARLY JUNE, the Tizard Committee had met in Oxford. Amongst those attending was the Deputy Chief of the Air Staff, Air Marshal Sholto Douglas. Also present was a tall young man with lean, rather striking features and named Reginald Jones, although known to all by his initials, 'RV'. Still only twenty-eight years old, RV had already secured a science Ph.D., and having worked as a Scientific Officer at the Royal Aircraft Establishment in Farnborough and at the Admiralty Research Laboratory was now part of Air Intelligence (AI 1c) within MI6; and therefore his views, despite his young age, were taken seriously.

The meeting, as ever, was convened to discuss the latest scientific developments and how they could benefit the RAF, but Sholto Douglas was hoping for something more from the assorted collection of Government and ministry boffins. 'Can anyone tell me,' he asked, 'what the Germans are up to?' He was bemused because for the past few days Manston, down on the tip of Kent, had been packed full of aircraft flown back from France. It had presented an ideal target, and yet no German aircraft had come near it. 'It confirmed my impression,' wrote RV, 'that the Germans had been surprised by their own success, and had no coherent plan for the imminent future.'

He was not far wrong. Hitler had *hoped* for a lightning-fast success in the west; so too had Halder and Guderian and everyone involved with the planning of the operation. They had believed it was *possible.* Few had thought it was likely, however, because of the bald statistics combined with the weight of history, which suggested that defending forces with greater fire- and manpower could not be easily beaten. Even Hitler must have had many moments when he wondered whether his dream would unravel before him. Count Galeazzo Ciano, the Italian Foreign Minister, had been witness to the talks between Hitler and Mussolini in Munich. 'Hitler is now the gambler who has made a big scoop,' he noted perceptively, 'and likes to get up from the table risking nothing more.' Ciano had probably hit the nail on the head.

The assault on the west had been a huge gamble that had paid off, but at least then his army and air force – his two strongest arms – had been fighting a Continental war. The Luftwaffe had been designed for precisely that, supporting the army, the spearhead for the land attack. In Poland, Norway and in the west it had repeatedly proved its effectiveness in that task. General Wever had advised having a strategic bomber force, but with his death the four-engine bomber programme had been put to bed. It had been given life again with the He 177 project, but now Udet, with the blessing of Jeschonnek and Göring, had put that on hold. It meant the Luftwaffe was now contemplating an air assault without the army beneath them and without the right tools to effectively do the job; the Luftwaffe did not have a heavy-bomber force, and it had rather fewer aircraft and crews than it had before the start of the offensive in the west.

Although Hitler was showing little appetite for a cross-Channel invasion, he had, however, instructed the Kriegsmarine to start making feasibility preparations for such an operation. This task had been given to Konteradmiral Kurt Fricke, Chief of the Naval Staff Operations. Fricke's first ideas had been put forward at the end of May and on their basis preliminary work on an invasion had begun – within the navy, at any rate. As a starting point, Fricke believed that no invasion could be accomplished until the RAF had been knocked out. He also favoured invading along either the south coast or the east coast, but not in the heavily defended narrows of the Channel. First, however, there were a number of tasks for the Kriegsmarine: minesweeping, minelaying, the assembly of suitable shipping, action against the Royal Navy, and the organization of protection for the transport fleet. Strategic surprise – as Admiral Forbes had correctly pointed out – would be hard to achieve.

A hunt for shipping had already started by scouring the coasts and rivers of Holland, Belgium and France for anything that might cross the Channel and even the North Sea. Germany had possessed no landing craft whatsoever at the beginning of the war, and by 14 June the

Kriegsmarine had managed to get its hands on just forty-five flat-bottomed barges suitable for landing troops. Ideas were being put forward for ferro-concrete tanks that could 'swim' across the Channel and then crawl off the flat beaches, and there were designs for super-fast landing barges. A more practical solution was to start requisitioning Rhine barges and other craft from Germany's inland waterways. Meanwhile, detailed studies were also made of Britain's southern coast-line and navigational conditions, her defences, ports and the proximity of airfields to these harbours. What was clear from these early investigations, however, was that the difficulties of such an operation were many indeed. And they were still just preliminary preparations, not yet part of any formal planning – because both Hitler and his commanders still hoped Britain would sue for peace.

As it happened, the chances of Britain doing the 'reasonable thing' seemed to have been given a boost at the end of June. On the 19th, von Ribbentrop had told Count Ciano that Germany now wanted peace with Britain and had alluded vaguely to contacts between London and Berlin through Sweden. This referred to comments made by 'Rab' Butler, a junior minister in the Foreign Office, to the Swedish envoy in London, Björn Prytz. Butler had told Prytz during an off-the-cuff meeting at the FO, that if reasonable conditions were offered, Britain would be open for talks. Apparently, halfway through the conversation, Butler was called in to see Halifax, who sent the message that 'Common sense and not bravado would dictate the British Government's policy.' This was Halifax still thinking with the same detached logic he had used at the end of May – an argument that had already been defeated and was, for the time being at any rate, a non-starter. However, Prytz sent a cable about his conversation with Butler back to Stockholm, from where it was then forwarded to the Germans by the Swedish Foreign Minister.

Both Butler and Halifax had their knuckles rapped by Churchill and that was pretty much the end of the matter as far as London was concerned. However, for the Germans, it suggested the British were secretly hoping for a peaceful settlement despite all the outward bluster to the contrary. Then, at the end of June, Pope Pius XII proposed mediating between Britain and Germany. Although Britain did not respond to the offer, it helped build a groundswell of opinion in Germany and on the Continent that Britain was about to seek terms – something that Hitler was all too eager to believe.

On 2 July, the Führer met with Goebbels to discuss his triumphant return to Berlin and his plans for a speech to the Reichstag in which he would make a peace offer to Britain. He told Goebbels he would return to Berlin on the 6th and make his speech a week after that. In other words, his own peace offer would be made nearly a month after he had told his secretary the same thing. It was not true to say he had no plan – he did; it was to let Britain stew, and then make her a peace offer which she would be mad not to accept.

He was still grappling with what to do when Count Ciano visited him in Berlin on 7 July. Ciano found Hitler in a kindly mood, still flushed with success. The Führer told Ciano that he was inclined to continue the struggle and promised to unleash 'a storm of wrath and steel' upon the British. 'But the final decision has not been reached,' jotted Ciano, 'and it is for this reason that he is delaying his speech.'

In the meantime, General Jodl, Chief of Operations at OKW, had issued an appreciation of the situation. Although he regarded Britain's position as hopeless and assumed she would come to her senses, he proposed a series of options should she stubbornly insist on battling it out. First and foremost was the destruction of the RAF, but combined with this was the strangling of Britain's war economy, terror bombing raids, and then a landing, which he viewed as being the death blow. He also suggested wider action such as the capture of Gibraltar in co-operation with Spain, and the Suez Canal with the Italians. 'Discuss basis for warfare against England,' noted Halder on 1 July. 'Prerequisite is air superiority.' Then he added what his superiors were also thinking, 'which might make landing unnecessary.' Britain might have been an island, but the strategy of knocking out the enemy's air force first, then sending in the army, had worked so far in the war, and was now the basis of Jodl's plans too.

In fact, Göring had already ordered a few raids over Britain. Hajo Herrmann and KG 4, for example, had been dropping mines at the mouths of British harbours, while raiders had attacked airfields in Britain for three nights from 5 June, then industrial works for two more nights on 18 and 19 June. None of these light attacks had caused much damage, however. Certainly there had been no sustained effort, no wholehearted commitment, against Britain yet.

That was fine by Göring, who felt no burning sense of urgency to launch an all-out air assault on Britain. Like the Führer, he remained convinced that the British would see the light and sue for peace. In any case, following the end in France, there was much reorganization to be done.

Units needed to move up to the north-east, others needed to be rested. Supply chains needed to be established. Some of the losses suffered since 10 May had to be made good. Aircraft needed to be repaired and new models sent to their *Gruppen*. Should Britain insist on fighting on, then at least his Luftflotten would have built up their strength ready to unleash the hammer blow.

Air Chief Marshal Dowding was also continuing to make good use of the respite, for with the rapidly changing situation since 10 May his defensive system had needed urgent and considerable modifications. This system, so carefully developed and refined ever since Dowding became C-in-C of Fighter Command, had become a highly efficient and effective means of co-ordinating all his resources to their best capabilities. A key facet was the radar chain, but this was only one cog in the system. Chain Home and Chain Home Low were an effective demonstration of the benefit of new science but it was when they were linked to other cogs that their benefit really came to the fore.

One of these other cogs was the Royal Observer Corps and its vast telephone network. Its roots went back to 1917, during the German Zeppelin and Gotha raids. Major-General Ashmore set up a warning system for London using various defence units which reported through a new telephone network to an Operations Room at Ashmore's headquarters. A few years after the war, Ashmore refined the system again, using volunteer civilians to man a series of experimental posts between Tonbridge and Romney Marsh in Kent. These proved successful, so he was authorized to set up an observer network that covered all of Kent and Sussex. Dividing the two counties into a number of zones, each zone was then given a number of observer posts, each connected by a direct telephone line to an observer centre, which was in turn linked to Air Defence HQ. Once again, Ashmore's system worked well, so the Home Office authorized the establishment of the Observer Corps, which gradually grew and grew into a network of 'Groups', which were then attached to nearby fighter stations. Thus No. 1 Group, based in Maidstone, for example, was attached to Biggin Hill.

By the summer of 1939, there were still gaps in the Observer coverage, in north-west Scotland, west Wales and Cornwall, but there were now more than 1,000 posts and some 30,000 observers, all managed by the police. Observers remained volunteers and trained on evenings and at weekends, but from 24 August, when the Corps was mobilized, they were expected to carry out round-the-clock manning of posts. They also came under the direct control and administration of the Air Ministry. Pay was introduced, although many never claimed their hourly rate, but apart from their tin helmets they were not issued with any uniform.

Each area was divided into groups. Within each group were a number of posts, whose observation area was a concentric ring around the post, and which overlapped with neighbours so that every part of the sky above was covered. These would be given a letter and a number dependent on where they were on the group grid, such as 'R2' or 'J3', for example. There were usually thirty to thirty-four posts in a group, each manned by around fourteen to twenty observers. Each post consisted of a hut, in which there were a telephone, binoculars, logbook, tea-making facilities and a pantograph that looked a bit like a giant sextant. With a height bar and sighting arm, it also had a device for correcting height estimates and was mounted on a gridded circular map of ten miles radius. When an aircraft was sighted, the observer manning the pantograph made his calculation, then another of the observers rang through to the group centre. Plots were then followed at the group centre and forwarded on to RAF Operations Rooms. Where radar warned of aircraft approaching Britain, the Observer Corps provided information inland, as well as a back-up to what was being provided by CH and CHL. It was also incredibly quick. By breaking the system down to area, group and post, and by having different people concentrating on different tasks, the Observer Corps network could manage over a million reports during a twenty-four-hour period, each of which could reach Fighter Command Headquarters in under forty seconds.

Information from the radar chain and the Observer Corps was all very well, but useless unless the controllers on the ground were able to use the information to direct fighters towards their targets. Radio telegraphy – R/T – was standard in most aircraft at this time and allowed pilots to communicate with each other once airborne. What had not been common practice, however, was for pilots to be able to communicate with ground controllers, or for ground controllers to be able to direct (or 'vector' as it was termed) fighters towards targets from a control room – but this is precisely what Dowding introduced. Not only did Fighter Command pilots have radios that enabled them to listen to ground controllers, but there were also networks of antennae radio receivers on the ground that picked up transmissions from the pilot. Cables ran from these antennae to the control room, where, on a cathode ray tube screen, the direction of the transmission could be picked up. With the receivers at the centre of the screen, a line would light up from the transmissions from the pilot, which would then indicate what bearing he was on. This was called High Frequency Direction Finding, or HF/DF (pronounced 'huff-duff'), while the automatic transmissions were christened 'Pip-Squeak'.

With information on enemy aircraft's position from radar and the Observer Corps, it was then a case of applying simple trigonometry. Drawing a line from the enemy to the fighters and making this the long base of an isosceles triangle, the fighter would then be vectored along an angle that was the same as that of the bomber. Where the two equal angles met to form the apex of the triangle would be where the two would meet, known as the interception point. If the bombers changed course, a new triangle would be visualized and if the fighter reached the apex before the bomber, he could circle and wait. A further refinement was the 'Pip-Squeak' system, by which a pilot's radio gave off transmissions automatically for fourteen seconds in every minute. In the control room there would be a clock with its face divided into four coloured quarters, with a hand that rotated once a minute. Four aircraft could thus be controlled in rotation, each pilot being told the quarter in which he was to set his control. The code word for Pip-Squeak was 'cockerel'; if a pilot forgot to switch it on, as often was the case, the controller could ask, 'Is the cockerel crowing?' It was simple but ingenious.

The final cog was the telephone network, which was run and maintained by the General Post Office, the GPO, then still part of the Government. GPO engineers were responsible for laying vast numbers of extra lines between 1937 and 1940. Most RDF stations, for example, were built on comparatively remote farmland, which provided a big logistical challenge. At each, two lines were needed for signalling between stations and the appropriate fighter group headquarters Filter Room. These also needed to be taken through different routes as an insurance against damage. Another line was needed for general operational control, while a further two lines were needed for communicating between neighbouring stations – thus each station needed five new and separate lines in all. At Bentley Priory, all lines went through the Stanmore exchange at the bottom of the hill, but, in case of damage there, an entire duplicate set of lines was built through to the Bushey exchange to the north.

In addition to this incredible and complex amount of engineering work to and from fighter stations, radar stations, Observer posts and so on, the GPO also created a separate network, authorized by the Treasury, called the Defence Teleprinter Network (DTN), as a back-up and an extra means of confirming signals. This linked and served all three home RAF commands, but was still run by the GPO, and maintained by its specially created War Group.

Clever science, ingenuity, common sense and the dedication of thousands of volunteers ensured that Fighter Command could call on a series of invaluable cogs in its defensive system. However, bringing all these together effectively and efficiently into a smooth and reliable machine was of vital importance were Fighter Command to reap the maximum benefit from what each of these strands had to offer. Fortunately, Dowding had managed exactly that.

Centralization and standardization were the key. Fighter Command was divided into operational groups, each of which had its own headquarters and Operations Room. The Groups were then divided into sectors, which were given a code letter. Each sector contained a principal fighter station and sector headquarters with its own Operations Room. Linked to this were the sector's direction-finding stations. Also within each sector were other satellite airfields. For example, Duxford was a sector station, and nearby Fowlmere was a satellite. All Operations Rooms, whether sector, Group, Fighter HQ, or Observer Corps centre, looked the same. In the centre of the room was a large plotting table with a map of Britain, on which were all the sectors and Observer Corps zones. It was large enough for anyone looking at it to see at a glance precisely what was going on. Around the table were the plotters, each equipped with telephone headsets and a croupier's rake. As a call came through, the information would be plotted on the map, with the marker pointing in the direction the aircraft were heading. Rectangular coloured counters were added to show height, size and whether they were bombers or fighters. RAF plotters were WAAFs, from the Women's Auxiliary Air Force, and were popularly known as the 'Beauty Chorus'.

Overlooking the plotting table on a raised dais were the men who would use the information being collated in front of them. At a sector station, there were usually about eight such people, with the Senior Controller at the centre, controlling the squadrons in his sector. Next to him were the Assistant Controller, and then the two Deputy Controllers. Either side of them was 'Ops A', who was in permanent contact with Group, and 'Ops B', whose job it was to ring through to the squadron dispersal and scramble the pilots. On the wall opposite the controllers would be the five-minute colour change clock. Each five-minute section of the clock was coded red, yellow or blue. When a plot came through, it was given the colour indicated by the minute hand at the time of its arrival. There were also a weather board, a list of barrage balloon squadrons and their heights, and a series of panels, at the top of which were written the Fighter Command squadrons in each, and beneath them their state of readiness, such as 'available', 'in position' or 'landing and refuelling'. The relevant state would be illuminated by a maximum of four lightbulbs, each reflecting the relevant colour of each squadron section, red, blue, yellow and green. Only when 'enemy sighted' was lit up would the bulbs all be coloured red. These state boards were known as 'totes' because they looked rather like the lists of horses and odds displayed at a race meeting. Below these there was also a list of the pilots and aircraft available to each squadron, which would be updated first and last thing each day. Thus with one glance a controller had a mass of information about the current state of play at his fingertips.

Dowding had also issued a series of very simple code words for various orders; they could be easily memorized and rarely misheard or mistaken for something else. Thus 'scramble' meant take off as soon as possible, 'orbit' to circle, 'vector 230' to fly on a course of 230 degrees; 'angels' meant height – 'angels 15' stood for 15,000 feet; 'bandits' was the code for enemy aircraft. It was simple and it was standardized.

The hub of this network – the nerve centre – was Fighter Command Headquarters at Bentley Priory. The *pièce de résistance*, however, was the Filter Room, which, since March, had been housed in a concrete bunker below the priory itself. All radar plots were received here, with a filter officer for each CH and CHL station. Information was checked and assessed and cross-referenced with other known flights. Another canny invention was Identification Friend or Foe (IFF), which was a small transmitter in all RAF aircraft that gave a distinctive blip if they flew near the coast and were picked up by radar. When it was not clear, plots would be labelled 'X'. This was the filtering process. Once this was done – and filter officers were highly trained to do this task quickly and accurately – the plot was given a number and passed to the Command Operations Room in the bunker next door, and simultaneously to the Group controllers, who then passed them on to the relevant sector stations. Sector stations then forwarded details of the plot back to Observer centres.

With all the different links in the chain and the mass of different telephone lines relaying information, any lesser system would have created utter chaos and mayhem. It worked, however, because in essence it was very simple and everyone knew precisely what their job was and did not deviate from that. Only at Bentley Priory was there a complete overview of what was going on, but Dowding did not then interfere with the operational and tactical control of his Fighter Groups. The Group Commander and his controllers decided what sectors and squadrons to use and when. Similarly, it was then left to the sector controllers to bring their squadrons into contact with the enemy. In Fighter Command there was no von Rundstedt sticking his oar in.

But that was not all Dowding had at his disposal. Directly under him was AA Command with its anti-aircraft guns and searchlights, although the number of guns available was woeful. Lieutenant-General Pile, C-in-C AA Command, had only 1,204 heavy ack-ack guns and a pitiful 581 light guns, as opposed to the 2,232 and 1,860 that it was agreed he should have. In other words, there were only half and one third the number of guns considered necessary – and many of these were obsolete. This was not good. Heavy defence of aircraft factories was necessary, but then airfields, ports and naval bases also needed defending, as did numerous other industrial plants. The buck supposedly stopped with Dowding, but, as he was well aware, such decisions were beyond his realm of experience and he found himself spending far too much time discussing which of these precious guns should go where. To get around this, he formed a committee representing the various different interests and let them thrash it out between themselves. It also helped that he had an excellent working relationship with General Pile, and whatever dispositions of guns there were could be immediately relayed to Groups and sectors and thus to the fighters in the sky.

He also had some 1,500 barrage balloons in Balloon Command under his orders, as well as control of the Air Raid Warning System, which was operated from Bentley Priory. Furthermore, he benefited from whatever information could be gathered by Air Intelligence and, indeed, from other intelligence branches via the Air Ministry. Permanently at Fighter Command HQ were General Pile as well as liaison officers from the other commands, from the Admiralty, and also the heads of the Observer Corps and Balloon Command. Each had his place on the dais in the Operations Room with a direct line to his organization.

There were flaws in the system. Neither radar nor the Observer Corps could accurately assess the height of an incoming raid – although they got it right more often than not – and with the exception of Bentley Priory not a single Operations Room was even remotely bomb-proof. Yet in all other respects it was genius. Dowding had been given truly awesome responsibilities, yet he had achieved what so few leaders ever properly manage, and that was the ability to delegate – to give each person in the chain a clearly defined role and then let them get on with it. And it was remarkably flexible too. Because of the standardization, squadrons could be added or removed from various sectors, sent into different Groups, and the system remained exactly the same. This allowed Dowding to rotate his squadrons; it also meant that if he needed to reinforce a particular Group, he could do so easily. The system also ensured that his squadrons did not waste time or energy with fruitless standing patrols. They were trained to be airborne in a matter of minutes, and could now be vectored towards the enemy as and when it arrived. Of course, it would never run 100 per cent smoothly all the time, but it was still the most sophisticated and comprehensive defence system in the world at the time.

By the beginning of July, Fighter Command was sufficiently ready to face the Luftwaffe. Dowding would have liked more aircraft and more pilots, but new machines and men were arriving with every passing day. His defence system was established, those under his command knew what they had to do, and his squadrons had benefited from the pause in the Luftwaffe's attention.

Every man was now waiting for Göring's air fleets to attack. Whether their preparations had been enough, however, only time would tell . . .

29

Trouble at Sea: Part 2

On 3 July, the *Hartlepool*, a 5,500-ton freighter, inched its way out of Southend-on-Sea. It was one of fifty-three slow, chugging merchant ships that made up convoy OA178. 'OA' for 'Outward Bound, Route A'; this was a large transatlantic convoy heading to Sydney, Nova Scotia. *Hartlepool* was near the front of the convoy, each of the ships progressing down the Thames estuary in a single line, one after the other. Nearly an hour later, Captain William Rogerson, looking back from the bridge, still could not see the tail of this long line of ships.

Protecting them was just one naval corvette, hardly armed to the teeth – just one four-inch gun and four anti-aircraft machine guns were all it could boast. Having now formed up into two columns, they inched their way towards the Channel, aircraft often buzzing overhead. Most were identified as German, clearly watching the convoy with interest. There were no attacks, however, and as afternoon wore on to evening, the convoy continued on its leisurely way, calmly, even serenely in the still summer night.

Convoys of merchant shipping had passed through the English Channel since the outbreak of war; London, especially, remained a hugely important port. Of course, some ships had been lost, but it had nonetheless remained a viable trade route. Even after Dunkirk, the Channel remained open, including the Straits of Dover. As June gave way to July, however, this was about to change, and the Royal Navy and British Merchant Navy would pay a harsh price for their complacency.

Captain Rogerson was out on the bridge again at 6.45 the following morning. Overnight, the convoy had manoeuvred again, this time into lines of eight ships abreast. Single aircraft were once more overhead, enemy reconnaissance planes watching the convoy, which had now passed through the Straits of Dover and was heading along the south coast of England, although, as Captain Rogerson noticed, somewhat further south of their supposed course. After a brief breakfast, he took double altitude positions and realized they were even further south than he had thought, almost parading past the newly conquered French coast. 'Good heavens!' he remarked to the Second Officer, 'We should be able to see Cap La Hague and Alderney.' With that, he left the Chart Room and went back out on to the bridge. Visibility was excellent – about fourteen miles – and without bothering with binoculars he could see Cap La Hague and the French coast and all the now German-occupied Channel Islands. It did not make him feel easy. 'In my opinion,' noted Rogerson, 'we should have wheeled almost 90 degrees as we were parading before the French coast.'

The reconnaissance aircraft – not to mention watchers on the French coast – had reported the movement of the convoy and shortly before 1 p.m. Stukas from St.G 2, led by Major Oskar Dinort, suddenly appeared overhead and in waves of six peeled off and began diving on the hapless ships below, their sirens wailing. Again and again they attacked, diving, releasing bombs, then climbing again for another diving run. Since his attack on British ships off Calais, Oskar Dinort and his crews had marginally improved – in any case, dropping bombs on freighters chugging along at ten knots was easier than hitting a speeding destroyer.

'The enemy aircraft appeared to drop straight out of the clouds,' noted Captain Rogerson on board the *Hartlepool*. Recently armed with a four-inch ack-ack gun and a twelve-pounder, his gun's crew immediately opened fire. Three salvoes of bombs were dropped near the ship, with ten in all falling horribly close by, huge spumes of water erupting into the sky. However, as one of the Stukas came out of his dive, Captain Rogerson's gunlayer managed to hit the aircraft, which then plunged into the sea. 'It was probably a lucky hit,' Captain Rogerson admitted, 'but the gunner was hot stuff with the 4 inch gun.' He had been practising every day and clearly this had now paid off.

Hartlepool escaped unscathed, but others were not so lucky. Captain Rogerson saw bombs hit the *Irene Maria* on his port bow; it immediately went up in flames and had to be quickly abandoned. He also saw the

Britsum and *Eastmore* hit, the former also flaming. Further along the convoy, another ship, *Dallas City*, was also burning; frantic messages for help were coming over the radio. Captain Rogerson decided to open up the engines and go through the rest of the convoy.

As *Hartlepool* cleared the leading ships, a signal now arrived from the convoy commodore for the ships to turn forty degrees north, towards the coast. Shortly after it wheeled, a second attack arrived. From the bridge, Captain Rogerson looked back and saw the remainder of the convoy being dive-bombed. Flaming ships floundered, diving sirens could be heard, columns of smoke and spray were rising into the air. Captain Rogerson ordered the ship to increase speed again, this time to full steam ahead at nearly fourteen knots. Making towards Bury Head, he wanted to try and find some protection by hugging close to the shore. Soon after, however, came another signal, this time for the convoy to head into Portland, where the commodore hoped the harbour defences might make a better fist of protecting them than the lone escort corvette.

This was a bizarre decision that reeked of panic. At Portland, Oskar Dinort's Stukas were nearing the edge of their range, and had they continued on their way the convoy would have been soon clear of the fray. By going into Portland, however, the ships would become sitting ducks. In any case, Portland could hardly offer them a wall of steel; the shortage of anti-aircraft guns had affected almost every port in Britain, but especially those further away from the vulnerable south-east, and which were naval as opposed to trade ports. In fact, Portland's sole protection was a lone naval anti-aircraft guardship, HMS *Foylebank*, an ageing freighter that had been requisitioned by the Admiralty and on which had been bolted a number of anti-aircraft guns.

On board *Foylebank* was Ron Walsh, a twenty-year-old from Lymington, in Hampshire. Although he came from a naval family, Ron had never really wanted to go to sea himself. After school he'd briefly joined the Merchant Navy, then switched to the Royal Navy, only to desert after a year, and go and work on a farm. All was well until war broke out; eventually, Ron had known that his past would catch up with him as he was obliged to register for service. For a while he thought about joining the army, but at the last minute decided to return to the navy after all. Immediately put on a charge for desertion, he was offered a King's Pardon with the promise that his desertion would be wiped from his record.

His first draft was to *Foylebank*, which he joined in Belfast after a rail and sea journey via Stranraer. The ship had only just been commissioned into the navy and almost immediately set sail for Portland. Ron's action station was as a range setter on the starboard 3.5-inch ack-ack gun near the stern in X Turret, which was about twenty feet above the deck. At Portland, he had soon been relieved of his gunnery duties, as he had volunteered to drive the motor launch that took the crew and mail back and forth between the ship and the port. However, just the day before, on 3 July, another seaman had taken over from him so he had returned to his position on the guns.

The ship's gunner had been quite active in the preceding days as various reconnaissance aircraft had come over. Clearly, the Luftwaffe had taken note, because a couple of evenings earlier Ron had been on the Mess Deck and had heard Lord Haw Haw come over on the radio from Berlin and warn the Admiralty to remove the anti-aircraft ship in Portland harbour or else the Luftwaffe would do it for them. 'We laughed,' says Ron.

Lord Haw Haw's promise was no idle threat, however. Shortly after 1 p.m., Ron was on the Mess Deck when he suddenly heard shouting and running about from the deck above. Deciding he should head to his station immediately, he had just stepped over the combing of the door when there was an enormous crash and he found himself flying across the canteen. When he looked up again, he saw the hammock nettings were burning, the double ladders were all twisted, and tables had been grotesquely bent and turned over. He and a friend began making their way along the port side when another bomb went straight down the funnel and blew out the side of the ship. Frantically, he and his mate turned back and saw a number of men try and scramble up stairs to the deck only to be machine-gunned and tumble backwards. Clambering over the bodies, the two of them managed to make their way to the aft end of the ship, where the sick bay was, and where all the non-combatants were. There was also a ladder there that led up to X Turret. Ron began clambering up it with his friend following when there was another huge crash. A further bomb had gone through the upper deck and into the sick bay, killing all the men sheltering there as well as Ron's friend, who had been only just behind him.

Dust and smoke was getting in his eyes and up his nose, but Ron eventually managed to climb through a hatch out on to the deck and bright sunshine. The summer sun could not hide the carnage, however. 'The guns were all bent to hell,' he says, 'and none of the crew to be seen.'

Above, he could see the bombs falling from a Ju 88. Someone shouted, and he turned and saw 'Badger' Otley, the captain of X Gun, miraculously still firing, even though the coconut matting around the gun was on fire. Despite this, Otley was screaming for more ammunition. Two sailors were yelling back at him, so Ron stumbled on, until he reached the front gun deck. Looking over, all he could see was bomb holes, bodies and twisted metal. A voice shouted up to him, 'Anyone there?' It was the First Lieutenant.

'Me, sir!' Ron replied.

'We're going to abandon ship shortly,' he called back. 'Get down here!'

Ron jumped down – the ladder had been mostly shot away – landing on his back on the kedge anchor. Although he had badly damaged several vertebrae in the fall, adrenalin hid the pain. Making his way forward down a ten-foot-wide passageway, he had nearly reached the starboard pom-poms – the 20 mm quick-firing cannons – when a pile of bodies blocked his way. Ahead, beside the guns, was the Petty Officer, who yelled at him. 'Clamber over them!' he shouted. 'They're all dead. Get up here!'

Ron did so, only to see one of the leading hands, Jack Mantle, sitting on the seat of the pom-pom, desperately trying to switch the change-over lever from electric to manual; it had become slightly bent. Mantle looked a mess. His leg was shattered and around him lay his gun crew, all dead. Evidently, he had managed to heave himself back on to the seat, but was now cursing as an Me 110 from VIII Fliegerkorps had turned out over the bay and was now coming back towards them. Just as Jack got the lever down, the Messerschmitt opened up with his machine guns. 'He fired four barrels of pom-pom,' says Ron. 'I don't know what happened to the plane, but Mantle flaked out on his gun. He'd been hit across the chest.'

The *Foylebank* was now low in the water and it was clear she would soon sink. The Petty Officer sent some men to get Mantle down off X Turret, and ordered the rest of them to get the wounded into a number of civilian craft that had come to their rescue. He also called for someone to accompany the First Lieutenant down below to look for any other survivors. Seeing the ship's Surgeon Lieutenant sitting on a bollard with his guts in his hand, Ron volunteered to go with the First Lieutenant. A lot of the ship was already flooded. They found one man slouching beside one of the bulkheads, so the First Lieutenant went over to him. 'He touched him on the shoulder,' says Ron, 'and he fell apart.'

Hurrying back up, he helped the others get Mantle down. Having helped lower him from the fo'c's'le on to a boat below, Ron then clambered down himself. Safely reaching the quayside, the survivors then mustered in the dockyard as *Foylebank* finally slid beneath the sea. Ron was one of the lucky ones. Sixty men had been killed and more would later die of their wounds, including Jack Mantle who, for his bravery that afternoon, was awarded a posthumous Victoria Cross.

While *Foylebank* had been heroically doing her best to stave off the Stukas, the terrible folly of sending the convoy into port had become quickly apparent, not least because three freighters were hit almost as soon as they reached the port. Not until much damage had already been done were the orders countermanded. For *Hartlepool*, the orders had been an infuriating waste of time. She had already had to turn around in an effort to make for Portland and now had to turn back again. It was dusk by the time she and three others were finally making headway once more, now out on their own and quite apart from the rest of the straggling ships. But at least the attackers had gone, and as the light began to fade they could have been forgiven for thinking their ordeal was, for the time being, over.

At 9.30 p.m., four *Schnellboote* of the 1st S-Boat Flotilla left their docks at Cherbourg and began speeding their way, one after another in line astern, across the Channel. There was a kind of feline beauty to the *Schnellboot.* Perhaps less so when docked in port, but out at sea, with her three Daimler-Benz MB 501 engines opened to full throttle, these lithe, pale 35-metre-long boats, scything through the water, had an appearance of awesome power. Third in the line was S26, hurtling through the water at more than forty knots. The prow of the boat was quite clear of the water, a huge storm of white spray following in her wake. Either side of the prow were two torpedo tubes, while on the forward deck was mounted an MG 34 machine gun and at the rear a rapid-firing 20 mm cannon.

Commander of S26 was Oberleutnant zur See Kurt Fimmen, known to all as 'Bobby'. Good-looking, with pale blue eyes and sandy-coloured hair, Bobby had turned twenty-nine in May. He had been born in Wittenberge, in Brandenburg, and had joined the Kriegsmarine in 1935, as an officer cadet, becoming a midshipman three months later. Two years later, he had joined the S-boat arm, a branch of the German navy that had very nearly been abandoned. A series of unreliable engines had dogged the S-boats that had been developed, but the OKM had persisted with them and by 1939 Daimler-Benz had produced the MB 501, a robust, reliable and powerful engine that soon proved ideal. Extravagant plans to dramatically increase production of S-boats never came to fruition – these died with the rest of the Z Plan – but the potential of these immensely quick inshore boats was realized and by the time the first victories in the Low Countries were taking place it became clear they could have an important role in harassing and destroying British merchant trade through the Channel. Although there were just two flotillas of nine and seven boats each, the S-boats had scored a number of victories during the Dunkirk evacuation, including the British destroyer HMS *Wakeful*. Bobby Fimmen and S26 had also scored their first victory when, in tandem with S23, they destroyed the French destroyer *Scirocco*, in a daring night-time attack. The ship had sunk in minutes, taking with her 480 soldiers.

With the fall of France, new opportunities had arisen. Because convoys passing through the Straits of Dover could be better protected by day than by night, the commander of S-boats, Korvettenkapitän Hans Bütow, realized that convoys would thus often be passing west of the Isle of Wight at night. This would provide great opportunities for his wooden-hulled S-boats, which could speed over magnetic minefields, smash the convoys, then speed back again. The ports of Cherbourg and Boulogne were ideal bases from which to launch such attacks.

The 1st and 2nd Flotillas had reached Boulogne on 25 June, and three S-boats from the 1st Flotilla, including Bobby Fimmen's S26, had then moved to Cherbourg three days later; the rest of the flotilla arrived on 1 July. Bütow believed his S-boats could wreak havoc on Allied shipping in the Channel if they worked closely in tandem with VIII Fliegerkorps, which was now based in Normandy. If von Richthofen's Stukas and Me 110 Zerstörers ('Destroyers') attacked by day, his S-boats could attack by night in a co-ordinated assault on British merchant shipping through the Channel.

Convoy OA178 had provided the perfect opportunity for Bütow to test his theories. Despite the pasting the convoy had received that afternoon at the hands of VIII Fliegerkorps, Bütow felt their effort had been somewhat half-hearted. However, as four S-boats sped across the Channel, the chance had come for the navy to show what they could do.

S-boat tactics were to cover the bulk of the distance in line astern, then, as they neared the enemy targets, they would split into pairs, or *Rotten*, as fighter aircraft also termed a pairing. The two pairs would then attack their targets together, having first slowed to around ten knots. This was necessary in order to fire the torpedoes; if they were going too fast, the speed would affect the trajectory of the torpedo. The second advantage was that at lower speeds the boats were considerably quieter.

It was around twenty minutes to midnight when the S-boats had a stroke of luck. From the shore a searchlight was casting a beam out to sea, and there suddenly silhouetted against it were four ships. In constant VHF radio contact with one another, the S-boats now throttled back and prepared to attack. Splitting into their pairs, Bobby manoeuvred beside S19, his adrenalin beginning to pump. From the bridge, he could see the pale grey forward deck stealing towards their targets. 'You don't actually realize the terrible power of the S-Boote until you come in contact with an enemy ship,' says Bobby. 'During the attack, the boat is literally one with her torpedo.'

At ten minutes to midnight, on board *Hartlepool*, Captain Rogerson saw the track of a torpedo pass before his starboard beam, then disappear under *Elmcrest* on their right. Fortunately, it did not explode, but then *Elmcrest* blew a quiet signal on her steam whistle, warning the other three in their group of the danger. Wasting no time, Captain Rogerson once again ordered full speed and turning sharply to starboard began to zig-zag frantically. It was too late for *Elmcrest*, however. S24 had fired the first torpedo and missed, but Bobby had now lined up for a shot in turn. On the signal to fire, the torpedo had burst out of its tube, speeding towards *Elmcrest* at forty-four knots. Immediately the boat whirled around to port with the sudden lightening of the load, but Bobby was able to glance back and see the torpedo had hit the large 12,000-ton vessel amidships. The ship had now stopped in the water as Bobby curved around for a second attack. She was a sitting duck, and Bobby made sure they did not miss. Most of the crew had already begun abandoning the ship and as the torpedo sped towards *Elmcrest*, it passed under one of the life rafts causing it to capsize. The torpedo struck the engine room, and tore the ship in two. Captain Rogerson watched, appalled, as the ship was silhouetted by the explosion. The tanker sank in less than two minutes.

Meanwhile, S24 had fired another miss. Leutnant Götz von Mirbach in S20 had also missed twice but his crew had now reloaded and was attacking *British Corporal*, and this time she hit. There was no huge explosion, but a high column of water, twisted metal, oil and debris shot into the air. Water began pouring into the engine room, the rudder was shot away, and although the ship was not listing, it was clear she would have to be abandoned.

One after another, the S-boats were doing their deadly work. S19, with S26 following, was pursuing *Csarda*, but it was S20 who now turned her attention to *Hartlepool*. Because of the increased speed, the ship was shaking and the bridge rattling loudly so that Captain Rogerson never heard the S-boats stealing towards them. But suddenly the Second Officer called out, 'Here's one for us!' It struck at the stern of the ship, blowing off her propeller. Now with no more torpedoes to fire, S20 raked the lifeboats and *Hartlepool* with machine-gun fire before opening her engines and disappearing into the night.

'The assault of 1st S-boat Flotilla was a complete success,' noted Kapitän Bütow proudly. Bobby Fimmen in S26 had claimed *Elmbank*, and Götz von Mirbach in S20, *British Corporal* and *Hartlepool*, a total of nearly 13,500 tonnes. No wonder they were feeling pleased with themselves.

Von Mirbach could have been forgiven for thinking he had sunk both vessels; after all, they had been hit and men were seen abandoning their ships. However, both had survived. Captain Rogerson had been loath to abandon ship, despite being repeatedly told to do so by the naval escorts that had arrived by first light. His judgement had been proved right, however. Both *Hartlepool* and *British Corporal* were towed back to Weymouth later that morning, where they were beached. They had somehow survived, but that was hardly the point; not only were they severely damaged, their cargoes would not be reaching Nova Scotia.

Winston Churchill was not the most patient of men at the best of times, but particularly not when there were urgent war matters to attend to. To ensure that key matters were dealt with as a matter of extreme urgency, he would mark 'Action This Day' on the top of certain memos. He wrote these three words on to a note he sent on 5 July to the Vice-Chief and Assistant Chief of the Naval Staff, in which he wanted to know, on a simple piece of paper, what they were planning to do about Channel convoys now that the Germans were along the French coast. 'The attacks on the convoy yesterday,' he wrote, 'both from the air and by E-boats,* were very serious.'

Sixteen ships from OA178 had been sunk or damaged and would never reach their destination. Three of those had been caused by just four

* The British called all Axis motor torpedo boats 'E-boats'.

S-boats; the rest had been hit by many more Stuka Ju 87s and Me 110 Zerstörers, whose hit ratio had not been anything like so high. For all the wailing of sirens, crashing of bombs and rattle of machine-gun fire, Oskar Dinort and the Stuka pilots were still finding it very difficult to actually hit and sink moving ships, even ones crawling along at under ten knots.

However, from the British perspective, it was clear that large ocean-going convoys could no longer travel through the Channel. A 30 per cent loss rate was too high, especially when the convoy had not yet even reached the hunting grounds of the U-boats. The answer to Churchill's question was that, from now on, ocean-going convoys to and from the Port of London would have to go the longer, more arduous, route up the east coast and over the top of Scotland.

That was a sensible but time-consuming solution for ocean-going shipping, but there was no way round the problem of getting coastal cargoes to and from London and to the south of England. Britain depended on coal: it was the lifeblood of the power stations which provided the electricity so that aircraft and almost every other war requirement could be made. The south coast alone needed as an absolute necessity some 40,000 tons of coal a week. Without coal, Britain would collapse. Yet the inland transport network – the under-developed road system and the railway network – simply could not cope with the demands that would be needed were the coastal convoys to stop. Despite the considerable threat from S-boats and U-boats, from the Luftwaffe and from mines, the colliers and trampers would have to keep going.

These crews would be performing a vital and heroic duty for Britain in the weeks to come.

30

Crooked Leg

BY THE END OF the French campaign, the whole of III/JG 52 had scored just ten victories. Supporting Army Group A as part of Luftflotte 3's Jagdfliegerführer 3, the pilots had seen little action, so it was perhaps something of a surprise that they had already been posted to Jever, near Wilhelmshaven, on Germany's North Sea coast. However, the pilots soon began to see why. Soon after arriving at Jever, they had handed over their Me 109 E1s and E3s and instead been given new E4 models. Leutnant Günther Rall, for one, was impressed. The E4 had improved armour plating around the pilot's head, and better armament with a German-built Oerlikon MG-FF 20 mm cannon in each wing which used an improved shell called a 'mine-shell' capable of carrying a much larger explosive charge – a very useful weapon when trying to knock aircraft out of the sky. The E4 also had an improved field of view and more storage space, which, as Günther soon discovered, could house one-man rubber dinghies. The penny really began to drop when they were also given new personal kit. The impractical brown flying combination gave way to a new lightweight flying jacket and loose, comfortable trousers with pockets large enough to hold various new life-savers: pocket knife, tins of concentrated Choco-cola, fishing lines and hooks and small bags of coloured dye. There were new yellow life-jackets too, flare pistols and a leather bandolier and cartridges that were worn around the leg. It did not take a genius to work out that soon they would be flying over water. 'The next opponents we are supposed to bring to their knees,' noted Günther, 'with the benefit of our new air-sea rescue equipment are to be the British.'

For the next few days, they carried out a number of coastal patrols and navigational exercises, all part of their preparation for their next move to the Pas de Calais. Günther found it disorientating at first. Flying over the sea it was easy to lose all sense of the aircraft's flying altitude and of visual distance. He was grateful that he had already mastered the art of flying by dead reckoning and had some night flying under his belt. Even so, he found himself listening a little more closely to the note of his engine, and more frequently scanning his instrument panel. It was a pity, he thought, that Göring had not flown in his *Schwarm*. 'By now,' he noted, 'he might be having second thoughts about his pompous statement that England is no longer an island.'

The third *Gruppe* of Jagdgeschwader 52 was not the only unit to be moved back to Germany. A large number were doing so. Dolfo Galland, now commander of the 3rd Staffel of JG 26, accompanied his new first *Gruppe* to Mönchengladbach in North Rhein–Westfalia, which, conveniently for him, was near his family. JG 52's first *Gruppe* had also been posted back to Germany, to Zerbst, some eighty miles south-west of Berlin. Günther Rall might have been sanguine about their move to the North Sea, but for Ulrich Steinhilper and the men of the 2nd Staffel the posting in early June had been a huge disappointment. They all felt they had hardly been given a chance to prove themselves.

For Ulrich, however, there was one benefit to the move. Like Stan Fraser, Ulrich was a keen amateur cine photographer, and on arrival at Zerbst had shown a roughly edited cut of his footage to the entire *Gruppe*. It had gone down well and so the I Gruppe commander, Hauptmann Wolfgang Ewald, suggested they start a movie war diary and get a new camera and some film for the purpose. In these times of heavy rationing, this was no easy task, but Ulrich called a dealer in Stuttgart and, with the help of his girlfriend Gretl's family, managed to get hold of a good one.

It was thus only fair that he should be the one to go and collect it. Taking the *Staffel*'s Me 108 four-seater Taifun, he was also charged with stopping at the town of Trier, on the banks of the Moselle near the Luxembourg border. There, in the monastery that had become a field hospital, was one of their wounded colleagues, Feldwebel Karl Munz. Ulrich was going to take him to hospital in Stuttgart instead, near to Munz's wife.

The experience of visiting the field hospital left a lasting impression on Ulrich. There were wounded and dying men everywhere. When they saw his uniform, one man cried out, 'To hell with you, Herr Leutnant! To hell with the whole bloody lot of you! Now we're wounded and not much use, we're on the scrap heap. Nobody cares!' Even Ulrich could see there were nothing like enough doctors and staff for the number of patients. He eventually found Munz near the roof of the old monastery. Munz was distraught and begged Ulrich to get him out of there. 'Please get me out, any way you can,' he pleaded. 'People are dying all the time.'

It was no easy task getting Munz away, not least because he was clearly not really fit to fly. The doctors objected, but by repeatedly lying through his teeth, Ulrich persuaded them to lend him an ambulance to take Munz to the airfield and with the help of a nurse managed to get the wounded man on to the Taifun. It was thus with some relief that Ulrich opened the throttle of the Messerschmitt and felt them gathering speed. 'A little of the glory that I youthfully saw in the campaign,' he wrote, 'was left amongst those stinking rows of blood-sodden mattresses.'

In Germany, Goebbels had made sure not a syllable about possible peace talks had made the German press, and at the same time warned them not to speculate as to when the full-scale attack on Britain might begin. However, Britain's attack on the French Fleet was to be used as a prime example of how low she had sunk. Britain had been France's ally; but some ally Britain had been to France. He also instructed the press to clearly support the continuation of Germany's ongoing struggle with Britain.

Convalescing in Leipzig, where he was recovering from the wound to his wrist, Siegfried Knappe had also noticed the mood of the people was very positive. Life seemed much the same as it had before the war, he thought. The people seemed relaxed and proud of Germany's achievements. Siegfried, however, sensed an attack on Britain would be no walkover. 'Although we had just thrown the British Army out of Europe,' he noted, 'we knew we would not be able to invade England without heavy losses.' With his soldier's knowledge, Siegfried was understandably cautious, but most Germans believed Britain was finished. Certainly, Berlin was agog with expectation. Else Wendel, like most Germans, was convinced that they would soon invade Britain. It would obviously be a walkover and then the war really would be over. 'We didn't hate the English so much now,' she noted, 'but just felt rather sorry for what was coming to them.' Germany, she believed, had clearly proved herself to be the greatest country in the world; as for England, she would no doubt one day be quite a valuable ally when she had swallowed her pride and acknowledged defeat. Goebbels would have been proud; his message was getting through.

'If and when Germany intends to invade Great Britain,' William Shirer broadcast to his CBS listeners in America, 'is still the chief topic of conversation here.' He had just returned from a week's rest in Geneva, with his family, where he had discovered much talk of the 'new Europe'. Switzerland, although neutral, was clearly pro-Germany. France had also announced an end to parliamentary democracy. She, too, was becoming a totalitarian state, albeit a puppet one. 'The Nazis,' noted William, 'are laughing.'

Then, on 6 July, Hitler returned to Berlin. Goebbels had issued more than a million swastikas to the crowds that lined the streets. On the radio, blaring out in factories, homes and the streets, was a running commentary from the moment *Amerika* pulled into the station until Hitler's arrival at the Reich Chancellery. The streets had been lined with crowds and flags and church bells had been rung as all of Berlin, it seemed, rejoiced in the return of their glorious Führer.

'What did I tell you?' said Else Wendel's boss, Herr Wolter, at the Department of Art. 'Don't you admit now that our Führer is the greatest man in the world?'

'Yes,' Else replied. 'I do and without reservations.'

Herr Wolter wondered whether Else could speak English. She could – she was almost fluent. 'Very well,' her boss told her, 'then I will take you with me when we go to England.' He already had plans to take the factory exhibitions to Britain.

'Feverishly,' noted Else, 'we waited for the invasion.'

It was not only Berliners who were waiting with bated breath; so too was General Kesselring, commander of Luftflotte 2. He and his fellow commanders at the front could not conceive how Hitler could hope to reach an agreement with Britain when day after day went by without anything of any significance happening. Some of the pilots were wondering the same. 'When nothing happened,' noted Hans-Ekkehard Bob, 'one wondered about our leadership.' Hans and III/JG 54 were now based at Bergen-aan-Zee in Holland from where they were providing cover for their own coastal convoys. Siegfried Bethke and JG 2 had remained in

France at Beaumont-le-Roger in Normandy. Supposedly still in the front line, he and the other pilots were becoming increasingly frustrated. They had heard on the radio that Britain was already being constantly attacked by bombers, but, if so, they certainly hadn't noticed. Rather, they were spending their time at cockpit readiness waiting to take off should British bombers arrive. Instead of taking the attack to England, JG 2 had been ordered on to the defensive. For the pilots it meant one day on, one day off. 'That is why one day,' he noted, 'I get up at 4.15 a.m., and sit from five until 2230, then go to bed at 2300. The next day I get up at 9 a.m. and have almost nothing to do.' The next day, he wrote: 'General situation: no-one knows anything!'

Göring had, in fact, on the last day of June, issued his 'General Directive for the Operation of the Luftwaffe against England'. Three Luftflotten were to be used, 2 and 3, as in the western campaign, but also 5 Luftflotte in Norway. The attack would begin just as soon as the new disposition of forces had been completed. The problem was that to attack Britain the Luftwaffe needed as many fighters, with their low range, as close to the coast as possible, which meant creating a large number of new airfields. Since a cleared field was sufficient for taking off and landing, this in itself was not much of a problem. Nor was finding billets, which could be requisitioned from the French at the click of an adjutant's fingers. More problematic was setting up the groundcrews, complete with spares, tools and other requirements, and establishing smooth lines of supply. Of equal importance to Göring was establishing anti-aircraft defences and sufficient defences for each of these new airfields. The campaign by the RAF's Bomber Command had not caused serious damage yet, but it had never once paused. In the first week of July, Bomber Command had flown thirteen separate missions to Germany, Holland and Belgium, including a number of attacks on coastal airfields; considerably more British bombers were over German territory than German bombers were over British. These were proving a considerable nuisance that was beginning to get on the nerves of the German command. Göring certainly expected British bombers to step up their campaign the moment the Luftwaffe started theirs. Hitler's indecisiveness was one reason for the continued pause in operations, but another important one was his determination to make sure his Luftwaffe was fully ready. 'The intensified attacks against the enemy air force can be ordered very soon,' he said on 21 July. 'Until then, careful preparations, maintenance and improvements of personnel and material readiness for battle should continue.' Göring and his Luftwaffe might have been outwardly confident, but they clearly shared Hitler's twitchiness too. Bomber Command had already played a crucial role in the battle to come.

Nonetheless, Göring had spelled out his aims in his directive. All three air fleets were to be given dates and targets simultaneously so that the 'well-developed defence forces of the enemy can be split and be faced with the maximum forms of attack'. First, he wanted to draw out smaller enemy formations and, with reconnaissance, firmly establish the strength and grouping of Fighter Command. This done, primary targets would then be the enemy air force, its ground organizations and its industry, but they would also concentrate on harbours and installations, merchant and naval shipping, and so sever Britain's lifelines.

'As long as the enemy air force is not defeated,' he concluded, 'the prime requirement for the air war is to attack the enemy air force at every possible opportunity by day or by night, in the air or on the ground, without consideration of other tasks.'

Luftwaffe squadrons, despite the losses suffered in the western campaign, now had plenty of experience to share around. Broadly, their tactics had been proved, and most pilots and crew believed they had aircraft that were better than those of their opponents. Confidence was high, as well it might have been. Ever since Spain, it had been one-way traffic with the Luftwaffe. Although the word 'panzer' now held connotations of military invincibility, it was the German air force, above all, that was still perceived around the world to be its most terrifying weapon. Certainly, the Luftwaffe had more than played its part in the great victories to date.

General Milch spent a great deal of his time hurrying from one *Geschwader* to another, talking to the pilots and commanders. So, too, did Kesselring; they understood the importance of listening to the views of the men in the firing line. There were few concerns. The Spitfire had been recognized as a formidable opponent, but the failure at Dunkirk had been largely explained away by the weather. It had been bad luck, that was all. In terms of equipment, and tactically and operationally, most pilots believed they were well served. 'The campaign had gone so well in our favour,' noted Ulrich Steinhilper, 'that there had been no need for complex tactical analyses and instructions.'

Yet the reason pilots such as Siegfried Bethke were sometimes spending all day at cockpit readiness – that is, sitting in their 109s waiting to be sent into action at a moment's notice – was because the Luftwaffe had not set up their sophisticated *DeTe* – radar – technology to support their front-line pilots. Nor were pilots supported by any air-to-ground radio telegraphy or Direction Finding system. Luftwaffe pilots and aircrew could communicate with their own units in the air, but a fighter pilot could not talk to a bomber pilot, for example. Pilots and crews were briefed on the ground and then expected to go and get on with the mission.

This was a cause of great frustration to Ulrich Steinhilper, who, since the beginning of 1939, had been his *Gruppe*'s communications officer, or *Nachrichtenoffizier*. This had been when I/JG 433 (as JG 52 had then been known) was being formed. Three 'Spaniards', including Dolfo Galland, had been the *Staffel* commanders, and the junior officers, such as Ulrich, were being given other positions within the *Gruppe*. Ulrich was appointed *Staffel* Adjutant under Galland, but the last position to be filled was that of communications officer. No-one wanted to do it, so it fell to Ulrich, as the youngest, along with his adjutant duties.

No-one seemed to have much idea what was involved. Ulrich dutifully carried out some research and discovered that he was supposed to have some seventy-five men under him, equipped and trained to operate two 1.5 kilowatt radio stations and two field telephone units, mounted on trucks with their own switchboard, cables and telephones. These were intended to be completely manoeuvrable and to accompany the *Gruppe* wherever it went and to provide the pilots with both ground-to-ground and ground-to-air communication. The idea was that the field telephone units would plug into the national circuit.

This was the supposed equipment and the theoretical use for the *Nachrichtenzug* – the Communications Unit. What was clear, however, was that no-one in JG 433 had given communications much thought. There were seventeen men rather than seventy-five, and although Ulrich battled hard to improve things, there was little enthusiasm amongst the other pilots, most of whom thought that any form of radio in an aeroplane was a waste of time and merely added extra weight. Leading the dissent was Dolfo Galland, who continually argued that they had managed fine in Spain using sign signals, and who was clearly becoming irritated by Ulrich's youthful over-zealousness.

But Ulrich had persisted, winning the support of the *Gruppe* commander, Hauptmann Graf Dietrich von Pfeil, and even an audience with General Martini, the head of Luftwaffe Signals. Gaining more equipment and his full complement of men, and having attended signals courses himself, Ulrich pressed ahead with his efforts to improve the *Gruppe*'s communications. His big moment came that summer when the *Gruppe* – now re-designated I/JG 52 – was involved in a large training exercise commanded by General Hugo Sperrle. The fighters were to 'protect' Stuttgart from an 'attack' by bombers. Each fighter was now equipped with a radio, and Ulrich and his communications unit were, with their radio units set up by the control tower, to direct the *Gruppe* to attack the bombers. Helping him were the *Luftnachrichten*, the German Observer Corps, of which there were some 1,200 people. It was a big responsibility for a young twenty-year-old pilot but his theories and persistence seemed to have paid off. The observers provided him with early warning of the arrival of the bombers, and he and his comms unit were able to then direct the fighters on to them.

Ulrich was feeling very pleased with himself when he attended the mass debrief afterwards, but this quickly turned to disappointment. No-one mentioned the communications and ground controlling at all. Eventually, he plucked up the courage to ask General Sperrle what he had thought, but Dolfo Galland cut in. 'Good, Steinhilper,' he said, 'you have reminded me. You were talking too much. You were just bothering us all of the time. As I've always told you, it would be best to throw out all of these damned radios! We don't need them.'

Humiliated and deflated, Ulrich realized that for the time being he had taken his communications crusade as far as it could go. Dolfo Galland had moved on soon after, but there was still little enthusiasm to improve matters. And this attitude was not unique to JG 52, but across the board. A junior officer was not going to change the outlook of the entire fighter force let alone the Luftwaffe as a whole. By the end of the French campaign, ground-to-air control remained virtually non-existent. Ulrich had heard about 'Freya' and 'Würzburg', but his tentative investigations got him nowhere. Debate had also begun over how many *Staffeln* should operate on the same frequency. Usual practice was for an entire *Gruppe* to use one frequency, but even this number could cause confusion, because no matter how often it was drummed into pilots to keep radio discipline, as soon as they found themselves in an action, the airwaves were swamped and all that could be heard was a high-pitched whistling.

Tentative debate there might have been, but there were certainly no dramatic changes about to take place. If and when the Luftwaffe launched its assault on Britain, it would be doing so with only very limited radio co-ordination. 'Our communications,' noted Ulrich, 'would continue to be fatally flawed.'

Instead, the Luftwaffe had concentrated on looking to use radar and radio technology to develop in-flight aids for navigation and bomb-aiming. In many ways, this was logical. After all, since the Luftwaffe had so far always been on the offensive there was less need for an early-warning system such as Dowding had established. They had thus, since the mid-thirties, been developing a series of three electronic bombing and navigational aids, and two of these were available for use in Göring's bombers.

Since joining Air Intelligence, Dr 'RV' Jones's brief had been to try and obtain early warning of any new weapons or methods used by the enemy. Although he had been spending time researching German self-sealing fuel tanks and magnetic mines, it was towards aids to navigation that RV had been devoting much thought. In early March, he got an interesting lead. Captured German aircrew were all interrogated, but also placed together in bugged cells. Air Intelligence's chief interrogator, Squadron Leader Denys Felkin, passed on to RV details of a conversation in which one prisoner was telling another about a device called *X-Gerät*, or 'X-Apparatus'. 'The beginning of a thriller,' noted RV, 'could hardly have had a more intriguing title.' This was potentially more exciting than the very best thriller, however. From what the prisoner was saying it certainly seemed that *X-Gerät* was a bombing apparatus using pulse radio technology, and the more RV thought about it, the more it seemed likely that it was a system of intersecting radio beams from German transmitters, and that where the intersection occurred was the target – hence the 'X'.

For the time being, however, RV got no further, but then, later in March, he was passed a scrap of paper, found on a downed Heinkel 111, on which was written: 'Radio Beacons working on Beacon Plan A. Additionally from 0600 hours Beacon Dühnen. Light Beacon after dark. Radio Beacon Knickebein from 0600 hours on 315 degrees.' It was the phrase 'Knickebein on 315 degrees' that really interested RV. Further interrogation by Felkin revealed that *Knickebein* was indeed a bomb-aiming aid a bit like *X-Gerät*, but, other than that, for the time being RV could make no further headway at all.

It was not until 12 June that RV got another lead. Group Captain Lyster Blandy, head of Air Intelligence's Y Service, passed on a message.

'KNICKEBEIN KLEVE, IST AUF PUNKT 53 GRAD 24 MINUTEN NORD UND EIN GRAD WEST EINGERICHTET.' There was the word *Knickebein* again – German for crooked leg. Kleve, RV thought, must be the German town, as in Anne of Cleves. This being so, the message would read: 'Cleves Knickebein is at position 53 degrees 24 minutes north, and 1 degree west.' The position referred to was in England, roughly on the A1 north of Retford. This was a decoded message, picked up by the cryptologists at Bletchley Park, then passed on to Blandy and then to RV.

That day, RV saw his old mentor, Professor Lindemann, and told him about *Knickebein* and that he was convinced it was an intersecting beam system for bombing England. Lindemann argued that this was not possible because it would necessarily be using short waves, which could not bend round the curvature of the earth. RV argued, however, that this was not necessarily so; he had recently seen a report by a leading scientist at the Marconi Company, T. L. Eckersley, who had proved that theoretically radio waves would bend around the earth to a surprising extent. The next day, RV gave Lindemann a copy of Eckersley's report. Now convinced RV was right, Lindemann wrote to Churchill informing him that the Germans had probably developed a targeting device. The Prime Minister passed this on to Sinclair, asking him to find out more.

The following day, 14 June, Squadron Leader Felkin told RV that another prisoner had confessed that *Knickebein* was indeed a bomb-dropping device involving two intersecting radio beams. Immediately, RV began thinking about the possibility of putting in a false crossbeam that would make the Germans drop their bombs before they reached their target. The prisoner revealed more, sketching a transmitting tower at the Luftwaffe's development centre at Rechlin. As RV instantly realized, it looked just like other towers in Germany that had been photographed by aerial reconnaissance.

By now, Sinclair had asked Air Marshal Sir Philip Joubert to investigate further. RV was called to a meeting with Joubert, Lindemann and even Dowding. All were agreed that *Knickebein* needed to be given all priority. So too did Churchill, when he was informed of their conclusions. RV was convinced that *Knickebein* had to be using Lorenz-type beams, a German invention that they had already discovered. Two beams were transmitted, pointing in slightly different directions but also just overlapping. One of the beams would be represented by a 'dot' signal, the other by a 'dash', which would be heard through the headset of the pilot or navigator on board an aircraft. The two beams would be set so that when the aircraft was flying on the correct course, the two sounds would merge into one continuous note. If the pilot deviated he would hear more dashes or dots depending on whether he veered left or right.

If RV was right, then *Knickebein* would be a further note that would be heard the moment the two beams actually intersected. This would thus be set at a specific target point. The Y Service was immediately put on the alert for any more information; interrogations were also targeted at finding out more. At Boscombe Down, near Salisbury, the Blind Approach Development Unit, which had been experimenting with Lorenz-type beams, was also called upon to help by sending up aircraft using captured Lorenz receivers and trying to pick up beams. It found nothing. RV was sure that one of the beams was coming from Cleves, but he needed to know the location of the second one. This was the key. By good fortune, a breakthrough came almost immediately from another piece of paper salvaged from a shot-down bomber. This fixed the second beam in Schleswig-Holstein. More pieces of the jigsaw were quickly found; Felkin was doing his work well. First, the team at the BAD unit discovered that the Cleves beam was set at 31.5 megahertz, then that Schleswig-Holstein was set at 30.0 megahertz. They now had hard information on the size of the two beams, so the next step was to confirm their existence by discovering and flying along them for themselves.

It was only eight days since the decoded Cleves message, but events had moved very quickly. RV now found himself urgently called to a meeting with the Prime Minister at Downing Street. It was already in progress when he arrived. Sinclair, Newall and Dowding were there, as were Lindemann and Beaverbrook. So too was Portal, C-in-C Bomber Command, as well as Watson-Watt and Tizard. RV had never met the Prime Minister or many of the other war leaders gathered there but straight away he correctly sensed there was tension in the air – before his arrival, Lindemann and Tizard had clashed, the latter insisting that 'bending' beams was not possible. As RV now listened for a few minutes to the continuing discussion, it became clear to him that none of them had really grasped the essence of what had been discovered. Eventually, when Churchill turned to him to ask him some points of detail, RV replied, 'Would it help, sir, if I told you the story right from the start?'

'Well, yes it would!' the Prime Minister answered after a moment's hesitation.

RV spoke for some twenty minutes. Every man there was both older than and vastly superior in rank to him, but he keenly felt that the threat of *Knickebein* was so serious that the facts needed to be properly grasped. Certainly, when he finished no-one was left in any doubt as to the serious danger posed by an enemy system that enabled bombers to accurately target their bombs. Churchill wanted to know what could be done. First, they needed to prove the existence of the beams, RV told him, then he planned to try to create some counter-measures. 'Churchill,' noted RV, 'added all his weight to these suggestions.'

There were still doubters, however, as he discovered at his meeting later that day with Air Commodore Nutting, the Director of Signals. RV was having doubts himself; he had begun to wonder whether perhaps he had fallen for a massive German hoax and had just wasted an hour of the Prime Minister's time when Britain was about to be invaded. However, in his heart of hearts, he felt sure his conclusions had been right. A hunch now made him suggest that the next investigative flight should assume the director beam was on Derby, the location of the Rolls-Royce works where Merlin engines were built.

'And what do we do if we find the beams?' Air Commodore Nutting asked.

'Go out and get tight!' RV whispered to the man sitting next to him.

RV's hunch proved right. On the next flight, on the night of 21/22 June, the beams were found, and they intercepted over Derby on a 400- to 500-yard-wide point. It was a stunning breakthrough with potentially far-reaching consequences for Britain's ability to withstand a future German bombing offensive. When RV returned to Nutting's office with the results of the flight, there was widespread jubilation; the Director of Signals even began skipping round the room with joy. 'All doubts were now removed,' noted RV, 'and plans for counter-measures could go urgently ahead.' That was the key – and in developing those counter-measures, there was not a moment to lose.

ÉDITION EN LANGUE FRANCAISE

Signal

PART III

KANALKAMPF

«*Alerte, des spitfires!*»

crie le mécanicien à bord du bombardier allemand qui survole l'Angleterre . . .

Voir notre reportage illustré à l'intérieur de ce numéro

31

First Combat

IT HAD BEEN A miserable day. The pilots of 609 Squadron had woken at their new base of Middle Wallop, near Salisbury, at 4.30 a.m., and had then flown down to a forward airfield at Warmwell, south of Dorchester. The weather had been terrible and when, at around 9 a.m., a report had come through that enemy aircraft were attacking shipping off Portland, David Crook and Peter Drummond-Hay had set off to investigate in low cloud. In fact, it had been so low it was actually covering the top of the hills. Spotting a gap where a road ran through a narrow valley towards the sea, they roared through it, at tree-top height, causing two cyclists below to throw themselves into a ditch in alarm. They found nothing out at sea, so, disappointed, had returned to Warmwell.

The rest of the morning and afternoon had been spent sitting inside their dispersal tent listening to rain pattering down on the canvas, smoking, reading and feeling increasingly bored and frustrated. David and Peter had made plans for their twenty-four-hour leave to London the following day, but otherwise there had been little chat between the men.

Much had happened to the squadron during the past few days. The attacks on Portland and convoy OA178 on 4 July had prompted swift action. Radar had clearly not been able to pick up German aircraft quickly enough for the fighter squadrons to intercept – at least not that far west at any rate – so 609 had been posted from Northolt to the sector station of Middle Wallop. From there it would move daily to Warmwell, near the Dorset coast.

Needless to say, Dowding deplored the use of his precious fighters to protect Channel convoys and requested that all merchant shipping, even coastal freight, be routed via Scotland and the west coast. This suggestion was turned down by the Admiralty with Churchill's support, not only because he argued that there was the urgent need for coal traffic to London and the south, but also, bizarrely, because they feared a loss of face should they abandon the east coast. Furthermore, they argued that the east-coast convoys acted as bait for the Luftwaffe north of London out of enemy fighter range. This was a somewhat spurious argument because Luftwaffe operations over the Channel were designed more as bait for Fighter Command than the other way round. By following this policy, they were merely playing into German hands. Unsurprisingly, Dowding vociferously disagreed with it, arguing that attrition over sea would not save Britain and pointing out that if too many squadrons were based on the coast, they would not be able to sufficiently protect inland targets such as airfields and factories. Furthermore, little provision had been made for air-sea rescue. Dowding had not expected his pilots to be operating much over the sea and this was one area that had been badly neglected.

His arguments fell on deaf ears, however. By order of the Air Ministry, Fighter Command was to meet any Luftwaffe attacks on Allied shipping. As a result a number of squadrons were moved to coastal airfields, both in the Middle Wallop sector and in the south-east in 11 Group. 609 Squadron was a part of this redeployment, along with two Hurricane squadrons, 238 and 501.

Yet to begin with it was only 609 Squadron that was ordered to use Warmwell as a forward base. The airfield had been a Bombing and Gunnery School and was not really kitted out to support fighter squadrons. 'Warmwell possessed,' noted John Dundas laconically, 'though in rather irregular proportions, the two chief characteristics of a forward station – action and discomfort.' What facilities there were lay the far side of the airfield away from where the squadron was operating. The focal point during times of readiness was the dispersal, usually a hut or building of some kind, in which there would be a telephone and usually a few chairs and beds. At Warmwell, this was a tent. Nor were there any toilets at their dispersal, but since a pilot would risk missing a scramble if trekking all the way to the main airfield buildings, most went in the hedge, between the edge of the airfield and the road. The station commander also insisted they eat their meals in the main building. The new CO, Squadron Leader George Darley, pointed out that they could neither leave dispersal nor stick to regular mealtimes, but this did not wash at all. Eventually, Darley complained to Air Vice-Marshal Quintin Brand, Air Officer Commanding 10 Group, who arranged for some mobile latrines and an assortment of primus stoves and crockery to be used at dispersal.

Discomfort aside, logistically, it was also impossible for 609's groundcrew to maintain the squadron at both Middle Wallop and Warmwell. The only solution was to send half the squadron, one flight at a time. Splitting the squadron in two, however, was far from ideal.

The pilots hardly needed any more disruption. As it was, the atmosphere in 609 Squadron was not up to much anyway. As David Crook had noticed on his return, the squadron had changed a great deal over the past few weeks. Darley's arrival had shaken things up. A 27-year-old regular who had been in the RAF since 1932, he had served in the Middle East and in France and had also had a stint as an instructor to two other Auxiliary squadrons. Darley had been unimpressed by the low morale he had found, and had told the pilots in no uncertain terms that they were a miserable and ignorant bunch who needed to pull their fingers out and start learning the lessons from Dunkirk very quickly indeed. The old prewar auxiliaries – the weekend fliers – had been shocked.

Now, by evening on this Tuesday, 9 July, the rain had stopped and the weather had begun to brighten slightly. At around 6.30 p.m., Green section was ordered to patrol Portland once more. David, Peter Drummond-Hay and Michael Appleby took off, with Peter leading. Once again, however, they saw nothing, and after three-quarters of an hour headed back to Warmwell and circled the airfield. In a rather irritated tone of voice, Peter asked for permission to land. They were told, however, to continue the patrol out over Weymouth at about 7,000 feet as a formation of Stukas had been reported approaching.

They did as they were ordered and David immediately saw a Stuka dive down through cloud some two miles away. He called up Peter on the R/T, and they manoeuvred into line astern and turned towards the enemy. Moments later, David spotted two more Ju 87s. Turning on his reflector sights, he switched his gun button to 'fire', his excitement mounting at the chance to pounce on these slow, rather helpless-looking machines. Last in line behind Peter and Michael, he quickly glanced behind him and was horrified to see at least nine Me 110s some 2,000 feet above beginning to dive down upon them.

Keenly aware that instead of attacking the Stukas they needed to get themselves out of there quickly, he shouted, 'Look out behind! Messerschmitts behind!' But to his horror, both Peter and Michael continued heading straight towards the Stukas. 'I have never felt so desperate or so helpless in my life,' noted David, 'as when, in spite of my warnings, these two flew steadily on, apparently quite oblivious of the fact that they were going to be struck down from the rear in a few seconds.'

Now the leading Me 110 opened fire and David saw cannon shells and machine-gun tracer hurtle over his head 'jolly close'. Turning violently left, he dived through a layer of cloud just below. As he emerged, now travelling at more than 400 mph, he saw a Ju 87 just ahead of him, and so opened fire. It was his first shots in action, but to his surprise, the Stuka seemed to fly straight through his bullets and then disappeared. Somewhat shaken and bemused, David now climbed back up through the cloud and spotted another Messerschmitt some distance above him, so pulling himself into a steep climb he opened fire again. He was too far away, however, and the Me 110 turned away and vanished into cloud.

But David was now aware of a spectral outline of another aircraft in cloud flying parallel to him. Stalking him through the cloud, as they emerged David saw it was a Stuka and that it was now directly in front of him. He pressed down on his gun button and pumped his remaining rounds at the machine. To his amazement, bits of the aircraft began flying off, smoke burst from the engine and then a great lick of flame. Just as suddenly, the Stuka began plummeting from the sky. David watched it tumble until the whole machine was engulfed in flames and eventually hit the sea with a great burst of white foam. The two crew had obviously been killed; David had often wondered what he would feel should such a moment ever occur, and was now rather surprised that a sensation of elation had swept over him – and bewilderment that it had been so easy.

Now out of ammunition and with the Messerschmitts seemingly having disappeared, he headed back to the coast, repeatedly calling up Peter and Michael over the R/T, but with no response. Then he suddenly spotted another Spitfire flying a very erratic course, the pilot obviously desperately looking behind him. Catching up, David saw it was Michael and together they dashed back towards Warmwell.

David made a poor landing, overshooting the runway badly and nearly flipping his Spitfire. When he finally unbuckled his leads and harness and jumped down on to the ground, he discovered his hands were shaking and that even his voice was unsteady. Catching up with

Michael, he learned what had happened. Michael had left his radio on 'transmit' instead of 'receive' and so had not heard David's warnings. Remembering just in time, he had heard David shout 'Messerschmitt' and had whipped round to see three Me 110s bearing down on him. Fortunately, he had managed to escape unscathed – but he had not seen what had happened to Peter, of whom there was still no sign.

As soon as their Spitfires were rearmed and refuelled, six of them took off again to look for Peter, but they saw nothing. Just a wide empty sea. Inexperience, and over-excitement at seeing the Stukas, had almost certainly led Peter to leave his R/T in transmit mode too. It had proved a fatal mistake.

Having returned to Warmwell, they then took off once more for Middle Wallop just before dusk. Arriving back, David went up to the room he had shared with Peter. Everything looked exactly as it had been left; Peter's towel still hung on the window where he had hurriedly left it eighteen hours earlier. 'But he was dead now,' noted David. 'I could not get out of my head the thought of Peter, with whom we had been talking and laughing that day, now lying in the cockpit of his wrecked Spitfire at the bottom of the English Channel.'

Just two months earlier, David had flown his first flight in a Spitfire with barely a care in the world; war had seemed so far removed from the experience. Now, however, the reality was beginning to bite. The next morning, before David had left for London, Pip Barran, the 'B' Flight commander, had been called to the telephone. It had been Peter's wife; the telegram had not yet reached her so she was ringing wondering what the arrangements were for his leave that afternoon. Of course, Pip had then had to tell her the news. 'It all seemed so awful,' wrote David. 'I was seeing for the first time at very close quarters all the distress and unhappiness that casualties cause.'

Later that day, David bade farewell to the rest of 'B' Flight and headed up to London on his own. He would not see either Pip or his other good friend, Gordon Mitchell, again. The following day, while David was with his wife, 'B' Flight was scrambled to go to the aid of another Channel convoy that was being attacked twenty miles to the south of Weymouth. Just five aircraft against a massive formation of Stukas and protective Me 110s never had much of a chance, although it seemed that once again, as three of the five had dived down on the Stukas, the pilots had not heard the warnings of the other two that Me 110s were diving down on them. What happened to Gordon Mitchell, no-one was sure. Pip had headed back to the coast, smoke trailing and his airscrew stopped. Bailing out, the surviving three had signalled his position, but by the time a naval launch found him, he had been in the water a long time, with bad burns and bullets through his legs. As he was lifted aboard, he died. Gordon's body eventually washed up on the Isle of Wight some ten days later. For David Crook, this had been a further double blow. Both men had been close friends; Gordon had been at school with David, while he had known Pip since first joining 609. Three of his best friends had been killed in as many days. All had been hugely popular. 'In a squadron,' David pointed out, 'there are so few pilots, and it really seems more like a large family than anything else, and therefore three deaths at once seems very heavy indeed.' The whole squadron, let alone 'B' Flight, seemed to have had its heart ripped out.

George Darley had been right, however. The squadron had not learned from Dunkirk. 'Beware the Hun in the Sun' was a mantra that would be drummed into every Fighter Command pilot, but was a lesson that the pilots of 'B' Flight had failed to adhere to during their first week of action on the south coast. That would all have to change very quickly. So, too, would operating in such small formations. Sending penny packets of fighters was neither an efficient nor an effective way of protecting the Channel convoys – but many of the ground controllers were inexperienced too. Like the pilots, they were learning on the job. Yet pilots also had to understand that three or five aircraft could not take on fifteen, twenty or even thirty enemy aircraft; they would have done well to follow Oberleutnant Kühle's more cautious approach with 3/JG 52.

This Darley recognized fully, and complained vociferously about the use of his squadron in such a way. Another problem was the method of attack. Pre-war practice had led the RAF to develop six types of formation attacks. They were based on the assumption that they would be made against unescorted bombers flying straight and level, but as France had shown, this scenario rarely occurred. When they had spotted the Stukas over Portland on the evening of 9 July, Peter Drummond-Hay had ordered Michael Appleby and David Crook into a classic Fighter Attack No. 1, calling them first into line astern, one behind the other, from which they were then supposed to peel down, one after the other, have a crack at the target, then pull up and climb again, ready for another attack if necessary. Neither Peter nor Michael had looked behind and above them and had paid the price. The other five Fighter Attacks were progressively more complicated and time-wasting, and completely inappropriate.

Pilots were distracted by thinking about their formations and the sequence of a particular attack, rather than keeping their wits about them.

Yet although a large number of Fighter Command's squadrons had seen action in France and over Dunkirk, the month's respite had not been used to collate and disseminate the lessons learned. Dowding may have developed a supremely advanced defence system, but in the crucial area of fighter tactics he had not been so forward thinking. This was because he believed it was too late in the day to start rewriting the tactic book. He was, however, underestimating the speed with which men in battle adapt.

Instead, it was left to individual squadrons, commanders and pilots to learn and change on their own initiative. Some did, others did not. Fortunately for 609 Squadron, George Darley was not going to let all his pilots be killed in such an unnecessary manner. He began drumming into them the importance of working as a team, of each pilot constantly looking out for enemy aircraft above, behind and below. In the days that followed, he was unable to persuade the ground controllers to use the entire squadron rather than individual flights and sections, but the kill–loss ratio did improve; at least, no-one was getting killed, although two of the pilots were shot down by a single, diving Ju 88. They both bailed out safely, returning to the squadron in one piece, albeit rather humiliated. John Dundas also improved his record from Dunkirk by sharing in the destruction of an Me 110 and the probable kill of a Dornier 17. Darley had not made himself popular with his plain speaking, but the men of 609 were quick to realize that he was a man worth listening to. David Crook, for one, soon began to admire him greatly. His experience, imperturbability, and sound good sense were precisely what the squadron needed.

Darley's plans to keep his squadron alive were given a boost on 13 July, when 152 Squadron was posted to Warmwell. Since it was a Spitfire squadron, the pressure on 609's groundcrew was at last alleviated. Most could now remain at Middle Wallop because there was enough support at Warmwell to house the entire squadron during the day. 'From now onwards,' noted David Crook, 'we generally flew as a complete squadron, which is a very much more formidable and powerful adversary than three aircraft only.'

In terms of numbers of single-seater aircraft, the Luftwaffe had only a small advantage over Fighter Command, but overall Göring's men had enormous numerical superiority. Even so, only two *Fliegerkorps* had been given the task of establishing air superiority over the Channel. General von Richthofen's VIII Fliegerkorps was now mostly based in Normandy between Cherbourg and Le Havre, while General Loerzer's II Fliegerkorps was slowly but surely arriving in the Pas de Calais. Plenty had yet to arrive, however. The entire Jagdgeschwader 26 was now part of II Fliegerkorps, but neither Dolfo Galland's new command, III/JG 26, nor the other two *Gruppen* had yet left Germany. A sense of urgency there certainly was not.

This meant that during the Channel attacks, the Luftwaffe did not have the kind of overwhelming superiority in numbers that it had on paper. However, it had the huge advantage of being able to choose when and where it would attack. Dowding rightly insisted on keeping his forces well spread, but that meant that Park in 11 Group and Brand, now in command of the newly formed 10 Group in the south-west, could only respond to attacks. The Luftwaffe could thus attack in strength at one or two points, rather as German field commanders had done at the start of the western campaign.

These main two points were the Channel and coastal ports of central and south-east England. In the latter, 32 Squadron was one of 11 Group's squadrons also now spending much of its time patrolling over convoys, taking off at dawn from Biggin Hill and heading to Hawkinge near Dover, or to Manston near Ramsgate. It had also been sent on patrols over to the French coast. Pete Brothers had flown to Le Havre on 4 July and to Calais-Boulogne two days later.

It was also being scrambled to intercept incoming raids. On the other side of the Channel, the principal bomber formation in II Fliegerkorps was KG 2, equipped with Dornier 17s, which was being sent over both during the day and at night. On the afternoon of 3 July, 32 Squadron had been vectored to attack a raid of twenty-one Do 17s along with 610 Squadron; on this occasion, the enemy had promptly turned back to France. Soon after, and while still in the air, they were vectored towards another raid, this time of thirty-four Dorniers that were bombing Kenley, just a short distance away from Biggin. Seeing the explosions and puffs of AA fire, they dived on the bombers, managing to shoot three down.

Now that German aircraft were flying over south-east England, Pete began to feel worried about his wife. He was unusually young amongst fighter pilots to be married. He had met Annette when the squadron had been based at Boscombe Down and had been instantly smitten. 'She was super, gorgeous,' says Pete. 'I was very lucky.' Annette had been only twenty when they became engaged, and perhaps not surprisingly her father was none too pleased at the prospect of her marrying so young, and especially a pilot. However, she was due to be twenty-one in April and told her father that then she could do as she pleased. Reluctantly, he agreed to the marriage. The next hurdle was for Pete to get the permission of the station commander. Generally, pilots had to be either a squadron leader or twenty-eight to be allowed to marry. 'You're a bit bloody young, aren't you?' the station commander told him. 'What if I said no?'

'It would be a bit difficult to send you an invitation to the wedding, Sir!' Pete replied. The station commander laughed and gave him his blessing. They married in March 1939, honeymooning in Cornwall during the Czech crisis. Then, the day before they returned, he received a telegram saying he had been promoted to Flight Lieutenant, which pushed his pay from fourteen shillings a day to twenty shillings and twopence. It made all the difference. To begin with they lived in a bungalow next to Biggin, but when war was declared he insisted she should move in with an aunt in nearby Westerham.

Now, in July, he had already begun to think he should move her out of danger when a bomb fell nearby and a piece of shrapnel flew through the window and smashed the mirror on her table as Annette was sitting at it. As far as Pete was concerned, that was it. He insisted on her going to Lancashire to stay with his parents. 'Got her away from the worst of it,' he says, 'which was good because she used to count us in. Every time I came back from a sortie, I had to whiz over the house to reassure her I was still around.' He would miss her, but at least he no longer had to worry about her so much.

The incident also marked a change in his attitude. Like many others, he had regarded the war as something of a game that was exciting, dangerous, but nothing personal. He felt differently now. 'I then said, "Right, these are a bunch of bastards. I don't like them any more. I am going to be beastly."' He was soon able to put his words into actions. On 19 July, the squadron was scrambled to intercept an attack by Stukas on Dover Harbour. In the ensuing scrap, he shot down an Me 109 from JG 51. The next day, whilst protecting yet another Channel convoy, he claimed another.

Yet although it was principally 10 and 11 Group squadrons that were in range of II and VIII Fliegerkorps and most called upon during these early days of July, other squadrons were seeing some action, albeit usually in negligible amounts. From Pembrey, for example, on 15 July, Tony Bartley had chased a Ju 88 that had been targeting a nearby TNT factory. A few days later, other members of 92 Squadron had shot down a lone Heinkel. Enemy bombers were also occasionally venturing further north, in part lured by the east-coast convoys as the Admiralty had predicted, but also by airfield and industrial targets. However, whether this enemy activity was worth the Luftwaffe 'bait' policy was another matter. Certainly, as far as Cocky Dundas was concerned, 616 Squadron was flying endless, tedious convoy patrols in which there was a conspicuous absence of the enemy. It had attacked a lone Dornier on 7 July, and Cocky had actually managed to score some hits, so shared in its destruction. That had been it, however, and he was conscious that his older brother had not only been involved in a number of scraps, but was also steadily increasing his personal score. Immensely proud of his older brother, Cocky was desperate to emulate John's success.

Sharing Leconfield was one of Dowding's new squadrons, 249. It had originally been formed during the last war, but had been disbanded after the armistice. In the middle of May, it had been re-formed at Church Fenton. For nineteen-year-old Pilot Officer Tom Neil, it was his first posting, as it was for most of the pilots. However, some more experienced men had also been drafted in – the Canadian 'Butch' Barton from 41 Squadron, 'Boozy' Kellett from 616; James Nicolson from 72; and John Grandy, still only twenty-six, as the new CO. Only Grandy held a regular commission. Four or five held short-service commissions, while the rest of the officers, like Tom, were Volunteer Reservists. Of the sergeant pilots, who made up slightly under half the total, only three were regulars. The average age was twenty-two; Tom, still a couple of months off his twentieth birthday, was among the youngest. The squadron was also equipped with Spitfires, much to Tom's great joy. His first flight had been on a perfect summer's day with unlimited visibility. Flying this machine of untold and awesome power, he was acutely aware that he had never been happier. His life's ambition had been fulfilled.

Tall, good-looking, with a floppy mop of strawberry blond hair that inevitably led to him being nicknamed 'Ginger', Tom had first become fascinated by aviation during a trip to London with his parents. His father was on the board of the Lancashire and Yorkshire Railway, and not infrequently had to go to London, but on this occasion, they had visited

Croydon aerodrome and there Tom had watched the Handley Page 42s with awe. Soon after, he had met a young airman and been so taken by the man's dash and glamour that at that point he had become determined to make it his career, much to the disappointment of his parents, both of whom remembered the Great War only too clearly.

In the years that followed, Tom had not been swayed from his goal, despite being rebuffed by 611 Auxiliary Squadron. However, having turned eighteen, he then applied to join the Volunteer Reserve and was accepted. For almost a year, however, his flying training had to fit around his daytime job as a clerk for the District Bank in Manchester, which he loathed. Then, on the outbreak of war, Tom was immediately called up. A few weeks later, to his relief, he was sent to an Initial Training Wing at Bexhill-on-Sea.

Having gained his wings and been marked out as a fighter pilot, Tom had joined 249 Squadron. He was hugely keen and enthusiastic, but otherwise was largely ignorant of what was expected of him. He knew nothing of high-frequency radio, of being moved around the sky by a ground controller, of IFF, or even technical matters, such as what a supercharger did. He had never worn an oxygen mask or a Mae West inflatable jacket, and had had almost no gunnery training. He and the other new boys in the squadron were thus very fortunate to have six weeks in which to learn all these things, and to have some longer-serving pilots on whose experience they could draw. In the first three weeks, Tom managed to add eighty hours on the Spitfire, by which time he was thoroughly at home with the machine. There was gunnery practice too, and formation flying, at which his flight commander, Boozy Kellett, was a stickler. It would not be much use in battle but improved his flying skills all the same. The squadron was also given a sympathetic and understanding medical officer, who stressed the importance of sleep and rest during times of stress. Tom had scoffed at the idea, but nonetheless the advice remained lodged in his mind. There were discussions, too, on how and when to bail out, and when to try to crash-land with the wheels up. The pilots were warned that neither the Hurricane nor the Spitfire would float on water; thus, if an aircraft was struggling out over the sea, it was best to bail out as soon as possible.

On 11 June, they had been transferred on to Hurricanes. Tom was not overly disappointed. It was true the Hurricane climbed at a slower speed, and Tom disliked the throttle, which he felt was a little flimsy. On the other hand, the controls felt balanced and the aircraft solid and steady. 'There was no question of converting,' noted Tom about the transition from Spitfires to Hurricanes. 'We flew our Hurricanes four times each day from the outset. With ease and comfort and feeling perfectly at home.'

The squadron became operational on 29 June, and just a few days later, now operating from Leconfield, Tom's section was scrambled at around 4.30 p.m.; a bandit had been picked up on the radar and they were to go and intercept it. Flying out some twenty miles to sea at around 13,000 feet, Tom felt excited but not the slightest bit apprehensive. Further reports from the ground controller were received and then to Tom's amazement he spotted the Dornier. He was so thrilled he forgot all about his radio, instead waving his arms and waggling his wings at the section leader, 'Dobbin' Young. Eventually, Dobbin realized what these frantic signals were and immediately led them into a No. 1 Attack, just as Boozy Kellett had taught them. However, rather than turning away and exposing himself, the German pilot headed straight between their legs, then making a dash for some cloud. The Hurricanes followed, losing him, then spotting him again, before losing him once more, this time for good. Tom returned exhilarated and disappointed in equal measure.

By the middle of July, Tom had flown more than 150 hours on Spitfires and Hurricanes. 'A' Flight, of which he was a member, was still flying tight wingtip-to-wingtip formations and practising the glaringly outdated Fighter Attacks, and there were other shortcomings too, such as in gunnery. In his first practice attacking towed drogues, for example, Tom reckoned he had fired some 10,000 rounds without scoring a single hit. During a second session, he had been marginally more successful, but his shooting had still not been up to much. However, impatient though he and the other pilots might have been to get into the action, this time in Yorkshire was proving invaluable. By keeping them out of the fray for the time being, Dowding was giving them a chance; a chance to become thoroughly familiar with the defence system and, more importantly, with their aircraft. When the battle began to heat up, as surely it now would, many new pilots would not be so fortunate.

Cecil Beaton's photograph of Tom Neil, a young Hurricane pilot with 249 Squadron. The squadron had been re-formed in May 1940 at Church Fenton in Yorkshire, and not until August was the squadron moved south, allowing Tom and many of the other pilots a crucial few months in which to build up flying and combat experience in a mostly quiet sector.

The Luftwaffe High Command became obsessed with dive-bombers. The Junkers 88 was originally conceived as a fast, long-range bomber, but lost much of its speed when it was decided to give it dive-bombing capability. This also massively set back production.

Above: The four-engine Heinkel 177 suffered the same fate. Dive-bombing properties simply could not be applied to such a big aircraft, something that was realized too late. It was one of the reasons the Luftwaffe had almost no heavy bombers.

Below: The Junkers 87, better known as the Stuka, the only operational aircraft conceived as a dive-bomber, but whose flaws were first exposed over Dunkirk. Here Feldmarschall Milch addresses Stuka pilots and crews on one of his many airfield visits.

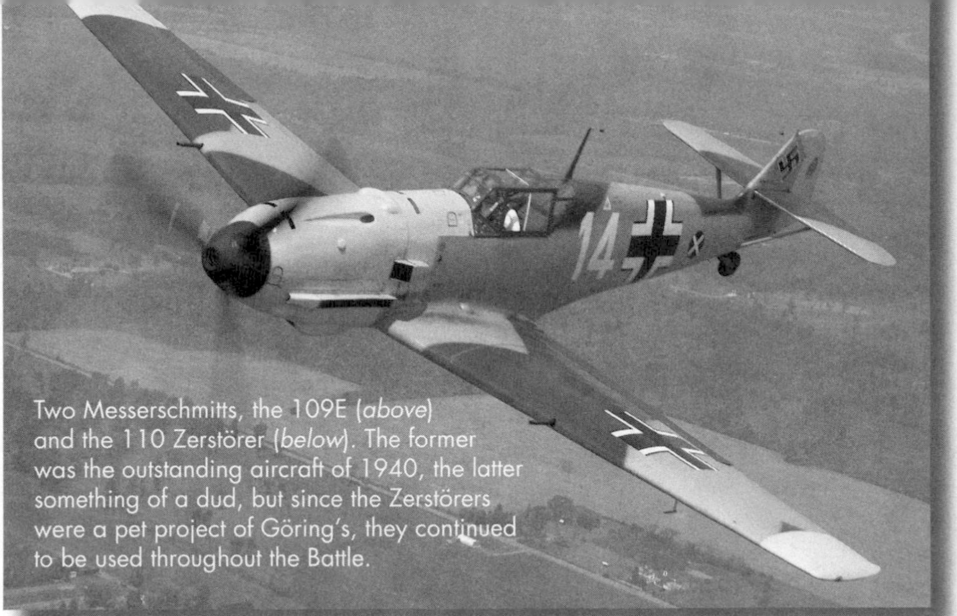

Two Messerschmitts, the 109E (*above*) and the 110 Zerstörer (*below*). The former was the outstanding aircraft of 1940, the latter something of a dud, but since the Zerstörers were a pet project of Göring's, they continued to be used throughout the Battle.

Below: Britain's two principle fighters were the Hurricane and Spitfire. The Hurricane was a direct descendent of Hawker's earlier biplanes, as can be clearly seen when compared with the Hart (*top*). The Spitfire (*right*), on the other hand, was something entirely new, and a superb aircraft even when still at the beginning of its development life in 1940.

Above: The Führer's triumph through Berlin in July 1940. This was possibly the greatest day of Hitler's career.

Above: Colonel Raymond Lee, the US military attaché, and, unlike the Ambassador, a confirmed Anglophile with an uncanny knack of predicting how events would play out.

Pont was a genius and in this cartoon brilliantly reflects the more phlegmatic mood of most in Britain by the time *Adlertag* was finally launched.

Pont.

". . . meanwhile, in Britain, the entire population, faced by the threat of invasion, has been flung into a state of complete panic . . ."

Right: Churchill with his great friend and Minister for Aircraft Production, Lord Beaverbrook. Not only did Beaverbrook give aircraft production (*below*) the kick up its backside that was needed, he also understood a thing or two about public relations – as did the Prime Minister. With Churchill's great oratory and Beaverbrook's schemes such as the Spitfire Fund (*bottom*), these two men gave Britain back its self-belief and galvanized the country.

Above: Me 109s of 9/JG 54 at Guines, tucked away under netting and by the trees at the edge of their makeshift airfield.

Right: A downed Heinkel 111 over England. It has been riddled with bullet holes – but it often took a great many .303 rounds to knock such an aircraft out of the sky.

Above: Paul Temme's Me 109 at Shoreham in Sussex.

Below: A downed Blenheim in Northern France being picked over by the Luftwaffe. The Blenheims were flying over France attacking German airfields every day.

Above: Me 109s of JG 27, taken by Julius Neumann, mid-flight.

Right: Julius was shot down over the Isle of Wight on 18 August and taken into captivity. This photograph of him, looking every inch the blond, good-looking and rather dashing archetypal German fighter pilot, was printed all around the western world.

Below: A Luftwaffe bomber crew are led away from the burning wreck of their aircraft. Downed RAF pilots could often fly again – and frequently that same day – but this was not the case for German crews shot down over England. For them, the war was over.

Above: An attack on Ventor Chain Home RDF station on the Isle of Wight. Although Ventor was temporarily knocked out, radar masts proved nigh-on impossible to destroy, and the Luftwaffe soon gave up trying.

Below: Cherbourg after an attack by British bombers. RAF Bomber Command never let up with their attacks on German targets, both along the continental coast, on airfields, and in Germany itself. It proved a major thorn in Hitler's side.

⊙ 32 ✠

Peace Offerings

After Hitler's triumphant return through the streets of Berlin, he had attended Goebbels's reception at the Reich Chancellery. There he was asked by his Propaganda Minister what his plans were for Britain. Hitler told him the British attack on the French Fleet had changed everything. His planned speech to the Reichstag, in which he intended to announce a peace offer, had been nearly finished but now had to be rewritten, because he was no longer sure he could offer peace with Churchill still Prime Minister. Goebbels was furious. He hated the British and Churchill especially, whom he thought was a raving lunatic, and urged Hitler against offering Britain any easy peace. 'We must not be guided by hatred,' Hitler told him, 'but by common sense.'

Over the next couple of days, surrounding himself with favourites, the Führer daydreamed about future plans. There would be new autobahns, including one from southern Austria all the way to the very northern tip of Norway; he was also going to build a vast naval base at Trondheim. A lengthy lunchtime discussion took place over what to call this giant new port. Himmler favoured 'Atalantis', but Goebbels suggested 'Stella Polaris'. This was the pinnacle of Hitler's career so far; never had his power been greater. For a precious few weeks, he had Europe in the palm of his hand. Within Germany he had never been more popular; his power was absolute. Adoring millions waved their flags, courtiers reminded him that he was the greatest warlord the world had ever seen.

Foreign leaders had fallen at his feet; his vision for the Reich was beginning to be realized. These were heady times indeed.

He had risked so much for these goals, and they had so nearly been entirely achieved; nearly – but not quite. Britain still remained, shouting defiance, sending aircraft to bomb the Reich, preventing him from finishing the war and then preparing to face the Soviet Union. It was so tantalizing: to have one's dreams at one's fingertips and yet not be able to grasp them fully. With every passing day it must have become clearer even to him that Britain would not now roll over. And that meant he had to attack her, swiftly and decisively, once and for all.

Dreams of future projects had to remain just that for the time being. Hitler still did not know what to do about Britain, so he told Goebbels he was going to leave Berlin and head to his favourite place in the world – the Obersalzburg, above the town of Berchtesgaden in the Bavarian Alps, where he had built his house, the Berghof. There he would see his commanders, hear their views on matters and mull things over. He left Berlin on 10 July.

Grossadmiral Raeder, C-in-C of the Kriegsmarine, visited him on 11 July, discussing with him the results of their preliminary investigations into an invasion of Britain. Raeder felt it should be attempted only as a last resort. However, he also believed Britain could be forced to sue for peace by a blockade and heavy air attacks, particularly on her ports, which would make a forced invasion unnecessary. High amongst his concerns was whether it would be possible to clear a large enough area of mines, and pointed out that this cleared stretch of the Channel would also need its own flanking minefields. Collecting the necessary transport vessels would also be no easy matter and would take time. Having listened carefully, Hitler agreed that invasion should be the last resort, Raeder suggested. He also accepted that air superiority was essential.

The next day, however, came Jodl's latest appreciation, which was approved by Keitel and was decidedly more bullish. Yes, the Royal Navy had command of the sea, but that could be locally resolved by command of the air at the necessary crossing point of the Channel. He accepted that most of Britain's army would be in the south-east of England so suggested treating an invasion as a river crossing in force, with a large number of troops on a broad crossing front. The first wave of landings had to be very strong, which meant making the narrow sea lane in the Dover Straits completely secure. Jodl had called the landing Operation LION.

Next in the stream of commanders trooping up to the Berghof were von Brauchitsch and Halder, who were to attend a joint meeting with Jodl, Keitel and Raeder. Leaving Fontainebleau in France at 8 a.m. on the 13th, they landed in Salzburg just over two hours later, then drove to the Berghof, arriving around 11 a.m. An hour later, Halder gave his briefing, outlining what they knew of Britain's defences, his own plans for organizing an invasion force, and suggesting, as had Jodl, that they treat it as a 'river crossing'. Separate raids on the Isle of Wight and Cornwall were suggested, as was bringing up all large guns to the Pas de Calais under the unified command of the Kriegsmarine to create artillery cover over the 'water lanes'. Hitler agreed with these plans in principle but made it clear he also wanted Spain drawn into the fight in order to build up a stronger, longer front against Britain. 'The Führer is greatly puzzled by Britain's persisting unwillingness to make peace,' noted Halder. 'He sees the answer (as we do) in Britain's hope in Russia and therefore counts on having to compel her by main force to agree to peace.' But Hitler was worried that if Britain was defeated then her Empire would disintegrate, which would only benefit Japan, the United States and others.

Two days later it was the turn of Admiral Canaris, head of the Abwehr. Listening to this latest conversation was Hitler's army adjutant, Gerhard Engel. 'Main point of conversation, as always in recent weeks,' noted Gerhard, 'Britain.' Hitler was bemoaning not having whisked the Duke of Windsor from France when he had had the chance. Now it was too late; the former King and Emperor was in Lisbon, in neutral Portugal. 'My impression,' noted Gerhard, 'is that F. is now more irresolute than ever and does not know what to do next.' After all the differing views over the previous few days, it was hardly surprising Hitler was feeling a little indecisive. Like most of his commanders, Hitler was inherently a Continental. The Wehrmacht had been designed for Continental war; and the Luftwaffe had evolved as an instrument of that Continental war. It could now use the Luftwaffe as the spearhead with the army following behind, but while the principle was the same, operationally it was a very different kettle of fish. The Channel changed everything. Germany was no longer on *terra firma*, literally and metaphorically.

How Hitler must have cursed during that week in the Berghof. If only Britain would see sense! Neither he nor Göring really understood the people or what it was like to be an island nation; what that narrow stretch of water that separated her from the Continent meant to the psychology of Britain's leaders, and indeed the nation as a whole. And nor did Hitler understand that, for all its shortcomings, parliamentary democracy and the basic rights of the common man were something that had been hard fought for and were highly valued both consciously and subconsciously by the vast majority of British people. Yes, there were fascists in Britain and there were communists too, but these were fringe parties; there was little appetite for either of their doctrines. For most, Nazism, with all its associated limitations on human rights, its warped ideologies and secret police, was abhorrent. What Hitler failed to grasp was that most British people felt strongly about this. It had taken just a couple of weeks after the armistice for France, apparently voluntarily, to discard democracy and become a puppet totalitarian state. Britain did not want to go the same way.

What was gnawing away at Hitler, however, at this moment of deep prevarication, was the possibility – however remote – that swift and decisive victory might not be possible. That was unthinkable, and yet he had to think of it, to prepare, to deal with the catastrophic consequences. How quickly the ecstasy of victory must have begun to fade.

The next day, 16 July, Hitler issued his War Directive No. 16, 'On Preparations for a Landing Operation against England'. 'Since England, in spite of her hopeless military situation, shows no sign of being ready to come to an understanding, I have decided to prepare a landing operation against England, and, if necessary, to carry it out,' he announced. 'The aim of this operation will be to eliminate the English homeland as a base for the prosecution of the war against Germany and, if necessary, to occupy it completely.' It would no longer be called Operation LION but, rather, Operation SEALION.

Next, he finally announced he would make his speech to the Reichstag at the Kroll Opera House in Berlin on the evening of 19 July. Within this speech would be his final offer of peace to Britain.

Two of the few German commanders to have visited Britain were Generals Milch and Udet. It had been in October 1937, during the time of the Anglo-German Naval Treaty and when showing a conciliatory approach to Germany had been the British policy. Milch had headed a German delegation and they had been shown around shadow aircraft factories that had just been established, had met Dowding, Churchill and the King, amongst others, and had even had a formal luncheon held in their honour at Bentley Priory. Milch had always been against war and particularly with Britain, not least because he was convinced the Luftwaffe was not yet ready in 1939; like many, he expected to have several more years' preparation. However, with the storm clouds building, he had, in July 1939, helped put together an intelligence appreciation on Britain, called *Studie Blau* (Study Blue), on which he had drawn on his visit to Britain. There were, however, plenty of gaps in his knowledge of British industry and so, on German Air Ministry notepaper, he had written to a London bookseller asking for copies of books about the subject. The witless bookseller had duly obliged. Heinkel 111s with civilian markings had also flown over taking comprehensive reconnaissance photographs, the British press had been scoured for information, and the German air attaché in London had also been ordered to obtain as much information as possible. The net result was that Study Blue became a fairly comprehensive reference source about British targets, from power plants to aircraft industry factories to airfields. It was still the major point of reference now as the Luftwaffe prepared to assault Britain.

British intelligence had its faults but at least all three services had their own branches within the intelligence service and at least each of those branches was sensible enough to recruit the best brains for the task in hand, which was why a brilliant young civilian scientist like RV Jones was able to work for Air Intelligence. There was also complete co-operation between different organizations. RV Jones would not have discovered the key to *Knickebein* without the help of the Admiralty Research Laboratory, the Y Service, the Blind Approach Development Unit, the codebreakers at Bletchley, the RAF Director of Signals and the Government itself. Such a scenario was inconceivable in Nazi Germany.

There was nothing comparable within the Nazi party or the Wehrmacht – no Joint Intelligence Committee, for example, where Group Captain Tommy Elmhirst met with his other service colleagues, nor an office where intelligence officers from different arms of the forces worked side by side. This was because different intelligence bodies in Germany viewed themselves as rivals. In a state where knowledge was power, it did not pay to surrender that knowledge to those rivals within the system. Thus Göring still had his listening service, the *Forschungsamt*, which was entirely separate from the Wehrmacht secret service, the Abwehr, and equally so from the Sicherheitsdienst, which included the Gestapo, the Nazi secret police.

Nor was there any co-ordination between inter-service intelligence departments. The result was that intelligence only really came together at the very top. Since Hitler was not a man who took kindly to unfavourable intelligence reports, and since giving him good news tended to improve the standing of the person who had given it to him, information was often spruced up to make it more palatable. Göring was of much the same mind as the Führer, as Oberst Josef 'Beppo' Schmid, head of 5th Abteilung within Luftwaffe Intelligence, was well aware.

There were a number of different organizations collecting air intelligence, so the remit of the 5th Abteilung, was limited to obtaining information about foreign air forces. And although 5th Abteilung was directly attached to Luftwaffe Operations, Beppo Schmid held a position far more privileged than his rank suggested because he was at the same time also a member of Göring's personal staff. Furthermore, as a veteran of the Beer Hall Putsch of 1923, he had both valuable status and protection in the dog-eat-dog world of Nazi politics.

Shrewd, cunning and charming, he had transferred to the Luftwaffe from the army in 1935, but knew little about aeroplanes or air warfare and had never learned to fly. Nor did he speak any languages, and like many Germans at this time had barely travelled – and certainly not to Britain. Known to be overly fond of drink, he gathered intelligence principally by scouring the foreign press – handed out to him by the SD – and garnering information from air attachés. Dolfo Galland, for one, thought he was useless. 'Beppo Schmid,' he said, 'was a complete washout as an intelligence officer, the most important job of all.' Milch also recognized that Schmid was a man who 'trimmed his sails to the wind' for fear of upsetting his boss. Certainly, Beppo knew which side his bread was buttered. He enjoyed his position, with its access to the highest in Nazi Germany, and the privileges that came with it. He was not prepared to jeopardize that by telling Göring home truths his boss did not want to hear.

The other prime intelligence source came from General Martini's 3rd Abteilung, which handled all signals intelligence. Any updates on Study Blue were largely thanks to Martini's team, rather than Schmid's, as the British press was less useful as a source of information once war began and because thereafter signals intelligence was the prime means of gathering information. There were, admittedly, also Abwehr spies sent to Britain by Canaris – the real Fifth Columnists – but these had so far proved abjectly bad at their task. Most had been caught almost as soon as they had arrived. The 3rd Abteilung did pass on daily intelligence summaries to Schmid's team, but when a new intelligence appreciation was asked for by Göring and the Luftwaffe General Staff, it was Schmid, a colonel, rather than Martini, a general, who was given the task.

His subsequent report, presented on 16 July, was riddled with misconceptions and wrong diagnoses. Although his estimation of operational fighter strength – 675 – was not far off the mark, he considerably underestimated how many new aircraft were being produced a month and claimed that British output would decrease because of damage by German air attacks. Time would tell on that score, but during July 385 Spitfires and Hurricanes had been built and that did not include the number that had been repaired – certainly, Schmid had not the first idea about the Civilian Repair Organization. He reckoned that a shortage of planes rather than pilots was the RAF's biggest headache, when in fact the opposite was the case. He also made no mention whatsoever of radar, or any other aspect of Dowding's defensive system. As far as aircraft were concerned, he pronounced that both the Spitfire and the Hurricane were inferior to the Me 109 – that was true, although the tone suggested there was a massive gulf, which was not the case with regard to the Spitfire. He also said that the Me 110 was superior to the Hurricane but inferior to skilfully handled Spitfires. The Me 110 was one of Göring's pet projects, so clearly it would not pay to belittle it. However, while the 110 was fast and had impressive firepower, it was nothing like as manoeuvrable as a Spitfire or Hurricane; a twin-engine aircraft could not possibly be.

Interestingly, there is no suggestion that Schmid knew that the RAF was split into different commands. However, perhaps his biggest misjudgement was his verdict on Fighter Command's structure and organization, which he claimed was rigid and inflexible, when that was precisely what it was not. In fact, it was ironic how much Schmid had perceived Fighter Command's weaknesses as strengths and its strengths as weaknesses. 'The Luftwaffe is clearly superior to the RAF,' he concluded, 'as regards strength, equipment, training, command and location of bases.'

So the Luftwaffe, then, should have no great trouble overwhelming Fighter Command. Neither Göring, nor Milch, nor Jeschonnek saw any reason to doubt Beppo Schmid's report, and it was on this appreciation and armed with Study Blue that the plans for the all-out assault on Britain were to be made. What was striking about both sides' intelligence, however, was that while Tommy Elmhirst and his team at the Air Ministry had somewhat overestimated Luftwaffe strength, Beppo Schmid had underestimated that of Fighter Command; indeed, he did not even know of Fighter Command's existence. Both were therefore wrong in their appreciations. The difference was that while one of those incorrect assessments would ultimately prove to have been an advantage, the other most categorically would not.

Hitler's speech, when it was finally delivered, was not what was expected. It went on for two and a quarter hours, the Führer speaking less dramatically than was usual; there was no ranting and raving, or as much gesticulating and spittle flying as usual. Sitting in the front rows were his commanders and senior Nazis, many of whom had been promoted. William Shirer, who was watching, had never seen so many gold-braided generals massed under one roof. There were twelve new field marshals announced, of whom Milch, Kesselring and Sperrle were three. Watching from the dais beside Hitler was Göring, elevated to Reichsmarschall, a six-star general. There was now no higher-ranking officer in the world. Thrilled with this latest promotion, he had had a new uniform designed specifically, one that would show he was a commander of all three services rather than just the Luftwaffe. A soft light grey was the colour of choice. When his valet suggested it was a woman's fabric, Göring replied, 'If I wear it, then it's for men.'

The Reichsmarschall beamed as Hitler saluted him then handed him the title deeds in a specially designed box encrusted with diamonds and emeralds. 'His boyish pride and satisfaction was almost touching,' observed William Shirer. He wondered why Göring should remain so popular, and concluded that it was because on occasions such as this he seemed so human, 'so completely the big, good natured boy'.

Finally, having extolled their great victories and spoken of Germany's new strength, and having announced the string of promotions, the Führer turned to Britain. Churchill was the object of his scorn, the man he blamed for continuing the war and for starting the bombing offensive. He then made one of his most prescient comments. 'I only know clearly,' he predicted, 'that the continuation of this struggle can end only with the entire destruction of one of the two opponents.'

He went on to add that it would be England. 'I feel obliged, in this hour, by my conscience, to direct one more appeal of reason to England,' he continued. 'I believe I can do this not as someone who has been defeated, but as a victor . . . I see no compelling reason for the continuation of this war.' Despite the usual euphoric *Sieg Heils* that followed the end of the speech, there was a sense of disappointment amongst Hitler's inner circle and commanders. There had been no firm offer, no outline of terms, merely an appeal to 'reason'. Göring sensed that they would now have to fight it out after all. All those weeks he had been thinking Britain would sue for peace. Suddenly, with the Führer's vague offer, those hopes seemed likely to have been dashed. As he commented later, Hitler's speech had thrown the 'fat into the fire'.

In London, at the Ministry of Information, Duff Cooper, along with Harold Nicolson and two others, sat around the wireless in the minister's office listening to Hitler's crackling voice and taking notes. They were all rather surprised that when it was finally over there had still not been any definite peace offer. 'Considering everything,' noted Harold, 'Hitler is really rather modest and temperate and he only starts screaming when he thinks of Winston Churchill.'

The object of Hitler's scorn was also receiving translated sections of the speech as it clattered over the teletyper. He made no comment that night. 'I do not propose to say anything in reply to Herr Hitler's speech,' he told Jock Colville, 'not being on speaking terms with him.' However, at Cabinet the next day it was decided some kind of response was needed. Churchill believed Halifax was the man to make it. After all, he was the Foreign Secretary. More than that, however, Berlin was quite aware that Halifax, above all, was the biggest British dove. A rejection from him would have greater impact than one from Churchill. Furthermore, Halifax had been due to make a routine broadcast on the evening of Monday, 22 July. This would be the perfect opportunity to make Britain's position clear once and for all.

Meanwhile, the day after his speech, Hitler met his commanders at the Reich Chancellery and reminded them once again that Britain's position was hopeless and that a political solution was still on the cards, although he would not wait for much longer. If Britain still refused to come to terms, then she would be destroyed by a combination of air and submarine warfare by mid-September at the latest, at which point the invasion would be launched. After telling them this, he left Berlin once again, not for the Berghof, but for Bayreuth, where the Wagner Festival was underway. Hitler had long since found that there were few things more calming than a Wagner opera. He needed it, for there was much on his mind.

*

Before Halifax broadcast his reply, Jock Colville heard of a dramatic new rumour coming from Washington. The British Ambassador, Lord Lothian, had been contacted by the German chargé d'affaires, Hans Thomsen, via an American third party. Thomsen told Lothian they could outline precise peace terms for Britain that Germany would find acceptable. General Halder also heard of this. 'British ambassador to Washington is quoted: Britain has lost the war. Should pay, but do nothing derogatory to her honour.' Of course, Lothian had said nothing of the kind and the offer had come from Thomsen and Berlin, rather than the other way round. Churchill told Lothian not to respond. The same day, a Dutch businessman, at Göring's behest, also offered to mediate between Berlin and London. There was also another attempt by the Pope.

Then, on Monday evening, Halifax made his broadcast as planned. 'Hitler may plant the Swastika where he will,' he announced in a line that was pure Churchill, 'but unless he can sap the strength of Britain, the foundations of his empire are based on sand.' The speech put an end to any further German hopes. 'England has chosen war,' ran the headline of Goebbels's paper, the *Völkischer Beobachter*. Goebbels had been monitoring public opinion in Germany carefully. Goaded by the Propaganda Ministry, which had urged editors to attack Britain with 'all possible might', the papers had referred to Britain's rejection as a war crime. 'German public opinion is boiling hot,' noted Goebbels with relish. 'The war against England will be a relief. That is what the German people want. The nation is aflame.'

William Shirer noticed a different mood. He thought Berliners seemed depressed rather than angry, although most seemed to be pinning hopes on a quick victory which would be won by autumn, and thus save them from another long, cold winter of war. At any rate, the peace with Britain that had been so assured would not happen just yet. As William wrote in his diary, 'The die seems cast.'

33

The Besieged

Cecil Beaton had left New York on the Cunard liner *Britannic*, on 2 July. As the ship sailed out, a German pleasure steamer, on a tour of the New York sights, crossed their bows. 'And as it passed close by,' noted Cecil, 'its crew grinned with macabre grimaces as it jabbed its thumbs down at us.' Despite this taunt, and regardless of however terrible the prospect might be, Cecil was impatient to get back home.

A few days later, after an eventless return trip in which no U-boats had been spotted, he was back at his home in south Wiltshire. Immediately, he found his spirits soaring once more. 'Any day now an invasion by the Germans could be expected,' he noted, 'the future might well be gruesome, but, somehow, to be in the midst of this maelstrom was far less painful than to hear of it from afar.'

Fear of invasion had never gone away. A report by the Chiefs of Staff on 4 July had accepted that an invasion might take place any moment. A few days later came another appreciation, this time on the 'Estimated Scale of Air Attack upon the United Kingdom', produced by Tommy Elmhirst and his team. 'I think that Hitler will probably invade us within the next few days,' jotted Harold Nicolson the day after hearing the Führer's speech. 'He has 6,000 aeroplanes ready for the job.' In Tadworth in Surrey, Daidie Penna could hardly keep up with the invasion rumours. It sometimes seemed that every day Hitler was about to attack them over the Channel. 'Today is one,' she noted early in July, 'but I haven't seen him yet.' A few weeks later, it appeared to be quieter on the war front, despite the aeroplanes that were flying over. 'Though it is reported,' she added, 'that Hitler is putting the last touches to his invasion plans.'

There might have been a continued expectation of invasion, but after the dramatic events of the Dunkirk evacuation and the French capitulation, the war seemed quieter again. Daidie was not alone in finding it hard to continually work herself up to a fever pitch of expectation only for nothing to then happen. It had led to a gradual acceptance of the threat of German bombers and invasion, and the hardships and inconveniences brought by war. Somehow, almost overnight, these things had become normal. When tea was rationed on 9 July, Daidie barely batted an eyelid; rather, she wondered whether people would come to appreciate their new abstemious habits before the war was over. The same day, she had some concrete blocks delivered, which were to form a blast wall at the front of the house. With the man who delivered the blocks, she discussed whether the Germans would continue bombing once autumn arrived; already she was thinking of a future beyond the next few days. They both thought English fog would help them. 'Still, whatever does come,' thought Daidie, 'I think people will be well prepared for it.'

Confidence was definitely mounting. At the end of June, Olivia Cockett was convinced that they could not possibly win. Three weeks later, her level of morale, she felt, was still much the same but she no longer felt the end of life as they knew it was nigh; she was still spending time doing things for the future both in the house and in her garden. 'I still feel that WE are bound to win the war,' she jotted, having forgotten her earlier pessimism, 'but I don't know why.'

It was Harold Nicolson's task, as a member of the Committee for Home Morale, to keep a close watch on the spirits of the people. Daily reports would reach him, taken from observers and pollsters around the country. Yet another invasion date had been predicted for 19 July, the date of Hitler's speech. 'People cheerful and optimistic at weekend when Hitler failed to invade Britain on Friday as threatened,' ran a report of 22 July. 'General feeling now that war will last a long time as invasion cannot succeed and we shall then settle down to hammering away at Germany by RAF.'

What was bothering 'all classes' was the new Government decision to prosecute people for defeatist talk or for spreading rumours under what was called the 'Silent Column Campaign'. Olivia Cockett and her colleagues at the Pay Office at New Scotland Yard were appalled. She felt that people liked a good moan. 'Opinion unanimous that it was much better to let people talk as they thought, instead of bottling up worries and grievances,' she noted, 'and that anyway, surely one of the things we're fighting to restore to Europe is FREE SPEECH.' The campaign had been a Ministry of Information initiative and had been launched with posters and advertisements. In the press there were even accusations that the Ministry had begun spying on the people. 'There is no doubt,' noted Harold Nicolson, 'that our anti-rumour campaign has been a ghastly failure. All together the M. of I. is in disgrace again.'

Although the Silent Column Campaign had clearly been misjudged, the criticism undoubtedly reflected the changing, more confident, mood of the nation. The Ministry, despite the criticism, had done good work, ensuring the public were well-informed, sending out clear messages, efficiently surveying morale and using well-known cartoonists and designers for a number of successful campaigns, such as 'Careless Talk Costs Lives'. Yet when it came to boosting the morale of the people it was not the Ministry but two particular individuals who seemed to have the magic touch. The first was Max Beaverbrook, the diminutive press baron turned king of aircraft production, who hit on the brilliant idea of asking the nation to donate pots and pans to make aeroplanes. On 10 July, Lady Reading, head of the Women's Voluntary Service (WVS), broadcast an appeal to Britain's women on Beaverbrook's behalf. 'Very few of us can be heroines on the battle-front,' she said, 'but we can still have the tiny thrill of thinking as we hear the news of an epic battle in the air, "Perhaps it was my saucepan that made part of that Hurricane."' The response was phenomenal and tapped brilliantly into the feeling that most British people had that they were besieged and all in it together. This was the people's war, and everyone could help. Equally successful was the Spitfire Fund, which had begun in Jamaica, where the people of Kingston began raising money for new planes to fight against the Luftwaffe. Other Dominions caught on to the idea and, recognizing a golden opportunity, Beaverbrook announced that £5,000 would buy a Spitfire (in reality it was nearer £12,000) and launched a more formal appeal. Again, the response was swift and enthusiastic. Soon there was not a town in Britain that did not have its own Spitfire Fund. It became a kind of national craze. Boy Scouts would do jobs to raise money; collections were made in church, in the pub, at work; town mayors launched campaigns, so too did newspapers. The Durham Miners, for example, raised £10,000 – that was two Spitfires! And Beaverbrook also correctly judged that it was the Spitfire, not the Hurricane, with its beauty, modernity and mean power, that best represented Britain's defiance in the air.

Beaverbrook may have had a nose for a good PR coup, but it was Churchill himself, more than anyone, who led the Government's propaganda effort. Since his hoedown with Halifax and the successful evacuation of the BEF, his position had been greatly strengthened. Although his energy and far-sightedness had been impressive, it was his resolve and spirit, conveyed so brilliantly in his oratory, which helped unite the country. He never shirked from revealing the harsh realities, yet he was also relentlessly positive; there were no limits as to what might be achieved. However formidable Hitler's Germany might seem, no matter how dire Britain's situation, these challenges were surmountable. Such ardent self-belief was infectious.

Nearly 60 per cent of the population had listened to his 'finest hour' speech; his next, on 14 July, had been heard by nearly 65 per cent. This was an incredibly high proportion of the population, especially when considering that seventy years down the line the most popular television programmes would only reach around 12 per cent of the population. This broadcast, to the English-speaking world as much as to Britain, had been another inspirational piece of oratory. 'But all depends now,' he told his listeners, 'upon the whole life-strength of the British race in every part of the world and of all our associated peoples and of all our well-wishers in every land, doing their utmost night and day, giving all, daring all, enduring all – to the utmost – to the end. This is no war of chieftains or of princes, of dynasties or national ambition; it is a war of peoples and of causes.' As his low, rumbling, distinctive voice came through the wireless sets of countless offices and households in Britain and around the world, he finished with another memorable flourish. 'This is a war of the unknown warriors,' he announced, 'but let all strive without failing in faith or in duty, and the dark curse of Hitler will be lifted from our age.' No wonder people felt inspired.

Churchill was certainly in an upbeat frame of mind, as General Brooke discovered on 17 July when the PM visited Hampshire and Dorset to see the troops and inspect coastal defences. 'He was in wonderful spirits,' noted Brooke, now back in his old post as GOC Southern Command, 'and full of offensive plans.' Large areas of the coast had now been designated 'Defence Areas'. Straggling coils of barbed wire and mines were a feature of most beaches, while piers and harbours were now lined with machine guns, sandbags and even some of the precious anti-aircraft guns. The same day, the US military attaché, Colonel Raymond Lee, had also been on a tour to the coast. The defences, he thought, looked impressive. He was struck by the apparent co-ordination: above, fighter aircraft roared over, while out at sea were patrol boats and other naval vessels. On the land were the LDV and the army. It looked good to him, so long as it could all work smoothly together. He wondered whether Hitler had some wonder weapon up his sleeve. 'Every day that he puts it off is immensely valuable,' he noted, 'and I should say that in another three weeks the coastline will be nearly impregnable to ordinary attack.'

There was something in what he said, although the calamity of leaving the vast majority of Britain's guns and army equipment stranded in France had in no way been resolved. There were now 1.3 million troops in Britain, including the LDV, 22,000 Canadians, and 16,000 Australians and New Zealanders. Monthly intake was around 50,000 from conscription and a further 27,000 volunteers. There was no shortage of manpower, just a shortage of equipment. Out of twenty-seven infantry divisions now in Britain, only four had their full establishment of rifles and mortars, and one of those was the 1st Canadian, which was also the only division to have the prescribed amount of field and anti-tank guns. The gun shortage was horrendous. By June, for example, just thirty-five twenty-five-pounder field guns were being produced a month, yet one infantry division required seventy such pieces, and many of the twenty-seven divisions had none whatsoever. In other words, not only were there dire shortages, but there was no immediate means of resolving the problem either. It was not just the aircraft industry that had needed a massive kick up the backside, but the British arms industry as a whole. How the old generals must have despaired. Just over twenty years before, the British army had been the best in the world – and the best-equipped too. Now it could not even arm its men with rifles.

One of those discovering how bad the British army's supplies were was Sid Nuttall. After his return from Dunkirk, Sid had eventually rejoined the Border Regiment at Crook in County Durham, and then was given a brief forty-eight-hour stint of leave back home to Halifax. Having made the most of this brief break by getting engaged to his girlfriend, he returned to Crook. 'We had no weapons, no transport,' he says. 'Nothing.' After a while, some Canadian rifles arrived, all Great War relics which fired clips of five .300 rounds rather than two clips of five .303 like the Lee Enfields. Some civilian vehicles were requisitioned, vans and trucks with names like 'John Smith Butchers' painted on the sides. It was a bit humiliating. New uniforms arrived as well as they worked themselves back up to full strength. A number of men and officers were still missing, presumed to be POWs in Germany. Towards the end of June a further 232 men and six officers arrived, all new recruits with between six and nine months' training. Then, on the last day of June, they had moved to Prudhoe near Newcastle. Their new role was to defend the coast, repelling any invaders, and to help them move around they were given a number of civilian Midland Red buses complete with Midland Red civilian drivers. As a mechanic, Sid had little to do so he asked to be trained as an infantryman instead. The new RSM, who had been the HQ Sergeant-Major in France, agreed.

Stan Fraser had also been busy, having been drafted in to help reorganize the 4th HAA Regiment. Based at Aberporth Camp in south-west Wales, Regimental HQ was based in marquees from where Stan drafted in new men and investigated rumours and reports of those still missing from France. He found the work rather interesting, but, as with the Borderers, the regiment was ready by the beginning of July. The men had been without any guns since ditching theirs in France, but having been posted to Whatton near Nottingham, they arrived to find enough 3.7-inch heavy AA guns for all three batteries. The reason for this apparent high prioritization of gun allocation soon became apparent when two of the batteries, 5 and 6, were sent to Derby to help protect the Rolls-Royce factory. The third battery, 18, remained with HQ, and together they were to form a mobile column for any place in the East Midlands which might be blitzed, as air attacks were now being called.

Five days later, however, they were posted, not anywhere in the Midlands, but to a tiny village in Norfolk near the airfield of Bircham Newton. The men were billeted in the granary. 'Using the sacks of grain as a mattress,' recalls Stan, 'I slept very well during the week which we spent at this lonely spot.' They usually moved after five days or so, fulfilling their new name, 'MacDuff Mobile Column'. Stan's job was to accompany the two 18th Battery surveyors, working out the known ranges at each gun site so that the range-finding instruments could be checked. He was enjoying himself well enough; after France and Dunkirk, a slightly less frenetic pace of life was not unwelcome.

Clearly, the army was in far better fettle than it had been six weeks earlier after the shock of Dunkirk. The shortage of weapons was certainly still critical, but American rifles, ammunition, machine guns and field guns had been enough to make a difference, and war production was speeding up too, thanks to an all-out effort from the war factories. What now concerned Churchill, however, was the army's defensive outlook. It had been trained to be defensive, which was one of the reasons there were so few tanks, for example. Yet the Prime Minister firmly believed that a defensive mindset was not the way forward. He had been much impressed by the Germans' offensive approach and wanted the British army to take a leaf out of their book. He suggested, for example, the creation of 'Storm Troops' or 'Leopards' as he fancifully termed them, who were trained to pounce within four hours on any place that should need them.

When General Ironside, GOC Home Forces, had first been given the thorny task of how best to prepare for invasion with large numbers of badly equipped men, his solution was to combine what few mobile units he had with static defences over a wide area. Inland, from Bristol, south around London then all the way to Richmond in North Yorkshire was what he called the GHQ Line. Making the most of natural obstacles such as rivers and escarpments, this would be lined with pillboxes and other defences. The idea was that troops around the coast would be able to hold off the enemy long enough until mobile troops could fall in behind the GHQ Line. It was unquestionably a defensive plan that was designed to make the best of a bad job. After all, infantry without guns or transport could not be expected to achieve much.

The Vice-Chiefs of Staff had criticized Ironside's strategy because to them it seemed crazy to make no real effort to halt the enemy until half the country had already been overrun. Churchill was equally critical because he felt that the army now had enough equipment to be able to put up a decent show, particularly if those involved were imbibed with enough offensive spirit. Rapid, resolute engagement was what he wanted; the defence of a stretch of the coast, he believed, should be measured not by the number of troops immediately available, but by the speed in which a counter-attack could be mounted.

On 20 July, Ironside was sacked for the second time since Churchill had taken over. This was hard on Ironside, but the right decision; he was out of date, a relic from a different age. Brooke took his place, with a firm remit for a more offensive outlook to Britain's land defences. But as he had noted during the PM's visit on 17 July, Churchill had other plans as to how to take the attack to the enemy. Prime amongst these was what Churchill called 'ungentlemanly warfare'. The seeds of Churchill's thinking may have been sown with the idea of an Allied redoubt in Brittany, but at the same time Hugh Dalton, the Minister for Economic Warfare, had also been thinking about 'black' propaganda and 'special', clandestine operations that could involve sabotage in enemy-occupied territory. After lengthy discussions with members of the Foreign Office, the War Cabinet and other officials, it was agreed that such an organization should be set up with a controller armed with almost unlimited authority. Late on the evening of 16 July, at around 11.30 p.m., Churchill told Dalton, who had been lobbying hard for the post, that he would become chairman of what would be called the Special Operations Executive. Lord Swinton was also recalled to head MI6, the secret intelligence operation within Britain and Ireland. As Chamberlain wrote to the War Cabinet once the decision had been ratified by them, SOE would conduct 'operations of sabotage, secret subversive propaganda, the encouragement of civil resistance in occupied areas, the stirring up of insurrection, strikes, etc.'. Churchill put it more succinctly. 'And now,' he told Dalton, 'go and set Europe ablaze.'

The Prime Minister had come to the conclusion that an imminent German invasion was unlikely. The increased coastal defences, the appointment of Brooke, in whom he had high hopes, the establishment of SOE, the performance so far of Fighter Command – all these factors had strengthened his belief that a corner had been turned. He found it hard to visualize an invasion all along the coast by troops in hundreds of small craft. There was, he pointed out to the War Cabinet, no evidence of large numbers of small craft being assembled. Furthermore, surprise seemed out of the question. The Admiralty had now amassed some thousand patrol craft, of which two or three hundred were always now at sea, and there were the destroyer flotillas all the way from Portsmouth to the Humber.

A more concrete strategy for the war was also beginning to evolve in his mind. In essence, this had always been to ride out the current storm and then gradually strike back, but as the days passed and still Germany did not launch her all-out attack, the way forward seemed clearer, more possible. Britain could impose its own economic blockade on Germany, helped by Bomber Command. Penning Germany in, combined with sustained bombing, could eventually starve Nazi Europe into submission. Allied to this was the firm belief, shared by his ministers, that the German economy had already peaked and would not be able to sustain a long, drawn-out war. By the winter of 1940–1, it was confidently expected,

Germany would be on the point of collapse. That was still a very long way off, but it represented an important psychological chink of light.

Germany's premature economic collapse was a line even Ambassador Joe Kennedy believed. As he pointed out in a letter to his youngest son, Bobby, there were millions of people in Nazi-occupied Europe who might well find it difficult to get enough food during the next winter. 'And when people are starving,' he wrote, 'there is no limit to what they will do.'

Kennedy remained sceptical about Britain's chances, however. With little access to Churchill, Beaverbrook had become his closest source, and told the Ambassador that Churchill believed that if they could get over the summer months, then the crisis would have passed. Beaverbrook confided to Kennedy that he now felt even more optimistic than that. More than just resisting invasion, he was beginning to feel that the RAF might be able to 'overcome' the Luftwaffe. 'I thought this optimism,' noted Kennedy, 'was a clever attempt to enlist more active United States support, and Beaverbrook admitted that they were doing an about-face to make their situation look as bright as possible.'

Kennedy might have been suspicious about this upbeat new line, but Raymond Lee believed Britain now had a real chance of holding out. Thanks to his earlier time as attaché, Raymond was already a well-known and popular figure amongst Britain's military hierarchy, and consequently found many doors open to him. In fact, he was often given greater access than Kennedy, and furthermore had a greater understanding of military matters. Like everyone, he was sure Hitler's all-out attack would begin any moment. 'I also believe,' he added sagaciously, 'that if he is not successful by the fifteenth of September, he will never be.'

Raymond's more positive reports were certainly a marked contrast with those of the Ambassador. 'I send plenty of cables home,' he jotted in his diary, 'in which I call 'em as I see 'em.' This had not gone unnoticed and coincided with Roosevelt's suspicions about Kennedy's judgement. Deciding he needed an independent opinion, the President sent to Britain one of his trusted old friends, Colonel William 'Wild Bill' Donovan, and the journalist Edgar Ansel Mowrer, to assess Britain's chances. Kennedy was incensed. Not only had he not been consulted, but his protests when he learned what was afoot had been ignored. Then, when Donovan and Mowrer did finally arrive on 20 July, Donovan persisted with the charade that he was there to try and understand how Britain's conscription law worked. 'They can do nothing,' grumbled Kennedy, 'but complicate the situation here.'

Raymond Lee spent a great deal of time with Donovan and Mowrer, taking them around the south coast defences, introducing them to Churchill, General Brooke and others. Lee had also organized a morale poll of his own and discovered that, with the exception of the City of London, morale was pretty high in Britain, and, to his surprise, highest among the workers in the industrial areas. On 2 August, he had a farewell breakfast with Donovan in which they had a 'free and frank' discussion. Lee was pleased that they seemed to be of much the same opinion as him: that Britain had better than even odds of surviving. Donovan also gave Kennedy a stinging rebuke. 'Well,' Donovan told Lee as he boarded his plane, 'I told him before I left that the American policy was to help in every way we can and it doesn't help these people any to keep telling them that they haven't got a chance.'

Churchill, of course, was delighted by Donovan's visit. By the time Wild Bill headed back to Washington, there were other small signs of encouragement too. On 19 July, Roosevelt had been nominated to stand for an unprecedented third term. Should he win, the chances of American entry into the war would receive a huge boost. Arms and munitions were also continuing to make their way across the Atlantic. Churchill had deliberately left Roosevelt alone since his last appeal for help before the fall of France, but with six weeks gone, with the arrival of Donovan and with the news of Roosevelt's nomination, the Prime Minister decided to once again ask for fifty or sixty old destroyers. Large construction work was underway building new ships but the fruits of these labours would not be ready until 1941. He needed the President's help to stop the gap now.

Kennedy remained deeply sceptical. 'Don't let anybody make any mistake,' he wired Roosevelt along with the Prime Minister's cable, 'this war, from Great Britain's point of view, is being conducted from now on with their eyes only on one place, and that is the United States. Unless there is a miracle, they realize that they haven't a chance in the long run.'

Kennedy was right to add a sober word of caution. Britain was in a better position than she had been at the end of June, but this was no time for becoming over-confident. The Luftwaffe, for all its shortcomings, was still a mighty foe, whilst, with the material benefits gained as a result of Hitler's lightning victories, Germany had far stronger economic legs than Churchill and his ministers realized. Britain's survival was not now a foregone conclusion. Not by any means.

34

Hotting Up

Just after 5 a.m., on Wednesday 24 July, the pilots of 87 Squadron were settling down at their dispersal hut for a nap before breakfast. They had recently moved to Exeter, in the south-west, and had been up since before first light on readiness. Suddenly, and much to their annoyance, the operations phone rang. A plot had been picked up and a section was needed to patrol Lundy Island off the north Devon coast at 8,000 feet.

Bee Beamont, along with Rob Voase Jeff and Harry Mitchell, took off, climbing through the grey morning cloud. Soon they were climbing through thick cumulus, the cloud's peaks gleaming with orange. Bee thought it was almost better than sleeping, flying amongst these wondrous sunlit shapes. Just as they cleared the Devon coast, with Lundy in the distance, the ground controller told them that the target should be right in front of them. Sure enough, moments later they spotted the dark silhouette of a Junkers 88 below them in a gap in the cloud.

Voase Jeff and Harry Mitchell peeled off towards the gap but Bee decided to dive down to the left of the cloud in order to cut the bomber off. Emerging through cloud, he came in directly behind the Junkers just as two Spitfires were hurtling down from the right. His two fellow Hurricane pilots, he now saw, were well behind. The lead Spitfire attacked with a burst then broke away, leaving Bee 200 yards behind exchanging fire with the German rear-gunner. A few moments later, the rear-gunner stopped firing, a trail of smoke began streaming from the fuselage, and the Junkers arced slowly downwards in a gentle dive. Bee followed it down, crossing back over the coast at just a few hundred feet.

Just as he thought none of the crew would escape, a white parachute opened, Bee nearly flying straight into it. Seconds later, the Junkers hit the ground, sliding across a field, through a hedge, over a road and into another field; then it slewed around, broke its back and finally caught fire. Bee hurtled over the top, throttled back and then circled around it, hoping to see some sign of life. He spotted the man with the parachute prostrate two fields away, but then, circling again, Bee now saw the rest of the crew, one standing up, another sitting, and the third either dead or unconscious. Fascinated by the scene, Bee continued buzzing around overhead, and watched an old Morris trundle towards the burning wreck and several members of the LDV clamber out and round up the crew, all of whom, in fact, had survived. 'We returned to breakfast,' noted Bee, 'with a considerably stimulated appetite.'

It had been a reasonable morning in south-west England, but it was filthy over the Channel. A little after one o'clock, the Me 109s of 8/JG 52 took off from Coquelles airfield for their first operational flight to England. It was drizzling and grey but, despite this, their orders were to climb to 2,000 metres and, with the rest of III/JG 52, join the Stukas of I/St.G 2 over Boulogne at 1.20 p.m., and then escort them to Dover. None of the pilots were happy about their orders. Fully laden with fuel and bombs, a Stuka could manage little more than 160 mph; fully laden, an Me 109 could only just about stay in the air at that horribly low speed. Günther Rall was not alone in strongly believing that the best way to escort Stukas was by securing their air space in a wide arc around them. To carry out the kind of direct support that had been ordered meant sacrificing both speed and manoeuvrability, two of the fighters' key advantages. 'But the bomber crews want to see us,' noted Günther. 'They cannot be convinced that a fighter escort which is not constantly within sight is their best form of life assurance.' There had already been bitter debates about this; the fighter boys had even been accused of being more interested in shooting down Spitfires than ensuring a Stuka crew made it safely back to base. It was hard to understand why the bomber crews could not see the validity of the fighters' arguments, or why the senior commanders kept siding with the bombers.

It was even harder to understand when it ran against tactical instructions given out by Göring himself. At a conference at Carinhall on 21 July, he had been quite specific in insisting fighters operated independently. 'Putting the majority of fighters and Zerstörer close to the bomber formations,' he said, 'will prevent them from being used as effectively as they might. They would be unable to achieve their full fighting capability and would inevitably have high losses.' He could not have been clearer, and yet, somehow, this order had not filtered down the chain.

The third *Gruppe* of JG 52 had reached Coquelles only two days before, touching down with the white cliffs of Dover clearly visible. There were now some nineteen airfields in the Pas de Calais area, and while some were old Great War aerodromes with proper facilities, a number, like Coquelles, were just rough fields. Over the previous weeks, the Luftwaffe had clearly done little preparation here; the rye had been cut by a resentful farmer, and the only building, a hay barn, had been turned into the Operations Room, orderly room and quarters all rolled into one, but that was about it. The three *Staffeln* of III/JG 52 were now to make their home here, their aircraft dispersed at various points around the edge of the field. Nor was their landing ground even flat: the ground rose slightly towards the centre and enough to prevent someone standing on one side seeing the other. This made massed scrambles a nerve-wracking process as pilots were never quite sure whom they might meet as they sped across the field.

Now, after just one orientation flight, it was time to head out over the Channel. As they climbed away from Coquelles, Günther could see the faint shape of Cap Gris Nez through the murk on his right. Already he had a terrible sense of foreboding. The weather and the stupidity of their orders, gave him a feeling of impending doom.

They met up with the Stukas and even at 160 mph they were nearing Dover in no time. Suddenly, without any warning at all, Spitfires of 610 and 54 Squadrons pounced down upon them as the Stukas began bombing Dover and the shipping below. Günther saw Lothar Ehrlich, their *Staffel* commander, turn in towards the enemy, but then as aircraft and bullets filled the sky, it was all he could do to save his own skin. In seconds, his *Schwarm* was separated, each man fighting entirely alone in a confused, twisting mêlée. There was no longer any question of protecting the Stukas; it was hard enough trying to defend themselves.

Somehow, Günther managed to extricate himself and make it back to Coquelles. Climbing down on to the ground, he joined some of the others who were already puffing on cigarettes and gesticulating wildly as they discussed the action. 'The Tommies caught us just as we had feared,' noted Günther, 'like proverbial clay pigeons.' None of them could understand how the Spitfires managed to find their formation in such poor weather and attack from such an advantageous position. Other planes were landing. Two pilots had claimed a Spitfire each, but there were several of their own pilots missing. As the minutes ticked by, hope began to fade. By evening, the 7th Staffel commander, Herbert Fermer, and one of his pilots, Erich Frank, had been declared missing. So too had Wolf-Dietrich von Houwald, the *Gruppe* commander. Both von Houwald and Frank were washed up near Dunkirk a few days later. For Günther's 8th Staffel, there was a massive blow: their CO, Lothar Ehrlich, was also missing. Günther's premonition had been proved right.

Although only twenty-two, Günther was told he would be taking over command of 8th Staffel with immediate effect. Suddenly, he was responsible for the pilots and eighty groundcrew. As he was discovering, promotions could come quickly during times of war.

Dolfo Galland had learned this already. Now a major, he had led his *Gruppe* to Caffiers, just a few miles south of Calais, on 21 July, having had the honour of patrolling over the Kroll Opera House as Hitler had made his Reichstag address. Caffiers was another rough field, with basic facilities. Most of the men were tented, although the pilots were billeted in houses nearby. Their Messerschmitts were dispersed under trees and between hedges around the edge of the field, beneath camouflage nets.

Although the *Geschwader Stab* (headquarters) had still not arrived, Dolfo had declared his third *Gruppe* ready for action on the 24th. It, too, had been sent over the Channel in the murky drizzle, Dolfo leading the *Gruppe*'s three *Staffeln* shortly after III/JG 52, this time, however, escorting eighteen Do 17s. Soon engaged by Spitfires of 54 Squadron, Dolfo had found it hard to shake off the British fighters and seeing the little red light of his fuel gauge light up had decided the only way to get out of the fray was to dive quickly away, the Spitfires seemingly unable to follow, then hurry back low across the sea.

He had not been impressed by his pilots' discipline, however. In the excitement of action, basic lessons had been forgotten; wingmen had not stuck to their leaders, pilots had fired from too far away, and had missed other firing opportunities. They had shot down one Spitfire from 54 Squadron and damaged another, but had lost two men themselves, including the *Gruppe*'s technical officer, a former test pilot, Oberleutnant Werner Bartels. Gathering his pilots together, Dolfo gave them a roasting.

Their performance, he told them, had not been good enough – not good enough at all. They needed to improve and fast, because as Dolfo knew, from now on they would be in the very thick of the action.

The next day, Thursday, 25 July, was fine for a change, warm with light haze in the Channel; the rain of the previous day had gone – which was bad news for the coastal convoy now forming up at Southend. Cloud at least offered them some protection. The large ocean-going vessels might have gone from the Channel, but there were still twenty-one colliers and trampers in CW8 (Channel Westbound 8), and although the smallest ship was just 351 tons, even the SS *Jolly Nights* would feel conspicuously large when enemy bombers began diving down upon them.

Inevitably, the convoy had been sighted before it had even left the Thames estuary, the news soon reaching VIII Fliegerkorps, and then the headquarters of Sturzkampfgeschwader 1. By half-past one French time, the whole of St.G 1 was airborne, including I/Stuka 1 based at Dinard, across the mouth of the harbour from St Malo in Brittany. Commanding the 1st Gruppe was 29-year-old Paul-Werner Hozzel, like Dolfo Galland also newly promoted to major. Stuka 1 had already gained something of a legendary status within the Luftwaffe. It had been the spearhead in Poland, then Norway, and although it had only reached France at the end of June, it was now leading the way with the Luftwaffe's attempt to secure air supremacy across the English Channel. Not only were its crews amongst the most experienced in operating with Ju 87s, but they were also amongst the most decorated – Paul had been one of four pilots from Stuka 1 to win the Knight's Cross back in May.

Despite being born and raised in Hamburg and having a shipbroker for a father, Paul's ambition had always been to join the army. As a concession to his parents he had even completed his shipbroking training when, in 1931, still aged twenty, he had applied and been accepted as an officer candidate in the artillery. He had only just passed his officers' examinations in January 1934 when he and his sixty fellow officer candidates were given the chance to join the clandestine air force. It had been a hard decision for Paul. He felt loyalty to the regiment and he was not sure he wanted to give up being a soldier. On the other hand, the increased pay plus the adventure of flying were highly tempting. In the end, it was the pay, above all, that lured him towards the Luftwaffe; a 75 per cent pay rise was not to be sniffed at.

He soon discovered he had a natural aptitude for flying and having completed his training was posted for fighter training. However, failure to take his theoretical work seriously enough led to him being transferred to reconnaissance instead and from there to Stukageschwader 162, which was training to dive-bomb, albeit with Heinkel 51s and then Henschel 123 biplanes. Not until the end of 1938 was it given the new Ju 87s, purpose-built as dive-bombers. There was no Stuka school at that time, but a Stuka Training Group had been formed in Pomerania, and it was there that I/Stuka 160, to which Paul now belonged as a *Staffel* commander, was sent.

First, however, the two-man crews needed to be formed. Paul chose his back-seater carefully and was still with him nearly two years later – the two trusted each other implicitly – but those not gelling were quickly separated. Having fully familiarized themselves with flying the Ju 87, they began diving training. There were various instruments and gadgets to help, such as a reflector sight, which enabled the pilot to keep the whole plane centred on the target and allowed for wind and velocity. A continuously adjustable red arrow was also mounted on the altimeter, set to local altitude above sea level, which enabled the bomb-releasing altitude to be set. When passing that altitude, a warning horn signal told the pilot to press the bomb-release button on the control column. The bomb release also automatically activated the hydraulic recovery device, which helped the pilot, already struggling from the effects of negative-g, to pull out of the dive.

Normally, bombs would be released at around 700 metres, but Paul reckoned it was possible to go as low as 500 metres – but no less than that. Too many trainee pilots had died through pulling out of a dive too late. Bombing accuracy had also been practised hard. The Ju 87 had been designed specifically for accurate bombing and pilots were expected to be able to hit a ten-metre circle. 'This was not achieved every time,' Paul admits. 'It is one thing dropping bombs in a training time without fear of being shot, and another doing this in war.' And it was quite another, as Oskar Dinort had discovered, hitting a moving ship.

By the time war began, Stuka 160 had been bedded into Sturzkampfgeschwader 1, and all of its crews were highly trained, tactically and operationally. But despite all this training on attacking pinpoint targets, they had not once practised bombing moving vessels out at sea; no-one then had thought that Stukas might be operating over open water.

Paul and the rest of Stuka 1 had gained some experience in this during the Norwegian campaign, however, where they had attacked British ships at Namsos and off the coast. The anti-aircraft fire from these naval vessels had been fearsome, but the pilots simply had to brace themselves and fly through it, hoping for the best. Paul discovered that it often took the efforts of a number of aircraft before a hit was scored. 'Every pilot,' noted Paul, 'was guided by the hits scored by the plane in front of him and had to adjust his point of aim accordingly.' The adrenalin rush – and fear – caused by performing such a potentially lethal operation was intense. Afterwards, as they headed back home, Paul and his men would often sing together over their R/T. It relieved the tension.

Although the Stukas were part of Luftflotte 3, it was Oberst Johannes Fink, commander of KG 2 in Luftflotte 2, who had been given the specially created title of *Kanalkampfführer* ('Channel Battle Leader') and the task of gaining air superiority over the Channel. At forty-five, Fink was one of the older pilots, and a veteran of the last war, too, although he had been an infantryman then, serving on the Western Front. Although not a flippant man, he had gone along with a joke about his new title, 'Chief Sewage Worker', a pun on *Kanal*, which meant drain as well as channel. He recognized the need for humour, and to look after the interests of his men. Devoutly religious, he liked to think of himself as an avuncular figure as well as a bomber commander, using his faith to offer solace to his crews.

Now he was responsible for many more men than those just in KG 2. Under his direct command for operations over the Channel were the Stukas and two *Gruppen* of Me 110 Zerstörers, plus the Me 109s now in the Pas de Calais.

At around 3 p.m., Paul Hozzel's entire first *Gruppe* from Stuka 1, escorted by Dolfo Galland's *Gruppe* from JG 26, began to attack the convoy as it passed through the Straits of Dover. In waves of between eighteen and twenty aircraft, Paul's Stukas peeled off and began their seventy-degree dives, sirens wailing. Over water, Paul found it best to drop bombs as low as possible – from 500 rather than 700 metres. Immediately, the convoy began to scatter, each skipper desperately beginning to weave, the white wakes of their veering vessels clear against the blue-green sea. Several ships were hit, however. One was ripped apart, and capsized before sinking. Others were stopped in the water and riddled with shrapnel. One Stuka was caught as it pulled out from its dive and plunged into the sea. Another ship, one of the smallest, was hit three times.

Meanwhile, both 54 and 64 Squadrons had been sent to protect the convoy from above. Spitfires from 64 Squadron had been vectored to a low height to catch the Stukas as they came out of their dives, while 54 Squadron tackled Dolfo Galland's Me 109s. Dolfo was soon on the tail of a Spitfire flown by Flying Officer Basil Way, twenty-two years old and an experienced pre-war pilot who had won the Groves Memorial Prize as best all-round pilot at RAF Cranwell. He was also 'B' Flight commander and had a number of claims to his name already. It seems likely Dolfo's burst of fire killed him right away. At any rate, his Spitfire turned away in a lazy arc then burst into flames and plummeted into the Channel.

When the Stukas disengaged, the German fighters followed. Incredibly, despite the mass of swirling fighters, Dolfo's men had destroyed only two Spitfires, while the RAF pilots had shot down just one Me 109.

Paul Hozzel's men had done their work for the day, but more Stukas attacked the convoy just after four o'clock. By the time they then turned for home, the losses from the two attacks were mounting. Five ships had been sunk and a further five were so badly damaged, they were now struggling to Dover and would not complete the treacherous journey.

Although the Stukas had finished with CW8 for the day, more dive-bombers were sent to attack two destroyers near Dover later that evening, and this time it was pilots of III/JG 52 who were sent as escorts including Günther Rall and his *Staffel.* Once again, they were forced to fly so slowly it was all they could do to stop their machines stalling. And, once again, there were Spitfires waiting for them, this time from 610 Squadron. By the time they landed back at Coquelles, just after 8 p.m., four more pilots had been lost, including Oberleutnant Keidel; the 7th Staffel had lost its second commander in just over twenty-four hours. The *Gruppe*'s adjutant had also been lost, as had one of Günther Rall's men. All had been good, highly experienced pilots – the more senior men from the *Gruppe* – and yet they were being mauled. Günther was in no doubt as to why. 'As a fighter pilot,' he says, 'it should be up to you to make a plan how best to protect the bombers. It was stupid to escort Stukas at their slow speed. We should have been higher and had the freedom to manoeuvre.'

Despite the losses suffered by the Luftwaffe – nineteen aircraft compared to Fighter Command's nine – the German airmen had certainly wreaked havoc upon British shipping. A destroyer – one of only two now remaining in the 1st Destroyer Flotilla – had been badly damaged by the evening attack. Nor was CW8's ordeal over. At Cherbourg, the 1st S-boat Flotilla had also been tracking the convoy, and with fine weather once more was hoping for a good night's work. The men had had a frustrating few days. Bobby Fimmen in S26 had sunk just one vessel since 5 July, and that only a 350-ton coaster. On several patrols they had spotted nothing; on another mission they had been forced to turn back because of poor weather, and on another had been beaten off by British destroyers. The previous night, S26 and three other S-boats from the 1st Flotilla had headed towards the Isle of Wight. Splitting into pairs as usual, Bobby and S20 had headed to the east of the island, while S19 and S27 sped further west, where they had spotted and sunk a 6,000-ton vessel. Only that morning, having safely returned to Cherbourg, did they learn that more than a thousand French troops being repatriated to France had gone down with the ship.

As Paul Hozzel's Stukas were attacking the convoy, the S-boat crews were getting ready. While Bobby was discussing the operation with Kapitän Bütow and the other commanders, and planning where they might try to find the convoy, the rest of his crew were getting the boat ready, loading torpedoes and ammunition, checking oil and filling the boat with fuel. Two hours before they left, the engines were turned on. 'They have to run perfectly,' says Bobby, 'which means that the mechanics have to check every detail.' It was even more important now; Bütow and his commanders were all getting worried about the strain on their engines caused by almost daily operations since the Norwegian campaign. Despite Bütow's pleas, new engines had not reached them, however.

His concerns proved justified. Bobby's engines had developed a problem – one that could not be rectified in time for the evening's mission. Much to his frustration, the flotilla would have to head out without S26. It was cruel luck, for there were rich pickings to be had that night. Departing at 9.30 p.m., three boats sped off out across the Channel, finding the convoy just south of Brighton. Three more ships were sunk, one was set on fire, and a fifth had to turn for port.

The carnage in the Channel continued. Two more precious destroyers were attacked at Dover two days later. One was badly damaged, the other, HMS *Codrington*, sunk. The barracks at Dover were also hit, and from then on it was accepted that Dover should no longer be used as an advance base for destroyers. In fact, Dover was becoming so pummelled that the Air Ministry issued Fighter Command with instructions to send its fighters out to sea whenever possible to meet raids heading towards the port – a tactic Dowding disapproved of.

That same day, 609 Squadron had been scrambled to intercept another raid heading towards Portland. The pilots were getting fed up with this shipping war. No more men had been lost since Pip Barran and Gordon Mitchell had been killed, but convoy patrols were wearing; and when the Luftwaffe showed up, they always seemed to come out of the sun, with the advantage of both height and numbers. It was the same on this occasion. John Dundas could see the enemy fighter escort high above them, but the squadron was in no position to take them on. Neither he nor David Crook even saw the bombers. In fact, the Stukas were below them, hidden by cloud and attacking the destroyer HMS *Delight*, which had just completed a refit and was heading to Liverpool. She would not be reaching her destination, however, as bombs from fifteen Stukas hit her repeatedly. By the time rescue ships arrived, she was ablaze.

Above and oblivious to this, David and Johnny Curchin were in a vic with James Buchanan leading. Both David and Johnny were scanning the skies, keeping an eye on the 109s some distance away and above. Then David looked behind him and when he turned back saw that 'Buck' Buchanan had disappeared. Back down at Warmwell again, neither David nor Johnny could understand what had happened, although when Buck never showed up, they came to the conclusion that he must have spotted the Stukas down below through a gap in the cloud and gone after them. Perhaps he had had some mechanical failure; whatever the reason, Buck had said nothing over the R/T and nothing was ever seen of him again. For John Dundas, it was a particular blow. 'It's uncommon,' he wrote to Margaret Rawlings that afternoon, 'how my own best friends in the RAF seem to have been lost right and left.'

David Crook and Johnny Curchin took off again and searched for over an hour out to sea, looking for any sign of Buck. They spotted something, but on closer inspection it turned out to be a downed barrage balloon and not a parachute. That evening, the mood in the mess had been grim. Everyone felt depressed and discouraged by Buck's loss. Like Günther Rall and the men in III/JG 52, they all felt these recent losses had been unnecessary and avoidable, and at the same time that they were not achieving very much. And, like Günther, they also believed it was their tactics that were at fault. Both John and David thought it was pointless chasing out to sea after the enemy when they were so outnumbered. David also realized that in an effort to try and hit the Stukas, they were never giving themselves enough height. Getting above the enemy, David now concluded, was the secret to successful air fighting.

Life was still quiet enough in the north of the country but in the south, and south-east especially, the air fighting had become quite intense. 'The excitement grew slowly and progressively,' says Pete Brothers, 'but by the end of July it was definitely getting interesting.' For every pilot in Fighter Command, each day was a long one. Most were up before dawn and ready to fly by first light. In the case of the 32 Squadron pilots, they would then fly to their advance airfield. Pete would regularly fly four sorties a day. On 25 July, during the massacre of the CW8 convoy, he flew six times. Four days later, he managed to shoot down another Me 109. On the last two days of the month he flew five times and then a further four, including six combat patrols. It was a lot of flying under any circumstances, but particularly when pilots were expected to operate from primitive airfields with minimal facilities, where food and beds and other comforts were in short supply.

Dowding was certainly worried. In addition to the combat losses, accidents were also mounting. In fact, they accounted for around a third of all losses that month. He now ordered that pilots should have at least eight hours' rest a day and twenty-four hours' leave a week.

There were no such concessions to the Luftwaffe pilots, who at least had the benefit of being able to choose when and where they flew. At the end of the month, their fighter tactics briefly changed. The fighter aircraft had been subordinated to new formations called *Jagdfliegerführer* – or *Jafü* as the Germans abbreviated them – which were effectively a fighter corps within each *Luftflotte. Jafü* 2, in Luftflotte 2, had been pressing hard to be allowed to carry out 'free hunts' rather than to be shackled to bomber escorts and, in the absence of any more convoys going through the Straits of Dover, had finally been given authority to do so. Dolfo Galland certainly thought this was the right way to use fighters, the idea being to lure British fighters into combat. So too did Günther Rall. And it seemed to work, although largely because Fighter Command was still flying patrols that were therefore already in the air when the Messerschmitts came over. Nonetheless, on 29 July, Günther flew three such free hunts. On the last, his 8th Staffel claimed three Hurricanes for no loss of their own.

Despite this success, however, III/JG 52 was about to become the first fighter unit to be withdrawn from the battle. The losses had been too great. On 1 August, it was posted to Zerbst to rest and refit. 'The high price paid for the experience of our six days on the Channel coast,' noted Günther, 'is not something we could have budgeted for in advance.' That was true enough; the fighting in July had been a warning shot to the Luftwaffe that the RAF was a better organized and more formidable opposition than it had been in France and the Low Countries.

The Luftwaffe had lost over 200 aircraft in July, Fighter Command half that, yet the battle had hardly begun. It soon would, however, for on 1 August Hitler finally gave his order for an all-out attack on Britain. 'The German Air Force,' he announced in his directive, 'is to overpower the English Air Force with all the forces at its command, in the shortest possible time.' This 'intensification' of the air war would begin on or after 5 August.

On 1 August, Dolfo Galland was awarded the Knight's Cross. Feldmarschall Kesselring visited him at Caffiers and presented him with the medal himself. As he did so, two reconnaissance aircraft flew over high above.

'What are those?' Kesselring asked.

'Spitfires, Herr Generalfeldmarschall,' Dolfo replied.

Kesselring laughed. 'The first to congratulate you.'

They may have been laughing that day, but they would soon have little time for such levity. On the shoulders of senior commanders like Kesselring and young fighter leaders like Dolfo Galland lay a huge responsibility: destroying Fighter Command and seizing the skies over Britain.

35

Bombs on Germany, *Bomben auf England*

AT BEAUMONT-LE-ROGER in Normandy, Siegfried Bethke was still flying very little – a few coastal patrols and just a couple of operations against Britain. For the rest of the time, the 1st Gruppe of JG 2 had largely been playing a defensive role, waiting to intercept forays by British reconnaissance planes and bombers. They had had some success too – a Blenheim on both 28 and 29 July, and another on 2 August. Siegfried even saw that one go down. 'That was the first kill I saw from the ground,' he noted.

It was the *Gruppe* adjutant, Oberleutnant Paul Temme, who had attacked the Blenheim. He had been flying in a *Kette*, or wide vic of three, circling over Le Havre, when he had seen the British plane suddenly appear out of the cloud base. It had immediately tried to dodge back into the cloud, but Paul had given chase, wondering whether it wasn't a Ju 88 after all. He soon spotted it again, however, and the Blenheim's gunner opened up, just as Paul opened fire too. Cloud hid it once more and then it emerged again and Paul fired again until, cursing, his cannon jammed. 'But at that moment,' noted Paul, 'the Englishman's right engine burst into flames.' Cloud hid it once again, but then he spiralled out of the sky, on fire. Paul followed it down and watched as it crashed into the centre of Le Havre, exploding and blazing fiercely; none of the three-man crew from 59 Squadron survived. Moments later, the bombs detonated, causing considerable damage.

At Beaumont-le-Roger, Siegfried had also heard that ten Blenheims had attacked Cherbourg and that five had been shot down. In fact, thirteen Blenheim bombers and ten Blenheim fighter escorts had attacked the airfield there, scoring hits on hangars and barrack blocks, with three failing to return. Attacks such as these were a real nuisance, and sometimes more than that. Almost daily, Blenheims were attacking airfields, coastal oil plants, and ports; an effort was also made to attack the *Schnellboote* bases, which had now been identified. It meant the Germans had to defend these targets, with fighter aircraft and flak, which was an annoying drain on resources. In any case, it was the Luftwaffe that was supposed to be doing the attacking, not the RAF. The raids by the Blenheims on the airmen waiting to assault Britain also had an important psychological effect. They helped underline the point that the RAF was a determined and defiant foe. 'The war against England will be more difficult for us than against France,' jotted Siegfried. 'Can't back down! Dedication!'

One of those Blenheim pilots causing so much irritation was Arthur Hughes, who had been passed fit for flying duties once more at the end of June. Immediately requesting a transfer to fighters, he'd been turned down and sent back to 18 Squadron, which was now part of 2 Group Bomber Command. It had been re-designated a medium-bomber squadron since he had been away, but he discovered he had missed little; most of the time the squadron had been rebuilding since being decimated in France. Still, there were a few familiar faces who had seemed genuinely pleased to see him back, and despite the isolation of the airfield – near the north Norfolk coast – he had been pleased to get back into the swing of things.

Poor weather over the Continent had hampered operations in the middle of July, most of which had been directed against Dutch barges and airfields in France. Despite the weather, however, there had still been a steady loss of pilots and crew. Then, at the end of the month, he received a great fillip when he and three others had all been awarded the DFC. 'I shall at least have something to show,' he noted, 'and P/O A Hughes DFC will look much more imposing in the casualty lists!' It was hard not to think of the dangers. Barely a mission went by without one of their Blenheims failing to make it back. There were now heavy flak concentrations over the enemy coast, and around any of the airfields, ports and industrial targets they visited as well the fighters held back to defend them. And they were still operating during daylight hours.

Arthur found his mood swung constantly. One moment he was

feeling daring and excited at the thought of being able to hit back; the next, overcome by the steady erosion of odds. 'The future stretches ahead in a dreary succession of nerve-wracking sorties,' he jotted on 2 August, 'from which there is no release save death or maiming – a future in which all the kindly gentle arts are subordinated to that one mad end: mutual destruction.' Earlier that morning, he had bombed Rotterdam, and within five seconds of dropping his bombs was being hammered at by German flak. On that occasion, however, he made it back unscathed, but any shard of exploding flak could prove lethal. It was a question of luck and odds. And every time one survived, the odds shortened.

It was not just the Blenheims that were making daily forays over German occupied territories. The so-called heavy bombers were also flying over, albeit at night. The RAF had still not really sorted out its bombing strategy; bombing was still a new form of warfare and it took time to work out the best way to conduct operations. What was clear, however, was that the current system was not working. It was the Air Ministry that decided what and where was bombed, while Air Marshal Portal, C-in-C Bomber Command, was left to provide the means, when really Portal should have been left to get on with it without interference. One of Portal's frustrations was that the Air Ministry kept changing its mind. One minute it wanted enemy ports and shipping to be attacked, then it decided it should be industrial targets once more. To its complaints that attacks had been too dispersed and 'patchy', Portal argued that inaccurate bombing was not wasted because of the 'moral effect' it had on Germany. The Air Ministry did not disagree but felt that specific material destruction still had to be the priority. Yet another directive was issued on 24 July, the third that month. 'Recent reports and information,' it ran, 'have confirmed that oil is the weakest link in Germany's war economy, and I am to say that the destruction of Germany's oil resources remains the basis of the main offensive strategy.' It clearly did not yet know about Germany's oil deal with Romania.

The nub of the matter was that a gulf had developed between what the Air Ministry would *like* to achieve, and what Portal and his men in Bomber Command could in *reality* achieve. The Air Ministry wanted accurate, decisive, strategic bombing against specific and legitimate war targets. Portal, however, knew that he had neither the numbers nor the equipment with which to achieve that aim. It was hard enough to find a target in daylight, but it was incredibly difficult, with only primitive navigational aids, to hit a target at night, especially when there was cloud and plenty of flak bursting all around. Photographic and intelligence analysis of the bombers' efforts consistently demonstrated the inaccuracy of their bombing. The solution was to adopt a more *laissez-faire* approach to targets. Of course, they should *aim* to hit specific targets, but if bombs were liberally splayed about, then the effort was not wasted because of the psychological effect it would have on the German people below.

'Getting bombs onto the target was difficult,' says Andrew Jackson, an observer with 115 Squadron. 'We did have bomb sights but they were not controlled by the gyro compass and therefore you relied entirely on the pilot keeping the aircraft straight and steady for the run-up to the bombing.' From Kippen, near Stirling in Scotland, Andrew had joined the Volunteer Reserve in early 1939. He had then been called up on 1 September, and had turned twenty-three two days after war had been declared. He had always been interested in flying, so the RAF was naturally his first choice. He had hoped to become a pilot, but as a trainee surveyor he had been singled out to become an observer, with the combined role of navigator and bomb aimer. During his training, he had managed to drop bombs at an average of 230 yards from the target, and his instructors had seemed really pleased with that. 'But that was at 2,000 feet,' says Andrew, 'and you didn't bomb at that height. You bombed at a minimum of 10,000 feet generally.' And from that height, it was far, far harder to drop them even remotely accurately.

His training had been somewhat deficient in other areas too. By the time he reached RAF Marham in the middle of May, he had only done twenty-three hours' night flying out of 155, and only three hours at his OTU. His first operation, admittedly, had been during the day, over St Valéry in support of 51st Highland Division, but thereafter every mission had been at night. And mostly to targets well inside Germany.

'On the whole,' he says, 'I was a pretty good navigator.' He needed to be, especially since dead reckoning was the main navigational tool. The navigator would plot a course between his airfield and the target and then, having calculated the speed of the aircraft and the effect of the wind, would lay off a course that would get them from base to target in a given time. The effect of wind had to be repeatedly and accurately taken into account and the course adjusted accordingly. Clearly, there were enormous opportunities for a plotted course to go wrong. Visual markers were always given, but these were obviously of no help at all when there was plenty of cloud about. Furthermore, the weather forecasts that the crews were given were often inaccurate. Nor did it help that they flew off on their own. At least when they flew together they could help one another.

The only other means of navigating was for the wireless operator to tune his radio receiver to any enemy or shipping beacons. Crews had been issued with a list of German frequencies so could, theoretically, tune into them and from that get a fix. Larry Donnelly had been promoted from tail-end Charlie to Wireless Operator/Air Gunner and on 24 July had set off for his first raid in his new role with his crew to bomb Hamburg. The weather had been terrible and with absolutely no visual fixes possible and with the weather worsening, Larry switched on the receiver and managed to get a good bearing from the Texel shipping beacon off the Dutch coast. Eventually, they had to abandon the mission, but Larry had managed to find two other German beacons, which had been perfect for making a cross-bearing to pinpoint their position. This he repeated as they droned over the Low Countries and finally headed back over the Channel. Larry was delighted when they landed safely. His radio navigation had proved far more effective than dead reckoning could ever have been.

Yet however inaccurate these night-time bombing missions were, there was no denying the effort. On 27 July, for example, Andrew Jackson and his Wellington crew bombed Hamburg; two days later, it was Mannheim. On 2 August, it was Hamburg again, and this time Andrew saw his bombs explode over the docks and fires raging where other bombers had already struck. Three days later, they hit Kiel, where the battleship *Gneisenau* was in dock. All this bombing – from the combined efforts of Bomber Command – was most definitely having an effect, not least upon the German High Command. Göring was incensed and urged Hitler to allow him to give the British ten bombs back for every one they dropped on Germany. Hitler, however, expressly forbade any such retaliation for the time being. Nonetheless, he referred to British bombing in his Reichstag speech. 'About six weeks ago,' he said of Churchill, 'he began to fight in the sphere in which he seems to think he is particularly strong, namely the air war against the civilian population, though under the pretence that the targets are important for the war effort.'

Goebbels was also quick to emphasize the loss of civilian life caused by British bombing. 'Churchill's answer – cowardly murdering of a defenceless population!' ran a headline in a Berlin paper following the rejection of Hitler's peace offer. Few civilians *were* being killed but air raids were becoming a feature of life in the industrial and Baltic cities of Germany. Ulrich Steinhilper's mother wrote to him towards the end of July telling him of two raids over three nights. She even heard the drone of the aircraft overhead. Yet when the American press claimed that Hamburg had been 'pulverized', he was livid and hastily arranged a press trip to the city, on which William Shirer was one of the journalists. He had to admit he could see little damage, but that was hardly the point. British bombing was annoying the Nazi High Command. More importantly, it was showing the world that it was possible to strike back at Germany. And in the summer of 1940 that was important.

When the Führer had expressly forbidden hitting civilians, he had meant it. Bomber crews were given their quite specific targets and were expected to hit them, not splay bombs all over the place. Admittedly, they had far superior navigation and bomb-aiming instruments compared with those of the RAF, but it was still never an easy task hitting a target from a considerable height, even with *Knickebein* and *X-Gerät*. As Hajo Herrmann points out, 'You had to see and recognize what it was you were trying to bomb.'

Earlier in July, on the 2nd, his 9th Staffel was given the task of bombing the Vickers Armstrong factory at Newcastle upon Tyne, where tanks, guns and other war materiel was made. The works stood right on the banks of the Tyne, close to the city centre, so accurate bombing would be a challenge. Having been fully briefed and having studied aerial photographs, Hajo was left to decide when to carry out the operation. With a waning half-moon and a forecast of cloud cover along the east coast of Britain, he decided to carry out the strike by day rather than at night. They set off from Schiphol in the afternoon, landing at Bad Zwischenahn further north over the border in Germany, where they refuelled; then, climbing high, they headed out over the North Sea in a loose formation and on radio silence, beautiful sunshine beaming down upon them.

As they approached the English coast, Hajo knew they could expect enemy fighters at any moment. Fortunately, just as the meteorological officer had predicted, he saw tall banks of cloud ahead. That was good; if any fighters appeared, they could dive straight for the cover it would offer. The cloud was spread like a carpet over the coast, then rose in layers like giant towers. It made him think of Valhalla, the Hall of the Gods, and he remembered what his father had told him as a boy: that it was to the sky that people went when they died.

Suddenly, from near the top of these towering clouds, two fighters appeared. Hajo saw the rest of his *Staffel* either side of him dive away, but he waited a little longer, then dropped down into the cloud himself. On the altimeter he could see 2,300 metres, then 2,000 metres and then he was clear and ahead was the green patchwork of northern England and Newcastle itself. Having seen enough to orientate himself, he climbed a little way again, into cloud once more, wondering where the fighters now were. Desperately scanning the skies, he heard his wireless operator shout, 'He's coming!' and then Hajo saw him too and dived once more. He emerged through the cloud at 1,800 metres, sweeping just over fat, bulbous barrage balloons. They had been lucky because there was a stiff wind and the balloons had been swept forward. 'The stiff wind,' noted Hajo, 'was laying them flat like a stream does to water weeds.'

The fighters had both gone so Hajo continued onwards, following the Tyne, sweeping left and right as flak began to open up. The really dangerous part of the operation was about to begin. Telling the rest of the *Staffel* to orbit, Hajo thought for a moment, and decided that a diving attack would be madness, because the slowness with which they pulled out of the dive after releasing their bombs would make them far too exposed. But by dropping from a greater height, more calculations needed to be made, not least the wind speed. This was crucial because their bombs would not fall vertically but at an angle, and wind could make a huge difference to this. These calculations took a nerve-wracking few minutes, in which Hajo's Ju 88 was completely exposed in the clear, open sky. Hajo was sweating now; down below, he could see the dark outline of Hadrian's Wall, but he was not interested in sight-seeing – he just wanted to get the job done, then get the hell out of there.

At last his observer was finished and miraculously not a single fighter had spotted them. Having broadcast the bomb settings to the rest of the *Staffel*, he turned to begin his bomb run, which would be along the river, flying east–west. As they reached the start point, he began his stopwatch and rose up into the cloud ceiling. Tensely waiting for the flak to open up, they flew on, the seconds ticking by, and then the cloud thinned and there below was the target, just as it had looked in the photographs he had examined. More barrage balloons, and now flak tracer whizzed past them. 'Come on!' thought Hajo, 'Drop the bloody things!' The observer looked completely calm, his eye glued to the eyepiece. And then at last, bombs away. Hajo hauled the plane into a climbing turn and was soon enveloped in the clouds. Drawing a deep breath he headed south to take one last look, peeping briefly out of the cloud. He could see smoke rising and then there was another bang of flak. Darting back into the cloud, he roared over the port at full throttle and calling out to the rest of the *Staffel* wished them good luck for the journey home.

They all made it back safely, and were writing their reports when a provost arrived and demanded to interview Hajo. According to the Führer Headquarters, word had reached them that German aircraft had just carried out a 'terror raid' on Newcastle and he had been ordered by 9th Fliegerdivision Headquarters to investigate. Scarcely concealing his anger, Hajo told him that he had no idea whether his bombs had hit the target and also explained that he had expressly ordered his men never to hang around after they dropped their bombs. He also pointed out that it took 20.7 seconds for their bombs to reach the ground from a height of 2,000 metres and that with fighters and flak around, that was a long time to loiter over a target in an attempt to see where the bombs landed. Hajo then advised him to report back that when they released their bombs, they did so with the target in their sights. Long-range reconnaissance crews would have to follow it up. 'I was reprimanded,' noted Hajo, 'for having prevented my crews from being questioned, for my disrespectful attitude, and, quite absurdly, because neither I, nor any of my crews, knew what we had hit.'

In fact, they had hit the grounds of the factory, and a little further on at Forth Street, and various warehouses near the King Edward and High Level bridges. They had missed the Vickers works, but not by very much as it happened. One man had been killed and five others wounded. Hajo was ordered to write up the entire episode, then long-range reconnaissance flew over, spotted the damage, and wrote a further report. Hajo then heard nothing more until eventually he received a letter complimenting him on his bombing accuracy, and ordering him to give a number of lectures to various bomber units in Luftflotte 2 on how to deliver a daylight bombing raid using cloud cover. It was signed by Generalfeldmarschall Kesselring.

What this showed was that very accurate bombing was extremely difficult. It also demonstrated that if bombers were really going to make an impact, lots of them were needed with as many bombs as possible. And despite their more sophisticated navigational aids, this applied to the Luftwaffe as well as to Bomber Command.

Massed bombing was what Hitler had in mind for *Adlerangriff* – the 'Eagle Attack' as the air war against Britain was dramatically called,

although there were still to be no bombings of civilians. However, he did add a caveat. 'I reserve to myself,' he wrote in his Directive No. 17, 'the right to decide on terror attacks as measures of reprisal.'

Hopefully, it would not come to that. Hopefully, the RAF would be defeated by heavy and overwhelming attacks on British aircraft, their airfields, ground installations, their supply organizations, and aircraft industry. Once that was done, then the Luftwaffe could turn on the ports and 'stores of provisions in the interior of the country'. The Kriegsmarine was also to intensify operations. That meant the U-boats were to head back out to sea and the *Schnellboote* were to continue their good work.

There is no doubting that in the Luftwaffe Hitler still had a mighty force. There were some 2,500 aircraft that could be brought to bear – a mighty armada indeed. Reports from the fighting so far suggested the RAF had already lost some 400 aircraft, more than half the force they had had at the beginning of July. The odds, then, looked good. The British army was also still in disarray. In Norway and in France and the Low Countries, the German armed forces had proved superior; indeed, British efforts had seemed disorganized, chaotic even. It was even possible to argue that the BEF's escape from Dunkirk had been largely down to luck.

But the Channel was more than a river. No leader, not even the arch risk-taker Adolf Hitler, would undertake an invasion lightly, and thus he viewed Operation SEALION more as a *coup de grâce*, to be put into force only once the RAF had been destroyed and the sea lanes secured. It was unclear, however, how long that might take. A few days? Weeks? Months even? Beyond the middle of September, it would be getting too late; equinoxial tides and poor weather would make a crossing too difficult, although there was a window at the end of September and the beginning of October. That gave him six to eight weeks only. In retrospect, his presumption that Britain would sue for peace had been wrong, yet if, in private moments, he regretted having waited so long for the peace talks that had never come, he never said so. His troubled mind, however, had, during these days of introspection, begun to think ahead.

At the Führer's Berghof conference with his senior commanders on 31 July, he made clear his thoughts. The intention was to bludgeon Britain into submission, with the air assault beginning now. 'Its results,' he said, 'will determine our ultimate relative strength.' He was confident of success and if the British began to crumble, then SEALION would go ahead. On the other hand, he had to consider the possibility that results might not be as hoped, in which case, an invasion would be put on hold.

But Britain had to be taken out of the war. That was key to all future plans, so alternative means of achieving this now had to be considered. Britain was clearly placing her hopes on Russia and the United States, he told them. This was the old paranoia returning: East and West; the fear that Germany would be penned in either side, consumed by the Western powers and the Soviet Union. However, he now argued, if Russia was out of the picture, then America would also be lost for Britain, because elimination of Russia would increase Japan's power in the Far East. This would threaten both British and American interests there. War between Japan and America would distract the United States from Europe.

Hitler had already begun to feel a little twitchy about Russian intentions. The Soviet Union had recently absorbed the Baltic States, as agreed in the Molotov–Ribbentrop Pact, but she had also occupied Bessarabia, an area to the south that bordered Romania. Intelligence also suggested that Russia was alarmed by the speed of Germany's victories. Britain knew this, he claimed, which was one of the reasons she now held so much faith in Soviet intervention. 'With Russia smashed,' Hitler told his assembled commanders, 'Britain's last hope would be shattered.' Germany would then be master of Europe and the Balkans. Therefore, Russia's destruction had to be part of the struggle to defeat Britain, and the sooner the better. Such an attack would only achieve its purpose if the Soviet Union could be 'shattered to its roots with one blow'. He now ordered planning for an attack on the Soviet Union to begin. The provisional date for this assault was May the following year.

Incredibly, Hitler was now dramatically suggesting that Germany turn on Russia far earlier than he had ever envisaged, purely to hasten Britain's exit from the war. General Halder, for one, was not convinced by this argument and believed a decisive blow could also be achieved in the Mediterranean and Middle East along with the Italians. At any rate, either option meant the continuation of war beyond the autumn, and would lead to a war on two fronts, which was precisely what Hitler had always feared; it was why he had gone for the all-out gamble against the West that May. Britain was frustrating his hopes, wrecking his plans. For Germany's sake, the Führer and his commanders had to pray that these new ideas remained plans only, a fall-back and nothing more, and that in the days and weeks to come Britain would be smashed and out of the war for ever.

LIFE

PART IV

BATTLE OVER BRITAIN

AIR-RAID VICTIM

SEPTEMBER 23, 1940 1

YEARLY SUBSCRIPTIO

36

The Wall of England

THE NEWLY PROMOTED Oberstgeneral Heinz Guderian had been having an easy time of it these last six weeks. His Panzer Group had been dissolved, although the staff had stayed on briefly in Paris, from where he had played the tourist, visiting Versailles, Fontainebleau and other sites. Then, at the beginning of August, since he was not involved in any way in invasion plans, he and his staff moved back to Berlin.

Nonetheless, Halder had allocated both Army Groups A and B to the invasion, although the main landings along the south-east were to be conducted by the former. A number of panzer divisions were included in Halder's planned second wave, including Rommel's 7th Panzer. The division had been transferred to the west of Paris and Major Hans von Luck was now living in a comfortable villa on a loop in the Seine, right opposite the American singer Josephine Baker. Along the river – rather than on the coast – they practised loading and unloading converted barges under combat conditions. Hans found it wearisome in the extreme.

What Halder was finding wearisome was the apparent diametrically opposed views of the army and Kriegsmarine over the planning of Operation SEALION. It was ironic that Germany, with the OKW, should have been enlightened enough to create the world's only tri-service high command, yet thanks to the Nazi practice of divide and rule was rarely able to reap its benefits. Thus for SEALION no joint planning team had been organized. Rather, the Kriegsmarine had been left to make its plans and OKH had been told to draw up its own, almost entirely independently of each other. From their headquarters, Halder and von Brauchitsch had decided that the invasion should take place on a broad front. Six divisions from General Ernst Busch's Sixteenth Army would cross from the Pas de Calais and land between Ramsgate and Bexhill-on-Sea, while four divisions from General Adolf Strauss's Ninth Army, embarking from Le Havre, would land between Brighton and the Isle of Wight. Three further divisions from the Sixth Army, departing from the Cherbourg Peninsula, would land between Weymouth and Lyme Regis. Some 90,000 men would be put ashore in the initial attack, increasing to 260,000 by the third day. Airborne troops would play a part at Lyme Bay or in the Portsmouth area. A second wave of panzer and motorized divisions would follow, along with further forces until some forty-one divisions in all were landed. Bridgeheads would be established, then they would thrust forward. After initial heavy fighting, it was reckoned, British resistance would crumble. The whole operation would take about a month.

But Halder had viewed the planning issues in terms of the land operation only, treating the English southern coast as merely the start line of an attack. Trifling issues such as how to get the men there was not the OKH's concern. It had made its plan, and it was up to the navy to get them there. Konteradmiral Fricke, on the other hand, could only see a mountain of difficulties in getting across this troublesome stretch of sea, not for nothing once described as the 'wall of England'. To start with, the scale of the OKH's operation was way out of proportion to the capabilities of the Kriegsmarine, which was just 15 per cent of the size of the Royal Navy. The OKH also wanted to land at dawn, which would mean travelling through the night. But the Kriegsmarine needed a certain amount of light – at least half a moon, rising at around 11 p.m., and clear skies and weather. It also had to have a tide that was just beginning to go out, so that barges could run on to the beaches easily. Combining these requirements meant the invasion would have to take place between 19 and 26 September, a bad time from the point of view of weather prospects.

Another difficulty was obtaining and preparing a sufficient amount of shipping. Fricke reckoned that for six weeks he would need to make use of all domestic harbours and any naval dockyards along the Rhine, and down the whole stretch of the Dutch and Belgian coasts, which would be crammed with barges. 'All repairs and construction of new boats,' he added, 'must be ceased at these docks during this time.' He also reported that the Ministry of Economic Affairs had explained that taking more than 1,000 barges and some 24,000 men from the German shipping industry would have seriously detrimental effects on the German military and civil economies, because it would mean domestic water-borne transport would all but cease. 'This would not only affect domestic shipping,' Fricke added, 'but also international shipping, and would also have an effect on the railways and this in turn will have very noticeable effects on the entire German economy.'

All this Raeder repeated at the Führer Conference on 31 July. He also suggested landing on a much shorter front, a proposal that was rather left up in the air. Yet despite Raeder's catalogue of difficulties and warnings, Hitler did insist full planning went ahead. Afterwards, he also told von Brauchitsch and Halder that they should continue to plan for a broad-front landing. Telling OKH this, whilst at the same time not disagreeing with the Kriegsmarine's narrow-front preference, was typical of Hitler, and thoroughly unhelpful especially when time was so tight. The other problem was that each party was working slightly at cross-purposes. Hitler was certainly serious about the landing in as much as it would be an absolute necessity should the RAF be beaten and Britain be on her knees. There could be no letting the British off the hook, and he foresaw that an invasion would be the only means of securing that, even if Britain did subsequently sue for peace. The army was also assuming air supremacy would have been achieved and that the threat of the Royal Navy could be dealt with by massed air attacks combined with submarine warfare. Certainly, there was confidence amongst the Luftwaffe crews that the Royal Navy's predominantly surface fleets could be destroyed, regardless of their current numerical advantage over the Kriegsmarine. 'I dreamed of bombing the *Rodney* or the *Nelson*,' says Hajo Herrmann, 'battleships that were thirty metres wide, and I think it would have been possible.'

The Kriegsmarine staff, on the other hand, with their inferiority complex with regard to the British navy, were less convinced this could be achieved. After all, the Luftwaffe's intensified air war was to be directed at the Royal Air Force, at the expense of attacks on the British naval and merchant fleets, which disturbed Fricke and his staff greatly, and led them to plan an operation in which the invasion fleet would be coming under heavy attack. They did not see the landings as quite the *coup de grâce* that Hitler did.

At a conference between navy and army staffs on 7 August, irreconcilable differences emerged. The Kriegsmarine was still insisting on a very narrow front from Folkestone to Beachy Head, while OKH was equally insistent that at sixty miles that was too narrow and most likely across the strongest defences. The argument was not solved that day. 'The issue,' noted Halder with evident frustration, 'must therefore be settled [at a] higher level.'

But there was another considerable concern for Konteradmiral Fricke and his team, and that was mines. A channel through enemy mines had to be cleared, whilst at the same time protective minefields big enough to protect German vessels from the British navy needed to be laid either side of this channel. The problem was that as soon as mines were swept, new ones were laid, and as soon as they were laid, the British swept them. Not completely, of course, but the Kriegsmarine would never be able to guarantee a passage free of mines or sufficient protection on its flanks. 'This fact,' wrote Fricke, 'must receive the greatest attention.'

Slipping quietly out of Immingham on the Humber at dusk on 1 August were seven British minelayers, heading for the East Coast Mine Barrier. Amongst them was HMS *Icarus*, armed with twenty-six Mk XVII and XX antenna mines. A deep and extensive minefield had already been laid around most of Britain, although through the Dover Straits and along the east coast the mines were particularly extensive. The idea was that they were far enough out to give any east-coast convoy a protective shield. They were obviously of no use at all against aircraft, and of limited use against highly manoeuvrable S-boats, but against other enemy shipping – not least barges – they posed a serious threat.

Icarus had been repaired and had been back out at sea by the third week in June, and since then had been carrying out a combination of minelaying duties and invasion patrols. One night in early July it had been suddenly ordered to hurry to Dover with all urgency. 'We went hell for leather that night,' says Andrew Begg, who was still one of the ship's engine room artificers, 'and it was a black night.' The rumour going round the ship was that the invasion had started, but when she reached Dover at dawn, there was nothing going on at all, so she headed back to Immingham. 'We never found out what that panic was about,' says Andrew, 'even our skipper never told us.'

Having sailed through gaps in the minefield, the convoy now headed down the eastern side of the barrier until it was off the east coast of

Norfolk. At around 10 a.m. on the 2nd, the minelaying operation began, each vessel heading in a steady straight line and dropping mines off the back of the ship. Each mine plunged to the bottom of the sea, where its weight, or 'sinker', moored it to the seabed and then the mine floated to the top, where in this case it was set to sit at a depth of around twelve feet. Others were set at different heights, and many floated, half submerged, like a buoy. If a vessel hit one of its contact horns, the charge exploded.

The minelaying did not take long. Between them, the minelayers laid some 300 mines along a fifteen-mile stretch, and after a few hours they headed back to Immingham. It was the comparative speed with which mines could be laid that bothered Fricke. He feared that the British would soon catch wind of any major mine-clearing operation, and then they would hastily lay some more.

The Germans had, meanwhile, been laying their own mines, although because of the lack of suitable ships, they were not as proficient at the task as the British. The S-boat flotillas had been roped into these duties, although each boat could only carry between six and eight at a time. The Luftwaffe had also been carrying out minelaying operations. This had largely been left to 9th Fliegerdivision, of which KG 4 was a part. Hajo Herrmann was involved in a number of such missions during the first ten days of August – not creating a protective barrier in the Channel, but trying to block up the mouths of harbours and ports by dropping mines from their bomb bays. Most were 1,000 kg magnetic or acoustic mines. He did not enjoy these missions at all. 'Minelaying and the positioning of the mines,' he says, 'was a very dangerous thing.' At Plymouth, for example, where he laid mines several times, there was only a narrow passage into the port, and underneath was one of the heavier concentrations of anti-aircraft fire. 'We had to go down to only 300 or 200 metres,' he says, 'and we had to pass slowly through this passage at just 180 mph or so. It was a terrible thing to pass through there.'

The Royal Navy did have specifically designed minesweepers, but most were converted trawlers from the Royal Navy Patrol Service, better known as Harry Tate's Navy. This had been formed on the eve of war at Lowestoft on the Suffolk coast with a call to all Royal Navy Reserve to hurriedly report to the holiday camp, Sparrow's Nest. Six trawlers and their crews were the first to arrive and report for duty at this eccentric new headquarters. They then sailed for Dover to be converted into minesweepers. Almost a year on, there were over a thousand drifters, trawlers and whalers in the Patrol Service, skippered by RNR men and crewed by fishermen, tugmen and lightermen. These men were tough, weatherbeaten and hard as nails. They cared little for naval rules and regulations, many of their ships had long ago seen better days, and they took pride in the fact that they were different from the regular navy; they even wore their own specific silver badge. Their preferred name said it all; 'Harry Tate' was slang for being incompetent and amateur. They were nothing of the sort, however. Rather, they were amongst the most resolute and courageous of those helping to protect Britain's seas.

Even so, Joe Steele had been appalled when he had first joined the service. A 23-year-old former dock worker from Liverpool, Joe had joined the RNVR before the war, and had been trained as a signalman. Called up into the navy before war broke out, in October he had been posted first to Sparrow's Nest and from there to North Shields on the north-east coast to join HMT *Dalmatia*, just one of the many trawlers that had been converted into minesweepers. It was a rough old vessel. The fish hold had become the Mess Deck, but that did not stop it from being filthy. There were ashes from the stoves all over the place, and half the food was mouldy. Joe was so aghast at what he'd come to he had actually wept. The skipper was RNR and a former fisherman, while the crew were mostly trawlermen from the Outer Hebrides. He came to like them well enough, but had great difficulty understanding what they were saying. Whenever they were in port, the crew would go out and get horrendously drunk. Soon after Joe's arrival, the mate had to be hauled off for being raving mad with rum. 'There wasn't a semblance of naval discipline,' says Joe.

Despite this, however, Joe had to admit they did a pretty good job minesweeping, often at the head of an east-coast convoy. And things improved. In the spring, Lieutenant Commander John Benson, an RNVR officer, had taken over as captain of *Dalmatia*, and had immediately instilled some much-needed discipline. In June, Benson had moved ships, taking over command of HMT *Darthema*, and with it command of the 29th Minesweeping Flotilla of four ships, including *Dalmatia*, based at Portsmouth. Joe had soon followed him, to his great relief. Although the crew were still mostly fishermen, they were better. The *Darthema* was a faster boat as well. 'With Benson,' he says, 'you had to be good.'

Their duties were sweeping by day and patrolling by night. They swept for moored contact mines by lowering a long loop of wire, kept at the right depth by a weight called a 'kite'. All along the wire, at regular intervals, were cutters. The wire would catch around the antenna, or chain, between the mine and its anchor (or sinker), and drag it until it reached one of the cutters, which would then sever the chain and bring the mine to the surface. This would then be detonated by firing at it with a rifle.

With minesweeping duties over, they would head out on anti-invasion patrols up and down the Channel as far as Eastbourne and back. 'There was an odd feeling of intenseness,' says Joe, 'because we all thought they would invade, and we would be listening out for the sound of motorboats, aircraft, anything at all which we'd all report.'

Now, at the beginning of August, the Patrol Service was also ordered to carry out convoy protection too, and that included *Darthema* and the 29th Minesweeping Flotilla. The mauling of convoy CW8 had shocked the Admiralty, but it was also apparent that morale amongst the crews of the colliers and coasters was plummeting. Something needed to be done and fast.

Improvisation and an ability to galvanize whatever resources were available were features of Britain's defence in the summer of 1940. When the next Channel convoy, CE8, left Falmouth on the afternoon of 5 August, the coasters were accompanied by two destroyers, three anti-submarine trawlers, various minesweeping trawlers and motor boats, and seven ships with barrage balloons tethered to them that had become a hastily devised Channel Mobile Barrage Balloon Flotilla. Specially trained teams of anti-aircraft gunners, called Channel Guards, were also added to the coasters' crews. *Darthema* joined the convoy from Portsmouth, helping lead the way to the Straits of Dover. Overhead, Spitfires and Hurricanes once again patrolled. It was an extraordinary combined effort, underlining just how precious these coastal cargoes and their crews were.

CE8 made it through without a single loss, although the next west-bound convoy was not so fortunate. Passing through the Straits of Dover on the afternoon of the 7th, it was picked up by German 'Freya' radar, and that night attacked by the 1st S-boat Flotilla, albeit without Bobby Fimmen, whose boat, S26, was still being repaired. Using new phosphorous cannon shells given to them from the Luftwaffe, they sank three ships. The Luftwaffe arrived next morning with a series of attacks all along the south coast. No fewer than six squadrons were scrambled to intercept them as the convoy struggled onwards, and despite repeated efforts by the dive-bombers not one more ship was lost. The extra effort had paid off.

Unbeknown to those struggling to keep these convoys going, the Channel Battle was over, however. The Luftwaffe had not managed to sever Britain's coastal lifeline. Despite the debris now being washed up on Britain's mine-strewn southern shores, only 24,000 tons of the 190,000 tons of merchant shipping lost around British waters between July and 8 August had been as a result of air attack. Sixty-seven ships had been lost in all, most of them to enemy mines. And 103 coasters and merchantmen had been successfully convoyed through. British waters were still an extremely dangerous place to be, but the coasters were now in for a comparative respite – from the screaming dive-bombers at any rate, which was no small mercy for the nerves of crews. Göring was now going to send his air forces inland.

All three of his air fleets, Luftflotte 3 in Normandy, Luftflotte 2 in northern France and the Low Countries, and Luftflotte 5 in Norway, were ready for the great air battle against Britain by 5 August. Certainly, his units were all in place by then. On 1 August, Ulrich Steinhilper had flown to Coquelles, which was to be I/JG 52's new base, taking over from the third *Gruppe*. Ulrich had flown over Dunkirk on his way and below him could still see row upon row of abandoned vehicles. 'I wondered how any army could lose so much and still be an army,' he noted. 'Was there really anyone left in Britain to fight?' On the morning of the 5th, the last fighter units also reached the coast. Julius Neumann and II/JG 27 had moved to Crépon in Normandy to join *Jafü* 3 in Luftflotte 3, while Hans-Ekkehard Bob and III/JG 54 moved to Guines just to the south of Calais, to complete the build-up of *Jafü* 2.

Two things were lacking, however. The first, incredibly, was an agreed plan of action. Such had been the expectation that Britain would come grovelling that no tactical plan had been put together. Once hopes had begun to fade, Göring then decided to wait until Hitler had issued his directive and he had learned what the Führer's requirements and also restrictions were. So it was not until 1 August that the Reichsmarschall asked his air fleet and corps commanders to submit their plans. These, when they came in, were all quite different, and so needed to be ironed out into a cohesive and co-ordinated plan.

Göring was now firmly ensconced back at Carinhall, and just as Hitler expected his commanders to make the trip to the Berghof, so the Reichsmarschall required his to trek back and forth between their front-line headquarters and his country pile north of Berlin. Several conferences had been held there over the ensuing days, as well as a co-ordinated map exercise, until by 6 August it seemed everything was at last agreed.

As Göring had breakfasted that morning, listening to jaunty opera excerpts by Daniel Auber, he believed he had every reason to feel optimistic. It was true that he had continued to hope Britain might yet be brought to the peace table, and behind Hitler's back had sent out further peace feelers through a Dutch businessman, Albert Plesman. These had come to nothing, dead-batted by London as had been all other appeals. So, an air assault it would have to be, and yet all the signs were that the Luftwaffe would be as successful in this as in all its other campaigns. Oberst Beppo Schmid had reassured him about the state of Fighter Command, having put the figure of British aircraft destroyed at more than 350 since the beginning of July. He believed there were only around 500 British fighters left. Schmid was equally reassuring about the state of British aircraft production, reporting that between 1 and 25 July just 240 aircraft of all types had been produced, of which a mere 133 were Spitfires, Hurricanes and Defiants. This meant, he told Göring, that his boys were already shooting them down faster than they were being built.

Milch, Jeschonnek, Udet, Kesselring *et al.* arrived later that morning, by which time Göring was fresh and changed into his new duck-egg blue uniform. The opening day of the *Adlerangriff* – the 'Eagle Attack' – would be called *Adlertag* – 'Eagle Day'. The July fighting had shown that the RAF had an organized defence system, but the Luftwaffe was still not quite sure precisely what it was or how it worked. Part of the battle plan, however, was to destroy the '*DeTe* devices' – the large numbers of pylons along the coast – as quickly as possible. Göring now even suggested that Stumpff send one of his Luftflotte 5 bombers over as a nuisance raider to destroy the VHF net protecting Scotland and the north of England.

'Everything depends on using all possible means to defeat the enemy's air force,' Göring told them. A tactical plan to support SEALION would come later. 'To achieve this,' he continued, 'our first aim is to destroy his fighters. If they avoid combat in the air, we shall attack them on the ground or force them to accept a fight by using bombers to attack targets within the range of our fighters. Moreover, we must constantly intensify the battle against enemy bomber units by attacking their ground support. When the enemy air force has been defeated,' he concluded, 'the Luftwaffe will continue its attacks on vital targets to be specified then.'

This was a perfectly sensible plan, drawn up and co-ordinated largely by Milch. Göring had serviceable and ready 2,422 aircraft with which to fulfil his aim, of which 949 were bombers, 336 dive-bombers, 869 Me 109s, and 268 Me 110 Zerstörers. Destruction of the RAF would take three days, but to be on the safe side Göring wanted four clear days of weather. The timing of the attack, then, was the only remaining sticking point. The next few days were not looking good, but from 10 August a ridge of high pressure from the Azores promised to give them the window they needed.

With everything now agreed and ready for the off, the Reichsmarschall led his commanders to see his latest toy: a vast model train set, complete with miniature farms, houses, stations and six-foot-high papier-mâché mountains. Beaming happily, Göring pressed a button and a flight of bombers running on wires whirred smoothly overhead.

The contrast between the Reichsmarschall and Air Chief Marshal 'Stuffy' Dowding could not have been greater. When Colonel Raymond Lee visited Bentley Priory the next day, Wednesday, 7 August, he found the C-in-C Fighter Command a tall, saturnine man who spoke clearly and calmly. 'He is the man,' noted Lee, 'who directs the force which, more than anything else today, stands between Britain and invasion.' Dowding took him down below to the underground Filter and Operations Rooms. Lee was struck by the quiet. Only a soft murmur could be heard as messages came and went over headsets, or plotters moved markers from point to point across the giant map table. Dowding carefully explained what was going on and how the system worked. Lee was deeply impressed. 'I had no idea,' he jotted, 'the British could evolve and operate so intricate, so scientific and rapid an organization, the tentacles of which reach out beyond the edges of the country.'

What neither Schmid nor the Luftwaffe command knew was that Dowding had been prudent with his squadrons during July, keeping plenty in reserve in the north. The pilots of 609 Squadron had been getting frustrated at being ordered up in small numbers, but both Park and the C-in-C had quite deliberately kept as many aircraft from operating over the open sea as possible, both well aware that they were probably being deliberately drawn out by the Luftwaffe. Fighter Command had more than 700 fighters, a marked improvement since the beginning of July. No fewer than 496 new fighters had also been built by Beaverbrook's workforces since then. By 8 August Dowding had fifty-eight squadrons with six more working up, including one Canadian squadron, two Polish and one Czech.

Of course he was apprehensive about the fighting to come. Although Fighter Command had acquitted itself well so far, it was obvious the Luftwaffe had yet to attack in full strength. Chief of his worries was the number of pilots. Sixty-four squadrons at their full establishment of twenty pilots meant 1,280 pilots. Dowding had 1,434 on 8 August, only a small excess, and there were nothing like enough coming through. Moreover, he would have to send some of those new pilots to squadrons in 11 Group, where the heaviest fighting would be taking place. There would be almost no time for them to acclimatize, to learn essential tricks and skills before being thrown against some of the best men the Luftwaffe had. It would, as he was well aware, be like throwing them to the lions.

There were other concerns too, chief of which was the lack of suitable night-fighters. It was one thing vectoring aircraft towards a target in daylight, but quite another doing it at night, when a pilot could not rely on eyesight to help. What was needed was airborne radar, but this was not available. A number of squadrons had been practising night-fighting. The two flights of 87 Squadron, for example, had been sent off in turn for a week's course, while 609 Squadron, amongst others, had sent its pilots up for night patrols. So too had 'A' Flight from 92 Squadron, which was posted to Bibury in the Cotswolds, much to the pilots' disgust, for night-fighter ops against raiders attacking Bristol, Swansea and Cardiff. Tony Bartley and the other members of the flight were really put out about it. 'This was the last straw,' noted Tony, 'when every day we heard on the news what our old friends in 11 Group were doing in the front line.' Night-flying in a Spitfire was not easy, not least because the flames from the exhaust stubs when the aircraft started were blindingly bright. Bibury was hardly ideal either – a small grass strip in which the only landing lights were paraffin flares and one Chance light. There were a number of accidents and mishaps. Norman Hargreaves got lost and had to bail out; Ronnie Fokes overshot into a brick wall; Geoff 'Boy' Wellum hit a wing on the Chance light, and Tich Havercroft ended up on his back in the middle of the flare path. Later, he was hit by a Ju 88's rear-gunner. They did not get a single enemy aircraft on night ops.

Of the 107 pilots killed between 10 July and 11 August, eighteen died in accidents, and mostly at night. Twin-engine aircraft were better for the task, because the engines were to the side, where their glare was not in the pilot's eyes. The Beaufighter, developed from the Blenheim, was the best prospect to take on night-fighting duties, but although it was coming into service, Fighter Command had not received sufficient numbers yet. So long as the Luftwaffe continued to concentrate its efforts during the day, this was not as much of a problem. But Dowding liked to be prepared, and on that score he was not.

Following the heavy attacks on the convoy on 8 August, the anticipated poor weather meant there was little activity over the next couple of days. There was a lot of cloud and rain about, while on 10 August it was squally and thundery. The next day, there was plenty of cloud in the afternoon, but during the morning it was bright and clear and soon heavy attacks developed.

The Luftwaffe's plan was to draw fighters out over the Dover area with harassing raids, and then deliver the main punch at Portland. This latter operation was a major task for Luftflotte 3. Many of the fighters of *Jafü* 3 were to be involved, some drawing out the British fighters, others escorting a comparatively small bomber force. Since it was a reasonable distance, co-ordination of these fighters into their formations needed to be quick and slickly carried out. It would be a good test – a kind of dress rehearsal, albeit for real.

Siegfried Bethke, now commanding the 2nd Staffel of JG 2, had attended a briefing the day before, when the pilots had been told that *Adlertag* would begin any day, just as soon as the weather was set fair. Siegfried was quite struck by the magnitude of what was about to unfold. They were about to take part in the biggest air battle the world had ever known, and his stomach had churned at the thought in a way it had not done before the Battle for France. He felt a bit unsure of himself too, wondering whether he had quite the right attitude. As a *Staffel* commander, he knew he should set an example, and yet the only thing that was giving him comfort was the thought of being part of such a large mass of fighters when they headed across the Channel. But the Channel worried him too. It was one thing flying over the narrow Straits of Dover, but quite another crossing all the way from Normandy. If any of them went down, he knew their chances of survival would be slim.

Now, at a little before 11 a.m., French time, he was taking off from Cherbourg, where the *Gruppe* had flown to earlier, and heading out over the Channel.

The growing plot over the Cherbourg peninsula had been picked up by radar early, giving the controllers at 10 and 11 Group Headquarters plenty of time to alert their squadrons. With no convoy currently in the Channel, it was also clear that the raiders must be heading for a coastal target, and as the plot developed it seemed likely that Portland was the target.

Already at Warmwell was 609 Squadron, which had been hastily scrambled and told to patrol over Weymouth Bay at angels 24. By ten, only five minutes after Siegfried Bethke had taken off, 609, along with 1 and 145 Squadrons, was already airborne. Within the next quarter of an hour, aircraft from five further squadrons were also scrambled, including 87 Squadron from Exeter.

As they headed out over the Dorset coast, 609 Squadron's pilots saw the armada heading across the Channel. John Dundas was astonished. 'More Huns than I ever imagined I'd see together in one piece,' he noted. In fact, there were around a hundred Me 109s and Zerstörers. Squadron Leader Darley took his squadron up to around 25,000 feet, then, with the sun behind them, and with a thousand feet of height to their credit, he gave the order to attack. 'We came down right on top of the enemy formation,' noted David Crook, 'going at terrific speed, and as we approached them we split up slightly, each pilot selecting his own target.' He now saw an Me 110 Zerstörer ahead, cutting across him. Opening fire, David realized he had not allowed enough deflection, but closing up he opened fire again, this time at almost point-blank range. Smoke burst from the German's port engine, then he turned to the right and stalled. David was so close, he only narrowly avoided hitting the Zerstörer's port wing, ducking instinctively as it flashed past him.

Below he could see Hurricanes also attacking, while above were many more enemy fighters. Unable to find another target in a good position to attack, and thinking it was a rather unhealthy spot to find himself in, he dived down out of the fray, and headed back to Warmwell. John Dundas, meanwhile, managed to hit another Me 110, but was then peppered himself. The squadron landed back in ones and twos, having left the fight in full swing as more squadrons arrived on the scene. To everyone's amazement, however, all the pilots made it back, even John, whose Spitfire was trailing white smoke from his glycol coolant and had an engine on the point of seizure.

Yet while this mass of German fighter aircraft engaged one squadron after another, the bombers, escorted by I/JG 2 amongst others, pressed on towards Portland. The bombers were immediately pounced on by Hurricanes of 213 Squadron. Above, Siegfried Bethke and his 2nd Staffel now dived in turn on Hurricanes of 87 Squadron as they arrived on the scene. Siegfried had seen them as he and his *Staffel* had been flying at around 4,000 metres. 'They were flying in pretty tight formation,' he jotted, 'almost peacefully.' Coming up behind without being spotted, he opened fire. 'It broke into pieces after the first shot,' noted Siegfried. 'I had to pull away hard to avoid hitting it.' This was Voase Jeff, Bee Beamont's flight commander, an ace and veteran of France. He had been due to be married in ten days' time. The Hurricanes now took evasive action and the Messerschmitts 'burst', breaking into their two-man *Rotten*. Siegfried, almost by chance, found himself behind another Hurricane, this time the Australian, Johnny Cock. A cannon shell hit the Hurricane and it caught fire. 'As I was turning away,' added Siegfried, 'I'm quite sure I saw the pilot bailing out with his parachute.' He was right; Johnny was later fished out of the sea, minus his trousers, which he had discarded to make it easier to swim, much to the great amusement of the rest of the squadron.

Siegfried had now had enough. One of his pilots had already gone down into the sea, another was hit and struggling back across the Channel. Feeling rather tense and nervy, he decided to head back home. Little damage had been caused at Portland, although smoke was now billowing into the sky. 'We had about eighty kills,' noted Siegfried later once they were back on dry land. It was, of course, a massive over-estimation; in fact, the RAF had lost twenty-eight aircraft during the entire day's fighting. That was still no small number – almost one and a half squadrons. Fighter Command, for its part, shot down thirty-eight German planes. This, however, had been just the prelude. Eagle Day was now almost upon them.

37

Adlertag

When Ulrich Steinhilper touched down at Coquelles for the first time, he soon discovered the groundcrew had been quick to plunder the large stocks of equipment abandoned by the British ten weeks earlier. They used British bell-tents, considered much better than German equivalents, which were erected in an orchard at one end of the airfield. Inside each tent, a hole around a metre deep had been dug and lined and, Ulrich thought, made for quite a comfortable billet. There were British Nissen huts too. 'Calais and Dunkirk were rather like vast military supermarkets,' noted Ulrich. 'Virtually anything you wanted could be found in or around the harbours or on the beaches.' Among other things, they had appropriated a Morris triple-axled truck and a large van which they converted into a mobile tool and parts store, and also discovered a plentiful number of barrels of wine floating in the harbour at Calais, which gave them an almost unending supply. Having hitched up the local electricity supply, they found their new home was reasonably comfortable, if a little primitive. They even had a record player.

Up the road at nearby Guines-South, Hans-Ekkehard Bob was also settling into his new surroundings. Like most fighter airfields in the Pas de Calais, Guines was another field, its crop only recently harvested. It was pretty rudimentary. The aircraft were penned in the woods at the edge of the field. Like Coquelles, there were bell-tents, a kitchen and Nissen huts, where the groundcrew lived, set up in the woods, and a large tent in which aircraft were repaired. 'The technicians' tent was really big,' says Hans, 'big enough to fit an aircraft in.'

Hans, along with the other pilots, found digs in the village. He also brought with him his dog, a fox terrier called Chica. She would always fly with him whenever they moved airfields, stowing away in the luggage hold behind his seat. 'She was a passionate flier,' he says. 'She always cried when she wasn't allowed to come with me.'

On 12 August, the *Gruppe* was in action, escorting bombers first to Dover, then Manston, Hans claiming a Spitfire. Ulrich Steinhilper had also flown his first missions over England. On 11 August, he had flown four in one day, and had helped shoot down a Blenheim over the Channel, something that prompted mixed feelings of elation and guilt at having caused the deaths of other human beings. On the other hand, the Blenheim had looked as though it was about to attack a Heinkel 59 seaplane that was searching for downed airmen. Ulrich was not alone in thinking that British attacks on these unarmed rescue planes were nothing short of murder. However, Dowding had made it clear via an official communiqué that he did not consider that military aircraft rescuing downed airmen could legitimately be marked with a red cross. 'They were engaged in rescuing combatants and taking them back to fight again,' he wrote, 'and they were also in a position, if granted immunity, to make valuable reconnaissance reports.' Pilots were often inured to the gory and violent realities of war; most will say they were always attacking the machine not the pilot. Disgust at shooting at rescue planes is therefore perhaps understandable. At the same time, notions of chivalry were somewhat misplaced. This was war: hard and brutal. Britain could not afford to observe noble niceties when she was fighting for her life. Ulrich, Hans, Siegfried Bethke and others may have been fundamentally decent, upstanding young men, but Hitler, Göring and the Nazi elite were not.

Ulrich flew several times again the following day, 12 August. The fighters were helping with the final prelude to *Adlertag*, trying to draw out the British fighters and providing cover for a series of attacks on '*DeTe* devices', those tall latticed masts which stood defiantly all along the coast on the other side of the Channel. As General Martini had realized, so long as these peculiar-looking masts were still operating, the Luftwaffe would never achieve any surprise.

Leading the attacks on the RDF Chain was Hauptmann Walter Rubensdörffer, commander of Erprobungsgruppe ('Experimental Group') 210. Swiss by birth, the thirty-year-old Walter was a Spanish veteran and former Stuka pilot. However, he was also something of a pioneer and had spent several weeks at the Luftwaffe experimental centre at Rechlin on the Baltic, trialling the Me 110 Zerstörer and Me 109 as precision bombers. Out of these trials, Erpro 210 had been formed, a force of twenty-eight hand-picked, highly skilled pilots. Brought into Luftflotte 2, their results during the *Kanalkampf* had been encouraging. Having been a sceptic, Kesselring had come to regard Erpro 210 as one of his most elite units.

Around 8 a.m., Walter was leading his three *Staffeln* over the Channel, the British coastline looming towards them. 'Calling 3 Staffel,' he said over the R/T, 'proceed on special mission. Good hunting. Over.' Oberleutnant Otto Hintze acknowledged and with his eight bomb-laden Me 109s headed straight towards the white cliffs of Dover, while Walter peeled off to port with the Zerstörers of 1st and 2nd Staffeln. They now separated themselves, each *Staffel* to attack different RDF stations at Rye, Pevensey and Dunkirk in Kent. Carrying two 1,000 lb bombs, each plane could pack a considerable punch as those manning the RDF stations now discovered. Flying in low one after the other, each aircraft waited until the targets filled their reflector sights, then dropped their bombs, before flying off again back over the Channel, dust smoke and debris left in their wake.

Back at Calais-Marck, Walter had good reason to be pleased. His men had reported scoring a number of hits. A number of Ju 88s also later attacked the RDF station at Ventnor on the Isle of Wight. Already, Pevensey was reportedly silent, bombs having sliced through the main electricity cable. At Dover, Oberleutnant Hintze had seen the towers clearly swaying and a number of buildings destroyed. Buildings had been destroyed at Rye and Dunkirk too.

Although some fifteen Ju 88s had peeled off to attack the RDF station at Ventnor, the main target of the sixty-three bombers from KG 51 and KG 54 was the naval dockyards at Portsmouth. In port after returning from another four-day mine-sweep and invasion watch was the converted trawler *Darthema*. Joe Steele had come ashore that morning to collect the ship's mail and had met up with a sailor from HMS *York*. The two were chatting when suddenly they heard the low rumble of aircraft and the sirens begin to wail. The bombers were upon them so quickly they had no time to head for a shelter, so instead they dived behind some sandbags outside the NAAFI shop, from where they had a grandstand view. The bombers arrived in waves, as each *Staffel* flew over and dropped their loads. Joe was amazed to see the railway tracks around the harbour twisting and contorting as they were wrenched into the air. 'It was the most tremendous sight,' says Joe. 'I'd never seen anything like it.' Then he saw the chimney on the cookhouse literally disintegrate. It was too much for his friend, who decided to make a dash for it, but Joe stayed put, reckoning he was safer where he was.

Two hundred yards away was HMS *Victory*, a ship which had not been surrounded by so much smoke and dust since the Battle of Trafalgar almost 135 years before. Directly in front of Joe was a destroyer, whose guns were now pumping away, as were other ack-ack guns. He watched an airman floating down in his parachute and men from the destroyer were firing at him. 'I heard the skipper shouting at them to stop,' says Joe, 'but there were still more shots.'

In just a few minutes, it was all over. The harbour was heavy with smoke, dust and the stench of cordite. The harbour railway station had been hit, the pier destroyed, a pontoon dock badly holed and fires were raging in several buildings, but miraculously, no ship had been hit. Joe wandered around, looking in wonder at the damage, and saw a dead German airman. Whether it was the same man he had seen coming down or not, he wasn't sure, but the man was riddled with bullets. 'It was sad,' he says, 'very sad. There was no need to shoot him like that.'

That afternoon, more bombers were sent over to attack airfields. Lympne was heavily attacked twice, and then, early in the afternoon, so too was Manston, Walter Rubensdörffer's Erpro 210 in action once again. Pitted with craters, the grass airfield was put out of action for the rest of the day. Workshops were also destroyed and two hangars damaged, although only one person was killed. Hawkinge, further to the south on the Kent coast, was also badly hit, with two hangars destroyed, but although equally riddled with craters, the airfield remained just about usable. Dowding had pressed hard for more concrete runways for Fighter Command, but there was one huge advantage in sticking with grass: with plenty of work teams, craters could be both easily and quickly refilled, not least because Dowding had also arranged for each airfield to have plenty of supplies of hard-core and rubble for just such a purpose before the war.

Despite their early confidence, by mid-afternoon General Martini was picking up pulses from nearly all the British listening posts once more. In fact, the transmitting and receiving blocks at Rye had been undamaged, Pevensey was up and running again within a few hours, no major damage had been caused at Dunkirk or Dover, and while Ventnor was badly hit and completely out of action, impulses were sent out from a mobile transmitter instead, not least to make the Germans believe it had been repaired. But while Martini had accepted that the British *DeTe* devices would be harder to destroy than had originally been expected, reconnaissance photographs suggested considerable damage had been caused. Neither Lympne, Manston nor Hawkinge, for example, were expected to cause the Luftwaffe too much trouble any more. Yet again, German intelligence was to prove woefully mistaken.

And so Tuesday, 13 August – *Adlertag* – finally dawned. Oberst Johannes Fink had been up early and had breakfasted well – as had all his pilots and crew. It was something he insisted upon before a morning mission, and now, at 7.30 a.m., his bomb-laden Do17s of KG 2 were climbing high up over northern France towards Cap Gris Nez ready to rendezvous with the fighter escort.

Yet there was no sign of the escort and ahead he saw a bank of cloud rolling over the Channel which most definitely had not been predicted by the met men. Already feeling puzzled, he quickly became irritated as a few Zerstörers passed in front of his nose in a series of short dives, rather than heading towards England. Then, his temper rising, he watched them dive away completely. Johannes could not make head or tail of it, but decided to press on anyway, with or without the fighter escort; at least the unexpected cloud would offer them some cover.

As they droned on, they fleetingly caught a glimpse of Margate before flying over yet more cloud. They were now approaching Eastchurch, their target, so Johannes ordered the formation to loosen out as they prepared to descend. As a former Luftwaffe Chief Accident Investigator, he was always mindful of safety precautions, and was concerned that none of the bombers should get too close to one another as they passed through the cloud. Suddenly, the sky cleared once more and down below, and just a few miles ahead, was Eastchurch. Yet just as Johannes's men were preparing to drop their bombs, Spitfires from 74 Squadron dived down out of the gleaming early morning sun on to the rear *Staffel* of Dorniers, shooting down one and damaging most others.

While the rear of the bomber formation was being attacked by the British fighters, the rest of the formation forged on, pasting Eastchurch with bombs. Climbing and banking, Johannes then led his formation back out over the Thames estuary, but now came under attack again, this time from 111 Squadron's Hurricanes. In a brief flurry of machine-gun chatter and darting tracer, four Dorniers were plunging to the ground and a further four limping back, smoking and riddled with bullet holes.

When Johannes finally touched down again at St Léger, near Cambrai, he was almost speechless with fury. Up until now, his *Kampfgeschwader* had suffered the least number of casualties in the western offensive, a statistic he was justly proud of, yet on one brief mission he had lost five aircraft and crew, with more badly damaged and wounded, and all because the fighter escort had not managed to join them. It was criminal negligence.

Hurrying to the crew room, he demanded to be put through to the 'Holy Mountain', Kesselring's bunker HQ at Cap Blanc Nez, just to the south of Calais.

'Where the hell were those fighters, then?' he asked angrily, as he heard the field marshal come on the line.

Calmly, Kesselring tried to explain. The weather had changed overnight; the high pressure from the Azores had dispersed. News of this sudden development had been sent to Göring's headquarters and on that basis the attacks had been postponed until 2 p.m. The decision had filtered back in time to stop the fighters but not the first bombers due to go into action, Johannes's KG 2. The Zerstörers he had seen had been trying in vain to warn him. Crazy though it may seem, the only way of getting through to the bombers once airborne had been to fly manically in front of them – and even then it did not work. How the Luftwaffe would have benefited from some form of ground control that morning.

It was not a great start to Eagle Day, but in fact it was going even worse than anyone realized. Once again, faulty intelligence was to blame. Despite the losses, KG 2 claimed ten Spitfires destroyed on the ground at Eastchurch, when in fact the aircraft they hit were Blenheims of Coastal Command; Eastchurch was not, and never had been, a Fighter Command airfield. Twelve people had been killed and forty injured in the attack, but despite the damage and bomb craters the airfield was fully operational again ten hours later. At Göring's headquarters, however, Oberst Beppo Schmid had already crossed it off his list as another airfield they no longer need concern themselves with. Schmid and his team had pored over aerial photographs in exacting detail yet, despite Martini's listening service and the large number of aerial reconnaissance missions that had been flown, the picture of where and how Britain's fighters were disposed remained sketchy, to say the least.

*

The unexpected cloud had not prevented Siegfried Bethke from leading his second *Staffel* over the Channel on a free hunt early that morning, joined by the *Gruppe* adjutant, Oberleutnant Paul Temme. 'Hurricanes near Brighton,' Siegfried noted later. 'Oblt. Temme stayed there. Shot down?' Paul had in fact been shot down, just as they were turning for home. Struck from behind, bullets had hit his engine and radiator cooling system. With his oil pressure rising, he had crash-landed, wheels up, in a cornfield within sight of the hangars at Shoreham airfield.

Still in one piece, Paul released his harness and clambered out, only to see a number of gunners from an ack-ack position guarding the airfield running towards him, rifles in hand. Feeling a sudden inexplicable need to urinate, he peed against the fuselage of his Messerschmitt, which seemed to have a calming effect on his pursuers. Instead of rough handling him, the gunners led him gently to the station commander at the airfield, who greeted him in perfect German, 'Oh, ein sehr früher Gast' ('a very early guest'), and then asked Paul whether he was ready for some breakfast.

Although Paul had not, in fact, eaten anything that morning, he politely declined the offer feeling it would not be right to eat from the enemy's table. However, when a steward arrived with ham, eggs, toast and tea, and the station commander insisted he tuck in, Paul had a change of heart. After all, he was feeling quite hungry. The CO at Shoreham was not really sure what he was supposed to do with captured German airmen, so their having finished breakfast, he sent for his car and had Paul taken to the Royal Artillery in nearby Brighton. Taken to the mess, he found the gunners there were busy eating breakfast and reading papers, and in no mood to be hurried. Intrigued by their unexpected guest, they invited him to join them. Settling down to his second plate of bacon and eggs, Paul admitted that he had no idea there was such protocol between services.

That was as may be, but the gunners didn't much want him either so passed him back to the RAF, this time at Farnborough, nearly fifty miles away. There he was briefly interrogated by an army officer before being handed back to the RAF. 'Take no notice of him,' the RAF officer reassured him, 'he isn't a pilot. And now, what about some breakfast?' At this rate, a surfeit of bacon and toast was beginning to seem more life-threatening than being shot down by Hurricanes.

*

The cloud did begin to clear as the day wore on. Shortly after midday, twenty-three long-range Zerstörers from Caen arrived over the Dorset coast. Although Dowding had ordered that his squadrons should not engage enemy fighters unless they had to, this plot was picked up as a bomber formation and so three squadrons were scrambled to meet it, just as the Germans hoped. The idea was that the Zerstörers would keep them busy for a while then, once the British fighters had headed back to their bases, the bombers would arrive as they were on the ground refuelling and rearming. It was a good plan in theory but depended on pinpoint execution. However, that kind of co-ordination was not really happening for the Luftwaffe that day, and unfortunately for the Me 110s sent as bait they reached England only to find the three Hurricane squadrons already high above and waiting.

Zerstörers had serious firepower, but lacking manoeuvrability could now only form a defensive circle, flying round and round, toe-to-tail, protecting each other's backs. Even so, this could not save them from diving attacks at speed and by the time the battered Me 110s broke off and made for home, one had plummeted to the ground and six into the sea, and a further seven had been damaged to varying degrees of seriousness. Thus of the twenty-three that had set off, just nine made it back unscathed. That was not good at all.

In any case, the bombers did not arrive back until later that afternoon, by which time the fighters were fully ready and waiting again. However, whether there were enough fighters to take on the numbers of German raiders was another matter. At Fighter Command Headquarters, more and more plots were being reported: twenty plus, fifty plus, thirty plus and another thirty plus, all heading towards Portsmouth and Portland. Similar-sized plots were developing across the Straits of Dover, too.

Amongst those now surging towards the southern English coast were two *Gruppen* of Stukas headed for Middle Wallop. Major Paul Hozzel had taken off from Dinard with his first *Gruppe* from Stuka 1, leading them out towards Guernsey, over which they had met their fighter escort. The day before, Paul had flown over to Guernsey to meet with Major Günther Freiherr von Maltzahn, the commander of II/JG 53, whose pilots were to escort them over England and were now stationed on the island. Despite Göring's very specific orders to the contrary, the fighters were still expected to stick like glue to the Stukas, although Paul was fully aware of the fighters' dislike of close escort. 'In our talk von Maltzahn made no bones about this,' he noted, 'though he promised to do his best for us and not to leave us alone.'

It was not helping the Luftwaffe to find itself in the middle of a tactical rift at this moment, and it should have been emphatically resolved without delay, and in the fighters' favour as Göring had instructed. But it was one thing making such a pronouncement from the far-off confines of Carinhall and quite another getting such a tactical order down the long chain of command to those actually operating on the front line, even if the originator was a six-star general.

Now, above the Channel, the weather was clear, but as the German aircraft neared England, a closed layer of cloud seemed to extend all the way across the country. Since the pilots could not guess the height at which the cloud layer began, Paul realized they had little choice but to press on and then dive blind through the cloud and hope they would emerge over the target. But, as he was well aware, the chances of that happening were slim indeed.

Listening to Paul Hozzel through his R/T was David Crook. The squadron was one of four that had been ordered into the air to meet the advancing raid, and now, just after four o'clock, the voice, which had been faint at first, was quite distinct. By chance the German raid was using an almost identical radio wavelength as 609 Squadron.

Suddenly, David saw them – dive-bombers, then Me 110s and finally, on top, the Me 109s, some sixty machines in all, he guessed – and heard a German voice say, 'Achtung, Achtung, Spit und Hurri.' He watched a Hurricane squadron tear into the Me 110s, then saw the fighters and Stukas pass beneath them. 'We were up at almost 20,000 feet in the sun,' noted David, 'and I don't think they ever saw us till the last moment.'

This was certainly true. Paul had assumed their attack would be a complete surprise and that they would hit Middle Wallop and the Spitfires and Hurricanes on the ground before they had been given a chance to take off. Now, however, the surprise was on him as 609's Spitfires dived down upon them. With a 250 kg bomb visibly suspended from beneath the plane each of the Stuka crews was literally sitting on a powder keg. As Paul flew on, he heard the first explosions as a Stuka was blown to bits mid-air. 'A sudden fire ball,' he recorded, 'and all was over.'

David's section was flying slightly above the rest of the squadron, protecting their tails, when he saw five Me 109s pass beneath them. Immediately breaking away, David dived on the last German fighter, and gave him a hard burst at close range. The Messerschmitt burst into flames and spun downwards through the clouds, a long line of smoke trailing behind. Following him down, he could not pull out in time to avoid going below the cloud himself. Emerging into the clear, he found himself about five miles north of Weymouth. Seeing a great column of smoke rising from the ground, he flew over and saw his Me 109 in a field, a great tangled pile of wreckage. People from the nearby village were already hurrying towards it.

Meanwhile, Paul Hozzel was still trying to extricate himself from disaster. The fighters had taken on some of the Spitfires and Hurricanes but more Stukas were being knocked out. There was only one thing for it, and that was to dive down through the cloud, drop their bombs and then make for the deck and head back across the Channel. As best he could, Paul tried to get his Stukas to stick together. By the time they cleared the cloud, they were over Portland. After they dropped their bombs, he ordered them home. He and a number of others made it safely, but others were not so lucky, a number being plucked off as they struggled south across the sea.

Back at Warmwell, David Crook had been one of the first to land. The groundcrew were in a state of great excitement, having heard the battle raging overhead clearly enough but been unable to see a thing. As usual there was the counting-in as more pilots landed. Four, six, then ten were down. Then the last three arrived – that was the lot. Not one man missing. Having clambered down from their aircraft the pilots stood around talking excitedly, and it soon became clear that in just four minutes of frenzied fighting, the squadron had had its best day ever. Every pilot put in at least one claim. John Dundas shot down one confirmed and another probable, adding to his mounting score. As they all now realized, thirteen pilots had shot down thirteen enemy planes on the 13th day of the month. It felt as though the squadron had reached an important turning point, as though they had somehow come of age. 'I shall never again,' noted David, 'distrust the number thirteen.'

Back at Dinard, the grim truth was revealed. Both Stuka *Gruppen* had lost about a third of their aircraft and crews, while nearly all had suffered some kind of damage. Incredibly, some Stukas had pressed on towards their target, although they hit the small satellite airfield at Andover rather than Middle Wallop and caused no serious damage. For Paul Hozzel, it had been a sobering and bitter experience. As he was well aware, the Stuka force would soon be gone if this rate of losses was continued.

To the east, the large afternoon raid had been aimed at Detling and Rochester. The former was another Coastal, rather than Fighter, Command airfield, and was badly mauled, but cloud meant Rochester was missed altogether. In the day's fighting, the RAF had lost fifteen aircraft and just four pilots; the Luftwaffe thirty-nine planes and sixty-six aircrew. No attempt had been made to attack the RDF stations again, and every raid had been met by British fighters. Of the comparatively small amount of damage that had been caused, it was Coastal Command that had come off worst; Fighter Command's ability to continue the fight had barely been dented.

Curiously, although *Adlertag* had been the official codename for the launch of the intensification of the air battle, few of the pilots were aware of it. Hans-Ekkehard Bob had no idea that 13 August had been anything special. Siegfried Bethke had thought the day before had marked the start of the battle. All in all, *Adlertag* had been a bit of a cock-up for the Luftwaffe. It was therefore no bad thing that, as far as most German airmen were concerned, Eagle Day had never happened.

38

The Biggest Air Battle

The previous Sunday, Harold Nicolson had been at home at Sissinghurst in Kent, and that lovely summer's afternoon the cottage garden had looked especially beautiful, a blaze of colour. As a large heron flew steadily away from the lake, Vita, Harold's wife, asked him, 'How can we possibly win?' It was not an unreasonable question, and one that Harold had been thinking himself but had dared not ask. Even if Britain did survive the German assault that was to be hurled at them, what then? For all Churchill's talk of setting Europe ablaze, what could Britain really do? She still had many worries, after all. The week before the Italians had invaded British Somaliland in East Africa, and looked certain to attack from Libya into Egypt. In the Far East, the Japanese had been making martial noises and had recently arrested a number of British subjects on spurious spying charges. There were still concerns over Spain. As far as Harold was concerned, it seemed as though Britain would shortly be assailed from all sides. He began to picture how matters might play out. The Italians would push on into Kenya and the Sudan and then Egypt and the Suez Canal. The Japanese would attack in the Far East, taking Singapore, Malaya and then even drive into India. Soon, German heavy bombers would come over and the pressure to sue for peace from within Britain and the United States would be intense. Churchill would come to symbolize a sullen obstinacy that was imposing tremendous suffering on the whole world – a suffering that could be eased if only Britain's leaders would face facts and accept Hitler and the new European order. 'We shall become,' wrote Harold, 'the most hated race on earth.'

This was a very real scenario. Really, who knew what toll German bombing would take? No nation had ever been attacked from the air as Britain was surely about to be assaulted by the Luftwaffe. What if Douhet, Baldwin *et al.* had been right all along? Aerial warfare was still so new; its potential was still unknown, even in August 1940.

Sir Samuel Hoare's missives from Madrid, where he was now Ambassador, were hardly encouraging. Living in a city of shadows and intrigues was not to his taste. One day Spanish radio announced he was negotiating with Hitler through the Windsors; the next British flags were torn from the Embassy cars. 'The rumours baffle description,' he told his old friend Neville Chamberlain. 'The trouble is that in a country where there is no free press, false reports are given far more credence than they would be if people knew even a little of the truth, and in a city like Madrid where the climate is very trying and the heat terrific, everybody's nerves are very jumpy.' Fortunately for Britain, Hoare was surrounded by somewhat less nervy people than himself, not least the naval attaché, Captain Alan Hillgarth, a cool-headed spook, who was playing a perfect game of carrot and stick with the Spanish, offering just the right amount of aid whilst reminding them that the Royal Navy would blockade Spain in an instant should she declare war. Still broke from the Civil War, Franco could not afford this. In fact, the Generalissimo had presented a number of demands to Hitler for Spanish entry on the Axis side, not least Vichy France's possessions in Africa. But with Britain's attack on the French Fleet, Hitler had hoped Pétain might declare war on Britain and so did not want to risk jeopardizing that by handing over French territories to the Spanish. Still, when Hoare wrote that the situation was on a knife edge, and a pretty sharp one at that, he was not far wrong. Spain remained a serious concern.

And what about Japan and the Middle East? Churchill had assured the Australian and New Zealand governments that should they be attacked by Japan he would abandon the Mediterranean and send the Fleet to help them as quickly as possible. Cool logic suggested the Middle East should be abandoned anyway; the Suez Canal was now unreachable since the Italian entry into the war, while nearly all Britain's oil no longer came through Persia and the Middle East, but from the USA. But cool logic had suggested Britain sue for peace at the end of May, and logic had not been right then and, as far as Churchill was concerned, was not right now with regard to the Middle East. It would mean abandoning Iraq,

Egypt, Palestine, Malta and Gibraltar. Fighting the Italians in the Mediterranean and in Africa at least offered Britain a chance to successfully fight back. The Italians were not the highly motivated, well-equipped force that the Germans were. Nonetheless, it was causing him much anxiety. He had not been impressed with General Wavell, the C-in-C Middle East, during a visit to London. Like most British generals, he lacked the kind of optimistic and offensively minded vision of the Prime Minister. And there were other considerations. 'The P.M. is very much on edge,' noted Jock Colville on Eagle Day, 'concerned with the quickest method of sending reinforcements to the Near East before the expected attack on Egypt.' There were two problems. The first was the severe shortage of war materiel and sending overseas arms and equipment that was still desperately needed in Britain, a gamble Churchill was prepared to take and to overrule all objections from his Chiefs of Staff to do so. In fact, no fewer than 150 precious tanks were sent to the Middle East, while a daring plan to fly in Hurricanes from an aircraft carrier from the western Mediterranean was also put into effect. The second problem was time. Getting men and materiel all the way round South Africa, or from India and the Dominions, was very time-consuming. Britain had to pray the Italians would not attack too soon.

For a young man like Jock Colville, just twenty-five years old, his proximity to Churchill and Britain's leaders at this momentous time was eye-opening to put it mildly. He was almost daily finding himself dining with Churchill, Beaverbrook, Eden, Ismay or the CIGS, General Dill, and other Chiefs of Staff. On the second weekend in August, he was at Chequers, the PM's country residence, and found a letter from Admiral Nelson in one of the rooms, written shortly after the Battle of the Nile in August 1798. 'My Lord,' Nelson had written to the First Lord of the Admiralty, 'was I to die at this moment, want of frigates would be found stamped on my heart.' Jock now suggested Churchill send this to Roosevelt. The Prime Minister smiled and assured him that they were now certainly going to get the destroyers from America. 'But it is curious,' noted Jock, 'how history repeats itself even in small details.'

Churchill had, by this time, already heard that Roosevelt and his Cabinet had agreed to the legislation for the sale of fifty or sixty old destroyers. What now had to be agreed was a quid pro quo that would be acceptable to Congress and the British. On the morning of 14 August, Ambassador Joe Kennedy, through gritted teeth, presented Churchill with Roosevelt's offer. Britain had to agree to send the Fleet to other parts of the Empire should British waters become untenable, and, second, to grant ninety-nine-year leases to establish US naval and air bases in the West Indies, Bahamas, Bermuda and Newfoundland. As ever, Churchill offered Kennedy a 'highball' on his arrival at Number 10. As ever, Kennedy declined. 'This war will go on till then unless Hitler is beaten,' Churchill told him on reading the terms about the ninety-nine-year lease. 'I think the more we get together with you people, the better it will be for the world.' Subject to approval – which would happen – the deal was, at long last, on. A week earlier, the US Secretary of State, Cordell Hull, had called for a massive build-up of arms; on the 11th, America accepted an order from Britain for 4,000 tanks. These would not be ready for another year, but one of Churchill's greatest attributes was his vision, and an ability to see a way through and beyond the current crisis, something many of his colleagues – Harold Nicolson included – did not share. British investment in the US arms industry was a powerful weapon. As Churchill was well aware, once American industry was producing thousands of tanks, planes, ships, vehicles and ordnance – and making herself rich as a result – her own road to war would seem ever more likely.

Despite anxieties in the Middle and Far East and elsewhere, Britain's current head-to-head with Nazi Germany remained very much Churchill's prime concern. He had told Jock Colville that there was only one aim: to destroy Hitler. Just as Hitler had singled out Churchill as the architect of British stubbornness, so the Prime Minister saw the Führer, rather than the German nation, as the cause of the current war and strife. 'Let those who say they do not know what they are fighting for,' he told Jock, 'stop fighting and they will see.'

On Eagle Day, it was the pilot shortage not the massed German raids that was particularly bothering him, just as it was Dowding. Training had already been snipped and trimmed back, Elementary Flying Training reduced to seven weeks from eight in summer and ten in winter, and the later intermediate and advanced stages of training also cut by a week. Specialization would now begin at an earlier stage and more pilots were accepted initially to allow for losses through 'wastage'. The really critical bit was the reduction of the OTUs from a month to a fortnight. This was the last stage of training, where pilots became operational on Spitfires or Hurricanes. Two weeks was no time to prepare raw and inexperienced pilots for battle. Nonetheless, the cuts were to have a dramatic effect on the numbers of pilots coming through, if not the quality, with a projected increase from 1,632 pilots in June to 2,108 in September.

However, there were other experienced pilots waiting in the wings, not only those transferred from the navy, but also those of other nationalities. There were, for example, forty Free French officers and NCOs at OTUs on 10 August, and 114 Czech, 443 Polish and 28 Belgian pilots already enlisted into the RAF Volunteer Reserve. Amongst these not inconsiderable numbers was Jan Zumbach.

Jan and his fellows had been kept at the detention centre in Blackpool for three long weeks, but eventually they were declared fit to fly. The first few were sent to existing British squadrons, but then eventually the Air Ministry decided to form two new Polish squadrons at Northolt. Jan was among those posted to what had been designated 303 Squadron by the RAF and Kościuszko Squadron by the Poles.

They arrived at Northolt on 2 August, yet despite its being a Polish squadron, 303 was still to have a British squadron leader and flight commanders, although these were paired with Polish counterparts. The new CO was Tom Neil's old flight commander at 249, Boozy Kellett, while also watching over the Poles was the Northolt station commander, Group Captain Stanley Vincent, a veteran of the Great War and a man not to be pushed around by impatient, truculent Polish pilots. 'I'm not having people crashing around the sky,' he warned them, 'until they understand what they're told to do.' So before Jan and his fellows were let off the leash, they were sent back to school. Every morning, they were put on a bus at Northolt and taken ten miles to Uxbridge to learn the basic vocabulary that would be used in flight. They had to be able to count, use the clock-face system of giving bearings, and understand the RAF code words such as 'angels', 'bandits' and 'pancake'.

After proving themselves in Magisters, they were finally introduced to the cockpit of the Hurricane, but before they were allowed to take to the air, Jan and the other Poles all had to get their heads round a quite different layout to what they had been used to. 'Everything here was back to front,' said Jan. 'In Poland and France, when you wanted to open the throttle, you pulled; here, you pushed. We had to reverse all our reflexes.' And that was not all. Now it was miles rather than kilometres, feet rather than metres, and gallons not litres. 'The units of pressure were even more eccentric,' added Jan. 'The British certainly had their own ways of doing things.'

All this was learned on the ground, the pilots cycling on out-sized tricycles fitted with radio, compass and an airspeed indicator. Needless to say, they found the indignity of these exercises deeply humiliating. 'The British were wasting so much of our time with their childish exercises,' noted Jan, 'when all of us had already won our wings.' They got their own back by partying hard at night and gaining a deserved reputation for unruliness. Jan didn't care. He just wanted to get in the air and shoot down Germans. Yet however undignified and however frustrating these seemingly puerile lessons were, they were essential all the same. The Dowding System depended on every man and woman knowing their role, and that included the pilots. Although the Kościuszko Squadron pilots were, by the middle of August, champing at the bit, they would soon get their chance, and then all painstaking ground training would quickly prove its worth.

Pete Brothers was convinced God was on their side. 'It's just one of those things,' he says. 'God was there and he was looking after us.' After almost non-stop action since the middle of May, countless tussles and near misses, Pete had good personal reasons to think so. Those believers in the Luftwaffe must also have sometimes wondered whether, or at least suspected that, the British had some untold influence on the weather. First the millpond Channel during the Dunkirk evacuation and now an almost unceasingly cloudy and wet summer. It was poor weather that had disrupted plans for *Adlertag*, and it was poor weather once again that scuppered any persistent heavy operations the next day. There was still activity, however. Successive large raids hit the south-east after midday, and amongst the raiders Walter Rubensdörffer's Erpro 210 hit Manston yet again, destroying two hangars, while above fighters tussled. Dolfo Galland added to his mounting score, shooting down another Hurricane – in fact, it had been a good day for all of JG 26, who claimed eleven downed aircraft. No less important, only one of the Stukas they had been escorting had been shot down.

Elsewhere, small groups of raiders pressed inland. Amongst their targets was Middle Wallop, hit far more successfully by one Junkers 88 than by two entire *Gruppen* of Stukas the day before. The pilots of 609 Squadron had been lunching in the mess for a change when the air raid warning sounded. Dashing out, they sped down the edge of the grass field to the square bungalow that acted as dispersal, grabbed their parachutes and flying helmets and dashed to their Spitfires. One section had already been up patrolling, but David Crook and several others now sat strapped into their planes waiting to be ordered off. Soon after, he heard the unmistakable unsynchronized thrum of German bombers above the clouds. Immediately signalling to his groundcrew to stand by, he then watched as a lone Ju 88 broke out of the cloud to the north of the aerodrome, turned slightly then dived at high speed. David watched four bombs dropped from around 1,500 feet. A moment later there was an earth-shaking boom followed by immense clouds of mushrooming smoke and dust.

David and the others took off immediately, but Sergeant Alan Feary, already up in the air, swooped down and attacked the Junkers as the German came out of his dive. Hit at close range, the aircraft crashed in flames soon after. 'I flew over to the crash and have never seen any aeroplane more thoroughly wrecked,' wrote David, 'it was an awful mess.' Later, both he and John Dundas chased after several Heinkels, David damaging two and John finishing off one of them. When the crash was subsequently investigated, two senior Luftwaffe officers were found dead on board. John hoped to get the silver wings and swastika from the tunic of one of the dead colonels. 'If so,' he asked Margaret Rawlings, 'would you like it?'

From their headquarters near the battle front, the *Luftflotten* and *Fliegercorps* commanders were tearing their hair out in frustration. That evening the forecast once again looked bad for the following day, and although elaborate plans had been drawn up, it seemed these would have to be postponed once again. Then orders had arrived for them to go to Carinhall the following morning for another conference with the Reichsmarschall.

Climbing through the early-morning haze, Kesselring, Sperrle and their air corps commanders had flown towards Berlin. It was true that the Reichsmarschall still maintained his other political offices of state and thus proximity to Berlin could be more than justified. Yet it was by no means necessary since most of his enterprises and operations were running themselves. Rather, most of his time was now being spent art-collecting and indulging other pastimes. Many of his directives to his commanders had so far been quite sensible, but if he were to play a large part in the battle he needed to be near the front, as he had been during the western campaign, not hamming it up at Carinhall. It was a costly waste of time dragging all his commanders to the forests north-east of

Berlin every time he wanted to talk to them, but it was a trick of Hitler's that he liked to ape; it suited his periodic bouts of indolence and reinforced his sense of power.

Although Luftwaffe claims remained wildly optimistic, there could be no denying it was not making the headway it had planned, and that the Stukas and Göring's beloved Zerstörers, in which he had placed so much faith, were getting a pasting. He decided there should be new tactics. From now on, each Stuka *Gruppe* would be escorted by an entire fighter *Geschwader*, with one *Gruppe* remaining with the Stukas and diving with them, the second flying overhead, and the third protecting the whole attack from above. What he was forgetting was that Me 109s and Me 110s could not dive with Stukas, because they were not dive-bombers and did not have air brakes. If they kept up, they would plough on into the ground. Göring also now insisted the Stukas should also be escorted on the way back. He berated his commanders as well for using the Me 110s as regular fighters. 'I have repeatedly given orders that twin-engine fighters are only to be employed where the range of other fighters is inadequate,' he scolded, 'or where it is for the purpose of assisting our single-engine aircraft to break-off combat.' He was now talking contradictory nonsense. Me 110s could not be used to support single-engine fighters if they were only allowed to be flown on long-range sorties. The real problem was that the Zerstörers were simply not manoeuvrable enough for fighter operations against Spitfires and Hurricanes. They were more suited to long-range, low-level ground attack; Walter Rubensdörffer's team were proving how effective they could be, given the right role.

Göring next underlined the priorities for targets. Until further notice, he told them, all operations were to be directed exclusively against the enemy air force, including targets in the aircraft industry. Shipping was only to be attacked when the opportunity was 'especially propitious'. Night attacks, he told them, were to continue, but were essentially to be nuisance raids, albeit also directed against air force targets. In fact, this was what the Luftwaffe was already doing, as outlined in his previous directive. Then there was the issue of the British aircraft *DeTe* chain. 'It is doubtful whether there is any point in continuing the attacks on *DeTe* sites,' he added as one of his final thoughts, 'in view of the fact that not one of those attacked has so far been put out of action.' This was an extraordinary decision. Clearly, Martini had been completely hoodwinked by the dummy pulses being sent out from Ventnor, which was still out of service. So far, just a handful of the RDF stations had been attacked. Yet determined and repeated attacks on these sites could and should have caused the kind of damage that had been suffered at Ventnor, which would have created a massive handicap for the British fighters. By abandoning attacks on them, Göring was giving Fighter Command an astonishing boost.

The Reichsmarschall had pulled all his senior commanders away from the battle front to tell them to use more fighters when escorting Stukas, to use the Zerstörers more sparingly, to stop attacking British RDF stations, and to carry on hitting the same targets they were already attacking. Why this could not have been put on a one- or two-page memo is not clear, but while they were sitting in his great hall, surrounded by antlers, great masterpieces and other trophies of war, Britain and the English Channel were basking in glorious sunshine.

It was therefore fortunate for the Luftwaffe that one staff officer had been prepared to put his neck on the line and order the planned operations for that day to go ahead.

Earlier that morning, Oberst Paul Deichmann, Chief of Staff at II Fliegerkorps, had wandered out of their farmhouse headquarters at Bonningues, near Calais, and realized that the early-morning cloud was, in fact, just haze, and that behind it breathed an almost perfect summer's day, and not a ridge of low pressure. The weathermen had got it badly wrong. By mid-morning, the haze had evaporated revealing nothing but blue skies up above and glorious sunshine. Of the wind, there was barely a breath.

It was certainly too good a day to waste. Aware that most of the bomber crews would be fuelled up and almost ready to go, Deichmann decided to issue his orders. Stukas were to attack Hawkinge and Lympne. Dorniers were to give Eastchurch another pasting while another *Gruppe* attacked Rochester. Erpro 210 could attack Martlesham Heath. Having had his orders acknowledged, Deichmann headed to the Holy Mountain, Luftflotte 2's HQ at Cap Blanc Nez.

It was ironic, when considering the thrusting, up-front approach to command adopted by Guderian, Rommel *et al.* during the western campaign, that Kesselring should have chosen to have his HQ in a dank, deep underground bunker of the type favoured by defeated French commanders. Presumably, fear of British bombs had driven him to use such a base, but while Kesselring was undoubtedly safe down there, he did miss things, such as the sun emerging through the morning haze.

So it was that when Deichmann reached the dimly lit underground command post, Oberstleutnant Herbert Rieckhoff, Kesselring's operations officer, said, 'Ah, Herr Oberst, I expect you have heard. The attacks have been called off because of bad weather.'

'My dear Rieckhoff,' Deichmann replied, 'are you mad? It's a glorious day. Come up and take a look.'

Together they clambered up to Kesselring's look-out post, a parapet dug out from the cliffs, and saw the sun-drenched Channel. Despite this, Rieckhoff disagreed with Deichmann's decision. The operations had been cancelled; it was not their place to go against the orders of their superior. He therefore insisted on countermanding Deichmann's decision. But as he reached for the telephone, Deichmann grasped his wrist. 'It would be madness,' Deichmann told him, 'and besides, it's too late – they've already taken off.' This was true enough, as they now heard. Suddenly, hundreds of aircraft appeared overhead, wave after wave, bombers, dive-bombers, fighters, all heading across the narrow Channel to England.

Fearing for his future, Rieckhoff tried to contact Kesselring at Carinhall, but was told the *Luftflotte* commander was not to be disturbed. 'Orders or no orders,' Deichmann told him, 'they are flying all the same.'

The pilots of JG 26 had already been flying the kind of three-way fighter escort outlined by Göring that morning, and up above the Stukas now heading for Hawkinge and Lympne were Dolfo Galland and his III Gruppe. It was around 11.30 a.m. as they flew over the Kent coast. From their position, some 5,500 metres high, England looked a tiny island. The entire shape of the leg of Kent could clearly be seen, as could the winding Thames estuary and the round bulge of East Anglia. To Dolfo's left, the south coast of England stretched away to the Isle of Wight. Towns were dotted across a balmy, peaceful-looking countryside marked with dark spreads of wood and forest and seemingly never-ending patchwork of golden and green fields. Behind, the distance between Britain and France looked so small one could almost leap across. It was tantalizing; invasion did not seem so very difficult from 18,000 feet.

Down below, Spitfires from 54 Squadron were in formation preparing to dive down on to the Stuka formation. Seeing this, Dolfo quickly dived down on to them, forcing them to quickly abandon their attack on the Stukas in a desperate fight for survival. With his wingman, Joachim Müncheberg, somehow managing to stick with him, Dolfo followed a Spitfire as it took a wide right curving dive. Closing in on the Spitfire's tail, he pressed himself forward to counteract the force of negative gravity, then opened fire, seeing his bullets knock out chunks of the aircraft. The Spitfire fell away, spiralling to the ground.

Pulling back towards the vulnerable Ju 87s as they were re-forming after their attack, he glanced down and saw smoke billowing up from the airfield. He called his three *Staffeln* together and they covered the retreat of the Stukas; then he led them back up to 15,000 feet ready for another brief attack on the British fighters. His decision paid off. Almost immediately, he spotted Spitfires re-forming after the mêlée, dived down on one, and without being seen opened fire at close range. Bits of the airframe once again began scattering across the sky before the machine burst into flames. Pulling clear, he now saw a Spitfire attacking one of his pilots, and dived towards it, peppering it with bullets. The Spitfire reared into a steep climb, out of Dolfo's reach. Glancing around him, he realized it was time to head back. With his ammo almost out and fuel low, he needed to get home fast. Reaching the French coast, Dolfo took out one of his preferred Mexican cheroots and lit it with the lighter he had had specially installed, along with an ashtray, in his Messerschmitt. A smoke after a fight like that was just the thing.

It was around noon, and Cocky Dundas and the pilots of 616 Squadron had been stood down from readiness and headed to lunch at Leconfield's mess as usual. Barely had they sat down, however, before the tannoy crackled with the order for them to scramble immediately. At first they thought the controller must have taken leave of his senses – they had never been scrambled before at thirty minutes' notice; in fact, they had hardly ever been scrambled at all, it had been so quiet up there on the east coast.

However, the order was repeated with greater urgency and then a telephone rang and, a moment later, a steward entered the dining room and told them they were to head to dispersal immediately. Downing tools and pushing back chairs, they ran out to their cars and sped off round the perimeter track only to see their groundcrew already running towards their Spitfires in a rush to have them running and ready.

Sprinting to his Spitfire, Cocky grabbed his parachute from the wing and with fumbling fingers fastened the buckle, then jumped up on to the wing and hurriedly clambered into the tight confines of the cockpit. Helmet on, leads in, a thumbs-up to the groundcrew and away. Speeding off in twos and threes, the pilots heard the controller repeatedly telling all available aircraft to head out to sea at top speed and to intercept many bandits heading their way. Giving his Spitfire maximum boost, Cocky set course. For once there was no squadron formation; some were ahead, some behind, and one by one they tore over the coast and out over the sea, climbing as they went.

Cocky was about fifteen miles east of Bridlington when he saw them, to his left and slightly below, the long, thin shapes of German twin-engine Junkers 88s, some seventy in all, flying a loose, scattered formation. And all on their own – not a enemy fighter in sight. Switching on his reflector sight and setting the range for 250 yards, Cocky switched the gun button to 'fire', then arced down in a diving turn, curving towards the nearest bomber so that he came in behind. Tracer pulsed towards him and sped past, then Cocky opened up with his eight Brownings and the return fire stopped immediately. Moments later, the Junkers banked and fell away, a gush of black smoke followed by a steady stream from its engines, and then it was diving headlong into the sea.

Now turning to look for another target, he saw his fellows diving down on to the German planes. Below him, a damaged bomber was turning back to sea so he decided to go after it and try to finish it off. This was a mistake; he should have looked for a fresh target, because by the time he caught up and fired the last of his ammunition, he was several more miles out to sea and the sky was suddenly empty.

Sweat ran over his head underneath the tight, hot confines of his leather flying helmet and oxygen mask, but with a feeling of elation he now headed for home. One by one, the squadron straggled back, and everyone seemed to have fired his guns – the tell-tale red patches to keep away the dust had been shot through and streaks of smoke ran across the wings. 'A very large number of Bosche disturbed our lunch,' Cocky wrote to his mother the next day, his excitement still palpable, 'and we bagged a very large proportion of them, along with other squadrons. I had the personal satisfaction of adding to my own private score – one definite with a good big splash in the old traditional "burning fiercely" style, and another with one engine out of action creeping home ten feet above the water. Altogether, quite a refreshing interlude in what was becoming a dull life.'

This had been Luftflotte 5's first major effort of the battle. Stumpff had only some 230 aircraft in his entire Norwegian-based air fleet, yet assuming all the British fighters would be in the south, he had launched a series of attacks using more than a hundred Junkers 88s, Heinkels and

Zerstörers to pulverize a number of airfields in the north-east. All were bomber airfields and only one was actually hit, Driffield, where four hangars were damaged and ten Whitleys destroyed on the ground. It was, however, a poor return. The unescorted bombers had proved rich pickings for Cocky and the other pilots scrambled with time to spare. Fifteen bombers were shot down, several more badly damaged, while the Me 110s had also taken a battering, with seven shot down and two more damaged. For the bomber crews, it had been a terrible shock to see Spitfires, Hurricanes and even Blenheims homing in on them, guns blazing.

While the northern squadrons were having their turkey shoot, the aerial battles were raging all over southern England, too. Never had so many enemy aircraft been seen over Britain's skies. Deichmann had not been chastised for his decision; in fact, the number of raids had been hastily stepped up, with more airfields and aircraft works the targets. German bombers headed once more to Dover, Lympne and Deal, while Walter Rubensdörffer's Erpro 210 Zerstörers attacked Martlesham Heath. Later in the afternoon, raids totalling some 300 aircraft hit the south coast between Portsmouth and Weymouth. Bee Beamont and 87 Squadron had been scrambled at around 4.30 p.m., and by the time they were airborne heard the soothing tones of the controller telling them, 'One hundred and twenty plus approaching Warmwell from the south – good luck, chaps.' Over Lyme Regis at some 12,000 feet they began to weave about searching the sky above and behind. And then Bee saw them, still out to sea – what looked to him like a gigantic swarm of bees all revolving round each other in a fantastical spiral from about 8,000 to 14,000 feet. If the CO had been worried, he did not say so; instead, he swung the squadron round, opened the throttle and urged his men to pack in behind him.

As they drew closer, Bee saw there were about fifty or more Stukas with Me 110s above and Me 109s above them. The CO shouted, 'Tally ho!', the attack signal, and then they were diving into the fray. In a brief, manic and confused action, Bee nearly hit a Stuka, then noticed he was under attack by Me 110s, managed to shoot one of those down instead, and then another one. In minutes the organized air armada had become a mass of swirling aircraft more like a swarm of angry bees than ever, tracer zipping and crossing the sky, sometimes an aircraft plunging down towards the sea, thick smoke trailing behind, an occasional parachute drifting down through the mad, frantic air fighting.

Hurricanes and Spitfires had just fifteen seconds' worth of ammunition and in a dogfight it soon ran out. With his guns empty, Bee rolled the already badly strained Hurricane into a diving 400 mph aileron turn and headed into cloud, emerging out over Chesil Beach. With the sudden release of tension, he now felt very hot and looking down saw his uniform was dark with sweat. Sliding back the canopy, cool air breathed over him. Glancing at his watch he was astonished to see he had been in the air a mere thirty-five minutes.

Bombers reached as far as Middle Wallop again, 609 Squadron getting airborne in the nick of time and attacking the mixed formation of Ju 88s and Me 110s. Curiously, the bombers caused less damage collectively than the lone aircraft had done the day before. Hurtling after them, David Crook managed to shoot down a Blenheim, mistaking it for a Ju 88. Fortunately the crew survived, although the rear-gunner got a bullet in his backside. 'The Blenheims had sometimes got in our way before,' noted David, 'and we had often remarked jokingly, "If one of the blasted Blenheims gets in our way again we'll jolly well put a bullet through his bottom." And now it had come to pass, and everybody was very amused (except possibly the rear-gunner).'

Despite the vast numbers of aircraft in action over southern England that glorious summer's afternoon, it was still possible not to see a thing. The day before, 249 Squadron had been sent south, to Boscombe Down, the RAF's Aircraft and Armament Experimental Establishment near Salisbury, and now a fighter base as well. Tom Neil had been boyishly excited at the prospect of finally entering the fighting, although by the time they got there and had paused for thought, different emotions had been swirling around. 'Everything was new, uncertain and a bit confusing,' he noted. 'But thrilling.'

With around twenty-four pilots and twenty Hurricanes, not everyone could fly every sortie and it was not until later in the afternoon that Tom finally found himself airborne. Climbing to 15,000 feet, and heading towards the Portland coast, Tom and his section were then vectored from one part of the sky to the other. It was beautifully clear and Tom felt he could see for ever. All of England seemed stretched out before him: the jagged coastline, the Isle of Wight, Portland Bill and Chesil Beach. It seemed impossible on such a day that he could not see a single other aircraft, but the skies were strangely empty. 'After further wanderings and long periods of silence from control,' noted Tom, 'we returned with nothing to show for our trouble other than eyes bloodshot from the glare and necks positively aching from swivelling about.'

Dolfo Galland and his men were in action again during the last major attacks of this extraordinary day, protecting raids aiming for Kenley and Biggin Hill – for once, fighter airfields. So too were Hans-Ekkehard Bob and the pilots of II/JG 52. No fewer than seventeen RAF squadrons were scrambled to intercept this raid, and it soon dispersed, the fighter cover quickly embroiled in another tangle of manic air fighting. As it neared Biggin, Hans's *Schwarm* was suddenly attacked by a lone Spitfire, although the pilot never opened fire; his guns must have jammed at the crucial moment. At any rate, Hans followed it in what became a hard-fought chase, the Spitfire weaving and turning relentlessly in an effort to shake off his pursuer. But Hans managed to keep on his tail, and eventually pulled close enough to open fire. With smoke gushing from the Spitfire, Hans watched the pilot bail out down into the Channel below.

The combination of British fighters and evening haze now lying like a blanket over England had knocked the attacks off course, however. Rather than hitting Biggin, the raiders attacked the satellite airfield of West Malling, while Walter Rubensdörffer and his elite Zerstörer pilots also had trouble finding Kenley. Walter had struggled to tell whether they were even over sea or land. Leading his *Gruppe* down to under 10,000 feet, he realized to his horror that they were over England but no longer with any fighter escort. The Me 109s had gone. A moment later, however, he spotted an airfield and, assuming it must be Kenley, prepared to attack.

As the Zerstörers began their dive, Hurricanes from 111 Squadron began to pounce down after them, putting Walter and his men completely off their stride. As they roared over the airfield, many of their bombs fell wide, hitting not hangars or aircraft, but factories around the perimeter – for this was not Kenley at all, but Croydon, London's primary civilian aerodrome and strictly off limits to German attack.

Walter and his men were now in deep trouble. As the Zerstörers and now bomb-free Me 109s pulled out of their dives, they had to somehow escape from the British fighters opening fire behind them. Walter also knew that he was now getting low on fuel. Somehow, he had to get away. Banking hard he turned and headed south, but there was a Hurricane on his tail and, no matter how hard he tried, Walter could not shake him off. Heading south, Walter dropped lower and lower, hoping to hedge-hop, but still the Hurricane was there and his bullets were now beginning to hit home.

Watching this last battle were Daidie Penna and her mother, who had just finished their tea and went out to watch the spectacle as the swirling mass of German and British planes rolled ten miles south-east from Croydon and passed right over Tadworth. Daidie enjoyed watching the aircraft come over, which in the last few days had become a regular feature of the day. To begin with they could not see anything, but then the planes emerged from behind the trees. Daidie was struck by the haphazard way in which they were flying. It was hardly surprising: she was watching the remnants of Erpro 210 desperately struggling home. One was flying very erratically, smoke gushing behind it.

'See that? Looks a bit odd,' she said to her mother.

'It's only his exhaust.'

At that moment there was a heavy explosion, followed by a number of Hurricanes diving down upon them. This was a flight of 32 Squadron, hastily scrambled from Biggin. The siren now went off in Dorking, and, rather reluctantly, Daidie called her children and led them indoors. She found it rather frustrating sitting inside with the roar of aircraft and chatter of machine guns going on around them, and wanted to go back out and watch.

Meanwhile, Walter Rubensdörrfer was losing his own personal battle. England was becoming larger again the lower he flew. Over the fields and oast houses of Kent, he limped on, but then a bullet punctured a fuel tank and flames began rippling along his wing and fuselage. He needed to find somewhere to land, and very quickly, but it was easier said than done, especially now the controls were like lead in his hands. The flames were growing, molten pieces of aluminium dripping from his stricken Zerstörer.

It was now too late. Suddenly the aircraft was falling, swooping down in a trail of smoke and fire. At around 7 p.m., Walter Rubensdörffer ploughed his aircraft into a tree-studded bank at Bletchinglye Farm, near Rotherfield. Both he and his crewman were killed instantly.

'Today there took place the greatest and most successful air battle of all,' scribbled Jock Colville. At No. 10, the Prime Minister had been fed with regular updates, and with the numbers of downed enemy aircraft apparently rising by the minute he finally decided to drive over to the nerve-centre itself, Fighter Command HQ at Bentley Priory, with General Ismay in tow. When they got there, every single available aircraft in 11 Group was airborne, with nothing at all left in reserve. Ismay felt sick with fear. As he watched in silence, the plotters and controllers as calm and measured as ever, his panic passed and the fighting died down. Afterwards, as they drove back, Churchill turned to Ismay and said, 'Don't speak to me; I have never been so moved.' Five minutes later, he muttered, 'Never in the field of human conflict has so much been owed by so many to so few.'

On returning to Downing Street, Churchill told Jock to ring Chamberlain, who was in the country recovering from a recent operation for his cancer.

'The Lord President was very grateful to you,' Jock told Churchill afterwards.

'So he ought to be,' the PM replied. 'This is one of the greatest days in history.'

39

The Hardest Day

ON 14 AUGUST, Generaloberst Halder had received a report from Luftwaffe headquarters on the air fighting to date. It all seemed to be going well as far as he could see. Fighter losses were 1:5 in the Luftwaffe's favour; eight major air bases had been virtually destroyed. 'We have no difficulty in making good our losses,' he noted. 'British will probably not be able to replace theirs.' The only concern really was the weather, which continued to look unpredictable.

It is hard to know whether whoever wrote this report for OKH was aware that it was a load of rubbish or whether the Luftwaffe truly did believe these wildly inaccurate figures. Certainly, Oberst Beppo Schmid claimed with confidence on the morning of 16 August in his daily situation report that Fighter Command now had just 430 aircraft left, of which only 300 could be considered serviceable. In fact, the RAF had 653 ready and waiting to fly that morning. Only three airfields were out of action. Of these, Martlesham, which Walter Rubensdörffer had reported as being little more than a smoking pile of rubble the day before, was already nearly operational again. By the end of the day, 99 per cent of its telephone system was working once more, and all water and electricity had been reconnected and bomb craters filled in. Elsewhere, such as Hawkinge, the station staff merely moved to a previously prepared house half a mile from the airfield. West Malling was unserviceable for five days, and it took forty-eight hours to get Lympne up and running once more. At the moment, however, there were still plenty of airfields that were fully operational. German bombing was certainly taking its toll, but not decisively so as yet.

The British were just as bad at over-claiming. The previous day had certainly been a good one for Fighter Command, but to say it was one of the greatest in Britain's history might have been overstating the case just a little, even if they had shot down 180 German aircraft as had been claimed; in fact, the figure was seventy-six. Many more, however, were damaged to varying degrees. German mechanics could repair minor damage at airfields, while more seriously damaged aircraft had to be taken away to workshops further afield. The Luftwaffe's repair network was certainly nothing like as efficient as that of the RAF. As Siegfried Bethke points out, losses were regularly higher than those official figures for aircraft lost in action. 'Sea rescue incidents were not counted as losses in our statistics,' he says, 'although the loss of the plane was total.' One pilot from his squadron returned with eighty-eight bullet holes in his machine, but not one had hit a vital part of the aircraft. 'But the plane had to be taken apart and transported back home to be repaired,' he adds. 'Very often the wool was pulled over the public's eyes in the communiqués of the High Command. Almost always!'

An important difference between British and German attitudes was that the Luftwaffe commanders believed the bilge Schmid produced, whereas Dowding remained more concerned with his own losses rather than those imposed on the enemy. When Sinclair asked him about the wild divergence between the claims of the two sides, Dowding replied that the truth would become apparent soon enough. If the Germans' figures were accurate, he told him, the enemy would be in London in a week. 'Otherwise they would not.' From the point of view of the conduct of the battle, Dowding's approach was definitely the more sensible one.

The Luftwaffe would never again fly so many sorties over Britain in one day, but a pattern had already developed of persistent and heavy attacks by massed raiders primarily targeting airfields, and accompanied by large formations of fighters. For the pilots a hectic, utterly exhausting period of intense flying had begun. Any kind of flying required considerable concentration, which was in itself tiring, but combat flying required considerably more. Pilots had to remain alert at all times, watching all parts of the sky, listening to instructions, making sure they were in the right position. At the moment of contact, a surge of adrenalin would see even the most exhausted pilot through, but as soon as the tension was released, fatigue would sweep over them. Three, four, or even five sorties a day was a lot, especially as pilots were usually expected to be up before dawn.

For the German pilots, flying over water was an added strain. 'Our conversations now revolve almost solely on the Channel and all that water,' scribbled Siegfried Bethke on 16 August. 'It is so terribly disagreeable to us all.' It was disorientating but no-one wanted to end up in the water and then not be found. The trouble was the shortage of fuel. Air fighting used up a great deal very quickly and it was all too easy to find oneself suddenly short but with a large stretch of the Channel still to cross to reach safety. Too many pilots had been pulled out by the air-sea rescue service, but that gave only a little solace. 'Nobody liked flying over the dark water,' agrees Julius Neumann, who with JG 27 was also operating from Normandy, 'especially with the sky full of clouds and no horizon. But you just did your best and got on with your job.'

One pilot with plenty of personal fuel still left was Tom Neil. Word had reached 249 Squadron of the rich pickings over the north-east coast the previous day. It was just his luck that the moment the squadron moved south, there should be a flurry of action up north. He was also annoyed to have been left off the 'slate' that morning as one of the pilots not required for duty. That meant another pilot using his plane, which he did not like.

Tom's own 'B' Flight was scrambled around half-past twelve. Hurrying back from the mess where he had been having an early lunch, he then hung around dispersal, pacing impatiently as he waited for their return. They had been sent to intercept a large raid heading for Portsmouth. In fact, the bombers were heading for the airfield at Gosport, which once again was not a fighter field, but belonged to the Fleet Air Arm. 'B' Flight missed the bombers but did run into some Me 110s and Me 109s. It was during this rather confused tangle that James Nicolson, one of the squadron's flight lieutenants, was attacked from behind whilst over Southampton. Four cannon shells slammed into his cockpit, the first bursting on his canopy and the second on the reserve petrol tank in front of his instrument panel, while the third struck James's foot.

With incredible wherewithal, he pulled his feet up away from the flames and dived down hard to his right, only to see an Me 110 heading towards him, so opened fire, knocking the machine down, then prepared to bail out. The first time, he forgot to push back the remains of the canopy and hit his head, the second time he was pulled back by his straps, and only at the third attempt was he free. Burned and wounded in the leg, he then suffered further ignominy by being shot in the backside by an overzealous member of the newly renamed Home Guard. For this action, Nicolson was later awarded Fighter Command's only Victoria Cross.

But James Nicolson was not the only 249 pilot shot down that afternoon. So too was the nineteen-year-old Pilot Officer Martyn King – who was flying Tom's Hurricane. And unlike Nicolson, King was dead.

The relentless interruptions to daily life caused by air raid sirens were quickly becoming a feature of everyday life in Britain. On 16 August, Cecil Beaton, now taking photographs for the Ministry of Information, was leaving London early in the afternoon, and heading home to Ashcombe, his house in the south-west corner of Wiltshire. The train had barely reached the outskirts of the city, however, when the sirens went. Calmly, the guard wandered along calling for all blinds to be put down. Above, Cecil and the other passengers heard thumps, bangs and distant crumps as the Luftwaffe bombed Biggin and Kenley. Barely anyone looked up or even batted an eyelid. In silence, they continued reading or staring into space. 'The English are an extraordinary people,' he jotted later. 'Their genius for understatement goes deep. They behave in an incredibly calm way in the face of disaster. Imagine a carriage as ours filled with Latins! The screams! The hysterics!'

Near Malden, Cecil pulled the blind and had a quick peep outside. All seemed quiet but a huge plume of black smoke was curling into the sky. When they then inched their way into Malden, the station was an untidy mess, with glass all over the place and the roof blown in. Nearby, a house was on fire. Then the all-clear sounded and Cecil watched those who had been taking shelter now emerge, laughing, waving and giving the thumbs-up. He followed a number of people who now got off the train and trooped on to the line to inspect the damage. 'The usual story of bricks, cement dust, broken glass,' noted Cecil, 'bomb craters amongst the runner beans and rambler roses.'

Cecil had already seen more bomb damage than most. The week before, he had been sent to Newcastle by the Ministry of Information to photograph bomb damage. A particularly powerful photograph had been of a three-year-old girl called Eileen Dunne, who had been hit by a bomb splinter. With a bandaged head and clutching her doll, her wide eyes showed a mixture of childish fragility and defiance. Now he had some more commissions, this time of troops on Salisbury Plain; it was a good assignment, since he could base himself at Ashcombe for a change.

Eventually, they got going again, although the train had to be routed via Southampton because of bomb damage at Basingstoke, caused when the raiders had attempted to hit Odiham. It was some four hours later that Cecil finally reached Salisbury.

It was the shock of the rapid defeat in the Low Countries and in France, and the seemingly invincible German armed forces, that had worried so many British people, but when the parachutists did not come and one, then two, then three potential invasion dates came and went, the phlegmatic attitude that Cecil Beaton discovered on his train from Waterloo seemed to take root once more. Even if people did still believe Hitler and his hordes would invade, they had now had time to get used to the idea. The vast majority of people were quite calm and able to carry on with their lives. People continued to go to work, play tennis and cricket, go dancing and to pubs. One of the country's best-loved cartoonists, Graham Laidler, known as 'Pont', summed up the prevailing view in his *Punch* cartoon that week. It showed two men sitting by the bar of a pub, looking supremely untroubled, smoking pipes and staring into space, their half-drunk pints beside them: '. . . meanwhile, in Britain,' ran the caption, 'the entire population, faced by the threat of invasion, has been flung into a state of complete panic . . .'

Yet Olivia Cockett found it hard now to avoid talk about air raids – the suburbs were being hit by stray bombs from the attacks meant for airfields around the city – and sirens were now going off several times a day. Rumours were once again rife, this time about where bombs had landed. They were usually nonsense. 'Atmosphere cheerful,' noted Olivia. 'People pull faces and say, "Pretty bad," and repeat rumours and facts and wonder when the next one's coming.' At her father's work, they had started having sweepstakes on when the next raid would arrive.

The press was having a field day now that plenty of German aircraft wrecks had begun to be scattered over the country. 'Something for Britain's scrap drive,' ran a headline in the *Daily Express*, with a picture of a downed Zerstörer beneath. 'BLITZKRIEG – BY THE RAF,' ran another headline, '69 down in one day!' 'Calm? Of course! It's just a nuisance,' ran a column beneath by Hilde Marchant, an *Express* correspondent who had stationed herself in a town on the south coast. 'People here,' she reported, 'the ordinary little householders and shopkeepers continue their ordinary little lives with a gesture of supreme indifference.'

Many people were also fascinated and rather thrilled by the aerial battles. Despite the rumours and despite the slowly mounting civilian casualties, few people were being killed. There was danger in the air, but not too much; enough to bring a frisson of excitement, but not so much as to cause major concern – not for the majority, at any rate. Douglas Mann had now broken up from Marlborough College, so had put away his OTC uniform and headed home to Hartfield on the Kent–Sussex border. There, he discovered his family farm was directly under much of the aerial battle now going on. 'It was extraordinary,' he says. 'There was machine-gun fire and empty shell cases cascading down, and aeroplanes, too, falling in flames.'

He was out on the terrace at the front of the house, sitting in a deckchair with his father, when they saw fighting begin overhead.

'What I need are my field glasses,' Douglas's father told him. He rang the bell and the butler appeared. 'Get my field glasses, will you?' Douglas's father asked him.

'Very good, sir,' replied the butler. A minute later he reappeared, the field glasses laid out on a silver salver. Douglas's father took them, put them to his eyes and leaned back. 'Ah,' he said, 'that's much better.'

Not so far away, Harold Nicolson, at home with his family in Sissinghurst, was about to go in for lunch when they heard the sound of aircraft and looked up to see 'twenty little silver fish in arrow formation'. These passed but whilst eating lunch they suddenly heard aircraft quite close and stopped to look. 'There is a rattle of machine gun fire,' noted Harold, 'and we see two Spitfires attacking a Heinkel. The latter sways off, obviously wounded.'

Jock Colville had headed to Stansted Park for the weekend to stay with his friends, the Bessboroughs, and had been hoping to see some aerial battles, most of which he had missed so far. But while Friday the 16th had been another day of heavy fighting, Saturday had been notably quiet. Jock and Moyra Bessborough had walked over to see a crashed Junkers 88, but had seen nothing above them.

But on the Sunday, 18 August, he got his wish. With another day of fine weather, the Luftwaffe came over in droves. After lunch, they were sitting out on the terrace looking towards Portsmouth and Thorney Island, the barrage balloons just visible. Suddenly they saw puffs of smoke in the sky followed by the sound of ack-ack fire. Moments later came the roar of engines.

'There they are!' exclaimed Moyra. Shielding their eyes against the glare of the sun, they saw twenty or so aircraft fighting, and soon a bomber plunged towards the ground, smoke billowing behind, and then, following after, a parachute drifted down. Jock spotted a dive-bomber scream towards the airfield at Thorney Island. Vast explosions followed, and huge plumes of smoke began rising from the airfield. It was all over in a few minutes, although another attack seemed to be going on near Portsmouth. 'When peace was restored,' noted Jock, 'Moyra, Jean Meade and I sat on the terrace in high spirits, elated by what we had seen.'

Siegfried Bethke was due to have been taking part on that raid, but his Messerschmitt had developed ignition problems and so he had returned. Julius Neumann, however, had been flying that afternoon, providing escort for twenty-eight Ju 87s of I/Stuka 77. Leading the 6th Staffel of III/JG 27, Julius spotted a number of tiny specks just as they crossed the coast. Recognizing them as British fighters, he led his *Staffel* towards them.

Julius always felt nervous before any sortie – it was a natural enough feeling – but once in the air such feelings soon disappeared; he had a job to do, and he found there was little time for feeling scared. Now, as he turned towards the British fighters, the adrenalin beginning to flow, he felt quite calm and in control of his machine. Yet it was not his aircraft at all. Back on the 15th, during the last of three sorties over southern England, his personal mount, Yellow 3, had been hit and on arriving back in France he had been forced to crash-land with his wheels up. Although he escaped unscathed, his Messerschmitt had not, and now he was flying a different plane, Yellow 6. Nor did he have his usual mascot with him. His girlfriend had given him a white silk scarf – which he was wearing – and a miniature teddy bear, which normally hung from the side of his cockpit. It had not, however, followed him into his borrowed machine.

It did not occur to him that somehow this mission was jinxed, but now both 43 and 601 Hurricane Squadrons were tearing towards both his *Staffel* and the Stukas they were supposed to be protecting. As they tussled with the Hurricanes, Julius and his *Staffel* were unable to go and help the Stukas. All he could do was try to inch the dogfight down lower towards them, and thereby give them some protection, but his efforts did not seem to be working. Rather, his *Staffel* was now completely split up as planes wheeled and dived.

Eventually emerging from the mêlée, but without his wingman,

Julius climbed and then over the Solent saw another tussle going on between Me 109s and Spitfires. Chasing after one of the British fighters, he got on its tail and opened fire. The Spitfire immediately turned away, but Julius followed, the two weaving ever lower over the Isle of Wight. At last, after one more burst from Julius's guns, the Spitfire began to smoke. With a sense of satisfaction, Julius now prepared to give the fighter the killer burst. Glancing behind to check there were no British fighters creeping up behind him, he was surprised to see two trails of smoke, one black and one white. But turning back to the enemy in front of him, he could see only one, a black trail from the Spitfire. With a sinking heart, he glanced down at his temperature gauge and saw his worst fears realized: the needle was stuck at its hottest limit. Somehow during the fighting, a stray bullet must have punctured his radiator, because he now had a glycol leak. The white smoke was his.

His mind raced as he pulled away from the Spitfire. There was no chance of getting home, and now the engine had begun to cough and splutter. His only chance was to try and gain as much height as he could and then bail out. As he pulled his Messerschmitt into a climb, the engine began to struggle more and more and then packed up entirely, flames suddenly spreading back from a joint in the cowling around the engine.

Julius jettisoned the canopy but he was still horribly low – maybe only thirty or forty metres high. He had no chance of bailing out now. He called up his *Gruppe* leader on the R/T and told him he was on fire and going to attempt to crash-land.

'Where are you?' came the reply.

'For a moment,' says Julius, 'I thought about saying something dramatic but I couldn't think of anything, so I said nothing. I did think this might be it, though.' Below him, the ground, rushing ever nearer, looked hopelessly unsuitable: all hills and woods and hedges. Opting for what he thought looked the least bad, he aimed for a sloping newly harvested cornfield. Suddenly the left wing touched the ground, but fortunately took the force of his landing rather than fatally cartwheeling him, and spinning around, Yellow 6 finally came to a halt with a jolt that made Julius knock his head hard against the metal frame of the windscreen. Dazed, he tried to gather his wits, unbuckled his harness, and clambered down.

Stumbling backwards he was struck by how intact it still looked despite ticking and smouldering. Heading back to the cockpit, he got his flare pistol and fired two shots into the radio. 'I suddenly felt rather lonely,' he says. 'So I took out a cigarette, had a smoke and waited to be taken prisoner.' He did not have long. Plenty of people had seen him come down, and at length two elderly members of the Home Guard hurried across the field. Rather to Julius's surprise, they immediately demanded a souvenir from him.

'What kind of souvenir?' he asked.

They weren't really sure. But something. Julius pulled out his sunglasses, but there was only one pair, so he broke them in half and gave the men half each, which seemed to satisfy them. And then he was marched away.

As Tom Neil had discovered, it was perfectly possible to be scrambled, climb up to 15,000 feet or more, and then see no sign of the enemy whatsoever, while forty miles away a huge swirling air battle was raging. On this Sunday, David Crook, John Dundas and the rest of 609 Squadron had flown off to investigate some trails of smoke, had been scrambled to patrol over Ringwood, and then again above Middle Wallop, but had seen nothing at all.

Pete Brothers and the men of 32 Squadron, on the other hand, had seen rather too many enemy aircraft that day – some forty bombers and sixty fighters at around 1.20 p.m., then a further fifty or so bombers and thirty fighters shortly after five o'clock. In the first, the men had been hastily scrambled when it seemed the bombers were heading straight for Biggin Hill. Speeding off, they climbed up to 16,000 feet and then dived down into the bombers in an effort to disperse the formation. In a flurry of frantic shooting, they claimed a number of bombers shot down, including another for Pete, who hammered a Ju 88 and watched it plunge earthwards. By tearing into the bombers they saved Biggin, but exposed themselves to the enemy fighters. 'Our casualties were P/O Pain,' ran the rather dispassionate report in the squadron record book, 'shot down and slightly wounded, in hospital. F/Lt Russell shot down and severely wounded. Sgt. Henson forced landed. Slightly wounded.'

During the second fight, north of Canterbury, another three of their aircraft were shot down, but once again all three pilots survived, two heading straight back to the squadron. It had, however, been a good day for Pete, who shot down his second confirmed enemy plane of the day, an Me 109 flown by Gerhard Müller-Dühe from Dolfo Galland's III/JG 26.

'His score was five,' says Pete. 'Curiously, he was my fifth. He should have known better.'

That Sunday was the Luftwaffe's last big effort for a few days, as a front of bad weather once again scuppered German plans. Yet the first week had shown that the Dowding System was working. There had been moments of extreme anxiety, yet on the whole Fighter Command had come through well. Dowding's rotation of squadrons was also allowing fresh squadrons to enter the fray. On the 19th, for example, 616 Squadron were sent south, to bomb-damaged Kenley, near Biggin Hill, to replace the battle-weary 64 Squadron.

Cocky Dundas was, like Tom Neil a few days earlier, excited by the move south, although the reality soon hit home when he reached Kenley and saw the ruins of the station. Wrecked aircraft and vehicles lay strewn around the perimeter, newly filled craters dotted the field, while a number of the buildings were blackened wrecks. Still there was 615 Squadron, which had lost one pilot killed and three wounded, as well as eight Hurricanes the day before, and many more during the past month. Cocky noticed the obvious strain on the faces of the 615 pilots; the tension and weariness in the mess were palpable.

Three days later, the Prime Minister arrived at the airfield. All the pilots lined up to shake his hand. No sooner had Cocky done so than Corporal Durham raced out of dispersal yelling to the pilots to scramble. As Cocky sprinted to his Spitfire, he wondered whether the whole thing had been put on especially for Churchill; certainly, it had been quiet since they had arrived with barely an enemy plane in sight.

Climbing to 12,000 feet, they were above Dover, and Cocky was thinking about going into London that evening, when several explosions suddenly burst around him. In seconds, the cockpit was filled with thick, hot smoke, blinding him entirely. Centrifugal force had pressed him back against his seat and he knew he was now spinning. Panic and terror consumed him fully. 'Christ, this is the end,' he thought, then told himself, 'Get out, you bloody fool. Open the hood and get out.' Using both hands, he tugged the handle where the canopy locked on to the top of the windscreen, but after he had moved it back an inch it jammed. Smoke gushed through the gap and suddenly he could see again – the earth and sky spinning round and round. Desperately he now tried to control the spin, but to no avail. Still plummeting at terrific speed towards the ground he knew that opening the canopy was his only chance. Giving it one more almighty heave, he at last wrenched it back. Pulling out his leads and unbuckling his harness, he now pushed the top half of his body up out of the aircraft, but with the aircraft spinning and with raw terror consuming him as the ground drew ever closer, he was unable to break clear. Sitting down again, time rapidly running out, he tried again, this time from the other side, and at last managed to slither out along the fuselage and fall free. 'Seconds after my parachute opened,' he noted, 'I saw the Spitfire hit and explode in a field below. A flock of sheep scattered outwards from the cloud of dust and smoke and flame.'

He landed moments later, rolling to a halt underneath a hedge. His leg was sticky with his blood and he had dislocated his shoulder, which hurt like hell. A farmer with a gun arrived, then soldiers, and then an army ambulance, and he was driven away to the Kent and Canterbury Hospital.

'Very sorry indeed to hear that a 109 – or rather 12 of them – inflicted grievous bodily harm on you,' his brother John wrote to him. 'Mummy sent me a wire yesterday and you were mentioned as wounded in an 11 Group Intell. Summary this morning. I haven't heard any details, but I do hope the damage isn't too bad.'

It was not; Cocky would soon recover and fly again. He had been lucky, very lucky. But Cocky's survival and that of the 32 and 615 Squadron pilots on 18 August demonstrated what an enormous home advantage Fighter Command held over the Luftwaffe. For Julius Neumann, the war was over. Having been interrogated, he was now at a camp in the Lake District and would eventually be sent to Canada. But for Fighter Command, downed pilots could fly again – that day if they were unscathed, or a few days or weeks later if their wounds were not too bad.

Because more new and repaired aircraft were being produced than were being shot down, the crucial factor for Fighter Command was the number of pilots being lost, rather than Spitfires and Hurricanes. Between 8 and 23 August, Fighter Command lost 204 aircraft, but more than 300 had been built and a further 260 repaired in that period alone. In the same period, the Luftwaffe lost 397 aircraft, of which 181 were Me 109s and 110s, so only a fraction less than the number lost by Fighter Command. However, throughout the whole of August only 184 new Me 109s were built and 125 Me 110s, while for the whole of August 476 British fighters were built. Fighter Command was comfortably winning in terms of aircraft numbers, but was emphatically so in terms of pilots.

Fighter Command lost 104 pilots killed in that same period; the Luftwaffe suffered 623 dead and around the same number again taken prisoner, permanent losses which were twelve times higher than those of Fighter Command. Despite the wrecked airfields, despite the numbers of British aircraft destroyed, and despite the visually overwhelming sight of vast armadas of German aircraft flying over Britain, in no way was the battle going well for the Luftwaffe. In fact, it was going really rather badly wrong.

40

Bombs on Berlin

HILDA MÜLLER MIGHT have loved dancing but second on her list of favourite pastimes was going to the cinema. Barely a week went past without her seeing a film, mostly stirring propaganda pieces. Beforehand, just as in cinemas throughout Britain, news reports would be shown. In Berlin that August, they would also repeatedly run a song, 'Bomben auf England', a suitably stirring march, and accompanied by footage of Stukas diving down on ships and Me 109s tearing over the white cliffs of southern England. The march was undeniably catchy, relying on mass-chanted repetition of the chorus and plenty of trumpets. 'Comrade! Comrade! Get the enemy!' it ran, 'Bombs on England! Do you hear the engines singing? Get the enemy! In your ears it is ringing! Get the enemy! Bombs! Bombs! Bombs on Eng-e-land!' It was played over the radio, too, full of crackly static, and over public tannoys. 'We used to add different refrains,' says Hilda, 'such as, we are swimming to England and so on.'

Hilda thought it quite fun, but it grated on the nerves of those it sought to glorify. 'We pilots,' wrote Dolfo Galland, 'could not stand this song from the very start.' Naturally, it did not help that neither their situation nor their mood was quite so relentlessly buoyant as the march. Dolfo had already been feeling decidedly disgruntled with what he viewed as faulty tactics when he and a number of other *Gruppen* commanders, as well as all senior commanders, were summoned away from the front to attend Göring's latest conference. Flying to Berlin on 17 August, Dolfo found himself transported to what seemed like a different world. The weather was beautiful and Germany seemed swathed in peaceful serenity. In Berlin, everyone appeared to be carrying on as normal. Interest in the war seemed to have taken a nose-dive, which he found upsetting. No doubt the air battles over Britain and the U-boat war did seem a million miles away to many – and hardly like a proper war at all; it was the Continental mentality that wars were fought on land by armies.

But as Dolfo saw civilians and soldiers swanning about enjoying the summer sun, he wanted to shake them from their complacency. 'Naturally,' he noted, 'we had no insight into the ramifications of this war, but we guessed fairly accurately that the battle we were fighting on the Channel was of decisive importance to the continuance and the final outcome of the struggle.' It seemed to him that suddenly the burden of the war's future now rested on the few hundred fighter pilots stationed on the Channel coast, and he felt their efforts were underappreciated. The contrast between the life and death struggle in the skies over England and the smug serenity of Berlin had a deeply depressing effect on him.

He had not shaken off this feeling of gloom by the morning of 19 August, when he was driven to Carinhall for the conference. There, in the luxurious and opulent surroundings of Göring's palace, and with Kesselring, Milch, Jeschonnek *et al.* in attendance, even the supremely self-confident Dolfo Galland felt somewhat overawed.

The Reichsmarschall's frustration with the way the battle was going was clear, even though all those present maintained they had inflicted large and crippling losses on the RAF. But they had not destroyed the British fighter force in three days as planned. Göring was still trying to look to tactical mistakes for the reasons, and had decided that it was the fighter force that was largely to blame. He reiterated his decision of four days before that three *Gruppen* of fighters should protect one *Gruppe* of bombers, and having singled out Dolfo and Werner Mölders (another young fighter leader and the leading German ace), to be invested with the Pilot Medal with jewels, announced that the older fighter leaders were going to be sacked and replaced with younger men – like Galland and Mölders, who, he announced, were to become fighter *Geschwader* commodores.

Dolfo's heart sank – he liked being a *Gruppe* commander and wanted to continue flying, but Göring reassured him. The *Geschwader* commander, he said, must lead his pilots in the air, not from a desk. His intention was that these young commanders would lead by example, and inject some youthful dynamism into the fighter forces.

It was not the fighter force that was the problem, however, but the bombers. Pulverizing airfields and the aircraft industry required heavy bombers and lots of them. Göring simply did not have enough aircraft, of the right kind, for the job. But ever since Wever's Ural long-range, four-engine bomber force had been scrapped, Göring and Jeschonnek had put their faith in the dive-bomber, convinced, as Udet had been, by its exciting potential.

Udet had become fixated with the idea of the dive-bomber during a trip to the United States in 1933. There, the aircraft designer Glenn Curtiss had developed his Hawk, a dive-bombing biplane that Udet had even been allowed to fly himself and then take two back to Germany. And, back home, Udet soon convinced his old friend Göring of the dive-bomber's merit. The result was the development of the Junkers 87.

There is no doubt that, to a cavalier like Udet, dive-bombing, which required daring, skill and panache, was far more appealing than a fleet of bombers flying horizontally and releasing bombs from high altitude. But there were also sound reasons for backing the dive-bomber. No adequate bombsight had been developed, and German radar was very much in its infancy, making high-altitude bombing seem a costly and ineffective method of bombing. It was therefore surely much better to destroy a target with one accurately placed bomb than to paste an area with lots of bombs dropped haphazardly. And in addition to being a more accurate means of bombing, it was also more economical: the more accurate the bombing, the fewer bombs and aircraft would be needed.

Early trials with the Ju 87 had been hugely encouraging and led to what can only be described as an obsession amongst the General Staff for dive-bombing. Jeschonnek, in particular, along with Udet, became a confirmed proponent and they now insisted that the Ju 88, currently being developed as a fast, long-range, highly diverse bomber, also be given dive-bombing capabilities. After a lot of teeth-sucking, Junkers agreed that this would be possible, but in being adapted to these new requirements it changed fundamentally, putting on massive weight and losing speed. And it took time. Redeveloping an aircraft into something quite different was no easy task, but it was why the bomber that was supposed to be the mainstay of the Luftwaffe was barely ready by the beginning of 1940. It was why the Luftwaffe now, in the summer of 1940, was mostly using older Dornier 17s and Heinkel 111s travelling at speeds of 160 mph. The Junkers 88 prototypes had flown at 320 mph carrying 2,000 kg loads. That was faster than a Hurricane. The whole point of the Ju 88 had been to have an aircraft superior to any other of its kind. Yet having completely ruined this exciting, modern new medium-bomber, Udet and Jeschonnek next decided the He 177 heavy bomber should have dive-bombing capabilities too. It was this new specification that led Heinkel to try combining two engines, tandem-fashion, to drive one propeller, instead of sticking with the more stable design of four independently functioning engines and propellers. It was a disaster, because the double engines kept catching fire and lots of planes and their crews – as many as fifty – were lost in the process. That was fifty good pilots who could not drop bombs on England. Eventually, it was decided to go back to the four-prop model, but by then the entire project had been irredeemably delayed.

And Jeschonnek and Udet had even insisted the new, upgraded Me 110 project, the Me 210, should also have dive-bombing performance. It was partly this requirement that ensured the Me 210 project failed. The huge amounts of time, money and resources wasted on these machines, for a specification ill-suited to their original design, were quite astonishing.

What was more, their obsession with the advantages of dive-bombing made them overlook its inherent disadvantage, which was that to enable such a dive in the first place meant the aircraft was all but standing still the moment it recovered from releasing its bombs. This did not matter when cowing Poles with swords or rusty Norwegian troops or even intimidated Frenchmen taking shelter in their bunkers, but it was a major problem when there were efficient modern fighters above waiting for just that moment.

A further problem was that although it was extremely accurate when compared with a high-altitude horizontal bomber, it was still not pinpoint enough to hit moving ships or small – in terms of footage on the ground – RDF masts and operating huts. The best – men like Paul Hozzel – could regularly hit a ten-metre-wide circle, but less often when under enemy fire. *The War Illustrated* weekly magazine ran an article in one of its August editions entitled 'Why the Bomber Often Misses the Convoy'. Undeniably intended to give its British readers heart, it nonetheless gave an informative and accurate explanation, pointing out that when attacking a 250-yard-long ship lengthways, a bomb aimer would have a window of around 1.5 seconds in which to release his bomb, a decision which had to take into account the speed of the moving ship as well as the path of the bomb, the time for the bomb to fall, and wind speed. In a cross-ways attack, that window would be a quarter of a second. In other words, it was very difficult.

These two fundamental problems with the Stuka had first really reared their heads during the air battle for Dunkirk, but such concerns, if voiced, had been swept under the carpet. They had then become increasingly apparent during the *Kanalkampf*, and since then the failings of the Stukas had been a major disaster. As of now, they were withdrawn from the battle entirely. The part of the Luftwaffe in which Udet, Jeschonnek and even Göring had placed so much faith, the terror of the world in 1939 and early 1940, was no longer fit for battle. It was a catastrophe, because it showed that much of their tactical and strategical thinking in the mid- to late 1930s had been fundamentally flawed.

Blaming the fighters was not the answer. Nor were the new measures going to miraculously turn things around – far from it. There were fewer Me 109s and 110s than bombers, but Göring now expected three fighters to protect every bomber. That meant the pilots would have to fly three times as much as the bombers during daylight operations, and to make matters worse, often at speeds that cancelled out their operational advantage. It smacked of panic. After all, it was he, the most senior officer in the world, who a month before had been insisting fighters should be allowed to operate to their strengths.

At his latest conference, Göring had also given new instructions for attacks on the enemy aircraft industry. During the day, he announced, these should be carried out by lone raiders making the most of cloud enabling them to carry out surprise attacks. How they were then to navigate their way to the target was not explained. Opportunistic attacks meant bombers could not really use *Knickebein* or *X-Gerät*, which needed to be fixed beforehand. Further attacks, Göring told his commanders, should be carried out at night. So far, his night-bombing raids had scarcely been more successful than those of Bomber Command. For example, between 14 and 23 August, the Bristol Aeroplane Company's factory at Filton had been selected for attack eight times, but bombs fell on it only twice. In the same period, the Westland, Rolls-Royce and Gloster works had also been picked out nine times but only twice had bombs landed within five miles of their target. In all this time only one night bomber claimed to have successfully hit the Rolls-Royce works at Crewe – and he had been mistaken.

The reason so few targets were being hit was that night bombers were coming over only in very small numbers, often even singly. Sophisticated navigational aids significantly helped a bomber get to roughly the right neck of the woods but it was still very difficult to drop bombs accurately. Hajo Herrmann's bombs meant for the Vickers works were very close – but they were still between 50 and 500 yards off their marker. One of the most effective attacks had been by a lone Junkers 88 on Middle Wallop on 14 August, because it had dropped its bombs from a very low height. Moments later, however, it had been shot down. Therein lay the crux of the problem: accurate bombing was extremely risky.

What all this showed was that precision bombing was not really possible. If the Luftwaffe wanted 'bombs on England' to make an impact, it needed to forget its obsession with precision bombing and send over massed formations instead, at night when the fighters were not around, and carpet-bomb whatever target it was going for with as many bombs as it could possibly drop. If it dropped enough, some would inevitably hit their mark. Then *Knickebein* and *X-Gerät* would prove their worth.

Of course, had Göring really wanted someone to blame, he could have first pointed the finger at his own General Staff, and then turned on his intelligence men, particularly Oberst Beppo Schmid. Not only had Beppo given him a completely false picture of RAF strength, but he had led the Luftwaffe commanders to expend invaluable numbers of men, aircraft and bombs on targets that made no impact on Fighter Command's ability to function. On 18 August, the four principal targets had been Croydon, Thorney Island, Ford and Poling. Croydon was justified as it was a fighter airfield in 11 Group, albeit not a sector station. Thorney Island, on the other hand, was Coastal Command, while Ford was Fleet Air Arm. Poling was an RDF station and was knocked out, although emergency mobile radar was installed later that day. Of the twenty-one biggest attacks on airfields and RDF stations since 13 August, nine, or just over 40 per cent, were nothing to do with Fighter Command. It is not entirely clear whether Schmid and the Luftwaffe High Command were aware they were frequently hitting non-fighter airfields, or whether they were consciously going for bomber and naval airfields as well as part of their attempt to destroy the RAF as a whole. However, at Göring's conference on 21 July, he had made it clear that the RAF's fighters were to be destroyed first before attacks on 'bomber formations' could begin. Whatever the truth, it was still a mistake.

The Reichsmarschall had hoped that a pep talk, combined with the appointment of some younger fighter commanders, and closer co-operation between fighter and bomber units – he demanded more telephones for his commanders – would give his Luftwaffe the impetus to now finish the job. 'We have reached the decisive period of the air war against England,' he told his assembled commanders. 'The vital task is to turn all means at our disposal to the defeat of the enemy Air Force.' Sadly for the Luftwaffe, however, Göring's new instructions would not give them that chance. Not yet, at any rate.

One person keenly aware of how effective massed German night bombing might be was Dr Reginald 'RV' Jones, the scientific adviser at Air Intelligence. Since his breakthrough with the German *Knickebein* beams, RV had learned much more about German use of radio technology. Decrypts of Enigma signals had alerted him to an instrument called 'Wotan'. RV had immediately turned to his friend, Frederick 'Bimbo' Norman, a professor of German literature, who told him Wotan was the king of the old German Gods and had only one eye. 'One eye – one beam!' Bimbo had suggested excitedly down the telephone to RV. 'Can you think of a system that would use only one beam?'

He could, and explained how. A plane could fly along a beam pointing over a target, and then something like a radar station could be placed alongside the beam transmitter, so that the distance of the bomber could be continually measured from the starting point of the beam. When it reached the target, the crew could be told. Soon after, RV discovered an apparatus called 'Freya'. Having bought a book on Norse mythology from Foyle's bookshop and bringing into the frame what he already knew, RV concluded that 'Freya' was most likely a form of mobile radar. Once again, he was bang on the money.

Further documents recovered from downed German bombers suggested that a new *Knickebein* beam was being installed at Cherbourg and that KG 54 would soon be using it for operations to Liverpool. At the same time, RV had begun bombing surveys to record the pattern of German bombing, and suggested Liverpool and Birmingham for particularly careful observation. Meanwhile, the RAF's 80 Wing under Wing Commander Addison, working with the Telecommunications Research Establishment at Worth Matravers in Dorset, had begun working on *Knickebein* counter-measures as suggested by RV. The first solution was to 'jam' the beams by transmitting a 'mush' of noise on the *Knickebein* frequencies. A more subtle solution, however, came in the form of transmitted 'dashes' that sounded very like the genuine *Knickebein* dash created when the two beams intersected.

The idea was that the bomber crew listening to it would think they had reached the target earlier than was the reality, so would drop their bombs, it was hoped, before they actually got to it. Since *Knickebein* beams had been coded 'Headaches', this new system was given the codename 'Aspirin'.

By the end of August, both the jamming and Aspirin systems had been tried and tested. RV had always felt it was only a matter of time before the Luftwaffe turned to massed night bombing, but was confident now that in the absence of effective night-fighters the RAF at least had some counter-measures in place.

On the night of 24/25 August, several German bombers, aiming for the aircraft factory at Rochester, mistook the Thames for the Medway, and instead flew over London and dropped their bombs, which exploded in Milwall, Tottenham and Islington. Although completely unintentional, it was still strictly *verboten* to drop bombs over central London, as decreed by both Hitler and Göring. The bombs were not numerous and did not cause huge amounts of damage, but the following morning Churchill and the War Cabinet were all anxious to retaliate and ordered Bomber Command to send aircraft to attack Berlin the next night.

When Tommy Elmhirst, at Air Intelligence at the Air Ministry, heard of this plan, he immediately thought a terrible mistake was being made. At present, Luftwaffe raids on airfields had not caused any serious problems for Fighter Command and he was inclined to encourage them to continue. Any full-scale attack on Berlin was bound to bring retaliatory raids on London, which he thought might prove disastrous. He told his fears to the Deputy Chief of the Air Staff, who, convinced Tommy was right, then put his case to the Prime Minister. Churchill, however, was not to be swayed. The attack was to go ahead.

Bomber Command had sent rather more bombers over Germany at night than the Luftwaffe had sent over Britain over the past couple of months. Bombs had continued to be splayed fairly loose and free but occasionally the crews had had triumphant successes, not least when they managed to block the Dortmund–Ems Canal on the night of 12/13 August. Ten days later the canal was still blocked, a major inconvenience.

The first assault on Berlin, however, was something of a damp squib. Around fifty bombers were sent to the German capital, which was swathed in cloud when they got there. Only a handful of bombs actually fell within the city, destroying a wooden summer-house and wounding one person. On the way back, having encountered heavy winds, the Hampdens, absolutely at the limits of their range, struggled to get back. Three were lost and three more fell into the sea on their return leg.

The bombers were sent there again on the night of 28/29 August, and this time some Wellingtons were included. Amongst those on this epic bombing raid were Andrew Jackson and his crew. 'Berlin,' says Andrew, 'was a hell of a long way.' At that stage, each bomber was still heading off, independently from the rest of the squadron or other bombers that were flying that night. 'You could go on your own, in your own times,' says Andrew. 'There was no restriction at all – the height you bombed at, for example, you chose that yourself.'

They were given little guidance about how best to get there because apart from a few Hampdens, no-one had flown the route yet, and not from their base or in a Wellington. Andrew and the pilot got together beforehand and plotted the route. The only major city on the way was Hanover, so they needed to avoid the flak defences around it, but otherwise they decided to head pretty much due east.

Because of the distance and because Berlin was at the extreme range of the Wellington as well as the Hampden, they flew first from Marham to Norwich, where they refuelled. Andrew always liked to have a last cigarette and a pee against the tail-wheel before clambering aboard; these rituals had quickly become an important part of any mission routine. Once aboard and rolling around the perimeter towards the runway, he felt a tightening in his stomach, but no intense fear, despite the importance of the mission and the distance they needed to cover. They took off again at 9.25 p.m., and once airborne there was much for Andrew to think about – it was his task to get them there and over their target then safely home again. It was a big responsibility and he could not afford to switch off for a minute.

To further conserve fuel, they began a very gentle climb over the North Sea, which that evening was covered with low cloud. Much to their annoyance, however, they were shot at by anti-aircraft fire from their own ships below. Fortunately, they were not hit.

During the long flight, they met both searchlights and flak, but over Berlin they encountered little of either. There was little cloud over the city and they could see it clearly, lying spread out beneath them. 'It was quite something to think you were flying over the capital of Germany,' says Andrew. 'Quite thrilling really.' They had been given a choice of two targets, either marshalling yards in the centre of the city or the Siemens factory where Hilda Müller worked. Having spotted the former, Andrew made his calculations, they dropped their bombs, and then they turned for home.

They landed back down at five past eight the following morning, having been flying for ten hours and forty minutes. Stiff and tired, they were immediately filmed by Movietone News, who were anxious to capture the first men to properly bomb the centre of Berlin. 'I suppose it helped destroy the myth of German invincibility,' says Andrew. 'And I guess it caused considerable anger to Hitler and Göring.'

Twelve people were killed in the attacks and twenty-nine wounded, and some damage was caused. William Shirer thought that Berliners were more affected by the fact that British planes had penetrated the city centre than they were about the casualties. 'For the first time,' he noted, 'the war has been brought home to them.' No doubt Dolfo Galland would have thought that no bad thing.

Hilda Müller was one of thousands who went over to Charlottenburg to see the bomb craters near the S-Bahn train station; Andrew and his fellow observers' bombs had not been so very wide of the mark. 'Everyone went to see,' says Hilda, 'and after that, there were gunners on the Siemens roof.'

Under Goebbels's direction, the German press denounced the 'cowardly' British attack. 'One paper achieves a nice degree of hysteria,' added William Shirer, 'it says the RAF has been ordered "to massacre the population of Berlin."' One of the first reactions to the bombs was for Hitler to order the construction of several flak towers – vast concrete and steel buildings housing a formidable array of anti-aircraft guns and with enough room beneath to shelter up to 18,000 people. And Flakturm 1 was to be built by Berlin Zoo, at the very heart of the city.

A number of British bombers flew over again two nights later, and Andrew Jackson was amongst the crews involved. This time they targeted the airfield of Tempelhof. In the big scheme of things, the damage was not great, but it proved an important point. Berlin was far from impregnable, and it reminded Germans that the war was not over after all. The idyll of the victory summer had been shattered, while Hitler and the Nazi elite had received an embarrassing slap in the face. And no-one, either in London or Berlin, expected them to turn the other cheek.

41

Tactics and Technicalities

WHILE THE LARGER bombers continued to fly nightly over Germany and even Italy, the Blenheims continued with their daily missions to hit German airfields and shipping all along the French and Dutch coasts. On 23 August, for example, nineteen Blenheims went over, the usual number employed. They all went off individually, unescorted, doing their own thing. Only one was shot down that day, by flak gunners at Guines near Calais, as it tried to bomb JG 52's airfield.

As the Blenheim crews were discovering to their great cost, it was hard to get the balance right. With the benefit of daylight it was obviously far easier to find and hit a target, but it was also suicidally dangerous. The losses in the Blenheim squadrons were appalling; it was why Arthur Hughes was occasionally struck by moments of deep despair. Debate about tactics raged endlessly, however. At the beginning of August, some Blenheims of 101 Squadron carried out some high-level raids at 20,000 feet which had reportedly been quite successful. They had also been experimenting with two aircraft. They would take off at the same time, one would climb to 20,000 while the other cruised at fifty feet, so it arrived at the target twenty to thirty minutes earlier. Approaching low, the aircraft would then climb to 700 feet, release its bombs and make off until the excitement had calmed down, then return to assess the damage. In the meantime, the second, high-level Blenheim would come over and 'lay his eggs'. 'It sounds all right in theory,' jotted Arthur, 'but against the sort of flak defence the Jerries have, and their almost instantaneous response, I doubt whether an aircraft climbing from 50 to 700 feet at relatively low speed would stand an earthly.'

Soon after this debate, a rumour reached 18 Squadron that it would soon be switched to night bombing. This was surely more sensible. 'Night ops,' pointed out Arthur, 'in good weather are seemingly less dangerous than daylight hit-and-run and perhaps more effective. At least it will keep the blighters awake.' By the third week of August, they had made this switch over to night operations, and on their first trip bombed Cap Gris Nez and the German fighter airfields of Guines, Caffiers and Coquelles amongst others. Arthur, however, was unable to find his targets, first because of low cloud, and then, when that cleared, because of high cloud hiding the moon. At least for a change, no-one was hit.

Such tactical debate underlined just how new this type of warfare was. Both sides were feeling their way. Necessity is the mother of invention and onboard radar and increasingly sophisticated bombsights were being developed, but they were not in widespread use in the summer of 1940. It was perhaps odd, though, that Göring, a former fighter pilot, should have been such a proponent of Douhet and the theory that the bomber is the principal tool in air warfare, especially when he had such a fine fighter force at his disposal.

As it was, by the latter end of August, many of the fighter units were beginning to feel decidedly underappreciated and frustrated at being made to operate with what they instinctively knew were the wrong tactics. At the smaller tactical level, the German fighter pilots had, with the pairs system and finger-four, developed a combat formation that has been used by air forces around the world ever since. Culturally, Luftwaffe pilots were also more open to discussion and debate than their British counterparts, who, after a hard day's fighting, tended to head to the mess or pub, where talking shop was not really on the agenda. Hajo Herrmann, for example, used to regularly write up papers on his theories of how bombing should be conducted, and, although he would not deny himself the odd glass of wine, spent most of his evenings in contemplative study. In I/JG 52, there was also much tactical discussion amongst the pilots. After supper, usually eaten in and around their bell-tents, they would then sit and talk, albeit with some of the wine retrieved from Calais harbour to loosen the throat. 'All of the pilots, NCOs and officers would gather,' noted Ulrich Steinhilper, 'and lively discussions would usually ensue. These were generally toned by the events of the day; losses would quieten us down and bring a mood of introspection, whereas success would bring with it a surplus of energy and excitement.'

They were all angry about the new rules with regard to bomber escort. Ulrich believed, rightly, that the Me 109s should try and destroy the RAF fighters not only in the air but also on the ground. On 19 August, his *Staffel* had carried out a ground attack on Manston. His heart had been hammering in his chest, but as he had pushed down the nose of his aircraft and sped towards the airfield, he had calmed down. Spotting a fuel bowser refuelling a Spitfire, he opened fire and it exploded destroying two Spitfires in the process. It made him realize how much power he had with his cannons and machine guns and how effective a low-level attack such as that could be, especially when they were streaming across at 300 mph, making themselves very difficult targets for the British flak gunners. He firmly believed that fighters should be used in a 'free hunt' mode at all times. 'I predicted that if we were to continue as we were,' he wrote, 'the losses would end up being higher because, slowly but surely, we were losing our pilots in a long drawn-out battle of attrition.' It was not so very different from the debate between the mobile-armour progressives and the conservatives before the campaign in the west. Guderian and his fellows had been right then as the fighter pilots were right now. An attritional war of any kind, whether on land or in the air, was bad news for Germany, even now with her improved resources. And what must have made these flying restrictions even more frustrating was that in the Me 109E the Luftwaffe had the best fighter in the world in the summer of 1940.

Since the end of the Battle of Britain, there has been almost endless discussion about the various merits of the fighters involved. Most conclude, however, that, on balance, there was not much in it between the Spitfire Mk I and the Me 109E series. On paper, the maximum speeds of the two were about the same, while the Spitfire could out-turn an Me 109E, something that has always been viewed as a key attribute in dogfighting. 'But who gives a bugger about turning?' says Tom Neil. 'You don't need to turn. All you need to do is go like a bat out of hell, catch the other fellow, fire your guns, and disappear. These things the Me 109 did very, very well. It could catch us and it could run away from us, almost at will.'

Tom is quite right. When compared with either the Spitfire or the Hurricane Mk Is, the Me 109E had a superior rate of climb and speed of dive, and most definitely vastly superior firepower. These were the key ingredients to successfully shooting down lots of the enemy in the summer of 1940.

The reason for its superb acceleration was a combination of its supercharger, fuel injection and electric variable pitch propeller, all of which also contributed to its swift rate of climb. Even after tests were made at Farnborough of two intact Me 109s captured in France, British fighters had two-speed propellers. The angle of the propeller varied. Coarse pitch meant its blades were angled so that as it rotated, it would 'bite' the air more effectively. At fine pitch, the propeller was at a flatter angle, which allowed the engine revs to be greater, but did not provide as much 'bite'. But getting the best from a plane meant striking a balance between performance and fuel consumption in a range of different flying altitudes, speeds and other scenarios such as, for example, diving or climbing. Thus having just two pitch options was somewhat limiting, especially when compared to a variable pitch propeller, which enabled a pilot to maintain a far more varied and subtle use of the interchange between thrust, engine revs and power. On the back of the Farnborough tests, however, first Spitfires and then Hurricanes were hurriedly converted to De Havilland variable pitch propellers. In another astonishing feat of production, over a thousand existing, repaired and new-build Spitfires and Hurricanes had been converted by 15 August, which did much to improve their performance.

The Me 109's ability to dive away from any mêlée quickly was largely due to the DB601's fuel injection, which Spitfires and Hurricanes did not have. Rather, the Merlin relied on a carburettor. Any sudden dive downwards created negative gravity, or negative-g, which not only pushed the pilot up against his straps, but also forced all the fuel to the top of the float chamber. If the negative-g was maintained, this would cause the carburettor to become flooded with fuel because the float was no longer controlling the fuel flow into the carburettor. This in turn then caused the engine to cut out (called a rich-cut), producing a large puff of black smoke as it did so. This only lasted as long as the duration of the negative-g, and might only take a few seconds, but it was in that moment that an enemy could make good his escape. This was not an issue for the Me 109 because with its pioneering Bosch fuel injection fuel was pumped into the engine consistently even when under negative-g. It was this feature of the Me 109 that saved Siegfried Bethke's life on 2 September. He had been around 12,000 feet above the eastern edge of London, and escorting bombers, when they were, as expected, attacked by British fighters. In a confused tussle, Siegfried was performing a very steep left turn, and glancing up in his mirror his blood suddenly chilled. Just behind him was a Hurricane with all of its eight machine guns spitting bolts of lightning at him. He knew that the 109 could out-dive the British fighters and that therefore his only chance of escape was by quickly diving away. The Hurricane followed after him, but could not catch up, having lost precious seconds.

The Me 109 also suffered little sideslip when banking, unlike the Spitfire and Hurricane. Sideslip occurred because of the change of airflow caused by the turn, which meant it would literally slide, or drop a bit of altitude. But by keeping this to a minimum, an attacker could keep an enemy aircraft in his sights with greater ease.

It is true that in the Daimler-Benz 601 the Me 109 had a beast of a powerplant, but in addition to its supercharger and airscrew, it was the thrust from this engine combined with superb airframe design and high wing loading that gave the Me 109E such high speed and aggressive handling. Wing loading refers to the weight of the aircraft divided by the area of the wing, and on the Me 109E was 32 lb per square foot, while that of the Spitfire Mk I was 25 lb per square foot – in other words, it was much higher on the Me 109 than on the Spitfire. This was because the Me 109E had comparatively small wings; the Spitfire had very thin wings, but their elliptical shape gave them quite a large surface area. The advantage of small wings is that speed is created by forward thrust countering drag; thus, the smaller the wings, the less the drag, and this contributed to greater speed.

There is, however, a pay-off for having high wing loading, namely that the aircraft will stall at higher speeds. A stall occurs when the airflow over the wing reaches a stage where it no longer provides lift, at which point the aircraft starts to drop out of the sky. This is not necessarily a problem when operating at height, but it can be when taking off and landing, when the aircraft would be necessarily travelling at low speeds. Inexperienced Me 109 pilots could find taking off particularly difficult because the propeller would be rotating one way, creating enormous torque. This meant that lift was being caused over one of the wings and prop-wash – airflow over the wing caused by the propeller – over the other. This needed to be corrected by use of the rudder and aileron, but if a pilot was not careful, he could over-correct, the aircraft would roll, and he would crash into the ground.

When coming in to land, the high stalling speed was lowered by slats at the front of the wing, which automatically extended from the leading edge of the wings at around 110 mph, and flaps at the back, thus giving the wings greater surface area and preventing the aircraft from stalling. Me 109 pilots, however, could use this capability in combat to help them achieve a tighter turn. The theoretically minimum turning circle of the Me 109E was 885 feet, while that of a Spitfire was 696 feet. Any aircraft will lose speed when turning, which is one of the reasons not to turn in the first place when in the middle of a dogfight. However, by pulling back on the stick, and allowing the slats to open – which would occur at around 120 mph – an Me 109 could, in fact, out-turn a Spitfire. In any case, as was revealed by the Farnborough tests, Spitfire and Hurricane pilots were often reluctant to push their aircraft in as tight a turn as possible because they were worried about stalling. A pilot could feel the aircraft nearing the stall as the control column would start to shake; it was what was called 'pre-stall buffeting'. It was easy to recover an Me 109E from a stall, but this was not always the case with the Hurricane, which, despite being a very forgiving aircraft, could flip over and go into a spin. 'The Hurricane would always drop a wing,' says Pete Brothers. 'It was notorious for it.' The Spitfire, despite its thoroughbred, silky handling, could also prove a handful if ever pushed to stalling point. Pilots were warned of this in the accompanying *Pilot's Notes.* 'Never attempt a "tail-chase" with an enemy aeroplane having a smaller turning circle than the Spitfire,' it noted. 'If stalling incidence is reached, the aeroplane usually does a violent shudder, with a loud "clattering" noise, and comes out of the turn with a violent flick. This would be a serious loss of advantage in a combat.'

Certainly, during the Farnborough tests, the pilots, despite being highly experienced combat and test pilots, were nervous about stalling both the Spitfire and the Hurricane. 'In a surprisingly large number of cases, however,' noted the report, 'the Me 109 succeeded in keeping on the tail of the Spitfire or Hurricane during these turning tests, <u>merely because our pilots would not tighten up the turn sufficiently from fear of stalling and spinning</u>.' It is interesting that those writing the report felt it necessary to underline this key part of their findings. In other words, what was comparable on paper did not really represent what was happening in the air. The Me 109E, on the other hand, was less likely to flip and spin in a stall, and its high stalling speed could be used by skilled pilots to good effect in combat, because a stall enabled it to lose sudden height very quickly, a useful trick when being pursued.

It was also true that the Me 109E had a comparatively narrow undercarriage, which made it less stable on the ground, potentially a hazard in the hands of inexperienced pilots when touching down. However, although its roots were much narrower than that of the Spitfire, its legs were splayed so that in fact, they were about the same width as that of the British fighter. The Hurricane, with its inward folding undercarriage, was the most stable of the three on the ground, but the great advantage of the Me 109 arrangement was that the legs were attached to the underside of the fuselage rather than the wing. This meant wings could be replaced with comparative ease without having to dismantle the wheels, legs and hydraulics. It is a myth, however, that it was the narrow undercarriage that made the Me 109 so potentially lethal to the inexperienced. Rather, it was its unforgiving nature at low speeds, more a result of its high wing loading and the enormous torque of its DB601 engine. At Guines, for example, there was a track running about two-thirds of the way across the airfield. 'It was only a slight dip,' says Hans-Ekkehard Bob, 'but it was just where you took off and where you landed back down again. If you didn't judge it right, it was very easy to jolt the plane as the wheels went over it. Then a wingtip would hit the ground, then the propeller, and before you knew it the machine had flipped. It never happened to me, but it did to lots of others.'

It is true that considerable numbers of Me 109s were lost or damaged in flying accidents, but there is little to suggest they were any higher than those of the RAF, which suffered its fair share too. Despite its wide and stable undercarriage, a staggering 463 Hurricanes, for example, were damaged as a result of accidents between 10 July and 31 October. Some of these were minor prangs, others were fatal. 'Landed with undercarriage retracted', or 'overshot', or 'hit rough ground' were common lines scrawled across the accident report cards. So too was 'failed to open quick enough – aircraft stalled'. 'Taxied wrong way after landing on a very dark night,' read another report, 'ran into ditch.' 'Carelessness. Unnecessary taxiing in the dark when out of touch with Aldis lamp.' There were also other non-combat-related losses: mechanical failure, mid-air collisions, navigation error, lack of fuel. In fact, it has been suggested that these contributed as much as 20–30 per cent of losses during the battle – on both sides. Most were caused by a mixture of inexperience, lack of concentration and fatigue.

Yet, interestingly, the Farnborough tests also revealed that the British pilots had no difficulties landing or taking off in the Me 109E once they got used to it. Nor did Hans-Ekkehard Bob, or Dolfo Galland, or Siegfried Bethke or Günther Rall. Ulrich Steinhilper dropped a wingtip and damaged his 109 when he took off and suddenly hit a strong cross-wind. He had also just had a few whiskies since he had not been expecting to fly. Clearly, he had not been concentrating as hard as usual. What this showed was in the hands of very good and experienced pilots the Me 109 held no terrors. It was the inexperienced who struggled with it. In contrast, most pilots found the Spitfire and Hurricane both very straight-forward and forgiving to fly. A really superb pilot flying a Spitfire could not get much more out of it than an average pilot. An excellent pilot flying an Me 109, however, could do all sorts of things in his machine that a pilot of lesser ability would never achieve. Already, the leading German aces – or *Experten*, as they were called – were amassing considerable scores, Dolfo Galland and Werner Mölders among them. In part this was because of the pairing system, with one man doing the principal shooting while the wingman watched his back. But it was also because all those men were excellent pilots and could get a performance from their Me 109Es that was significantly superior to anything the enemy could manage.

The other key factor was firepower. Both the Spitfire and Hurricane had eight machine guns, four spread in each wing, that simultaneously fired 1,200 rounds per minute. The problem was that they only carried ammunition drums of 300 rounds, which meant they had just fifteen seconds' worth of firing time. Most pilots found this was very quickly used up. The second problem was that to bring the full effect of these machine guns to bear, the target needed to be hit at the point at which the bullets all converged. And since most of these bullets were ordinary .303 that could have been used in a Bren or a Lee Enfield rifle, on their own they did not pack that much of a punch. The advent of De Wilde incendiary ammunition improved matters a bit. 'When it hit an aeroplane,' says Tony Bartley, 'it flashed and you could see the flash as it hit, which was good.' But De Wilde rounds only ever made up a small proportion of the bullets used. Dowding and the Air Ministry – and Beaverbrook especially – had recognized that cannon-armed Spitfires were the way forward, but although some Spitfires had been trialled with cannons, jamming and seizure were recurring problems that had yet to be ironed out.

In contrast, both the Me 109E3 and E4 had two MG17 machine guns and two MGFF 20 mm cannons, one in each wing. The E4 had the

MGFF/M, which fired a new and more powerful explosive shell. Both machine guns were mounted on the engine cowling so there was no need to worry about bullet convergence – a pilot simply pointed his plane at a target and fired. Each of these high-velocity machine guns had 1,000 rounds, that is, more than three times as many rounds as each of the Brownings. Since the MG17s also had a slightly lower rate of fire, that meant German fighter pilots had around 55 seconds' worth of ammunition, almost four times as much as their British counterparts. It was true that the cannons only had sixty rounds each, and that even though they had a far slower rate of fire they were worth just seven seconds of firing time. However, the cannons and machine guns had different firing buttons – a thumb button on the top of the control column grip fired the cannons, while a finger trigger fired the MGs – so the cannons could be used once the machine guns had already found their mark. And while just one 20 mm high-explosive cannon shell could mean instant destruction for a British fighter, it often took a lot more .303 bullets to shoot down anything, as 74 Squadron discovered when between them they fired 7,000 bullets at a Do 17 and still failed to knock it out of the sky. Stand at 250 yards and fire a single .303 bullet into a piece of aluminium and the result is a tiny neat circle. Do the same with a 20 mm cannon shell and a hole the size of a fist is the result. Add something on the other side against which the shell can explode and the mess is astonishing. Allan Wright once saw a Spitfire hit by a German cannon shell. 'The cockpit blew up,' he says. 'You could see the canopy disappear and presumably the bloke as well because there was such an explosion.'

Unsurprisingly, most pilots when asked which they would rather have, the German or British armament, opt for the cannon and machine-gun combination. 'They had much more ammunition than we did,' says Tom Neil, 'and it was effective. Their cannon shells exploded.' Pete Brothers agrees. 'Cannon gave them a tremendous advantage,' he says. 'You certainly envied them their cannon.'

The Me 109 was thus a better fighter aircraft than the Spitfire in 1940, and a far superior one to the Hurricane. It has been endlessly pointed out that the Hurricane shot down more aircraft than the Spitfire in 1940, but there were many more of them than Spitfires, which makes this something of a false argument. Compare the profile view of the Hurricane with its biplane predecessors such as a Hawker Hart or Fury, for example, and the genealogy is immediately apparent. All three have almost identical fuselages, tail-planes and cowlings. The fuselage of the

Hurricane was also made of doped Irish linen like the earlier biplanes. Another big drawback of the Hurricanes and Spitfires was fuel tanks that had not been treated with any kind of flameproof sealant. This was partially remedied, as those in the wings were treated with a sealant called Linatax, but the reserve tank in the fuselage was left uncovered. The best that could be done for the large fuel tank sitting the other side of the instrument panel was to put up a metal bulkhead in between. This very probably saved Cocky Dundas's life, but even with Linatax the wing tanks in the Hurricane were especially susceptible to flame, which, thanks to the draught caused by the gun holes, soon spread along the hollow wings and engulfed the cockpit. The problem was that once the cockpit was on fire, the pilot had seconds to get out, because opening the hood once the fire took hold only fanned the flames further. Many of those who did get out suffered horrific burns.

Hurricanes had their merits. They were a stable gun platform and certainly bullet holes through the fuselage were easy and quick to repair. They were also faster than all the German bombers and infinitely more manoeuvrable. Pete Brothers did everything he could to improve the performance of his Hurricane. He took the mirror off the top and bought a curved car mirror and had it fixed inside the windscreen, and when he was waiting to be scrambled, he and his rigger would often sit on the wing with a bit of sandpaper, filing down the pock rivets to help reduce the drag. 'I reckon we got an extra seven miles per hour out of it,' he says. 'No-one else bothered but I thought it was worth doing and it gave me something to do on the ground.'

The Germans also had Me 110 Zerstörers, which had greater firepower than any of the single-engine fighters and were faster than Hurricanes, which made them a dangerous opponent. Plenty of Spitfires and Hurricanes, especially, were shot down by Me 110s, although this did not hide their fundamental weakness as a fighter – their lack of manoeuvrability. The Zerstörer was another pet project of Göring which, like the Stuka, was horribly shown up once they were confronted with half-decent single-engine fighters. Unlike the Stukas, the Zerstörers would continue to play a part in the battle, albeit a reduced one, but the losses of Me 110s were horrendous. Twenty-one were destroyed on 15 August, and a further thirteen three days later. Since Göring had puffed up the status of the Zerstörer units, its pilots were often both highly skilled and experienced. The loss of men like Walter Rubensdörffer, for example, could not be readily made up for. The tactical short-sightedness with which Göring and his staff viewed the Zerstörers meant far too many potentially highly skilled pilots who might have been far better used in single-engine fighters were lost to the Luftwaffe.

Yet despite this, numbers of German Me 109s still roughly matched those of their British counterparts. It was true that Fighter Command pilots held some home advantages. They had their early-warning system and if they survived being shot down, they could return to fly again. Nonetheless, it was the British fighters who had the harder task. First and foremost, they had to shoot down German bombers, but at the same time they had to try to avoid being shot down themselves by German fighters. But although a bomber presented a bigger target, it was harder to destroy than a fighter, not least because most bombers had plenty of armour plating. A Heinkel 111, for example, had some 600 lb of armour plating; a Ju 88 was even better protected. With just fifteen seconds of bullets rather than fifty-five and no high-explosive cannon, British pilots often found they were short on firepower. It meant the pilots often had to keep their fingers on the firing button for long periods of time to achieve any results. This required keeping the aircraft fairly steady, which in turn made it more vulnerable to enemy fire. Also, every bullet fired at a bomber was a bullet that could not then be used against an attacking Me 109 or 110.

Nor did it help that so little time had been spent on gunnery. Both sides had neglected this aspect of training, but at least the Germans had begun the summer understanding that the best results were achieved by taking the enemy by surprise and hitting him from close range. In May, Fighter Command was setting the harmonization range at 400 yards. By July, 250 yards had become the prescribed distance. Pete Brothers had his guns harmonized even closer than that, even though, strictly speaking, it was against RAF rules. He was not alone; many of the more experienced pilots did the same. 'You needed to get up jolly close,' he says. 'Fifty yards if you could; as close as possible and then you really did hammer it.' Tom Neil soon reset his guns at 150 yards.

Getting in close had now filtered down to the training of new pilots coming through, who were now told to get in behind the enemy and shoot them from dead astern. In early August, Sergeant Jimmy Corbin had been sent to the fighter OTU at Hawarden. A 23-year-old metalwork and maths teacher from Tonbridge in Kent, Jimmy had been hooked on flying ever since seeing Sir Alan Cobham's Flying Circus as a boy. Refused entry into the RAF at seventeen, he had later, in December 1938, been accepted into the RAFVR, although because of the short provision of training places it was not until November, more than two months after the outbreak of war, that he was finally called up to begin his EFT course.

Nine months later, he was at his OTU training to go operational on Spitfires. There was no more mention of ordered formation attacks, although he did practise flying vic formations, which struck him as counter-productive. 'It was bloody silly,' he says. 'If you are flying in a really tight formation, wing inside wing, there was only one person looking for the enemy and that was the commander.' The course highlight was the gunnery training, which involved air-to-ground firing only and against fixed targets. That was it, and was no preparation at all for the mad, frenetic air-to-air combat that was to come.

'We couldn't shoot for toffee,' says Tom Neil. After the war, he attended the School of Land Air Warfare and became associated with operational research. 'It was deduced that of every hundred bullets fired by us,' says Tom, 'ninety-seven missed.'

Pete Brothers had the unfortunate experience of being shot at by one of the squadron's new boys. Chasing an Me 109, Pete banked only to see in his mirror that his number two's guns were firing across him. 'I was a bit rude to him,' says Pete. 'Told him to desist!' Back on the ground, Pete hauled him off for some one-to-one gunnery practice, and took him off ops for five days. 'That was a great blow to his pride,' says Pete, 'but it taught him a sharp lesson.'

Some people mastered deflection shooting, but very few – the leading aces only. It was no accident that the most successful fighter pilots so far – men like Dolfo Galland, Mölders and Helmut Wick – were Condor Legion veterans, with a bucketload of combat experience behind them already. Dolfo Galland was also a fine shot on the ground; he understood the principles of deflection shooting and was a skilled marksman.

Sometimes aircraft came down because of a catastrophic mechanical failure. The Hurricane, for example, also had a habit of leaking oil from a seal around the propeller. 'It would cover your windscreen,' says Tom Neil, 'and you couldn't see out.' The canopy of both the Spitfire and the Hurricane also tended to steam up if they lost altitude quickly. How many pilots were lost because they could not see properly will never be known, but it was certainly a proportion. Others were hit by stray bullets streaking across the sky as aircraft tangled and turned in a dogfight.

Without doubt, however, most people were shot down without having ever seen the enemy. 'It was always the one you didn't see,' says

Pete Brothers, 'that shot you down.' This was how 609 Squadron lost so many pilots in July; by turning the tables they then got their own back once the August battles began.

This was why altitude was the most important tactical advantage of all for the attacker. With height, a pilot could position himself in the best possible position to attack – that is, with the sun behind him, making him blind to the aircraft below. The Me 109, above all other aircraft, was ideal for this. A pilot could swoop down, hammer an unsuspecting flight of Spitfires or Hurricanes with a big punch, then quickly climb away again out of danger and repeat the process.

In contrast with the men of Fighter Command, all the Luftwaffe fighters had to do was shoot down Spitfires and Hurricanes, and they had the very best aircraft with the right armament to do the job. They could – and should – have been winning hands down, but by denying their natural advantages Göring was effectively forcing them to fight with their hands tied behind their backs. They were becoming the hunted rather than the hunters.

Their primary role was no longer to shoot down British fighters, but to protect the bombers. Fighters, designed to be offensive weapons, were being made to play a defensive role instead. In their panic – and because of their lack of tactical understanding – the Luftwaffe High Command failed to realize that by shooting down Spitfires and Hurricanes their fighters *would* have been protecting the bombers. It was an unforgivable mistake.

42

Breaking Point

In Churchill's speech to the House of Commons on 20 August, he repeated the line he had muttered to Ismay a few days earlier about how much was owed to 'the few', although he was careful to include all those in Bomber Command. 'On no part of the Royal Air Force,' he added, 'does the weight of the war fall more heavily than on the daylight bombers.' Certainly their losses were proportionally the highest, as Arthur Hughes was uncomfortably aware. Since 10 May, Bomber Command alone had lost 693 aircraft, and that included 191 since the fall of France. Just in August, 235 men had been lost, 150 of whom had been killed, with the rest either wounded or now POWs. The Prime Minister also pointed out that the current battle against Germany was different from the 1914–18 war in other ways. 'The whole of the warring nations are engaged,' he said, 'not only soldiers, but the entire population, men, women and children. The fronts are everywhere. The trenches are dug in the towns and streets. Every village is fortified. Every road is barred. The front line runs through the factories. The workmen are soldiers with different weapons but the same courage.'

Yet there were also many risking their lives at sea. There were men like Joe Steele on board *Darthema* and Andrew Begg on *Icarus* still carrying out anti-invasion patrols and sweeping for, and laying, mines. There were the men still manning the colliers that were hacking their way around the British Isles. And there were also the many men daring to cross the Atlantic to bring vital food, supplies and armaments to Britain.

Now even neutral shipping was no longer safe; on 17 August, Hitler had declared a total blockade of Britain. From now on any ship steaming in the direction of the British Isles was liable to be attacked and sunk by the U-boats.

With the Western Approaches still largely undefended, the U-boats were continuing to have a field day. Thirty-eight ships and 195,825 tons of shipping were lost in July to German submarines, while in August that figure rose to fifty-six ships and 267,618 tons. These were crippling losses, and on top of that the Germans now had a few precious four-engine long-range reconnaissance aircraft – not the ill-fated He 177, but the Focke-Wulf 200, or Condor, as it was known – which were now operating from the French Atlantic coast. Not only were they proving superb ship and convoy spotters, but they could also attack shipping too. The Condors managed to sink a further fifteen vessels worth 53,283 tons during August. Against them, Britain had almost nothing – not until 16 August was a U-boat damaged by an aerial depth charge dropped by a Coastal Command aircraft.

Günther Prien and U-47 had left Kiel on 27 August for their ninth combat patrol, and, although they had not been at sea since July, were soon back to their successful best, sinking a 7,000-ton ship on 2 September, another one two days later and three ships on 7 September. It augured well for another bumper month, for getting ready to join U-47 and U-65 already out in the Atlantic were twelve more U-boats, including seven now based at Lorient in France, which meant saving a week's sailing time to reach the Atlantic, which in turn enabled the U-boats to remain hunting out at sea for longer.

Admiral Dönitz's delight at his U-boats' continued success was, however, tempered by his frustration at the still small numbers of ocean-going submarines. 'The results we could have obtained during these months had we had more boats,' he wrote, 'are obvious.' Hitler had vowed to build hundreds of U-boats but these had been empty promises. The army and Luftwaffe, especially, had taken precedence over the navy when it came to supplies of steel and other materials. It was soul-destroying for Dönitz. Typical of the kind of production bottlenecks that were hampering all areas of German war production, twenty-three ocean-going U-boats had been delayed because of a shortage of torpedo tubes. Dönitz remained absolutely convinced that his U-boats could bring Britain to her knees, but he envisaged being able to send a hundred or more U-boats into the Atlantic at any one time, rather than between nine and twelve, the best he could manage at present.

In fact, had Dönitz been able to send triple or even double the amounts of U-boats into the Atlantic, the inevitable losses would have been hard to sustain. As it was, they were sinking more ships than were being newly produced by British shipyards. 'Losses have been very heavy,' it was soberly reported in the War Cabinet's weekly review on 29 August. The next evening, Churchill confessed to Jock Colville that one of the things that was really beginning to worry him was the 'startling shipping losses in the North-West Approaches, where lay the seeds of something that "might be mortal" if allowed to get out of hand'. In fact, shipping losses were about to get even worse. Dönitz's band of brothers were about to bring new tactics to bear – tactics that would bring even greater destruction upon the cold, grey waters of the Atlantic.

In the towns, villages and fields of southern England, people continued to watch the aerial battles with a sense of excitement and wonderment. Swirling con-trails were left high in the deep blue summer sky, and occasionally what had been a glinting pinprick one minute would become a thrillingly low-level chase the next. Douglas Mann had a friend from school staying and they spent their days helping out on the farm, watching the aerial battles and collecting spent cartridge cases that used to clatter down from above. One day, the fighting seemed to get a little too close. They were loading trusses of hay but with machine guns going off and aircraft falling in flames they decided to take cover behind the hayrick. The horse was getting frightened and restless so they let him free then took cover once more. 'We crouched behind the hayrick,' says Douglas, 'while assorted bits of metal came down from above.'

John Wilson had also returned to Kent at the end of Marlborough's summer term, but unlike Douglas he had now left school. Still seventeen, he nonetheless offered his services to a retired admiral who was organizing the LDV in Hawkhurst. Given an armband and a rifle with five rounds, he spent a number of nights sitting on the top of a hill watching out for parachutists. 'Very dull,' he says. 'No roadblocks.' More fun was taking to the roof of his parents' house armed with an air rifle. One time a Messerschmitt roared over so low he had to duck. 'That chap went so bloody fast,' he says, 'I didn't even have the rifle to my shoulder.'

There had been few opportunities for taking pot-shots at low-flying

Messerschmitts between 19 and 23 August, however. The bad weather had been a much-needed breather for RAF Fighter Command. Airfields were further patched up and squadrons rotated, exhausted pilots had a chance to catch up on some sleep, while groundcrews and CRUs performed miracles in repairing damaged Spitfires and Hurricanes. And while Göring was addressing his commanders at Carinhall on 19 August, Air Vice-Marshal Park also took the opportunity to circulate new instructions to his ground controllers in 11 Group. High on the list were orders not to venture far from land – gliding distance from the coast was the absolute limit. 'We cannot afford to lose pilots,' he wrote, 'through forced landings in the sea.' As a rule of thumb, Park had ordered that Spitfires be directed against enemy fighters and Hurricanes against the bombers, although now, against mass attacks inland, only a minimum number of squadrons were to engage the enemy fighters. The main object was to attack the bombers. Controllers were also not to be shy about calling on 12 Group to help patrol 11 Group airfields should all the squadrons around London be airborne. There was also encouragement for 303 Kościuszko Squadron, which was to be allowed to patrol over inland airfields, especially when the 'older squadrons' were on the ground refuelling.

The Luftwaffe was back with a vengeance on Saturday, 24 August, however. Manston was so heavily bombed that it was decided necessary to evacuate all administrative personnel permanently, while nine people were killed and ten wounded on an attack on North Weald. The next day, Warmwell was one of the main targets. Bee Beamont was just coming back from a forty-eight-hour leave and drove straight around the perimeter track to see how 'B' Flight were getting on before heading into Exeter to change. But no sooner had he stepped into the dispersal hut just after 5 p.m. than the squadron was scrambled. Hastily putting on his Mae West and harness over his No. 1 uniform, he dashed to his Hurricane and took off along with the rest of the pilots, some sixteen aircraft in all.

As they hurried as fast as they could towards Warmwell, Bee suddenly spotted eight little dots, which developed into twin-engine bombers. Then another five appeared, then another six and a further five, before they realized there were as many as a hundred plus. Desperately scanning the skies above for enemy fighters, the squadron tore into the leading bombers, Bee opening fire on a Do 17, which, much to his satisfaction, rolled over after just one burst.

Also diving down upon the formation was 609 Squadron. David

Crook was almost last in line. 'I shall never forget seeing the long line of Spitfires ahead,' he noted, 'sweeping down and curling round at terrific speed to strike right into the middle of the German formation. It was superb!' With the twin advantage of height and the sun behind them, they were in the perfect position, and helped to split up much of the German formation. David chased after an Me 110 but dived too fast and in the heat of the moment forgot to throttle back and overshot badly. Instead of the Zerstörer being knocked down, the German rear-gunner managed to plant a line of bullets across David's wing. 'I learnt not to be over enthusiastic after this show,' noted David, 'and always took my time. Much better – and safer!'

Meanwhile, Bee Beamont was considering whether to use the speed of his dive to make a split turn and then head back into the fray, but glancing back at the lines of tracer he saw the Me 109s were already amongst them, so continued diving and, when he eventually pulled out, briefly blacked out as a result of the negative-g. He was now at around 5,000 feet above Dorchester. Up above, a confused action was still going on. A burning Hurricane suddenly hurtled past, a livid ball of flame, followed by a wheel leg from a bomber. Climbing back up again, he then saw an Me 109 dart from a cloud, evidently intent on heading back home. As Bee turned on to his tail, the German pilot spotted Bee and broke left. Firing across the turning circle, Bee saw his De Wildes strike the fuselage. Half rolling, the German dived. Following, Bee unleashed another burst as he rolled out of the dive, which proved a crippling blow. Slowing dramatically, he tried one more turn, but seeing Bee positioned for the kill, he deliberately stalled and dropped, which took Bee's sights off him. He then dived down and sideslipped into a field near Abbotsbury, a thick trail of smoke following him down. Bee watched him hit the ground, the Messerschmitt slewing amidst a cloud of dust and smoke. Circling, Bee saw the pilot on the wing, firing into his machine. Flames licked from the cowling, then the German raised his hand as Bee roared over him. The pilot was Gefreiter Bröcker of 1/JG 53, and he had been attacked by one Spitfire and two Hurricanes, of which Bee was the second.

Bee landed back down at Exeter to find most of the squadron already back, and talking excitedly. Then more sobering news: Sergeant James Cowley had been shot down and wounded, and then they saw a Hurricane, that of Peter Comely, the last man back, approaching the airfield. Suddenly, his plane flipped over and dived towards the ground.

When it was found, the aircraft was discovered to be riddled with bullet holes and Peter had had most of his hand shot away. He had probably passed out through loss of blood.

Siegfried Bethke had led his *Staffel* over to Warmwell, but a barrel burst in one of his cannons, badly damaging his wing so he had been forced to turn for home. The first *Gruppe* had claimed three kills that day, two going to Helmut Wick. The next day, during a large raid on Portsmouth, he claimed another two, bringing his score to twenty-two and making him one of the leading aces in the battle. Two days later, Wick was awarded the Knight's Cross, usually awarded when a pilot had twenty victories to his name. *Ritterkreuz* winners definitely acquired kudos and respect that set them apart. Fêted relentlessly by Goebbels's propagandists, they became media darlings and were household names throughout the Reich, featuring in magazines and newsreels and across the airwaves. Wick was summoned to Carinhall to receive his medal in person from Göring, another media opportunity that did not go begging.

Julius Neumann insists that working as a unit and carrying out the orders given them were uppermost in the pilots' minds, but because so much emphasis within the Reich was placed on individual heroism, it was not surprising that a number of fighter pilots strove to win the kind of fame and accolades won by the *Experten*. Anyone flaunting such ambition was, of course, ribbed for it. A pilot might be accused of having a sore throat. 'The Knight's Cross ties around the throat,' explains Hans-Ekkehard Bob, 'so saying someone has a sore throat means they are desperate to win one.' Such men were also called a *Dödel*. 'It's a joke,' says Hans. 'A *Dödel* is a rude name for a penis – like a dick.' Or they might be accused of being *Kanalkrank* – 'Channel sick', the urge to get across to England to shoot down more aircraft. That there were no fewer than three nicknames for such ambition rather underlines its prevalence. Most German pilots looked the part too; and knew it. This originated at the very top: Göring was determined his men should have wonderful uniforms, and so they did. Fighter pilots, especially, could call upon an astonishing number of different jackets, tunics, trousers and hats. Some were highly practical, such as the special *Fliegerhose* trousers that had large pockets for maps and leg bandoliers for flare cartridges. There were also lightweight and heavyweight leather jackets, heavily lined cotton jackets, dress trousers, pantaloons, overalls, special sunglasses and several types of everyday tunic, all of which were beautifully and intricately tailored. They looked fantastic, but they did not need half these items. It was an extravagant waste at a time when the German economy could ill afford to be expending needless costs on elaborate uniforms.

In contrast, the RAF pilots had one uniform – a blue tunic and trousers. One set which they wore every day and the other for smart occasions. If they wanted a warm jacket, then they had a sheepskin Irvin. Apart from flying boots and gloves, that was it.

There was ambition in the RAF too, but striving to improve personal scores was deeply frowned upon. 'We weren't interested in scores,' says Bee Beamont. 'What you were doing was knocking up a record for the squadron. We were a team.' Any kind of boasting was deplored, and anyone who did was immediately accused of 'shooting a line'. Unofficially, a pilot became an 'ace' when he had five confirmed kills. It was an important marker and usually earned a pilot the Distinguished Flying Cross, but a DFC could be earned without a pilot having reached five kills. Certainly there was no cult of the individual. A few were known to the wider public – Douglas Bader, the legless pilot, for example – but rather than focusing on individuals, fighter pilots as a whole were considered rather special. It was customary for them not to do up the top button of their tunics – a touch of dash that set them apart – and because of the need to constantly turn their heads, a relaxed view to uniform was taken. Most pilots did away with their neckties and opted for soft, silk scarves instead or roll-neck sweaters. Pete Brothers, for example, had a dark blue polka-dot scarf given to him by his wife, which doubled up as something of a mascot. But although scarves and the like were adopted for practical purposes, it added to the glamorous image, as most pilots were well aware. Tony Bartley, for one, enjoyed this special status very much. 'We were heroes to the people,' he says, 'and we were greeted as such and treated as such and bought drinks.'

The 10 Group pilots did not know it, but the big raid on Warmwell on 25 August was the last of its kind over Dorset. The two principal *Luftflotten* did not have enough aircraft to attack with sufficient numbers in south-east England and the south-west at the same time, especially now that Göring was insisting that each bomber *Gruppe* should be escorted by an entire fighter *Geschwader*. Consequently, most of *Jafü* 3's fighters were transferred to the Pas de Calais, while von Richthofen's VIII Fliegerkorps, which contained most of the Stukas, was withdrawn from the battle, to be kept back until the invasion. Still, concentration of force is just as valid

Ulrich Steinhilper. An intelligent and thoughtful young man, Ulrich began the summer eager to enter the fray and to put his pre-war training to the test. Over the long ensuing months, however, he became increasingly disillusioned, frustrated by the Luftwaffe's shortage of aircraft and properly trained pilots, and by what he perceived to be the wrong fighter tactics. As summer turned to autumn he also began to struggle against the demons of combat fatigue. He was far from alone.

Above: Jan Zumbach (*left*). His was a long journey from Poland to Britain, but when he and his fellow Poles finally joined the great air battle, they very quickly proved both their courage and skill as fighter pilots.

Left: Andrew Jackson, a navigator in Bomber Command. He and his crew were among the first sent to bomb Berlin in August.

Right: HMT *Darthema*, a pre-war trawler given a few guns and converted as a mine-sweeper. She was one of the many civilian vessels that made up the Royal Navy Patrol Service, better known as Harry Tate's Navy.

Below: One of her crew, Joe Steele. A pre-war member of the Royal Navy Volunteer Reserve, Joe joined *Darthema* as a signalman, operating in the Channel throughout the Battle of Britain.

Some of the Few. Allan Wright (*above, standing*) and Tony Bartley (*right*) of 92 Squadron, veterans of Dunkirk who later found themselves in the thick of the battle when they were posted to Biggin Hill in early September. Jimmy Corbin (*below*) joined 66 Squadron in 11 Group straight from training in August, but was quickly sent north to a quieter sector to gain crucial flying hours and experience.

Right: Keith Park, a brilliant fighter commander who was both tactically and operationally astute, and who led 11 Group with consummate skill and in perfect tandem with his C-in-C, Air Chief Marshal Dowding.

Below: Middle Wallop. Men of 609 Squadron watch a flight of Spitfires take to the sky.

Above: A reconnaissance photo of invasion barges at Dunkirk. Despite the RAF's best efforts, Germany had enough barges along the continental coast by mid-September to meet their invasion plans, but not all in the right place.

Above: Men of Erpro 210, the 'experimental unit' of mostly Me 110 Zerstörers. All were highly skilled pilots, specializing in precision bombing. They suffered a heavy toll, however, as this photograph of the 1st Staffel shows: the men with crosses above their heads were all lost in the Battle.

A German sentry stands guard beside one of the heavy guns ranged across the Channel. On clear days, with the White Cliffs in easy site, Britain must have seemed tantalizingly close.

Right: Peter Stahl at the controls of his Ju 88. Like most bomber pilots and crews, Peter was expected to fly over Britain day after day, and later, night after night.

Pilots of 32 Squadron at dispersal. Laughing in the centre is Pete Brothers, with one of their Hurricanes standing behind them. Like all the Squadron's pre-war regulars, Pete survived the Battle. Experience, properly managed, was the key to survival.

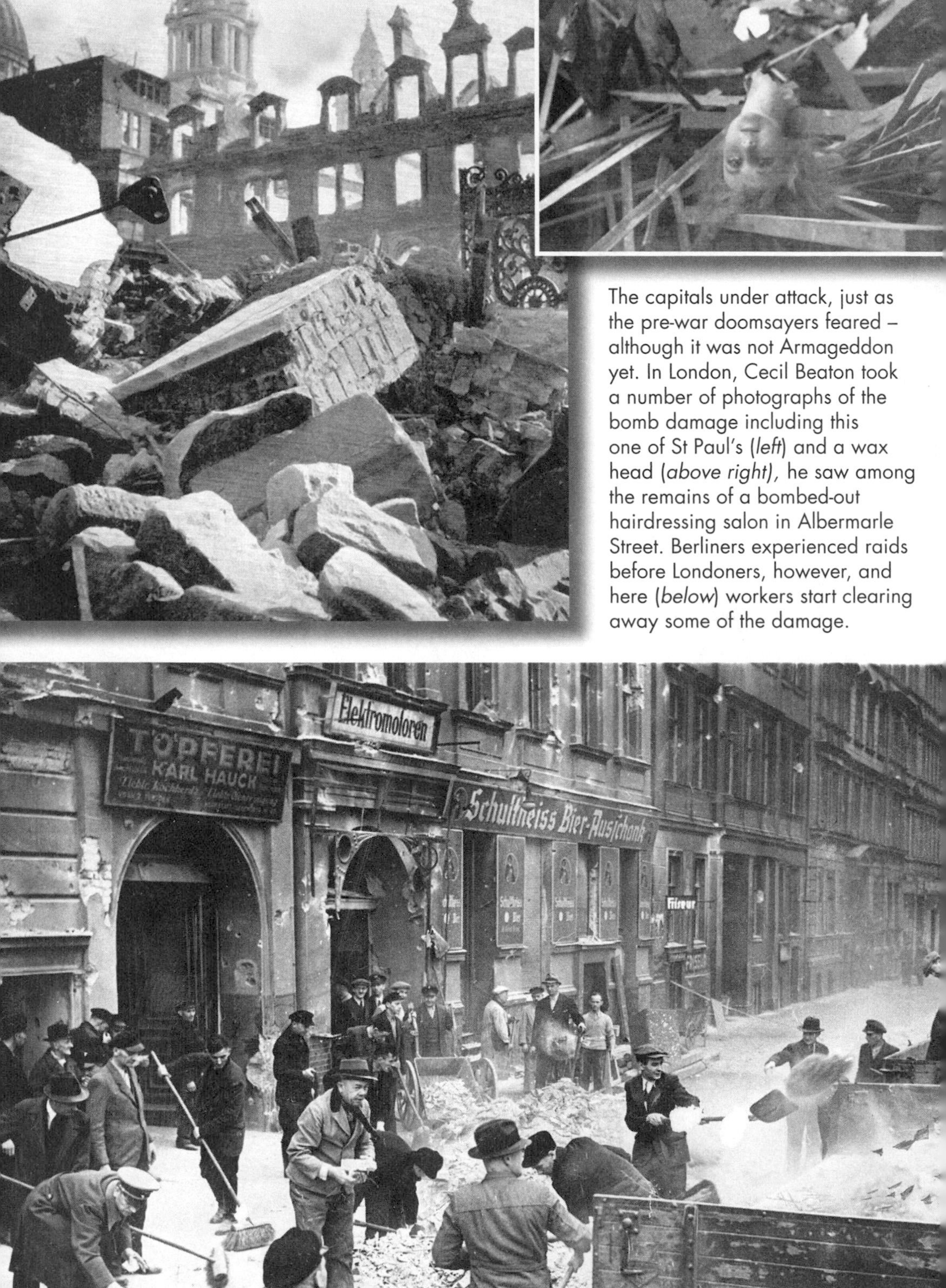

The capitals under attack, just as the pre-war doomsayers feared – although it was not Armageddon yet. In London, Cecil Beaton took a number of photographs of the bomb damage including this one of St Paul's (*left*) and a wax head (*above right),* he saw among the remains of a bombed-out hairdressing salon in Albermarle Street. Berliners experienced raids before Londoners, however, and here (*below*) workers start clearing away some of the damage.

Above: The crew of U-48. The summer of 1940 was known as the 'Happy Time' by the U-boat crews, who carried out a slaughter of Allied Atlantic shipping. Had they had a hundred, or even fifty ocean-going submarines, as Dönitz had demanded, rather than a maximum of fourteen, the U-boats really might have brought Britain to her knees.

Below: Prien's U-47, with her snorting bull logo on the conning tower, leaves for another mission.

The Dundas brothers – John on the left, and Hughie, or 'Cocky' as he was known in the RAF, on the right.

a principle in offensive air operations as it is on the ground. Bringing to bear most of their forces against 11 Group was undoubtedly a sensible policy. General Loerzer, in II Fliegerkorps, also came up with a cunning plan to confuse the British early-warning system, by sending over numerous formations, some simply to patrol the Channel and others to occasionally deliver feint attacks. All would appear on the British radar screens and all would have to be dealt with, but not all would then develop into real raids. It was simple and effective and immediately put a considerable added strain on 11 Group.

In fact, Park had already started to worry that his fighters were not making enough successful interceptions when compared with the number of sorties flown. This was because of cloud and inaccuracies of plotting, but he felt his squadrons were stretched so thin they could ill afford such mistakes. It also worried him that single squadrons were often engaging large formations because the other fighters scrambled had not arrived in time or at all. He now ordered fighter leaders to make a visual report of size, height and direction of any enemy formation they spotted, which could be immediately relayed to other fighters already airborne.

The next day, 27 August, he issued another instruction to his Group controllers. It had been agreed that should heavy enemy raids be heading for 11 Group airfields within easy reach of 10 and 12 Group squadrons, then these neighbouring units could be called upon to help. Park felt that 10 Group had been co-operating magnificently. 'Up to date, 12 Group, on the other hand,' he wrote, his frustration all too apparent, 'have not shown the same desire to co-operate by despatching their Squadrons to the places requested.' The result, he stated, was that on two occasions in recent days, they had not patrolled the airfields as asked and that these stations had been heavily bombed as a result. This being so, Park now instructed his sector controllers to make any future requests for reinforcements direct to the Controller at Fighter Command HQ.

It was a direct criticism of AVM Trafford Leigh-Mallory, the commander of 12 Group, although Park cared less about upsetting colleagues than ensuring the safety of his squadrons and their airfields. The two men had never got on well, and Park certainly did not have a high opinion of Leigh-Mallory's understanding of modern fighter tactics. One of the reasons for 12 Group's no-show was Leigh-Mallory's desire to bring a maximum strength of fighters to bear against the approaching enemy formations. Rather than sending a squadron or even a flight against the attackers, Leigh-Mallory believed it was better to try and meet such raids with two or three squadrons, operating at wing strength. To bring these squadrons into one formation, however, took time – too much time, as had been proved already. The raiders had been and gone before Leigh-Mallory could get his formations together over Park's airfields.

As the Germans had discovered during the campaign in the west, personality spats between commanders were not helpful, and the emergence of Park and Leigh-Mallory's tactical disagreement at a time when Fighter Command was more under the cosh than at any other time was unfortunate to say the least.

On 28 August, 32 Squadron bid farewell to Biggin Hill. It had been based there for nearly eight years. Already, the place looked a wreck, with craters all over the place. Pete Brothers' 'B' Flight office had had its roof smashed in and all of the pilots were in need of a rest; they had been in the thick of the action since the middle of May. Pete had been at Biggin since first joining the squadron. 'Bye, bye, Biggin, after 4 years,' he scribbled in his logbook. They were sent north, to Acklington in Northumberland, well out of the fray now that Luftflotte 5 had all but withdrawn from the day battle. Pete was greatly relieved. 'I thought, this is nice,' says Pete. 'I am going to enjoy this.'

But 32 Squadron had escaped from Biggin before the worst of the raids reached it. The Luftwaffe was still hitting Coastal Command stations, but more 11 Group airfields were coming under increasing attack. Biggin was smashed twice on 30 August, when massive damage was done to buildings and equipment. The workshops, transport yard, stores, barrack stores, armoury, met office and station office were all rendered useless. Gas and water supplies were severed as were a number of telephone lines. On top of that thirty-nine people were killed and a further twenty-six injured. The next day, the Germans were back, causing further and extensive damage to hangars and buildings, including the operations block, Officers' Mess and Officers' Married Quarters. The same day, Croydon and Hornchurch were also heavily attacked. In the fighting, it was Fighter Command's worst day, with forty-one aircraft destroyed and nine pilots killed. The Luftwaffe lost thirty-nine aircraft; for once, more British planes were downed than German. In one week, Fighter Command had lost sixty-four pilots dead and a further eighty-one wounded. Six of those had come from 616 Squadron; Cocky Dundas had been well out of it on 26 August, when two of the pilots had been killed and four more badly wounded.

It was perhaps not surprising, therefore, if Park was feeling a little tetchy at times. The sudden increased attacks on fighter airfields since 24 August were beginning to be keenly felt. It was true that Dowding had set aside materials to help fill in craters, but Park felt that the Air Ministry had not made enough provisions for the supply of labour. His complaints to this effect seemed to be going unheeded so he began recruiting whole battalions of soldiers to help with the work. He was severely criticized by the Air Ministry for taking matters into his own hands, but fortunately, he found a useful ally in the Prime Minister. Churchill had visited Manston on 28 August and was appalled to discover that although four days had passed since it was last attacked, most of the craters remained unfilled and the airfield remained largely unserviceable. 'I must protest emphatically,' he told Newall and Sinclair, 'against this feeble method of repairing damage.' He demanded more men be employed and that all craters from henceforth be filled within twenty-four hours. Had he known that a number of men had refused to work at Manston for fear of being hit, he would have been even more appalled.

But at least some much needed experienced pilots were now being brought into the battle for the first time. The Poles of 303 Squadron had been tearing their hair out with frustration at Dowding's unwillingness to let them enter the battle. Instead, they had been patrolling their sector in north-west London and endlessly practising simulated attacks against old Blenheims.

On 30 August, however, their chance finally came. Patrolling at 10,000 feet at around 4.15 p.m., Flying Officer Ludwik Paskiewicz suddenly spotted a large formation of bombers and fighters above them. But although he warned his flight commander, Boozy Kellett did not bother to respond; their job was not to go chasing after the enemy. Impatience getting the better of him, Paszkiewicz decided to break formation and chasing after a Zerstörer closed almost to collision and opened fire. The Me 110 burst into flames and spun down to the ground, where it exploded in a ball of flames. Returning to Northolt, he performed a victory roll over the airfield and landed.

He was immediately summoned to see Group Captain Vincent. Having been emphatically reprimanded, he was then congratulated for scoring the squadron's first kill. Later, Kellett rang Fighter Command and recommended the squadron be made operational. Dowding and Park agreed – after all, they desperately needed determined, motivated and skilled pilots such as these. Almost exactly a year after their country had been invaded, the Kościuszko Squadron entered the battle.

AVM Park's 11 Group might have now found itself under intense pressure, but so too were the German *Jagdflieger*. On 28 August, Siegfried Bethke and JG 2 moved to the Belgian border, close to Dunkirk, the first and second *Gruppen* basing themselves at Mardyck, while III/JG 2 went to Octeville. Siegfried flew no fewer than three operational sorties on 30 August. The British fighter pilots might not have been the finest shots, but they earned the respect of the Luftwaffe for their flying prowess. 'Those brothers are good,' noted Siegfried Bethke. 'Nice tactics.' The next day, he flew another three, two more on 1 September and another two the following day. They were shooting down Spitfires and Hurricanes but they were losing aircraft and pilots too, the latter at a greater rate than Fighter Command. By the end of August, Fighter Command had around 1,100 pilots; the Luftwaffe had just 735 operational fighter pilots.

On 2 September, Siegfried was awarded the Iron Cross First Class, but was envious of Wick's Knight's Cross. 'I will never get that far,' he complained to his diary. 'At least not against the English fighters. We can almost never surprise them. They are always inferior in number because we never fly in a force less than a *Gruppe*. However, a *Gruppe* should be fifty planes. I only have five planes here; the other *Staffeln* only have six to seven machines at the moment.'

Other fighter units were suffering the same problem. British fighter squadrons were losing experienced men, but so far there was never a shortage of aircraft. The Luftwaffe fighter units, however, were losing experienced pilots *and* suffering a shortage of aircraft. On 1 September, Hans-Ekkehard Bob's 9th Staffel had just five aircraft fit for duty, and only six the next day. 'There were definitely not enough machines,' says Hans, 'and as the battle progressed there were even fewer.'

Twenty-year-old Gefreiter Rudi Miese had joined 4/JG 2 on 24 August along with two other pilots. Rudi had assumed they would be flying against the Tommies right away, but he was much mistaken. Despite the ever-lowering number of fighter pilots, there were still not enough aircraft to go round, and in II/JG 2 the new boys were not going to be given mounts ahead of one of the combat-tested and experienced pilots. Nonetheless, it was a severe blow to Rudi, made worse when the rest of the *Gruppe* were posted to Mordyck and he and the two other new boys were told to remain in Beaumont-le-Roger. Some new barrack blocks needed building and it was decided that with the shortage of aircraft they would be better off helping with that task than sitting around not flying at Mordyck.

But just as the new pilots arriving at Fighter Command squadrons were horribly green, so too were the fresh intake to reach German fighter units. Rudi was typical of the new breed of wartime-trained pilots being sent to the front. Having been accepted into the Luftwaffe in December 1938, Rudi had not then begun his basic training until April 1939, but even then, because of the shortage of flying training schools, he had been sent to a civilian *Reichssportfliegerschule* near Bielefeld. He thoroughly enjoyed it, especially the relaxed civilian environment, but having completed a basic training that included around sixty bumps and circuits by the end of August, he was told that, for the time being, there were no more places available at the official Luftwaffe training schools. Instead, he and the others on his course were packed off to do basic military training instead. Not until the beginning of January was he sent to do his A/B training. Then, on 14 May, having been awarded his wings, Rudi was finally sent to complete his fighter pilot training. After eight weeks, in which he flew the Me 109 for the first time and did some clay pigeon shooting, he was sent to the *Ergänzungsjagdgruppe* – the equivalent of the British OTU – in Merseburg, where he flew the Me 109, practising bumps and starts, and carried out a tiny amount of air-to-ground gunnery on fixed targets. It was no better than the RAF gunnery training.

Certainly, Dolfo Galland, new *Geschwaderkommodore* at JG 26, was concerned at the level of training of the new pilots he was getting. As in England, most were undercooked but, such were the demands on his *Geschwader*, he did not feel he had the aircraft or time to bring their training up to speed. Nor did he want to send them over to England in the hope that they would live long enough to learn on the hoof. When Feldmarschall Milch visited him on 22 August, Dolfo pleaded for at least thirty more experienced officer pilots. Milch promised to do what he could, but a gift of a box of Brazil cigars was the best that he could do in the immediate term, and a week later the pilot and aircraft shortages were worse than ever. On 31 August, Dolfo only just managed to get enough aircraft in the air for two missions and one free hunt over England. Later in the day, he was rung up by *Jafü* 2 asking for a previously unscheduled further operation. It meant sending all three *Gruppen* over for a fourth mission in one day. This was a lot – more than could be reasonably expected. Fighter Command pilots were by now automatically given forty-eight hours' leave every two weeks, and, of course, were rotated out of the front line. Very few German units were withdrawn for rest and refit – not now, at any rate, and there was certainly no system of weekly or fortnightly leave. German pilots were expected to simply keep going. Moreover, British pilots were mostly flying over their own country. The culture within Fighter Command was such that getting away from it all once stood down for the day was actively encouraged. They could head to a pub, where they would be greeted as heroes. The German pilots were operating on foreign turf, however. Most got on well enough with the French and Belgians, but it was not the same. Siegfried Bethke noticed that the Belgian people employed in the kitchen and elsewhere around Mordyck were noticeably quiet. He wondered what they thought of it all. 'Before, there were lots of English here,' he mused, 'and then all those Stuka attacks nearby, huge fires and destruction, and now the Germans who take off from here fly towards London.'

The stress and strain of keeping up that level of intense air fighting was immense, and as well as flying over England three or four times a day, they were still regularly being bombed by marauding Blenheims. On their second morning at Mordyck, Siegfried Bethke and his fellows were shaken when a Blenheim came over early and dropped a number of bombs over them. As Hans-Ekkehard Bob points out, there was another meaning to *Kanalkrank*. 'It also means your nerves are shot,' he says, 'and you simply cannot fly any more.' At Coquelles, Ulrich Steinhilper noticed that the evening debates were becoming increasingly heated and that tempers had started to fray. One evening, Hinnerk Waller, one of their pilots, became so upset he stormed out of the tent, threatening to shoot himself. 'The strain of unrelenting front-line flying,' noted Ulrich, 'was beginning to show.'

43

Black Saturday

On 28 August, Colonel Raymond Lee accompanied Admiral Robert Ghormley and his US naval 'observation' team to Dover as guests of the Prime Minister. It was Lee's second trip in a week to what the journalists had christened 'Hellfire Corner', and once again he felt it did not seem quite so dangerous or knocked about as the press were making out. The children had long ago been evacuated, but the shops and pubs were still open and he could only see a few destroyed houses and buildings.

Fighting had developed above them, however. They could clearly see aircraft droning and whirling about the sky, machine guns occasionally sputtering. Then one German plane dived down almost vertically with a high-pitched whine, finally crashing with a dull 'whoomph', followed by a pilot drifting down in his parachute. At the same time, a German bomber hurtled into the sea with a large splash.

They lunched at Dover castle, from where they could clearly see Calais. 'It seemed queer to observe the long stretch of French coast,' noted Lee, 'and think that along it are strung the hordes of Hitler, crowding up against the Channel for a pounce upon England.'

A few days later, Ambassador Kennedy invited Churchill and Admiral Ghormley and his team to dinner at the Embassy. The Prime Minister suggested they call it the 'Destroyers Dinner' since the deal was due to be signed the next day. The Ambassador was still feeling sidelined and humiliated, having been completely ignored in the negotiations.

Over dinner, however, Kennedy learned that the Prime Minister knew almost nothing about the ships that were to be handed over and was learning very little from Admiral Ghormley. 'Will they be able to come across the ocean on their power?' Beaverbrook eventually asked impatiently.

'Perhaps,' Kennedy replied.

'Well, I always expected that if I made such a gesture,' said Churchill cheerfully, 'you would have to give us something, and, of course, I believe that something is going to be, sooner or later, big financial credits or gifts.'

'Don't let America,' added Beaverbrook, 'think she is settling for these bases with these old worn-out destroyers.'

Having always suspected that the deal was more about drawing the US into the war than the need for ships, Kennedy now felt Churchill and Beaverbrook were revealing their true hands.

In fact most of the ships did require significant work and modification before they could be used operationally, and although the deal was finally signed on 3 September, they would not be reaching British ports in a hurry. But in many ways Kennedy was right; privately, Roosevelt was doing increasingly more to help Britain. A secret British mission to the US had also secured sixty new merchant ships to be built by a massively expanding American Maritime Commission. Mass production of simply built, welded, 440-foot, 11,000-ton merchantmen was underway. Labelled 'EC-2 Emergency Cargo' ships, they would later be known as 'Liberty' ships.

In return for this clandestine help, Britain agreed to share some of her technological and scientific advances, including RDF, aerial depth charges, Huff-Duff, the Rolls-Royce Merlin, and a power-driven gun turret. Another secret mission, headed by Henry Tizard, set sail for Washington in late August, carrying with them examples of many of these items. The two countries also began negotiations to exchange code-breaking information. Churchill's long-held plans to bring American muscle to bear were beginning to take fruit.

Across the Reich, planning for Operation SEALION continued. A compromise had finally been agreed between the OKH and Kriegsmarine. There would be no landing at Lyme Bay, but a single crossing of light forces from Le Havre to Brighton would be carried out in addition to the main landing between Eastbourne and Folkestone. It was now proposed that 4,500 paratroopers from the 7th Fallschirmjäger Division should be dropped on to the South Downs in support of the Brighton crossing. Like most compromises, it pleased no-one. Raeder and Fricke still felt this was too broad a front, Halder and von Brauchitsch that it was too narrow. Both OKH and OKW were now agreed that the invasion could now only be viewed as a *coup de grâce* – exactly as Hitler had earlier envisaged.

Yet when Raeder suggested that SEALION be converted to an operation of bluff and nothing more, Hitler rejected the idea out of hand and insisted genuine preparations should continue, including the build-up of shipping regardless of the detrimental effect on the economy. There was also talk of launching large-scale terror raids on London on the eve of an invasion, with the intention of causing mass panic. It was hoped that streams of people would flee London, blocking roads in the process and hampering British moves to meet the invasion.

Having returned to Berlin for this critical period in the battle against Britain, Hitler told Jodl on 30 August that he would decide on SEALION on or around 10 September. Since it was accepted that at least ten days' notice would be needed, a timetable was now drawn up and issued on 3 September. This made the earliest sailing date 20 September, with troops landing early the following morning.

Göring made it clear that he had little faith in SEALION, but Hitler was becoming more optimistic, ironically because at last the Luftwaffe now seemed to them to be emphatically winning the air battle currently raging. At a conference with the Reichsmarschall in The Hague on 29 August, Beppo Schmid confirmed that British fighter strength had dropped to around one hundred, although with the lull up to the 23rd, they probably had an actual strength of around 350. Kesselring reported that according to Generalmajor Theo Osterkamp, the commander of *Jafü* 2, Germany 'already had unconditional fighter superiority now'. Only Sperrle was prepared to add a note of scepticism. By the first week of September, the situation looked even more favourable. Fighter units were reporting that the RAF was attacking with between five and seven aircraft rather than full squadrons of twelve to fifteen aircraft. 'English fighter defence hit hard,' it was reported to OKW. 'Ratio of kills has changed much to our favour.' There was now a feeling of confidence that September's fighting would see the end of British fighter defence – admittedly, later than had been scheduled, but air superiority over Britain at last appeared to be assured.

*

Some refreshed Luftwaffe units had now arrived at the front. Kampfgeschwader 30 'Adler' had been moved to southern Belgium. For Unteroffizier Peter Stahl, in the 2nd Gruppe, the new posting was no surprise; after all, it had seemed odd that they should have stayed in Germany and Denmark kicking their heels while other bomber crews were fighting to exhaustion. At least he was refreshed, having managed to get four weeks' home leave. A young NCO pilot, Peter had been a civilian test pilot before the war, and in August 1939 had been newly married and living a very contented life near the Baltic coast in northern Pomerania. Ever an optimist, he had been stunned by the outbreak of war. He had been immediately called up, but although he had dreamed of joining fighters, after a stint of instructing blind flying had been posted to KG 30 and had flown his first operational sorties over France only in June.

He was under no illusions about what lay in store. 'It is being said,' he jotted in his diary, 'that the British are already on their last legs, but when one hears what the operational pilots – and, in particular, bomber crews – have to report, we're obviously still a long way from victory. The losses suffered by our bomber units must be terrible.' Their new airfield was yet another series of harvested fields at Chièvre near Mons, and for Peter his first landing did not augur well, as touching down he had a blow-out in one of his tyres and only narrowly avoided crashing his Ju 88. 'Not the most pleasant of arrivals,' he noted.

Tommy Elmhirst had been promoted to Air Commodore and posted to Fighter Command HQ at Bentley Priory, where he was to be one of three men who were to keep a twenty-four-hour watch in the vast underground Operations Room. There was not a moment's relaxation whilst on watch and this was exhausting work, with rotas of a straight eight-hour watch, then sixteen, then a further eight, then a day off. Hugely impressed by the calm, cool efficiency of the staff involved, he nonetheless found it an alarming experience. It seemed to him that counters being shuffled around the plotting table represented the highest stakes imaginable: the destruction of Great Britain and her Empire.

His last task before leaving Air Intelligence had been to make an assessment of how long the battle might continue. His figures for downed German aircraft were inaccurate but they had a fairly clear understanding of German production levels. He therefore predicted that if current German fighter losses continued, the Luftwaffe would probably give up around the third week of September. But at the beginning of the month, after the worst week for Fighter Command since the battle began, this was of little comfort. 'The great query was, however,' noted Tommy, 'whether our fighters could continue their present volume of effort and sustain their present rate of losses for another three weeks.'

The seriousness of the situation was underlined to him on his arrival at Bentley Priory. AVM Douglas Evill, Dowding's deputy, thought their prospects looked grim, but welcomed Tommy's paper and hoped they might be able to hang on for another three weeks. From their point of view, 11 Group's airfields were in turmoil, they were struggling to keep squadrons at strength, and their pilots were, between them, flying between fifty and sixty hours a day to meet the hordes of enemy aircraft that continued to come over. The reality was that Fighter Command squadrons were often in better shape than most Luftwaffe units and their pilots were getting more chance to rest. The Luftwaffe strength seemed so formidable because it could choose when it attacked and was able to concentrate its forces, but in fact, in terms of total numbers of aircraft, the gap between the RAF and Bomber Command was closing, rather than widening as the Luftwaffe High Command thought. Hypothetically, the RAF could have mounted a thousand-aircraft raid on the Pas de Calais. Logistically, it would have been impossible, but it is interesting to think what the German reaction might have been. Dumbfounded shock, probably.

But that was not the point. To those in charge of Britain's defence, it seemed as though they were reaching crisis point. There was no let-up in the number of enemy raids on the plotting tables at Bentley Priory and Uxbridge, and now photographs by Coastal Command and reports by Bomber Command's Blenheims warned of huge concentrations of barges and ships suddenly filling harbours all the way from Holland to Le Havre. Dowding had for some time wondered when the Germans might begin delivering massed raids that could not be parried. From the pictures of Continental ports, and the known build-up of Luftwaffe units in the Pas de Calais, the strong suggestion was that the hammer blow was about to come. What worried Dowding was that they would not be able to meet that blow.

On the morning of Saturday, 7 September, Dowding called a meeting with Park, Evill and Sholto Douglas, the Deputy Chief of the Air Staff. He explained that they needed to think about what to do should Fighter Command 'go downhill'. His assumption was that they would soon be unable to keep squadrons fully equipped with pilots. Certainly, if things continued as they were, his policy of rotating squadrons would become impossible. It also worried him that the Germans might discover how hard hit they were – he had no idea they already believed Fighter Command to be a spent force. He was therefore determined to keep 11 Group at full strength come what may, but was unable to increase the numbers of squadrons in the south-east because of the damage to airfields, the limited number of existing airfields, and other logistical issues of maintenance, airfield protection and infrastructure. Already, he said, Park was demanding more pilots for five of 11 Group's squadrons, which were now under-strength but had been in the front line for just a short period.

Sholto Douglas insisted that Dowding was being too pessimistic, and reeled off pilot figures that suggested they had ample numbers of new men coming through. But Dowding retorted that it was one thing to be a trained pilot, and quite another to be a *combat-ready* fighter pilot. At current rates, they were losing 120 pilots a week, a rate that could not be sustained. Losses were now outstripping those coming through the OTUs and the course had already been cut to two weeks. This meant that some pilots were being sent to squadrons with as little as ten hours on Spitfires and Hurricanes. Park now backed up Dowding, pointing out that he had already been forced to put together composite squadrons, a practice to which Dowding was vehemently opposed. 'You must realize,' Dowding said to Douglas, 'that we *are* going downhill.'

Park had been dealing with the problem of under-trained pilots by insisting they were given further training with the squadron before being made operational. This, he said, was no longer possible, but he now suggested a new scheme. New pilots could be sent to squadrons in the north for extra training, while only fully trained pilots from the north would be sent to squadrons in the south. Dowding pointed out that he needed fresh operational squadrons to exchange with 11 Group's battle-exhausted squadrons. The two schemes could run in tandem, Park replied. He was only suggesting importing individual pilots, not entire squadrons, and proposed this should take effect only when a squadron's quota of pilots fell below fifteen. Dowding – and Douglas, for what it was worth – agreed to Park's proposal. From now on, squadrons were to be given categorization. Class A were those squadrons in 11 Group and some in 10 and 12 Group like 609 and 87 Squadrons, for example, which were fully operational and had their quota of sixteen or more combat-ready pilots. Class B squadrons would contain up to six non-operational pilots in a quota of sixteen, while Class C squadrons would retain at least three fully operational pilots. Most Class C squadrons would be in 13 Group, although there would be some in 10 and 12 Groups too. It was the best they could do in the circumstances. They now had to hope that, in the days to come, it would be enough.

The day before, Reichsmarschall Herrmann Göring arrived in Holland aboard *Asia*, bringing with him the news that he was now going to take over personal command of the battle. RAF Bomber Command had been back to Berlin again on the nights of 3 and 4 September. For Hitler, these raids were an abomination. Despite the urgings of many senior Nazis, he had insisted on showing restraint, but now the British had pushed him a step too far. At a speech at the Sportsplatz on 4 September, he had vowed revenge. 'And if the British Air Force drops two, three or four thousand kilos of bombs,' he railed, 'then we will now drop 150,000, 180,000, 230,000, 300,000 or 400,000 kilos, or more, in one night. If they declare that they will attack our cities on a large scale, we will erase theirs! We will put a stop to the game of these night-pirates, as God is our witness. The hour will come when one or the other of us will crumble, and that one will not be National Socialist Germany.'

But now it was Göring, who just ten days earlier had been champing at the bit to attack British cities, who had cold feet. He hoped Britain might yet be brought to the peace table. Attacking London, he knew, would shatter those hopes. Reaching the front, he visited his commanders and summoned a number of his new fighter commodores, including Werner Mölders and Dolfo Galland.

The Reichsmarschall was not in good spirits. Wracked with indecision about the mass attacks on British cities that Hitler had now at long last authorized, he felt that it was the fighters that had let him down and told his fighter commanders so in no uncertain terms. Protecting bombers, he told them, was more important than securing record bags of enemy fighters. Then, softening, he asked them what he could do to improve matters for them. 'I should like an outfit of Spitfires for my squadron,' blurted Dolfo.

'We have the best fighter in the world!' Göring retorted.

Dolfo tried to explain what he meant. Of course he preferred the Me 109. As a fighter it was much better because it could accelerate, climb and dive quickly. But because of its lower wing loading, the Spitfire was more suited to slower manoeuvres, which was what was needed when protecting the bombers. Göring had no answer. Growling, he turned away and left.

Certainly many of the Luftwaffe were anxious to begin massed daylight raids. Despite formations of up to a hundred plus, bombers had rarely been used in numbers of more than that, and usually they were considerably smaller. Dolfo Galland was convinced that really large bomber attacks were the way forward and the only tactic likely to persuade the British fighters to come out into open battle. General von Richthofen was of a similar mind. 'This afternoon the decision comes to raid London,' he recorded. 'Let's hope the Reichsmarschall stands firm. I've got my doubts on that score.'

Von Richthofen need not have worried. The following afternoon, Göring stood on Cap Gris Nez with his assembled commanders and entourage watching the largest Luftwaffe formation ever assembled pass over his head. There were some nine hundred aircraft – three hundred bombers and six hundred fighters – stepped up between 14,000 and 23,000 feet. It was a vast armada, the like of which had never, ever been seen before.

Tom Neil had sensed something was up. Already he had been on two sorties that morning, the first for around fifteen minutes, the second for almost an hour and a half, during which they had patrolled the Thames estuary and as far east as Canterbury. He couldn't quite put his finger on it, but it was almost tangible. All of south-east England had been spread before him, basking in the glorious sunshine of a perfect Indian summer, and yet they had not spotted a thing. As his Hurricane had thrummed rhythmically over a silent world, he had felt as though they were the only people alive.

The squadron was now based at North Weald, in 11 Group, a fighter airfield to the north-east of Epping Forest in Essex. Since their arrival five days before they had had plenty of scrambles but Tom, for one, had still not seen much action. Having landed back at the airfield, Tom had headed to the crew room and slept, fully dressed, his Mae West round his neck, until suddenly, at 4.30 p.m., they were scrambled, and ordered to patrol Rochester–Maidstone.

They had climbed to 18,000 feet when they spotted puffs of ack-ack bursting and then immediately saw the armada of Germans – a wedge of Heinkel 111s, then Dornier 17s and above a huge cloud of fighters.

Tom heard the attack cry, 'Tally ho!', and then they were turning towards the enemy, twelve Hurricanes against more than a hundred. Attacking from the beam, Tom watched the Heinkels fill his gunsight. 'Like slugs,' he thought. 'Huddled together as though for warmth.' Checking his gun button was ready to fire, he glanced either side of him and saw Hurricanes rocking and bunching eagerly. Banking more sharply to give himself a clearer run, he closed towards the bombers, which seemed to surge towards him. Now he was firing, the noise like thick, coarse fabric being ripped, the guns shaking the aircraft. Smoking fronds of tracer sped towards their target and he saw the De Wilde bullets sparking as they hit, and then he was speeding beneath their pale, curved bellies.

Turning on his back, dust from the cockpit floor falling around him, he pulled hard and then began climbing back up, searching the sky. Aircraft were now moving in every direction. He pulled harder on the stick, turning and climbing. Suddenly the bombers had gone, but there were the 109s. One was away to his right, heading towards him but from the opposite direction. Tom turned towards it and fired but the Messerschmitt curved away in a slight dive. Following, Tom dived after him, straining the Hurricane and willing it to catch up. Giving it another burst, he again saw bright sparks and then a brief puff of dark smoke, followed by a thin plume of white and a thicker trail of grey.

The Messerschmitt suddenly looked tired as Tom fired again – and again. Lilting almost lazily, the aircraft appeared to give up. A puff of debris exploded into the air, and then, like a dying animal, the Messerschmitt fell away, the angle of its dive steepening, the trail of smoke thickening. Tom had his first kill.

But he had been guilty of watching his victim and not his back, a cardinal sin. Realizing this with a start, he began to climb once more and spotted a squadron of Hurricanes, Canadians of the newly operational 1 Squadron RCAF. Tagging on behind, Tom followed them as they climbed, flying north-east. Then, roughly parallel and heading in an easterly direction was another huge formation of enemy aircraft, the bombers some 1,500 feet below, the fighters about the same level. They were now flying on a convergent course. Drawing closer, Tom sensed the Canadians were about to attack but then suddenly half a dozen yellow-nosed Me 109s peeled off to the right and came around the rear of the Hurricanes.

The Canadians now dived, and Tom followed. He felt as though he were part of a cavalry charge of the wildest kind, hurtling in a thirty-degree dive towards the bombers, and then, as they drew near, all the Hurricanes appeared to open fire at once. 'Then, when a collision seemed inevitable, we were through,' recalled Tom, 'a chaos of wings, engines, and fuselages with black crosses.' In an instant, the bombers were gone and so were the yellow-nosed 109s, and Tom was diving, the engine screaming, the controls rattling in his hand, his ammunition spent. Below him the Thames, with pillars of smoke rising into the sky. He began to pull out, huge forces pressing him into his seat, and his vision beginning to grey. Slowly, gradually, he straightened out, and caught back his breath. He was still alive.

It was time to go home.

The yellow-nosed Messerschmitts were from JG 52; almost every German fighter was in the air that late Saturday afternoon. Ulrich Steinhilper thought it an unbelievable sight. Flying top-cover, he marvelled to see the sky thick with German aircraft, the various levels stacked up one upon another as far as the eye could see. By the time he was within sight of London, he could see many oil tanks already burning brightly with huge clouds of smoke reaching high into the sky. He was also surprised to see so many Spitfires and Hurricanes – if the intelligence being told them by the High Command was correct, he reckoned there should have been minimal fighter opposition. As it was, he soon realized he could not afford to take his eye off the ball for a moment. 'Everywhere was danger,' he noted, 'from the British fighters, from the heavy flak and from loose barrage balloons.' One had become detached and was now floating around near their altitude, burning brightly amidst a cloud of thick, dark smoke.

Also in the thick of it was Siegfried Bethke and his 2nd Staffel. Diving down on to a squadron of Hurricanes that were attacking the bombers, Siegfried managed to get on to the tail of one. They had nicknamed the Hurricanes *Hurenkähne*, literally 'whore barges', and now he opened fire and saw bullets and cannon strike and then it burst into flames. He watched the pilot bail out and float downwards as the *Hurenkähne* dived, scything through the air, a mass of flame and smoke.

Also entering the fray were the Hurricanes of 303 Kościuszko Squadron. The Poles had impressed in the first few days in action, but much to his great frustration Jan Zumbach had still to open his account and had begun to worry that he was somehow jinxed. Ordered into the air around the same time as 249 Squadron, they had climbed to 20,000 feet, patrolling the north of London. It was the cotton wool bursts of flak over the Port of London that had alerted Jan to the attackers. Beneath them, to their right, he now saw the large formation of bombers and their fighter escorts. Jan expected to dive down upon them immediately in an effort to break up the bombers before they began dropping their bombs, but Boozy Kellett ordered them to fly on.

Writhing with irritation, Jan then heard a Polish voice telling them to attack. It was Paszkiewicz, swooping down with the other sections – and Kellett – following. Jan's heart began pounding so much he could hardly breathe. Spitfires were attacking as well and now a huge swarm of diving, wheeling aircraft buzzed and twisted across the sky, tracer criss-crossing murderously. Two blazing Dorniers dived in front of him, then parachutes puffed open. Jan followed the others in a glancing frontal attack but as he pressed down on the gun button, nothing happened. Cursing wildly he realized he had failed to turn off the safety catch.

Wrenching his Hurricane into a tight turn, he doubled up over the stick from the force of negative-g, and then a Dornier sprang up in front of him, growing until it filled his sights. The tail-gunner opened fire and then Jan pressed down again and this time bullets sped from his guns, the Hurricane shuddered, but smoke began streaming from the Dornier's port engine. Another burst, and a flash of flame. 'Just like that,' noted Jan, 'it all seemed easy.'

English and Polish voices filled his headset. Jan dived after another Dornier, getting so close it was a sitting duck. When he opened fire, it blew up with his first burst, debris clattering against his own machine. A voice now shouted, 'Watch out, Messerschmitt!' and in the same moment, Jan saw a 109 on the tail of a Hurricane, but he was too late to help. And now he was fighting for his own life as a dozen Me 109s seemed to be drawn on to him by Jan's attempt to intervene. With lines of bullets criss-crossing over him, he steep-turned hard to the left and blacked out. When he came to, he had lost some 12,000 feet and was all alone in the sky and with a few holes gaping in his port wing. Only as he set course back to Northolt did he realize his oxygen lead had come detached; no wonder he had passed out.

Arriving back over Northolt it was now his turn to perform a victory roll. He was not alone – the squadron made claims for eleven Dorniers and three more damaged and two Me 109s and two damaged. They had paid a price, however. Athol Forbes, one of their flight commanders, had been shot down and wounded, another pilot lost half his buttock, and a third bailed out and landed in a suburban garden.

In London that afternoon was RV Jones, who had been working at the Air Intelligence office at 54 Broadway, between Victoria and St James's Park, when the sirens began to wail. Making no immediate rush for the shelter, RV remained where he was but soon heard bombs and machine-gun fire. Even so, they did not appear to be very near, so he and his boss, Fred Winterbotham, joined others who were already watching from the roof. Against the clear blue late-afternoon sky, they watched bombs bursting, and smoke billowing from fires that were already raging from the docks in the East End. High above, formations of German bombers, RAF fighters weaving and diving around them like angry wasps. Occasionally a parachute would drift down.

Colonel Raymond Lee was also at work that Saturday afternoon, trying to catch up on his correspondence. At first, he paid no attention to the sirens, but then, when he heard anti-aircraft guns begin to pound followed by a series of heavy explosions, he began to take note. When he heard aircraft he went outside on to Grosvenor Square and, straining his eyes, looked up and saw tiny glinting specks of aircraft high in the sky. Then McDonald, one of his Embassy colleagues, came down from the roof and reported huge fires raging in the docks. Now, massive mushrooms of smoke were rising high into the sky, blotting out a number of barrage balloons, which themselves were around 5,000 feet high.

Meanwhile, Tom Neil had landed back at North Weald, where he had clambered down wearily from his plane and had begun tramping back across the field, only for the siren to start before he had even reached the dispersal hut. Moments later, enemy bombers could be seen approaching. Fighter Command groundcrew had, by now, refined the art of refuelling and rearming in a matter of minutes, so as soon as his Hurricane was ready, Tom took off again, his fourth sortie of the day. Climbing to 8,000 feet, he saw the enemy was by now too far away. Straining to catch them, he felt utterly hopeless – he was one solitary Hurricane chasing fruitlessly after hundreds of the enemy. Even so, by the time he had climbed to angels fifteen, he managed to catch up with a straggling Dornier. It was still a bit too far away, however, while puffs of ack-ack were now bursting worryingly close by. Firing several long bursts from too far away, Tom could only watch the Dornier continue calmly on its way. 'I flew back,' noted Tom, 'my guard down. Totally spent. Since breakfast, I had been in the air for more than four hours.'

Back in the Pas de Calais, the pilots were excitedly discussing the mission. At Mordyck, Siegfried Bethke learned that his wingman, Feldwebel Rudorrfer, had shot down three Hurricanes in addition to his one. Some of his pilots had returned with flak damage to their aircraft, others with bullet holes. One of Siegfried's friends had been rammed and forced to bail out and had been taken prisoner.

Ulrich Steinhilper had been shaken to see a 109 latch on to the tail of another and shoot it down by mistake. He had also seen pilots falling, their parachutes on fire, but not a single one of their own *Gruppe* had been shot down – all had safely returned. They had also been delighted by radio intercepts of the British radio which had revealed numerous references to an elite 'yellow-nosed' wing. Ulrich had not shot down anything himself, but he knew he would not forget that afternoon in a hurry. The aerial battle over London had been a beautiful but awe-inspiring sight. 'The pure azure-blue of the sky,' he wrote, 'with the sun dimmed by the sinister smoke penetrating to extreme height; this interwoven and cross-hatched by the contrails of fighters locked in their life and death struggles. In amongst this the burning balloons and the few parachutes in splendid and incongruous isolation.' Like many pilots, he had not failed to realize the significance of what had happened that day.

Raymond Lee, meanwhile, seeing the bombers had gone, had hailed a taxi and hurried towards the fire. As he drove through London, people already seemed to be carrying on as normal, people reading papers or wandering through St James's. Finally, he reached the Tower of London and from Tower Bridge he looked down the Thames and saw immense fires raging on both sides of the river. Leaving his taxi, he walked down through Wapping, the streets crowded with fire engines and hoses, police and soldiers forming picket lines. 'Tremendous fires were raging within a block of where these crowds were,' noted Lee, 'but they displayed little excitement and no signs of panic.'

Having touched down for the last time that day and staggered back to dispersal, Tom Neil learned that the squadron had taken a hammering.

George Barclay had force-landed somewhere, Pat Wells was missing, 'Boost' Fleming had been shot down in flames, although he had been spotted bailing out; Sergeant Killingback had bailed out but was badly wounded, and so too was Sergeant Smithson. Sergeant Beard had also been shot down but had bailed out. Pat was later reported to be in hospital but Boost Fleming had been killed. Landing by parachute, he had been on fire. Burns and shock did for him. Fighter Command lost twenty-five aircraft and sixteen pilots killed that day, the Luftwaffe forty-one aircraft and fifty-two aircrew dead. But for 249 Squadron, six pilots shot down in one afternoon was a big loss – more than a quarter of the squadron down in a stroke. 'The dispersal hut,' noted Tom, 'seemed empty that night.'

Later that evening, RV Jones went back home to Richmond, wondering whether this was the end of everything. 'The fires in the docks were enormous,' he wrote, 'they could never be put out before nightfall. Even if we jammed the beams completely, the night bombers would have perfect markers, for the flames in the docks could be seen from the coast.' It seemed to him that all the Luftwaffe had to do was keep the fires stoked with successive raids, while the main force pulverized the rest of central London.

Certainly, the Luftwaffe was not finished that day, and as RV Jones had correctly judged, the fires had not been put out by nightfall. A further raid had arrived after 8 p.m., but although this was still in daylight, no attempt was made to intercept it; Fighter Command was spent for one day, it seemed. More bombers, in smaller numbers, flew over the city throughout the night, right up until four the following morning, adding to the difficulties of the population and firemen below. One of the night raiders was Hajo Herrmann, leading his 9th Staffel. Incredibly, it was already his sixty-ninth combat mission of the war. He regretted the turn on London but had a clear conscience. He was convinced that they had done everything possible to conduct the war as a struggle between combatants rather than civilians. Yet British bombers had been indiscriminately bombing Germans for some time without any retaliation, conducting what Hajo viewed as a war of terror. He hoped that by their answering like with like, the British might be compelled to return to warfare according to the rules. 'That was preached by our leaders at every level,' noted Hajo, 'and I, from bitter personal experience, never had any reason to doubt it.'

Raymond Lee had gone out to dinner that night – with the writer Somerset Maugham amongst other guests – since no-one had thought to cancel because of the bombings. Afterwards, he walked back to his club, and found many of the staff sleeping awkwardly on sofas and on chairs, evidently feeling safer on the ground floor. He had known the 'hard pounding' was bound to come at some point, but he sensed there would now be no let-up and that a new phase of the battle had begun. 'The Boche has failed to knock out the RAF by attacking the airdromes,' he wrote to his wife, 'has failed to cripple industry by random and wide-spread bombing, and has made no impression whatever upon the British civil morale.'

⊙ 44 ✠

Summer Madness

SATURDAY, 7 SEPTEMBER, had also been the day on which the Joint Intelligence Committee advised the Chiefs of Staff that an invasion was once again imminent. Hundreds of invasion barges were now stacked up the other side of the Channel, and numbers were increasing daily. They also had intelligence on German troop movements and had picked up the fact that von Richthofen's dive-bombers had been moved near to the Pas de Calais. Four German spies had also been caught landing from a rowing boat on the south-east coast, and they confessed that their job had been to report troop movements of British reserve forces. Furthermore, the conditions of the tide and moon, not to say the weather, were highly favourable between 8 and 10 September. It all seemed to point heavily to one thing. With enemy bombers already over London, the Chiefs of Staff accepted the JIC's advice and at 5.20 p.m., issued an official alert.

The army was already at eight hours' notice, but General Brooke's Chief of Staff, General Bernard Paget, now gave the 'immediate action' to all troops in Eastern and Southern Commands, and then, at 8.07 p.m., Brooke issued the signal 'Cromwell', the code word that warned all troops to go at once to their invasion battle stations. Although only a warning, however, the 'Cromwell' signal was issued to all Home Guard commanders, many of whom interpreted it to mean the invasion was already happening. Across countless towns and villages, church bells were rung, calling the Home Guard to arms. In no time, reports were flooding in of German parachutists landing and fast motor boats approaching the coast. Of course, nothing of the sort was happening. Although the British had spent most of the summer expecting German parachutists to descend at any moment, Göring had still not even pledged his precious *Fallschirmjäger* to the invasion operation, despite OKH's plans for them.

There were plenty of boats out at sea, but none transporting German infantry to England. All local naval commands had been put at immediate notice by night and short notice by day. The 29th Minesweeping Flotilla, for example, had been ordered to lie offshore at Eastbourne as a first anti-aircraft line. 'We made up a barrage line,' says Joe Steele, 'about eight trawlers stretched across the harbour and as planes came over we'd open fire with our 12-pounder and twin .5s.' As Joe admits, it was not very effective – the 12 pounder was not designed as an anti-aircraft gun and neither were the .5-inch machine guns – but the trawlers were cannily placed should the invasion have been mounted.

Churchill had personally rung Park to inform him of the invasion warning, but had not seemed unduly concerned himself. Nor was Park, who was confident Fighter Command could stave off the enemy fighters while Bomber and Coastal Commands attacked any invasion shipping.

In fact, much to his annoyance, Park had still been in his meeting with Dowding when the bombers had arrived over London so had not been in the Operations Room at Uxbridge. Hurrying there, he had arrived before the raiders passed, conferred with his controllers and then dashed to Northolt, where he kept his Hurricane. Rather like Feldmarschall Milch, Park made sure he flew regularly, seeing the lie of the land for himself, and speaking to as many of his squadrons as possible.

Flying over London, he had been appalled by the sight of so many fires, but he sensed that the attack on the capital was unlikely to have been a one-off. Rather, he suspected it marked a major switch in Luftwaffe policy, and, if so, it would give him a chance to bring his airfields back to some kind of order. In short, the Luftwaffe might have thrown him a lifeline.

Churchill had been at Chequers, but at noon on Sunday, 8 September, he left for London taking General Ismay with him, and headed straight to the worst parts of the East End. More than 300 had been killed and more than 1,300 seriously injured, but one of the first places they had been taken to was an air raid shelter that had suffered a direct hit. About forty people had been killed, and now, the afternoon after the night before, the place was still heavy with those searching for trapped people and belongings. As the Prime Minister got out of the car, people rushed around him crying, 'It was good of you to come, Winnie!' and 'We thought you'd come!' Others shouted out in defiance, 'We can take it! Give it 'em back!'

Churchill was profoundly moved; when he had supported plans to attack Berlin, he had been aware of the probable German reaction but was equally firm in his belief that Britain and her people had to be prepared to accept losses in the struggle against Nazi Germany. Now, however, he sobbed quite openly, the tears streaming down his cheeks. As Ismay struggled to get him through the press of people, he heard an elderly lady say, 'You see, he really cares, he's crying.'

As they continued their tour, they saw many Union Jacks flying on piles of rubble that the day before had been houses and homes. Others were little more than skeletons. Fires still burned and before Churchill left much later it was evening and the bombers were returning once more. Ismay tried again and again to get the Prime Minister to leave, but he was in a defiant and obstinate mood and insisted on seeing everything. As Churchill finally agreed to head back to Downing Street, a shower of incendiaries fell just in front of them. It was a long journey, the entourage struggling to get back through the narrow streets, many of which were blocked by houses and buildings having been blown across them.

At around the same time that Churchill was struggling through the streets of London's East End, across the sea at the Biscay port of Lorient, the newly refurbished U-48 was slipping from her moorings and heading out on patrol in the Atlantic. The submarine was one of the most famous of all U-boats, with record-breaking numbers of ships to her name. She also had a new skipper, her third in a year, Kapitänleutnant Heinrich Bleichrodt, who, aged thirty, was new to command and had only one combat patrol to his name. He had a lot to prove. So did all Admiral Dönitz's U-boats. They had to prove that even if SEALION could not be launched, there was still a way of bringing Britain to her knees.

Also on board was a new 1st Radio Operator, or *Funkgefreiter*, Rolf Hilse. Just eighteen years old, Rolf had only recently been promoted having been on a course to Pilau – signal school – where he had learned about the latest radio and sonar equipment and how to operate it. Like Hans-Ekkehard Bob, Rolf was from Freiburg in the Black Forest, about as far away from the sea as any point in Germany. His father, however, had been in the navy in the last war, where he had served on the battleship *Friedrich der Grosse* at the Battle of Jutland. All the same, Rolf might never have joined the navy at all. In August 1939, he had been called up and posted to the 214th Anti-Tank Regiment near Frankfurt. One morning, whilst on parade, all those who were single and under five foot eight inches were asked to step forward. Since Rolf was both, he did as he was told. Only then were they told they just 'volunteered' to join the U-boat arm. 'Nobody was keen,' says Rolf. 'We knew what was coming.'

After training on U-67 and having completed his signals course, he was sent to Lorient towards the end of August along with another new member of the crew. Spotting an officer down at the harbour they asked to be directed to U-48. In fact, the officer was their new captain, Heinrich Bleichrodt, who shook hands and directed them to see the *Oberbootsmann*, the Ship's Mate. On board they were allotted bunks and Rolf had a chance to look around his new boat. He was impressed; with the refit, U-48 could have been a brand-new submarine.

Now, with dusk turning to night, U-48 was heading back to sea. Two minesweeper escorts led them out of the harbour and out into the Bay of Biscay, but after an hour and three-quarters, they turned back. 'They flashed their lights,' says Rolf, 'and wished us good luck and good hunting.'

The bombers returned to London the next day, Monday, 9 September. Amongst those attacking the capital was Peter Stahl. He had been forced to sit around kicking his heels waiting for his Junkers to be repaired, but although it was still not ready, he had been given the oldest 'sledge' in the *Gruppe* and told to fly in that. Taking off from Chièvre, they climbed through cloud, the machines scattering somewhat. His canopy was icing badly but when they emerged into the sun he realized he was leading the *Gruppe* and so remained in that position. They then formed up with the other bomber units over Lille until there were at least 200 bombers, and then later, as they reached the French coast, the fighters joined them too. Peter found that flying an individual plane amongst such a large formation gave him a sense of security. 'Wherever one looks are our aircraft,' he noted, 'all around, a marvellous sight.'

As they crossed the Channel, the formation began to sort itself out. Fighters zig-zagged beside and above them, and then, as they passed over the British coast, flak rose up to greet them. Visibility was good and soon he spotted great pillars of smoke rising 5,000 metres into the sky, which he took to be coming from London. Soon they had reached the outer belt of London flak. The British gunners, he thought, were shooting unpleasantly well and the formation became restless. Peter found it hard to hold his position and he had to concentrate hard just to avoid colliding with another aircraft. He felt unprepared for this; no-one had warned him of the difficulties of flying in a large formation with flak bursting all around them. It was a terrifying experience.

Somehow, he had reached the city unscathed. The first bombs were already falling and then it was his turn to press the red release button. Bombs away, and the Junkers made its usual jump of relief. Below, Peter saw the curving Thames and the city spread out like a giant map. They watched the bombs explode as they made a wide banking turn. 'It must be terrible down there,' he scribbled. 'We can see many conflagrations caused by previous bombing raids. The effect of our own attack is an enormous cloud of smoke and dust that shoots up into the sky like a broad moving strip.'

The impressively co-ordinated formation had now disintegrated, and Peter was glad he was in a Ju 88, with speed and acceleration enough to be able to easily change position and altitude. But suddenly British fighters were amongst them. 'Hein,' he told his gunner, 'keep your eyes open, they are Tommies.' Tracer criss-crossed the sky, but while the bombers lumbered on, Peter was conscious of fighters locked in combat, twisting and turning around them. Hein suddenly opened fire with his machine gun, which made Peter jump and then, moments later, shouted, 'They have turned away!' Below, some parachutes drifted downwards and ahead of him, Peter saw a Heinkel 111 diving, trailing smoke. Soon after, he overtook another, flying with one engine dead.

Having escaped into the clear, Peter pulled out a sandwich which he had kept in his knee pocket and which he always found helped to calm him down. He had barely taken a bite, however, when Leo, his navigator, tapped him on the shoulder and pointed to an oil slick running over his starboard engine. A glance at the dials revealed the truth: he had already lost eighty litres of oil, leaving just ten. A bullet, or simply an old engine? He wasn't sure, but he now had no choice but to shut the starboard engine down to avoid it seizing.

They staggered on. Ten-tenths cloud cover helped conceal them, but once again icing up of the canopy was causing Peter problems. Now dependent on his instruments, he gently dived down through the cloud.

As it darkened, he knew he was near the base, and they emerged only 400 metres from the ground. Immediately they spotted an airfield – Amiens, which would do – so Peter restarted the starboard engine, hoping there was just enough oil to enable him to land. To their great relief, all went well. 'We touch down,' he wrote, 'the wheels rumble over the airfield until we come to a stop and I can switch off the engines. Our first trip to London is over.'

Later that night, the Luftwaffe hit the City and West End. The next day the planes were back again; Portsmouth and Southampton were also hit. Once again, London was bombed at night.

Air Vice-Marshal Park's hunch had been right. A clear pattern was now emerging and on 11 September he issued another instruction order to his controllers. The enemy, he pointed out, had stopped the practice of carrying out two or three separate attacks by up to 300 aircraft a day, and instead was now concentrating three or four hundred planes in two or three waves following in quick succession, the entire engagement lasting between forty-five minutes and an hour.

Before, he had been forced to meet the large numbers of disparate raids with whatever he could scramble, fighting over a wide area, but now he recognized that it should be possible to meet the enemy at maximum strength, employing squadrons not in large wing formations, but in pairs, each independent of the other but operating in tandem, and rendezvousing over a base decided upon by the Group controller. Sector controllers were to inform the Group controller the moment a pair of squadrons had rendezvoused. The Group controller would then lead those two squadrons to a raid, leaving the remaining squadrons in a sector to the sector controller. Spitfires were to attack the high fighters, Hurricanes the bombers and close escort. Learning from the Germans, Park also told his squadrons to dispense with the vic, and to fly in a more loose, line-abreast formation of four instead. In issuing these new orders, Park was demonstrating just how adaptable he was, revealing a commander who was prepared to make decisive operational and tactical changes according to how the battle evolved. Surprisingly few shared this attribute.

However much Park and Dowding may have viewed the change of German effort as a respite for their airfields, it did not feel that way to the men flying to meet these colossal German raids. On 7 September, 92

Squadron was posted to Biggin Hill, now one of the world's most bombed airfields. Tony Bartley had been on leave and returned to Pembrey to find everyone gone, and with them his V8 car. It was too late to head to Biggin that night so he stayed at Pembrey, too excited to sleep. It never occurred to him that he might be killed.

He was flown up the following morning, 13 September, in an Anson. Circling over Biggin he saw a bomb-scarred mess – roughly patched craters on the grass and tarmac runway, and ruined, blackened buildings. The ferry pilots landed and rolled over towards some Spitfires, which, Tony realized, belonged to 92 Squadron. Without even turning off the engines, the pilot bustled him out of the Anson, which then sped off again as quickly as possible.

Several of the pilots greeted him cheerfully, including his friend Brian Kingcombe. 'We shoot Huns all day, dear boy,' Brian told him, 'and get bestially drunk at night.' The station stores had been hit so they had all begun helping themselves to whatever they wanted. Brian had taken two of everything for a rainy day and advised Tony to do the same.

Just then, ack-ack guns opened fire as a lone Ju 88 emerged through cloud and disappeared to the south, on this occasion ignoring Biggin.

'What does one do on these occasions?' Tony asked. Being at an airfield coming under regular attack was a new experience.

'Just put on a tin hat and strike a hostile attitude,' Brian suggested.

His car, Tony now discovered had been wrapped round a tree a couple of days earlier by Norman Hargreaves. He'd been drunk but had been let off with a one-pound fine.

'I'll fix him for this,' Tony told Brian.

'Been fixed already, poor chap,' Brian replied, 'on the dawn patrol yesterday.' In fact, there had been quite a few changes already. Another pilot had been killed the day before and a further one shot down. On the 9th, Allan Wright had been badly shot up but had spluttered back, and two others had been shot down and wounded. Bob Stanford Tuck had been posted to command 257 Squadron, and Allan had taken over Tuck's flight. The new CO, Squadron Leader Philip Sanders, was also out of action, having set fire to himself accidentally with his cigarette lighter. A quick lunch in the crew room at dispersal was interrupted by another lone raider. Everyone dived for cover apart from Brian. 'This gives me the most terrible indigestion,' he muttered.

They were stood down later, having not flown, so Tony found his new digs. The mess had been bombed out, so they were in army buildings a bit further down the road. Tony raided the stores as suggested, taking various items including a spare parachute, and making sure he chatted up a WAAF packer first to make sure she did a good job. Dinner was in the old army mess and, as they ate, the German bombers roared overhead on their way to London.

After dinner, they decided to go to the White Hart pub at Brasted, a couple of miles down the hill. Allan was the only one not to join them, preferring, quite sensibly, to remain sober as far as possible and to get his sleep. The rest headed off in the squadron truck, everyone yelling in unison, 'Ninety-Two Fighter Squadron!' at the tops of their voices in response to the sentry's challenge. Through the gate, they drove at breakneck speed down the narrow roads to Brasted.

In the pub were two identical and striking twins, who were quickly introduced to Tony as the MacNeal sisters. They seemed to know all the pilots and in no time pints were being poured and liberally handed out.

'Who's paying for all this?' Tony asked.

'Don't know. Who cares as long as I'm not,' replied Brian. 'The natives are very friendly.'

After they had downed a number of pints the landlord called time. One of the twins suggested they head to the Red House. Everyone seemed to be keen on that idea. Tony was game, although he hadn't the faintest idea what the Red House was. They piled back into the truck and after a short drive pulled up in front of a fine old manor house. At the door, the twins were already waiting for them. Tony was shown into the drawing room and given a very large whisky. Someone put on the radiogram and another pilot grabbed one of the twins and began to dance.

Several hours and bottles of whisky later, Tony thought perhaps they should be heading back. Geoff Wellum had been sick, all of them were drunk. Tony could not help wondering how on earth they were going to make dawn readiness.

He was woken by his batman at 4.30 a.m. with a cup of tea. In the corridor, he bumped into 'Wimpy' Wade, who had put his uniform on over his pyjamas. Outside, it was cold and still dark. Somehow, the pilots managed to converge in the barrack block wearing an assortment of jackets, pyjamas, roll-neck sweaters and scarves. Silently, they clambered into the truck and rumbled up to dispersal. Spitfires stood silently silhouetted against the thin dawn sky. In the middle of the dispersal hut was a stove which had already been lit by the duty ops telephone operator. Around the walls were the pilots' day cots, iron single beds.

Tony put on his Mae West then went over to his own aircraft and chatted to his fitter, Wallace, who was already checking her over. Each pilot had a fitter and rigger to look after his plane. Complete trust in these men was essential and usually justifiably earned. Wallace assured him his Spit was running like a bird.

He wandered back to dispersal, where he spent the next few hours waiting to be scrambled, trying to catch up on his sleep and hoping his hangover would wear off. He was eventually scrambled three times that day, but it was in the last sortie that the squadron intercepted the large enemy raids heading for London. Two more of their pilots were shot down and wounded, but that night, having been stood down, they had dinner and then once again headed to the White Hart.

Every squadron had its own culture, usually dictated by the character of the squadron leader and two flight commanders, but since there were few fighter pilots over the age of twenty-seven, it was understandable that these young men should want to relax by drinking in the evening. Some pilots never drank a drop, others, like Allan Wright, were sufficiently of their own mind not to be swayed by any kind of peer pressure, and would only join in when they felt like it. It was true that 92 Squadron were particularly fond of playing hard in the evening, but they were not the only ones by any means. Bee Beamont and the 87 Squadron pilots would be down the pub most nights, as would those in 32 Squadron. 'We used to booze dreadfully,' says Pete Brothers. One day they were stood down because of low cloud and rain, so they went to the mess and got pissed. By early afternoon, however, the sun had come out and they were suddenly called to readiness and then scrambled. 'I shall never forget taking off and thinking, "That button . . . turn it that way . . . switch on gunsights . . ." We were all absolutely tanked. Mind you, when you saw black crosses, you were instantly sober.'

There was always Benzedrine, which some medical officers would hand out more liberally than others. In 92 Squadron, Bob Holland was notorious for taking the drug in order to get himself going in the morning, although most pilots with sore heads found that a few deep inhalations of oxygen were enough to clear the head. For Pete Brothers, as for others, the boozing was done because it was fun and they were young and because they could. But it also helped them not to dwell on things too much. The camaraderie of wartime is something that cannot be understood by someone who has not experienced it. A squadron – or *Staffel* – was a very close, tight-knit bunch of young men. Most preferred to put the losses out of their mind, but it was not always that easy, especially when it was particularly close friends or even family. On 12 September, Arthur Hughes learned that his brother, Dave, a Hurricane pilot with 238 Squadron, was missing. Two days earlier, Arthur had been given an overseas posting, to help a Free French squadron in West Africa. In the knowledge that he had miraculously survived the current battle, he had been looking forward to his sister's wedding that coming weekend. He knew this meant his 'dear brother' was dead. 'Poor Kathleen, poor parents,' he scribbled. His brother would have been twenty-three in two weeks' time. 'This is the end of my youth, and who knows what the future will bring?'

Arthur did not record whether he drowned his sorrows that night, but certainly the drink helped most people. 'You anaesthetized yourself with a good old jar of beer,' says Tony Bartley. 'You flew all day and fought all day and then you played all night.'

Bomber crews would spend a fair amount of time drinking too. Andrew Jackson and his crew would invariably head to the pub once they knew they would not be flying that night. Arthur Hughes would often go to parties in King's Lynn or there might be a big drinking session in the mess. One evening in August, a spontaneous mess party developed and they all got so drunk they began playing 'High Cock-a-Lorum', which involved one team getting in a line, each man's head between the legs of the man in front, and then members of the other team taking a running leap and trying to land as far along the backs as possible. Inevitably, there were injuries, one of them cracking his skull open, which required three stitches. 'This morning he was very perky,' jotted Arthur the next day, 'and claimed never to have felt better.'

Luftwaffe pilots would drink in the evening but by and large there was not quite the same degree of careless abandon about their drinking sessions as there was in the RAF. Siegfried Bethke felt there was an important difference between the two sides that summer. 'They knew exactly what was at stake that summer,' he says. 'Our motivation and conviction was of a different dimension. We wanted to be successful but we didn't have a national goal.' The Luftwaffe pilots and crews were also more disciplined, more sober in their approach. Luftwaffe *Staffeln* would not have been allowed to go out on benders if they knew they would be flying the following morning; it would not have even occurred to them to do so.

This did not mean they were completely abstemious, however. Ulrich

Steinhilper and his fellow *Gruppe* members would be on the wine most nights, but they tended to talk shop, discussing tactics, the day's events and other flying matters, which was not really the done thing in the RAF. In Ulrich's case, he drank wine as a tension-reliever and also to help him sleep, but not with the intention of getting blind drunk. Hans-Ekkehard Bob says there was some drinking in the evening, but usually they would wait until they had a night off and then they would head into Lille, where there were lots of bars and good restaurants. They had a commandeered black Citroën they would use. 'And there were very, very nice girls in Lille,' says Hans. Like all the officers, Hans was now living in a requisitioned house a short distance from the airfield in order to get away from the attacks by Blenheims and ensure he got a good night's sleep. 'For us pilots,' he says, 'if there was a pretty girl in one spot, you tended to stay there.'

Julius Neumann says he rarely drank in the evening and neither did anyone else in II/JG 27. Nor did his *Staffel* ever head out together for an evening in a bar or local restaurant. 'We never did that,' he says. Instead they would eat their meal and go to bed, or write letters or be writing up combat reports. Anyone who claimed to have shot down an enemy plane had to write one of these reports, and describe in some detail the action and circumstances and what they saw, rather like a police witness statement. For men like Hans-Ekkehard Bob, who already had thirteen victories to his name, this could be a time-consuming business. Hajo Herrmann and his *Staffel* would go into the village where they were billeted and chat up girls and have a drink, but there was not much opportunity for letting their hair down. 'I was a *Staffel* captain and I tried to improve things,' says Hajo. 'I used my spare time to write reports, I didn't waste time.' He lived in reasonable comfort, sharing a house with five or so other officers. They had another house that acted as a mess, complete with Luftwaffe furniture. There was also, of course, the sea. The French beaches were not mined and covered with barbed wire like the beaches were in England. Mordyck was almost amongst the sand dunes and Siegfried Bethke enjoyed regular evening swims at La Panne, followed by dinner out in the town.

For the British pilots, the waiting around was difficult. 'There was a lot of tension in sitting around in dispersal,' says Bee Beamont. 'You jumped a foot when the telephone went.' Bee slept as much as he could. 'If you'd been fighting during the day and you'd gone off down the pub with the lads at night and then had a little bit more than you should have,' he says, 'by four o'clock in the morning when you were woken you probably had a bit of a hangover and so as soon as you got to dispersal you'd find a bed and lie down and go to sleep till somebody woke you up.'

Some people read but Bee never did. Nor did Allan Wright. He greatly enjoyed reading but he couldn't whilst waiting to be scrambled. 'If you're immersed in a book,' he says, 'and you are suddenly called out, it takes a few seconds, or a minute or so to readjust and I thought that might slow me up.' Instead he preferred to talk to his fitter and rigger, check his aircraft and simply watch what was going on.

Time between missions was different for Luftwaffe pilots because they usually knew when they would be flying – normally only a couple of pilots would be kept at cockpit readiness in case of intruders. 'Very often it was decided in the evening before the mission what every pilot had to do the next day,' says Hans-Ekkehard Bob, 'whether it would be a free hunt, or close escort.' Pilots still felt tense waiting around to fly, however, but would spend the time in much the same way their British counterparts did. 'Writing, reading, playing chess, eating, sleeping etc,' scribbled Siegfried Bethke, 'passing the hours, each in his own way.' Hans used to play a German card game called Skat a fair amount, and like Siegfried would swim in the sea whenever he got the chance.

Relaxation was crucial to a pilot's chances of survival, and those who were able to switch off and turn their minds to other things would tend to live longer. There was a balance, however. Getting blind drunk and flying still half-inebriated was obviously not a good idea, but nor was living and breathing the war every minute of the day. A cool, calm head was also essential. In times of intense pressure and stress, the body tenses, the muscles shorten, and the heart rate quickens. In these circumstances it is harder for the brain to make calm, informed decisions, so panic takes over and the brain works irrationally. By keeping calm and measured, the effects of pressure lessen: the heart rate remains at a steadier pace, the body feels more relaxed and so those split-second decisions that can mean the difference between life and death are more likely to be the right ones. Hajo Herrmann, for example, was superb under pressure, able to control his fears and think clearly at all times. 'My crew always said that I was extraordinarily calm in the plane,' he says, 'even when there were fighters and flak around us, but you had to be like this.'

Certainly all the best pilots shared this attribute. Hans-Ekkehard Bob says he always felt in complete control in his aircraft and that adrenalin prevented him from feeling scared. Pete Brothers reckoned experienced pilots developed a kind of sixth sense. 'You'd get the feeling that someone was looking at you,' he says, which would make him look round in time to take evasive action. The difficulty for the sprogs – as new pilots were known in the RAF – was that flying these machines was still a comparatively new experience. When Pete Brothers or Hans-Ekkehard Bob got into their planes they knew precisely what their machines were capable of and in the heat of battle could manoeuvre their aircraft without having to think about what they were doing. For men new to action it was a completely bewildering, frightening and alien experience, and apart from the especially cool-headed most tended to panic, then not to be able to make informed decisions, so they were invariably shot down.

Familiarity with one's aircraft combined with experience also helped the better pilots to get more from their machines. Pete Brothers was fortunate enough to be taught by a First World War ace who told him that when he was about to black out he should put his head on his shoulder, which stopped there being such a direct flow of blood from the head. 'It slows the blacking-out process down,' says Pete. 'Enables you to pull another couple of g before you pass out. I used to tell the chaps in the squadron.' He also learned other tricks. 'Suppose you see tracer passing on your left,' he says. 'The instinct is to turn away from it. The chap who is shooting will have noticed that he is flying to the left of you and he will be correcting his aim. Trick him – go through where he is firing and you'll collect a few holes but you'll throw him off his aim.' Pete always used to wind a bit of rudder trim, so that his Hurricane was always yawing, or crabbing, slightly. He felt it helped put any would-be attacker slightly off his aim.

Pete believes that experience was the key to survival and points out that in 32 Squadron not a single pre-war pilot lost his life that summer. 'People were shot down,' he says, 'but no-one was killed. It was always the new boys that got the chop.' In many ways he was right, but battle fatigue was also a merciless killer. 'Fighting was tiring,' says Bee Beamont. 'It was all cumulative. The weeks went by and the pressure never stopped, and then there was the loss of your colleagues.' It was precisely this cumulative effect that was now beginning to seriously take hold of the Luftwaffe pilots especially. The new boys arriving were green and under-trained, but the experienced ones were being flown into the ground. This was because commanders like Kesselring and Sperrle had no choice but to keep them flying. It was true that there was little proper understanding of combat fatigue, and this did not help the pilots' cause, but the main reason for pushing the pilots so hard was that the Luftwaffe had been given the task of destroying the RAF, a job that required a force far larger than was currently available. The increasingly desperate shortage of new and repaired aircraft made the situation progressively worse because no sprog would be given an aircraft above a more experienced pilot. So the older hands had to fly on and on and on, every day, without let-up. Only bad weather would spare them from combat sorties, and even then, if the weathermen thought the skies might be clear over England, they might still be sent over. These missions would be called *Mülleinsatz* – a 'rubbish action'. 'We used the phrase to refer to actions that were not only unreasonable,' recorded the 9/JG 52 diarist, 'but also pointless because the weather was so bad.'

'We began to feel the fatigue and the tiredness that comes with living under constant threat,' noted Ulrich Steinhilper. Adrenalin would keep them going during combat. 'We would feel the relief of returning to base, but would then have to cope with the emotions of having lost friends and colleagues, knowing also that within minutes we would have to do it all again.'

It was the relentlessness that was so difficult to deal with – the lack of time off, and the lack of any real release of tension. It was true that the German pilots did not have quite the same anxiety of waiting to be scrambled, but this was small consolation. There was the exhaustion of combat flying married to an anxiety on every sortie of not having enough fuel to get home. 'We only had ten minutes to fight,' says Julius Neumann, 'and then we had to go back.' It was all too easy to misjudge that narrow window. Many a pilot flew back with his fuel gauge on empty, every passing second wracked with tension that he might not make it. Plenty did not.

45

The Crux

'THERE'S NO WORD I can start off with,' jotted Olivia Cockett, 'to give the mood of these ghastly days and nights of bombs on London.' Even so, she was managing to keep a grip on herself; only once had she broken down and had a good cry. She also felt better having seen one big, strong fellow crumple up and sob like a child. Her home in Deptford was frighteningly close to the London docks, and overnight she had found herself on the front line of the war. On Sunday night she had put out an incendiary that landed beside her coal cellar. These were small bombs containing an explosive charge which would ignite some incendiary material inside the casing and start a raging fire, and were thus potentially lethal if not quickly extinguished. The following night a high-explosive bomb at the end of her garden brought all the garden walls down and left a crater ten feet deep and thirty wide, and smashed a lot of windows in the process. She had since replaced the glass with cardboard and done the same for the lady living opposite.

Every night had been spent in the cellar. 'I cannot sleep,' she wrote, 'especially since I was the only one awake to hear the incendiary bomb . . . I daren't sleep now.' She had ten sheltering with her, including a cousin of forty with his mother of seventy, and her sister-in-law and two-year-old nephew. 'Brother a hero in the AFS,'* she added, 'doing rescue work and laughing and joking and looking 20 years older in three days, during

* Auxiliary Fire Service.

which he had seven hours off duty.' Her brother, like all those involved in civil defence, had been fully mobilized.

On the 13th, Cecil Beaton was glad to escape London and get back to his house in the country. Every night he had listened to the German bombers from the basement of his South Kensington home. They sounded to him like a slow swarm of bees. 'Jerky bees – buzz-er-buzz-er-buzz,' he scribbled. He noticed that many normal household sounds, such as the banging of a door or the crackle of wood on a fire, had now become noises of destruction. On Monday, the third day, he had been taking pictures of bomb damage when the sirens had gone again. 'I wander deserted streets,' he noted, 'that, until the sirens had sounded, had been a hive of business activity.' The all-clear siren was, he thought, more penetratingly shrill than the warning. 'And so another raid had ended, and we buy more evening papers to learn what damage has been done.' Friends told him of bombs that had fallen nearby but in just a few days he confessed he had already become something of a bomb snob, only impressed when he met someone who had been actually grazed by bomb blast.

He had spotted a wax head lying among the debris of a former hairdressing salon in Albemarle Street, and later returned to try and find it again, this time armed with his camera. As he arrived, a demolition party was pulling down a large top-heavy facade. Watching the walls collapse with a mighty 'whrump', he waited for the dust to settle then clambered over the rubble and found a new wax head among the cracked mirrors, shards of glass and other wreckage. Cecil asked the men whether they had seen a head with golden hair flying wild, and to his surprise they had. Unearthing it, they handed it to him, and he then photographed it against the backdrop rubble. 'I felt thoroughly sad and somewhat unnerved as I walked down the havoc of Savile Row,' he scribbled later, 'where scarcely a window-pane remains intact. And the East End is far worse.'

Harold Nicolson had driven back to London on Sunday the 8th, his journey interrupted by some craters in the road near Maidstone. 'When we get nearer London,' he wrote, 'there is a great pillar of smoke rising like it used to when an oil well was aflame in Persia or Iraq.' The Ministry of Information now braced itself to face one of its toughest tests: heavy air raids over London and the prospect of an imminent invasion. Harold and Duff Cooper urged Churchill to broadcast to the nation, to which the Prime Minister agreed, and Harold prepared a speech for him, which he ignored. However, as Harold admitted, the speech was nonetheless 'effective'.

If the enemy were to try an invasion, it could surely not be much longer delayed, he warned. They had therefore, he said, reached a pivotal moment in Britain's history, one that ranked with the days when the Spanish Armada approached, and when Nelson alone seemed to stand between Britain and the French armies at Boulogne. 'But what is happening now,' he said, 'is on a far greater scale and of far more consequence to the life and future of the world and its civilization than these brave old days of the past.' It was a time for everyone to stand together, and hold firm, which they were already doing. 'This effort of the Germans to secure daylight mastery of the air over England is, of course,' he told the nation, 'the crux of the whole war. So far it has failed conspicuously.'

Harold Nicolson's Home Intelligence reports on morale suggested there was no major cause for concern. There was shock at the bombing of London, but little sign of defeatism. The people who were taking it the worst were the elderly women of the East End. 'Old women and mothers are undermining morale of young women and men by their extreme nervousness and lack of resilience,' it was reported on the Monday. A more general national survey suggested there was bitterness but increased determination to 'see it through'. There was dismay that there were not enough anti-aircraft guns – in fact, there were only a third of the guns that had been planned pre-war, most siphoned off to the navy. It was also clear more rest centres, mobile canteens and improvements to public shelters were urgently needed. A mass exodus from the East End was causing concern, as were reports of rising anti-Semitism and class feeling because the bombs had mostly landed in working-class areas.

As the week wore on, however, morale improved noticeably. General Pile had had sleepless nights over what to do to improve AA fire over the capital and on the 11th ordered his gunners that night not to worry about aiming or accuracy, but to simply fire as much as possible. That night, his thirty-five gun sites launched 13,221 rounds of heavy ack-ack – around one every two seconds. It worked – the bombers pushed noticeably higher that night and in many cases avoided flying over the city at all. More importantly, the population were delighted. 'Morale has jumped to new level of confidence and cheerfulness since tremendous AA barrage,' ran the morale report on the 12th. 'This is true of every district contacted, including East End.' Growing class resentment was diffused when on Friday the 13th the grounds of Buckingham Palace were hit by three bombs whilst the King and Queen were at home. After a week of heavy bombing, British morale was showing no sign of cracking whatsoever.

Göring had suspected this all along. It was one of the reasons he had been reluctant to launch these massed attacks on London. Based at his mobile headquarters aboard *Asia*, the Reichsmarschall had asked Jeschonnek, one of the foremost advocates of terror bombing, 'Do you think that Germany would cave in if Berlin was wiped out?'

'Of course not!' replied the Chief of Staff. He then realized what he had said and quickly added, 'British morale is more brittle than our own.'

'That's where you are wrong,' said Göring.

Before 32 Squadron had left Biggin Hill, a downed German fighter pilot had been picked up by the police and put in the guard room at the airfield. The pilots found out and brought him down to the dispersal hut. He spoke good English and they gave him a drink and then took him over to the mess for some more. Eventually he asked for a pen and piece of paper. The pilots asked why. 'Tomorrow, when the Luftwaffe blackens the sky and you lose the war,' he replied, 'I want to write all your names down to make sure you are all well looked after.'

'We laughed and laughed,' says Pete Brothers. 'He couldn't understand it. "Why are you laughing?" he asked us, and we said, "Oh, you poor fellow! *You* are going to lose!" The arrogance of it – charmingly put over all the same.'

German attitudes were changing, however. Group Captain Felkin and his team were still in charge of interrogating all POWs and found that a useful way of gleaning information was to put several men together and bug their cell. Results showed that some still believed the invasion would happen any moment and that Britain would be defeated. A fair number had also accepted the German intelligence reports about the strength of Fighter Command. 'I estimate that at the most they have only 150 front-line fighters left,' said one *Oberleutnant*, who then explained, 'Production is rather poor.' But others were not so convinced. 'The English certainly have many more aircraft than is assumed by us,' said one bomber pilot. 'I'd like to know where the English get all their fighters from,' said another.

Also increasingly common was a growing concern that they might have missed the bus. 'If we have to wait until spring,' said one prisoner, 'the whole blessed affair must be started over again.' 'Well, if the landing does not materialize and we have to wait here till next year,' muttered a *Feldwebel*, 'it will be damnable.' 'I simply cannot see how we are to win this war,' said one pilot on 11 September. 'At any rate, we must finish the war somehow soon,' said another. 'If we are not in a position to force England to make peace, it might develop into a kind of thirty years' war. That is what I am afraid of.'

Even more apparent were the growing concerns about shortages of pilots and aircraft. One pilot reckoned losses over England were three times higher than they had been during the western campaign. 'The Germans have too few pilots,' said another. 'We have nothing but new crews,' said a bomber *Gruppenkommandeur*, who then complained that his *Gruppe* had not been given one new aircraft since the beginning of the war. 'Not a single one! What a state of affairs!'

Certainly those still flying over to Britain were feeling the aircraft shortage terribly. On 5 September, Siegfried Bethke's 2nd Staffel had just three planes. 'That is my whole squadron,' he noted. The entire *Gruppe* had just eighteen aircraft, while the second and third *Gruppen* had only twelve. They were supposed to have thirty-six. Siegfried had heard that one Zerstörer *Geschwader* had only a dozen aircraft left, rather than the supposed establishment of eighty-one. 'There is currently a crisis with planes,' he recorded starkly. Out to sea, they watched convoys continue to pass through the Channel in front of their noses.

Ulrich Steinhilper was struggling to keep his flagging spirits up. His friend Hinnerk Waller had been shot down and then a few days later a lone Me 109 landed and came to a halt right in the middle of the airfield. Ulrich hurried over along with some of the groundcrew only to find the lifeless body of an *Oberleutnant* in the cockpit. Taking him out, they discovered he had been badly wounded in the abdomen, and had bled to death, dying the moment he touched down. 'It was a shattering reminder,' noted Ulrich, 'of what waited for all of us, every day we flew.' Neither he nor anyone else in the *Gruppe* had had any leave since arriving at Coquelles six weeks before. Siegfried Bethke had not had any since May. 'We've been away since January,' complained one German sergeant pilot, 'and have had no leave at all and yet we have these flights every day.' As a rule of thumb, most squadrons in 11 Group were there for three weeks before being rotated. Dowding and Park were also worrying about their squadrons falling below sixteen pilots, that is, to less than 75 per cent of their strength. Many German fighter *Staffeln*, however, were operating at levels of under 50 per cent.

Nor was there any let-up from Bomber Command, who continued to carry out harassing raids on German airfields just as lone Ju 88s or Dorniers were doing to British bases. Blenheims had attacked JG 2 at

Mordyck the same night as the bombing began on London. 'At St Omer,' complained another bomber pilot, 'these fellows came over our aerodrome every night. I'll never forget those bombs! None of us was wounded, but they hit a lot of aircraft. Every night they were there. Every morning the ground had to be levelled again.'

Clearly, if anyone needed to worry about morale, it was Reichsmarschall Göring.

The new plan devised by Park was proving inspired, because it meant many freshly trained pilots were now being given a chance of survival, while front-line squadrons were kept at reasonable strength. One of the beneficiaries was Sergeant Jimmy Corbin. He and three others from his OTU had been posted to 66 Squadron at Kenley, near Biggin Hill. They all now had around 160 flying hours, which was a reasonable amount, but Jimmy only had twenty-nine hours on Spitfires and no proper combat training at all. Although Jimmy and the other sprogs were keen to join the rest of the squadron in the air, they were fortunate that Squadron Leader Rupert Leigh was clearly a humane man and had refused to let any of them fly operationally. Then, the day after Dowding's meeting on 7 September, Jimmy and one other had been temporarily posted to 610 Squadron, now Category C under the new system, and based in Acklington in Northumberland. The other pilots commiserated, and both Jimmy and his friend Nick felt very depressed about it, but it was the best thing that could have happened to them. A few days after their arrival at Acklington, Jimmy finally flew operationally, scrambled to intercept a German raider from Luftflotte 5. The aircraft, when they eventually found it, turned out to be a Heinkel 115 seaplane down on the water. Jimmy and the other pilots circled above it, preventing it from taking off until a naval launch arrived and took the crew prisoner. 'I touched down on the aerodrome,' noted Jimmy, 'and felt a rush of euphoria. It was good to be back. It was good to be alive.' It was the ideal first operational sortie. Jimmy had been given a taste of the nerves and adrenalin rush that come with combat flying whilst not ever being in great danger himself.

It was thanks to the new Park Plan that Pete Brothers now found himself being sent back down to 11 Group, with the purple and white ribbon of the DFC sewn on to his tunic. He had been lifted from 32 Squadron and posted to 257 at Martlesham, to replace one of the flight commanders who had been killed. Bob Stanford Tuck had also joined from 92 Squadron as the new CO. It was hard on Pete, but at least he had enjoyed a fortnight away from the fray – it was more than any of his German counterparts had been given. It was also sad to say goodbye to the squadron. 'It seems incredible to me to say goodbye to Peter B,' the CO wrote in the squadron diary. 'He's been with us for years and years. He's shared our laughs and shared our tears and now he's gone – new friends to meet. So long, old pal, we'll miss you Pete.'

Time was now fast running out for Germany, as Hitler was well aware. If he was going to strike, he had to strike soon. The navy was now almost ready. For all the earlier pessimism of the Kriegsmarine, its plans had been going well. Weather had hampered some minesweeping operations, but on 6 September Raeder had reported that flank mine barrages had now been successfully laid, the *Schnellboote* playing their part in these operations. All the transportation shipping was now assembled, although as landing craft the hastily gathered barges were hardly ideal. Only half the barges even had engines, and these were not powerful enough to get them across on their own. Tug boats were the solution, and some 350 had been found for the purpose. Each one would tow two barges, one without an engine, and one with. Just before they reached the English coast, those with engines would be cut loose and then expected to make the last stretch under their own steam. The whole shipping operation was clearly fraught with potential problems, but Raeder, rather surprisingly, now seemed more optimistic about the entire plan. 'If air supremacy is increasingly established,' Raeder told Hitler, 'it will be possible to be ready by the new date.' Having been one of the biggest sceptics, Raeder now believed that with the air supremacy proviso, SEALION could succeed. Von Brauchitsch and Halder were of much the same mind, and confident that should they get a foothold in England, their forces would prevail. All now depended on the Luftwaffe.

The tension was mounting with every day and every hour. Hitler knew he had to make a crucial decision. To go ahead and then fail would be catastrophic, but to abandon the invasion would also be disastrous. It would mean the war going on through the winter, on into the following year, Britain getting stronger, America increasing its military output to levels Germany could not hope to match, whilst in the east Russia built up her strength too. War on two fronts. Hitler would *have* to attack in the east after all, another operation fraught with danger.

But the Luftwaffe had yet to clear the skies. On 10 September, Hitler still held back, deciding to postpone his decision until the 14th. In between, however, poor weather once again prevented the kind of full-scale daylight operations the Luftwaffe needed. Nonetheless, on the 13th, Hitler was still optimistic. Reports on British morale being fed back by the German military attaché in Washington suggested English morale was crumbling under the weight of the air attacks. At OKW operations, it was rumoured that Hitler believed a revolution in Britain was about to erupt. Luftwaffe reports also suggested that fighter superiority had by now almost been achieved. The directive for SEALION had also been drawn up and handed to Jodl. Everything was ready to go; Hitler only needed to give the word.

On the 13th, he seemed to be placing his hopes on defeating Britain through continued air assault and internal revolution to bring about victory, but the next – decision – day, he seemed more inclined to go ahead once more. 'A successful landing followed by an occupation,' he said, 'would end the war in a short time.' This, of course, was exactly what everyone in the Reich wanted. The temptation, therefore, to go ahead with one last final gamble must have been huge. But still, even a gambler like Hitler recognized that one prerequisite above all remained: air superiority, and however encouraging the signs, they still did not quite have it. 'Four to five days of good weather are required to achieve decisive results,' Hitler told a conference of his commanders on 14 September. 'There is a great chance of defeating the British; already the effect up to now has been enormous.' Just one last push was needed – a maximum effort and some sunshine. Operation SEALION was not to be abandoned yet.

Despite a misty, hazy start, Sunday, 15 September, promised to develop into a fine day, ideal conditions for the Luftwaffe to begin to deliver its *coup de grâce* on the RAF. The problem for Kesselring was that his maximum effort was not as impressive as it had been a month earlier. Leading the way for the first big raid of the day were only around forty Dorniers drawn from KG 76 and KG 3. Leading the formation was III/KG 76, which had only nineteen aircraft left in the *Gruppe*; the first *Gruppe* had even fewer – just eight. Kesselring also now had fewer fighters to call on since most of *Jafü* 3 had returned to Normandy, part of the increasingly confused tactical thinking of the High Command. A number of replacement aircraft over the past week had eased the aircraft shortage a bit, but even so *Jafü* 2 was well below its establishment of around 600 aircraft; certainly, Kesselring could not call on much more than around 400 Me 109s and a hundred Zerstörers.

At Biggin Hill, most of 92 Squadron were once again recovering from a heavy night of boozing. In the dispersal hut, some were trying to sleep, others fidgeting nervously. On the wall were enemy identification charts and a warning poster with 'Remember the Hun in the Sun' written on it. One of the pilots began pacing about, muttering about how much he hated the waiting.

By mid-morning, the haze was beginning to thin; a fine day was emerging, which meant the Hun would inevitably be over before long. Then, at five past eleven, after six and a half long hours of being at readiness, the phone rang and everyone jumped, waiting for the orders. It was a scramble. Angels 25, rendezvousing with 72 Squadron over base then patrolling Canterbury. Everyone rushed for the door and ran to their Spitfires. Reaching his, Tony grabbed his parachute, clambered into the cockpit, strapped himself in, attached his leads and then started his engine. Suddenly the airfield was alive with the roar of twelve Merlins. Following behind Brian Kingcome, he took off, climbing over the strange valley that hung off the north-east edge of the airfield. As they climbed slowly in a left-hand circuit, he saw London away to his right, the Thames winding and silvery, the city, though, shrouded in mist, largely a result of the previous week's bombing. The sun was now breaking through, its rays glinting off the barrage balloons that seemed to sprout oddly from the ground. He started having fanciful ideas about how their twenty-four Spitfires were all that was barring the ruthless enemy from London, then realized the effects of the previous night's drinking were still with him. It was not a good idea to fly and daydream at the same time.

At Bentley Priory and Uxbridge, the commanders and controllers were in position; there were no strategy meetings this Sunday morning. Good warning of the developing raid had been picked up by the RDF chain, giving Park plenty of time to scramble eleven squadrons from his Group, all but one in pairs, while 609 Squadron had also been sent from Middle Wallop to patrol over Windsor, and a wing of five squadrons led by Douglas Bader from 12 Group was instructed to patrol over Hornchurch. By 11.30, all were in the air, heading to their attack positions – since enemy raids were now invariably headed for London, it was possible to stagger the interceptions from the moment the enemy crossed the Channel all the way to London.

Park had sensed something was up; the invasion talk and the promise of good weather had made it inevitable. He had even forgotten his wife's birthday that morning, although she had assured him that a good bag of German aircraft would be present enough. Over breakfast at Chequers, the Prime Minister had also had a feeling the weather would be good for the enemy, so with his wife, Clemmie, and bodyguard in tow drove to 11 Group Headquarters. There, he assured Park, he had no wish to disturb any station but Uxbridge, and had called by on the off chance that something was up. Park led him to the underground Operations Room, a bunker a couple of hundred yards from the main Headquarters in Hillingdon House. Painted green with a lead roof, it was an unprepossessing and shallow block, offering a tiny target from the air. Steps led down to the entrance, a latticed iron gate, which then opened the way to a longer set of steps going down some thirty feet, the air conditioning system whirring loudly overhead. As the steps turned sharp left and descended another thirty feet, Park tried tactfully to explain that the underground air conditioning could not really cope with cigar smoke.

They continued down a long corridor, lined with thick, rubber-coated wiring, then Park took the Prime Minister up a short staircase into the viewing room. There, through a screen of curved glass designed to reduce the glare and reflection and to cut out the sound from those below, Churchill looked down on the Operations Room with its map table, tote board, clocks, WAAF plotters and Ops staff. The viewing gallery was quiet save for the now soft, background whistle of the bunker's ventilation system

As it happened, he had arrived just in time. Churchill and his wife – he with an unlit cigar clenched between his teeth – stood watching the plots being shuffled across the plotting table, and, along the tote board, the lights being lit up as squadrons took to the air, and then turning from the four colours of their sections to all red as they engaged.

'Hello, Gannic Leader! Gannic Leader!' Tony Bartley now heard in his headset. 'Carfax calling! Two hundred plus coming in over Red Queen. Vector 120, angels 22.'

'Hello, Carfax, Gannic Leader,' Tony heard Brian Kingcombe reply. 'Message received. Over.'

'Hello, Gannic. Gannic Leader. Carfax calling. Watch out for snappers above. Many snappers above. Hear me?'

'Loud and clear, Carfax. Over and out.'

They were now high over Kent, the finger of south-east England spread out before them, and there to intercept the approaching raid well before it reached London. Moments later, as he glanced over his starboard wing, Tony spotted puffs of ack-ack and then huge Vs of bombers. Above, he could just see the 'snappers' – visible by the contrails. *Jesus*, Tony thought. He wondered where they would begin. Luftflotte 2 might have been severely under-strength but being just one of twenty-four Spitfires against nearly 200 aircraft was a sobering proposition. In no time the formation had grown, and then they seemed to be hurtling towards each other.

'Tally ho, right, here they come, chaps,' someone said and then Brian led them in, half rolling and tearing into the approaching enemy. Tony was conscious of Brian opening fire and then a Dornier filled his sights and he pressed down the gun button himself, the De Wilde bullets clearly striking the machine. Hastily dropping its bombs, the Dornier had begun to burn. Sweeping round, Tony drew his bead on a second, and as his guns blazed saw bits of engine cowling flying off the German bomber. Caught in the Dornier's slipstream as he passed, his Spitfire was bucked to one side. Already he was out of ammunition, his fifteen seconds up, but a second later his ailerons jolted and two Me 109s flashed by. Shouting a warning, he then dived away out of the swirling mass and bolted for home, managing to safely land despite his crippled aileron.

With 92 and 72 Squadrons now heading for home, 603 Squadron joined the attack, followed by 253 and 501. Meanwhile, six more squadrons had been scrambled, including 249 Squadron from North Weald. As Tom Neil headed to join the battle, he found himself flying in and out of cloud before bursting through at around 15,000 feet over the east of London, condensation dripping from the canopy. While they were being vectored up to 17,000 feet, 66 and 41 Squadrons had continued the attack, pecking away at the German formation, and then, as the bombers approached London, 257 and 504 joined in. This was Pete Brothers' first serious engagement since joining the squadron and in the ensuing mayhem he managed to shoot down first a Dornier and then a Ju 88. Like Tony twenty minutes before him, however, he was also hit himself, a bullet causing an aileron wire to snap. He was preparing to bail out but found he could still just about fly the Hurricane, even with the aileron now hanging down, so ducking out of the fight headed for his old base, Biggin Hill. Opening his hood as he came in to land, he was horrified to find his lucky navy blue polka-dot scarf had come loose and was now whistled out of the cockpit, seemingly gone for ever. Having made it safely back down, he jumped out and was inspecting the damage when, to his delight, he saw his scarf fluttering from the elevator. A good omen, it seemed.

It was now 249 and 46 Squadrons' turn. Tom Neil spotted the bombers, feeling a flutter of exultation and raw fear, and then moments later they were in amongst them. A Dornier filled his gunsights and he opened fire, feeling horribly exposed as he did so and wondering where the 109s were. There were aircraft everywhere, including Spitfires, but still no Me 109s. He saw one struggling Dornier being attacked by a pack of Hurricanes, 'wolves worrying a flagging deer', then turned to see a Spitfire attacking him. Turning out of the way, and with ack-ack bursting in the distance, he headed for home.

Both Pete and Tom had been surprised by the small number of enemy fighters, but it had been at this point that the so-called Duxford Wing of five squadrons had entered the battle, some fifty Spitfires and Hurricanes attacking the 109s. Amongst these was I/JG 52, with its yellow-nose Messerschmitts that seemed to be making such an impression on the Fighter Command pilots. Ulrich Steinhilper had just turned twenty-two and as an unintended present had been allotted one of the new Me 109E4s to have reached the *Staffel*, already christened Yellow 2. He was flying it now, with its new improved cannons, and hoped that with this increased hitting power he would finally open his score and start shooting down some enemy aircraft. Ulrich was sure the RAF must now be in its death throes so had been taken aback by the number of Tommy fighters that now met them. 'Over there we met amazingly strong fighter opposition,' he wrote to his mother. 'I believe that the British are concentrating everything they have left around the capital.'

While Ulrich was fending off the Duxford Wing, more squadrons were engaging the bombers, including 303 Kościuszko Squadron. Jan Zumbach had hit a Dornier before coming under fire from some of the 109s. Dodging in and out of cloud, he felt disorientated and frightened by this game of hide-and-seek but managing to eventually get on the tail of one of his pursuers he opened fire, shooting it down, and then ran out of ammunition and saw he was dangerously low on fuel, so landed at Kenley, where he was refuelled and rearmed within minutes.

Meanwhile the bombers had finally dropped their loads, most falling ineffectively over south-eastern suburbs, although bombs did hit bridges between Victoria and Clapham and a further one landed in Buckingham Palace gardens. Even so, the damage was slight compared with the raids of the past week. The retiring bombers now met the latest squadrons on their tortuous route.

David Crook was away on leave, but twelve pilots of 609 Squadron were waiting for the scattered remnants of the formation. John Dundas was now one of the squadron's leading aces, his marksmanship improving with every sortie. So too was his tactical nous, for although he had received no orders to dive down on the bombers, he decided to lead his section into attack before the enemy fighters could intervene. He did so in the nick of time, for the 109s were quick to follow, and having shot down one of the bombers, he found himself being attacked by two Messerschmitts. Shaking them off, he then managed to open fire on another Dornier, raking its belly from underneath before being pounced on by a further three 109s. Fortunately for him, they gave themselves away by opening up at too great a range – clearly they were new, inexperienced pilots. Easily escaping, John headed back to Middle Wallop.

Jan Zumbach had meanwhile taken off again and instead of flying off home to Northolt decided to chase after more enemy aircraft as they retreated back towards the coast. He soon spotted a solitary Dornier and homed in for the kill. Watching it fill his sights, he was about to press the gun button, when suddenly there was an ear-splitting crash and a shattering explosion and most of his cockpit was blown away. Bailing out of the shattered remains of his aircraft, he remembered the rumours of Germans opening fire on parachutes so, with remarkable coolness, waited until he was passing through some cloud to pull the ripcord. Expecting to land in the Channel, he quickly inflated his Mae West, but then was whisked along by the wind, carrying him spinning until he glimpsed the coast. But was it England or France? Landing safely on a beach, he began folding his parachute, by now convinced that he would shortly be in the hands of the Germans.

Some men appeared, firing every time Jan made a slight movement. Eventually, they came to a halt except for one man who approached him with an odd weaving walk. Jan thought he must be drunk but then saw the man was British.

'Allied fighter!' shouted Jan. 'Polish pilot!'

The man kept coming towards him until Jan could see his Coast Guard's badge. 'Sorry I fired,' said the man. 'I had to stop you moving. You're standing in the middle of a minefield.'

'I zigzagged out on the sergeant's heel,' wrote Jan, 'and recovered my composure with the assistance of a large Scotch.'

The morning raid had barely died down when the next one began massing. In fact, the first raid had primarily been a means of wearing down the defenders. More than double the size of the previous effort, there were over a hundred in this formation, although Kesselring had been forced to put two *Gruppen* together to achieve the normal strength of one. There were also more fighters as well, some 350 in all, including Dolfo Galland and his *Geschwader* and all of JG 53.

At Uxbridge, Churchill was still intently watching the unfolding events. Just after 2 p.m., the spotter, sent up to patrol the coast at 26,000 feet, reported in. This was Allan Wright. 'The idea,' noted Allan, 'is to get up really early and plot the position of the blitz as it comes in. Lonely job.' It was an idea of the Controller's at 11 Group HQ, and 92 Squadron had been chosen to provide the pilot since it was a Spitfire squadron, and Allan had volunteered. Unfortunately, he had not been scrambled early enough for the first raid and had missed it, but this time he had made it in time, although only just, because the raiders were passing almost as he was sending in his report. He had also been spotted in turn by two Me 109s. After firing a good burst at one, he dived vertically, dropping from 28,000 to 7,000 feet and blacking out in the process. Recovering from the dive in time, he recovered his wits and headed back to Hawkinge.

Squadrons were once again scrambled, although this time Park aimed to have most of his forces attacking the bombers as they turned back for home. They were also scrambled in pairings of one Spitfire and one Hurricane squadron. By 2 p.m., both Pete Brothers and Tom Neil were once again taking off. Five minutes later, so too was 92 Squadron. At 2.15 p.m., 238 Squadron from 10 Group was asked to take over 609's earlier role, and 12 Group was asked to bring its big wing in to cover Hornchurch.

Once again, the Prime Minister watched the plots moving on the table and the lights moving to 'engaged'. Conscious of Park's growing anxiety, he asked, 'What reserves have we got?'

'There are none,' Park replied. All his available squadrons were now airborne.

An enormous aerial battle was now taking place. The bombers were doing their best to reach their targets but the number of Tommy fighters was putting them off, just as it had Peter Stahl a few days earlier. Plenty of bombs were scattered over Kent and Sussex, but most fell on south-east and east London. The fighters were having their own private battles. Tony Bartley was caught up in a dizzying swirl of aircraft over east London. Tom Neil attacked a vic of eight Dorniers, aiming for the last on the right of the formation. Somehow, everything fell into place and he found himself dead astern and just below, buffeted about in its slip-stream. He opened fire at close range and bits of aircraft immediately fell off. He fired again, worried he was almost too close, and then two objects hurtled towards him too quickly for him to evade, and as they shot past his head he realized they were two of the crew bailing out. 'I veered away,' he noted, 'shocked at what I had just achieved.'

Dolfo Galland suffered no such feelings of remorse as he led his *Geschwader* down on to Bader's big wing. It was a perfect bounce, an attack with the benefit of height and sun, and Dolfo set the tone by tearing down upon the Czechs of 310 Squadron, hitting one Hurricane so hard huge pieces of metal were torn from it. At the last moment, he leapt over the stricken machine and straight through the formation, hitting a second Hurricane. By the time Bader's force realized what was happening, Dolfo and his 109s had sped on past. Dive, attack and run – it was the most effective way of taking on fighters. Glancing back, he saw two parachutes drifting downwards – his thirty-third and thirty-fourth victims. Climbing again, he made for the stream of bombers heading back from London, which were being mercilessly snapped at by Park's fighters.

Meanwhile, Hans-Ekkehard Bob, recently promoted *Staffelkapitän* of the 7th Staffel, had been hit in the cooling system and, quickly disengaging, turned for home. With his engine temperature rising alarmingly, he switched off, knowing that his engine would otherwise seize. Refusing to even consider ditching in England, he now attempted to glide home. But having put his 109 into a gentle glide, he saw that his propeller was still turning – or 'windmilling' – because of the wind. This, he realized, would be cooling his engine, so after a while, he restarted the engine, climbed a little bit, then switched off again. 'I was determined not to ditch in the Channel,' he says. 'It was all about timing. The trick was to turn off the engine before everything seized.' Fortunately for Hans, his timing was spot on. All too many pilots had failed to make it back across the sea, but by carefully nursing his machine Hans was able to land back safely at Guines and lived to fight another day.

Churchill was still watching as the enemy returned home. One by one, the confused tangle of counters were moved clear from the map table. On the tote board, the lights showed the squadrons had landed back down, refuelling and rearming once more. He waited for a few minutes but no new plot appeared, so the Prime Minister and his wife climbed the stairways to the surface and stepped out into a beautiful late-summer evening. All was calm, all was clear. Puffs of white cloud hung seemingly motionless against the blue, betraying not a sign of the enormous air battles that had taken place that day.

46

Wolfpack

As it happened, the fading plots Churchill had witnessed had not been the last of the day. Around 6 p.m., twenty Zerstörers from Erpro 210 attacked the Supermarine works at Woolston in Southampton, accompanied by fighters from *Jafü* 3, including Siegfried Bethke and 2/JG 2. Siegfried heard on the radio about the large-scale attacks on London. 'Sixty kills, twenty losses. Submarines have again sunk a good number of ships.' He was still sure the invasion must go ahead soon, aware, as they all were, of the massive build-up of shipping around the Channel ports. They were speculating among themselves as much as the British were across the sea, with the rumour mill working overtime. 'I also "heard" yesterday,' he scribbled, 'that we will go over a few days after the first landing. How everything will develop, and if everything will go according to plan, no-one can say.'

That same day, Monday, 16 September, Göring summoned his commanders once more to his train headquarters near Beauvais. He was not pleased, and blamed the fighters once again for the lack of a more decisive day's fighting. It was true that many fighters had left the bombers to take on the British fighters – Dolfo Galland for one – and so left them exposed, but what was the point of the attack? To bomb London into submission or destroy Fighter Command? Dolfo was a highly competitive person and his victory score counted a great deal to him. Even so, the Luftwaffe High Command was still agreed that attaining air superiority was the prime objective and that could only be achieved by destroying the British fighters. As it happened, Dolfo's two victories were effectively worthless, since one of the Czech pilots bailed out unhurt and the other only slightly hurt his foot. Killing and badly injuring RAF pilots was the only way now the Luftwaffe had any hope of clearing the skies.

It was Generalmajor Osterkamp, commander of *Jafü* 2, who spoke out, complaining once more about the faulty tactics and shortage of replacement aircraft. 'The English have adopted new tactics,' he said. 'They are now using powerful fighter formations to attack in force. From our radio-intercept service we know that their orders are strictly to attack our bombers. Yesterday, these tactics took us by surprise.'

'That's just what we want,' Göring replied. 'If they come at us in droves, we can shoot them down in droves!'

Once again, German intelligence was faulty. The arrival on the scene of the Duxford Wing was certainly something new, but Fighter Command was by no means purely attacking the bombers. The latest assessment of enemy strength was another piece of fiction from Oberst Schmid. He reported that the RAF had begun the previous day with 288 fighters, and that morning with just 177. In fact, Fighter Command began the day with 659 serviceable aircraft ready to take to the skies. 'Göring believes the English are gathering their last forces,' noted Milch. It was the same story the Luftwaffe High Command had been peddling all month: all that was needed was one last push; victory, they felt sure, was tantalizingly within reach. The fighters, it was agreed, were to be reinforced with eight *Staffeln* from other areas and VIII Fliegerkorps was to transfer to Luftflotte 2; new instructions were issued. From now on, Luftflotte 2 was to attack British fighters during the day and London at night; Luftflotte 3 was to assault Southampton during the day and London by night. Meanwhile, 9th Fliegerdivision, which included Hajo Herrmann and KG 4, was to continue nuisance raids on London, and to begin dropping aerial mines on the capital.

It showed just how woolly Luftwaffe thinking had become. What *had* been the point of attacking London two times the day before? Just what were they trying to achieve? The subjugation of the British people or the destruction of the RAF? Why had *Jafü* 3 been sent back to Normandy when it would have been better to concentrate forces against England in the south-east, where the distance across the Channel was smaller? How could they have recognized this at the end of August and forgotten it two weeks later? And why Southampton? It seems that no-one was really sure. Operationally, the Luftwaffe was in a mess, short of aircraft and lacking the infrastructure needed to continue a battle of this intensity. Tactically, the thinking was faulty, as the High Command failed to use either bombers or fighters to their best capabilities. Operationally, it was struggling. And strategically, it had lost sight of what it was supposed to be achieving. Believing the German air force was within sight of victory was a fool's dream. The Luftwaffe was not on the verge of triumph; rather, it was further away than ever.

Across the Channel, the pilots had celebrated and so had the media, with radio news bulletins quick to gleefully announce record numbers of downed German aircraft. A photograph of a Dornier plunging vertically near Victoria Station, its fuselage severed, was printed in many papers. '175 SHOT DOWN' ran the headline in the following morning's *Daily Express*. Later the official figure was given as 185 destroyed for the loss of only twenty-five aircraft and eleven pilots. In fact, the RAF lost thirty-one aircraft and sixteen pilots.

Out in the Channel, HMT *Darthema* and the 29th Minesweeping Flotilla had been clearing the German flank minefield near Eastbourne and continuing their invasion watch at night. That evening, after the fighting died down, they picked up a downed German pilot and told him that 185 Luftwaffe aircraft had been shot down that day. 'This fellow spoke good English,' says Joe Steele, 'and he looked at me and said, "Half that!"' In fact, it was a third of the claimed figure – just sixty-one, and ninety-three pilots and aircrew and a further sixty-three taken prisoner. It was still a lot for the Luftwaffe to lose, the worst day's tally over England since 18 August, and the second-highest losses they had suffered since 11 May. In addition, there were another twenty aircraft that made it back but were either badly damaged or had to be written off. Unlike the RAF, the Luftwaffe could not make good these losses.

Not everyone was pleased with Fighter Command's effort, however. Park had admitted to Churchill that his men had not intercepted as many raiders as he would have liked, and knew perfectly well that the high claims were nonsense. The following day, he had made the most of yet another lull in Luftwaffe attacks by issuing another set of instructions to his controllers. Park was not being an over-zealous taskmaster; he was quite rightly trying to hone and improve a system that was proving not as effective as it might be. He was annoyed that squadrons were not rendezvousing correctly, and were being patrolled too far forward, at too low a height, and too late. From now on, he wanted the Spitfires from

Hornchurch and Biggin to be sent as high as 25,000–30,000 feet to attack the highest enemy fighter screen. He also wanted to improve controllers' ability to make the correct response to the size and make-up of an incoming raid, by sending up squadrons on shorter patrol lines at higher altitudes. Getting squadrons operating higher was, he believed, key. It meant they could maintain the height advantage and see more clearly. Furthermore, by holding back and waiting until the enemy drew inland, his fighters would have more time to get to these heights while at the same time making the German fighters operate to the limit of their fuel. He increasingly wanted to attack the enemy as they turned back for home, a very sensible policy. Unlike the Luftwaffe High Command, Park had a very clear picture both operationally and tactically and was using his available resources to make the most of their potential.

There had been almost no daylight activity on 16 September and not a great amount the day after. Squally showers, localized thunder and a few bright intervals were not conducive to heavy air attacks, especially when the wounds were still being licked from the previous effort.

Hitler continued to prevaricate over Operation SEALION. Around him, his commanders were still trying to find a way of keeping their options open. Raeder now suggested 8 October as a potential invasion date, to allow the Luftwaffe a bit longer. Jodl, on the other hand, noted that by keeping all the troops and transports along the Channel coast, they would continue to draw the RAF's bombers, which would expose them to fighter attacks under conditions more favourable to the Luftwaffe. Furthermore, with the RAF bombers so occupied, their raids over Germany would diminish, which would help improve German civilian morale. It is hard to think of a more spurious reason for keeping an invasion force at readiness.

Yet with 15 September so obviously failing to finish off the RAF, and with the 16th a day of no action, Hitler could not possibly give the go-ahead, because he could not guarantee that the right conditions would be in place in the ten days needed between giving SEALION the green light and it being launched. It was just too big a risk, so on the 17th he postponed the operation again. That he refused to cancel the operation, however, showed not his unwillingness to undertake the invasion, but rather his reluctance to abandon the project. Defeating Britain was still of tantamount importance. A successful invasion still offered him his best hope of achieving that, as he well knew.

*

However, there was some cause for cheer. The Luftwaffe's efforts might be proving disappointing, but the same could not be said for Dönitz's U-boat arm. There were now fourteen U-boats in the Atlantic, most in the Western Approaches to the coast of Ireland, waiting to pounce on any incoming convoys. Having had another successful patrol with a further six ships to her name, U-47, with just one torpedo left, was now loitering at a weather-reporting station some way to the west.

At 11.52 a.m. on 20 September, Rolf Hilse, on board U-48, received a coded message from Günther Prien in U-47. He had spotted a large eastbound convoy heading to Britain, and since U-48 had the latest most advanced radio equipment, he asked her to report this news to Dönitz at his command post in Lorient. 'We reported to Lorient,' says Rolf, 'and the message we got back was, "Proceed to beacon."' This meant U-47's beacon – U-48 was to converge with Günther's boat and operate together. Then, at 5.15 p.m., they received another signal, directing four more U-boats towards U-47. 'Received wireless message,' noted Rolf. 'U-48, 65, 43, 99, 100 assume attack formation.'

Dönitz was ordering them to form a wolfpack. This tactic was not new, but problems of communicating out at sea had made them difficult to co-ordinate successfully. However, radio technology had greatly improved in recent months, and by the following morning all six submarines were converging on U-47 ready to hunt together as instructed.

The mood aboard U-48 was already buoyant. The new skipper had more than proved he was up to the task, sinking four merchant ships on 15 September, and then, just after midnight on the 18th, sank two more, including the largest ship in the convoy, an 11,000-ton liner. The crew had been delighted, yet at the time they had no idea that the liner, the *City of Benares*, had been carrying some ninety British child evacuees to Canada, all members of an initiative set up by the Children's Overseas Reception Board (CORB). Two hundred and forty-eight of the 406 passengers drowned, including seventy-seven of the evacuees. The men on U-48 were not to know – it had not been marked as a Red Cross vessel, and neither had there been any indication that there had been children and civilians on board. As far as they were concerned, they had simply aimed for the largest ship in the convoy. What had really surprised them was the lack of any escort – the convoy was completely defenceless. 'We were pleased,' says Rolf. '11,800 tons – that's an enormous ship.' They had then sunk a further ship just after 5 p.m. the following day, making a total of seven ships sunk since leaving Lorient. It was not a bad bag for Kapitänleutnant Bleichrodt's first patrol in charge.

At 3.16 a.m. on the morning of 21 September, U-48 had the convoy HX72 in sight. Just over two hours later, Rolf picked up an SOS from a ship called *Elmbank*, a large freighter, carrying timber and sheet metal, which had been hit by U-99. Peering through the periscope, Bleichrodt had seen flashes and the sound of dull explosions. Half an hour later, they were also in position to fire. Their first torpedo missed, fired at too far a range, but the second, fired twenty minutes later, hit, with huge detonation columns erupting into the air. Almost immediately, Rolf picked up another SOS signal – they had hit the *Blairangus*. Fires now broke out on the ship as her cargo began to explode. Lifeboats were hurriedly launched but the skies were grey with squally showers and after a while, the stricken ship disappeared from view. U-48 now turned her attention to a tanker, although, again, the torpedo missed. Another immediate shot was not possible because they discovered one of the torpedo fins had been dented. Turning around they now took over from U-47 as the convoy shadow, radioing position reports to the other U-boats.

All day, U-48 kept up with the convoy, waiting for darkness, as were the others in the wolfpack. Several were low on torpedoes, U-47 and U-48 included, but at twenty minutes before midnight Bleichrodt attacked with his last tube, hitting *Broompark*, which soon began to lilt.

That night the carnage really began as HX72 struggled on, the wolfpack snapping at its heels. U-99 sank two, including a 9,200-ton tanker. U-47 then surfaced and with U-99 finished off the *Elmbank*, which had limped on all day, using their guns. In an extraordinary feat of daring, U-100 then manoeuvred into the heart of the convoy and sank three more. All through the next day, the wolfpack continued to keep up with the convoy, picking off one ship after another, U-100 sinking a further four. By the time both U-47 and U-48 turned for home, eleven ships had been sunk and a further two badly damaged. That was more than a quarter of the entire convoy.

A further 295,335 tons of Allied shipping were sunk by U-boats that month, and 56,328 tons by long-range Focke-Wulf Condors. The wolfpack mauling of HX72 proved indisputably the value of concentration of force; this principle that held true for the army and Luftwaffe applied equally to the U-boat arm, just as Dönitz had long been arguing.

'We lost another large number of ships off the Bloody Foreland last night as well as the night before,' noted Jock Colville on Sunday the 2nd. 'These losses are assuming serious proportions and the PM is very displeased with the Admiralty.' So too was Admiral Sir Charles Forbes, the C-in-C Home Fleet. Ever since Dunkirk he had repeatedly argued that placing unnecessarily large numbers of his ships in the south of the country was both unnecessary and pointless. He also strongly believed that using the Fleet to launch offensive blows against the enemy-held coast would force the Germans to disperse their forces and unsettle enemy invasion plans. He was almost certainly right.

What seemed to concern him even more, however, was that by insisting so many ships remain in the south-east on anti-invasion duty, the Admiralty was preventing him from protecting the convoys. It was no wonder the U-boats were having such a field day. On 28 September, he wrote again to the Admiralty pleading with them to let him be freed to carry out what he felt was the proper function of the Fleet – acting offensively against the enemy and defending Britain's trade. His appeal fell on deaf ears. The First Sea Lord and the other Command chiefs viewed invasion prospects very differently, especially Admiral Drax, who commanded the Nore Command, which would most likely face any invasion. As far as they were concerned, there could be no question of giving up the vigil. Forbes argued again that while the RAF was still holding off the Luftwaffe any invasion was out of the question no matter what intelligence was offered to the contrary. He had hit a brick wall, however. For those in the south, living underneath the great sky battles and being fed daily reports of the German invasion build-up, it was proving impossible to stand back and look at the situation with anything like a calm and logical approach.

So the convoys continued to cross the Atlantic virtually unescorted. The slaughter by the U-boats would continue.

In the absence of any Royal Navy offensive operations, it was left to Bomber Command to frustrate German invasion plans in what the bomber boys had christened the 'Battle of the Barges'. By 18 September, the Channel ports were packed with some one thousand barges, with a further six hundred waiting further up the River Sheldt. Day and night the bombers were over. Andrew Jackson and his crew had attacked Channel ports on four different nights up to 20 September. They had to fly through increasingly heavy flak in order to drop their bombs at low level, but so far had come through unscathed. On 13 September, they had made a particularly successful trip to attack the barges massed at

Antwerp. The following day, Konteradmiral Fricke's planning team reported that the RAF's raid had resulted in six naval vessels being damaged, three tugs and fifteen barges sunk, and three steamers sunk or put out of action. The report added that bomber and torpedo attacks on barges, trains, shipping and harbours had already caused severe delays to their plans, as had the amount of mines sown along the coastal route from the north German ports and the effects of long-range British naval shells being fired into 'excessively crowded harbours and roadsteads'.

German naval planners had worked out that, in all, 1,133 barges were needed for the first crossing. There were 1,491 by 21 September, but these were not all in the right ports. By this time, 214 had already been lost or damaged – which was not in itself disastrous, but the uneven distribution combined with losses meant, for example, that there was a 30 per cent deficit in Boulogne. And that was a problem, because there was no way the invasion could start with such a large shortfall at one of the key invasion ports.

Bomber Command was also continuing to bomb Germany. Larry Donnelly had made a number of trips to hit the invasion barges, but on the night of 24/25 September he and his Whitley crew were sent to bomb Berlin. It was the second night in a row after nearly a fortnight's break, and the target for Larry's crew was once again Tempelhof. Over the city, they found broken cloud but were unable to spot the aerodrome. They did, however, see the main railway station clearly enough so dropped their bombs on that instead. With flak coming up thick and fast, they climbed into the cloud and finally got home at around 5.20 a.m. They had been airborne ten hours and forty minutes.

Still in Berlin, William Shirer noticed that most Berliners were quite shocked by the renewed attacks. Goebbels once again whipped the press into a new frenzy. 'NEW NIGHT ACT OF THE PIRATES' announced the *Nachtausgabe*. The *Börsen Zeitung* reported that 'last night Churchill continued the series of his criminal blows against the German civilian population. Frankly, Churchill belongs to that category of criminals who in their stupid brutality are unteachable.'

The German press response was quite different to that of the British; rather than shouting defiance, it merely raged against British criminality. 'It does indicate,' noted William, 'that the Germans can't take night bombing as the British are taking it.' In this he was quite wrong, but certainly the night attacks were adding to the darkening mood of many Germans. The euphoria of midsummer had worn off. People wanted to know why the invasion had not happened, and it was beginning to dawn on them that the war might not be over soon after all. Else Wendel felt this mood keenly at her sister's engagement party. 'We can't get away from the war, you know,' the mother of the groom-to-be announced. 'It's no use pretending. It's here right in the midst of our happiness.'

In Berlin, William Shirer caught up with an old friend of his who was a bomber pilot in the Luftwaffe and had been flying over London. Somehow, his friend had managed to get some leave, and presented a far more realistic picture of what was happening at the front than that offered by the Nazi media. He confirmed that the night bomber crews were certainly very tired and expected to fly four nights a week. He also told William that the British bombers were pounding the French and Belgian coasts every night. 'And often they swoop down,' relayed William, 'and machine-gun the German bomber bases just as the German planes are taking off.' How often this was happening and how much it was mere rumour is not clear; yet it showed just how much the Bomber Command attacks were contributing to the battle. 'The British are slowly getting on our nerves at night,' Ulrich Steinhilper wrote to his mother. 'Because of their persistent activity our AA guns are in virtually continuous use and so we can hardly close our eyes. But there is nothing else we can do about that other than curse.' Doubts were also beginning to creep in about the invasion. He and his fellow pilots were aware that a good stretch of fine weather was needed but that the chances of getting this window were diminishing as autumn approached. 'I think we all felt,' noted Ulrich, 'that if the army didn't get their fingers out before long, much of what we had done and suffered might go to waste.'

Invasion anxiety was still very much at the front of the minds of Britain's leaders. Photographs clearly showed massed barges at Antwerp and the various Channel ports. Even the President of the United States was passing on invasion rumours. On Sunday, 22 September, he sent a message to Churchill warning him that he had heard from a 'most reliable source' in Berlin that the invasion was to begin at 3 p.m. that afternoon. Churchill, although rather sceptical, rang a number of people about it, including Lord Gort, who told the Prime Minister he thought it very unlikely. '12.50 p.m.: The prospects do not look good for invasion,' Jock Colville hastily scribbled in his diary that same Sunday. 'Pouring rain and a gale brewing up.' Not for the first time that summer, the weather seemed to be very much favouring the defenders.

Siegfried Bethke would have agreed. 'Days too quiet, always waiting,' he jotted on 18 September, 'weather always too unfavourable.' Three days later he wrote, 'Yesterday no mission because of weather. Bad again today.' On the 23rd the weather had forced him to land at Le Havre after a brief local flight. Finally, on the 24th, he flew two missions, on the first encountering nothing and the second a 'light encounter' with Spitfires.

But whenever it was dry, there was still plenty of aerial activity. On 18 September, three large raids had come over from the Pas de Calais. That day, Tony Bartley was shot down. He was firing at a Dornier, pressing down on the gun button rather longer than he should have in an effort to shoot the bomber down, and forgot the cardinal rule about watching his back. A cannon shell suddenly exploded behind his armour plating, a bullet tore through his leather helmet, grazing his head and smashing into the gunsight, and several more punched into his oil and glycol tanks, and then an Me 109 flashed past him.

With fumes quickly filling his cockpit, he knew that his plane was doomed and prepared to bail out. But as was doing so he saw his attacker lining up again and, realizing his adversary could well shoot him as he tumbled free, quickly sat back down in the seat and turned towards him. The ruse worked, and having fired a burst for good measure, he saw the Messerschmitt turn away. By this time, however, he was too low to jump so picked out a field and hoped for the best.

He was still a hundred feet off the ground when the engine seized. Blinded by oil, Tony hit the ground moments later, was catapulted out and landed in a haystack completely unhurt, apart from the graze to his head. He had had a remarkably close shave, actually and metaphorically. Releasing the buckle of his parachute he discovered he had been even luckier. As his parachute fell to the ground, the pack burst open, shredded silk billowing across the ground. 'If this fellow hadn't come at me again,' he says, 'I would have jumped and I would have killed myself because one of his shells had ripped my parachute to pieces.' Soon surrounded by several locals, he was escorted to the pub, plied with beer and then whisky and finally driven back to Biggin Hill, where he learned that Roy Mottram had been killed and Bob Holland wounded.

Five days later, a massive free hunt by some 200 Luftwaffe fighters had swept over. No fewer than twenty-four squadrons were scrambled to meet them. Certainly, for those in Fighter Command waiting to be scrambled, these were still long, tense days interspersed with frenetic action. Even on a quiet day, a pilot might end up fighting one of the toughest engagements of his life. Aircraft were still being shot down, pilots were still losing their lives.

Some were still able to enjoy euphoric moments of victory, however. On 26 September, Allan Wright was leading Green Section from his flight and managed to intercept a formation of Dorniers in perfect fashion. 'Most glorious fun,' he noted. He shot down one of the bombers, which dived into the ground and exploded. The next day he shot down a further Dornier and damaged a Junkers 88. 'Two squadrons met 20 Ju88s with many 109s,' he wrote in tiny neat writing in his logbook. 'Latter very shy.' In fact, 27 September marked the biggest day's fighting for nearly a fortnight. In the morning, bomb-carrying Zerstörers had attacked London, and were followed close after by formations of Dorniers and Ju 88s. These latter raids were largely split up by British fighters.

Ulrich Steinhilper was leading the entire *Gruppe* that day although such were their losses they were just thirteen planes from the three *Staffeln*. As they neared London, as many as forty Spitfires and Hurricanes were tearing towards them from seemingly nowhere. Deciding that the best form of defence was attack, he ordered the *Gruppe* to turn and climb. Ulrich could feel the stick against his leg as he brought his Yellow 2 into a hard aileron turn. Negative-g was pressing him into his seat, and his arms were heavy and his head felt as though it were crushing down on his neck as he increased the turn and climb, but his slats were snapping out automatically as his speed slowed, giving him an even tighter turn. With his vision greying, it would have been far easier to cut and run but with the British fighters diving down upon them at high speed he knew there was no way they could now cut inside their tight upward spiral. The Spitfires now hurtled past and then pulled up trying to climb back up for another attack, but still Ulrich ordered his men to keep climbing in their tight upward turn. Occasionally a Spitfire would cross their sights but they were so close to stalling that firing their guns might have caused them to drop out of the sky. It took them ten minutes of intensely stressful flying to climb some 10,000 feet, but eventually Ulrich was able to order them to roll out at the top of their climb and set course for home, which was effectively downhill all the way. By holding their nerve and keeping their discipline, not one of them had been lost.

Amongst those British fighters entering this latest fight were the Spitfires of 616 Squadron, now part of Bader's Duxford Wing. Cocky Dundas had rejoined the squadron on 13 September, by which time they had already been withdrawn from Kenley after two harrowing weeks and sent to Kirton in Lindsey in Lincolnshire. Five days later, however, they were ordered south to Fowlmere, a satellite of Duxford, to join the 12 Group big wing, although they were to fly back to Kirton each evening.

Cocky had been understandably wracked with fear at the prospect of combat flying once again, but on the first sortie with the wing he had been astonished to hear Douglas Bader calmly call down to the ground controller to arrange a game of squash. Cocky could not believe that someone with tin legs, leading five squadrons, could have been thinking about anything other than the job in hand. Yet the conversation had a very calming effect on him; he noticed his nerves finally begin to settle.

Now, on 27 September, Bader was leading them again. 11 Group squadrons had already set amongst the enemy formations by the time Bader brought them in high, still flying a tight, solid wedge. 'We came together with the Messerschmitts in a monstrous explosion of planes,' noted Cocky, 'and there developed immediately a dogfight of exceptional size and fury.' Collision seemed likely at any moment. Cocky turned and twisted, sweating with both exertion and excitement and sick with fear. Then – that strange phenomenon that never failed to surprise him – the sky was suddenly clear again, and Cocky dived down and headed back to base.

While Cocky was fighting for his life over the Thames estuary, his brother John was attacking a simultaneous raid towards Bristol. John's prowess as a fighter pilot was growing. With more than ten confirmed victories to his name, he had shot down one a day for the past three days, and now got another as 609 Squadron intercepted the enemy over Swanage. For David Crook it was a traumatic engagement. They had dived down on a formation of bomb-carrying Me 110s, which, seeing their attackers, had flung themselves into a defensive circle. David was flying just behind Mick Miller and watched as his friend flew head on into one of the Zerstörers. 'There was a terrific explosion and a sheet of flame and black smoke seemed to hang in the air like a ball of fire,' wrote David. 'Many little shattered fragments fluttered down, and that was all.' The two had been friends for over a year, and had been at FTS together.

There was fine weather on the last day of September and the Luftwaffe made the most of it to deliver a number of heavy and concentrated raids towards both London and the south. Siegfried Bethke flew two missions over England that day, the first a free hunt over Dorset and Hampshire. The Germans were intercepted by 609 Squadron, who had been sent up to 27,000 feet and were able to dive down on them with the sun behind. Spotting them only at the last moment, the 109s dived, but with the momentum of his dive David was able to catch up with his target, hurtling down at speeds approaching 600 mph and dropping some 23,000 feet in a matter of seconds. With an intense pain in his ears and the sea hurtling towards him, he managed to pull out at about 1,000 feet, latch on to his quarry and open fire at close range. 'The effect of a Spitfire's eight guns has to be seen to be believed,' he wrote. 'Hundreds of bullets poured into him and he rocked violently, then turned over on his back, burst into flames and dived straight down into the sea.'

He then spotted another 109 heading back out to sea, so chased after it, managing to catch him surprisingly easily. Another short, sharp burst, and the Messerschmitt swerved slightly, the canopy burst off and nearly hit David, and then the 109 dived, flattening out on the sea, smoke trailing behind. For the first time in the war, David found himself feeling rather sorry for a German pilot. He knew he could catch him up easily, and that if he attacked him at that height the pilot would die. But if he let him go, he would be back over England another day. 'The last few moments must have been absolute hell for him,' noted David. 'I could almost feel his desperation as he made this last attempt to get away.' Catching up, David fired his remaining ammunition and watched him plunge into the sea.

Hans-Ekkehard Bob had already flown twice that day, and on both occasions he had made it back to Guines with his tanks running on empty. In the afternoon the *Geschwader* was ordered to escort Ju 88s of KG 77, but after rendezvousing over Cap Gris Nez they could see that southern England was now covered with cloud. Unfortunately, the leading bomber erred with his navigation, crossing the Channel in a wide bow which made the escorting fighters use more of their precious fuel than was necessary. Over Brighton, they were intercepted by Spitfires and Hurricanes, by which time the Messerschmitts were already low on fuel. Extricating themselves, the 109s of JG 54 now made a dash for home, led by the *Geschwaderkommodore*, Hannes Trautloft. Ahead, they had a worryingly long flight over cloud and after a few minutes one of the pilots shouted, 'My red lamp is on!', which meant he had just ten minutes' flying time left. Trautloft immediately snapped back that they were to keep radio silence; the last thing they needed was the RAF alerted to their critical situation.

The cloud dispersed, but all they could see was water. Hans began to worry that they were flying in the wrong direction. One agonizing minute after another followed but then at last Hans caught sight of the coast. Unable to hold back, he called out, 'Cape Horn ahead!'

'Who was that?' demanded Trautloft. But Hans kept quiet.

David Crook got a third Me 109 later that afternoon, although, since he lost it in cloud, he could not claim it as a definite. It had been a good day for the squadron; 609 had come a long way since the dark days of early July. That night David and a number of the pilots went into Winchester to celebrate. They were alive and able to enjoy a good dinner and plenty of drink – someone even stood them a bottle of champagne and toasted their health. 'It was one of the best days I ever had in the squadron,' noted David. 'And thus ended that eventful month, September 1940.'

47

Exhaustion

On 19 September, Churchill had suggested Chamberlain leave London for the country. The former PM's operation had not gone as well as hoped, and he was now a very sick man indeed, although the cancer had not yet been confirmed. He had, however, been valiantly soldiering on, but with the advent of the raids he was finding both his treatment and periods of rest were being interrupted by the Luftwaffe. Utterly exhausted, he agreed and left London for what would be the last time. Having made it home, he then collapsed and spent the next couple of days in bed. Realizing his illness was most probably terminal and accepting that he could no longer be of any use, he offered his resignation. Churchill refused it. 'Let us go on together through the storm,' he told him. 'These are great days.'

Historic days, certainly. There was still much to worry the Prime Minister and his colleagues. The Italians had invaded Egypt and the British colony of Kenya, while one of Churchill's first offensive strikes, a British-backed Free French invasion of Dakar in French West Africa led by Général de Gaulle, had failed. Then, on 27 September, Japan signed a tripartite pact with Germany and Italy. Although she had not yet declared war, the move further threatened British interests in the Far East.

Yet, in other respects, the pact offered hope. Each member of the Tripartite Pact had promised to aid one another with all political, economic and military means, should one of them be attacked by a 'power not involved in the European war'. This was clearly directed at

America. The United States was becoming ever more wedded to the Allied cause, just as Churchill had hoped she would. And there was further cause for cheer from the United States. On 16 September, Congress had passed the Selective Training and Service Act, the first peacetime draft in her history. National Guard units – the US's territorials – had also been called up. Americans were also responding to Britain's defiance. A number of American volunteers were now flying for the RAF – there were three in 609 Squadron alone – while broadcasts from men like Ed Murrow were eagerly listened to. For some months, the Ministry of Information had been advised by various Americans to get more pictures in the US press. Back in August, Raymond Lee had urged Duff Cooper to do just this, but the Minister had told him that he could not get the pictures released from the service departments. On 23 September, however, Cecil Beaton's photograph of the three-year-old Eileen Dunne had been the front cover of *Life* magazine and was accompanied by a spread of his pictures of bomb damage. It all helped. American public opinion was changing; slowly but surely, the isolationists were losing ground.

Certainly, the message coming from Americans in London was that Britain was going to survive. Raymond Lee had said so in his reports, and so too did Ed Murrow and every other US journalist in town. On 23 September, Brigadier-General George Strong gave an interview in which he said that if the Germans invaded they would have a nasty surprise. Strong was Chief of the Army War Plans Division and had accompanied Admiral Ghormley on his visit to Britain – hence his views counted and were widely reported both sides of the Atlantic. Even Ambassador Kennedy had been forced to admit that the RAF seemed to be winning. On 17 September he had called on Chamberlain. 'I still think this war won't accomplish anything,' Kennedy told him. 'We are supposed to be fighting for liberty and the result will be to turn the last of the Democrats into Socialist, Communist or Totalitarian states.' He had learned nothing during his time in Britain, doggedly sticking to the same mantra – one driven by self-interest and excessive stubbornness. It was no wonder that both Churchill and Roosevelt barely acknowledged him any more. 'Kennedy,' noted Raymond Lee, 'has the speculator's smartness but also his sharp-shooting and facile insensitivity to the great forces which are now playing like heat lightning over the map of the world.' How right he was, as usual.

On his travels around the coastal defences, Lee had discovered that most soldiers seemed anxious to have a crack at the Germans. John Wilson certainly fell into that camp, and his eagerness to play his part in defending Britain against the enemy had been one of the reasons why he had joined up. Originally planning to take up a place at Oriel College, Oxford, he had since been written to and told that there was no point while the war was on, so on 11 September he had persuaded his mother to drive him to Maidstone and there signed up, joining a Young Soldiers Battalion. 'We were blistered on to another battalion called the 8th Home Defence Battalion,' says John. 'They were frightful old chaps – all about fifty, and a terribly motley crew.' It was hard not to feel disappointed; there had been more excitement taking pot-shots from the roof at home.

Douglas Mann, meanwhile, had returned to Marlborough College in Wiltshire to start the autumn term. Summer was over. The leaves in the trees were beginning to turn and the days shortening, which meant later starts and earlier finishes for the pilots of Fighter Command. Both sides were exhausted. The big air battles of 27 and 30 September had been costly. In the last four days of the month, Fighter Command had lost seventy-four aircraft and forty pilots, the Luftwaffe 180 aircrew and a further 125 aircraft, of which seventy-six had been Messerschmitt 109s and 110s.

Tony Bartley had missed the 30 September battle with severe toothache, but Allan Wright had flown twice that day. He shot down a 109 in his first sortie and another in the second but then was surprised and hit by two others. Even an experienced ace like Allan could get caught out by the aircraft he had not seen. Managing to chase them off, however, he limped back towards England, both his Spitfire and leg in a bad way. With half his rudder and elevator shot away, it had been quite a feat to get home, but he somehow managed to land at Shoreham. 'When I took my boot off,' he says, 'it was half filled with blood.' Taken off to hospital, he would not fly again for two months.

Tony Bartley recovered from his toothache but when he went back up in the air again, something snapped, and suddenly he was really, truly afraid. That night he drank half a bottle of brandy at the White Hart and finished it off at the Red House, where he was eventually put to bed by the MacNeal twins, and, with his head spinning, began weeping uncontrollably with fatigue and grief for his dead friends. The next day, he was grounded and two days after that, having been awarded a DFC, was ordered to take seven days' leave.

John Dundas was now on leave too. 'It's really good to be alive up here,' he wrote to Margaret Rawlings. 'And I feel I've earned it. We went for Jerry hammer and tongs four days running before I left Middle Wallop.' Luftwaffe pilots were given leave, but usually only after a number of months in the front line. By the second week of October, Siegfried Bethke was one of only four pilots remaining from those far-off days of May, and one of those was home on leave. Several of the new pilots he had sent back for being 'too soft'. One of the other originals was struggling with *Kanalkrankheit* – the combat fatigue version. 'Rothkirch is not adding up,' he noted – he had flown just eight missions in two months. 'He's always "sick". A pathetic figure.' A few days later, Hauptmann Helmut Wick returned from Berlin, where he had been awarded the *Eichenlaub* – 'Oak Leaves' – to his Knight's Cross, an award given for forty victories. Hitler himself had placed it around his neck. Wick reported back all that he had been told. Both Hitler and Göring, he said, still hoped the Luftwaffe would completely destroy the British fighters in a few days of good weather. Siegfried thought that impossible. 'It is also hoped,' he noted, recording much of what Wick had told him, 'that through the blockade, there will be serious disruptions to supplies in England. Unfortunately, not enough submarines off the west coast of England.'

At Coquelles, as losses mounted, the evening debates were becoming increasingly tense. It was not helping these young pilots to endlessly discuss tactics at night. With leave so infrequent, they needed to use the time off from operations to try and put the fighting to one side and relax – but there was little chance for that, it seemed. The biggest complaints came from the NCO pilots, who felt strongly that too many of the commanders were glory hunters only interested in getting medals. It did not seem fair to them that awards should only be handed out for aerial victories, when it often took more bravery to sit at the back of the formation, keeping watch over the glory boys' backsides. Ulrich had quite a lot of sympathy – he had never thought much of the special treatment given to men like Dolfo Galland.

Of greater concern to him as a senior member of the *Staffel* was the loss of pilots as well as the shortage of aircraft. At the beginning of the western campaign, their *Gruppe* had had thirty-six experienced pilots with at least three years in the Luftwaffe under their belts. Now they were getting new boys straight from fighter school, and unlike in Fighter Command, there was no structure in place by which they could be given further training before being thrown into the front line. He and Kühle did their best to take care of these fledglings until they had acquired a bit more experience but this was not always possible.

At the end of September, a new NCO pilot arrived with minimal flying time and only a tiny amount of air-to-ground gunnery. He had never flown using oxygen and had no idea how to use his radio. Ulrich gave him around ten hours of extra 'tuition', taking him and some of the other new boys out across the Channel to shoot at shadows or at the old lighthouse at Dungeness. But they could not be kept off operations for ever so Ulrich took his particular charge and made him his wingman. Climbing out over the Channel, the *Gefreiter* struggled to keep up and it was clear he had no idea how to manage his propeller pitch control. Eventually, Kühle ordered him home, but instead of heading for France, the new boy made for Dover. Ulrich raced after him, catching up just before they reached the balloon barrage. Only by violently rocking his wings did Ulrich manage to make him understand, and then he led him back. It was one of only two missions he missed all through the battle. 'They were supposed to be replacements,' noted Ulrich, 'but in the event they were more of a problem for us than reinforcement for the *Staffel*.'

This simply put greater pressure on the more experienced ones. There were increasingly more cases of *Kanalkrankheit* in the 2nd Staffel too. Ulrich had noticed that Oberfeldwebel Grosse, a Condor Legion veteran, had begun to fly back home more and more frequently with 'engine trouble'. 'It seemed you could just wear out like any other machine,' noted Ulrich. 'And that is where things were going wrong; we just weren't getting a break.'

It was much the same for the bomber crews. Hajo Herrmann bombed the port at Great Yarmouth on 5 October, then London three nights later, and the night after that, and the night after that. And again two nights later and for another three nights on the trot. By 18 October, he had carried out twenty-one attacks on London alone, and nearly ninety combat missions since the start of the war, a truly astonishing number, and way, way more than his British counterparts would ever have been expected to fly. That night, as he took off with two 1,000 kg bombs beneath him, his left tyre shredded on some bomb splinters that had not been cleared after an earlier attack by Bomber Command, and he crashed, wrecking the aircraft. Fortunately the bombs did not explode, but Hajo was pulled from the wreckage unconscious. He had broken a lumbar vertebra and strained another and suffered some cuts and concussion. When he came to he wept uncontrollably. 'Why, I don't know.' Then he spotted a Knight's Cross on the bedside lamp. The doctor told him the Reichsmarschall had personally awarded it to him three days earlier. He had forgotten the occasion completely.

Peter Stahl was flying over London almost as often as Hajo, and often three nights running, something that would never have been demanded of Bomber Command crews. His *Staffel* was also struggling with inexperienced new crews. On 16 October, during yet another night attack on London, four crews failed to return and two crashed on landing, although the men escaped alive. But six aircraft out of nine was a terrible night of losses. In the bus back to their quarters afterwards they discussed what point there was in sending out hundreds of aircrews every night without any hope of reasonable results. 'And tomorrow,' noted Peter, 'the communiqué of the OKW will state that our brave aircrews have flown another major operation and despite bad weather conditions, have inflicted devastating blows on various vital targets. Our own losses were only "minimal"!'

There was no leave for Hans-Ekkehard Bob either, who as a *Staffel* commander was very much expected to lead the way. On constant front-line duty since the opening of the western campaign, he had now been given even greater responsibilities, for on 2 October Kesselring had visited JG 54 and ordered Trautloft to form one of his *Staffeln* from each *Gruppe* into a *Jagdbomber* – fighter-bomber – unit, and from the third *Gruppe* had chosen Hans's 7th Staffel for the task. The *Jabo* pilots – as they were known – of Erpro 210 had all been carefully trained in such operations, but Hans and his pilots had never ever carried out such a task; many doubted it was really possible. There was only one way to find out, and Hans opted to be the first to try and fly with a 250 kg bomb strapped underneath the plane. It was a nerve-wracking experience, but worked. The key now was to get the men trained as *Jabos* as quickly as possible. On 4 October, four of Trautloft's best pilots, Hans included, took off for a practice mission to Dungeness – the ruined lighthouse was becoming a favoured marker for the Luftwaffe pilots. The results were not encouraging, but after more practice it was decided that attacking in a low, shallow dive produced the least inaccurate results. Hans later bombed Tilbury Docks in London, but the *Jabos* were not really very effective. The Me 109 was simply not designed for such a role and the pilots had not been given enough training. Even experienced *Experten* like Hans could not suddenly become fighter-bomber marksmen overnight.

*

The fighting continued – the Luftwaffe lost 379 aircraft in October and Fighter Command 185 – but the Germans were further away than ever from achieving air superiority. On 4 October, after all the blistering air battles of September, Fighter Command had, for the first time, more than 700 fighters ready to take to the skies. The Germans could keep coming over all they liked, but they were not going to win. Neither Göring nor Hitler had any idea of the true strength of Fighter Command, but they now began to accept that the great battle against Britain had failed – for 1940, at any rate. On 12 October, Hitler finally postponed SEALION until the following spring. Naval personnel and shipping were to be released, tugs and barges returned to their normal, much-needed roles, although many of the divisions allocated for the invasion were to remain along the coastal areas. All that effort, all that cost; it had come to nothing. Air operations over Britain would continue, especially the night bombing, but Hitler was now ever more set upon his next course of action. If Britain could not be brought to heel now, then she would once the Soviet Union had been absorbed into the Third Reich.

Yet at this moment of great triumph for the RAF, and especially Fighter Command, the release from the stranglehold prompted not celebration but acrimony, jealousy and the worst kind of ugly political jostling. In some ways, Air Chief Marshal Dowding had been on borrowed time. His original three-year tenure at Fighter Command had been up in June 1939, but had then been extended until the following April. By then, with the war about to boil over, Newall asked him to stay on a bit longer, until July. But by July there had been no question of retiring Dowding. He was asked to remain until the end of October, which he accepted. Yet when Churchill heard that Newall was even considering removing the C-in-C Fighter Command, he angrily wrote that Dowding should remain in office as long as the war lasted and could even be promoted to take over as Chief of Air Staff.

Despite this rebuke, however, a month later Sinclair and Newall still had not confirmed Dowding's future. When he discovered this, Churchill was incensed. 'It is entirely wrong to keep an officer in the position of Commander-in-Chief, conducting hazardous operations from day to day, when he is dangling at the end of an expiring appointment,' Churchill wrote angrily to Sinclair. 'Such a situation is not fair to anyone, least of all to the nation.' At this, both Newall and Sinclair bowed to their Prime Minister's wishes and told Dowding he was now to remain in office for the foreseeable future.

This did not make his position impregnable, however. During his long career, Dowding had never been much interested in politicking and had no qualms at all about arguing with those at the Air Ministry whenever he thought it necessary. Quite single-mindedly he had pursued his task of strengthening Fighter Command and Britain's defences, encountering endless hurdles of opposition as he had done so. This had made him some notable enemies, and while his position had been safe during the frantic scrabble to get Britain ready for war and again when the nation was facing untold peril, it was not so secure the moment that threat diminished.

Park, too, despite his brilliance, was another interested only in winning the war rather than playing any kind of political games. Throughout the summer his mind had been fully occupied with the battle, of how to marshal his forces correctly, and how to evolve tactics; he was not interested one jot in the ambitions and jealousies of his fellow commander in 12 Group, or about walking roughshod over Air Ministry red tape if it meant saving some of his precious fighters.

This attitude was entirely understandable, but even in wartime office politics plays its unattractive part. Slowly but surely, the movement to remove both men was taking hold. Two of its architects were Leigh-Mallory, the commander of 12 Group, and Air Marshal Sholto Douglas.

Brother of the more famous George – lost whilst attempting to climb Everest in 1924 – Trafford Leigh-Mallory was a barrister by training, had repeatedly proved his bravery as a soldier and then a pilot in the Great War, and since then in his post-war career with the RAF had shown himself to be an intelligent, energetic organizer, popular with his men, although less popular with his commanders. He had no experience with fighters, however, and Park, for one, had always thought him incompetent in his role as head of 12 Group. He was also incredibly ambitious. Throughout the summer, Leigh-Mallory had bristled with resentment at the way Park and 11 Group were always given priority and seen as the senior Group in Fighter Command. The concept of the big wing, however, put forward by Douglas Bader, offered a means of getting his 12 Group more directly involved in the battle. Furthermore, it was very obviously a different tactical approach to anything Park had been trying. If it worked, then Leigh-Mallory would be able to get one over his rival.

In Bader he had the perfect accomplice. This fearless fighter commander was well known for having overcome horrific injuries, and with two tin legs had still returned to flying. He had incredible energy, determination and drive and his courage was unquestionably an inspiration. But he was also something of a bully with an ego almost as big as Leigh-Mallory's. Bader was delightful and charming and enormous fun just so long as he was the boss, and people played by his rules and accepted that he was right at all times; in some ways, he was cut from the same cloth as Dolfo Galland.

Bader's big-wing idea was that as soon as a large raid was seen to be building up, he would form up a wing of three to five squadrons to intercept the enemy as they crossed over the Channel. 11 Group fighters would then harry the departing raiders as they headed back to home. This tactic would have given the big wing the primary role rather than 11 Group's fighters, which is exactly how Bader wanted it; like Leigh-Mallory he was frustrated at being kept out of the action. Unfortunately, his ego was getting in the way of sound tactical sense.

As the Duxford Wing was finally put into practice, Bader and Leigh-Mallory repeatedly put in monstrous claims, gleefully picked up at the Air Ministry, which did much to curry support for their new ideas. Park, however, found both Leigh-Mallory and Bader irksome in the extreme. The big wing was taking too long to form up, frequently missing the action, and by following this wasteful enterprise they were not properly protecting 11 Group airfields, which was their primary function. The claims, Park said, were absolutely risible. He also knew that there was no way the big wing could meet a large German raid as it crossed the coast, as Leigh-Mallory and Bader were proposing. Duxford was much further away from Canterbury, for example, than Cap Gris Nez. At the very least it would take half an hour from the moment a raid was picked up over the Pas de Calais to reach south-east Kent, and that was not even taking into account forming-up time. The Germans would take just fifteen minutes.

Park's appreciation of the big-wing theory was spot on. Bader's men *were* massively overclaiming. Even Cocky Dundas, who had been quite awed by Bader during 616 Squadron's brief stint with the wing, had admitted that he had not seen anyone actually shoot anything down during the big air battle on 27 September; and that was the only time they had ever properly engaged the enemy at all while he was involved. So absurd were these inflated notions about big wings, Park had assumed he could dismiss them with a few withering explanatory comments. But he was wrong. Leigh-Mallory had the support of Sholto Douglas and a number of other highly influential players within the RAF and Air Ministry, men like Marshal 'Boom' Trenchard, long retired but whose views still counted, and a former Chief of the Air Staff, Sir John Salmond. These were men who had long wished to see the back of Dowding, and they now sensed their moment to strike was coming. A coup was being staged, one that would rid them of both Dowding and Park.

The first bone of contention was Park's supposed tactical rigidity and his reluctance to embrace the big wing. Few commanders were more tactically astute than Park, but in a meeting on 17 October chaired by Sholto Douglas, and at which Squadron Leader Bader, bizarrely, was present, he was forced to defend himself against a largely united front of Douglas and Leigh-Mallory in which it was quite clear they had no intention of listening to a word he was saying.

The second cause for criticism was over the difficulties of night interception. Dowding was working on a system in which fighters would rely entirely on their instruments to fly and would be guided to the target by radar. This he had reported in a paper, which Churchill had described as 'masterly'. Many, however, thought this would be impossible, Douglas included, and that, even if it could be achieved one day, it would take too long to develop. Amongst those critical of Dowding's plans were Sir John Salmond, who had been asked to chair a committee into night defence. It was not the first time Dowding had been on the receiving end of such criticism. He had received a copy of Salmond's report, but had thought little of it. Certainly, no committee was going to deter him from what he believed to be the right course.

In all but dismissing Salmond's report, however, Dowding had made a big mistake. The man who had instigated Salmond's committee in the first place was none other than Lord Beaverbrook, Dowding's supposed ally. So he had been, but Beaverbrook, displaying the kind of unsentimental ruthlessness that had been a hallmark of his career, had correctly recognized that night-fighters had now dramatically become the key to Britain's future defence against the Luftwaffe. It did not matter that he had the utmost respect for Dowding and what he had achieved; as far as he was concerned, the C-in-C Fighter Command was not tackling night defence with the kind of urgency he felt was needed. This was not true, but Beaverbrook felt the time had come for a change and a fresh approach. When Dowding saw Salmond's report, he ticked three of the eighteen points, put question marks by five, and crosses by the other nine. It was precisely the dismissive reaction Beaverbrook had expected, but now gave him the leverage needed to ease Dowding from office. Dowding had thought that after Churchill's open backing in the summer his position was pretty much impregnable. This was a big miscalculation, because it was not. Dowding might have been able to defy Trenchard, Salmond, Douglas *et al.*, but not Beaverbrook.

In the short term, however, Dowding and Park agreed to try and bring the big wing into play more often. It did not work, largely because of its fundamental flaw – it simply took too long to assemble. Repeatedly, Bader's forces arrived too late. Investigations by the Air Ministry confirmed the ill-feeling between Park and Leigh-Mallory, which everyone knew about already. At the end of October, Douglas told Dowding to sort out the problem once and for all and to make better use of the big wing. Dowding replied, rebutting the criticism and suggesting that Bader suffered from 'an over-development of the critical faculties', and should be posted where he could be kept under better control. Bader was not posted, work continued with Dowding's night-fighter plan, and Park continued intercepting the ever-decreasing daytime raids as he saw fit. Thus the situation was left largely unresolved – for the time being at any rate.

The night bombing continued, but there was no break in British morale. Olivia Cockett was no longer so apprehensive about the air war – it was not proving as bad as she had feared. No-one she knew had been killed, although she knew of a couple of homes that had been destroyed. If anything, the Blitz – as it was being called – had given her a new feeling of self-confidence. She realized that if she had the guts to put out an incendiary, then she could stand up to most things. 'This has resulted in a general boldness of thought and action,' she scribbled, 'a kind of sparkle on my usual cheek, which I have been quite surprised (and pleased) about.'

Most people had adjusted amazingly well to finding themselves a nation under siege. There was no prospect of the war ending, but the terrible peril of the summer had passed. 'Life around here proceeds in its quiet way,' wrote Daidie Penna. 'Air-raids and the proximity of bombs are still being taken for granted and even the whacking of a house or two seems to have done nothing to disturb the Tadworth phlegm.' Daidie could have been speaking for much of Britain that Tuesday in October 1940.

48

Last Flight

On the last Sunday in October, the 27th, Ulrich Steinhilper woke up early. His tent smelled musty, and it was cold; winter was on its way. With some effort, he pulled back the blankets and got up, staggering over to the makeshift washstand. He looked tired, he knew, his eyes dark, his cheeks thin. But he *was* tired. He had flown over 150 combat missions over England. On one day he had even flown seven sorties, excessive even by Luftwaffe standards.

He was on Early Alarm, which meant being at dispersal by dawn, mercifully later now that the days were rapidly shortening. Having shaved, he dressed, putting his trousers and shirt straight over his pyjamas, then with two others drove over to dispersal. A low mist hung over the greying stubble fields that were their runways. Smells of coffee and food came from the tented camp at one side of the airfield. Groundcrews stamped feet and rubbed hands to keep warm, while pilots smoked cigarettes.

Helmut Kühle, Ulrich's *Staffelkapitän*, suddenly drove up in his car, having been to the morning briefing. 'Protect the fighter-bombers,' he told the waiting pilots. 'Target London. Take off 09.05 hours.'

Ulrich now hurried over to his plane, Yellow 2, with its five stripes on the tail, one stripe for each of his victories. His mechanic, Peter, was already waiting for him on the port wing. Clambering up, Ulrich put on his harness with Peter's help, then clambered into the tight cockpit. Reaching for the starter lever, he felt the aircraft rock gently as Peter began to wind up the eclipse starter before it could be engaged, so turning over the Daimler-Benz 601 engine. Pulling the starter, Ulrich felt the engine roar into life and then set the throttle lightly forwards so that he could complete his start-up checks. The other eight remaining Me 109s were all running now, then they began to emerge from their camouflaged dispersal pens. This was all that could be mustered from the entire *Gruppe*.

As he finished his taxi, Ulrich glanced around him, then pushed the throttle on to full power and felt the Messerschmitt surge forward. He lifted the tail as the machine bumped over the rough field, Yellow 2 bounced a little, then suddenly the jolting stopped as the plane became airborne. Retracting the undercarriage, he waited a few moments whilst his speed increased, then eased back the control column and began to climb away. Looking either side of him, he watched the position of the others and then they began to tighten up for the climb.

They met cloud over Kent, but as they approached London the sky cleared, just as the met officer had predicted. Everyone began scanning the sky, but nothing could be seen – yet. The engine in front of him throbbed rhythmically. It was noisy in any fighter, but with his headphones strapped close to his ears it became such a constant background thrum that he might as well have been flying in silence; and the silence in his headset only added to the tension he felt as he waited for the moment the British fighters would be spotted.

Ulrich continued searching the sky behind, in front, either side, below, but especially above. Suddenly a voice full of static crackled in his ear, 'Raven calling! Raven calling! Eleven o'clock high! Eleven o'clock high. Condensation trails, same course.' Ulrich looked up and saw them now, about 3,000 feet above, to their left, the vivid white contrails clear against the deep blue. The fighting had got higher in recent weeks. The *Gruppe* were already at 32,000 feet, which meant the Spitfires were now at 35,000, an incredible height. It was hard flying at those heights. The 109 did not like it and the pilots had to constantly change the propeller pitch and throttle to improve performance: with a fine pitch, they could increase the RPM and get more pressure from the engine's supercharger, but by then switching to coarse pitch they could make up some speed, which was essential if they were to keep up with the rest of the formation.

But there was something up with Yellow 2. Ulrich was struggling to change pitch. Most probably condensation had begun to collect in the grease of the pitch-changing gear during the cold nights of the past week, and now, at 32,000 feet, it had frozen, which had affected the pitch control. For a moment, Ulrich thought about turning back but then dismissed the idea, opting instead to keep the pitch fine and run the engine at high revs and rely on the supercharger to help maintain speed. It meant the engine would be running at a level higher than the recommended RPM, but that happened all the time in combat. In any case, having made his decision to fly on, he did not have any other choice.

A pattern had emerged in this latest phase of the air battle. The Luftwaffe's planes would assemble and set course for London. The Tommies, meanwhile, warned of the approaching raid, would climb up high and wait for them. They would then patrol the sky, and just as the German formations turned for home at their tactically weakest point and at the limit of the fighters' range, they would pounce, from height with the sun behind them. Now, as the moment to turn for home approached, Ulrich waited for the order with increasing trepidation.

The *Jabos* began their attack, the radio suddenly full of chatter until there were so many different voices that the noise merged into a jarring whistling. Moments later and the formation was turning, but to the left, rather than the right, as they had been expecting. The eight machines of I/JG 52 quickly manoeuvred into their *Rotte* position, Ulrich's wingman, Lothar Schieverhöfer, moving in beside and behind him. Suddenly someone shouted, 'Out of the sun! Out of the sun!' and Ulrich swivelled and craned his neck upwards to see a number of Spitfires diving down towards Lothar. Ulrich shouted out a warning and tried to move to protect his tail, only to see him doing the same. Behind, at least four Spitfires were stepped up, each lining up to fire. Ulrich now dived away, his revs way too high, so at 22,000 feet he levelled out, eyeing a safe-looking bank of cloud below. He was wondering whether Lothar had got away when suddenly there was a loud bang as something exploded on the left side of his machine, and as something clattered into his elevator his stick shook in his hands. Frantically looking around, he could see no sign of the enemy so decided it must have been his supercharger that had blown. Glancing at his instrument panel, he saw everything still appeared to be working, but his oil pressure was dropping dramatically. Air speed was around 400 mph in his shallow dive and he was still able to weave from side to side, so he pushed the stick forward, put the nose down, and dived down towards the cloud layer, reaching the milky mass at around 6,000 feet. Moments later he was out into the blindingly bright sun, but at least it enabled him to get a fix. If he was on course for home, the sun should have been ahead and slightly to the right, and so it was, so he slipped back into the protective shroud of the cloud.

He checked his instruments again and everything still seemed to be in order apart from the oil loss, but just as he was beginning to breathe a little more easily, he slid out of the cloud again and was horrified first to see the Thames estuary below – he thought he had made more distance – and then in front and slightly below him a formation of Hurricanes. Deciding attack was his only option, he checked the lights that told him his guns were armed and ready, then seeing four green lights switched on the gunsight. But this was not working – there was too much ice on the windscreen from his long dive. He would have to use the metal emergency sight, but as he removed his oxygen mask, he was suddenly gripped with fear – his engine was beginning to boil and if it came to a tussle he was not sure how long his machine would keep flying. Gently, and very slowly, he climbed back into the cloud.

His engine temperature was now 130 degrees. He could not understand why it was so high; his engine was losing oil, but that would not affect the cooling system. He was sure he had dived before the Spitfires had opened fire, but a bullet in the radiator seemed the only cause of his rapidly rising temperature gauge. 'This is Owl 2a,' he called over the radio, 'have been hit in the radiator, will try to reach the Channel. Taking course from Thames to Manston. Please confirm.' But there was no reply – just a hiss of static.

At 6,000 feet once more, and still in cloud, he switched off the engine, so that he was now gliding and blind flying. At 4,000 feet he emerged through the cloud once more, but still he continued his glide and decided to try another radio call. This time the ground station in the Pas de Calais replied. 'Understood Owl 2a. Air-Sea Rescue will be notified. Only go into the water when absolutely necessary.' He now heard Kühle's voice too, telling him he would start searching the Channel immediately while the others would return, refuel then continue the search if necessary. Ulrich felt his spirits lift.

Now, at around 1,600 feet, he began to attract some light flak, so he decided it was time to restart the engine. It whirred into life immediately and he began to climb once more, the oil temperature still under control. In the clouds, he transmitted another fix to the ground station, but by now the temperature was beginning to rise alarmingly again so he cut the engine once more, hoping to repeat Hans-Ekkehard Bob's trick of 'bobbing' back across the Channel.

But the engine's power was fading, and he was soon struggling to gain any height at all. He had to open the throttle further – there was no alternative – but as he did so, the engine seized. There was no bang, no sudden explosion – just silence. With his machine dead, he knew he would have to jump. Having sent a last message, he briefly wondered whether he should perhaps try and crash-land instead but then madly decided he must not let his machine fall into enemy hands. No, bailing out was the only option. He ran through the emergency procedures: oxygen off. Throat microphone off. Remove flying helmet and headset. Reaching for the canopy jettison lever he pulled but it broke off in his hand. Trying desperately not to panic he shot a glance at his altimeter – he was now at only 800 feet. He needed to get out of there quickly – very quickly. He now tried to open the canopy as normal and as he pulled the lever and pushed, it burst open with a sudden rush of wind and cold air that forced the Perspex hood off its hinges so that it clattered noisily down the side of the fuselage. Gasping from the cold, he released his belts and pushed himself up into the incredibly strong 130 mph draught, but as he did so was buffeted backwards, wedging his parachute under the rear part of the canopy and catching his legs under the instrument panel. Frantically, he tried to claw his hands back down on to the control column in an effort to flip the machine over, but he could not reach. And now Yellow 2 was beginning its final dive. There was nothing for it: he would have to risk tearing his parachute or die. Leaning over to the right, with one last effort he pulled his legs free and up towards his body and suddenly he was rolling through the air, somersaulting past the tail of his Messerschmitt.

Still tumbling he pulled the parachute release but for a moment nothing happened, and in panic he began groping helplessly at the pack, only for the silk to burst out. As the main parachute opened, the secondary 'chute managed to get tangled around his left leg causing him intense pain so that he was hanging upside down, his leg feeling as though it was being pulled from his hip. Somehow, he managed to right himself and was relieved to discover his leg was still intact, although the pain was excruciating. Ahead he now saw Yellow 2 dive into the ground in the middle of a field of cows, which were scattering in all directions. He heard a soft thump as it hit the ground and then the ammunition began exploding.

The ground was now rising up to meet him, but fortunately he landed on his right leg and the ground was soft, and he was able to release the parachute harness with ease. He was lying beside a canal embankment. A short distance away, although out of sight, ammunition was still exploding. Looking around, he could see no-one. He felt desperately alone and helpless, and his throat began to tighten. He thought he might cry.

But then the moment passed as he began to discard his rubber dinghy, flare pistol, and sea water dye container. Suddenly a shot rang out and he quickly lay flat, pressing his head into the damp ground. Carefully raising his head again he saw a man in civilian clothes approaching him, an armband around his left sleeve and clutching a shotgun.

'Get up!' he yelled.

'My leg is hurt!' Ulrich replied. He tried to get up, but collapsed in pain.

'I'll come round to you,' called out the man.

Ulrich sat there on the wet grass, waiting for his captor. Depression swept over him. He was twenty-two and a prisoner of war. The battle was over.

Postscript

LATER ON THE AFTERNOON of Wednesday, 28 November, Siegfried Bethke was flying over England for the second time that day. Leading the entire *Gruppe* was the recently promoted Major Helmut Wick, who now had a staggering fifty-five victories to his name and was the youngest *Geschwaderkommodore* in the Luftwaffe. Flying over the Isle of Wight at about 25,000 feet, they suddenly spotted a formation of Spitfires, yet although they were both travelling at about the same height, Wick decided to lead his Messerschmitts away.

Ten minutes later, however, at around ten past five, having climbed much higher, the German fighters found the Spitfires again and dived down towards them. Spotting the attack, the pilots of 609 Squadron turned to fly directly underneath the German formation, but seeing this Wick detached three aircraft, including himself, and dived out of the sun in close formation. As the three Me 109s sped towards them, the Spitfires began breaking into sections, and then suddenly the Me 109s were flashing by, guns flashing bullets and cannon shells. In the brief tussle, Wick shot down his fifty-sixth victim, Pilot Officer Baillon, but then, just moments later, was attacked in turn by John Dundas.

'Whoopee!' shouted John over the R/T. 'I've got a 109.' It was the last words anyone heard him say, for a moment later Rudi Flanz, one of the *Stab* pilots, opened fire and John's Spitfire began plummeting down towards the sea. Like Wick, he made no effort to bail out. In just a few seconds, two of the best aces on each side had been killed. Few saw what had happened, and certainly not Siegfried Bethke – the formation had already broken up and spread out. Both the pilots of 609 Squadron and JG 2 spent long hours of desperate search the following morning. Nothing was found. Nor was there any sign of Pilot Officer Baillon, who had been seen bailing out into the sea. Like Wick, his wife had been expecting a child. His body was eventually washed up in France six weeks later, but of John and Helmut Wick, nothing was ever seen again.

For his beloved younger brother, Cocky, John's death was a shattering blow. He had just been given some leave and having borrowed a car had reached his home in Cawthorne at teatime on 1 December, shortly after the telegram announcing that John was missing had arrived. 'So it has happened at last,' he wrote in his diary. 'I suppose it had to happen. I suppose that we were inordinately lucky to have survived intact as long as we did.' Seven weeks later, just before Christmas, he confessed that since then his time in the squadron had been a blur of unhappiness and restlessness. 'It affected my life deeply,' he admitted many years later. 'I think hardly a day has gone by since then when I have not thought of John.' How many other brothers, sisters, parents, wives, husbands, lovers and friends would have echoed his thoughts after that long summer? Too many, and yet, of course, so much worse was to come: the war would spread into a global conflict, the worst the world had ever seen. Sixty million would be dead by the time it finally came to an end five long years later.

Göring left France in November, having lost interest in the air war against Britain and feeling somewhat humiliated by the Luftwaffe's failure. None of his senior commanders were sacked, not even Beppo Schmid, unlike the victorious Dowding or Park. The architect of Britain's defence was finally eased from office on 25 November, having been asked to head a mission to the United States. Park left at the same time. It must have been galling to them that their jobs were taken by Sholto Douglas and Leigh-Mallory respectively; it was this usurpation by their detractors as much as anything that has ever since left something of a sour note in the British view of the battle. It should not, however. By November, Dowding was exhausted. He had rarely had more than a few hours' sleep a night all summer and since the autumn even less, as almost every night he had been driven to Kenley or Redhill to observe night interception tests and experiments with radar. In fact, his plans were beginning to work. On

19 November, John Cunningham,* a night-fighter pilot, shot down a Ju 88 using airborne radar just as Dowding had claimed would be possible. There were still some refinements and many improvements to be made, but in this, as in many things, Dowding had proved Beaverbrook, Salmond and his other doubters utterly wrong.

Nonetheless, Beaverbrook had surely been correct in thinking that Dowding should move on. The time had come for a change, for an injection of new energy and blood. He had achieved almost all that could have been achieved and had both Churchill's and the nation's gratitude. But if Dowding went, then Park had to go too. He could not have carried on under Douglas and with Leigh-Mallory breathing down his neck. Personality counts for so much in every walk of life, and that includes high command in a time of war. Dowding and Park understood and respected each other greatly. As a team, they worked seamlessly in a way that Douglas and Park could never have done. Awarded a knighthood for his efforts, Park later showed his brilliance again during the RAF's second-biggest air battle – over Malta in 1942. Then he replaced Air Vice-Marshal Lloyd, a man who knew nothing of fighters or fighter tactics. Ten days after Park's arrival, the air battle for Malta was over, achieved, in no small part, by using several squadrons operating together and intercepting the enemy forward of the island. It wasn't that Park was ever against big wings *per se*; it was just that he did not think they could be effectively used over south-east England in 1940. However painful their departure may have been in November 1940, they both lived long enough to know the respect and admiration history would accord them, which is more than could be said for Leigh-Mallory, who was killed in a flying accident in November 1944. Sholto Douglas is now largely forgotten, having commanded Fighter Command during a period of endless fighter sweeps over France in 1941 and 1942, which achieved very little and cost far too many lives and aircraft. In pursuing this strategy, he ensured that as few Spitfires as possible were sent overseas where they were really needed. On the other hand, Dowding and Park remain deeply – and justifiably – revered. It is Dowding's and not Douglas's office that has been preserved at Bentley Priory, while a statue of Park has even stood on the Fourth Plinth in Trafalgar Square.

* John Cunningham became the most famous RAF night-fighter of them all, nicknamed 'Cat's Eyes' Cunningham and scoring twenty victories, of which nineteen were at night.

*

Hans-Ekkehard Bob still insists that the Luftwaffe did not lose the Battle of Britain, and prefers to think of it as more of a draw. After all, he points out, the Luftwaffe was not destroyed. Ulrich Steinhilper disagrees. He thinks the RAF broke both the back and the spirit of the Luftwaffe in the summer of 1940, and that they never again recovered. Certainly, by June the following year, when Hitler invaded the Soviet Union, the Luftwaffe was a smaller force than it had been the previous May, unable to fully recover from the heavy losses it suffered during the summer of 1940, in terms of both aircraft and experience.

Perhaps Hans does have a point, but in earlier days it did not require the utter destruction of a force to win or lose a battle; after all, the French were not destroyed at Waterloo, but they were still beaten. By the end of October 1940, the Luftwaffe had lost 3,701 aircraft irredeemably destroyed, yet it had begun the summer with 3,578. In other words, it had losses of more than 100 per cent. Certainly, it had had replacements, but because production was not keeping up with losses, its combat strength by the end of October 1940 was somewhere in the region of 75 per cent less than it had been before the western campaign. By then, almost every *Gruppe* was operating with a fraction of its supposed establishment and many of the men were utterly exhausted, showing clear signs of combat fatigue, and struggling to maintain morale. That would constitute defeat by most people's standards.

This is not really the point, however. In the summer of 1940, Germany faced Britain and France, and had to defeat both. That was the gamble Hitler took. He beat France, but he did not beat Britain, and at the end of the summer Germany was significantly worse off than she had been in May, and facing a long, attritional war on two fronts, which was precisely what the Führer had so desperately wished to avoid. It has been fashionable in recent years to play down the importance of the Battle of Britain, but to do so is wrong. It was a key – if not *the* key – turning point in the war because it meant that instead of the conflict being a European war which one day would escalate into a clash between Germany and Russia, it became a global conflict in which the Third Reich was unlikely to ever realistically emerge victorious. Britain's defiance *did* save the world from Nazism.

When Göring heard Britain had declared war on 3 September 1939, he had telephoned von Ribbentrop. 'Now you've got your ******* war!' he shouted down the phone. 'You alone are to blame!' Like so many leading Nazis, Göring did not want war in 1939, not because he thought war was wrong but because he knew Germany was not ready and that it would lead to unmitigated disaster – and he had been right. He had not wanted to attack Britain in the summer of 1940, either, recognizing that while Britain's army might not be up to much, she still had a powerful navy, a half-decent air force, and in America and the Dominions both powerful and very useful friends.

First and foremost, Germany lost the battle against Britain because she really was not ready for war. Her economy could just about cope with a few short, sharp conflicts such as Poland, and Norway, and as the western campaign had proved to be, but nothing more. However over-mighty a formation of Junkers, Dorniers and Heinkels might appear to those watching the giant raids over southern England, the Luftwaffe was not big enough to do what it set out to achieve. Nor was the U-boat force. A staggering 352,407 tons of Allied shipping were lost to the U-boats in October – the highest toll so far. It would not always be so easy; once the Home Fleet was released from anti-invasion duty and once the Royal Navy grew some more, the convoys would be better protected. Yet what an opportunity had been missed. If between nine and fourteen submarines could wreak that much havoc, what would fifty or a hundred have done? Churchill was worried enough as it was. Had Dönitz had the boats he had been earlier promised then perhaps Britain might have been brought to her knees. Massed U-boat attacks combined with a more sensibly handled air battle could have been devastating.

The truth was that the crushing victory in France hid many of Germany's deficiencies. Hitler was lucky to have had such inspired commanders in men like Guderian and, frankly, even Halder, who understood the potential of modern mobile warfare and the principles of concentration of force. The western campaign had come off in lightning-quick fashion because of the genius and vision of a few men and the high training of a key proportion of the army. Contributing to that success was the Luftwaffe, a large aerial force that had developed tactics and methods of directly supporting the ground troops in a way that no other nation had considered at that time. And it succeeded because the French crumbled so badly. Operationally, tactically and strategically, the French had been woeful. Their leadership was too old, too dated. Morale was poor and they made lots and lots of really bad mistakes. On paper, Germany should never have won.

It must have seemed, in June 1940, that momentum alone would force victory over Britain. Hitler never knew how close he was to achieving his goal in the last days of May, but the halt order was the first of many missed opportunities that summer. From Dunkirk onwards, when the Luftwaffe's shortcomings were first exposed, the Germans made a catalogue of mistakes. Hitler prevaricated too long, they had no clear strategy, and they constantly, persistently, depended on incredibly faulty intelligence; the roguish Beppo Schmid had a lot to answer for. At no point did they ever have a clear picture of Fighter Command's strength or an understanding of the Dowding System. They also singularly failed to exploit the strengths of what resources they did have. The handling of the fighter arm, for example, was grossly incompetent. Nor did they look after their most precious asset of all: the men. Finally, they suffered from what in modern military parlance is known as mission creep. Their primary stated aim was to destroy the RAF, yet the constant switching of tactics, the differing uses of aircraft, and the move from targeting airfields to London were all indicative of a high command that had no real strategic idea of how it was to achieve its goals. Only for around two weeks, towards the end of August and at the beginning of September, did it really make any attempt to do this. Sending over a multitude of small and medium-sized raids stretched Fighter Command to its limits, but these raids were unable to make a big enough impact. Massed raids could deliver that impact, but with increased scale the quantity of raids had to be sacrificed, and suddenly Fighter Command could anticipate the attacks more effectively and consequently bring more fighters to bear. Had the Luftwaffe had many more aircraft, it would have been a different matter. But it did not.

Luftwaffe failings, however, should not detract from the achievement of the RAF in the summer of 1940. Had it not had such a superb defensive system, and had it not had such inspired and brilliant leaders, the Luftwaffe would still have prevailed, no matter how valiant or skilful the pilots. The Luftwaffe's shortcomings were only revealed because the RAF was handled so much better. 'The Few' have rightly been considered heroes – they were to a man – and as the first line of defence their stand against the Luftwaffe was every bit as magnificent as the myth would have it. Yet it is a mistake to view the Battle of Britain in isolation as RAF Fighter Command versus the Luftwaffe. It was a far more collective effort that saved Britain in 1940. The fledgling performance of Bomber Command, for example, has traditionally been viewed as being so ineffective to have been almost risible, yet it played a crucial part in the battle, taking the fight into Germany, showing the world that German invincibility was a sham, and contributing to the battle to grind down the Luftwaffe. The relentless attacks on German airfields wore down Luftwaffe crews far more than has ever been appreciated.

But everyone played their part: the navy, the army, the auxiliary services, the Home Guard, the groundcrews, the Observer Corps, the civilian repair units – Britain's defiance in the summer of 1940 was a collective effort. The pilots of Fighter Command may have been the first line, but there were many thousands more who contributed to Britain's victory.

Neville Chamberlain died on 9 November, after losing his fight with cancer. He had finally resigned from the Cabinet a month earlier, accepting he was too ill to be of any further use to Churchill. History has been too unkind to Chamberlain. Thanks to him, the RAF received the funding it needed in the 1930s when he was still Chancellor of the Exchequer, while no matter how distasteful the Munich agreement may have been, the postponement of war certainly gave Britain the chance to fight back in 1940. Nor, after Munich, did Chamberlain appease any more. He was not the right Prime Minister for war, however, yet once forced from office he proved an invaluable colleague to Churchill and, at the end of May, helped ensure that Britain fought on. At his funeral at Westminster Abbey, Churchill delivered a eulogy that even today can still bring a lump to the throat. 'The only guide to a man is his conscience,' he said, 'the only shield to his memory is the rectitude and sincerity of his actions. It is very imprudent to walk through life without this shield, because we are so often mocked by the failure of our hopes and the upsetting of our calculations; but with this shield, however the fates may play, we march always in the ranks of honour.' Chamberlain, he said, never failed to act with anything other than perfect sincerity and with the very best of ideals. 'Herr Hitler,' the Prime Minister concluded, 'protests with frantic words and gestures that he has only desired peace. What do these ravings and outpourings count before the silence of Neville Chamberlain's tomb?'

It was oratory like this that helped Churchill win over the nation and stem the panic wrought by Germany's incredible victory in France. From the moment he became Prime Minister, Churchill's leadership was superb. He alone had the vision, drive and energy to deliver Britain from the mire of France and Dunkirk. While Hitler dithered, Churchill showed steely resolve. It is hard to think of another man who could have given

Britain the will to carry on during those dark days of May and June. He was a great man, but never more so than during the summer of 1940, Britain's darkest and finest hour.

In 1940, Britain won the Battle of Britain, but she had not yet won the war. There was still a very long way to go. Although Roosevelt had gained his third term, it was another thirteen months before the United States finally joined the fight, and in that time Churchill and Britain faced one disappointment after another. Not until the end of 1942 had the tide begun to turn, by which time the grotesque folly of Hitler's invasion of the Soviet Union had become apparent. The Battle of Britain had forced Hitler to act against Russia sooner than he had originally planned – before he was ready. Once again, his gamble failed, and Germany's fate was sealed.

It was over the Soviet Union that many Luftwaffe pilots began to amass truly astonishing scores. Günther Rall went on to become the third-highest-scoring fighter ace of all time, with 275 victories, and later became a general in the post-war Luftwaffe. He died in October 2009. Dolfo Galland also survived the war, by which time he was a general with 104 victories – he had reached his fiftieth at the end of October 1940. Like Günther Rall he joined the post-war Luftwaffe and became friends for life with Douglas Bader and Bob Stanford-Tuck. He died in 1996. Siegfried Bethke remained on the Western Front, but in the summer of 1942 suffered serious injuries in a flying accident that halted his flying career. Surviving the war, he died in 2003. Another high-scoring ace was Hans-Ekkehard Bob, who amassed sixty victories, and ended the war flying Me 262 jets under Dolfo Galland. He became a successful post-war businessman, returning to Freiburg, where he lives to this day. He also still flies, and drives a convertible VW Beetle with 'JG 54' on the number plate.

Both Julius Neumann and Ulrich Steinhilper remained POWs in Canada until the end of the war, although Ulrich made two escape attempts. After the war, Julius was reunited with his teddy bear mascot, and became a lawyer. He died in 2009. After his return to Germany, Ulrich joined IBM, becoming a pioneer of the word processor. He died in October 2009. Rudi Miese was also shot down, only a month after finally becoming operational, and spent the rest of the war as a POW. He died in March 2009.

Hajo Herrmann later joined the Luftwaffe staff and then established the *Wilde Sau* – 'Wild Boar' – night-fighter unit. Flying single-engine FW

190 fighters, they provided a very effective night defence over Germany towards the end of the war. He was later captured by the Russians and imprisoned for ten years, after which he returned to Germany and became a lawyer, defending many former Nazis accused of war crimes. He lives in Düsseldorf. Peter Stahl went on to serve in Russia, where he bailed out sixty miles behind lines and made it back to safety. He was then posted to the Mediterranean and served in North Africa and Italy, before ending the war as a commander in KG 200, the Luftwaffe's sabotage wing.

Of the British pilots, Bee Beamont went on to become one of the RAF's most successful fighter pilots, pioneering the Hawker Typhoon, later commanding 609 Squadron, and becoming a leading ace at shooting down V1 and V2 rockets. He developed the trick of tipping German rockets by knocking them with a wing and thus making them hit the ground early, away from London. After the war, he continued in the RAF, later becoming a successful test pilot. He died in 2001. Billy Drake also had a highly successful wartime career, and was present at the German surrender in Reims on 7 May 1945. He remained with the RAF, retiring first to Portugal and then later returning to England. He lives in Devon. No less successful was Tom Neil, who later survived a long tour on Malta, then went on to command 41 Squadron. After a brief spell instructing, he was seconded to the US air force, took part in the Normandy invasion and then briefly saw action in Burma. Post-war, he became a test pilot and then later served at the British Embassy in Washington. He retired to Norfolk, where he still lives.

Tony Bartley later commanded 111 Squadron in North Africa and married the actress Deborah Kerr. Moving to Hollywood, he spent some years as a scriptwriter and producer, having his own production company as well as working as an executive for both CBS and Associated Rediffusion. Later remarrying, he moved back to his native Ireland with his second wife. He died in 2001. Pete Brothers also had a successful wartime career, and post-war remained in the RAF, rising to the rank of Air Commodore. He died in December 2008. Jimmy Corbin rejoined 66 Squadron in October 1940, was later commissioned and flew in North Africa. After the war he returned to teaching and still lives in Maidstone.

Sadly, David Crook did not survive. After leaving 609 Squadron in November 1940, he became an instructor. In December 1944, however, he began training for high-level reconnaissance and it was during a flight off the coast of Scotland on the 18th that his Spitfire suddenly dived down from 30,000 feet straight into the North Sea. It is not known for sure what caused his death, but his body was never recovered.

No squadron shot down more German aircraft in the battle than 303 Kościuszko Squadron. The Poles became legendary fighters – as did the Czechs – and continued to fight with the RAF until the end of the war. Jan Zumbach survived, but with no Poland to return home to continued flying, mostly as a mercenary in Africa. He passed away in 1986.

Of the bomber pilots, Arthur Hughes survived the war and remained in the RAF, retiring as a Group Captain. He died in 1993. Larry Donnelly went on to win the DFM and, towards the end of the war, won his pilot's wings. He remained in the RAF for a further twenty years before retiring to Cumbria, where he died in 2007. Andrew Jackson completed three tours on bombers, was demobbed in 1946 and returned to his pre-war career as a surveyor in Edinburgh. He was still living there when he passed away in January 2009.

Günther Prien and his crew of U-47 were lost at sea on 7 March 1941, having sunk over thirty Allied ships at more than 200,000 tons. Rolf Hilse, however, survived – one of only very few U-boat crewmen serving in 1940 to make it through the war. After the glory days of 1940 and 1941, German submarine losses began to mount – their golden opportunity had passed, as Allied tactics, numbers and anti-submarine devices steadily improved. From being highly effective hunters, the U-boats became the hunted. Not for nothing were they known as 'Iron Coffins'. Of around 40,000 who went to sea in the U-boats, 30,000 never returned. The *Schnellboote* crews fared somewhat better, and amongst those who survived the war was Bobby Fimmen, who ended up a Korvettenkapitän on the Kriegsmarine staff. After the war, he joined the family electrical business in Wittenberge, which his son now runs. He died in May 2001.

Of those serving in the Royal Navy, Joe Steele left after the war, becoming a dock worker in Liverpool and then London before retiring back to Merseyside. He died in March 2010. Andrew Begg also survived the war, including one of the most notorious convoys of them all, Operation PEDESTAL, to relieve the besieged island of Malta.

Of those in the army, Siegfried Knappe went on to fight in Russia and Italy and then served on General Helmuth Weidling's staff in Berlin during the final days of the war. Captured by the Russians, he was released in 1949 and emigrated to the United States. He died in December 2008. Hans von Luck took part in the invasion of the Soviet Union and later served with Rommel in the Western Desert and fought on throughout the North Africa campaign. He also served in Normandy during the invasion in 1944, and won the Knight's Cross. Captured by the Russians at the end of the war, he eventually returned to Germany and published his memoirs. He died in 1997.

Stan Fraser was posted overseas to Malta before the end of the Battle of Britain and later commissioned in the Middle East before returning to north-west Europe towards the end of the war. Demobbed in 1946, he rejoined his pre-war firm of paint manufacturers in Liverpool, and eventually ran his own business in north Wales. He lives there still. Sid Nuttall later joined the 1st Airborne Division, serving in North Africa and Italy and then joined the SAS in north-west Europe. He survived the war. Norman Field also later served in the airborne forces in North Africa and Italy, although having recovered from his wound at Dunkirk, he was initially recruited to join and develop the Auxiliary Units in Kent, a clandestine force of saboteurs trained to harass the enemy should the invasion have taken place, and then served on Montgomery's staff. Later he was involved in the planning of the airborne landings for D-Day and Arnhem, before being asked to join General Matthew Ridgway's staff for the Rhine crossing, and later took part in the liberation of Copenhagen. Retiring from the army as Lieutenant-Colonel in 1948 owing to ill-health, he set up a highly successful mushroom farm and became an acclaimed sculptor. He died in September 2009.

Douglas Mann later joined the army, landing on Gold Beach on D-Day, commanding a 'DD' Sherman tank squadron. He was almost immediately shot, but recovered and went out to north-west Europe again, only to be wounded a second time. After the war, he returned to farming, eventually settling on a farm in south-west Wiltshire, where he still lives. John Wilson also survived the war, despite also being twice wounded. He fought through most of the Italian campaign, and remained in the army after the war, finally retiring in 1973. He now lives near his old school in Marlborough.

In Germany, Else Wendel remarried, was reunited with her children and briefly found happiness, only to lose her husband in the dying days of the war. She remained in Berlin after the war and returned to her pre-war career as a social worker. Hilda Müller continued working for Siemens and also remained in Berlin right to the very end of the war. After the war, she became a kindergarten teacher and lives in Berlin to this day. William Shirer left Berlin in December 1940, and headed back to the United States. Returning to Europe to report on the Nuremberg

Trials, he later wrote his masterpiece, *The Rise and Fall of the Third Reich*, which was published in 1960.

In Britain, Harold Nicolson left the Government in 1941, remaining a backbencher for the rest of the war until losing his seat in the July 1945 election. He continued to write a number of books, and contributed journalism to various newspapers and magazines. Olivia Cockett remained in London throughout the war. She never did marry Bill Hole, but the two did become partners, retiring to Dorset, where she changed her name by deed poll to 'Hole'. She died in 1998. After the war, Daidie Penna trained as a teacher and taught art at a school in Epsom until she retired. Daidie passed away in 1969. RV Jones remained in intelligence until the end of the war. He introduced the dropping of metal foil – or 'chaff' – from aircraft to confuse German radar and later headed a team to target German long-range weapons, developing what became known as the Double Cross system. After the war, he left intelligence and became Professor of Natural Philosophy at Aberdeen University. He died in 1997. Cecil Beaton continued to work for the Ministry of Information and then returned to his pre-war career as a fashion photographer. He also designed a number of theatrical sets as well as costumes for films, including those for *My Fair Lady*. Later knighted, he died in 1980.

Seventy years on, the Battle of Britain remains an important moment in British history, and 1940 a key date alongside 1066, 1588 and 1805, when Britain was imperilled as never before. Over the years, books, films and television programmes have continued to propel an image of Britain as David and Germany as Goliath. It wasn't quite like that, but that does not mean the efforts of the RAF – or of Britain as a whole – in the summer of 1940 should in any way be belittled. And the myth does largely hold true. Britain was staring down the barrel in the summer of 1940 and her survival dramatically changed the course of the war. However, it is important, seventy years on, that the battle should be seen from both sides and in its wider context. In his despatch, Dowding wrote that the Battle of Britain really began in September 1939. He had a point, but certainly by the start of the western campaign, in May 1940, Britain's struggle for survival against Germany, and Germany's all-or-bust attack on Britain, had begun.

No other veterans of the Second World War are as hallowed as the Few, but equally no aircraft is as hallowed as the Spitfire. This aircraft, above all others, has gained an iconic reverence not given to any other.

The Me 109E might have been better for air-to-air fighting than the Spitfire Mk I in 1940, but Mitchell's plane was only at the beginning of its development back then. Subsequent models, complete with fuel injection, cannons and ever more powerful engines, were quite superb. No wonder that generations of children have built models of this beautiful aircraft, or that thousands still flock to air shows every summer to watch them fly. Certainly, watching the silhouette of those elliptical wings and hearing that deep roar of the Merlin never fails to be a highly moving experience.

There are some fifty still flying or close to flying, but there is one model, above all, that has special reverence for me. My fascination with the battle began with David Crook's wartime memoir *Spitfire Pilot*, and since then I have always had a special interest in his old squadron, 609 (West Riding). One of the squadron's Spitfires from the Battle of Britain remains. It was not flown by David Crook, but by that other 609 Squadron hero, John Dundas. Go to the Imperial War Museum in London and it can still be seen, suspended by wires from the ceiling. A favoured spot is on the second floor, along the balcony overlooking the atrium. From there it is possible to look down upon it, at its sleek, curving lines, and into the cockpit. It is always very still and quiet up there, but with a bit of imagination it is possible to see the Spitfire, not in some hall, but high in the burning blue above southern England, pirouetting and swirling, guns spitting bullets, and in a deadly duel with an Me 109. In fact, half close your eyes and one can even see John Dundas sitting in the cockpit, leather flying helmet around his head, leaning forward despite the straps of the harness, concentration etched on his face. He is not dead at the bottom of the English Channel, but suddenly very much alive.

Glossary

Abwehr	Wehrmacht Counter-Intelligence Service
CIGS	Chief of the Imperial General Staff
DeTe	*Dezimator Telegraphie Gerät* – early name for German radar
Erpro	*Erprobungsgruppe* – experimental wing
Fallschirmjäger	German parachute troops, and part of the Luftwaffe
Freya	type of German radar
He	Heinkel
Jafü	*Jagdfliegerführer* – German fighter division
JG	*Jagdgeschwader* – German fighter unit
Ju	Junkers
KG	*Kampfgeschwader* – German bomber unit
Mae West	inflatable life jacket
Me	Messerschmitt
MT	motor transport
OKH	*Oberkommando der Heeres* – the Army High Command
OKM	*Oberkommando der Marine* – the Navy High Command, also the Kriegsmarine
OKW	*Oberkommando der Wehrmacht* – the combined Armed Forces High Command
RDF	Radio Direction Finding
R/T	Radio Telegraphy
SNO	Senior Naval Officer
St.G	*Sturzkampfgeschwader*, or *Stuka-Geschwader* – Stuka unit
Wehrmacht	the German Armed Forces, i.e. army, navy and air force
Würzburg	type of German radar

Notes

Abbreviations

AFRHA	Air Force Research Historical Agency, Maxwell Air Force Base, Alabama
AHB	Air Historical Branch, Northolt
BA-MA	Bundesarchiv-Militärarchiv, Freiburg-im-Breisgau
BBK	Lord Beaverbrook Papers, House of Lords Archives
BfZ-SS	Bibliothek für Zeitgeschichte, Sammlung Sterz, Stuttgart
CAC	Churchill Archive Centre, Churchill College, Cambridge
CBP	Cecil Beaton Papers, St John's College, Cambridge
DTA	Deutsches Tagebucharchiv, Emmendingen
HND	Harold Nicolson Papers: Diary, Balliol College, Oxford
IWM	Imperial War Museum, London
JPK	Joseph P. Kennedy Papers, John F. Kennedy Presidential Library, Boston, Massachusetts
LHCMA	Liddell Hart Centre for Military Archives, King's College, London
MHI	Military History Institute, Carlisle Barracks, Pennsylvania
MO	Mass Observation Archive, University of Sussex
NCP	Neville Chamberlain Papers, University of Birmingham
NHB	Naval Historical Branch, Portsmouth
RAFMA	RAF Museum Archives, Hendon, London
TNA	The National Archives, Kew, London
WS	*War Speeches*, Winston S. Churchill
WSC	Winston S. Churchill, *The Second World War*, Vol. II

Private papers

In addition, the private papers of the following have been used:

Bartley, Anthony, 92 Squadron
Bob, Hans-Ekkehard, III/JG 54
Bethke, Siegfried, I/JG 2 (c/o Chris Goss)
Brothers, Pete, 32 and 257 Squadrons
Corbin, Jimmy, 66 Squadron
Dundas, Hugh, 616 Squadron
Dundas, John, 609 Squadron
Hughes, Arthur, 18 Squadron
Field, Norman, 2nd Royal Fusiliers
Fraser, Stan, 4th HAA Regiment
Jackson, Andrew, 149 Squadron
Neil, Tom, 249 Squadron
Neumann, Julius, II/JG 27
Rawlings, Margaret, civilian
Wright, Allan, 92 Squadron

Author interviews

I have not cited the following author interviews, all of which can be found on either www.secondworldwarforum.com or in the Sound Archives at the Imperial War Museum:

Beamont, Roland, 87 Squadron
Bob, Hans-Ekkehard, III/JG 54
Brothers, Pete, 32 and 257 Squadrons
Corbin, Jimmy, 66 Squadron
Drake, Billy, 1 Squadron
Field, Norman, 2nd Royal Fusiliers
Herrmann, Hajo, III/KG4
Jackson, Andrew, 149 Squadron
Mann, Douglas, Marlborough College, LDV
Miese, Rudolf, II/JG 2
Müller, Hildegard, civilian
Neil, Tom, 249 Squadron
Neumann, Julius, II/JG 27
Rall, Günther, III/JG 52
Steele, Joe, HMT *Dalmatia* and *Darthema*
Wellum, Geoffrey, 92 Squadron
Wilson, John, Marlborough College, LDV
Wright, Allan, 92 Squadron

References

Introduction

1 **'The Battle of Britain . . .'** TNA AIR 8/863

Part I: Miracles

1. First Flight

8 **'Practically everybody . . .'** This description comes from Crook, *Spitfire Pilot*, pp. 19–20, but also from: Clive Denney, a latter-day Spitfire pilot; Moss and McKee, *Spitfires and Polished Metal*; Price and Blackah, *Supermarine Spitfire: Owners' Workshop Manual*; and *Pilot's Notes Spitfire IIA and IIB* published by the Air Ministry

2. The Eve of Battle

10 **'grand evening'** Crook, *Spitfire Pilot*, p. 20
11 **'The battle which begins . . .'** Cited in Below, *At Hitler's Side*, p. 57
12 **'What now?'** Cited in Schmidt, *Hitler's Interpreter*, p. 158
12 **'Our enemy Number One'** Cited in Speer, *Inside the Third Reich*, p. 239
12 **'England is our enemy'** Cited in Ian Kershaw, *Hitler: 1936–1945*, p. 193
12 **'They are nerve food'** Cited in Eberle and Uhl (eds.), *The Hitler Book*, p. 55
15 **'Out this morning . . .'** MO diarist 53967, 7/5/1940
16 **'If we allow him to remain in office . . .'** Ibid.
16 **'"You know how obstinate old people can be . . ."'** Ibid.
18 **'The Prime Minister looked stunned . . .'** JPK, diary, 9/5/1940
18 **'A terrible world . . .'** Ibid.
21 **'I think I shall . . .'** Cited in Martin Gilbert, *Finest Hour*, p. 305
22 **'My nose is much too big . . .'** Schroeder, *Er war mein Chef*, p. 100
22 **'Have you all got . . .'** Ibid.
23 **'The French and British . . . of the division'** Luck, *Panzer Commander*, p. 37

3. The Go-for-Broke Gamble

28 **'We had achieved surprise . . .'** Herrmann, *Eagle's Wings*, p. 59
28 **'Meine Herren . . .'** Schroeder, *Er war mein Chef*, p. 102
29 **'air and sea war against England'** Cited in Frieser, *Blitzkrieg Legend*, p. 61
33 **'Surprise may now be regarded'** Halder, *Diary*, 18/2/1940
34 **'And then what . . . in any case'** Guderian, *Panzer Leader*, p. 92
34 **'You will be creeping by . . .'** Cited in Frieser, *Blitzkrieg Legend*, p. 98
36 **'It was a very long day . . .'** Knappe, *Soldat*, p. 164
38 **'To our surprise . . .'** BA-MA MSg2 2574

4. Hook, Line and Sinker

40 **'The last we saw of the planes . . .'** Fraser, wartime diaries, 10/5/1940
41 **'Here we go again . . .'** Cited in Bond, 'Gort', in Keegan (ed.), *Churchill's Generals*, p. 38
45 **'pursuit of the common object . . . before executing that order'** Cited in L. F. Ellis, *The War in France and Flanders*, pp. 11–12
46 **'impenetrable . . . Europe's best tank obstacle'** Cited in Frieser, *Blitzkrieg Legend*, p. 139

47 **'But of course it can be done . . .'** Pownall, *Chief of Staff*, 17/11/1939
47 **'If we can get there . . .'** Alanbrooke, *War Diaries*, 19/11/1939
48 **'It was hard to believe . . .'** Ibid., 10/5/1940
48 **'Well, Fraser . . .'** Fraser, wartime diaries, 30/4/1940
49 **'These precautions . . .'** Ibid., 10/5/1940
50 **'Oh, I don't know about that . . .'** Cited in Martin Gilbert, *Finest Hour*, p. 306
50 **'Now we could give the Huns . . .'** Crook, *Spitfire Pilot*, p. 21
50 **'Now they'll be wishing . . .'** MO diarist 53967, 10/5/1940
51 **'I asked Chamberlain . . .'** Cited in Martin Gilbert, *Finest Hour*, p. 313

5. The First Clash in the Air
57 **'Among the high command . . .'** BA-MA RL 3/2
59 **'Ack ack – 'ell! . . . got away with it'** Beamont, *My Part of the Sky*, p. 25
60 **'When we began at 8.10 . . .'** Hughes, diary, 10/5/1940
60 **'He also saw . . .'** Ibid.
61 **'Plots all over the board'** Richey, *Fighter Pilot*, p. 38
63 **'And you will take over . . .'** Kesselring, *Memoirs*, p. 51
63 **'I breathed a sigh of relief . . .'** Ibid., p. 55
65 **'Two out of three!'** Hughes, diary, 10/5/1940
65 **'It was an interesting experience . . .'** Beamont, *My Part of the Sky*, p. 26

6. Breakthrough
70 **'Morning reports show . . .'** Halder, *Diary*, 12/5/1940
71–2 **'Held up by artillery fire . . . a job for the infantry'** Luck, *Panzer Commander*, pp. 37–8
72 **'Hardly had the first boats . . . came to a standstill'** Ibid., p. 38
78 **'My whole attack . . .'** Guderian, *Panzer Leader*, p. 101
78 **'The flyers were doing . . .'** Ibid., p. 102
79 **'We're almost disappointed'** Bethke, memoir, DTA 652.9
79 **'All we saw . . .'** Drake and Shores, *Billy Drake*, p. 27
80 **'You British are mad . . .'** Cited in Richards, *Royal Air Force 1939–1945*, Vol. I, p. 117
80 **'And I am next . . .'** Hughes, diary, 12/5/1940
81 **'By now I was covered in petrol . . .'** Drake and Shores, *Billy Drake*, p. 28
81 **'With a little difficulty . . .'** Ibid.
82 **'Joy riding in canoes . . .'** Guderian, *Panzer Leader*, p. 102
82 **'Something that is easy today . . .'** Cited in Frieser, *Blitzkrieg Legend*, p. 167
84 **'The order from Luftflotte 3 . . .'** Cited in Deichmann, *Der Chef im Hintergrund*, p. 100

7. Inside the Third Reich
86 **'The shadow of Nazi fanaticism . . .'** Shirer, *Berlin Diary*, 27/9/1939

87 **'The people in Berlin . . .'** Shirer, *This is Berlin*, 10/5/1940
87 **'a new record . . . Hitler has taken'** Shirer, *Berlin Diary*, 10/5/1940
88 **'There are lots . . . this is war!'** Wendel, *Hausfrau at War*, pp. 18, 38
89 **'Nonsense. Of course it will be over . . .'** Ibid., p. 39
89 **'This wicked man . . . individual responsibility at all'** Ibid., p. 64
90 **'The truth is that . . .'** Shirer, *Berlin Diary*, 28/10/1940
92 **'We did not lose the war . . .'** Cited in Noakes and Pridham (eds.), *Nazism*, Vol. 2, Doc. No. 267
93 **'He must be very busy . . .'** Wendel, *Hausfrau at War*, p. 36
94 **'Propaganda means repetition . . .'** Cited in Irving, *Goebbels*, p. 582
94 **'getting nearer . . .'** Boelcke, *The Secret Conferences of Dr. Goebbels*, 10/5/1940
95 **'Make clear that we are engaged . . . polemics against France'** Noakes and Pridham (eds.), *Nazism*, Vol. 4, Doc. Nos. 1223 and 1224
95 **'All we want . . . the last war'** Wendel, *Hausfrau at War*, pp. 50, 51

8. Crisis and Dilemmas

96 **'at this extremely grievous and formidable moment . . . inspiration to all'** NCP, WSC to NC, 10/5/1940
96 **'I must say that Winston . . .'** Self (ed.), *Chamberlain Diary Letters*, 11/5/1940
98 **'All the hatred . . .'** Nicolson, HND, 10/5/1940
98 **'I have nothing to offer . . . no survival'** Churchill, *WS*, 13/5/1940
99 **'Profound anxiety'** Nicolson, HND, 13/5/1940
99 **'I spent the day . . .'** Colville, *The Fringes of Power*, 13/5/1940
100 **'Definitely'** JPK, diary, 13/5/1940
100 **'There could be no illusions . . .'** TNA AIR 8/863
101 **'The continued existence . . .'** James, *The Growth of Fighter Command*, p. 73
103 **'I have never accepted . . .'** Dowding Papers, RAFMA
106 **'All I want to know . . . retracting undercarriage'** Cited in Mitchell, *R. J. Mitchell*, p. 299

9. The Battle is Lost

110 **'All the Belgians . . .'** Pownall, *Chief of Staff*, 13/5/1940
110 **'It is not yet possible . . .'** Cited in Frieser, *Blitzkrieg Legend*, p. 143
111 **'Our front has been . . .'** Ibid.
113 **'A second was as good . . .'** Bethke, diary, 14/5/1940
114 **'Is it always . . . *nicht kleckern!*'** Guderian, *Panzer Leader*, pp. 105, 106
114 **'"Is Rommel immune?"'** Luck, *Panzer Commander*, p. 38
114 **'Keep going . . .'** Ibid.
115 **'The men were wide awake . . .'** Guderian, *Panzer Leader*, p. 108
116 **'We have been defeated . . .'** *WSC*, p. 38
120 **'In this region . . .'** Cited in Frieser, *Blitzkrieg Legend*, p. 146
121 **'I don't see how . . . we are *bust*'** Pownall, *Chief of Staff*, 16/5/1940

10. Emergency Measures

122 **'Preparing a hot reception . . .'** *The War Illustrated*, 24/5/1940
122 **'German parachute troops . . .'** Cited in Graves, *The Home Guard of Great Britain*, p. 10
123 **'The parachute troops . . .'** MO diarist 53967, 15/5/1940
123 **'I want to speak . . . will be armed'** Cited in Graves, *The Home Guard of Great Britain*, pp. 13–14
124 **'I hope they . . . discussing him'** MO diarist 53967, 15/5/1940
126 **'A paradox ball . . .'** *The Times*, 18/5/1940
127 **'Security Measures . . .'** TNA CAB 80/11
127 **'We have today . . .'** Nicolson, HND, diary, 22/5/1940
128 **'Evidently this battle . . . method and morale'** Ismay, *Memoirs*, p. 129
128 **'Today the news is worse . . .'** NCP, diary, 16/5/1940
128 **'He is definitely . . .'** JPK, diary, 16/5/1940
129 **'It could make the difference . . . and fight on'** JPK, memoir
130 **'We expect to be attacked . . .'** Cited in Martin Gilbert, *Finest Hour*, p. 345
130 **'It is not beyond the realm . . .'** JPK, memoir
131 **'We must expect . . .'** Cited in Martin Gilbert, *Finest Hour*, p. 356
131 **'That would mean . . .'** *For the President, Personal and Secret*, p. 428, 16/5/1940
132 **'Terrible message from Winston . . .'** NCP, diary, 16/5/1940

11. Learning the Lessons

133 **'Sign here . . .'** Herrmann, *Eagle's Wings*, p. 25
136 **'Come on, defend youself . . .'** Galland, *The First and the Last*, p. 13
137 **'Young pilots . . .'** Bethke, memoir, DTA 652.9
137 **'I had a friend . . .'** Rall, *My Logbook*, p. 33
138 **'The demands of this powerful machine . . .'** Ibid.
144 **'In a war of the future . . .'** Suchenwirth, *Command and Leadership*, p. 12
146 **'I'm a flier . . .'** Cited in Bartz, *Swastika in the Air*, p. 41
146 **'Then I can commit suicide . . .'** TNA WO208/4347
147 **'flying barn door'** Suchenwirth, *Command and Leadership*, p. 76

12. What to Do for the Best

151 **'I now felt . . .'** Donnelly, *The Whitley Boys*, p. 103
152 **'What I saw . . .'** Ibid., p. 110
153 **'So far as I can see . . .'** Shirer, *Berlin Diary*, 19/5/1940
153 **'Oddly, I was no longer scared'** Hughes, diary, 14/5/1940
155–7 **'I was having quite a difficulty . . . spasmodic shifts for meals'** Beamont, *My Part of the Sky*, p. 35
158 **'I want the Fighter Command . . .'** Cited in James, *The Growth of Fighter Command*, Appendix 10
158 **'If they do not come . . .'** TNA CAB 73/4

159 **'I believe that . . .'** James, *The Growth of Fighter Command*, Appendix 11
159 **'a time will arrive . . .'** Ibid., Appendix 12

13. New Appointments
161 **'I am exhausted . . .'** IWM 78/52/1
161 **'It seemed . . .'** Pownall, *Chief of Staff*, 19/5/1940
162 **'But the withdrawal . . .'** Ibid.
162 **'There are many most distressing sights . . .'** Ibid., 18/5/1940
162 **'Keep going . . .'** Luck, *Panzer Commander*, p. 39
163 **'La guerre est finie . . . was the cry'** Ibid.
165 **'We seem to be holding . . .'** MO diarist 53967, 21/5/1940
166 **'The situation is terribly obscure'** Nicolson, HND, 21/5/1940
166 **'I have a nice . . .'** Ibid., 19/5/1940
166 **'It must be remembered . . .'** TNA INF 1/250
167 **'When I talk to him . . .'** Cited in Taylor, *Beaverbrook*, p. 399
170 **'They are all captains of industry . . .'** Ibid., p. 420

14. Decisions
172 **'Not bad . . .'** Guderian, *Panzer Leader*, p. 113
172 **'attacking all enemy forces . . .'** Cited in L. F. Ellis, *The War in France and Flanders*, p. 83
172 **'A scandalous (ie Winstonian) thing to do . . .'** Pownall, *Chief of Staff*, 20/5/1940
173 **'Nobody minds going down fighting . . .'** Ibid., 20/5/1940
173 **'a critical moment . . .'** Cited in Liddell Hart, *The Rommel Papers*, p. 34
174 **'We are down to about . . .'** Pownall, *Chief of Staff*, 22/5/1940
175 **'Here are Winston's plans . . .'** Ibid., 22/5/1940
176 **'Other candidates . . .'** Knappe, *Soldat*, p. 168
176 **'Dead cattle and other livestock . . .'** Ibid., p. 169
176 **'The experience was impossible to forget . . .'** Ibid., p. 170
176 **'We are seeking . . .'** Halder, *Diary*, 21/5/1940
177 **'indicate clearly the object of this war . . .'** NHB EDS/Apprec/6: *The German Plans for the Invasion of England*
179–80 **'There were no camp duties . . . they're killing one another'** IWM 021116
181 **'We were utterly speechless . . .'** Guderian, *Panzer Leader*, p. 117
182 **'I have a good idea . . .'** Halder, *Diary*, 23/5/1940
182 **'He was livid with anger . . .'** Liss, *Westfront*, p. 196
183 **'Our spirits rise and fall . . .'** Pownall, *Chief of Staff*, 24/5/1940
183 **'Can this be the turn . . .'** Ibid.
185 **'I must not conceal from you . . .'** TNA WO 197/138

15. Fighter Command Enters the Fray
186 **'They ordered extra food . . .'** Hughes, diary, 20/5/1940

187 **'To say that I was scared . . . gory mess suggested'** Ibid., 23/5/1940
188 **'The Spitfires . . .'** TNA AIR 8/863
188 **'Stick to my tail . . .'** Bartley, *Smoke Trails in the Sky*, p. 11
189–90 **'Look out, 109s . . . pints of beer'** Ibid., p. 13
190 **'It has been . . .'** TNA AIR 27/743
191 **'I am doing very well . . .'** Steinhilper and Osborne, *Spitfire on My Tail*, p. 239
191 **'It was immediately clear . . .'** Ibid., p. 244
192 **'As we wheeled . . .'** Ibid.
193 **'Yesterday we reached . . .'** MO diarist 53967, 23–4/5/1940
194 **'The meetings . . .'** Elmhirst Papers, 'An Airman's Life'
194 **'if one really noticed the weather'** MO diarist 53967, 25/5/1940
195 **'The information given us . . .'** NCP, diary, 25/5/1940
195 **'It is probable . . .'** Delpla (ed.), *Les Papiers secrets du Général Doumenc*, Annexe 6
195 **'If France went out . . .'** TNA CAB 69/1
196 **'Down the ages . . . merit of candour'** *WSC*, p. 107
196 **'Once such a discussion . . .'** TNA CAB 66/7

16. Crisis

197 **'You have to see the German army . . .'** Shirer, *Berlin Diary*, 24/5/1940
198 **'The only effect . . .'** Churchill, *WSC*, p. 72
198 **'The answer is no . . .'** Cited in Guderian, *Panzer Leader*, p. 118
199 **'Apparently again . . .'** Halder, *Diary*, 24/5/1940
200 **'Expanding on the directives . . .'** Cited in Frieser, *Blitzkrieg Legend*, p. 298
200 **'This is a complete reversal of the plan . . .'** Halder, *Diary*, 25/5/1940
200 **'This is a wonderful opportunity . . .'** Cited in Cooper, *The German Air Force*, p. 117
201 **'Our air force . . .'** Cited in Irving, *Göring*, p. 290
201 **'The army always wants . . .'** Cited in Irving, *The Rise and Fall of the Luftwaffe*, p. 90
201 **'I pointed out . . .'** Kesselring, *Memoirs*, p. 59
201 **'Impression: G. successfully stirred it up . . .'** Engel, *At the Heart of the Reich*, 25/5/1940
202 **'It is all a first-class mess-up . . .'** Pownall, *Chief of Staff*, 25/5/1940
203–4 **'What are the prospects . . . not with France but with England'** The minutes of this entire War Cabinet meeting are held at the National Archives, CAB/65/13/20, or can be found online at http://filestore.nationalarchives.gov.uk/pdfs/small/cab-65-13-wm-40-139-20.pdf
205 **'The dream of all Germans . . .'** Martin Gilbert, *Finest Hour*, p. 403
208 **'If France could not defend herself . . . conquer this country'** The entire War Cabinet minutes are at TNA CAB 65/13/21 or online at http://filestore.nationalarchives.gov.uk/pdfs/small/cab-65-13-wm-40-140-21.pdf

209 **'I feel physically sick . . .'** Cited in Ismay, *Memoirs*, p. 133

17. Black Monday

210 **'Calais has fallen . . .'** Shirer, *Berlin Diary*, 26/5/1940
210 **'On the [left] wing . . .'** Halder, *Diary*, 27/5/1940
212 **'The Boche has got as far as Gravelines . . .'** Cited in Richard Collier, *The Sands of Dunkirk*, p. 31
213 **'No, Herr Generaloberst . . .'** Cited in Bekker, *The Luftwaffe War Diaries*, p. 163
214 **'Attack by *Gruppen* . . .'** Ibid., p. 159
215 **'Only fishing boats are coming over . . .'** Engel, *At the Heart of the Reich*, 27/5/1940
217 **'Saw England for the first time . . .'** Bethke, diary, 25/5/1940
218 **'The blackest day of all . . .'** Self (ed.), *Chamberlain Diary Letters*, 26/5/1940
218 **'Fear not the result . . .'** Cited in Martin Gilbert, *Finest Hour*, p. 406
219–20 **'This was perhaps . . . to consider them'** TNA CAB 65/7
221 **'I can't work . . . full of affection'** Dilks (ed.), *Diaries of Sir Alexander Cadogan*, 27/5/1940

18. Dunkirk: The Beginning

223 **'We now are receiving very little news . . .'** MO diarist 53967
223 **'Macfarlane tells us in blunt language . . .'** Nicolson, HND, 27/5/1940
224 **'Much of the town was in flames . . .'** Pownall, *Chief of Staff*, 28/5/1940
226 **'Whereat he went . . .'** Ibid.
226 **'So ended the meeting . . .'** Ibid.
227 **'Von Luck you will . . .'** Luck, *Panzer Commander*, p. 42
228 **'BEF FIGHT HEROIC BATTLE . . .'** *Daily Express*, 28/5/1940
228 **'I replied that it was best . . .'** Self (ed.), *Chamberlain Diary Letters*, 28/5/1940
229 **'I have only one thing to add . . .'** *WS*, p. 187
229 **'rather a steamy discussion'** Self (ed.), *Chamberlain Diary Letters*, 28/5/1940
229 **'The French are trying . . .'** TNA CAB 65/13
230 **'It's not a question . . .'** Cited in Lord, *The Miracle of Dunkirk*, p. 98
231 **'There are at present . . .'** NHB, Admiralty War Diary, 28/5/1940
232–3 **'And we dashed off to Dover . . . one of those'** IWM 10782
234 **'We shall go on . . .'** Cited in Dalton, *Second World War Diary*, 28/5/1940
234 **'I cannot recall . . .'** TNA CAB 65/13

19. Dunkirk: In the Balance

235 **'And so here we are . . .'** Pownall, *Chief of Staff*, 28/5/1940
236 **'Whacking great guns they were . . . and "C" Company'** IWM 021116
240 **'God helped our retreat . . .'** Fraser, wartime diaries, 29/5/1940

240 **'Apparently the lack of news . . .'** MO diarist 53967
243 **'Dear Mummy . . .'** Hugh Dundas papers
244–5 **'She just erupted . . . warm enough there'** IWM 10782
245 **'A regular officer came down . . .'** IWM 021116
246 **'The destroyers were being dive-bombed . . .'** Ibid.
247 **'When the bombs . . .'** Fraser, wartime diaries, 30/5/1940. Note that there is at this stage a slight discrepancy in Stan's dates. His diaries record this being the 30 May, but in fact he was a day ahead of himself

20. Dunkirk: The Middle
248 **'You looked . . . strokes a minute'** Rawlings papers, letter, 31/5/1940
250 **'My contacts with the Churchill Cabinet . . .'** JPK, memoir
251 **'Just think, all this death and destruction . . .'** Ibid.
251 **'We lost time . . .'** Halder, *Diary*, 30/5/1940
252–6 **'When we moved . . . his body before'** BA-MA MSg2 2574
260 **'Now, this is where . . .'** Fraser, wartime diaries, 31/5/1940
260–1 **'Very quiet night . . . It was bloody awful'** Norman Field Papers

21. Dunkirk: The End
262 **'On political grounds . . .'** *WSC*, p. 95
263 **'I don't know what day . . .'** Bethke, diary, 30/5/1940
263 **'The black smoke rose . . .'** Hugh Dundas, *Flying Start*, p. 30
264 **'Where the hell were you?'** Ibid., p. 32
265 **'The vessel didn't catch fire . . .'** Herrmann, *Eagle's Wings*, p. 60
266 **'I'd made it . . .'** Ibid., p. 61
271 **'We saw a piece . . . inside the boat'** IWM 021116
272 **'Things are getting . . .'** Gardner, *Evacuation from Dunkirk*, Appendix R
272–3 **'There was no thought . . . soldiers panic'** IWM 021116
274 **'BEF evacuated . . .'** Gardner, *Evacuation from Dunkirk*, Appendix T

Part II: Respite

22. What Next?
277 **'We silenced all six . . .'** Bartley, *Smoke Trails in the Sky*, p. 16
277 **'but the wretch'** John Dundas papers, letter, 9/6/1940
278–9 **'In our view therefore . . . to the imminent danger'** TNA CAB 80/12
280 **'miracle of deliverance . . . never surrender'** *WS*, 4/6/1940
280 **'The House was deeply moved'** Nicolson, HND, 4/6/1940
280 **'It was a magnificent oration'** Colville, *The Fringes of Power*, 4/6/1940
280 **'I thought it was . . .'** MO diarist 53967
281 **'The French are hysterical . . .'** Chamberlain, *Diary Letters*, 2/6/1940
282 **'The British Army? . . . it will be too late'** TNA WO 208/4340
282 **'Had I had these four divisions . . .'** Cited in Irving, *Göring*, p. 92
285 **'Captain, your breakfast'** Luck, *Panzer Commander*, p. 43
286 **'And what do you command? . . .'** Cited in Blaxland, *Destination Dunkirk*, p. 374

286 **'Dearest Lu . . .'** Liddell Hart (ed.), *The Rommel Papers*, p. 66

23. The End in France

288 **'One through the calf . . .'** Frank, *Enemy Submarine*, p. 89
289 **'Hit almost amidships . . .'** Ibid., p. 92
290 **'All that I found on my return . . .'** Alanbrooke, *War Diaries*, p. 74
291 **'Winston is justifiably . . .'** Colville, *The Fringes of Power*, 6/6/1940
291 **'It is embarrassingly . . .'** Engel, *At the Heart of the Reich*, 10/6/1940
292 **'People who go to Italy . . .'** Colville, *The Fringes of Power*, 10/6/1940
292 **'You mark my words . . .'** MO diarist 53967
293 **'To say that I was . . .'** Donnelly, *The Whitley Boys*, p. 133
295 **'At my command . . . was in Paris'** Knappe, *Soldat*, p. 183
295 **'If the French will . . .'** Colville, *The Fringes of Power*, 14/6/1940
296 **'I replied . . . I agree with you'** Alanbrooke, *War Diaries*, p. 81
297 **'Your signal based on error . . .'** Guderian, *Panzer Leader*, p. 130
297 **'Reply will be held . . .'** Halder, *Diary*, 17/6/1940
297 **'But if we suffer . . .'** Chamberlain, *Diary Letters*, 21/6/1940

24. Hitler's Dilemma

298 **'I observed his face . . .'** Shirer, *Berlin Diary*, 21/6/1940
299 **'How many mothers . . .'** Schroeder, *Er war mein Chef*, p. 80
299 **'What stupendous . . . of the world'** Wendel, *Hausfrau at War*, p. 81
299 **'They thought only of their skins . . .'** Cited in Eberle and Uhl (eds.), *The Hitler Book*, p. 57
300 **'F. talked again'** Engel, *At the Heart of the Reich*, 26/6/1940
300 **'as he fully appreciates the unusual difficulties . . .'** NHB EDS/Apprec/6: *The German Plans for the Invasion of England*
300 **'What he has in mind . . .'** BA-MA MsG2/5830
301 **'If they will not quit . . .'** Schroeder, *Er war mein Chef*, p. 80
306 **'We have nothing to lose . . .'** Cited in Tooze, *The Wages of Destruction*, p. 316; also Maier *et al.*, *Germany and the Second World War*, Vol. II, p. 842
306 **'Looks like a great deal of blood . . .'** Cited in Speer, *Inside the Third Reich*, p. 235
307 **'We cannot win the war . . .'** BA-MA RW19/205
308 **'Führer has again emphasized . . .'** IWM EDS 1571

25. All Alone

310 **'Think before you act . . .'** *If the Invader Comes*, TNA INF 1/250
310 **'I am quite lucidly aware . . .'** Nicolson, HND, 15/6/1940
311 **'He felt we should give in . . .'** Cockett, *Love and War in London*, 18/6/1940
311 **'Although I will grant . . . wouldn't it?'** MO diarist, 53967
312 **'But this was due solely . . .'** Hughes, diary, 21–2/6/1940
312 **'Hitler knows that . . .'** *WS*, 18/6/1940

313 **'I call for effort, courage, sacrifice . . .'** Dallek, *Franklin D. Roosevelt and American Foreign Policy*, p. 228
313 **'I send you my heartfelt thanks . . .'** Loewenheim, Langley and Joans (eds.), *Roosevelt and Churchill*, Churchill to Roosevelt, 11/6/1940
314 **'England is next . . . England from destruction'** JPK, memoir
315 **'Well, it boils down to this . . .'** Raymond Lee, *The London Observer*, 4/6/1940
316 **'Every hour the radio bulletins . . .'** Beaton, *The Years Between*, p. 31, and CBP, diary, 2/7/1940
316 **'like a death . . . possible capacity'** CBP, diary, September 1939
317 **'England will probably . . .'** Beaton, *The Years Between*, p. 31
318 **'The moment the Germans . . .'** Self (ed.), *Chamberlain Diary Letters*, 15/6/1940
318 **'All this . . . finished eating'** Zumbach, *On Wings of War*, p. 39, 59
320 **'So he took a chance . . .'** Ibid., p. 64

26. Getting Ready

323 **'I cannot get information . . .'** Beaverbrook Papers, BBK/D/414
323–4 **'Beaverbrook was an unpleasant bastard . . .'** Cited in McKinstry, *Spitfire*, p. 151
324 **'I hope there won't be any trouble . . .'** Cited in Suchenwirth, *Command and Leadership*, p. 86
325 **'All this planning is garbage'** Cited in Irving, *Göring*, p. 291
325 **Luftwaffe monthly production figures:** BA-MA ZA3/304
325 **'We're all very fatigué! . . .'** Bethke, diary, 25/6/1940
326 **'We were really glad . . .'** Bartley, letter to father, 25/6/1940
326 **'The old easy-going outlook . . .'** Crook, *Spitfire Pilot*, p. 22
328 **'We now have an embryo'** Cited in Orange, *Dowding of Fighter Command*, p. 80

27. Trouble at Sea: Part 1

332 **'Tomorrow at dawn . . .'** Colville, *The Fringes of Power*, 2/7/1940
333 **'This was a hateful decision . . .'** *WSC*, p. 206
333 **'You are charged with . . .'** Cited in ibid., p. 209
333 **'unlikely to take place before . . .'** TNA CAB 66/9
334 **'In general, I find myself in agreement . . .'** Ibid.
335 **'If so we should welcome . . .'** NHB ND10
335 **'The JIC have appreciated . . .'** Ibid.
337 **'He would ensure that . . .'** Doenitz [Dönitz], *Memoirs*, p. 42
341 **'Prien's opinions were shared . . .'** Ibid., p. 89
341 **'No sight of the enemy . . .'** NHB, logbook of U-47

28. Bringing It All Together

343 **'Can anyone . . . imminent future'** Jones, *Most Secret War*, p. 90
344 **'Hitler is now the gambler . . .'** Ciano, *Diary*, 18–19/6/1940

346 'a storm of wrath and steel . . . delaying his speech' Ibid., 7/7/1940

29. Trouble at Sea: Part 2

355 'Good heavens! . . . the French coast' TNA ADM 199/2133

357–8 'We laughed . . . and he fell apart' This entire account comes from IWM 27308

361 'You don't actually realize . . .' NHB

362 'Here's one for us!' TNA ADM 199/2133

362 'The assault of the 1st S-boat Flotilla . . .' NHB, *Kriegstagebuch des Führers der Torpedoboote*, 4/7/1940

362 'The attacks on the convoy . . .' *WSC*, p. 566

30. Crooked Leg

364 'The next opponents . . .' Rall, *My Logbook*, p. 49

365 'By now he might be having . . .' Ibid., p. 50

366 'To hell with you . . . blood-sodden mattresses' Steinhilper and Osborne, *Spitfire on My Tail*, p. 254

366 'Although we had just thrown . . .' Knappe, *Soldat*, p. 189

366 'We didn't hate the English so much . . .' Wendel, *Hausfrau at War*, p. 82

367 'If and when Germany intends . . .' Shirer, *This is Berlin*, 10/7/1940

367 'The Nazis are laughing' Shirer, *Berlin Diary*, 8/7/1940

367 'What did I tell you?' Wendel, *Hausfrau at War*, p. 81

367 'When nothing happened . . .' Bob, *Betrayed Ideals*, p. 97

368 'That is why one day . . .' Bethke, diary, 11–12/7/1940

368 'The intensified attacks . . .' BA-MA RL 2-II/30

369 'well-developed defence forces . . . other tasks' BA-MA RL 2-II/30

369 'The campaign had gone so well . . .' Steinhilper and Osborne, *Spitfire on My Tail*, p. 262

371 'Good, Steinhilper . . .' Ibid., p. 180

372 'Our communications . . .' Ibid., p. 263

372 'The beginning of a thriller . . .' Jones, *Most Secret War*, p. 84

Part III: *Kanalkampf*

31. First Combat

380 'Warmwell possessed . . .' TNA AIR 27/2102

382 'Look out behind! . . .' Crook, *Spitfire Pilot*, p. 29

383 'But he was dead now . . . casualties cause' Ibid., p. 30

384 'In a squadron . . .' Ibid.

385 'From now onwards . . .' Ibid., p. 34

390 'There was no question . . .' Neil, *A Fighter in My Sights*, p. 99

32. Peace Offerings

391 'We must not be guided by hatred . . .' Goebbels, *Diaries*, 7/7/1940

393 'The Führer is greatly puzzled . . .' Halder, *Diary*, 13/7/1940

393 **'Main point of conversation . . .'** Engel, *At the Heart of the Reich*, 15/7/1940
394 **'Since England, in spite of . . .'** Trevor-Roper (ed.), *Hitler's War Diaries*, No. 16, 16/7/1940
396 **'Beppo Schmid was a complete wash-out . . . trimmed his sails to the wind'** both cited in Mitcham, *Eagles of the Third Reich*, p. 106
397 **'The Luftwaffe is clearly superior . . .'** Cited in Wood and Dempster, *The Narrow Margin*, p. 110
398 **'If I wear it, then it's for men'** Irving, *Göring*, p. 293
398 **'His boyish pride . . .'** Shirer, *Berlin Diary*, 19/7/1940
398–9 **'I only know . . . of this war'** Cited in Lukacs, *The Duel*, p. 190
399 **'fat into the fire'** Cited in Irving, *Göring*, p. 293
399 **'Considering everything, Hitler . . .'** Nicolson, HND, 19/7/1940
399 **'I do not propose . . .'** Colville, *The Fringes of Power*, 24/7/1940
400 **'British ambassador to Washington . . .'** Halder, *Diary*, 22/7/1940
400 **'Hitler may plant the Swastika . . .'** Cited in Roberts, *The Holy Fox*, p. 249
400 **'all possible might'** Boelcke, *The Secret Conferences of Dr. Goebbels*, 22/7/1940
400 **'German public opinion . . .'** Goebbels, *Diaries*, 23/7/1940
400 **'The die seems cast'** Shirer, *Berlin Diary*, 23/7/1940

33. The Besieged

401 **'And as it passed close by . . .'** Beaton, *The Years Between*, p. 32
401 **'Any day now . . .'** Ibid.
401 **'I think that Hitler . . .'** Nicolson, HND, 20/7/1940
401 **'Today is one but . . .'** MO diarist, 2/7/1940
402 **'Though it is reported . . .'** Ibid., 31/7/1940
402 **'Still, whatever does come . . .'** Ibid., 9/7/09
402 **'I still feel that WE . . .'** Cockett, *Love and War in London*, 21/7/1940
402 **'People cheerful and optimistic . . .'** TNA INF 1/264
402 **'Opinion unanimous . . .'** Cockett, *Love and War in London*, 20/7/1940
403 **'There is no doubt that . . .'** Nicolson, HND, 21/7/1940
403 **'Very few of us . . .'** Cited in Gardiner, *Wartime*, p. 307
404 **'But all depends now . . .'** *WS*, 14/7/1940
404 **'He was in wonderful spirits . . .'** Alanbrooke, *War Diaries*, 17/7/1940
405 **'Every day that . . .'** Raymond Lee, *The London Observer*, 17/7/1940
405 **'We had no weapons . . .'** IWM 021116
406 **'Using the sacks of grain . . .'** Fraser, wartime diaries
408 **'operations of sabotage . . .'** TNA CAB 66/8
408 **'And now go and set'** Dalton, *Second World War Diary*, 22/7/1940
409 **'And when people . . .'** Amanda Smith (ed.), *Hostage to Fortune*, p. 451
409 **'I thought this optimism . . .'** JPK, memoir
409 **'I also believe . . .'** Raymond Lee, *The London Observer*, 15/7/1940
409 **'I send plenty of cables home . . .'** Ibid., 30/7/1940
409 **'They can do nothing but complicate . . .'** JPK, diary, 17/7/1940

410 **'Well, I told him before . . .'** Raymond Lee, *The London Observer*, 3/8/1940
410 **'Don't let anybody . . .'** JPK, diary, 31/7/1940

34. Hotting Up

412 **'We returned to breakfast . . .'** Beamont, *My Part of the Sky*, p. 49
413 **'Putting the majority . . .'** BA-MA RL 2-II/30
416–17 **'This was not achieved . . . aim accordingly'** AFHRA, K239.0512-1838 C 1
419 **'They have to run perfectly . . .'** Cited in Dallies-Labourdette, *S-Boote*, p. 42
420 **'It's uncommon how . . .'** John Dundas papers, letter, 27/7/1940
422 **'What are those? . . .'** Galland *The First and the Last*, p. 19

35. Bombs on Germany, *Bomben auf England*

423 **'That was the first . . .'** Bethke, diary, 2/8/40
423 **'But at that moment . . .'** Cited in Weal, *Jadgeschwader 2*, p. 47
424 **'The war against England . . .'** Bethke, diary, 6/8/1940
424 **'I shall at least have something to show . . .'** Hughes, diary, 26/7/1940
425 **'The future stretches ahead . . .'** Ibid., 2/8/1940
425 **'Recent reports and information . . .'** Cited in Webster and Frankland, *The Strategic Air Offensive*, p. 151
427 **'About six weeks ago . . .'** Cited in Noakes and Pridham (eds.), *Nazism*, Vol. 3, p. 571
429 **'Come on! Drop the bloody things!'** Herrmann, *Eagle's Wings*, p. 63
430 **'I was reprimanded . . .'** Ibid., p. 65
431 **'I reserve . . . relative strength'** Trevor-Roper (ed.), *Hitler's War Directives*, No. 17
432 **'With Russia smashed . . .'** Halder, *Diary*, 31/7/1940

Part IV: Battle Over Britain

36. The Wall of England

436–7 **'All repairs and . . . German economy'** BA-MA RM 7/8/97
438 **'The issue . . .'** Halder, *Diary*, 7/8/1940
438 **'This fact must receive . . .'** BA-MA RM 7/897
438 **'We went hell for leather . . .'** IWM 15583
440 **'There wasn't a semblance . . .'** IWM 028665
441 **'There was an odd feeling . . .'** Ibid.
442 **'I wondered . . .'** Steinhilper and Osborne, *Spitfire on My Tail*, p. 270
443 **'*DeTe* devices'** BA-MA RL2/II/30
443 **'Everything depends . . .'** Maier *et al.*, *Germany and the Second World War*, p. 385
444 **'He is the man . . .'** Raymond Lee, 7/8/1940
445 **'This was the last straw . . .'** Bartley, *Smoke Trails in the Sky*, p. 21
447 **'More Huns than I ever imagined . . .'** John Dundas papers, letter to Margaret Rawlings, 11/8/1940

447 **'We came down right on top . . .'** Crook, *Spitfire Pilot*, p. 42
448 **'They were flying . . .'** Bethke, diary, 11/8/1940

37. *Adlertag*
449 **'Calais and . . .'** Steinhilper and Osborne, *Spitfire on My Tail*, p. 272
450 **'They were engaged . . .'** TNA AIR 8/863
451 **'Calling 3 Staffel . . .'** Cited in Bekker, *The Luftwaffe War Diaries*, p. 186
454 **'Where the hell . . .'** Cited in Richard Collier, *Eagle Day*, p. 56
455 **'Hurricanes near Brighton . . .'** Bethke, diary, 13/8/1940
455 **'Oh, ein sehr . . . breakfast'** Cited in Richard Collier, *Eagle Day*, p. 62
456 **'In our talk . . .'** Hozzel, 'Recollections and Experiences . . .', p. 55
457 **'Achtung, Achtung . . .'** TNA AIR 4/21
457 **'We were up at almost 20,000 feet . . .'** Crook, *Spitfire Pilot*, p. 47
457 **'A sudden fire ball . . .'** Hozzel, 'Recollections and Experiences . . .', p. 56
458 **'I shall never again . . .'** Crook, *Spitfire Pilot*, p. 49

38. The Biggest Air Battle
460–1 **'How can we possibly win? . . . race on earth'** Nicolson, HND, 11/8/1940
461 **'The rumours baffle description . . .'** NCP, NC7/11/33/101
462 **'My Lord, . . . small details'** Cited in Colville, *The Fringes of Power*, 10/8/1940
463 **'This war will go on . . .'** JPK, diary, 14/8/1940
463 **'Let those who say . . .'** Colville, *The Fringes of Power*, 10/8/1940
464 **'I'm not having people . . .'** Cited in Olson and Cloud, *For Your Freedom and Ours*, p. 117
464 **'Everything here was . . .'** Zumbach, *On Wings of War*, p. 65
465 **'The British were wasting . . .'** Ibid., p. 65
466 **'I flew over to the crash . . .'** Crook, *Spitfire Pilot*, p. 50
466 **'If so would you like it?'** Rawlings papers, letter, 18/8/1940
467 **'I have repeatedly . . . out of action'** AHB, Translation No.VII/39
469 **'Ah, Herr Oberst, . . . all the same'** Cited in Richard Collier, *Eagle Day*, pp. 80–1
471 **'A very large number . . .'** Hugh Dundas papers, letter, 16/8/1940
473 **'The Blenheims had sometimes . . .'** Crook, *Spitfire Pilot*, p. 53
473 **'Everything was new . . .'** Neil, *A Fighter in My Sights*, p. 112
473 **'After further wanderings . . .'** Ibid., p. 113
475 **'See that? Looks a bit odd . . .'** MO diarist 53967
476 **'Don't speak to me . . .'** Ismay, *Memoirs*, p. 182
476 **'The Lord President . . .'** Colville, *The Fringes of Power*, 15/8/1940

39. The Hardest Day
477 **'We have no difficulty . . .'** Halder, *Diary*, 14/8/1940
478 **'Sea rescue incidents . . .'** Bethke, memoir, DTA 652.9
478 **'Otherwise they would not'** TNA AIR 8/863
479 **'Our conversations now revolve . . .'** Bethke, diary, 16/8/1940

480 **'The English are an extraordinary people . . .'** CBP, diary, 16/8/1940
480 **'The usual story of bricks . . .'** Ibid.
481 **'. . . meanwhile, in Britain . . .'** *Punch*, 14/8/1940
481 **'Atmosphere cheerful . . .'** Cockett, *Love and War in London*, 17/8/1940
481–2 **'People here, the ordinary . . .'** *Daily Express*, 14/8/1940
482 **'twenty little silver fish . . .'** Nicolson, HND, 18/8/1940
483 **'There they are!'** Colville, *The Fringes of Power*, 18/8/1940
485 **'Our casualties were . . .'** TNA AIR 27/300
486 **'Christ, this is the end . . . smoke and flame'** Hugh Dundas, *Flying Start*, p. 50, and *Evening Standard*, 6/1/1960
487 **'Very sorry indeed to hear . . .'** Hugh Dundas papers, letter, 25/8/1940

40. Bombs on Berlin
489–90 **'We pilots . . . the struggle'** Galland, *The First and the Last*, p. 39
495 **'We have reached . . .'** AHB, Translation No.VII/39
495 **'One eye – one beam!'** Jones, *Most Secret War*, p. 120
498 **'For the first time . . .'** Shirer, *Berlin Diary*, 29/8/1940

41. Tactics and Technicalities
499 **'It sounds all right in theory . . .'** Hughes, diary, 11/8/1940
500 **'Night ops in good weather . . .'** Ibid., 12/8/1940
500 **'All of the pilots . . . battle of attrition'** Steinhilper and Osborne, *Spitfire on My Tail*, p. 283
504 **'Never attempt a "tail-chase" . . .'** Air Ministry, *Pilot's Notes*
504 **'In a surprisingly large . . .'** TNA AVIA 6/2394
505 **'Landed with undercarriage . . .'** AHB, Hurricane Accident Report Cards 10 July–31 October 1940
506 **'When it hit . . .'** *The Few* (2000), ACO/Film/CO Film Channel 5
507 **'The cockpit blew up . . .'** Ibid.

42. Breaking Point
512 **'On no part of the Royal Air Force . . .'** *WS*, 20/8/1940
513 **'The results we could . . .'** Dönitz [Dönitz], *Memoirs*, p. 112
514 **'Losses have been very heavy'** TNA CAB 66/11
514 **'startling shipping losses . . .'** Colville, *The Fringes of Power*, 30/8/1940
515 **'We cannot afford . . .'** No. 11 Group Instructions to Controllers, No. 4, private collection
516 **'I shall never forget . . .'** Crook, *Spitfire Pilot*, p. 60
516 **'I learnt not to be over-enthusiastic . . .'** TNA AIR 4/21
518 **'We were heroes . . .'** *The Few* (2000), ACO/Film/CO Film Channel 5
519 **'Up to date . . .'** Cited in James, *The Battle of Britain*, Appendix 10
521 **'I must protest emphatically . . .'** *WSC*, p. 585
522 **'Those brothers are good . . .'** Bethke, diary, 2/9/1940
522 **'I will never get that far . . .'** Ibid.

524 'Before, there were lots of English . . .' Ibid., 30/8/1940
524 'The strain of unrelenting . . .' Steinhilper and Osborne, *Spitfire on My Tail*, p. 287

43. Black Saturday

525 'It seemed queer . . .' Raymond Lee, *The London Observer*, 29/8/1940
526 'Will they be able . . . worn-out destroyers' JPK, diary, 2/9/1940
527 'already had unconditional fighter superiority now' BA-MA RL2/II/30
527 'English fighter defence hit hard . . .' Schramm (ed.), *Kriegstagebuch des Oberkommandos der Wehrmacht 1940–1941*, 3–4/9/1940
528 'It is being said . . .' Stahl, *The Diving Eagle*, p. 58
529 'The great query was . . .' Elmhirst Papers, 'An Airman's Life'
530 'You must realize . . .' Cited in Orange, *Park*, p. 105
531 'I should like an outfit . . .' Galland, *The First and the Last*, p. 38
531 'We have the best fighter in the world!' Cited in Caldwell, *The JG 26 War Diary*, p. 71
532 'This afternoon the decision comes . . .' Cited in Irving, *Göring*, p. 295
534 'Everywhere was danger . . .' Steinhilper and Osborne, *Spitfire on My Tail*, p. 293
535 'Just like that . . .' Zumbach, *On Wings of War*, p. 71
537 'I flew back . . .' Neil, *A Fighter in My Sights*, p. 135
537 'The pure azure-blue . . .' Steinhilper and Osborne, *Spitfire on My Tail*, p. 293
537 'Tremendous fires . . .' Raymond Lee, *The London Observer*, 8/9/1940
538 'The dispersal hut . . .' Neil, *A Fighter in My Sights*, p. 135
538 'The fires in the docks . . .' Jones, *Most Secret War*, p. 128
538 'That was preached . . .' Herrmann, *Eagle's Wings*, p. 66
539 'The Boche has . . .' Raymond Lee, *The London Observer*, 8/9/1940

44. Summer Madness

541 'We made up a barrage line . . .' IWM 028665
542 'It was good of you to come . . . he's crying' Cited in Ismay, *Memoirs*, p. 185
543 'Nobody was keen . . .' IWM 26952
543 'They flashed their lights . . .' Ibid.
543 'Wherever one looks . . .' Stahl, *The Diving Eagle*, 9/9/1940
544 'It must be terrible down there . . .' Ibid.
544 'We touch down . . .' Ibid., p. 63
546–7 'We shoot Huns all day . . . very friendly' Bartley, *Smoke Trails in the Sky*, pp. 26–30
549 'Poor Kathleen, poor parents . . .' Hughes, diary, 12/9/1940
549 'You anaesthetized yourself . . .' *The Few* (2000), ACO/Film/CO Film Channel 5
549 'This morning he was very perky . . .' Hughes, diary, 13/8/1940
549 'They knew exactly what . . .' Bethke, memoir, DTA 652.9

551 **'Writing, reading, playing chess . . .'** Bethke, diary, 25/8/1940
553 **'We used the phrase . . .'** BA-MA RL 10.546
553 **'We began to feel the fatigue . . .'** Steinhilper and Osborne, *Spitfire on My Tail*, p. 294

45. The Crux

554–5 **'There's no word I can start off with . . . seven hours off duty'** Cockett, *Love and War in London*, 11/9/1940
555 **'Jerky bees . . .'** Beaton, *The Years Between*, p. 38
555 **'I wander deserted streets . . .'** CBP, diary, September 1940
555 **'I felt thoroughly sad . . .'** Beaton, *The Years Between*, p. 38
555 **'When we get nearer London . . .'** Nicolson, HND, 8/9/1940
556 **'But what is happening now . . .'** *WS*, 11/9/1940
556 **'Old women and mothers . . .'** TNA INF 1/250
556 **'Morale has jumped . . .'** Ibid.
557 **'Do you think . . . you are wrong'** Cited in Irving, *Göring*, p. 295
557–8 **'I estimate that . . . state of affairs'** TNA AIR 40/2400
558 **'That is my whole . . . crisis with planes'** Bethke, diary, 5/9/1940
558 **'It was a . . .'** Steinhilper and Osborne, *Spitfire on My Tail*, p. 294
558 **'We've been away since January . . .'** TNA AR 40/3071
559 **'At St Omer . . .'** Ibid.
559 **'I touched down . . .'** Corbin, *Last of the Ten Fighter Boys*, p. 96
560 **'If air supremacy . . .'** NHB EDS/Apprec/6: *The German Plans for the Invasion of England*
561 **'A successful landing . . . been enormous'** Ibid.
563–4 **'Hello, Gannic . . . chaps'** Bartley, *Smoke Trails in the Sky*, pp. 32–4
565 **'Over there we met . . .'** Steinhilper and Osborne, *Spitfire on My Tail*, p. 297
566 **'Allied fighter! . . . a large Scotch'** Zumbach, *On Wings of War*, p. 76
567 **'The idea is to get up . . .'** Allan Wright, logbook
567 **'What reserves have we got?' 'There are none'** *WSC*, p. 296

46. Wolfpack

570 **'Sixty kills, twenty losses . . .'** Bethke, diary, 16/9/1940
571 **'The English have adopted new tactics . . .'** Cited in Bekker, *The Luftwaffe War Diaries*, p. 226
572 **'This fellow spoke good English . . .'** IWM 028665
574 **'We reported to Lorient . . .'** IWM 26952
574 **'Received wireless message'** NHB, U-48 log, 20/9/1940
574 **'We were pleased . . .'** Ibid.
575 **'We lost another large number . . .'** Colville, *The Fringes of Power*, 22/9/1940
577 **'excessively crowded . . .'** NHB EDS/Apprec/6, *The German Plans for Invasion of England*, p. 118
577 **'It does indicate . . .'** Shirer, *Berlin Diary*, 23/9/1940

578 **'We can't get away from the war . . .'** Wendel, *Hausfrau at War*, p. 88
578 **'And often they swoop down . . .'** Shirer, *Berlin Diary*, 23/9/1940
578 **'12.50 p.m. . . .'** Colville, *The Fringes of Power*, 22/9/40
578 **'The British are slowly getting . . .'** Steinhilper and Osborne, *Spitfire on My Tail*, p. 298
578 **'I think we all felt . . .'** Ibid., p. 299
579 **'Days too quiet . . .'** Bethke, diary, 18–23/9/1940
579 **'If this fellow . . .'** Bartley, *The Few* (2000), ACO/Film/CO Film Channel 5
581 **'There was a terrific explosion . . .'** Crook, *Spitfire Pilot*, p. 75
582 **'The effect of a Spitfire's eight guns . . .'** Ibid., p. 81
582 **'The last few moments . . .'** Ibid., p. 82
582–3 **'My red lamp is on! . . . Who was that?'** Cited in Bergström, *Hans-Ekkehard Bob*, p. 26
583 **'It was one of the best . . .'** Crook, *Spitfire Pilot*, p. 84

47. Exhaustion
584 **'Let us go on together . . .'** Cited in Colville, *The Fringes of Power*, 24/9/1940
585 **'I still think this war . . .'** JPK, diary, 17/9/40
585 **'Kennedy has the speculator's smartness . . .'** Raymond Lee, *The London Observer*, 17/9/1940
586 **'It's really good to be alive . . .'** Rawlings papers, letter, 29/9/1940
587 **'Rothkirch is not adding up . . .'** Bethke, diary, 10/10/1940
587 **'It is also hoped . . .'** Ibid., 16/10/1940
588 **'They were supposed to be . . .'** Steinhilper and Osborne, *Spitfire on My Tail*, p. 304
588 **'It seemed you could just . . .'** Ibid.
589 **'And tomorrow . . .'** Stahl, *The Diving Eagle*, 16/10/1940
594 **'This has resulted . . .'** Cockett, *Love and War in London*, September 1940
594 **'Life around here proceeds . . .'** MO diarist 53967, 24/10/1940

48. Last Flight
595 **'Protect the fighter-bombers . . .'** This account comes from Steinhilper and Osborne, *Spitfire on My Tail*, pp. 9–19 and pp. 324–5

Postscript
601 **'Whoopee! I've got a 109'** John Dundas papers
602 **'So it has happened at last . . .'** Hugh Dundas papers, diary, 1/12/1940
604 **'Now you've got your ****** war!'** Cited in Irving, *Göring*, p. 268
607 **'The only guide to a man . . .'** Cited in Stewart, *Burying Caesar*, p. 448

Sources

Personal testimonies

Author Interviews

In addition to those listed in the Notes, the following were used:

Doe, Bob, 234 Squadron
Leigh, Joe, 64 and 72 Squadrons
Maxwell, Wendy, civilian secretary to Colonel Ian Jacob
Mounsdon, Maurice, 56 Squadron
Naumann, Johannes, I/JG 26
Seeger, Günther, I/JG 2 (interview by Stefan Körlin)
Sparks, Ken, civilian
Spreitzer, Karl, I/St.G 2
Wunderlich, Albert, civilian

Imperial War Museum, London

Begg, Andrew, HMS *Icarus*
Bell MacDonald, A. M., 32nd Field Artillery, RA
Colville, Jock, Secretary to Prime Minister
Cox, Gwladys, civilian
Martel, Ludvik, 54 and 603 Squadrons
McLaren, R. I., 8th Battalion Durham Light Infantry
Neary, Tom, 1st Battalion East Lancashire Regiment
Nuttall, Sidney, RAOC and 1st Border Battalion
Sparks, Ken, civilian
Steele, Joe, HMT *Dalmatia* and *Darthema*
Wedding, Ernst, KG 55

Winterbotham, Fred, Air Intelligence
Wright, Julian, 2nd Battalion Sherwood Foresters

The Second World War Experience Centre, Leeds

Brown, Eric, FAA

RAF Museum, Hendon

Smyth, Anthony, 115 Squadron

Private papers

Eden, Anthony, University of Birmingham
Elmhirst, Thomas, Churchill Archives Centre, Churchill College, Cambridge
Jacob, Ian, Churchill Archives Centre, Churchill College, Cambridge

Select bibliography

Official histories

Butler, J. R. M., *Grand Strategy*, Vol. II (HMSO, 1957)
Collier, Basil, *Defence of the United Kingdom* (HMSO, 1957)
Court, W. H. B., *Coal* (HMSO, 1951)
Department of State, Washington, *Peace and War: United States Foreign Policy 1931–1941* (HMSO, 1943)
Ellis, L. F., *The War in France and Flanders, 1939–1940* (HMSO, 1953)
Hinsley, F. H., *et al.*, *British Intelligence in the Second World War*, Vol. 1 (HMSO, 1979)
James, T. C. G., *The Battle of Britain* (Frank Cass, 2000)
—, *The Growth of Fighter Command 1936–1940* (Frank Cass, 2002)
Maier, Klaus A., *et al.*, *Germany and the Second World War*, Vol. II: *Germany's Initial Conquests in Europe* (Oxford University Press, 2003)
Naval Staff History, *British Mining Operations, 1939–1945*, Vol. 1 (Ministry of Defence Director of Naval Warfare, 1973)
Postan, M. M., *British War Production* (HMSO, 1952)
Richards, Denis, *Royal Air Force 1939–1945*, Vol. I: *The Fight at Odds* (HMSO, 1953)
Roskill, Captain S. W., *The War at Sea 1939–1945*, Vol. I: *The Defensive* (HMSO, 1954)
Savage, C. I., *Inland Transport* (HMSO, 1957)
Scott, J. D., and Richard Hughes, *The Administration of War Production* (HMSO, 1955)

Memoirs, biographies

Alanbrooke, Field Marshal Lord, *War Diaries 1939–1945* (Weidenfeld & Nicolson, 2001)

Allen, Wing Commander Dizzy, *Fighter Squadron: A Memoir 1940–1942* (William Kimber, 1979)
Allingham, Margery, *The Oaken Heart* (Hutchinson, 1959)
Avon, The Rt. Hon. The Earl of, *The Eden Memoirs: Facing the Dictators* (Cassell, 1962)
Bailey, Jim, *The Sky Suspended: A Fighter Pilot's Story* (Bloomsbury, 2005)
Baker, David, *Adolf Galland* (Window & Greene Ltd, 1996)
Balfour, Harold, *Wings Over Westminster* (Hutchinson, 1973)
Bartley, Tony, *Smoke Trails in the Sky* (Crécy, 1997)
Batten, John, *Dirty Little Collier* (Hutchinson, 1943)
Baumbach, Werner, *Broken Swastika* (George Mann, 1974)
Beamont, Roland, *My Part of the Sky: A Fighter Pilot's First-Hand Experiences 1939–1945* (Patrick Stephens Limited, 1989)
Beaton, Cecil, *Air of Glory: A Wartime Scrapbook* (HMSO, 1941)
—, *Ashcombe: The Story of a Fifteen Year Lease* (Batsford, 1949)
—, *History Under Fire: 52 Photographs of Air Raid Damage to London Buildings, 1940–41* (Batsford, 1942)
— (ed. Richard Buckle), *Self Portrait with Friends: The Select Diaries of Cecil Beaton* (Pimlico, 1991)
—, *The Years Between: Diaries 1939–44* (Weidenfeld & Nicolson, 1965)
Beck, Alfred M., *Hitler's Ambivalent Attaché: Lt. Gen. Friedrich von Boetticher in America 1933–1941* (Potomac Books, 2006)
Below, Nicolaus von, *At Hitler's Side: The Memoirs of Hitler's Luftwaffe Adjutant 1937–1945* (Greenhill Books, 2004)
Bergström, Christer, *Hans-Ekkehard Bob* (Air Power Editions, 2007)
Birkenhead, The Earl of, *Halifax: The Life of Lord Halifax* (Hamish Hamilton, 1965)
Bob, Hans-Ekkehard, *Betrayed Ideals* (Hans-Ekkehard Bob, 2008)
Bolitho, Hector, *Combat Report: The Story of a Fighter Pilot* (Batsford, 1943)
Bond, Brian, 'Gort,' in *Churchill's Generals* (ed. John Keegan), (Abacus, 1991)
Brickhill, Paul, *Reach for the Sky: The Story of Douglas Bader* (Collins, 1954)
Brittain, Vera, *England's Hour* (Continuum, 2005)
Bryant, Ben, *One Man Band* (William Kimber, 1958)
Buchheim, Lothar-Günther, *Das Boot* (Cassell, 1999)
—, *U-Boat War* (Collins, 1978)
Bullitt, Orville H. (ed.), *For the President Personal and Secret: Correspondence Between Franklin D. Roosevelt and William C. Bullitt* (André Deutsch, 1973)
Cave Brown, Anthony, *Wild Bill Donovan: The Last Hero* (Michael Joseph, 1982)
Channon, Sir Henry, *Chips: The Diaries of Sir Henry Channon* (Phoenix, 1996)
Cheshire, Leonard, *Bomber Pilot* (Hutchinson, 1944)
Churchill, Winston S., *The Second World War*, Vol. II: *Their Finest Hour* (Cassell & Co. Ltd, 1949)
—, *War Speeches*, Vol. 1 (Cassell, 1951)
Ciano, Galeazzo, *Diary, 1937–1943* (William Heinemann, 1947)

Clark, Kenneth, *The Other Half: A Self-Portrait* (John Murray, 1997)
Cockett, Olivia, *Love and War in London: The Mass Observation Wartime Diary of Olivia Cockett* (The History Press, 2008)
Collier, Basil, *Leader of the Few* (Jarrolds, 1957)
Colville, John, *The Fringes of Power: Downing Street Diaries*, Vol. 1: *1939–October 1941* (Sceptre, 1985)
—, *Man of Valour: Field Marshal Gort VC* (Collins, 1972)
Corbin, Jimmy, *Last of the Ten Fighter Boys* (Sutton, 2007)
Crook, David, *Spitfire Pilot* (Faber & Faber, 1942)
Dalton, Hugh, *The Second World War Diary of Hugh Dalton 1940–45* (Jonathan Cape, 1986)
Deere, Allan C., *Nine Lives* (Crécy, 1999)
Deichmann, Paul, *Der Chef im Hintergrund* (Munich and Hamburg, 1979)
Delpla, François (ed.), *Les Papiers secrets du Général Doumenc* (Olivier Orban, 1991)
D'Este, Carlo, *Warlord: A Life of Churchill at War, 1874–1945* (Allen Lane, 2009)
Dilks, David (ed.), *The Diaries of Sir Alexander Cadogan 1938–1945* (Cassell, 1971)
Doe, Bob, *Bob Doe Fighter Pilot* (CCB Associates, 1999)
Doenitz [Dönitz], Grand Admiral Karl, *Memoirs: Ten Years and Twenty Days* (Da Capo, 1997)
Donald, William, *Stand By for Action: The Memoirs of a Small Ship Commander in World War II* (Seaforth, 2009)
Donnelly, G. L. 'Larry', *The Whitley Boys: 4 Group Bomber Operations 1939–1940* (Air Research Publications, 1991)
Drake, Billy, with Christopher Shores, *Billy Drake, Fighter Leader* (Grub Street, 2002)
Dundas, Hugh, *Flying Start* (Penguin, 1990)
Dutton, David, *Neville Chamberlain* (Hodder Education, 2001)
Edwards, Squadron Leader Ralph, *In the Thick of It: The Autobiography of a Bomber Pilot* (Images Publishing, 1994)
Elmhirst, Air Marshal Sir Thomas, *Recollections* (privately published, 1991)
Forbes, Wing Commander Athol, and Squadron Leader Hubert Allen (eds.), *Ten Fighter Boys* (Collins, 1942)
Forrester, Larry, *Fly for Your Life* (Panther, 1959)
Frank, Wolfgang, *Enemy Submarine* (New English Library, 1977)
Freidel, Frank, *Franklin D. Roosevelt: A Rendezvous with Destiny* (Little, Brown & Co, 1990)
Galland, Adolf, *The First and the Last* (Fontana, 1971)
Genoud, François (ed.), *The Testament of Adolf Hitler* (Cassell, 1959)
Gilbert, G. M., *Nuremberg Diary* (Da Capo, 1995)
Gilbert, Martin, *Finest Hour: Winston S. Churchill 1939–1941* (Minerva, 1989)
Glancey, Jonathan, *Spitfire: The Biography* (Atlantic Books, 2006)
Goebbels, Josef, *The Goebbels Diaries 1939–1941* (Sphere, 1982)
Gregory-Smith, Captain Frank, *Red Tobruk: Memoirs of a World War II*

Destroyer Commander (Pen & Sword, 2008)
Grossjohann, Georg, *Five Years, Four Fronts* (The Aberjona Press, 1999)
Guderian, Heinz, *Panzer Leader* (Penguin, 2000)
— (foreword), *Blitzkrieg in Their Own Words* (Zenith Press, 2005)
Häberlen, Klaus, *A Luftwaffe Bomber Pilot Remembers* (Schiffer Military History, 2001)
Halder, Franz, *The Halder Diary, 1939–1942* (Greenhill Books, 1988)
Hall, Roger, *Clouds of Fear* (Bailey Brothers & Swinfen, 1975)
Hastings, Max, *Finest Years: Churchill as Warlord 1940–45* (Harper Press, 2009)
Henderson, Sir Neville, *Failure of a Mission* (Hodder & Stoughton, 1940)
Henshaw, Alex, *Sigh for a Merlin: Testing the Spitfire* (Crécy, 1996)
Herrmann, Hajo, *Eagle's Wings: The Autobiography of a Luftwaffe Pilot* (Airlife, 1991)
Hillary, Richard, *The Last Enemy* (Macmillan, 1942)
Hodgson, Vere, *Few Eggs and No Oranges: The Diaries of Vere Hodgson 1940–45* (Persephone Books, 2002)
Hollowood, Bernard, *Pont: The Life and Work of the Great Punch Artist* (Collins, 1969)
Hozzel, Paul-Werner, 'Recollections and Experiences of a Stuka Pilot' (unpublished)
Irving, David, *Goebbels: Mastermind of the Third Reich* (Focal Point, 1996)
—, *Göring* (Macmillan, 1989)
—, *The Rise and Fall of the Luftwaffe: The Life of Erhard Milch* (Weidenfeld & Nicolson, 1973)
—, *The Trail of the Fox: The Life of Field Marshal Erwin Rommel* (Book Club Associates, 1977)
Ismay, Hastings, *The Memoirs of General Lord Ismay* (Viking, 1960)
Jackson, Robert, *Before the Storm* (Cassell, 2001)
Jenkins, Roy, *Churchill* (Pan, 2002)
Joseph, Michael, *The Sword in the Scabbard* (Michael Joseph, 1942)
Jones, R. V., *Most Secret War* (Penguin, 2009)
Keitel, Wilhelm, *The Memoirs of Field Marshal Wilhelm Keitel, Chief of the German High Command, 1938–1945* (Cooper Square Press, 2000)
Kennedy, Ludovic, *Sub-Lieutenant: A Personal Record of the War at Sea* (Batsford, 1942)
Kershaw, Ian, *Hitler 1889–1936: Hubris* (Penguin, 1999)
—, *Hitler 1936–45: Nemesis* (Penguin, 2001)
Kesselring, Field Marshal, *The Memoirs of Field-Marshal Kesselring* (Greenhill Books, 1988)
Kessler, Ronald, *The Sins of the Father: Joseph P. Kennedy and the Dynasty He Founded* (Warner Books, 1996)
Kingcome, Brian, *A Willingness to Die: Memories from Fighter Command* (Tempus, 2007)
Knappe, Siegfried, with Ted Brusaw, *Soldat: Reflections of a German Soldier, 1936–1949* (Dell, 1992)

Lanchbery, Edward, *Against the Sun: The Story of Wing Commander Roland Beamont* (Cassell, 1955)
Langley, J. M., *Fight Another Day* (Collins, 1974)
Leamer, Laurence, *The Kennedy Men 1901–1963* (Harper Perennial, 2001)
Lee, Asher, *Goering: Air Leader* (Duckworth, 1972)
Lee, Raymond, *The London Observer: The Journal of Raymond E. Lee, 1940–1941* (Hutchinson, 1972)
Liddell Hart, B. H. (ed.), *The Rommel Papers* (Collins, 1953)
Liss, Ulrich, *Westfront 1939/40: Erinnerungen des Feindbearbeiters im OKH* (Neckargemund, 1959)
Loewenheim, Francis L., Harold D. Langley and Manfred Joans (eds.), *Roosevelt and Churchill: Their Secret Wartime Correspondence* (Barrie & Jenkins, 1975)
Luck, Hans von, *Panzer Commander* (Cassell, 2002)
MacGregor Burns, James, *Roosevelt: The Soldier of Freedom 1940–1945* (Weidenfeld & Nicolson, 1971)
Manstein, Field Marshal Erich von, *Lost Victories* (Zenith Press, 2004)
Mares, Frank, *Mission Accomplished* (Grub Street, 2007)
McKinstry, Leo, *Spitfire: Portrait of a Legend* (John Murray, 2007)
Middleton, Drew, *The Sky Suspended: The Battle of Britain May 1940–April 1941* (Secker & Warburg, 1960)
Mitchell, Gordon, *R. J. Mitchell: Schooldays to Spitfire* (The History Press, 2009)
Morris, Richard, *Guy Gibson* (Penguin, 1995)
Murrow, Edward R., *This is London* (Cassell, 1941)
Neil, Tom, *A Fighter in My Sights* (J&KH Publishing, 2001)
Nicolson, Harold, *Diaries and Letters 1939–1945* (Collins, 1967)
Norwich, John Julius (ed.), *The Duff Cooper Diaries 1915–1951* (Weidenfeld & Nicolson, 2005)
Olson, Lynne, and Stanley Cloud, *For Your Freedom and Ours: The Kościuszko Squadron – Forgotten Heroes of World War II* (William Heinemann, 2003)
Orange, Vincent, *Dowding of Fighter Command: Victor of the Battle of Britain* (Grub Street, 2008)
—, *Park* (Grub Street, 2001)
Overy, Richard, *Goering* (Phoenix, 2000)
Pownall, Henry, *Chief of Staff: The Diaries of Lieutenant-General Sir Henry Pownall*, Vol. 1: *1933–40* (Leo Cooper, 1972)
Prien, Günther, *U-Boat Commander* (Tandem, 1969)
Priestley, J. B., *Postscripts* (William Heinemann, 1940)
Pyle, Ernie, *Ernie Pyle in England* (Robert M. McBride & Company, 1941)
Quill, Jeffrey, *Spitfire* (Arrow, 1985)
Rall, Günther, *My Logbook: Reminiscences, 1938–2006* (Editions Twentynine Six, 2006)
Rice, Joan, *Sand in My Shoes: Coming of Age in the Second World War: A WAAF's Diary* (Harper Perennial, 2007)

Richardson, Charles, *From Churchill's Secret Circle to the BBC: The Biography of Lieutenant General Sir Ian Jacob* (Brassey's, 1991)
Richey, Paul, *Fighter Pilot: A Personal Record of the Campaign in France* (Batsford, 1941)
Ringlstetter, Herbert, *Helmut Wick* (Schiffer Military History, 2005)
Rivaz, R. C., *Tail Gunner* (Jarrolds, 1943)
Roberts, Andrew, *The Holy Fox: The Life of Lord Halifax* (Phoenix, 1997)
Ross, David, *Richard Hillary* (Grub Street, 2000)
Sawyer, Group Captain Tom, *Only Owls and Bloody Fools Fly at Night* (William Kimber, 1982)
Schmidt, Dr Paul, *Hitler's Interpreter* (William Heinemann, 1951)
Schroeder, Christa, *Er war mein Chef: Aus dem Nachlaß der Sekretärin von Adolf Hitler* (LangdenMüller in der F. A. Herbig Verlagsbuchhandlung GmbH, 1985)
Self, Robert, *Neville Chamberlain* (Ashgate, 2006)
— (ed.), *The Neville Chamberlain Diary Letters*, Vol. 4: *The Downing Street Years, 1934–1940* (Ashgate, 2005)
Sereny, Gitta, *Albert Speer: His Battle with Truth* (Picador, 1996)
Sherwood, Robert E., *The White House Papers of Harry L. Hopkins*, Vol. I: *September 1939–January 1942* (Eyre & Spottiswoode, 1948)
Shirer, William L., *Berlin Diary* (Hamish Hamilton, 1942)
—, *This is Berlin* (Arrow, 2000)
Slessor, Sir John, *The Central Blue* (Cassell, 1956)
Smith, Amanda (ed.), *Hostage to Fortune: The Letters of Joseph P. Kennedy* (Viking, 2001)
Speer, Albert, *Inside the Third Reich* (Phoenix, 1995)
Sperber, A. M., *Murrow: His Life and Times* (Freundlich Books, 1986)
Spitzy, Reinhard, *How We Squandered the Reich* (Michael Russell Publishing Ltd, 1997)
Stahl, Peter, *The Diving Eagle: A Ju88 Pilot's Diary* (William Kimber, 1984)
Steinhilper, Ulrich, and Peter Osborne, *Spitfire on My Tail* (Independent Books, 2006)
Stevenson, William, *A Man Called Intrepid* (Sphere, 1978)
Swift, Will, *The Kennedys amidst the Gathering Storm: A Thousand Days in London 1938–1940* (JR Books, 2008)
Taylor, A. J. P., *Beaverbrook* (Hamish Hamilton, 1972)
Thorpe, D. R., *Eden* (Chatto & Windus, 2003)
Toliver, Colonel Raymond F., and Trevor J. Constable, *Fighter General: The Life of Adolf Galland* (AmPress, 1990)
Vann, Frank, *Willy Messerschmitt* (Patrick Stephens Limited, 1993)
Vansittart, The Rt. Hon. Lord, *Lessons of My Life* (Hutchinson, 1943)
Vickers, Hugo, *Cecil Beaton* (Weidenfeld & Nicolson, 1985)
Vigors, Tim, *Life's Too Short to Cry* (Grub Street, 2006)
Walker, Oliver, *Sailor Malan* (Cassell, 1953)
Warlimont, Walter, *Inside Hitler's Headquarters 1939–45* (Presidio, 1964)
Webley, Nicholas (ed.), *Betty's Wartime Diary 1939–1945* (Thorogood, 2002)

Wellum, Geoffrey, *First Light* (Viking, 2002)
Wendel, Else, *Hausfrau at War: A German Woman's Account of Life in Hitler's Reich* (Odhams, 1957)
Werner, Herbert A., *Iron Coffins: A U-Boat Commander's War, 1939–1945* (Cassell, 1999)
Whalen, Richard J., *The Founding Father: The Story of Joseph P. Kennedy* (Hutchinson, 1965)
Wheeler, Edwin, *Just to Get a Bed* (Square One Publications, 1990)
Wright, Nicholas, *The Bump* (RAF Biggin Hill, 1980)
Wyndham, Joan, *Love Lessons* (Virago Press, 2001)
Young, Desmond, *Rommel* (Cassell, 1950)
Zumbach, Jan, *On Wings of War* (André Deutsch, 1975)

General

Addison, Paul, and Jeremy A. Crang (eds.), *The Burning Blue: A New History of the Battle of Britain* (Pimlico, 2000)
Admiralty, *The Protection of Seaborne Trade by the Royal Navy*, Vol. I: *Organization for Control and Protection of British and Allied Merchant Shipping by the Admiralty* (Admiralty, 1950)
Air Ministry, *Coastal Command* (HMSO)
—, *Pilot's Notes Spitfire IIA and IIB Aeroplanes Merlin XII Engine* (Air Publication 1 56 5 B)
—, *The Rise and Fall of the German Air Force (1933 to 1945)* (Public Record Office, 2001)
Anderson, Janice, *The War Years: Life in Britain during 1939 to 1945* (Futura, 2007)
Anon., *Documents on German Foreign Policy 1918–1945, Series D, Volume IX* (HMSO, 1956)
—, *Documents on German Foreign Policy 1918–1945, Series D, Volume X* (HMSO, 1957)
Ansel, Walter, *Hitler Confronts England* (Cambridge University Press, 1960)
Arthur, Max, *There Shall be Wings: The RAF from 1918 to the Present* (Hodder & Stoughton, 1993)
Asser, Roy, *The Battle of Britain: The Camera's View* (The Battle of Britain Historical Society, 2003)
Atkin, Ronald, *Pillar of Fire: Dunkirk 1940* (Sidgwick & Jackson, 1990)
Barker, A. J., *Dunkirk: The Great Escape* (J. M. Dent & Sons Ltd, 1977)
Barnett, Correlli, *Engage the Enemy More Closely* (Penguin, 2000)
Bartz, Karl, *Swastika in the Air: The Struggle and Defeat of the German Air Force 1939–1945* (William Kimber, 1956)
Bédoyère, Guy de la, *The Archaeology of the Air War* (Tempus, 2000)
Bekker, Cajus, *The Luftwaffe War Diaries* (Corgi, 1972)
Bell, P. M. H., *A Certain Eventuality* (Saxon House, 1974)
Benoist-Méchin, J., *Sixty Days That Shook the West* (Jonathan Cape, 1963)
Bishop, Patrick, *Bomber Boys: Fighting Back 1940–1945* (Harper Press, 2007)

—, *Fighter Boys: Saving Britain 1940* (Harper Press, 2003)
Blair, Clay, *Hitler's U-Boat War: The Hunters 1939–1942* (Cassell, 2000)
Blaxland, Gregory, *Destination Dunkirk: The Story of Gort's Army* (Military Book Society, 1973)
Blythe, Ronald, *The Age of Illusion: England in the Twenties and Thirties 1919–40* (Penguin, 1963)
Boelcke, Willi A., *The Secret Conferences of Dr. Goebbels 1939–43* (Weidenfeld & Nicolson, 1967)
Brendon, Piers, *The Dark Valley: A Panorama of the 1930s* (Pimlico, 2001)
Brewer, Susan A., *To Win the Peace: British Propaganda in the United States during World War II* (Cornell University Press, 1997)
Brooks, Robin J., *Hampshire Airfields in the Second World War* (Countryside Books, 1996)
—, *Kent Airfields in the Second World War* (Countryside Books, 1998)
Brown, Malcolm, *Spitfire Summer: When Britain Stood Alone* (Carlton Books, 2000)
Brown, Squadron Leader Peter, *Honour Restored: The Battle of Britain, Dowding and the Fight for Freedom* (Spellmount, 2005)
Bryant, Arthur, and Edward Shanks, *The Battle of Britain, The Few* (Withy Grove Press, 1944)
Bungay, Stephen, *The Most Dangerous Enemy: A History of the Battle of Britain* (Aurum Press, 2000)
Burleigh, Michael, *The Third Reich: A New History* (Pan, 2000)
Caine, Philip D., *American Pilots in the RAF: The WWII Eagle Squadrons* (Brassey's, 1998)
Calder, Angus, *The Myth of the Blitz* (Pimlico, 1991)
—, *The People's War: Britain 1939–1945* (Pimlico, 1992)
—, and Dorothy Sheridan (eds.), *Speak for Yourself: A Mass Observation Anthology 1937–1949* (Oxford University Press, 1985)
Caldwell, Donald, *The JG 26 War Diary* (Grub Street, 1996)
Cannadine, David, *In Churchill's Shadow: Confronting the Past in Modern Britain* (Allen Lane, 2002)
Cardozier, V. R., *The Mobilization of the United States in World War II* (McFarland, 1995)
Chorley, W. R., *Royal Air Force Bomber Command Losses of the Second World War,* Vol. 1: *Aircraft and Crews Lost during 1939–1940* (Midland Publishing, 2005)
Chorlton, Martyn, *Scottish Airfields in the Second World War,* Vol. 1: *The Lothians* (Countryside Books, 2008)
Clarke, Peter, *Hope and Glory: Britain 1900–1990* (Allen Lane, 1996)
Clayton, Tim, and Phil Craig, *Finest Hour* (Hodder & Stoughton, 1999)
Collier, Richard, *Eagle Day* (Hodder & Stoughton, 1966)
—, *The Sands of Dunkirk* (Collins, 1961)
Cooper, Matthew, *The German Air Force 1933–1945: An Anatomy of Failure* (Jane's, 1981)

Cornwell, Peter D., *The Battle of France Then and Now: Six Nations Locked in Aerial Combat September 1939 to June 1940* (After the Battle, 2007)
Corrigan, Gordon, *Blood, Sweat and Arrogance and the Myths of Churchill's War* (Weidenfeld & Nicolson, 2006)
Cowling, Maurice, *The Impact of Hitler: British Politics and British Policy 1933–1940* (Cambridge University Press, 1975)
Cull, Brian, *249 at War: The Authorized History of the RAF's Top-Scoring Fighter Squadron of WWII* (Grub Street, 1997)
Cull, Nicholas John, *Selling War: The British Propaganda Campaign against American Neutrality in World War II* (Oxford University Press, 1995)
Dallek, Robert, *Franklin D. Roosevelt and American Foreign Policy 1932–1945* (Oxford University Press, 1995)
Dallies-Labourdette, Jean-Philippe, *S-Boote: German E-Boats in Action, 1939–1945* (Histoire & Collections)
Davis, Brian L., *Uniforms and Insignia of the Luftwaffe*, Vol. 1: *1933–1940* (Arms & Armour, 1995)
Davis, Kenneth S., *The American Experience of War 1939–1945* (Secker & Warburg, 1967)
Davis Biddle, Tami, *Rhetoric and Reality in Air Warfare: The Evolution of British and American Ideas about Strategic Bombing, 1914–1945* (Princeton University Press, 2002)
Deichmann, Paul, *Spearhead for Blitzkrieg: Luftwaffe Operations in Support of the Army, 1939–1945* (Greenhill Books, 1996)
Deighton, Len, *Blitzkrieg: From the Rise of Hitler to the Fall of Dunkirk* (Pimlico, 2007)
—, *Fighter: The True Story of the Battle of Britain* (Pimlico, 1996)
—, and Max Hastings, *Battle of Britain* (Jonathan Cape, 1980)
Demarne, Cyril, *The London Blitz: A Fireman's Tale* (After the Battle, 1991)
Dierich, Wolfgang, *Kampfgeschwader 'Edelweis': The History of a German Bomber Unit 1939–1945* (Ian Allan, 1975)
Dobinson, Colin, *AA Command: Britain's Anti-Aircraft Defences of the Second World War* (Methuen, 2001)
Donnelly, Larry, *The Other Few* (Red Kite, 2004)
Earnshaw, James Douglas, *609 at War* (Vector Fine Art, 2004)
Eberle, Henrik, and Matthias Uhl (eds.), *The Hitler Book: The Secret Dossier Prepared for Stalin* (John Murray, 2005)
Ellis, John, *The Sharp End: The Fighting Man in World War II* (Pimlico, 1993)
Engel, Major Gerhard, *At the Heart of the Reich: The Secret Diary of Hitler's Army Adjutant* (Greenhill Books, 2005)
Faber, David, *Munich: The 1938 Appeasement Crisis* (Pocket Books, 2009)
Felton, Monica, *Civilian Supplies in Wartime Britain* (The Ministry of Information, 1945)
Ferguson, Niall, *Empire: How Britain Made the Modern World* (Penguin, 2004)
Fleming, Peter, *Operation Sea Lion* (Pan, 1975)

Foreman, John, *Fighter Command War Diaries: September 1939 to September 1940* (Air Research Publications, 1996)
Franks, Norman, *Air Battle for Dunkirk 26 May–3 June 1940* (Grub Street, 2006)
—, *Aircraft versus Aircraft: The Illustrated Story of Fighter Pilot Combat from 1914 to the Present Day* (Chancellor Press, 2001)
Frieser, Karl-Heinz, *Blitzkrieg Legend: The 1940 Campaign in the West* (Naval Institute Press, 2005)
Gardiner, Juliet, *Wartime: Britain 1939–1945* (Headline, 2004)
Gardner, W. J. R. (ed.), *The Evacuation from Dunkirk: Operation Dynamo, 26 May–4 June 1940* (Frank Cass, 2000)
Garfield, Simon, *We are at War: The Diaries of Five Ordinary People in Extraordinary Times* (Ebury Press, 2006)
Gelb, Norman, *Scramble: A Narrative History of the Battle of Britain* (Michael Joseph, 1986)
German Foreign Office, *Documents on the Events Preceding the Outbreak of War* (German Library of Information, 1940)
Gilbert, Martin, *Churchill and America* (The Free Press, 2005)
Gillies, Midge, *Waiting for Hitler: Voices from Britain on the Brink of Invasion* (Hodder & Stoughton, 2007)
Goodman, Susan, *Children of War* (John Murray, 2005)
Goss, Chris, *Brothers in Arms: The Story of a British and German Fighter Unit, August to December 1940* (Crécy, 1994)
—, *The Luftwaffe Bombers' Battle of Britain* (Crécy, 2000)
—, *The Luftwaffe Fighters' Battle of Britain* (Crécy, 2000)
Graves, Charles, *The Home Guard of Great Britain* (Hutchinson, 1943)
Graves, Robert, and Alan Hodge, *The Long Weekend 1918–1939: A Social History of Great Britain* (Abacus, 1995)
Gretzyngier, Robert, *Poles in Defence of Britain* (Grub Street, 2001)
Griehl, Manfred, and Joachim Dressel, *Luftwaffe Combat Aircraft: Development, Productions, Operations, 1935–1945* (Schiffer Military History, 1994)
Grunberger, Richard, *A Social History of the Third Reich* (Phoenix, 2005)
Gunston, Bill, *The Illustrated Dictionary of Fighting Aircraft of World War II* (Salamander Books, 1988)
Hammerston, Sir John (ed.), *ABC of the RAF* (The Amalgamated Press, 1943)
Handel, Michael I. (ed.), *Intelligence and Military Operations* (Frank Cass, 1990)
Harrison, Tom, and Charles Madge, *War Begins at Home by Mass Observation* (Chatto & Windus, 1940)
Harrison Place, Timothy, *Military Training in the British Army, 1940–1944* (Frank Cass, 2000)
Hastings, Max, *Bomber Command* (Book Club Associates, 1980)
Hewitt, Nick, *Coastal Convoys 1939–1945: The Indestructible Highway* (Pen & Sword, 2008)
HMSO, *The British War Blue Book* (The Musson Book Company, 1939)

—, *The Penguin Hansard, 1: From Chamberlain to Churchill* (Penguin, 1940)
Hooton, E. R., *Eagle in Flames: The Fall of the Luftwaffe* (Brockhampton Press, 1997)
Horne, Alistair, *To Lose a Battle: France 1940* (Papermac, 1990)
Hough, Richard, *The Longest Battle: The War at Sea, 1939–45* (Cassell, 2001)
—, and Denis Richards, *The Battle of Britain* (Penguin, 2001)
Hunt, Roger (trans.), *Death's Head: Combat Record of the SS Totenkopf Division in France 1940* (Roger Hunt, 1979)
Hylton, Stuart, *Their Darkest Hour: The Hidden History of the Home Front 1939–1945* (Sutton, 2003)
Irving, David (ed.), *Breach of Security: The German Secret Intelligence File on Events Leading to the Second World War* (William Kimber, 1968)
Ishoven, Armand, *The Luftwaffe in the Battle of Britain* (Ian Allan, 1980)
Julian, Marcel, *The Battle of Britain, July–September 1940* (Jonathan Cape, 1967)
Kaplan, Philip, *Spitfire: The One* (Vine House International, 2008)
—, and Richard Collier, *The Few: Summer 1940, the Battle of Britain* (Seven Dials, 1990)
—, and Jack Currie, *Wolfpack: U-Boats at War, 1939–1945* (Aurum, 1997)
Kay, Anthony L., and J. R. Smith, *German Aircraft of the Second World War* (Putnam, 2002)
Kennedy, John F., *Why England Slept* (Hutchinson, 1940)
Kershaw, Alex, *The Few: The American Knights of the Air Who Risked Everything to Fight in the Battle of Britain* (Da Capo, 2006)
Kershaw, Ian, *Fateful Choices: Ten Decisions That Changed the World, 1940–1941* (Allen Lane, 2007)
Koa Wing, Sandra (ed.), *Our Longest Days: A People's History of the Second World War* (Profile Books, 2008)
Lampe, David, *The Last Ditch: Britain's Secret Resistance and the Nazi Invasion Plan* (Cassell, 1968)
Lee, Cyrus A., *Soldat*, Vol. 1: *Equipping the German Army Foot Soldier in Europe, 1939–1942* (Pictorial Histories Publishing Co., 1992)
Le Tissier, Tony, *The Third Reich Then and Now* (After the Battle, 2005)
Liddell Hart, B. H., *History of the Second World War* (Cassell, 1970)
—, *The Other Side of the Hill* (Cassell, 1948)
Longmate, Norman, *The Bombers: The RAF Offensive against Germany, 1939–1945* (Hutchinson, 1983)
—, *The Real Dad's Army: The Story of the Home Guard* (Arrow, 1974)
Lord, Walter, *The Miracle of Dunkirk* (Penguin, 1982)
Lukacs, John, *The Duel: Hitler vs Churchill 10 May–31 July 1940* (Phoenix, 2000)
—, *Five Days in London May 1940* (Yale University Press, 1999)
Lund, Paul, and Harry Ludlam, *Trawlers Go to War* (New English Library, 1972)
Mallmann Showell, Jak P., *Hitler's Navy: A Reference Guide to the Kriegsmarine, 1935–1945* (Seaforth, 2009)

Marix Evans, Martin, *The Fall of France: Act With Daring* (Osprey, 2000)
Mason, Francis K., *Battle Over Britain* (McWhirter Twins Ltd, 1969)
Mazower, Mark, *Hitler's Empire: Nazi Rule in Occupied Europe* (Allen Lane, 2008)
McKee, Alexander, *The Coal-Scuttle Brigade* (New English Library, 1973)
McLaine, Ian, *Ministry of Morale: Home Front Morale and the Ministry of Information in World War II* (George Allen & Unwin, 1979)
Middlebrook, Martin, and Chris Everitt, *The Bomber Command War Diaries: An Operational Reference Book 1939–1945* (Penguin, 1990)
Milner, Marc, *Battle of the Atlantic* (Tempus, 2005)
Ministry of Information, *British Coaster 1939–1945: The Official Story* (HMSO, 1947)
—, *Front Line 1940–41: The Official Story of the Civil Defence of Britain* (HMSO, 1942)
—, *Land at War* (HMSO, 1945)
—, *Merchantmen at War: The Official Story of the Merchant Navy, 1939–1944* (HMSO, 1944)
Mitcham, Samuel W., *Eagles of the Third Reich* (Airlife, 1989)
Mosley, Leonard, *Backs to the Wall: London Under Fire 1940–1945* (Victorian and Modern History Book Club, 1972)
Moss, Graham, and Barry McKee, *Spitfires and Polished Metal* (Airlife, 1999)
Murray, Williamson, *Luftwaffe: Strategy for Defeat 1933–45* (Grafton, 1988)
—, and Allan R. Millett (eds.), *Military Innovation in the Interwar Period* (Cambridge University Press, 1996)
Nagorski, Tom, *Miracles on the Water* (Robinson, 2007)
Nauroth, Holgar, *Jagdgeschwader 2 'Richthofen'* (Motorbuch Verlag, 1999)
Neillands, Robin, *The Bomber War* (John Murray, 2001)
Nielsen, Generalleutnant Andreas, *The German Air Force General Staff* (USAF Historical Studies No. 173, Arno Press, 1968)
Noakes, J., and G. Pridham (eds.), *Nazism 1919–1945*, Vol. 2: *State, Economy and Society 1933–1939* (University of Exeter Press, 2000)
—, *Nazism 1919–1945*, Vol. 3: *Foreign Policy, War and Racial Extermination*
—, *Nazism 1919–1945*, Vol. 4: *The German Home Front in World War II*
Oberkommando der Wehrmacht, *Fahrten und Flüge gegen England* (Zeitgeschichte-Verlag Berlin, 1941)
Ogley, Bob, *Ghosts of Biggin Hill* (Froglet Publications, 2001)
Otter, Patrick, *Yorkshire Airfields in the Second World War* (Countryside Books, 1998)
Overy, Richard, *The Battle* (Penguin, 2000)
Pallud, Jean-Paul, *Blitzkrieg in the West Then and Now* (After the Battle, 1991)
Parkinson, Roger, *Blood, Toil, Tears and Sweat: The War History from Dunkirk to Alamein, Based on the War Cabinet Papers of 1940 to 1942* (Hart-Davis MacGibbon, 1973)
Ponting, Clive, *1940: Myth and Reality* (Cardinal, 1991)

Porton, Edward P. von der, *The German Navy in World War II* (Arthur Baker Limited, 1969)
Postan, M. M., D. Hay and J. D. Scott, *Design and Development of Weapons* (HMSO, 1964)
Price, Alfred, *The Hardest Day: 18 August 1940* (Book Club Associates, 1979)
—, *Instruments of Darkness: The History of Electronic Warfare* (Macdonald & Jane's, 1967)
—, and Paul Blackah, *Supermarine Spitfire: Owner's Workshop Manual* (Haynes, 2007)
Probert, Air Commodore Henry, and Sebastian Cox, *The Battle Re-Thought: A Symposium on the Battle of Britain* (RAF Historical Society, 1991)
RAF Manston History Club, *RAF Manston Album* (Sutton, 2005)
Ramsey, Winston G. (ed.), *The Battle of Britain*, 5th edn (After the Battle, 1989)
—, *The Blitz Then and Now*, Vol. 2 (After the Battle, 1998)
Rankin, Nicholas, *Churchill's Wizards: The British Genius for Deception 1914–1945* (Faber & Faber, 2008)
Raymond, Squadron Leader R., and Squadron Leader David Langdon, *Slipstream: A Royal Air Force Anthology* (Eyre & Spottiswoode, 1946)
Reader, W. J., *Metal Box: A History* (William Heinemann, 1976)
Rendall, Ivan, *Spitfire: Icon of a Nation* (Weidenfeld & Nicolson, 2008)
Reynolds, David, *The Creation of the Anglo–American Alliance 1937–1941: A Study in Competitive Co-operation* (The University of North Carolina Press, 1982)
—, *In Command of History: Churchill Fighting and Writing the Second World War* (Allen Lane, 2004)
Richards, Denis, *RAF Bomber Command in the Second World War* (Penguin, 2001)
Roberts, Andrew, *Eminent Churchillians* (Phoenix, 1995)
—, *Masters and Commanders: How Roosevelt, Churchill, Marshall and Alanbrooke Won the War in the West* (Allen Lane, 2008)
Robinson, Anthony, *RAF Fighter Squadrons in the Battle of Britain* (Brockhampton Press, 1999)
Robinson, Michael, *Best of the Few: 92 Squadron 1939–40* (Michael Robinson, 2001)
Royal Institute of International Affairs, *Review of the Foreign Press 1939–1945: United States (Research) Memoranda*, Vol. I, Nos. 1–97 (Kraus International Publications)
Sarkar, Dilip, *A Few of the Many* (Ramrod Publications, 1995)
Schramm, Percy E. (ed.), *Kriegstagebuch des Oberkommandos der Wehrmacht 1940–1941*, Teilbände I and II (Bernard & Graefe Verlag, 1982)
Sebag-Montefiore, Hugh, *Dunkirk: Fight to the Last Man* (Penguin, 2007)
Sharp, Lee, *The French Army 1939–1940: Organisation, Order of Battle, Operational History*, Vol. III (Military Press, 2003)
Shaw, Frank and Joan, *We Remember Dunkirk* (Hinckley, 1990)
Shepperd, Alan, *France 1940: Blitzkrieg in the West* (Osprey, 1990)

Shirer, William L., *The Rise and Fall of the Third Reich* (Secker & Warburg, 1960)
Smart, Nick, *Biographical Dictionary of British Generals of the Second World War* (Pen & Sword, 2005)
Smith, Graham, *Devon and Cornwall Airfields in the Second World War* (Countryside Books, 2000)
Smithies, Edward, *Aces, Erks, and Backroom Boys* (Cassell, 2002)
Smurthwaite, David, *et al.*, *Against All Odds: The British Army of 1939–40* (National Army Museum, 1990)
Spender, Stephen, *Citizens in War – and After* (Harrap & Co., 1945)
Spick, Mike, *Aces of the Reich: The Making of a Luftwaffe Fighter-Pilot* (Greenhill Books, 2006)
—, *Allied Fighter Aces of World War II* (Greenhill Books, 1997)
—, *Fighter Aces: The Jagdflieger and Their Combat Tactics and Techniques* (Greenhill Books, 1996)
Stedman, Robert F., *Jagdflieger: Luftwaffe Fighter Pilot 1939–45* (Osprey, 2008)
—, *Kampflieger: Bomber Crewman of the Luftwaffe 1939–45* (Osprey, 2005)
—, *Luftwaffe Air & Ground Crew 1939–45* (Osprey, 2002)
Stevenson, John, *British Society 1914–1945* (Penguin, 1984)
Stewart, Graham, *Burying Caesar: Churchill, Chamberlain and the Battle for the Tory Party* (Phoenix, 2000)
Suchenwirth, Richard, *Command and Leadership in the German Air Force* (USAF Historical Studies No. 174, Arno Press, 1969)
—, *The Development of the German Air Force, 1919–1939* (University Press of the Pacific, Honolulu, 2005)
—, *Historical Turning Points in the German Air Force War Effort* (University Press of the Pacific, Honolulu, 2004)
Tangye, Squadron Leader Nigel, *Teach Yourself to Fly* (The English Universities Press, 1942)
Terraine, John, *The Right of the Line* (Hodder & Stoughton, 1985)
Time-Life Books, *The Luftwaffe* (Time-Life Books, 1982)
Tooze, Adam, *The Wages of Destruction: The Making and Breaking of the Nazi Economy* (Penguin, 2007)
Townsend, Peter, *Duel of Eagles: The Struggle for the Skies from the First World War to the Battle of Britain* (Cassell, 1970)
Townshend Bickers, Richard, *The Battle of Britain: The Greatest Battle in the History of Air Warfare* (Salamander Books Ltd, 1990)
Trevor-Roper, H. R. (ed.), *Hitler's War Directives 1939–1945* (Pan, 1966)
Tyrer, Nicola, *They Fought in the Fields* (Mandarin, 1997)
Vasco, John, *Messerschmitt Bf 110: Bombsights Over England – Erprobungsgruppe 210 in the Battle of Britain* (Schiffer Military History, 2002)
War Illustrated, The, Vols. II and III (six-month bound editions)
Walmsley, Leo, *Fishermen at War* (Collins, 1941)
Warwicker, John, *Churchill's Underground Army: A History of the Auxiliary Units in World War II* (Frontline Books, 2008)

Weal, John, *Jagdgeschwader 2 'Richthofen'* (Osprey, 2000)
—, *Jagdgeschwader 27 'Afrika'* (Osprey, 2003)
—, *Jagdgeschwader 52: The Experten* (Osprey, 2004)
Webster, Sir Charles, and Noble Frankland, *The Strategic Air Offensive against Germany 1939–1945*, Vol. I: *Preparation* (HMSO, 1961)
Wells, Mark K., *Courage and Air Warfare: The Allied Aircrew Experience in the Second World War* (Frank Cass, 1997)
Wheatley, Ronald, *Operation Sea Lion: German Plans for the Invasion of England, 1939–1942* (Oxford University Press, 1958)
Wheeler-Bennett, Sir John (ed.), *Action This Day: Working With Churchill* (Macmillan, 1968)
Whitley, M. J., *German Coastal Forces of World War Two* (Arms & Armour, 1993)
Williamson, Gordon, *Luftwaffe Handbook 1935–1945* (Sutton, 2006)
Wilson, Patrick, *Dunkirk: From Disaster to Deliverance* (Leo Cooper, 2002)
Wood, Derek, and Dempster, Derek, *The Narrow Margin* (Hutchinson, 1961)
Woodman, Richard, *The Real Cruel Sea: The Merchant Navy in the Battle of the Atlantic, 1939–1943* (John Murray, 2005)
Wragg, David, *Royal Navy Handbook, 1939–1945* (Sutton, 2005)
Wynn, Kenneth G., *Men of the Battle of Britain* (Gliddon Books, 1989)
Zeng, Henry L. de, and Douglas G. Stankey, with Eddie J. Creek, *Bomber Units of the Luftwaffe, 1933–1945*, Vol. 1 (Midland Publishing, 2007)
Ziegler, Frank H., *The Story of 609 Squadron: Under the White Rose* (Crécy, 1993)
Ziegler, Philip, *London at War 1939–1945* (Mandarin, 1996)
Zweiniger-Bargielowska, Ina, *Austerity in Britain: Rationing, Controls, and Consumption 1939–1955* (Oxford University Press, 2000)

Articles, pamphlets, essays

Air Ministry, *The Battle of Britain – August–October 1940* (HMSO, 1941)
Andrew, Wing Commander Dean, 'Strategic Culture in the Luftwaffe – Did It Exist in World War II and Has it Transitioned into the Air Force?', *Defence Studies*, Vol. 4, No. 3 (Autumn 2004)
Baker, David, 'The Views of Adolf Galland', *Aeroplane*, July 2000
Bungay, Stephen, 'The Battle of Britain: An Anthem for Doomed Youth', *Everyone's War*, No. 10 (Autumn/Winter 2004)
Caddick-Adams, Peter, 'Anglo-French Co-operation during the Battle of France', in Brian Bond (ed.), *The Battle for France & Flanders Sixty Years On* (Pen & Sword, 2001)
—, 'The British Army in France 1940' (private paper)
—, 'The German Breakthrough at Sedan', in *The Battle for France & Flanders Sixty Years On*
Clark, Major Gregory C., 'Deflating British Radar Myths of World War II: A Research Paper Presented to the Research Department Air Command Staff College', www.radarpages.co.uk

Ellis, Ken, 'First of the Many', *Hurricane – A Fly Past Special*
—, 'Turning Rubble into Gold', *Fly Past*, October 2009
Gretzyngier, Robert, 'The Polish Few', *Battle of Britain – A Fly Past Special*
Jones, R. V., 'RAF Scientific Intelligence', in *Air Intelligence Symposium* (Bracknell Paper No. 7)
Kester, G. P., 'HMS *Wakeful* at Dunkirk – May 1940', Imperial War Museum
Orange, Vincent, 'The German Air Force is Already "The Most Powerful in Europe": Two Royal Air Force Officers Report on a Visit to Germany, 6–15 October 1936', *Journal of Military History*, Vol. 70, No. 4 (October 2006)
Page, Kirby, *How to Keep America Out of War* (published co-operatively, 1939)
Pugh, Cathy, 'A Really Vital Part of Our Essential Defence: The Local Defence Volunteer and the Home Guard', *Everyone's War*, No. 15 (Spring/Summer 2007)
Prince, Stephen, 'Air Power & Evacuations' *The Royal Navy and Maritime Power in the Twentieth Century* (ed. Ian Spiller) (Frank Cass, 2005)
Reynolds, David, 'Churchill and the British "Decision" to Fight on in 1940: Right Policy, Wrong Decisions', in Richard Langhorne, *Diplomacy and Intelligence during the Second World War* (Cambridge University Press, 1985)
Roodhouse, Mark, 'Feeding Britain: Food Control, 1939–45', *Everyone's War*, No. 15 (Spring/Summer 2007)
Schmider, Klaus, 'The Last of the First: Veterans of the Jagdwaffe Tell Their Story', *Journal of Military History*, Vol. 73, No. 1 (January 2009)
Thomas, Andrew, 'Battle Honour Battle of Britain 1940', *Hurricane Salute – A Fly Past Special*
Wright, Nicholas, 'Spitfire or Messerschmitt?', *Fly Past*, August 2006

DVD/Video/CD

Channel 5, *The Few* (ACO/Film/CO Film, 2000)
Craig, Phil (producer), *Finest Hour* (Brook Lapping/BBC, 2004)
Isaacs, Jeremy, *The World at War* (Thames Television 1973, Pearson Television DVD, 2001)
Saunders, Stephen, *Spitfire: Birth of a Legend* (ASA Productions, 2007)
Various, *The Battle of Britain July–October 1940: Extracts from the Imperial War Museum's Collection of Recorded Interviews* (Imperial War Museum)
Warwicker, John, *Secret Army* (ITV Meridian, 2003)

Internet

www.raf.mod.uk: Battle of Britain Campaign Diary (2000)

Acknowledgements

This book has been a long time in the making and inevitably a number of people have given me a considerable amount of help along the way. First of all, I would like to thank Malcolm Smith, former Secretary of the Battle of Britain Fighter Association, who was a great help ten years ago in putting me in touch with a number of veterans of the Battle of Britain. I would also like to thank the late Squadron Leader Joe Leigh, Maurice Mounsden, and Wing Commander Bob Doe, who were amongst the first Battle of Britain pilots to give me their time and to talk to me at length. I would also like to particularly thank Group Captain Allan and Barbara Wright, who have taken the trouble to talk to me numerous times over the years, and Squadron Leader Geoff Wellum, who has similarly recounted his memories of those days at great length as well as becoming a good friend. I also have Geoff to thank for prompting me to begin a career as a historian.

Similarly, Wing Commander Tom and Eileen Neil have allowed me to pester them a number of times over the years and Tom has shared not only his memories but also his wider knowledge and understanding of those days, for which I am extremely grateful. Our conversations have been both great fun and absolutely fascinating. I am also very grateful for all the time and help given to me by the other British veterans and their families and would like to particularly thank the late Air Commodore Pete Brothers, Vicky Bartley, Norman Field, Andrew Jackson, Jimmy and Jeanne Corbin, Lady Robbie Dundas, Jamie Dundas, Stan Fraser, Sandy Ellis, Jane Sacchi and her daughter, Camilla, Joe Steele, John Penna, Robin Penna, Ken Sparks, Wendy Maxwell, Wendy Kyrle-Pope, Douglas Mann, Daphne Hughes, and John and Patricia Wilson. My especial thanks also go to Norman Field's son, Richard Field, who has given help beyond what could be reasonably expected of anyone.

In Germany, I would like to thank Sarah Rivière for her considerable help in helping to locate German citizens who had been in Berlin in 1940, and also to her husband, Michael, for the hospitality both gave me over there. In Berlin I would like especially to thank Hilda Müller, but also Albert Wünderlich. I must also thank Sean Whyte of the excellent SWA Fine Arts for putting me in touch with Stefan Körlin in Aachen. Stefan, thank you for all your huge help. I shall never forget that extraordinary week driving around Germany interviewing Luftwaffe veterans. Thank you also for all your subsequent help as well. I am also, of course, extremely grateful to those German veterans who were willing to talk so freely and openly: Hajo Herrmann, Hans-Ekkehard Bob, Julius Neumann, the late great General Günther Rall, Johannes Naumann, the late Rudi Miese and Günther Seeger, and, in Austria, the late Karl Spreitzer. I am also very grateful to Kurt Dahlmann and Erich Rudorffer.

I owe thanks to a number of people in the various archives in Britain, Germany and the United States. At the Bundesarchiv-Militärarchiv in Freiburg, I would particularly like to thank Frau Jena Brabant, but also all the staff there who helped. I would also like to thank the staff at the Deutsches Tagebucharchiv, Emmendingen, and at the Bibliothek für Zeitgeschichte, Stuttgart. At the Imperial War Museum in London, I am particularly grateful to Richard Hughes in the Sound Archive, but also Roderick Suddaby and his team in the Department of Documents, and to the staff in the Photographic Archive. My thanks also to the staff at the National Archives in Kew, London; the archive there has been transformed in recent years and it is now one of the best equipped and most user-friendly archives there is. Thanks also to the staff at the Royal Air Force Museum, St John's College, Cambridge, the House of Lords and Birmingham University Archives. In Leeds, I would also like to thank Cathy Pugh and her fellows at the Second World War Experience Centre. It is a fantastic resource and Cathy, you are always incredibly generous with your time and help. Thank you. In America, I must thank Tami Davis Biddle for her help and advice and at Maxwell, Alabama, Richard Muller. My thanks also to Stephen Plotkin and Sharon Ann Kelly at the John F. Kennedy Presidential Library in Boston.

I must also thank a number of good friends, who have given considerable help along the way: Antony Beevor, who encouraged me to write the book in the first place, and whose advice has been greatly appreciated. Seb Cox, as the head of the Air Historical Branch, has also provided incredibly helpful advice, is a font of wisdom and knowledge, and has patiently put up with too many of my inane questions. I am also particularly grateful to him for painstakingly reading through and checking the manuscript. I am very grateful as well to Dr Peter Caddick-Adams, who was particularly helpful with the western campaign in May–June 1940 and steered me in the right direction on lots of different matters. He has also been an incredibly helpful sounding board, and someone with whom I can chat about these matters both at great length and with complete enjoyment. Thank you, Peter. I must also thank two other great buddies, Guy Walters and Rowland White, with whom it is always similarly good to talk through ideas and from whom encouragement is always given at just the right moment. Thanks are also owed to another dear friend and travelling companion, David Walsh, who accompanied me through northern France and the Low Countries, and to Germany. Thank you, too, to Professor Jeremy Black, a tutor of mine at Durham and now Professor of History at Exeter and a good friend. His advice and counsel have been an enormous help. My thanks, too, go to Clive and Linda Denney. Clive is a brilliant latter-day pilot and has been very helpful with both technical matters and in giving me an aerial tour of southern England and of a number of the Battle of Britain airfields, not least Biggin, North Weald, Duxford, Manston and the Pas de Calais. I also want to thank my brother, Tom, who has always been an enormous inspiration. My respect for him as a writer, academic and historian knows no bounds, and it is as a devoted younger brother that I am able to dedicate this book to him. Thanks, Bro.

No-one, however, has given me more help than Professor Rick Hillum. Not only does Rick have an encyclopaedic knowledge of the period, but he is also a technical wizard. His understanding of all scientific matters from flight to radar is incredible and he has patiently explained what were, to me, very complicated issues and translated things into clear, layman's terms. Rick has been with me all the way through the writing of this book, and it truly could not have been written without him. Rick, I shall be eternally grateful – thank you.

I also want to thank Lalla Hitchings, who has, as ever, been brilliant, transcribing numerous interviews, and Ute Harding, who both translated and transcribed my conversations with German veterans. I am also very grateful to the following for their help along the way: Giles Bourne, Chris Goss for the loan of much hard-garnered archive material, and Peter Osborne and Independent Books for so generously letting me cite from his book with Ulrich Steinhilper and for the use of photographs.

Thank you, too, to Patrick Walsh and to Claire, Alan, Jake, Alex and Alexandra, and all at Conville & Walsh. I am also really grateful to all those who have helped at Bantam Press. To Madeline Toy, Steve Mulcahey, Sheila Lee, Larry Finlay, Katrina Whone, Vivien Garrett, Mark Handsley and everyone else who helped on the book. My especial thanks, however, go to Bill Scott-Kerr, who has, as ever, been a joy to work with and whose enthusiasm and support have been just fantastic. Thank you.

Finally, I must thank my Rachel, Ned and Daisy. Writing books such as this are a great privilege, but they mean lots of time away and even more time spent locked in a study furiously writing. I am conscious that they have lived this war and in particular the Battle of Britain for longer than was the reality back in 1939–45. But I am very, very grateful to you. Thank you.

Picture Acknowledgements

All photographs have been kindly supplied by the author except those listed below. Every effort has been made to trace copyright holders; those overlooked are invited to get in touch with the publishers.

Endpapers in the hardcover edition only are taken from a German map of central London entitled 'Savoy Hotel and Somerset House' highlighting places not to be bombed, September 1940.

ILLUSTRATION SECTIONS:

Section 1

Page 1
David Crook: Frontline Books.

Pages 2 and 3
Lord Halifax and Joseph Kennedy, 27 August 1939: Popperfoto/Getty Images; Sir Winston Churchill with Neville Chamberlain, London, c. 1939: © Hulton-Deutsch Collection/Corbis; Gort and Pownall: Imperial War Museum/O 358; Franz Halder, 1938: akg-images; Hitler and von Brauchitsh, 1939: Imperial War Museum/MH 13148.

Pages 4 and 5
Erwin Rommel, May-June 1940: Bundesarchiv, Bild 146-1972-045-02; Heinz

Guderian, France, spring 1940: Imperial War Museum/MH 9404; German troops with radio, France, 14 May 1940: Bundesarchiv, Bild 146-1991-045-07/ Lohmeyer; German tanks near Sedan, 13/14 May 1940: ullstein bild-SZ Photo; German officer on a horse; German soldiers with a Panzer Mk I: both Dr Peter Caddick-Adams; German troops advance through Belgium, 11 May 1940: Bundesarchiv, Bild 146-1990-100-32A; German troops advance with bicycles through Compiègne, 13 June 1940: Bundesarchiv, Bild 146-2010-0027/ v. Hausen.

Pages 6 and 7
Bombing of Rotterdam: courtesy Julius Neumann; Hajo Hermann, January 1944: Bundesarchiv, Bild 146-2005-0025; Günther Rall: courtesy Günther Rall; Ulrich Steinhilper and pilots of JG52: Peter Osborne/Independent Books; Adolf Galland: Imperial War Museum/HU 4128; Siegfried Knappe: Deutsches Tagebuch Archiv, Emmendingen; Stan Fraser: photo courtesy Stan Fraser; Arthur Hughes: courtesy Daphne Hughes; Billy Drake: Imperial War Museum/ C 1296; Hurricane Mk I aircraft of 85 Squadron in flight: Imperial War Museum/CH 1510.

Page 8
Douglas Mann: photo courtesy Douglas Mann; Hilda Müller: photo courtesy Hilda Müller.

Section 2

Page 1
Hans-Ekkehard Bob and Chica: both photos courtesy of H-E. Bob.

Pages 2 and 3
The Royal Ulster Rifles on the beach at Bray: Imperial War Museum/HU 1137; abandoned trucks at Dunkirk: Dr Peter Caddick-Adams; Norman Field: photo courtesy Richard Field; evacuation of Dunkirk, June 1940: © Illustrated London News Ltd/Mary Evans Picture Library; burning oil tanks at Dunkirk: Imperial War Museum C 1721.

Pages 4 and 5
George VI and the Queen with Sir Hugh Dowding, 6 September 1940: Imperial War Museum/CH 1233; Chain Home Bawdsey CH station, Suffolk: Imperial War Museum/CH 15337; Observer Corps Post: Imperial War Museum/CH 2477;

Filter Room, HQ Fighter Command, Stanmore: Imperial War Museum/MH 27894.

Pages 6 and 7
English freighter in the sights of a German U-boat, from *Fahrten und Flüge Gegen England* by 'Oberkommando der Wehrmacht', 1941; Günther Prien, 1940: Bundesarchiv, Bild 183-2006-1130-500/Annelise Schulze (Mauritius); Germans bomb British ship in a harbour on the south coast of England, from *Fahrten und Flüge Gegen England* by 'Oberkommando der Wehrmacht', 1941.

Page 8
Hitler and Göring in conversation: Bundesarchiv-Militärachiv, Freiburg-am-Brieisgau; William L. Shirer, Compiègne, France, June 1940: Getty Images.

Section 3

Page 1
Tom Neill: photo by Cecil Beaton.

Pages 2 and 3
Junkers Ju 88: Bundesarchiv, Bild 101I-409-0885-30A/Kahler; Me 177: Imperial War Museum/HU 2965; Ernst Milch: Bundesarchiv, Bild 101I-760-0165N-26/Lange; Junkers 88, 1940/41: Bundesarchiv, Bild 101I-409-0885-30A/Kahler; Me 109: Eric Dumigan; Zerstörer setting out for England, from *Fahrten und Flüge Gegen England* by 'Oberkommando der Wehrmacht', 1941; Hawker Hart: © Chiltern Image Service/Alamy; Spitfire: Richard Paver Photography.

Pages 4 and 5
Victorious soldiers enter Berlin, 18 July, 1940: Bundesarchiv, Bild 183-L07586/Eisenhardt; '. . . meanwhile, in Britain, the entire population, faced by the threat of invasion, has been flung into a state of complete panic . . .' cartoon by Pont, *Punch*, 14 August, 1940; Churchill and Beaverbrook: Popperfoto/Getty Images; Spitfire Assembly Hall, Castle Bromwich: Hugh W. Cowin/Rex Features; Oxford Street, 1940: George Rodger/Magnum Photos.

Pages 6 and 7
Me 109s at Guines: photo courtesy H-E. Bob; Julius Neumann at Euston; Neumann's Me 109: both courtesy Julius Neumann; German airmen, 12 September 1940: Getty Images.

Section 4

Page 1
Ulrich Steinhilper: Peter Osborne/Independent Books.

Pages 2 and 3
Andrew Jackson: photo courtesy Andrew Jackson; Joe Steele: photo courtesy Joe Steele; Allan Wright; Tommy Bartley: both photos courtesy Vicky Bartley; Jimmy Corbin: photo courtesy Jimmy Corbin.

Pages 4 and 5
German soldier on watch, Channel coast, France, from *Fahrten und Flüge Gegen England* by 'Oberkommando der Wehrmacht', 1941.

Pages 6 and 7
London bomb damage: both Cecil Beaton; Berlin bomb damage: Bundesarchiv Bild 183-L09712; crew of U-48: Imperial War Museum/HU 54070; U-47 at surface: Imperial War Museum/HU 105585.

Pages 8
John and Cocky Dundas: photo courtesy Lady Robbie Dundas.

Index